EMPLOYMENT RIGHTS

EMPLOYMENT LAW AND HUMAN RIGHTS

SECOND EDITION

ROBIN ALLEN QC

RACHEL CRASNOW

ANNA BEALE

OXFORD
UNIVERSITY PRESS

OXFORD
UNIVERSITY PRESS

Great Clarendon Street, Oxford OX2 6DP

Oxford University Press is a department of the University of Oxford.
It furthers the University's objective of excellence in research, scholarship,
and education by publishing worldwide in

Oxford New York

Auckland Cape Town Dar es Salaam Hong Kong Karachi
Kuala Lumpur Madrid Melbourne Mexico City Nairobi
New Delhi Shanghai Taipei Toronto

With offices in

Argentina Austria Brazil Chile Czech Republic France Greece
Guatemala Hungary Italy Japan Poland Portugal Singapore
South Korea Switzerland Thailand Turkey Ukraine Vietnam

Oxford is a registered trade mark of Oxford University Press
in the UK and in certain other countries

Published in the United States
by Oxford University Press Inc., New York

© Robin Allen, Rachel Crasnow and Anna Beale, 2007

The moral rights of the author has been asserted
Database right Oxford University Press (maker)

Crown copyright material is reproduced under Class Licence
Number C01P0000148 with the permission of OPSI
and the Queen's Printer for Scotland

First published 2007

British Library Cataloguing in Publication Data

Data available

Library of Congress Cataloging in Publication Data

Allen, Robin, QC.
Employment law and human rights / Robin Allen, Rachel Crasnow, Anna Beale.—2nd ed.
    p. cm.
Includes bibliographical references and index.
ISBN-13; 978-0-19-929963-8 (alk. paper) 1. Labor laws and legislation—Great Britain.
2. Human rights. I. Crasnow, Rachel. II. Beale, Anna. III. Title.
KD3095.A955 2007
344.4101—dc22   100626104 3 T
                                                                                    2007024700

Typeset by Cepha Imaging Private Ltd., Bangalore, India
Printed in Great Britain
on acid-free paper by
Biddles Ltd., King's Lynn, Norfolk

ISBN 978–0–19–929963–8

1 3 5 7 9 10 8 6 4 2

PREFACE

This book has been written for employment law practitioners who want to know more about employment law and human rights. It has been a privilege to write, as human rights law is concerned above all else with the legal protection of human dignity. We believe that all of us, whether employer or employee, judge or tribunal member, witness or party, legislator or practitioner, have a personal stake in the adequate protection of human dignity. We hope that in the chapters that follow we have been able to convey some of our enthusiasm for the protections that the Human Rights Act 1998 brings to employment law, for we believe that by protecting and respecting the dignity of others our own dignity is enhanced.

The protection of human dignity in the workplace is a major task, not in any way to be underestimated. Only rarely do very foolish employers set out deliberately to demean the human rights of their workers. Motives and intentions are not necessarily grounded in bad faith. It is not only employers who violate the rights of others in the workplace. Fellow employees can also be deliberately cruel. The pressures on employer and employee, whether economic or as a result of hierarchy or peer pressure, can all too easily have an impact on dignity at work. The nature of these pressures changes over time but remains a constant presence. Therefore the task of protecting human rights is never-ending, even in a world which is more conscious than ever before of these rights.

It is an intriguing fact that, for by far the majority of the time since the European Convention on Human Rights was first agreed, the workplace has not been subject to any serious audit by the courts or tribunals against human rights norms. This might be understandable in the early years of the Convention, but it has also been true since the start of the modern era of employment law.

This is usually said to have begun with the Donovan Report (the Report of the Royal Commission on Trade Unions and Employers' Associations (1965–1968), (Cmnd 3623), June 1968). The Donovan Report was the source of the statutory right to protection from unfair dismissal but, as much or more so, it was concerned with collective rights of employers and trade unions. The period since its publication has been characterised by a growing and deepening emphasis on individual rights of workers, by reference to their employers, trade unions, and co-workers, and against the state. Indeed, a growing desire to protect the dignity of the worker has been a key theme of the statutory process in employment law over the last 30 years. In retrospect it might be thought that the European Convention on Human Rights would have played a part in that process. However, such protection as there has been has largely been driven by the need to secure a consensual rights based legal structure for industry, free from strikes and collective industrial unrest, and by the search for a new deal of lighter and more efficient regulation. Over all this the developing protection of workers' rights under European law has been a complicating and often contradictory factor.

What is surprising is how very rarely there has been an appeal to the protection of human dignity found in the European Convention on Human Rights. This can be seen by a simple analysis of the cases reported in the Industrial Case Reports, which, beginning in 1973 not long after the Donovan Report and shortly after the Industrial Relations Act 1971, record modern employment law cases. In the period of 26 years from their commencement to the end of 1997, there were only 11 reported cases in which there was any reference to the ECHR. However, in the much shorter period since the beginning of 1998 to the beginning of 2007 there has been as many as 49 reported cases in which the Convention has been referred to. Thus, the potential of the European Convention on Human Rights and the Human Rights Act to affect employment law is amply demonstrated by the change that occurred from the moment its implementation was anticipated.

Yet these statistics can be seen from another perspective. During the whole of this period employment law has in fact been deeply involved in the consideration of special but important human rights issues. There are literally hundreds of discrimination cases in the reports. Moreover, employment is the context in which the human right to equality has been almost exclusively explored. Indeed, the number of race, sex, and disability discrimination cases that have been heard by Employment (and before them Industrial) Tribunals far outstrips any other forum.

We sometimes separate equality from human rights issues because the Convention gives such a weak protection of equality. Yet this is the exception in a world context. International instruments and most other states see them as inextricably linked.

Our domestic equality law cases are just as much human rights cases as a dispute about private life or access to justice. So, in fact, employment lawyers have long had to be human rights lawyers, of a kind! They have had to grapple with equality in all its forms. The Employment Tribunals have needed to reconcile employees' expectations about dignity with opposing arguments concerning utility, economic necessity, and of course sometimes pure prejudice. Employment lawyers know about justification arguments and genuine occupational requirements.

They understand that some rights are so important they cannot be removed save by express statutory provision, and then only in a specific context. So all employment law practitioners of any experience will have some knowledge of some human rights issues. Of course many, maybe most, will not have realised that they do have such a basis for developing their knowledge of the consequences of the Human Rights Act 1998. It is for all those that we have written this book.

The Human Rights Act 1998 has been said to require a quite new way of thinking for many lawyers. In this respect it can be said that employment law practitioners are only a little different. While there is much to learn in relation to Convention case law and the application of the Human Rights Act, all employment law practitioners should have some understanding of some of the core concepts of human rights law—simply by reason of having been involved in a process in which the balance between the interests of the individual and those of the employer or collective interests of a greater group have to be balanced. In this way a part of the core concept of proportionality is already well understood. However, the way in which that balance is to be struck, and the limits to which considerations are assessed to be relevant, must be considered afresh against the more stringent tests of ECHR law.

The aim of this book is therefore to assist the employment law practitioner to understand more deeply the relevant ECHR jurisprudence and to use it with some confidence in an employment law context. It assumes a certain amount of knowledge in relation to employment law but little knowledge of the ECHR. We have tried to consider how the key provisions of the ECHR might affect the way in which employment law generally, and employment disputes in particular, might be resolved. We have not set out all the ECHR jurisprudence either in the European Court of Human Rights or indeed in this country, as our principal aim has been to look for the principles which must be understood and applied in relation to employment. We have therefore been selective in our citations. Nevertheless, we believe we have provided much more than a framework for understanding what impact the ECHR has through the Human Rights Act.

We certainly hope that the book will provoke all those involved with employment law to reconsider their work from this perspective, because since the Human Rights Act 1998 we all have to be human rights lawyers.

The first edition of this book was a long time in gestation and there are many people who contributed to the development of our thinking in this area. In the first edition our apologies went to those who suffered when the book had to take first place, especially Robin's children Kit and Luke. Since then Rachel has acquired two children, Esther and Noah who have suffered similarly! The authors of the first edition are delighted that Anna Beale, who assisted them on the first edition, has joined as a full author.

Our thanks go to Gay Moon, Matthew Dodd, and Will Garrood for their tolerance and encouragement, constructive criticism and more, over a long period. We are also grateful to John Mehrzad for help with proofreading.

Without naming any of them individually, we must thank all our colleagues in Cloisters where the pursuit of dignity in employment is a cardinal rule for whichever side we are acting.

There is never a good time to finish writing a book like this since there is always a new development on the way or a case which seeming once to clarify an issue is suddenly and unexpectedly overruled. Nevertheless, we have tried to state the law as at January 2007. Some changes since then have been picked up in the process of proof reading and amendments to the text made accordingly.

We apologise in advance for the inevitable mistakes that will be spotted by those more eagle-eyed than we are. We would welcome any comments or suggestions for improvements were we to write another edition.

Looking further (but not much further) into the future we welcome the government's commitment to a single Equality Bill and urge them to consider the full implementation of Protocol 12 to the ECHR. These are the necessary next steps to the protection of human rights in the workplace.

We believe that human dignity and, in particular, dignity at work is now better secured than ever before. Our task as employment law practitioners is to ensure that these gains are maintained and that our understanding of what is necessary next is based on informed human rights principles. We hope that in a small way we have contributed to achieving that.

Robin Allen
Rachel Crasnow
Anna Beale
April 2007

CONTENTS—SUMMARY

CONTENTS

ABBREVIATIONS

CEDAW	Convention on the Elimination of All Forms of Discrimination Against Women
CEHR	Commission for Equality and Human Rights
CPA 2004	Civil Partnership Act 2004
DDA 1995	Disability Discrimination Act 1995
DPA 1998	Data Protection Act 1998
EA 2002	Employment Act 2002
EA 2006	Equality Act 2006
EAT	European Appeal Tribunal
ECHR	European Convention for the Protection of Human Rights and Fundamental Freedoms
ECJ	European Court of Justice
ECRC	enhanced criminal record certificate
ECtHR	European Court of Human Rights
ERA 1996	Employment Rights Act 1996
FOIA 2000	Freedom of Information Act 2000
GOQ	genuine occupational qualifications
HRA 1998	Human Rights Act 1998
IBB	Independent Barring Board
ICCPR	International Covenant on Civil and Political Rights
ICERD	International Convention on the Elimination of All Forms of Racial Discrimination
ILO	International Labour Organisation
ET3	Notice of Appearance
para	paragraph
PCaW	Public Concern at Work
PCP	provision, criterion or practice
PIDA 1998	Public Interest Disclosure Act 1998
RIPA 2000	Regulation of Investigatory Powers Act 2000
RRA 1976	Race Relations Act 1976
s	section
Sch	Schedule
SDA 1975	Sex Discrimination Act 1975
UDHR	Universal Declaration of Human Rights

TABLE OF CASES

TABLE OF PRIMARY LEGISLATION

PRIMARY LEGISLATION (EC)

TABLE OF SECONDARY LEGISLATION

TABLE OF INTERNATIONAL INSTRUMENTS

1

AN INTRODUCTION TO HUMAN RIGHTS AND EMPLOYMENT LAW

A. Introduction

Human rights at work are concerned with the relationship between employer and **1.01** employee being based on humanity and not merely being an economic relationship. The starting point for an analysis of this relationship is human dignity;

a concept which is at the heart of the United Nations Universal Declaration of Human Rights ('the Universal Declaration'). The Preamble to the Declaration states that:

> . . . recognition of the inherent dignity and of the equal and inalienable rights of all members of the human family is the foundation of freedom, justice and peace in the world.

Articles 22 and 23 of the Universal Declaration emphasise the close connection between work and dignity.

Article 22.
Everyone, as a member of society, has the right to social security and is entitled to realization, through national effort and international co-operation and in accordance with the organization and resources of each State, of the economic, social and cultural rights indispensable for his dignity and the free development of his personality.

Article 23.
(1) Everyone has the right to work, to free choice of employment, to just and favourable conditions of work and to protection against unemployment.
(2) Everyone, without any discrimination, has the right to equal pay for equal work.
(3) Everyone who works has the right to just and favourable remuneration ensuring for himself and his family an existence worthy of human dignity, and supplemented, if necessary, by other means of social protection.
(4) Everyone has the right to form and to join trade unions for the protection of his interests.

1.02 So it can truly be said that employment and human dignity should go hand in hand in any modern democracy. An American judge put the point succinctly in the following way:

> . . . a man or woman usually does not enter into employment solely for the money: a job is status, reputation, a way of defining one's self-worth, and worth in the community. It is also essential to financial security, offering assurance of future income needed to repay present debts and meet future obligations . . . in short, 'in a modern industrialised economy, employment is central to one's existence and dignity.'[1]

1.03 The common law has developed to recognise this close relationship. Newman J pointed out in *Horkulak v Cantor Fitzgerald International*,[2] when discussing whether an employee must put up with foul abuse from a boss, that:

> The law has developed so as to recognise an employment contract as engaging obligations in connection with the self esteem and dignity of the employee.[3]

---

[1] *Per* Broussard J in *Foley v Interactive Data* [1988] Cal Rptr 211, cited with approval by Lightman J in *BCCI v Ali* [1999] IRLR 508 at para 1.
[2] [2004] ICR 697, [2003] EWHC 1918.
[3] [2004] ICR 697, [2003] EWHC 1918 [17].

The relationship between employment and human rights is the subject matter of **1.04** this book. The relationship between human rights and employment as worked out at home through our own domestic courts and tribunals has come about as a result of the Human Rights Act 1998 (HRA 1998) because it gives direct effect to the major provisions of the European Convention on Human Rights (ECHR) in the United Kingdom. The Act can be found at Appendix 1.

(1) The impact of the ECHR on UK employment law prior to the HRA 1998

Even before the implementation of the HRA 1998, the ECHR had already had **1.05** one major impact on employment law in the United Kingdom in that it was responsible for the end of the closed shop. Under 'closed shop agreements' between a trade union and an employer, the employer agreed to employ only those who were already, or who were willing to become, members of the relevant trade union. These provisions were outlawed as a result of the ECHR's judgment in *Young, James and Webster v UK*[4] long before the HRA 1998 was even thought of.

To appreciate the utility of the HRA 1998 it needs to be remembered that in order **1.06** to achieve that result these men had to litigate at great length domestically and then take the case to the European Court of Human Rights. That was the problem with the ECHR: it had potent force but it was only remotely accessible, but now, as a result of the HRA 1998, access to these rights has changed radically.

However, as the HRA 1998 does not have retrospective effect; decisions of courts **1.07** or tribunals before 2 October 2000, when the HRA 1998 came into force, cannot ordinarily be impugned on appeal by reference to the HRA 1998.[5]

(2) A changing approach

The HRA 1998 has already had a major impact. Over the period of almost seven **1.08** years since it came into effect, it has been cited in nearly 60 cases in the Industrial Case Reports, but the HRA 1998 has not only changed the way we litigate. It has also changed people's approach to their rights and responsibilities. Although the Act has its most immediate effect on public authorities (which include employment tribunals), it undoubtedly has an indirect effect on the way in which we relate to one another; whether employer or employee, trade union official or officer of an employer's organisation, lawmaker, judge, or tribunal member.

---

[4] (1982) 4 EHRR 38.
[5] *R v Lambert* [2002] 2 AC 545, [2001] UKHL 37 at paras 10, 111, 116, 143, 169–176; see also the powerful dissenting opinion of Lord Steyn in *R v Lambert* at paras 27–31.

1.09 Even before the Act came into force it had raised questions as fundamental as the way in which members of both the employment and employment appeal tribunals were appointed (*Smith v Secretary of State for Trade and Industry*;[6] see also *Link v Secretary of State for Trade and Industry*[7]) and had led to new terms of appointment.[8]

1.10 The Act affects employment law at almost every level: from decisions about what is reasonable in an unfair dismissal context to the procedure in the employment tribunal; from decisions about e-mail policies at work to discrimination against persons of different religious faiths, and in many other areas.

B. The aim of this book

1.11 This book has been written to help the busy practitioner understand how the HRA 1998 may affect employment law. It seeks to make the principles accessible and clear. It is not a guidebook to all employment law, or a comprehensive overview of every aspect of employment law, but it does seek to show how the Act has worked in practice and is likely to work in the future.

1.12 The aim is to show when the Act might be relevant, what it can and cannot do, and when and how a point under the Act might be taken. Overall it aims to help those who are suddenly confronted with such a point to understand how it should be approached. The reader should be able to understand how the Act could affect any aspect of employment law, both in a non-contentious situation and where a dispute has arisen.

1.13 The reader is urged to read Chapter 2; this outlines how the HRA 1998 works and which of the relevant Articles of the ECHR are that apply directly in the UK. Armed with this knowledge it will be easier to find the relevant parts of the chapters which deal with those Articles.

C. The European Convention on Human Rights

(1) Background

1.14 The HRA 1998 is based on the ECHR, so it is important to know a little about the Convention's origins. The starting point is the period immediately after

---

[6] [2000] ICR 69.
[7] [2001] IRLR 416.
[8] See the announcement by the Lord Chancellor in the House of Lords: *Hansard* HL vol 616, col WA 71–72 (27 July 2000).

the Second World War, when the importance of stating universally accepted human rights was recognised as having a high priority for the international community.

As a result, in 1948, the United Nations adopted the Universal Declaration, **1.15** referred to above at 1.01. This is not a binding legal instrument at the domestic level; however, it is recognised as part of the law of the United Nations. The Declaration has had a vital inspirational role in the development of human rights instruments ever since. One of the first of these instruments was the ECHR.

The ECHR was signed in Rome on 4 November 1950. It was drafted by the **1.16** Council of Europe, which included the major European states. The UK was very much involved in the drafting of its provisions and was one of the first to ratify the Convention.

(2) Democracy

In the context of the aftermath of the Second World War it was thought essential **1.17** to provide a basic structure to democracy to ensure that there was a common observance of rights which would help prevent the horrors that Europe had seen twice over. Democracy is therefore a key theme of the ECHR. It appears in the recitals to the Convention and in many of the Articles. The whole purpose of the ECHR is to strengthen democracy. It supports a pluralist, tolerant, political system, that permits diversity and does not allow the most powerful groups to ride roughshod over the rights of those less powerful. It is important to bear this in mind whenever the rights in the ECHR are applied.[9]

(3) Rule of law

Inevitably, in any democracy, rights do come into conflict from time to time. This **1.18** requires principles of law to determine how those competing rights are to be resolved. This is the second key theme of the ECHR: rights cannot exist without the rule of law. So the ECHR imposes a requirement that the state in all its manifestations secures that there are legal rules which determine when and how any rights can be abrogated.

The ECHR has been amended by a number of Protocols. These are as much a **1.19** part of the Convention as the original provisions and the HRA 1998 refers to a number of them.

What has made the ECHR so significant is the fact that it has had its own mecha- **1.20** nism for the determination of alleged failures by member states to afford respect

---

[9] See eg *Smith and Grady v United Kingdom* (2000) 29 EHRR 493 para 87.

to the rights enshrined in its Articles (see further 4.74–4.77). This has enabled a body of human rights jurisprudence to be built up over the years. The principal bodies with which this book is concerned are the European Court of Human Rights (ECtHR), and the European Commission on Human Rights ('the Commission'), though it should be noted that the Commission no longer exists.

D. Why the Human Rights Act 1998 was passed

1.21   The UK was one of the first signatories to the ECHR, and many cases have been taken to the institutions of the Convention: the Commission, the ECtHR, and the Council of Ministers.[10] As the caseload of these institutions increased, the time taken to conclude a case lengthened considerably. Attempts were made to persuade the domestic courts to take into account the provisions of ECHR. However, the Convention operated in the sphere of international law, and accordingly it had been held that it did not apply so as to overrule domestic law (*R v Secretary of State for the Home Department, ex parte Brind*[11]).

(1) The need for incorporation

1.22   With the growing recognition of the importance of respect for human rights, courts devised different ways in which such rights might be taken into account in developing standards for judicial review[12] and the common law (see, eg, *In re KD (A Minor) (Ward: Termination of Access)*;[13] see also *Derbyshire County Council v Times Newspapers Ltd*[14]), but it was not uncommon for them to find that they were constrained or that their judgments did not meet with the approval of the ECtHR (for example, in relation to telephone tapping compare *Malone v Metropolitan Police Commissioner*[15] with *Malone v UK*[16]).

1.23   At the same time the European Court of Justice and the institutions of the European Community were becoming increasingly aware of human rights norms and the standards set by the institutions of the ECHR. (See, eg, *Johnston v Chief*

---

10   The Commission ceased to exist from November 1998 as a result of Protocol 11 to the Convention.

11   [1991] 1 AC 696.

12   See in particular the approach taken by the Court of Appeal in *R v Ministry of Defence, ex parte Smith* [1996] QB 517, at 554, where it was held *per* Lord Bingham LCJ: '… The more substantial the interference with human rights, the more the court will require by way of justification before it is satisfied that [a] decision is reasonable …'

13   [1988] AC 806.

14   [1992] QB 770, 812 and 830.

15   [1979] Ch 344.

16   (1984) 7 EHRR 14.

Constable of the Royal Ulster Constabulary;[17] and *Elliniki Radiophonia Tilorassi AE and Panellinia Omospondia Syllogon Prossopikou v Dimotiki Etairia Pliroforissis and Sotirios Kouvelas and Nicolaos Avdellas and others.*[18])

Accordingly there was a growing call for direct incorporation of the Convention into domestic law.[19]   **1.24**

(2) Models for incorporation

The critical issue became how incorporation should be effected: should incorporation operate as a constitutional provision which would permit the courts to strike down statutes made by Parliament, or should Parliament retain its sovereignty? Irrespective of the constitutional objections to the first approach, the lack of legal certainty that it would engender in relation to pre-existing legislation was a powerful objection. It was important that rights under the ECHR should be accessible to all, so it was not enough that the rights should be available only to those who could persuade a higher court to strike down legislation which was incompatible with Convention rights.   **1.25**

The Bill that was ultimately presented to Parliament was universally recognised as a very subtle piece of drafting, which retained parliamentary sovereignty but combined it with a very strong requirement on courts, tribunals, and other 'public authorities'[20] to act compatibly with key Convention rights. As a result, the fundamental nature of those rights has been emphasised, and as much legal certainty as can be consistent with such an important change has been secured.   **1.26**

It is this concept which is at the heart of the HRA 1998—that the courts and tribunals and all other public bodies should act compatibly with Convention rights whenever possible.   **1.27**

E. Implementation of the Human Rights Act 1998

There was a gap of two years between Royal Assent (9 November 1998) and the date on which the HRA 1998 was to be brought into force (2 October 2000; although certain criminal provisions came into effect earlier).   **1.28**

---

[17] [1987] QB 129.
[18] [1991] ECR I-2925, para 41.
[19] See the Consultation Paper *Bringing Rights Home* (December 1992). For an excellent short synopsis of the campaign for incorporation, see, eg, J Wadham and H Mountfield, *Blackstone's Guide to the Human Rights Act 1998* (2nd edn, London: Blackstone Press, 2000) 6–11.
[20] Defined in s 6 of the HRA 1998 and discussed further at Chapter 4 below.

1.29 There were two reasons for this delay: (i) to allow sufficient time for the largest judicial training exercise that had ever taken place on a single topic; and (ii) to allow public authorities to prepare for implementation.[21]

(1) Preparation for the Human Rights Act 1998

1.30 Every major department of state was required to prepare an action plan in relation to the HRA 1998. There were many different training courses implemented by or for public authorities. The Local Government Association, the Law Society, the Employment Lawyers Association, the Employment Law Bar Association, the Institute of Public Policy Research, Justice and Liberty have all carried out training.

1.31 The Government spent about £1m on publicity for the Act in 2000. A target was set that 80 per cent of the adult population should know that there is a Human Rights Act 1998. This by itself has created an expectation in the workplace that human rights will be respected and will be available.

1.32 In the spring of 2000, almost every full-time or part-time chair of employment tribunals underwent a full-day training course in relation to the Act. This book draws on some of the experience gained in drafting this training.

1.33 Six years have now passed since the implementation of the HRA 1998. The Act has been cited and relied upon in a huge variety of cases, and is frequently discussed in depth in the media. Accordingly, employment practitioners need to be aware that whether or not they know themselves, the public know something about the Act, the tribunal members know something about the Act, and it is likely that their opponents will too.

F. The international context

(1) Employment law and international instruments

1.34 Since the HRA 1998 gives effect to an international human rights instrument, it must be seen in its international context.[22] It is standard practice in the interpretation of international treaties to consider what other relevant texts there are. This is particularly important in the field of employment law where there are

---

[21] The lead was taken by the Home Office, which set up a special Human Rights Act Task Force. The Task Force was chiefly concerned with training and was wound up in April 2001.

[22] As a treaty the ECHR's interpretation is governed by the Vienna Convention of 23 May 1969 on the Law of Treaties (Cmnd 4818). Arts 31–33 are particularly important in establishing a good faith and purposive construction. For a full discussion of the principles arising from the Convention, see texts such as B Emmerson and J Simor, *Human Rights Practice* (London: Sweet & Maxwell, 2000).

numerous international human rights instruments dealing directly or indirectly with employment matters. Their role has been to set standards for the international community.

For instance, the International Labour Organisation by Recommendation **1.35** No 119 (1963) was to effect that termination of employment should not take place without a valid reason. This formed a background to the development of the law in relation to unfair dismissal.[23]

Such instruments are also relevant in helping the courts[24] and tribunals of the **1.36** UK to decide how they should approach difficult issues of construction or the development of the common law.[25] This book does not discuss any of these other instruments in detail,[26] but it is important to remember that they provide a background for the application of the Convention to employment law in the UK.[27]

European Community law has a paramount role in this context. The most impor- **1.37** tant of the other instruments are the European Social Charter and those made by the International Labour Organisation. Article 4 of the ECHR, which prohibits all forms of slavery or forced labour, must be seen against the historic campaign to abolish slavery which has resulted in international agreements (see further, Chapter 5).

(2) The role of the law of the European Community in enforcing human rights

The European Community has looked at the way in which it can incorporate **1.38** the jurisprudence of the ECHR as part of its own common law (known as the *acquis communitaire*) over a number of years. With the enlargement of the

---

[23] See also the Commission on Trade Unions and Employers' Associations 1985–88 (the Donovan Commission) (Cmnd 3623).

[24] Historically the courts have not placed much reliance on these treaties: see, eg, *Williams v National Theatre Board Ltd* [1981] ICR 248, or *Blackpool and the Fylde College v National Association of Teachers in Further and Higher Education* [1994] ICR 648.

[25] Thus in *Sawyer v Ahsan* [2000] ICR 1, the Employment Appeal Tribunal considered the International Covenant on Civil and Political Rights (1977) and the International Convention on the Elimination of All Forms of Racial Discrimination (1969) in construing s 12 of the Race Relations Act 1976, together with the European Convention itself. *Sawyer v Ahsan* was overruled by the Court of Appeal on 7 February 2002, by the decision in *Triesman v Ali and Sohal* [2002] [IRLR] 489. *Sawyer v Ahsan* is now under appeal to the House of Lords, when this point may be revisited.

[26] For a detailed consideration see BA Hepple, 'European and International Standards' in 'Part A, Institutions and Sources of Labour Law', in R Upex (ed), *Sweet & Maxwell's Encyclopedia of Employment Law* (London: Sweet & Maxwell, 1992); BA Hepple, 'New Approaches to International Labour Regulation' (1997) 26 ILJ 353.

[27] For instance, the start of modern employment law in the UK can be traced from the formation of the National Industrial Relations Court in 1971. A founder member of the Court was the UK's then representative on the International Labour Organisation, Mr C Henniker-Heaton.

Community to include states in Eastern Europe this has become ever more important. In 1998, a *Comité des Sages*[28] reviewed the European Union's existing human rights protections and said:

> A European Union which fails to protect and promote human rights consistently and effectively will betray Europe's shared values and its long-standing commitment to them. However, the Union's existing policies in this area are no longer adequate. They were made by and for the Europe of yesterday; they are not sufficient for the Europe of tomorrow. The strong rhetoric of the Union is not matched by the reality. There is an urgent need for a human rights policy which is coherent, balanced, substantive and professional.[29]

1.39 Human rights have long been an important part of the norms of the European Community through the jurisprudence of the European Court of Justice (ECJ) and also as a common aspiration of the member states.[30] The ECJ treats human rights norms as an essential tool for the interpretation of Community law.[31] Thus, in *European Parliament v Council of the European Union*[32] it stated that:

> 35 Fundamental rights form an integral part of the general principles of law the observance of which the Court ensures. For that purpose, the Court draws inspiration from the constitutional traditions common to the Member States and from the guidelines supplied by international instruments for the protection of human rights on which the Member States have collaborated or to which they are signatories. The ECHR has special significance in that respect (see, inter alia, Case C-260/89 *ERT* [1991] ECR I-2925, paragraph 41; *Opinion 2/94* [1996] ECR I-1759, paragraph 33; Case C-274/99 P *Connolly v Commission* [2001] ECR I-1611, paragraph 37; Case C-94/00 *Roquette Frères* [2002] ECR I-9011, paragraph 25; Case C-112/00 *Schmidberger* [2003] ECR I-5659, paragraph 71; and Case C-36/02 *Omega* [2004] ECR I-9609, paragraph 33).
>
> 36 In addition, Article 6(2) EU states that 'the Union shall respect fundamental rights, as guaranteed by the [ECHR] and as they result from the constitutional traditions common to the Member States, as general principles of Community law'.

1.40 The decision of the ECJ in *Johnston v Chief Constable of the Royal Ulster Constabulary*,[33] demonstrates how Community law made an industrial tribunal conform to the Convention. The ECJ had to rule on a reference from a Northern

---

[28] Judge Antonio Cassesse, Mme Catherine Lalumière, Professor Peter Leuprecht, and Mrs Mary Robinson. See 'Leading by Example; A Human Rights Agenda for the European Union for the Year 2000', published by the Academy of European Law, European University Institute, Florence, 1998.

[29] Paragraph 2, *op cit* at n 28 above.

[30] See HG Schermers and DF Waelbrook, *Judicial Protection in the European Communities* (5th edn, Deventer: Kluwer, 1992) paras 63–69, for a detailed description of the development of the fundamental rights perspective of the ECJ.

[31] See *Internationale Handelsgesellschaft mbH v Einfuhr- und Vorratsstelle für Getreide und Futtermittel* [1970] ECR 1125.

[32] Case C-540/03 (ECJ 27 June 2006); [2007] All ER (EC) 193.

[33] Case C-222/84 [1986] ECR 1651 para 18, [1987] ICR 83, 101.

Ireland industrial tribunal. The tribunal wished to know whether a Ministerial Order which purported to oust its jurisdiction was contrary to the Equal Treatment Directive.[34] The ECJ ruled thus:

> The requirement of judicial control stipulated by [the Equal Treatment Directive] reflects a general principle of law which underlies the constitutional traditions common to the member states. That principle is also laid down in Articles 6 and 13 of the European Convention for the Protection of Human Rights . . . As the European Parliament, Council and Commission recognised in their joint declaration of 5 April 1977 (*Official Journal* 1977 No. C103, p. 1) and as the Court has recognised in its decisions, the principles on which that Convention is based must be taken into consideration in Community law.

(3) The relationship between the ECHR and Community law

In recent years human rights have played an important part in the amendment of the treaties that form the basis of the European Union. The Treaty on European Union (made at Maastricht on 7 February 1992) specifically included Article F(2), which required:

1.41

> The Union [to] respect fundamental rights, as guaranteed by the European Convention for the Protection of Human Rights and Fundamental Freedoms . . . and as they derive from the constitutional traditions common to the member states, as general principles of law.

Thereafter the ECJ was asked to give an opinion as to whether the European Community as a whole could accede to the Convention, but it ruled that the Community had no competence: see *Opinion 2/94*.[35] However, at the conclusion of the Intergovernmental Conference at Amsterdam European Council on 19 June 1997, it was agreed that this provision would be brought into the main EC Treaty. Now that the Amsterdam Treaty has taken full effect, the jurisprudence set out by the ECJ much earlier is clearly enshrined in the body of the EC Treaty.

1.42

(4) The Charter of Fundamental Rights of the European Union

The Charter of Fundamental Rights of the European Union was agreed at Nice on 7 December 2000.[36] It was proposed to incorporate the Charter as Part II of the European Constitution, which would have made it a binding text (see Article I-9(1) of the proposed draft Constitution). The Constitution has not yet been ratified as a result of referendum defeats in the Netherlands and France.

1.43

---

[34] Council Directive (EC) 76/207 on the implementation of the principle of equal treatment for men and women as regards access to employment, vocational training and promotion, and working conditions [1976] OJ L39.

[35] [1996] ECR I-1759.

[36] [2000] OJ C364/1.

The Charter therefore remains a 'solemn proclamation' only. However, this does not mean it has no relevance. For example, in *Vilho Eskelinen and others v Finland* Application no 63235/00, 19 April 2007, the wider ambit of Article 47 of the Charter (which broadly corresponds to Article 6 ECHR) was referred to as a basis for expanding the field of Article 6.

1.44 Its current significance was emphasised by Advocate General Tizzano, who said in *Broadcasting, Entertainment, Cinematographic and Theatre Union (BECTU) v Secretary of State for Trade and Industry*[37] that the Charter:

> ... includes statements which appear in large measure to reaffirm rights which are enshrined in other instruments. In its preamble, it is moreover stated that 'this Charter reaffirms, with due regard for the powers and tasks of the Community and the Union and the principle of subsidiarity, the rights as they result, in particular, from the constitutional traditions and international obligations common to the Member States, the Treaty on European Union, the Community Treaties, the European Convention for the Protection of Human Rights and Fundamental Freedoms, the Social Charters adopted by the Community and by the Council of Europe and the case-law of the Court of Justice of the European Communities and of the European Court of Human Rights.'

> I think therefore that, in proceedings concerned with the nature and scope of a fundamental right, the relevant statements of the Charter cannot be ignored; in particular, we cannot ignore its clear purpose of serving, where its provisions so allow, as a substantive point of reference for all those involved—Member States, institutions, natural and legal persons—in the Community context.

(See also *Max Mobil Telekommunikation Service GmbH v Commission*[38].)

1.45 The Charter is often referred to in the Preamble to modern Directives. The ECJ has also re-emphasised the important role that the Charter plays in the law of the European Communities in *European Parliament v Council of the European Union*[39] thus:

> 38 The Charter was solemnly proclaimed by the Parliament, the Council and the Commission in Nice on 7 December 2000. While the Charter is not a legally binding instrument, the Community legislature did, however, acknowledge its importance by stating, in the second recital in the preamble to [this] Directive, that the Directive observes the principles recognised not only by Article 8 of the ECHR but also in the Charter. Furthermore, the principal aim of the Charter, as is apparent from its preamble, is to reaffirm 'rights as they result, in particular, from the constitutional traditions and international obligations common to the Member States, the Treaty on European Union, the Community Treaties, the [ECHR], the Social Charters adopted by the Community and by the Council of Europe and the case-law of the Court ... and of the European Court of Human Rights.'

---

[37] Case C-173/99; [2001] IRLR 559.
[38] Case T-54/99 (CFI 30 January 2002); [2002] ECR II-313; [2002] 4 CMLR 1356, paras 48 and 57.
[39] Case C-540/03 (ECJ 27 June 2006); [2007] All ER (EC) 193.

From the opposite approach the ECtHR has also acknowledged the importance **1.46** of the Charter when addressing the question whether a decision by Ireland to apply Community law was compatible with the ECHR (*Bosphorus Hava Yollari Turizm ve Ticaret AS v Ireland* [40]).

The relevant paragraphs of the Charter are set out in Appendix 3. **1.47**

(5) New European discrimination laws

The EC Treaty affirms the importance of equality in relation to the activities of **1.48** the Community in Article 3(2) EC. The Amsterdam Treaty made an important further human rights amendment to the EC Treaty, introducing a new Article 13 EC,[41] which provides:

> Without prejudice to the other provisions of this Treaty and within the limits of the powers conferred by it upon the Community, the Council, acting unanimously on a proposal from the Commission and after consulting the European Parliament, may take appropriate action to combat discrimination based on sex, racial or ethnic origin, religion or belief, disability, age or sexual orientation.

A number of steps have already been taken to combat discrimination on the given **1.49** grounds. Foremost amongst the new legislative developments are the Race Directive, the Framework Employment Directive (which deals with each of the other grounds in Article 13 EC save for sex), and the amendments made to the Equal Treatment Directive under Directive 2002/73. Thus discrimination on grounds of age, disability, religion, and sexual orientation are now the subject of European legislation, along similar lines to the updated sex and race provisions.[42]

In the UK, these changes have been implemented through amendments to the Race **1.50** Relations Act 1976 and Sex Discrimination Act 1975, the Sexual Orientation[43] and Religion and Belief Regulations,[44] and the Age Regulations.[45] Inevitably the legislation arising out of these Directives will affect the way in which a court or tribunal will approach issues under the HRA 1998, but the relationship is not entirely predictable.[46] They are discussed further below in context, particularly in relation to Articles 9 and 14 of the ECHR in Chapters 9, 13, and 14.

---

[40] (App no 45036/98) ECHR 30 June 2005; (2005) 19 BHRC 299; (2006) 42 EHRR 1.
[41] This Article has been subsequently amended to allow for qualified majority voting in some circumstances.
[42] Council Directive (EC) 2000/78; see Appendix 5.
[43] The Employment Equality (Sexual Orientation) Regulations 2003, SI 2003/1661.
[44] The Employment Equality (Religion or Belief) Regulations 2003, SI 2003/1660.
[45] The Employment Equality (Age) Regulations 2006, SI 2006/1031.
[46] For a discussion of the difficulties see R Allen, 'The Contribution of International and Transnational Regulation in the Search for Substantive Equality in the Workplace: Clarity or Confusion' in H Collins, P Davies and R Rideout (eds), *Legal Regulation of the Employment Relationship* (The Hague: Kluwer, 2001).

(6) European employment law

1.51   As there is a huge and growing body of employment law [47] that derives from the UK's membership of the European Community, the potential for human rights issues to arise is great. This has already affected the rest of the European Community through the Community Charter of the Fundamental Social Rights of Workers. [48]

1.52   At Maastricht, 11 of the 12 member states wishing to continue down the path set by this Charter, agreed to a Protocol which was annexed to the EC Treaty. By Prime Minister John Major's famous 'opt-out', the UK was not a party to this Protocol. However, at the Amsterdam summit in 1997 the UK agreed to bring the text of this Protocol into the main part of the EC Treaty. As a result, an amended Article 117 EC, introducing the social provisions of the EC Treaty, reads as follows:

> The Community and the Member States, having in mind fundamental social rights such as those set out in the European Social Charter . . . and in the 1989 Community Charter of the Fundamental Social Rights of Workers, shall have as their objective the promotion of employment, improved living and working conditions . . .

1.53   The main provisions of the Community Charter cover: freedom of movement (see also Article 39 EC and Regulation 1612/68); employment and remuneration; improvement of living and working conditions; social protection; freedom of association and collective bargaining; vocational training; equal treatment for men and women; information, consultation, and participation for workers; health protection and safety at the workplace; protection of children and adolescents, elderly persons, and disabled persons. Thus, the body of European employment law which is affected by human rights norms is set to grow even further.

1.54   Much of Community law is already either directly enforceable between employee and employer, [49] or directly enforceable between employee and emanations of the state (see, eg, *Marshall v Southampton and South West Area Health Authority* [50]). In any event, pursuant to Article 5 EC courts must attempt to interpret municipal provisions so far as possible in a way which is consistent with Community law

---

[47]   See, for instance, B Bercusson, *European Labour Law* (London: Butterworths, 1996), or C Barnard, *EC Employment Law* (2nd edn, Oxford: OUP, 2000).

[48]   Made by 11 member states (excluding the UK) at the European Community Meeting at Strasbourg on 9 December 1989.

[49]   By Art 249 EC, Regulations have direct effect *inter partes*. Some of the main Articles have direct effect between employers and employees: Art 39 EC on the free movement of workers (Case 41/74 *Van Duyn v Home Office* [1974] ECR 1337; Case C-415/93 *Union Royale Belge des Sociétés de Football Association Asbl v Bosman* [1995] ECR I-4921); Art 141 EC on equal pay (Case 43/75 *Defrenne v Sabena* [1976] ECR 455).

[50]   Case 152/84 [1986] ECR 723.

(see *Marleasing*[51]). Indeed, in *Amministrazione delle Finanze dello Stato v Simmenthal SPA*,[52] the ECJ said:

> ... in accordance with the principle of the precedence of Community law, the relationship between provisions of the Treaty and directly applicable measures of the institutions on the one hand and the national law of the member states on the other is such that those provisions and measures not only by their entry into force render automatically inapplicable any conflicting provision of current national law but— insofar as they are an integral part of, and take precedence in, the legal order applicable in the territory of each of the member states—also precludes the valid adoption of new national legislative measures to the extent to which they would be incompatible with Community law provisions.

This jurisprudence of the ECJ is particularly important because, as developed below (see Chapter 3), there are limits to the extent to which the HRA 1998 will apply Convention rights in the determination of rights and obligations. **1.55**

If the employment context is one in which Community law applies then it will almost always be appropriate to examine a human rights issue in the light of both Convention and Community law. There are two main reasons for this—boldness and speed: **1.56**

(a) The ECJ can look at other human rights instruments and is not tied to the black letter of the Convention. Accordingly, it could be bolder and a more rigorous defender of human rights than the ECtHR.

(b) Questions can be referred to the ECJ by municipal courts and tribunals whenever they arise (see Article 234 EC). On the other hand, the ECtHR will not normally accept a complaint until domestic remedies have been exhausted (Article 26 ECHR). A reference to the ECJ should be made after the relevant facts have been found, but this may be well before the conclusion of the case. This can be very important in employment law, where there are three appellate courts after the initial fact-finding hearing. If there is to be a reference in a matter that has been heard by an employment tribunal, it is better that it is made earlier, before the Court of Appeal or the House of Lords. There is also a potential cost saving. While the case is before the employment tribunal or the Employment Appeal Tribunal costs are not usually awarded against the unsuccessful party.

The ECJ has also made it clear that national courts enjoy the widest discretion in deciding when and what questions should be referred. Because of the doctrine of supremacy of Community law, it is clear that an inferior court or tribunal may **1.57**

---

[51] Case C-106/89 [1990] ECR I4135.
[52] Case 106/77 [1978] ECR 629.

make a reference even if there is an apparent precedent in municipal law which appears to decide the issue in question (*Rheinmühlen Dusseldorf v Einfuhr- und Voratselle für Getreide*;[53] and *Chacón Navas v Eurest Colectividades SA*[54]).

(7) European Social Charter

1.58 The European Social Charter[55] was made at Turin on 18 October 1961 by the Council of Europe. This is the same body that made the ECHR, and it is not an organ of the European Community. The Charter sets minimum social policy standards in relation to employment law issues and contains 19 key rights, all of which are connected directly or indirectly with the employment relationship.

The key rights are the rights:

- to work;
- to just conditions of work;
- to safe and healthy living conditions;
- to fair remuneration;
- to organise;
- to bargain collectively;
- to protection for children and young persons;
- to protection for women;
- to vocational guidance;
- to vocational training;
- to protection of health;
- to social security;
- to social and medical assistance;
- to benefit from social welfare services;
- for physically and mentally disabled persons;
- to protection for the family;
- to protection for mothers;
- to engage in gainful occupation in the territory of other contracting parties;
- to protection for migrant workers and their families.

The UK has abstained in part from some of these rights.[56]

---

[53] Case 166/73 [1974] ECR 33.
[54] Case C-13/05 (ECJ 11 July 2006); [2007] All ER (EC) 59; [2006] 3 CMLR 1123; [2007] ICR1; [2006] IRLR 706.
[55] TS 38 (1965); Cmd 2643. For an early but still authoritative text on the Charter, see DJ Harris, *The European Social Charter* (Charlottesville: University Press of Virginia, 1984).
[56] See L Samuel, *Fundamental Social Rights: Case Law of the European Social Charter* (Strasbourg: Council of Europe Publishing, 1997), which is an excellent guide, for a discussion of how these rights may be given effect.

The Charter is an important point of reference for the interpretation of any **1.59**
Convention provision that affects employment law. The preamble to the Charter
makes it clear that it is to be read with the Convention.

However, unlike the rights under the ECHR, these rights cannot be enforced **1.60**
directly.[57] Complaints must be made through specified labour organisations to a
committee of experts who decide whether the member states have complied with
the relevant norms.

Of particular importance is that the contracting parties to the Charter (including **1.61**
the UK) have expressly recognised (for the first time in an international human
rights instrument) the right to strike:[58]

> The right of workers and employers to collective action in cases of conflict of inter-
> est, including the right to strike, subject to obligations that might arise out of collec-
> tive agreements previously entered into. (Article 6(4))

(8) The International Labour Organisation

The International Labour Organisation (ILO) was first set up by the League of **1.62**
Nations before the Second World War. It has played a pivotal role in the development of norms in the field of employment law.[59]

Seven core ILO Conventions (though not all have been ratified by the UK) address **1.63**
issues of fundamental rights in employment.[60] These cover freedom of association
and collective bargaining,[61] forced labour,[62] non-discrimination,[63] and minimum
age in employment.[64]

The ECJ and the ECtHR have been prepared to consider generally the standards **1.64**
set by the ILO. An employment tribunal will not need to have provisions of
the relevant Conventions cited to it often, but they form a background against
which any application of the Convention to employment law must be seen.
Occasionally this may be important.

---

[57] See also BA Hepple 'European and International Standards' in 'Part A, Institutions and Sources
of Labour Law', in R Upex (ed), *Sweet & Maxwell's Encyclopedia of Employment Law* (London: Sweet
& Maxwell, 1992) at paras 1.1156 *et seq.*

[58] See also Art 8(1)(d) of the International Covenant on Economic, Social and Cultural Rights
1966 and ILO Conventions Nos 87 and 105.

[59] For a wider discussion of the role of the ILO, see R Blanpain (ed), *International Encyclopaedia
for Labour Law and Industrial Relations* (Deventer: Kluwer, 1977).

[60] Some commentators have emphasised the importance of other Conventions: see BA Hepple,
'New Approaches to International Labour Law Regulation' (1997) 26 ILJ 353, 358 *ff.*

[61] Conventions 1948 No 87 and 1949 No 89 (not ratified by the UK). Conventions 1930 No 29
and 1957 No 105.

[62] Conventions 1930 No 29 and 1957 No 105.

[63] Conventions 1951 No 100 and 1958 No 111.

[64] Convention 1973 No 138 (not ratified by the UK).

(9) International Covenant on Economic, Social and Cultural Rights

1.65   In 1966, the United Nations adopted an International Covenant on Economic, Cultural and Social Rights. This Covenant came into force on 3 January 1976. The UK has ratified this Covenant but has not brought it into force domestically. The key provisions in relation to employment are Article 6, which contains a recognition of the right to work; Article 7, which refers to the recognition of the right to just and favourable conditions of work, including fair wages and equal remuneration without discrimination; and Article 8, which recognises the right to form and join trade unions.

(10) International Covenant on Civil and Political Rights

1.66   The International Covenant on Civil and Political Rights was adopted at the same time as the International Covenant on Economic, Social and Cultural Rights (see 1.65). It has many provisions similar to those found in the ECHR, but includes an important, free-standing, non-discrimination provision in Article 26. It is relevant to the approach taken by the ECJ also (see 1.48). This instrument was very relevant to the debate over a new Protocol to the ECHR. The new Protocol 12 was agreed on but has not been ratified by the UK. This is discussed further in Chapters 13 and 14.

(11) International Convention on the Elimination of All Forms of Racial Discrimination and the Convention on the Elimination of All Forms of Discrimination Against Women

1.67   Other relevant international provisions include the International Convention on the Elimination of all Forms of Racial Discrimination and the Convention on the Elimination of all Forms of Discrimination against Women. These and other such texts can be found in standard books such as *Basic Documents on Human Rights*.[65]

(12) Disability

1.68   The United Nations is currently considering a Convention on disability issues. This may be particularly relevant to the development of ECJ case law on disability since the ECJ takes into account international norms and has made it clear that disability has an autonomous meaning in European law (see *Chacón Naras v Eurest Colectindades SA*[66]).

---

[65]   Prof I Brownlie (ed), *Basic Documents on Human Rights* (4th edn, Oxford: OUP, 2002).
[66]   Case C-13/05 (ECJ 11 July 2006); [2007] All ER (EC) 59; [2006] 3 CMLR 1123; [2007] ICR1; [2006] IRLR 706.

2

CONVENTION RIGHTS UNDER THE HUMAN RIGHTS ACT 1998

A. Introduction

This chapter aims to give the reader an overview of the Convention rights found **2.01** in the HRA 1998. It is not intended to be a definitive or comprehensive guide[1] to the Act but to provide the employment law practitioner with sufficient background to understand which of the ECHR rights applies in the employment law context and the basic structure by which this is achieved.

The aim of the HRA 1998 is compliance with the ECHR. To that end, it operates **2.02** in two principal ways. First, it imposes an interpretative obligation in respect of all legislation, whether primary or secondary, and, secondly, it imposes a specific duty on public authorities to comply with the ECHR. These duties are discussed further in Chapters 3 and 4.

---

[1] For a more detailed guide to the HRA 1998, see J Wadham, H Mountfield, and A Edmundson, *Blackstone's Guide to the Human Rights Act 1998* (4th edn, Oxford: OUP, 2006). This work is a useful practical guide to the Act but does not seek to be a general textbook on all the ECHR jurisprudence.

2.03 Both mechanisms impose a requirement to act compatibly with 'Convention rights'. Not all the rights found in the ECHR are Convention rights for the purpose of the HRA 1998. The practitioner needs to understand this concept at the outset.

B. Convention rights

2.04 The HRA 1998 defines only certain rights in the ECHR as Convention rights (HRA 1998, s 1 and Sch 1). This is a key concept since it is those rights which are given domestic effect by the Act. It encompasses Articles 2–12 and Article 14[2] of the ECHR, Articles 1–3 of Protocol 1, and Articles 1–2 of Protocol 6. These have to be read with Article 16 ECHR, which restricts the political activity of aliens in relation to Articles 10, 11 and 14, and Articles 17 and 18 ECHR, which are non-abuse provisions. Article 16 is probably not very relevant to employment law. Articles 17 and 18 are discussed at 2.07–2.10 below.

2.05 The main rights contained in the Convention itself[3] are set out in Table 2.1 below.

Table 2.1 The principal Convention rights

Article	Right
2	Right to life
3	Prohibition of torture
4	Prohibition of slavery and forced labour
5	Right to liberty and security
6	Right to a fair trial
7	No punishment without law
8	Right to respect for private and family life
9	Freedom of thought, conscience and religion
10	Freedom of expression
11	Freedom of assembly and association
12	Right to marry
14	Prohibition of discrimination
1 of Protocol 1	Protection of property
2 of Protocol 1	Right to education
3 of Protocol 1	Right to free elections
1 of Protocol 6	Abolition of the death penalty
2 of Protocol 6	Death penalty in time of war

---

[2] This right is a prohibition on discrimination in the enjoyment of the rights and freedoms set forth in the ECHR. It is an accessory and not a free-standing right.

[3] The provisions of principal importance that have been omitted are Articles 1 (the obligation to respect human rights) and 13 (the right to an effective remedy), which the provisions of the HRA 1998 are intended to provide.

The Convention rights are subject to certain derogations or reservations **2.06**
(see HRA 1998, ss 14–17 and Sch 3). The effect of these derogations or reservations can be important in cases concerned with terrorism and education. For
a more detailed discussion of the reservations, reference should be made to other
works.[4] Where they might affect employment law, they are considered further
below.

C. Articles 17 and 18—the non-abuse provisions

As well as the rights set out in Table 2.1 above, Articles 17 and 18 ECHR are con- **2.07**
tained in Schedule 1 to the HRA 1998. These Articles are particularly important
as they set the scope of the Convention as a whole. Practitioners need to be aware
of them since they ensure that the provisions set out in the ECHR cannot be used
in a way which is destructive of the purpose of the Convention.

Article 17 ECHR provides:

Article 17
Prohibition of abuse of rights

Nothing in this Convention may be interpreted as implying for any State, group or person any **2.08**
right to engage in any activity or perform any act aimed at the destruction of any of the rights
and freedoms set forth herein or at their limitation to a greater extent than is provided for in
the Convention.

Article 18 ECHR applies to the restrictions that are contained in many of the **2.09**
main rights. These restrictions enable the rights to be enjoyed in a way which is
not destructive of the policy behind the Convention. It is vital to understand that
the restrictions cannot be used for purposes which are not consistent with this:

Article 18
Limitation on use of restrictions on rights

The restrictions permitted under this Convention to the said rights and freedoms shall not be
applied for any purpose other than those for which they have been prescribed.

The purposes of the restrictions are mostly self-evident, affecting, for instance, **2.10**
the enjoyment of rights by others and the security of the state. Thus, the right to
freedom of expression in Article 10 ECHR could be invoked to campaign for a
fascist, anti-democratic scheme.[5]

---

[4] See, eg, S Grosz, J Beatson, and P Duffy, *Human Rights—The 1998 Act and the European
Convention* (London: Sweet & Maxwell, 2000) 366 *et seq.*
[5] See *Redfearn v Serco Ltd t/a West Yorkshire Transport Service* [2006] EWCA Civ 659, [2006]
IRLR 623, where the argument was raised (though not finally decided by the Court of Appeal) that
it would be contrary to Art 17 for an avowed racist to rely on the Race Relations Act 1976.

D. Articles relevant to employment law

2.11   This book concentrates on the rights which have most direct relevance to employment law. These are Articles 4, 6, 8, 9, 10, 11, and 14 ECHR and Article 1 of Protocol 1, each of which is the subject of a separate chapter. However, practitioners should not forget the other rights, such as the rights to free elections (Article 3 of Protocol 1) and to education (Article 2 of Protocol 1), since these can have an unexpected relevance. Thus, in *Sawyer v Ahsan*,[6] the Employment Appeal Tribunal (EAT) considered Article 3 of Protocol 1 in deciding how to construe section 12 of the Race Relations Act 1976. The EAT had to decide whether the section should apply to discrimination in relation to the choice of a candidate to stand in an election for a political party.[7]

2.12   In the context of a case about employment at a school it is perfectly possible that the rights under Article 2 of Protocol 1 might come into conflict with the rights of the employee.

2.13   For example, parents might argue that a female nursery school teacher who wears the jilbab to work is jeopardising the education of her pupils as it is important for young children to be able to see their teacher's mouth in order to improve their verbal communication. The teacher could argue that refusal to allow her to wear the jilbab amounts to a breach of her Article 9 rights.

2.14   The right to marry (Article 12 ECHR) might come into play in a case which concerns a job only open to a single person, though this is likely to be unlawful marital discrimination contrary to the Sex Discrimination Act 1975. Article 3, which prohibits torture and inhuman or degrading treatment or punishment, could arise in particularly severe bullying at work cases (see 14.140–14.141).

E. Qualified rights

2.15   Giving effect to the duty to act compatibly with Convention rights or to secure an appropriate interpretation is by no means straightforward, for two key reasons. First, not all Convention rights are absolute;[8] most are qualified (and some are

---

   6 [2000] ICR 1.
   7 This judgment was later overruled by the Court of Appeal in *Triesman v Ali and Sohal* [2002] EWCA Civ 93, [2002] IRLR 489. However, an appeal to the House of Lords is now pending in *Ahsan v Sawyer No 2*.
   8 The absolute articles are Arts 3, 4, 7, 12, and 17 ECHR, and Article 1 of Protocol 6.

limited, such as Article 5, the right to liberty),[9] so a critical question will be the extent to which any qualification applies.

Where rights are qualified the person or body who must act compatibly will **2.16** need to consider whether any interference is 'prescribed' or 'in accordance with law', has a legitimate aim, and is 'necessary in a democratic society'. In particular, any interference must be proportional; it must not use a sledgehammer to crack a nut. These are all necessary requirements for a legitimate interference with a Convention right. They are discussed with relevance to specific Articles in later chapters in this book.

Secondly, Convention rights frequently come into conflict. Thus the right to **2.17** respect for private life under Article 8 may come into conflict with the right to freedom of expression under Article 10 (see 10.58–10.60). These conflicts are often difficult to resolve, and it is here that a thorough understanding of human rights law becomes so important for any lawyer, whether judge or practitioner, who has to help to resolve them.

F. Convention rights and the margin of appreciation

In many cases before the European Court, the Court has not upheld the com- **2.18** plaint because it considers that the approach taken by the relevant state is within the 'margin of appreciation'. It is important that employment law practitioners understand what this concept is, since it has been used in domestic case law to imply a discretion or flexibility as to how a domestic legal person may act.[10] However, the ECtHR's concept of a margin of appreciation is concerned with the interpretation of an international treaty by different sovereign states. In any event, the Council of Europe has remarked (see the explanatory memorandum to Protocol 12, at 13.105):

> The scope of the margin of appreciation will vary according to the circumstances, the subject-matter and its background[11] . . . For example, the Court has allowed a wide margin of appreciation as regards the framing and implementation of policies in the area of taxation.[12]

---

[9] These limited rights are not of great relevance to employment lawyers.

[10] See, eg, *London Underground v Edwards (No 2)* [1999] ICR 494, *per* Potter LJ at 505, where, in a case concerning indirect discrimination, he stated that 'an area of flexibility (or margin of appreciation), is necessarily applicable to the question of whether a particular percentage is to be regarded as "substantially smaller" in any given case' for the purposes of s 1(1)(b)(i) of the Sex Discrimination Act 1975.

[11] See, eg, the judgment of 28 November 1984 in the case of *Rasmussen v Denmark* Series A No 87, para 40.

[12] See, eg, the judgment of 23 October 1997 in the case of *National and Provincial Building Society and others v United Kingdom* (1998) 25 EHRR 127.

Accordingly, practitioners should be astute to ensure that neither judges nor employment tribunal chairmen nor wing-members seek to read across such a margin of appreciation into their duty under section 6 of the Act. The duty to act compatibly with Convention rights does not imply a margin of appreciation for domestic courts.

G. Frequently asked questions

2.19   **Are all the rights in the ECHR within the HRA 1998?**

No, only those set out in Schedule 1 to the HRA 1998. The main rights which are relevant to employment law are Articles 4, 6, 8, 9, 10, 11, and 14 ECHR and Article 1 of Protocol 1. All these are in Schedule 1 to the HRA 1998.

Are all rights in the ECHR absolute?

No, most of the rights are qualified. This is necessary since they are written in general terms and sometimes address complicated circumstances in which other rights or obligations may come into conflict with them.

What happens when rights come into conflict?

The court or tribunal has to carry out a balancing exercise to ensure that the invasion of one right is no more than is proportionate.

What is the 'margin of appreciation'?

The ECtHR recognises that the ECHR is an international treaty which has to be applied in very different circumstances. It recognises that democratic states will not all run in exactly the same way. Accordingly, it permits states to have a discretion within which they may apply the rights in the ECHR. This is called the margin of appreciation. The ECtHR controls the limit to the margin. In some cases the margin is drawn very tightly, while in instances where there is an emerging consensus as to what the nature of a right is, it may be drawn less narrowly.

How does the margin of appreciation relate to the duty to act compatibly in the HRA 1998?

Strictly the duty to act compatibly in section 6 of HRA 1998 means that public authorities must act with the right in any Article. It does not mean that public authorities have a further margin beyond that which the ECtHR permits.

3

INTERPRETING DOMESTIC LEGISLATION

A. Introduction

The interpretative obligation imposed by the HRA 1998 is the overarching **3.01** mechanism by which Parliament sought to make domestic law compliant with the standards of the ECHR. The interpretative obligation is in section 3 and states that:

> . . . So far as it is possible to do so, primary and subordinate legislation must be read and given effect in a way which is compatible with the Convention rights . . .

3.02   This obligation is underpinned by an obligation in section 6 of the HRA 1998 on public authorities to comply with Convention rights. These two obligations work in tandem to secure Convention rights within the UK. Where it is not possible to give effect in a way compatible with Convention rights then an application to the court for a declaration of incompatibility may be made under section 4 of the HRA 1998 (see 3.54–3.61).

3.03   The ability of the common law to adapt to new principles and currents is not in doubt. However, the Act goes further than that by seeking to mould statute law into compliance with Convention rights through section 3. In approaching the interface between common law, statute and old authorities, the courts and tribunals are now under an obligation as public authorities to give effect to Convention rights as a result of the duty laid on them by sections 3 and 6.

3.04   The principal way in which the Act gives effect to Convention rights without at the same time overriding inconsistent domestic legislation, and therefore causing an unnecessary lack of legal certainty on overturning the supremacy of Parliament, is by this interpretative requirement set out above. Section 3 of the HRA 1998 imposes this interpretative obligation on all courts and tribunals so that it affects the use of all legislation. It has a quasi-constitutional status.

B. Quasi-constitutional status

3.05   This quasi-constitutional status was explained by Lord Hoffmann in *R v Secretary of State for the Home Department, ex parte Simms*:[1]

> Parliamentary sovereignty means that Parliament can, if it chooses, legislate contrary to fundamental principles of human rights. The Human Rights Act 1998 will not detract from this power. The constraints upon its exercise by Parliament are ultimately political, not legal. But the principle of legality means that Parliament must squarely confront what it is doing and accept the political cost. Fundamental rights cannot be overridden by general or ambiguous words. This is because there is too great a risk that the full implications of their unqualified meaning may have passed unnoticed in the democratic process. In the absence of express language or necessary implication to the contrary, the courts therefore presume that even the most general words were intended to be subject to the basic rights of the individual. In this way the courts of the United Kingdom, though acknowledging the sovereignty of Parliament, apply principles of constitutionality little different from those which exist in countries where the power of the legislature is expressly limited by a constitutional document.

---

[1] [2000] 2 AC 115, 131.

C. The strength of the interpretative obligation

Before considering the impact of section 3 upon the construction of legislation **3.06** in the employment context, it is important to emphasise its strength as a key interpretative tool of the HRA 1998. It is necessary to note that section 3(1) requires both that legislation is to be read in a way which is compatible with Convention rights and that it is also to be given effect in a way which is compatible with those rights. Even though the heading of section 3 is 'Interpretation of legislation', the content of the section goes beyond interpretation to cover the way that legislation is given effect.

Section 3 requires that all legislation must be read and given effect to in a way **3.07** which is compatible with the Convention rights 'so far as it is possible to do so'. But the word 'possible' along with sections 3(2) and 4 make it clear that Parliament envisaged that not all legislation would be capable of being made Convention-compliant by application of section 3.

Such problems should be rare. The major departments of state have all attempted **3.08** to review the legislation for which they are the lead department to see if it is necessary to make any amendments. They have sought to check that where compliance might not be possible they are alert to the dangers, and in some cases important changes have been made.

Merely to utilise section 3 to resolve ambiguities would give it too narrow a scope. **3.09** Rather, section 3 may require a court to depart from the unambiguous meaning of the legislation and its operation need not depend upon the particular form of words adopted by the parliamentary draftsman in the statutory provision under consideration. Section 3 can require a court to read in words which change the meaning of the enacted legislation, so as to make it Convention-compliant.

Lord Woolf stated in *Poplar Housing and Regeneration Community Association* **3.10** *Ltd v Donohue*:[2]

> It is difficult to overestimate the importance of section 3. It applies to legislation passed both before and after the Human Rights Act 1998 came into force. Subject to the section not requiring the court to go beyond that which is possible, it is mandatory in its terms. In the case of legislation predating the Human Rights Act 1998 where the legislation would otherwise conflict with the Convention, section 3 requires the court to now interpret legislation in a manner which it would not have done before the Human Rights Act 1998 came into force. When the court interprets legislation usually its primary task is to identify the intention of Parliament. Now, when

---

[2] [2002] QB 48 at para 75.

section 3 applies, the courts have to adjust their traditional role in relation to interpretation so as to give effect to the direction contained in section 3. It is as though legislation which predates the Human Rights Act 1998 and conflicts with the Convention has to be treated as being subsequently amended to incorporate the language of section 3. However, the following points, which are probably self-evident, should be noted.

(a) Unless the legislation would otherwise be in breach of the Convention section 3 can be ignored (so courts should always first ascertain whether, absent section 3, there would be any breach of the Convention).

(b) If the court has to rely on section 3 it should limit the extent of the modified meaning to that which is necessary to achieve compatibility.

(c) Section 3 does not entitle the court to legislate (its task is still one of interpretation, but interpretation in accordance with the direction contained in section 3).

(d) The views of the parties and of the Crown as to whether a 'constructive' interpretation should be adopted cannot modify the task of the court (if section 3 applies the court is required to adopt the section 3 approach to interpretation).

(e) Where, despite the strong language of section 3, it is not possible to achieve a result which is compatible with the Convention, the court is not required to grant a declaration and presumably in exercising its discretion as to whether to grant a declaration or not it will be influenced by the usual considerations which apply to the grant of declarations.

3.11 A similar approach was taken by the House of Lords in *R v A (No 2)*,[3] by Lord Steyn thus:

> . . . the interpretative obligation under section 3 of the 1998 Act is a strong one. It applies even if there is no ambiguity in the language in the sense of the language being capable of two different meanings. It is an emphatic adjuration by the legislature: *R v Director of Public Prosecutions, Ex p Kebilene* [2000] 2 AC 326, per Lord Cooke of Thorndon, at p 373F; and my judgment, at p 366B. The White Paper made clear that the obligation goes far beyond the rule which enabled the courts to take the Convention into account in resolving any ambiguity in a legislative provision: see Rights Brought Home: The Human Rights Bill (1997) (Cm 3782), para 2.7. The draftsman of the Act had before him the slightly weaker model in section 6 of the New Zealand Bill of Rights Act 1990 but preferred stronger language. Parliament specifically rejected the legislative model of requiring a reasonable interpretation. Section 3 places a duty on the court to strive to find a possible interpretation compatible with Convention rights. Under ordinary methods of interpretation a court may depart from the language of the statute to avoid absurd consequences: section 3 goes much further. Undoubtedly, a court must always look for a contextual and purposive interpretation: section 3 is more radical in its effect. It is a general principle of the interpretation of legal instruments that the text is the

---

[3] [2002] 1 AC 45, [2001] UKHL 25 at [44].

primary source of interpretation: other sources are subordinate to it: compare, for example, articles 31 to 33 of the Vienna Convention on the Law of Treaties (1980) (Cmnd 7964). Section 3 qualifies this general principle because it requires a court to find an interpretation compatible with Convention rights if it is possible to do so. In the progress of the Bill through Parliament the Lord Chancellor observed that 'in 99% of the cases that will arise, there will be no need for judicial declarations of incompatibility' and the Home Secretary said 'We expect that, in almost all cases, the courts will be able to interpret the legislation compatibly with the Convention': Hansard (HL Debates), 5 February 1998, col 840 (3rd Reading) and Hansard (HC Debates), 16 February 1998, col 778 (2nd Reading). For reasons which I explained in a recent paper, this is at least relevant as an aid to the interpretation of section 3 against the executive: 'Pepper v Hart; A Re-examination' (2001) 21 Oxford Journal of Legal Studies 59; see also Professor J H Baker, 'Statutory Interpretation and Parliamentary Intervention' (1993) 52 CLJ 353. In accordance with the will of Parliament as reflected in section 3 it will sometimes be necessary to adopt an interpretation which linguistically may appear strained. The techniques to be used will not only involve the reading down of express language in a statute but also the implication of provisions. A declaration of incompatibility is a measure of last resort. It must be avoided unless it is plainly impossible to do so. If a clear limitation on Convention rights is stated in terms, such an impossibility will arise: *R v Secretary of State for the Home Department, Ex p Simms* [2000] 2 AC 115, 132A-B, per Lord Hoffmann.

D. The limits of section 3

Of course section 3 recognises that it may not be possible to give effect to Convention rights in every case, since it uses the phrase 'so far as it is possible'. What is the boundary over which the section 3 interpretative obligation must not stray? The answer is that the court or tribunal should not adopt a meaning inconsistent with a fundamental feature of the legislation being construed. It is vital to consider carefully the essential principles and scope of the legislation being interpreted. If the insertion of one word contradicts those principles or goes beyond the scope of the legislation, impermissible amendment occurs. **3.12**

This point emerged in *Bellinger v Bellinger*[4] where recognition of Mrs Bellinger, a male to female transsexual, as female for the purposes of section 11(c) of the Matrimonial Causes Act 1973, would have had excessively wide ramifications, raising issues unsuitable for court determination.[5] The House of Lords declined to read down the relevant legislation to such an effect. **3.13**

---

[4] [2003] 2 AC 467.
[5] See other examples such as *R (Anderson) v Secretary of State for the Home Department* [2003] 1 AC 837 at [30] and *Re S (Minors) (Care Order: Implementation of Care Plan)* [2002] 2 AC 291.

3.14 Conversely in *Ghaidan v Godin-Mendoza*[6] the Rent Act 1977 was rendered Convention-compliant as the underlying social policy was not changed by the proposed reading down of the text. The House of Lords decided that security of tenure under the Rent Act 1977 to the survivor of a couple living together as husband and wife was equally applicable to the survivor of a homosexual couple living together in a close and stable relationship. In this case the relevant section of the Rent Act was able to be read as though the survivor of such a homosexual couple were the surviving spouse of the original tenant so that cohabiting hetero-sexual couples and cohabiting homosexual couples could be treated alike for the purposes of succession as a statutory tenant.

E. What happens where compatible interpretation is not possible?

3.15 Where practitioners consider that it is not possible to read and give effect to legislation in a way which is compatible, there are three possible approaches that can be taken which are discussed below. The first is to seek an amendment of the law by consulting the relevant Department (see 3.53); the second is by a claim for a declaration of incompatibility (see 3.53–3.61); and the third is by a complaint to the ECtHR (see 3.63 and 4.74–4.77).

F. 'Giving effect'

3.16 It should be noted that the obligation in section 3 of the HRA 1998 is to 'read and give effect' to Convention rights. That is not the same as slavishly following the jurisprudence of the Convention. It means seeing what the Convention right provides in the context in which it is raised. It means understanding the context of the Act and the Convention and realising that these rights are fundamental. It also means realising that rights will come into conflict and that the rule of law requires that these conflicts are to be resolved in a way that follows established principles.

3.17 Courts and tribunals have already worked hard to understand this by training, by 'walk-throughs', and by their own self-education. The role of the practitioner will be to help the court or tribunal to understand the relevant Convention right, to identify the conflicting rights, if any, and to provide the arguments appropriate to the resolution of this task.

---

[6] [2004] 2 AC 557.

G. Compliance as a minimum requirement

Clearly, for courts or tribunals to afford better protection than the Convention **3.18** requires would be to act compatibly, so section 3 of the HRA 1998 is sometimes said to provide a floor for, not a ceiling on, the way in which fundamental human rights are to be afforded. This is important since the ECHR is by no means a comprehensive statement of all the rights that might be thought to be fundamental or basic human rights. For one thing the absence of a strong, free-standing equality clause in the ECHR is a critical fault. Domestic employment legislation and rights emanating from Europe provide much better protection of the human right to be treated equally (see Chapters 13 and 14). Likewise, workers' rights in relation to consultation or fair disciplinary procedures at work go much further than the ECHR specifically requires.

The aim of the provision is therefore to force, where possible, all legislative provi- **3.19** sions into the mould set by the Convention rights, while not reducing any better protection that might have been given.

H. Protection for existing human rights

It should be noted that the HRA 1998 explicitly protects *existing* human rights **3.20** (see s 11).

This provision will have most effect for the employment lawyer at the interface **3.21** between discrimination or equality law and other rights contained in the Act. The right to equality has long been recognised as a fundamental human right. The ECJ has called it a 'superior rule of law' for many years (see *Aktien Zuckerfabrik Schöppenstedt v Council of the European Communities*,[7] where this was first discussed) and it has found its way into many international human rights texts.[8]

So the protection of existing human rights means that the application of the **3.22** interpretative obligation to any discrimination legislation will be subject to this qualification. See Chapter 13, where this is discussed further in relation to equality.

---

[7] Case 5/71, [1971] ECR 975, at para 11.
[8] Perhaps most notably Art 26 of the International Covenant of Civil and Political Rights; but see also the equality conventions such as the International Convention on the Elimination of All Forms of Racial Discrimination (ICERD) and the Convention on the Elimination of All Forms of Discrimination Against Women (CEDAW) (see Chapter 13).

I. Autonomous concepts

3.23 Experience from training members of Employment Tribunals has shown that one of the most common mistakes in relation to the ECHR is to assume that it can be read like a British statute. Though Great Britain was heavily involved in the original drafting of the Convention, it does not follow that each provision can be read in such a way. There are at least two key reasons for this.

3.24 The Convention has to be seen in its international context. It was created by the agreement of different states having different laws, even if they had some legal traditions in common. It is not therefore to be interpreted in the way that it might be thought, simply by reference to the common law. It operates at a superior level. This idea of an autonomous concept, ie a concept having a meaning which is not owned by any one state that is party to the relevant international instrument, is key to understanding how these instruments work.

3.25 It is in any event a living instrument (see *Tyrer v UK*;[9] and see 3.28 below) which is to be interpreted in the light of modern understanding of the needs of society and the role of law.[10]

3.26 There are many examples of the way in which an autonomous meaning can affect the content of a Convention right (see in particular the discussion in relation to Article 6 ECHR in Chapter 6). The extent to which a tribunal or court will consider that it is restricted to the autonomous meaning when domestic law does not recognise the same constraints as might be found in other legal orders is as yet unclear. It is certain that a larger effect could be given in the UK under the HRA 1998 to a Convention right than might be given in a different legal order in another country. Equally, it is clear that a lesser meaning could not be given.

J. The relevance of ECHR jurisprudence in relation to Convention rights

3.27 The rights set out in the ECHR are paramount; by contrast, the jurisprudence of the institutions of the ECHR has a very important but secondary importance. This is because the HRA 1998 does not require courts or tribunals slavishly to

---

9 (1979–80) 2 EHRR 1.

10 The impact of this can be seen in the 'gays in the military' case, where in the Court of Appeal Sir Thomas Bingham MR recognised how time changes an approach to human rights for gays and lesbians: *R v MOD, ex parte Smith* [1996] 1 QB 517, at 554, and see also 583.

follow Convention jurisprudence but only to take it into account (see HRA 1998, s 2).

This reflects the way in which the institutions of the Convention have themselves **3.28** operated. In particular they have treated the Convention as a living instrument (see *Tyrer v UK*;[11] *Marckx v Belgium*;[12] *Dudgeon v UK*[13] and more recently *Johnston v Ireland*[14]) to be used and applied in a modern context and to give practical and effective rights (*Marckx v Belgium*, above). Accordingly, the context of any application is very important.

K. The ECHR is *not* to be read as a 'black letter' legal text

This is an important point about the way in which the ECHR is to be read. It **3.29** definitely should not be read as a 'black letter' law text. It is an international treaty whose text is authentic in more than one language. Its subject matter is rights and the treatment of individuals in a manner which respects, above all else, their dignity.

This is critical in understanding the Convention's provisions. It is sometimes **3.30** hard for those trained in the common law to follow. It might be thought that an international treaty would be construed in a strict way, so that anything that was not immediately obvious from the wording of the Convention was outside its ambit. But the ECHR must also be interpreted in accordance with good faith (Article 31 of the Vienna Convention on the Law of Treaties).

L. Positive obligations implied from the text of the ECHR

It should be noted that where the ECHR specifically prevents interference it **3.31** may also imply (even though it does not say so) that the state has positive obligations to secure compliance with the provisions of the Convention. Equally, where there are negative obligations it may be that positive obligations on the state are implied. The way in which such obligations can occur is discussed below in respect of each of the rights that are likely to have a substantial effect on the employment relationship.

---

[11] (1979–80) 2 EHRR 1.
[12] (1979) 2 EHRR 330.
[13] (1981) 4 EHRR 149.
[14] (1986) 9 EHRR 203.

M. Relationship with other interpretation rules

3.32 The obligation to read legislation compatibly applies to all legal persons, whether private or corporate, and to all courts, tribunals, ministers, civil servants and other office holders, and to all legislation. It has very important consequences for anyone taking decisions by reference to a statutory framework, because it means that all old common law rules of construction (including, for example, the *ejusdem generis* rule[15]) are now subordinated to it. This applies equally to the purposive construction of an Act of Parliament.

N. Purposive not literalistic approach needed

3.33 The House of Lords in *Ghaidan v Godin-Mendoza* also warned against an excessive concentration on linguistic features of the particular statute. Lord Steyn said[16] that:

> . . . nowhere in our legal system is a literalistic approach more inappropriate than when considering whether a breach of a Convention right may be removed by interpretation under section 3. Section 3 requires a broad approach concentrating, amongst other things, in a purposive way on the importance of the fundamental right involved.

He also described section 3 as the linchpin of the legislative scheme to achieve the purpose of bringing rights home.

3.34 This purposive construction is not of course unique to section 3. Since accession to the European Communities Treaties the domestic courts have been obliged to construe UK legislation in line with EU law; see *Pickstone v Freemans plc*[17] and *Litster v Forth Dry Dock & Engineering Co Ltd*.[18] As Lord Oliver of Aylmerton noted in *Litster*,[19] *Pickstone* had established that:

> . . . the greater flexibility available to the court in applying a purposive construction to legislation designed to give effect to the United Kingdom's Treaty obligations to the Community enables the court, where necessary, to supply by implication words appropriate to comply with those obligations . . .

---

[15] 'As the Latin words of the label attached to it suggest, the rule applies to cut down the generality of the expression "other" only where it is preceded by a list of two or more expressions having more specific meanings and sharing some common characteristics from which it is possible to recognise them as being species belonging to a single genus and to identify what the essential characteristics of that genus are' (*per* Lord Diplock in *Quazi v Quazi* [1980] AC 744, at 807).

[16] [2004] 2 AC 557 [41].

[17] [1989] 1 AC 66.

[18] [1990] 1 AC 546.

[19] [1990] 1 AC 546, 577A–B.

In both Community law and the Convention context, it is the effect of the words   **3.35**
implied rather than their number which matters.

O. Interpreting words such as 'just and equitable' and 'reasonable'

The interpretative obligation also means that phrases such as 'just and equitable'   **3.36**
and 'reasonable' have to be read in a way which is fully compatible with Convention
rights. Since these expressions appear in numerous places throughout employment law, it can be seen that this obligation is going to have an impact on many
occasions and not just when the state in any form is a party to the proceedings.[20]

There are many places in statutory employment law where 'just and equitable' or   **3.37**
'reasonable' appears. When section 98 of the Employment Rights Act 1996 (ERA
1996) requires the employment tribunal to determine an unfair dismissal case
'in accordance with equity and the substantial merits of the case', the tribunal
will need to interpret that expression in accordance with the HRA 1998. Thus
the question 'what are the substantial merits of the case?' will have to take into
account issues such as the right to respect for private and family life in Article 8
ECHR, and the right to respect for freedom, thought and conscience in Article 9
ECHR.[21]

So decisions that turn on the way in which a person has been afforded, for   **3.38**
instance, respect for his or her private and family life will immediately require the
tribunal to engage with the HRA 1998. In this very practical way the Act will
affect the way in which the tribunal will look at the facts. This in turn will affect
the way in which employers and employees will need to present them, and in turn
how employers and trade unions will develop policies. For instance, a firm which
offers no respect for private or family life, or respect for religious belief, is likely to
find that this will weigh against them where the case turns on, say, religious
observance or an interception of private correspondence.

This approach was taken in *X v Y*[22] and *Pay v Lancashire Probation Service*[23]   **3.39**
where the claimants were dismissed due to their activities outside work. It was
argued in both cases that such a dismissal was unfair under the ERA 1996 because

---

[20] For a wider discussion of such so-called 'horizontal effect' see M Hunt, 'The Horizontal Effect
of the Human Rights Act' [1998] PL 423.
[21] See the discussion in *X v Y* [2004] 1 ICR 1634 [64], and more generally in *Copsey v WWB
Devon Clays Ltd* [2005] EWCA Civ 932, [2005] 1 ICR 1789, [2005] IRLR 811.
[22] [2004] 1 ICR 1634.
[23] [2004] 1 ICR 187.

it involved a breach of their Article 8 right to respect for their private life and their Article 10 right of freedom of expression.

3.40   Both claimants sought to rely upon the interpretative legislation in section 3 of the HRA 1998 for the approach of the employment tribunal to section 98(4) of the ERA 1996. In *Pay* the European Appeal Tribunal (EAT) said[24] the impact of section 3 was that:

> It was not enough to judge the action of the employer simply by reference to what a reasonable employer would do in the circumstances without bringing into account the expectation that the reasonable employer would respect the fundamental rights of the individual and act proportionately to those rights.

3.41   Whilst in both cases the dismissal was found to be fair on the facts of the case, the EAT in *Pay* and the Court of Appeal in *X v Y* agreed that when deciding whether an employer has acted reasonably in dismissing an employee, the employment tribunal should interpret the words 'reasonably or unreasonably' in section 98(4) of the ERA 1996 as meaning 'reasonably or unreasonably having regard to the applicant's Convention rights'.

3.42   The impact of this was said by the Court in *Pay* to be that 'the circumstances' envisaged by section 98(4) should include those matters weighted in the balance in assessing first whether there had been an interference with a claimant's Convention rights and then points advanced by the employer as justification for an interference.

3.43   In *X v Y* the Court of Appeal said that the effect of this was that it would not normally be fair for an employer to dismiss an employee for a reason which was an unjustified interference with the employee's private life. Accordingly, in most cases a public authority employer will not act reasonably under section 98(4) if it violates an employee's rights guaranteed by the ECHR. For further discussion of the specific facts in *X v Y* and *Pay*, see Chapter 8 at 8.37–8.43 and Chapter 14 at 14.02–14.12. In particular, the guidance given by the Court of Appeal in applying Articles 8 and 14 and their relationship with section 3 in the context of an unfair dismissal case is set out in full at 8.41–8.43.

3.44   In *Foley v Post Office*[25] the range of reasonable responses test for unfair dismissal was reaffirmed. In *Pay* the EAT commented that in a case involving misconduct, the rules on unfair dismissal clarified by the Court of Appeal in *Foley* need to be considered in the light of Convention rights. If such clarification is carried out it

---

24 [2004] 1 ICR 187 [26].
25 [2000] 1 ICR 1283.

would be prudent to apply the interpretative obligations as explained by Lord Woolf in *Poplar* and *Re A (No 2)* (see 3.10–3.11 above).

In *B v BAA*[26] section 3 was applied to section 10(1) of the ERA 1996 which pro- **3.45** vides a legislative defence to a complaint of unfair dismissal where the dismissal is for the purpose of safeguarding national security concerns. The employment tribunal dismissed the complaint of unfair dismissal of an airport security guard as having no jurisdiction and on appeal it was argued that in order to comply with Convention rights section 10(1) had to be construed as only applicable to a Crown employer who can prove the requisite facts. The appellant submitted that Article 6 ECHR was engaged.

These arguments were rejected, but the EAT allowed the appeal on the basis that **3.46** section 10(1) had to be interpreted to include the impact of the section 98(4) (of the ERA 1996) test of fairness: that is whether the employer acted reasonably in dismissing the employee. This was a forthright example of section 3 of the HRA 1998 being used to overturn the national security exclusion.

So whilst employers can rely on section 10 of the ERA 1996 to oust unfair **3.47** dismissal claims in these circumstances, before the dismissal takes place such employers must apply the ordinary principles of fairness, including consultation and redeployment. Whether a court would read the fairness requirement into the context of a claim of someone who did not have jurisdiction due to age, work location, or lack of continuing service is perhaps unlikely.

Exclusory defences such as section 10(1) specifically prevent questions of reason- **3.48** ableness arising where dismissals take place for certain policy reasons. On one view the EAT's interpretation of section 10(1) ignores the intended purpose of the section and if so such an argument would be irrelevant. Thus, in *Ghaidan v Godin-Mendoza*,[27] Lord Steyn warned of the problems concerned where 'a judicial reading down, or reading in, under section 3 would flout the will of Parliament as expressed in the statute under examination'.

P. Citing ECHR jurisprudence

Section 2(2) of the HRA 1998 provides that rules may be prescribed for the giv- **3.49** ing of evidence in relation to any judgment, decision, declaration, or opinion of which account may be taken. There are no rules about the way in which the jurisprudence of the ECHR is to be taken into account in the employment tribunal,

---

[26] [2005] 1 ICR 1530.
[27] [2004] 2 AC 557 [40].

though it would be wise to note that the Civil Procedure Rules 1998 (CPR) do provide some guidance.[28]

Q. Statements of compatibility

3.50 Because compatibility is so important, and to underline the constitutional nature of this legislation, the HRA 1998 requires Ministers to make statements of compatibility in relation to any Bill of which they have charge in either House of Parliament (see s 19). Thus a Minister will have had to have thought about the implications of the legislation before it is introduced and to have kept them in mind as it proceeds. In practice this has not yet worked as well as it might, since the Race Relations Act Amendment Bill, when introduced, contained such a statement yet excluded the concept of indirect discrimination from its purview. Fortunately this was put right later. Nevertheless, this indicates the extent to which a cultural change in Whitehall (as well as everywhere else) has been required.

3.51 The government announced that it would set up a joint Human Rights Committee of both Houses which would assist the supervisory work of Parliament in this respect. This has performed an additional role of supervision since it started work at the beginning of 2001.

3.52 In those cases where the Minister cannot make a statement of compatibility, he or she must say so and state that the government nevertheless wishes the relevant House to proceed with the Bill (see HRA 1998, s 19(1)(b)). Hence in future, where there is an issue of compatibility, practitioners will want to consult the debates in Parliament, including any discussion of the Ministers' statements by the Joint Committee.

R. Consultation with departments

3.53 Where practitioners find what they consider is an incompatibility in a primary or secondary legislative measure, it would be sensible to raise this with the relevant department as soon as possible. This is likely to be the Department of Trade and Industry (responsible for tribunals), the Department for Work and Pensions (responsible for some legislation), the Home Office (responsible for some equalities issues, though not usually employment issues), the Department for Communities and Local Government (responsible for some equality matters), or the Ministry of Justice (responsible for the courts).

---

[28] No rules have been made; but see also *Barclays Bank v Ellis* The Times, 24 October 2000, in which the Court of Appeal said copies of decisions should be made available.

S. Declarations of incompatibility

If legislation cannot be interpreted compatibly with the ECHR, a court may **3.54**
make a 'declaration of incompatibility' (see HRA 1998, s 4). This is the second
route to a remedy for a deficiency in legislation. Once such a declaration is made
it will trigger certain remedial powers pursuant to section 10 of the Act. The exercise of these powers lies principally in the hands of the government. Applications
for such a declaration are likely to be made by way of application for judicial
review to the Administrative Court, but they do not have to be. They could
be made in relation to another claim, and could be the subject of a claim for a
declaration in ordinary civil proceedings.

However, there are no provisions for employment tribunals or for the EAT to **3.55**
make such declarations.[29] This seems a mistake, and it is to be hoped that in due
course this will change. In practice what is likely to happen is that the employment tribunal will express a view that it is bound by the words of a legislative
provision and so cannot give effect to Convention rights in the context before it.
Since the tribunal is under an obligation to give reasons for its judgment pursuant
to rule 30 of the 2004 Rules of Procedure,[30] it is likely that this will be quite clear
from the reasoning that it employs. However, the decision of the employment
tribunal will not by itself give rise to the remedial power.

An example of this problem is provided by *Younas v Chief Constable of the Thames* **3.56**
Valley Police,[31] where the EAT was asked to find that section 200 of the ERA 1996
(which precluded a police officer from bringing a claim for unfair dismissal), was
incompatible with Articles 6 and 14 ECHR. The EAT held that it had no power
to make a declaration of incompatibility and had to apply section 200 of the ERA
1996 as its meaning was clear, regardless of whether it was incompatible with
Convention rights. While this appeal ended positively for the appellant, in that his
appeal succeeded on another ground, the HRA 1998 was of no assistance to him.

Similarly, in *Whittaker v P and D Watson (t/a P and M Watson Haulage)*,[32] the **3.57**
applicant argued that the small employer exemption under the Disability
Discrimination Act 1995 was incompatible with Article 6 rights to a fair trial.

---

[29] However, the EAT Practice Direction 2004 recognises that where such a declaration is sought
it may provide a special reason for the appeal to be heard and indeed heard swiftly so that the matter
can go to the Court of Appeal which could make such a declaration: [2005] ICR 637.

[30] See Sch 1 to the Employment Tribunals (Constitution and Rules etc) Regulations 2004,
SI 2004/1717.

[31] [2001] All ER (D) 14.

[32] [2002] ICR 1244.

Lindsay J found that the drafting of the HRA 1998 did not give the EAT jurisdiction to issue a declaration of incompatibility, and called upon the legislature to consider amending the HRA 1998.

3.58 There is no reason of principle why declarations of incompatibility should not be determined by the EAT, which is a superior court of record with a key appellate function. It is therefore to be hoped that this deficiency will be remedied in the future.

3.59 Certain steps are necessary before a court with jurisdiction can make such a declaration. Section 5(1) of the HRA 1998 provides that 'where a court is considering whether to make a declaration of incompatibility, the Crown is entitled to notice in accordance with rules of court'. It is intended that the Crown should be notified at the earliest time, rather than just before a declaration is made, but that the notification should be by the court. In practice, an application for judicial review will put the Crown on notice at an early stage. Indeed, if the process of consultation referred to above has taken place this will have happened even earlier. While there is a requirement for the Crown to be notified, it should be noted that there is no requirement for the Crown to intervene.[33]

3.60 The relevant person for notification is likely to be the person named in the list published by HM Treasury under section 17 of the Crown Proceedings Act 1947. The notice should contain sufficient details to identify the claim, the parties to the claim, the court, the Convention rights under consideration, and a short statement of the issues that have led to the court considering making a declaration of incompatibility.

3.61 Once the court gives notice,[34] however, it will need to allow the Crown a minimum period of time to determine whether it wishes to be joined.[35] It is likely that

---

[33] In its consultation document the Lord Chancellor's Department has said that '. . . Under Section 5(1), we propose that it will be the Court that provides notice to the Crown once it begins to consider making a declaration of incompatibility, rather than the parties. This is because it is the Court that is considering making the declaration and it is the Court that will be best placed to provide useful information to the Crown to enable it to determine whether it wishes to be joined as a party. This approach gives the Court prime responsibility for managing the case, as encouraged in the Civil Procedure Rules.'

[34] The Lord Chancellor's Department has said that '. . . Where the Minister has nominated a person to be joined as a party the notice must be accompanied by the written nomination. Notice should be given to the relevant Government Department (or if none, or if the court is uncertain which is the relevant department, the Attorney General) even where the Crown is already party to the proceedings in some other capacity. This is to ensure that the specific issue of the fact that the Court is considering making a declaration of incompatibility is considered appropriately by the Crown . . .'.

[35] Section 5(3) of the HRA 1998 provides that notice by the Crown under s 5(2) that it wishes to take up its entitlement to be joined as a party can be given at any time during the proceedings.

the Crown should be allowed 21 days in the first instance to state whether it wishes to be joined as a party, *unless* the circumstances of the case mean that the court orders otherwise, but that the Crown would be able to apply, if necessary, for an extension of the time limit.

T. Quashing or disapplying subordinate legislation

Regulations and orders which cannot be interpreted in a way which is compatible with the ECHR may be quashed unless it is necessary that such subordinate legislation be made as a result of the wording of the primary legislation. Difficult issues can arise as to the effect of and proper way to deal with subordinate legislation which was made within the scope of the primary legislation prior to 2 October 2000 but which has since become unlawful.[36]   **3.62**

U. Applying to the ECtHR

Ultimately, where a person cannot achieve an adequate remedy under the procedures available under the HRA 1988, he or she will have the right to complain to the ECtHR. This is discussed further at 4.74–4.77. Practitioners should note that there is a time limit.   **3.63**

V. Frequently asked questions

How can UK law be read as being compliant with the standards of the ECHR?   **3.64**

By applying section 3 of the HRA 1998 which provides for an interpretative obligation. The courts must try to give effect to domestic legislation in a way which is compatible with Convention rights, so far as it is possible to do so.

How powerful is the interpretative obligation in section 3 of the HRA 1998?

Section 3 is regarded as having quasi-constitutional status and it may require a court to go as far as reading in words to the legislation to make it Convention-compliant.

---

[36] For more detailed consideration of these issues, see AW Bradley, R Allen, and P Sales, 'The Impact of the Human Rights Act 1998 upon subordinate legislation promulgated before 2nd October 2000' [2000] PL 358.

Is there a limit beyond which the powers enacted in section 3 should not stray?

No meaning should be adopted which goes beyond the scope of the legislation being construed.

What happens if legislation cannot be construed compatibly with the HRA 1998?

Where a compatible reading is not achievable via section 3, possible solutions are:
- *seeking an amendment by consulting the relevant government department;*
- *claiming a declaration of incompatibility;*
- *making a complaint to the ECtHR.*

What role does the HRA 1998 play regarding existing human rights?

Compliance with the HRA is a minimum requirement for domestic legislation. Existing human rights are to be protected by section 11 of the HRA 1998: including the right to equal treatment.

How is the ECHR to be read in today's society?

The ECHR is to be interpreted with reference to contemporary society in a practical and effective way. Accordingly, Convention jurisprudence should not be followed slavishly nor should the ECHR be read as a 'black letter' law text. The state may have positive obligations to secure compliance. Common law rules of construction are subordinated to the section 3 interpretative rule. Section 3 requires a purposive approach.

How should phrases which commonly appear in an employment law context such as 'just and equitable' and 'reasonable' be interpreted?

These phrases should be read with regard to an individual's Convention rights (see X v Y[37]), but section 3 cannot oust statutory defences such as national security exclusions or jurisdiction thresholds.

When will a court make a 'declaration of incompatibility'?

Where it is believed there is a deficiency in legislation, the most common route to seeking such a declaration is by way of an application of judicial review in the administrative court. The EAT has not been given powers to make such declarations to date.

---

[37] [2004] 1 ICR 1634.

4

THE DUTY TO GIVE EFFECT TO CONVENTION RIGHTS

A. Introduction

4.01 The second key mechanism by which the HRA 1998 operates is to impose a duty to give effect to Convention rights. This duty is placed directly on public authorities; though indirectly it will affect almost all companies or individuals. The duty on public authorities is to be found in section 6(1):

> It is unlawful for a public authority to act in a way which is incompatible with a Convention right.

4.02 Section 7 of the HRA 1998 enables section 6 to be relied upon in proceedings. It allows a person who considers that a public authority has acted unlawfully in breach of section 6 to bring proceedings against that authority if he or she is a victim (see 4.61 below).

4.03 Section 6 of the HRA 1998 is the gateway through which Convention rights permeate the actions of all public authorities. It is therefore as important as section 3 in bringing the Convention rights set out in Schedule 1 to the HRA 1998 into life in the domestic context.

4.04 The key questions about section 6 relate to the extent of its reach. The concept of a public authority is not at all simple and has led to some confusing and surprising jurisprudence. This chapter aims to help understanding of how section 6 should work in an employment context.

B. The nature of the duty on public authorities under section 6

4.05 This duty works with the interpretative obligation in section 3 of the HRA 1998, to reinforce it and to ensure that effect is given to Convention rights at all times, not only when there is a relevant piece of pre-existing legislation. It imposes a strong obligation on any person or body which carries out state functions to ensure that Convention rights are respected.

4.06 This obligation to give effect to Convention rights is stronger than the interpretative obligation in section 3, since it does not have the formula 'so far as it is possible' found in section 3(1). Nevertheless, section 6(2) does not require public authorities to give a different effect to legislation than that required by section 3. So where a public authority has a discretionary power, it must be exercised in a way which is compatible with Convention rights, but not where the authority is under a conflicting legislative duty.[1]

---

[1] See 3.12–3.14 above as to when the limits of s 3 are reached.

Since public authorities have many powers and discretions, the full extent of the **4.07** reach of this enactment has been very hard to predict: see *Parochial Church Council of the Parishes of Aston Cantlow and Wilmcote with Billesley, Warwickshire v Wallbank*;[2] *R (on the application of Heather and another) v Leonard Cheshire Foundation*;[3] and *R (A and others) v Partnerships in Care Limited*.[4] The key question is to identify a public authority within section 6.

C. Who are 'public authorities' for the purposes of the HRA 1998?

The definition in section 6(3) is not straightforward since it extends potentially **4.08** to companies and authorities that might not have been thought, at first sight, to have been included. Secondly, it is a new concept that sits rather uneasily with the Community law concepts with which employment law practitioners will be familiar.

Public authorities come in two sorts: obvious public bodies and hybrid bodies. **4.09** Thus the HRA 1998 defines public authority in section 6(3) as including:

(a) a court or tribunal; and
(b) any person certain of whose functions are functions of a public nature.

In the latter case the body is only to be treated as a public authority when the relevant act or omission which is under scrutiny has a public nature (s 6(5)).

The House of Lords considered when a body was acting as a public authority **4.10** in the *Aston Cantlow* case and held that a 'public authority' could be either a core public authority exercising governmental functions all of a public nature, or a hybrid public authority some of whose functions were of a public nature. Its emphasis was on the question whether the act (or omission) in question was governmental.[5]

The House of Lords did not discuss the other leading cases at a lower level on this **4.11** point, particularly the *Leonard Cheshire* case which took what might be described as a more restrictive view on the test to be applied. There is therefore a potential dichotomy in the jurisprudence and this is discussed further at 4.21 onwards.

---

2 [2003] UKHL 37, [2004] 1 AC 546.
3 [2002] EWCA 366, [2002] 2 All ER 936.
4 [2002] EWHC 529 (Admin), [2002] 1 WLR 2610.
5 It is noteworthy that in this context it had to consider the role of the Church of England. It held that although the Church of England, as the established church, had special links with central government and performed certain public functions, it was essentially a religious organisation and not a governmental organisation, even when seeking to enforce a repairing obligation to a church.

(1) Excluded bodies

4.12 Some public authorities are expressly and clearly excluded from these provisions:

(a) Parliament (but not the House of Lords in its judicial capacity) (s 6(3) and (4));

(b) a person exercising functions in connection with proceedings in Parliament (s 6(3)); and

(c) a tribunal exercising a jurisdiction in which legal proceedings are not concerned, ie in relation to purely spiritual matters (see the definition of 'tribunal' in s 21(1)).

(2) A functional test

4.13 Whatever view is taken about the right way to identify when a hybrid body is acting as a public authority it is clear that a body is not a 'public authority' unless it has a public function. Therefore the concept has a meaning that encompasses more than just the state and local authorities. It includes others exercising statutory or prerogative powers, and by reason of section 6(3)(b) even includes some privatised companies.

4.14 During the passage of the HRA 1998 through Parliament the Lord Chancellor said in the House of Lords[6] that a privatised company such as Railtrack Ltd, which then had both commercial functions in relation to railway property and public functions as a safety regulator, would be included within the definition of 'public authority' in section 6(3)(b).[7] Such bodies are referred to below as 'non-exclusively public bodies' or hybrid authorities.

4.15 The ambit of section 6 is less clearly limited in relation to those bodies which are within the definition of a public authority 'by virtue only' of section 6(3)(b). When the act (or omission) of such a body under scrutiny is 'private', it is not a 'public authority' in relation to that act (see 4.16 below). In this way the HRA 1998 has not brought directly within the section 6 duty the private acts of bodies who would not normally be treated as public authorities but for section 6(3)(b).

(3) Private acts

4.16 It must be remembered that the process of employment is not usually considered as an essentially governmental or public law activity. Most acts in relation to

---

6 *Hansard*, HL col 811 (24 November 1997); and see also the Home Secretary, *Hansard*, HC col 775 (16 February 1998).

7 Although see *Cameron and others v Network Rail Infrastructure Ltd* [2006] EWHC 1133, [2007] 1 WLR 163 decided following the loss of Railtrack's regulatory responsibilities, where it was held no longer to be such a public body.

individual employment are treated by the courts as 'private' acts. Judicial review will not normally be available in relation to individual employment issues (*R v East Berkshire Health Authority, ex parte Walsh*[8]), but it may be available in relation to collective decisions such as mass redundancies (*R v Liverpool CC, ex parte Ferguson*[9]).

Accordingly, complaints of breach of the Convention by hybrid authorities in relation to individual employment matters will not normally be within section 6 of the HRA 1998. They will have to be brought in other ways. Notwithstanding this, the interpretative obligation in section 3 will still apply to any court or tribunal concerned with other complaints between the parties. So this limitation on the scope of section 6(1) will principally have the effect of immunising such non-exclusively public bodies from claims for remedies directly caused by a failure to afford Convention rights.   **4.17**

D. When is a hybrid authority a public authority for the purposes of section 6?

This question is proving very difficult to answer with complete certainty. However, there are certain pointers. If the body's activities under scrutiny are regulated in some way that may be an indicator but will not be decisive, since they may have been allocated those functions by another body which is a public authority in all that it does: see *R (on the application of Heather and another) v Leonard Cheshire Foundation.*[10]   **4.18**

In that case it was also held that 'while the degree of public funding of the activities of an otherwise private body is certainly relevant as to the nature of the functions performed, by itself it is not determinative of whether the functions are public or private'.[11]   **4.19**

In the end the best test for determining when a hybrid body is acting as a public authority is perhaps to ask whether they are acting solely as a contractor or in a way which is properly characterised as governmental. This still somewhat restricted view of section 6, given in *Aston Cantlow,* and at the heart of *Leonard Cheshire,* has led to much discussion of its implications.   **4.20**

---

8 [1984] ICR 743.
9 The Times, 20 November 1985.
10 [2002] EWCA 366, [2002] 2 All ER 936.
11 See para 35 of the Court of Appeal judgment.

E. Implications of a limited interpretation of when a hybrid body has 'public functions'

4.21   First, it is argued that the aim of the HRA 1998 to 'bring rights home' will be eroded by the current trend of increasing privatisation and contracting-out a risk, unless a broad scope is given to the term 'public authority'. This was very much the argument (that was unsuccessful) in *Leonard Cheshire*.

4.22   The Joint Committee on Human Rights in 2003–2004 carried out an inquiry into the possible consequences of the courts' interpretation of 'public authority' for human rights protection in the UK. This inquiry explored how human rights accountability could be assured, in the context of increased delegation from the public to the private and voluntary sectors.

4.23   The context for the inquiry was the decision of the courts (such as *Leonard Cheshire*; see above) which had interpreted section 6 of the HRA 1998 so as to exclude from responsibility under the HRA 1998 many of the increasing number of private or voluntary sector organisations active in the provision of public services.

4.24   Whilst during the pre-HRA 1998 debates on the Human Rights Bill, Parliament took the view that responsibility to comply with Convention rights under section 6(3)(b) would depend on the nature of the functions a body performed; a line of cases regarding the application of section 6(3)(b) appeared to reject this approach, instead suggesting that a private organisation will often only fall within the ambit of section 6(3)(b) where its structures and work are inextricably 'enmeshed' with the delegating state body. See on this point the following:

- *Poplar Housing and Regeneration Community Association v Donoghue*:[12] a housing association providing rented accommodation on behalf of a local authority did, in performing that function, fall within section 6(3)(b). However, the court held that 'the fact that a body performs an activity which otherwise a public body would be under a duty to perform cannot mean that such performance is necessarily a public function'.[13] The most important factor in the court's conclusion was that the role of the housing association in providing accommodation for D was so closely assimilated to that of the local authority (or 'enmeshed' in the local authority's activities) that it was in this respect performing public functions.

---

[12] [2001] EWCA Civ 595.
[13] See judgment of Lord Woolf at para 58.

- *R (Heather) v Leonard Cheshire Foundation [2002] 2 All ER 936*: a charity managing a care home for the elderly was not exercising public functions albeit that it was doing so under a statutory arrangement (and the claimants' places were publicly funded). The court relied on the following facts:
  - there was no material distinction between the nature of the services provided to publicly and privately funded clients;
  - the Foundation was not 'standing in the shoes' of the local authority and was not exercising statutory powers in performing functions for the claimants.

- *R (A) v Partnerships in Care Ltd [2002] 1 WLR 2611*: a private provider of mental health care, in making a decision to change the focus of the ward on which the claimant was housed, was a hybrid authority exercising a public function. The Court of Appeal in A's case focused on the particular decision and function in question. The decision related to the question of whether adequate staff and facilities would be provided to enable A to receive the appropriate treatment. The hospital was directly responsible for providing staff and facilities as the registered person under the Registered Homes Act 1984. There was a public interest in ensuring that A received the appropriate treatment and care. The hospital was compared with a prison in this respect; the court also noted that A's admission to hospital was similarly compulsory.

- *R (Beer) v Hampshire Farmers' Markets Ltd*:[14] a private company set up to run a farmers' market was performing a public function in refusing to grant a farmer a licence. In reaching this decision, the court relied on the following facts:
  - the power to control access to the market had a public element or flavour;
  - there was a very strong institutional link with the county council: the company owed its existence to the council, was set up by that council, had stepped into the shoes of the council in this area and was assisted by the council in a number of ways.

4.25

Accordingly, the concern arose that the narrower the interpretation given under section 6, the less expansive the scope of the HRA 1998. The Committee concluded in February 2004 that:

> ... application of the functional public authority provision in section 6(3)(b) of the Human Rights Act leaves real gaps and inadequacies in human rights protection in the UK, including gaps that affect people who are particularly vulnerable to ill-treatment. We consider that this deficit in protection may well leave the UK in breach of its international obligations to protect the Convention rights of all those in the jurisdiction and to provide mechanisms for redress where those rights are breached.

---

[14] [2004] 1 WLR 223.

4.26 A whole range of possible solutions were considered and ultimately rejected by the Committee. These included:

— Not to recommend the amendment of s 6 since it was too soon since the HRA had come into force and amendment could hinder the HRA's flexibility.

— Not to specify the bodies whose activities fall within the ambit of HRA, particularly since it is the function of the body which determines whether the body falls within the ambit of s 6(3)(b) on any particular occasion.

— Not to introduce a 'horizontal' application of the HRA's provisions, through the duty on the courts to act compatibly with Convention rights and to interpret the law so far as possible in compliance with those principles.

— Not to make public authorities remain responsible for the actions of those to whom they delegate the discharge of their functions thought to provide sufficient redress.

— Not to include terms guaranteeing human rights protection in contracts between private or voluntary bodies delivering public services and the contracting authority or individual user nor to impose best practice in the formulation of contracts via government guidance.

4.27 Instead, the Joint Committee decided the government needed to intervene in the public interest as a third party in cases where it could press the case for a broad, functional interpretation of the meaning of public authority under the HRA 1998.

4.28 The principles which would close the gap in protection resulting from some of the early decisions on the application of the 'public function' test were those which set out a wide category of 'functional' public authorities identified on the basis of public function.

4.29 The Joint Committee believed this to be consistent with House of Lords' interpretation of section 6 in *Aston Cantlow and Wilmcote Parochial Church Council*,[15] which they summarised as concluding that a narrow category of 'pure' public authorities should be complemented by a wide category of 'functional' public authorities identified on the basis of public function.

4.30 In particular, Lord Nicholls held that a 'generously wide' scope should be given to the expression of 'public function' in section 6(3)(b), and further said that the factors to be taken into account in deciding whether a function was public should include:

> . . . the extent to which in carrying out the relevant function the body is publicly funded, or is exercising statutory powers, or is taking the place of central government or local authorities, or is providing a public service ([11]–[12]).

---

15 [2004] 1 AC 546.

The Committee concluded that a body should be defined as a functional public **4.31** authority performing a public function under section 6(3)(b):

> . . . where it exercises a function that has its origin in governmental responsibilities, in such a way as to compel individuals to rely on that body for realisation of their Convention human rights.[16]

There are mixed indications as to whether the Committee's 'interpretation' strat- **4.32** egy is likely to be successful. In *R (Beer) v Hampshire Farmers' Markets Ltd*, the Court of Appeal explicitly stated that it did not consider the House of Lords to have disapproved *Leonard Cheshire* or *Donoghue*.[17]

In *R (on the application of West) v Lloyd's of London*,[18] the Court of Appeal cited **4.33** both *Leonard Cheshire* and *Donoghue* at length, and although it also referred to *Aston Cantlow*, did not quote Lord Nicholls' comments in favour of a wide reading of section 6(3)(b). It is fair to say, however, that Lord Nicholls' approach would probably have made little difference to the conclusion that, in approving minority buy-outs in underwriting syndicates of which the claimant was a member, Lloyd's Business Conduct Committee was not exercising a public function.

In a more recent case, *R (Mullins) v The Appeal Board of the Jockey Club and The* **4.34** *Jockey Club*,[19] Stanley Burnton J decided that a key determinant of whether or not a function is public and thus subject to judicial review and the HRA 1998 is whether that function is integral to the discharge of statutory or other governmental functions as opposed to the activity being conducted merely under contract.

In reaching this conclusion, he quoted from the opinions of Lord Hope and Lord **4.35** Rodger in *Aston Cantlow*. From their speeches, he extracted the principle that the question is whether the body 'carries out, either generally or on the relevant occasion, the kind of public function of government which would engage the responsibility of the United Kingdom before the Strasbourg organs'. This approach appears much closer to that advocated by the Joint Committee.

On the facts of the case, Stanley Burnton J concurred with the previous decision **4.36** of the Court of Appeal in *R v Disciplinary Committee of the Jockey Club, ex parte Aga Khan*,[20] that Jockey Club decisions were not amenable to judicial review as the Club had not been woven into any system of governmental control of horse racing. Its functions could be described as public, in that they affected the public

---

[16] Joint Committee On Human Rights — Seventh Report dated 23 February 2004 [Session 2003–04] see www.publications.parliament.uk.

[17] *Per* Dyson LJ at [25].

[18] [2004] EWCA Civ 506, [2004] 3 All ER 251.

[19] [2005] EWHC 2197 (Admin); Times Law Reports 24 October 2005.

[20] [1993] 1 WLR 909.

and were exercised in the interest of the public, but not governmental. It is not entirely clear whether Stanley Burnton J's understanding of 'governmental' functions accords with the wide definition given to the term by Lord Nicholls in *Aston Cantlow*.[21]

4.37 Two very recent cases provide further evidence of continuing confusion. In *Cameron v Network Rail Infrastructure Ltd*,[22] Sir Michael Turner focused on the speeches in *Aston Cantlow*, but again moved away from the emphasis on 'functions', suggesting that this could result in circularity. He referred in particular to an article by Dawn Oliver,[23] and focused on 'acting altruistically and in the public interest' as key indicators of public functions. This analysis, together with the loss of Railtrack's regulatory functions, led him to conclude that it did not fall within section 6(3)(b).

4.38 In *R (on the application of Johnson and others) v Havering London Borough Council*,[24] Forbes J considered whether section 6(3)(b) led to the conclusion that the HRA 1998 would apply directly against a private sector operator of care homes for the elderly.

4.39 He held that he was bound by the decision in *Leonard Cheshire*, which he said was a similar case on the facts, as he did not consider that the principles to be derived from *Aston Cantlow* and Strasbourg authorities cited to him[25] justified a departure from Lord Woolf's approach in *Leonard Cheshire*. He specifically rejected an argument that *Aston Cantlow* required a wider construction of the section.

4.40 Partly as a result of the interpretative difficulties arising out of these cases, Paul Burstow MP introduced a private members bill under the ten minute rule seeking (amongst other things) to amend section 6(3) of the HRA 1998 so as to define 'public authority' to include 'a care home within the meaning of section 3 of the Care Standards Act 2000'. This 'Care of Older People (Human Rights) Bill' did not go to second reading since on 20 October 2006 the Bill came before the House but was not moved.[26] However, the proposals garnered a certain amount of publicity and helped to draw attention to the perceived loophole.

---

21 At [9].

22 [2006] EWHC 1133 (QB), [2007] 1 WLR 163.

23 'The Frontiers of the State: Public Authorities and Public Functions under the Human Rights Act' [2000] PL 476.

24 [2006] EWHC 1714, (2006) Lloyd's Rep Med 447.

25 *Van der Mussele v Belgium* (1984) 6 EHRR 163 at 170–1, paras 28–30; *Costello-Roberts v United Kingdom* (1995) 19 EHRR 112 at 131–3, paras 25–8; *Wos v Poland* Application 22860/02 (1 March 2005) paras 52–78; *Buzescu v Romania* Application 61302/00, (24 May 2005) para 78; *Sychev v Ukraine* Application 4773/02 (11 October 2005) paras 52–6, for discussion of the principles of state responsibility for violations of Convention rights by 'private' bodies.

26 See *Hansard* report at <http://www.publications.parliament.uk/pa/cm200506/cmhansrd/cm061020/debtext/61020-0003.htm#06102037000862>.

(1) Questions to ask to help identify whether a body is a public authority

With these points in mind the following list of questions is intended to help identify   **4.41**
whether a person or body is a 'public authority' for the purposes of the HRA 1998.

If the answer to any or all of the following questions is 'Yes', it is possible that the
Act will apply directly to the work of the body, even though it is a limited com-   **4.42**
pany or a partnership, or a charity or an organisation working under a Royal
Charter, or just an ordinary person doing some business.[27]

However, in considering the examples below, it is important to bear in mind that
the answer to the question may vary, depending on whether the wider *Aston*   **4.43**
Cantlow approach, or the narrower *Donoghue/Leonard Cheshire* approach is
applied by the court. The position will hopefully be clarified by the pending
House of Lords decision in Y. L.

Q   Does the body perform work or operate in the public domain as an integral part of a
   statutory system which performs public law duties?
   Example: A body carrying out a school inspection for OFSTED.

Q   Does the body carry out work of public significance?
   Example: A body which sets, monitors, and controls professional standards.

Q   Will legal rights or obligations be affected in the performance of the duty?
   Example: A private school providing special education to a child for whom there is a
   statement of special educational needs (although in *Donoghue*, the Court of Appeal
   stated that if a local authority, in order to fulfil its duty, sent a child to a private school,
   this would not mean the private school was performing public functions).

Q   Could an individual be deprived of some legitimate expectation in performance of the
   work of the body?
   Example: A professional body might act in a way which deprived a professional of an
   expectation that he or she would be able to practise his or her profession (see by analogy
   the decision in *R (Beer) v Hampshire Farmers' Markets Ltd*).

Q   Are there legal provisions which particularly cover the work that is done by the body by
   imposing powers and duties on it?
   Example: A charity providing family planning and abortion advice (although see *R (on
   the application of West) v Lloyd's of London*, where the power to enable minority buy-outs
   was conferred under a private Act of Parliament via the Major Syndicate Transactions
   Byelaw, but was not a public function).

Q   Even if not a statutory body, is the body established under the authority of any national
   or local government body?
   Example: A company set up under local authority economic development powers.

Q   Is the work supported by statutory powers and penalties?
   Example: A company under contract to run a failing school (although see again the
   decision in *Leonard Cheshire*[28]).

---

[27] See also the Core Guidance for Public Authorities published by the Home Office at <http://
www.scotland.gov.uk/Resource/Doc/1097/0000654.pdf>.
[28] At para 35.

Q Does the body do work that national or local government would otherwise perform? *Example:* A private hospital which undertook to carry out health care for a local health authority (although this may be in doubt following the *Leonard Cheshire* decision). Also a body like the Press Council might be considered to have public functions.

Q Is the body under a duty to act judicially in exercising what amount to public powers? *Example:* Although a body like the Jockey Club might have been considered to have public functions, Stanley Burnton J came to the opposite conclusion in *R (Mullins) v The Appeal Board of the Jockey Club and The Jockey Club.*

If the answer to any of these questions is 'Yes', it is possible that some of the work will be as a public authority within the scope of the HRA 1998. It will need to be assessed for the possible implications of the Act.

(2) Examples of public functions of otherwise private bodies

4.44 There follow some more examples of how section 6 of the HRA 1998 will work.

(i) A security company running a private prison

This may seem fairly straightforward. Nobody can be detained in this country without the authority of law. The private security company will probably have entered into a contract with the government to run the prison, and will receive prisoners only because they have been sent there by the Prison Service either after conviction, or because bail has not been granted. But in running that prison the company is clearly carrying out public functions. The Act applies to it.

(ii) Store security officers

4.45 A private security company will not just run prisons; it might install security devices in premises. That probably is not a public function. But sometimes security firms provide security in department stores. The security personnel will be responsible for arresting suspected shoplifters. The criminal process is essentially of a public nature, so a private security guard whose job involves making arrests is likely to be carrying out work of a public nature.

(iii) Regulatory bodies

4.46 This is a good example of a body that would once have fallen within section 6(3)(b) changing in nature such that it is no longer caught by the Act. As originally constituted, Railtrack had regulatory duties as a privatised company, which included the regulation of safety on the railways. These were public functions which were covered by the HRA 1998. However, when the Railways (Safety Case) Regulations 2000[29] came into force, Railtrack lost its regulatory function.

---

[29] SI 2000/2688.

In *Cameron v Network Rail Infrastructure Ltd*,[30] the High Court held that, as a result, it no longer had 'public functions', and was not a public authority within section 6 of the HRA 1998.

(iv) The privatised utilities

When they carry out public functions, the privatised utilities will certainly be **4.47** responsible under the HRA 1998.

(v) A firm under contract to provide car tow-away services

When the meter runs out and the car is no longer lawfully parked, the company **4.48** that comes and takes the car to the pound is carrying out public services and must comply with the HRA 1998.

(vi) A charity cafe in a hospital

This is a more difficult example, but it is possible that the cafe could be providing **4.49** a public function to assist the health authority with the care of its patients while they are waiting to be treated. However, if the approach in *Poplar Housing Association Ltd v Donoghue* is adopted, the cafe would in all probability not fall within section 6(3)(b). This example appears similar to that of a small hotel providing bed and breakfast accommodation as a temporary measure at the request of a housing authority, to which the Court of Appeal in *Donoghue* said the Act would not apply.

(vii) A housing association

Whilst it might be thought that a housing association, operating under a **4.50** statutory framework, would undoubtedly be covered by the HRA 1998, some doubt has been cast on this general proposition by *Poplar Housing Association v Donoghue*. If the test in that case is to be followed, the particular facts of each case will have to be examined closely.

F. What are private acts of non-exclusively public bodies?

An example might be where a charity is raising money for its funds; in such a case **4.51** it is probably acting privately. Decisions about employment, such as who to employ and what the terms of that employment might be, are likely to be seen as private acts. The critical point is whether the act is one which is fulfilling a public function. Thus, in a registered care home the delivery of the care plan is likely to be a public function; the recruitment of the staff is not. When a company

---

[30] [2006] EWHC 1133 (QB), [2007] 1 WLR 163.

running a private school is taking a decision about who will supply it with services such as telecommunications or stationery, it is acting in a private way. When it is making decisions about the way it will provide the services in the school it is carrying out public functions.

G. The relationship between the concept of a public authority under the HRA 1998 and the Community law concept of the emanation of the state

4.52 These provisions raise difficult issues at the interface with European Community law. Employers who are non-exclusively public authorities may well be emanations of the state within Community law. If so, employees can directly rely on Directives against them (*Foster v British Gas*[31]).[32]

4.53 Community law does not differentiate between the public and private acts of emanations of the state; neither does it distinguish between those emanations of the state that are exclusively exercising public functions and those that have both public functions and private powers. So there is potential for confusion here.

4.54 The doctrine of supremacy of Community law requires that a person invoking Community law rights shall have no less favourable a remedy than that accorded to equivalent municipal law rights (*Factortame IV*[33]). Accordingly, it is arguable that since an employee of an exclusively public authority could claim a direct remedy for a breach of the Community law which was also a breach of a Convention right, so ought an employee who was able to rely on the horizontal effect of a Directive against an emanation of the state which was not an exclusively public authority.

4.55 This argument would mean that in certain cases the European Communities Act 1972 might cause the HRA 1998 to have a greater effect on the employment rights of non-exclusively public bodies.

4.56 Even if a body is a non-exclusively public body, it must be emphasised that it can be indirectly affected by the HRA 1998 through the interpretative obligation in section 3 and because tribunals (being themselves public authorities) will be bound to give effect to it. This provides a powerful extra reason why in any case in which a tribunal has a discretion in relation to any matter, it must exercise that discretion to give effect to any Convention rights.

---

[31] (Case C-188/89) [1991] ICR 84 (ECJ), [1991] ICR 463 (HL).
[32] See also S Prechal, *Directives in Community Law* (Oxford: OUP, 2005).
[33] (Joined Cases C-46/93 and C-48/93) [1996] 2 WLR 506, para 90.

H. The common law and section 6

There is no doubt that section 6 will require courts and tribunals to revisit **4.57**
common law rules and precedents. This is the clear effect of the obligation under
section 6, which, as has been noted, is stronger than that under section 3 (see
4.06 above).

This effect can already be seen at work in cases decided before the HRA 1998 **4.58**
came into general effect. Thus, the decision of the European Court in *Osman v
UK*,[34] a case concerning public policy and actions in negligence against the police,
led the House of Lords in *Barrett v Enfield London Borough Council*[35] (a case concerned with the duty of care owed by local authorities to persons in care), to
revisit its approach to applications to strike out cases where it was argued that on
public policy grounds there was no duty of care. Lord Browne-Wilkinson was
aware that a strike out could be a disproportionate response (see *Barrett*[36]).[37]

In turn, this approach was then taken up and followed in a number of other **4.59**
House of Lords cases, most notably *Waters v Metropolitan Police Commissioner*.[38]
That case concerned a claim that Ms Waters had suffered psychiatric injury as a
result of bullying by fellow police officers over a number of years. The case had
been struck out at every level prior to the House of Lords on grounds of public
policy, in particular that the police should not be subject to such an investigation
by the courts under the law of tort. However, following *Barrett* (and inferentially
Osman), their Lordships allowed the appeal.

I. The consequences of a public authority failing to act compatibly with Convention rights

In a case where a public authority can act compatibly with Convention rights but **4.60**
fails to do so, the HRA 1998 provides what are called 'judicial remedies' to anyone who is a 'victim'. Both of these concepts are technical and need to be
understood.

---

[34] (2000) 29 EHRR 245.
[35] [2001] 1 AC 550.
[36] At 557–60.
[37] The debate as to whether or not a strike out is an exclusionary rule has continued: see Lord
Hoffmann, 'Human Rights and the House of Lords' (1999) 62 MLR 159; and *Phelps v Hillingdon
Borough Council* [2001] 2 AC 619.
[38] [2000] IRLR 720.

(1) Victims

4.61   Only a person who is or would be 'a victim of the unlawful act' may bring proceedings against a public authority for breach of section 6(1), or rely on the Convention rights in any proceedings brought under section 7(1) such as judicial review. 'Victim' has a specific meaning (set out in s 7(7)) under Article 34 of the Convention. The person concerned must either have been actually and directly affected, or there is a risk that they will be affected (see *Klass v Germany*[39]) by a breach of the Convention. Where a person is a 'victim', it is conclusively presumed that he or she has sufficient interest (see s 7(3); see also s 31(3) of the Supreme Court Act 1981 and Ord 53, r 3(7), Sch 1 to Section A of the Supreme Court Practice) to seek permission to apply for judicial review. In practice there should be little difficulty in identifying who is a victim in an employment law context.

(2) Proceedings for breach of section 6

4.62   Section 7(1) of the HRA 1998 provides that a person who claims that a public authority has acted (or proposes to act) in a way which is made unlawful by section 6(1), can bring proceedings against the authority under the Act in the appropriate court or tribunal. Which is the appropriate venue is to be determined in accordance with rules (see s 7(2)). No rules have been made to permit a complaint to be made in the employment tribunal for breach of section 6(1), or an appeal to the EAT. Accordingly, reference should be made to CPR, Part 16 in relation to statements of case and CPR, Part 52 in relation to appeals.

(3) Judicial remedies

4.63   The HRA 1998 provides for what are described in section 8 as 'judicial remedies'. A court or tribunal may grant such relief or remedy as is within its jurisdiction in relation to any actual or proposed act by a 'public authority' which is (or would be) 'unlawful' (see s 8(1) and (6)). It is not yet clear whether this power arises only where there is jurisdiction under section 7 for breach of section 6(1). Section 8 does not expressly say so, whereas section 7 does; and it is arguable that if the tribunal considers, incidentally to its main determination that there has been an unlawful act, it can give such judicial remedy as is within its own jurisdiction.

4.64   This means that a tribunal could interpret the power to make a compensatory award for unfair dismissal so as to include compensation for breach of a Convention right in an appropriate case, pursuant to section 123 of the ERA 1996. Likewise, it could include such an award in a discrimination case in accordance

---

[39] (1978) 2 EHRR 214.

58

with section 65 of the Sex Discrimination Act 1975, section 56 of the Race Relations Act 1976, and section 8 of the Disability Discrimination Act 1995 as well as the Regulations stemming from the Framework Directive covering Sexual Orientation, Religion and Belief, and Age. However, in a case which solely concerned redundancy, where the precise sum due is to be calculated by the statute, this would not be possible (see s 170 of the ERA 1996). The better view is that the word 'unlawful' in section 8 refers to section 6(1), and is therefore concerned only with proceedings brought under section 7(1).

(4) Damages

In any event, section 8(2) of the HRA 1998 specifically states that a court may **4.65** award damages or compensation only if it otherwise has that power. Thus damages could be awarded by the tribunal in a case under its contractual jurisdiction set out in the Employment Tribunals Extension of Jurisdiction (England and Wales) Order 1994.[40]

Section 8(3) sets limits on the power to award damages:

(3) No award of damages is to be made unless, taking account of all the circumstances of the case, including—

(a) any other relief or remedy granted, or order made, in relation to the act in question (by that or any other court), and

(b) the consequences of any decision (of that or any other court) in respect of that act, the court is satisfied that the award is necessary to afford just satisfaction to the person in whose favour it is made.

The concept of 'just satisfaction' derives from Article 41 ECHR and rule 60 of the European Court of Human Rights Rules of Procedure. This is made even clearer in the HRA 1998, which requires both the decision whether to award damages and the amount of the award to take into account the principles applied by the ECtHR in relation to awards of compensation under Article 41 (see s 8(4)). In practice this is likely to mean that damages and compensation will be moderate.

It has been remarked that there is an absence of clear principles in the decisions **4.66** of the ECtHR which would enable lawyers to work out how just satisfaction should be secured in other cases.[41] The aim is always full restitution (ie *restituto in integrum*). Both pecuniary and non-pecuniary loss may be recovered, as may costs and expenses. Interest may form a part of pecuniary loss. Loss in relation to anxiety, distress, and frustration may also be awarded. The seriousness of any

---

40 SI 1994/1623.
41 Law Commission (Law Com No 266, Cm 4853, 2000) at paras 3.04–3.15.

violation of human rights will always be considered. However, the court looks to see if there is a clear causal link between the damages claimed and the interference which is in issue.

4.67 The Strasbourg Court adopts the general aim of restoring the applicant to the position that he would have been in had there not been a breach of his Convention rights: *Papamichalopoulos v Greece;*[42] *Kingsley v UK;*[43] and *R v Mental Health Tribunal & Secretary of State for Health ex parte KB and Ors.*[44]

4.68 A full review of the case law in relation to damages is outside the scope of this book. However, the Law Commission has published a report entitled *Damages Under the Human Rights Act 1998.*[45] This analyses the relevant cases in great detail in order to try to define what are the relevant principles by which the ECtHR determines what sums would constitute just satisfaction.

(5) Restrictions on judicial remedies

4.69 Special provision is made in relation to claims under section 7(1) of the HRA 1998, in relation to judicial acts. This is because by section 6, courts and tribunals are themselves public authorities (see 4.09 above). These claims are most likely to occur at the interface of civil and criminal law, for example, in cases where a person has been deprived of his or her liberty contrary to Article 5 ECHR, since in those cases only it is not necessary to prove a breach of good faith. However, they might also arise in cases where a person has not had a fair trial contrary to Article 6 ECHR, if that breach was not an act in good faith pursuant to section 9(3) of the Act.

4.70 In cases where damages are sought in relation to judicial acts which are done in good faith, damages may not be awarded otherwise than to compensate a person to the extent required by Article 5(5) ECHR (see HRA 1998, s 9(3)). This Article provides that anyone who has been the victim of arrest or detention in contravention of Article 5 shall have an enforceable right to compensation. This is unlikely to arise in the context of employment law; but it could occur where, for instance, a security guard detained an employee.

4.71 If a tribunal were to fail to afford a person his or her Convention rights then it would be possible to seek a remedy against that tribunal. However, since it is very unlikely that the tribunal would have acted in bad faith, this will not be a common occurrence. Where this does occur, for instance, where there has been a manifestly biased hearing, this remains a possibility.

---

[42] (1995) 21 EHRR 439, 451 at para 34.
[43] (2002) 35 EHRR 10, 177 at para 40, p 190.
[44] [2003] EWHC 193 (Admin), 13 February 2003, *per* Stanley Burnton J at para 28.
[45] Law Com No 266, 2000. Available online at <http://www.lawcom.gov.uk/docs/lc266.pdf>.

(6) Time limits for judicial remedies

Subject to any stricter rule in relation to time limits for the proceedings in question,[46] proceedings against a public authority must be brought within one year beginning with the date on which the act complained of was done, or such longer period as the court or tribunal considers equitable having regard to all the circumstances (see HRA 1998, s 7(5)). **4.72**

(7) Forum

Any claim where the statement of case or a notice of appeal includes a claim under section 7(1) and section 9(3) of the Act in respect of a judicial act which would be heard in the county court can be transferred to the High Court (CPR, Part 16). The Practice Direction to CPR, Part 19 provides for the Lord Chancellor to be joined as a party where the claim is in respect of a judicial act (see s 9(3)–(5)). This is so that the proper Minister responsible for the court concerned may be before the court which is hearing the claim under section 7(1). In some cases it may be that the evidence heard in the court in question may be reconsidered in these proceedings pursuant to CPR, Part 33. **4.73**

(8) Complaints to the institutions of the ECHR

This is the third way in which a complaint can be made about an incompatibility between Convention rights and domestic legislation, or a failure to afford those rights. Article 13 of the Convention, which is not a Convention right for the purposes of the HRA 1998, provides a right to an effective remedy. The Act assumes it does so in its own way. If, however, the Act fails to provide an effective remedy, the possibility of a complaint to the ECtHR remains. **4.74**

Under Article 25 ECHR a complaint to the ECtHR can be made only by a victim (see 4.61 above) and only when all domestic remedies have been exhausted. This will mean that an application for a declaration of incompatibility will have to be made first in most cases.[47] Complaints must be made within six months of the date on which the final decision was taken. Practitioners should be aware of, and may wish first to visit, the website for the ECtHR.[48] This is updated regularly and contains much useful information. **4.75**

Where it is considered that a complaint concerns one of the rights guaranteed by the Convention or its Protocols, and all possibilities of domestic remedies have **4.76**

---

[46] Thus the three-month time limit for judicial review is not extended by this provision.
[47] It is possible that such a declaration will provide an effective remedy. However, this will depend on the steps taken by the government in the light of such a declaration.
[48] <http://www.echr.coe.int>.

been exhausted, a victim should first fill out an application form containing key information and send it to the Registrar of the ECtHR.[49] The application form can be downloaded from the website of the Council of Europe (see below), or alternatively, a victim may send a letter setting out clear details of the complaint to the Registrar, and an application form will then be sent to him/her. The application form must contain the following information:

(a) It should give a brief summary of the complaints.
(b) It should indicate the Convention rights alleged to have been violated.
(c) It should list the remedies already used.
(d) It should have attached to it copies (since documents will not be returned it is not appropriate to send originals) of the decisions given in the victim's case by all the public authorities concerned.
(e) It should bear the applicant's signature, or the signature of his/her representative.

The approved application form for an application to the ECtHR is at Appendix 7 together with the notes published by the Council of Europe as to how to fill in the form.[50]

4.77 The Registrar will reply to the letter. The complainant may be asked for more information or documents, or for further explanation of the complaints. The complainant may be informed how the Convention has previously been interpreted in similar cases; and if it appears that there is an obvious obstacle to the admissibility of the complaint, the complainant may also be advised of this.[51] If it appears from the correspondence with the Registrar that the complaint is one which could be registered as an application, the Registry will send the necessary documents on which to submit the formal application. After this has been completed and submitted, it will be brought to the attention of the Court. The complainant will be informed by the Registrar of the progress of the case. The proceedings are in writing at the initial stage.[52]

---

[49] The application form should be addressed to: The Registrar, European Court of Human Rights, Council of Europe, F-67075 STRASBOURG CEDEX.

[50] To check for any amendments to the form go to the Council of Europe website <http://www.echr.coe.int/ECHR/EN/Header/Applicants/Information+for+applicants/Application+form/>.

[51] The Registrar *cannot* advise about the law of the state against which complaint is made.

[52] At a later stage in the proceedings, if the complainant has insufficient means to pay a lawyer's fees, he or she may be eligible for free legal help. But legal help cannot be granted at the time when the application is lodged.

J. Frequently asked questions

What is the purpose of section 6 of the HRA 1998?   **4.78**

It places a duty upon public authorities to give effect to Convention rights and obliges bodies or people carrying out state functions to ensure that such human rights are respected.

How does section 6 act alongside section 3 of the HRA 1998?

The duty acts alongside the section 3 interpretative obligation to ensure that effect is given to Convention rights where there is pre-existing legislation and when relevant bodies are exercising public functions.

What is a public authority within the meaning of section 6?

It is a court or tribunal or a body whose functions are of a public nature (s 6(3)). Bodies which are specifically not public authorities include Parliament and non-legalistic tribunals (s 21(1)). Case law has found that a public authority can either be a core public authority exercising governmental functions all of a public nature or a hybrid public authority. Where private companies exercise public functions they will fall within the ambit of section 6.

Can workplace disputes be remedied by virtue of section 6 complaints about employers?

Usually behaviour relating to an individual contract of employment amounts to a private act and will not therefore be within section 6. So where a private employer fails to afford a Convention right to workers no remedy can be sought purely for such a failure. However, the interpretative obligation still applies to courts and tribunals hearing complaints between private parties.

When will a party which only has some public functions qualify under section 6?

The case law as to when a hybrid authority is a public authority is still developing. The broader the approach to defining a public authority, the wider the protection given by the HRA 1998. Pertinent questions to ask include whether the body is exercising governmental functions, whether its role is enmeshed with that of a core public authority such as a local authority, whether the power exercised by the body has a public element or flavour, and whether the body's function is integral to the discharge of statutory or other governmental functions. Further examples of how to identify public authorities can be found at 4.41-4.50.

How do Community law and section 6 interrelate?

Employers who are hybrid public authorities may well be emanations of the state for the purposes of Community law, which does not distinguish between public and private acts when determining what bodies are emanations of the state. Remedies under EU law are to be no less favourable than those under domestic law.

What remedies are available if a body is in breach of section 6?

Judicial remedies are available to 'victims' of unlawful breaches of section 6. A victim must be actually and directly affected by the breach and is empowered by section 7 to bring proceedings against the authority in question to the appropriate court (generally the county court or High Court). Damages may be awarded pursuant to section 8 if the court would otherwise have that power. It must have regard to the ECtHR concept of 'just satisfaction'. In practice this will mean that damages and compensation will be moderate. Proceedings against a public authority must be brought within one year of the act complained of.

Are any remedies restricted?

Unlawful acts of courts and tribunals committed in good faith only sound in damages where security issues are involved (HRA 1998, s 9(3)).

Who can complain to the Strasbourg Court?

Such a complaint can only be made by a victim where all domestic remedies have been exhausted. This usually means applying for a declaration of incompatibility from the domestic courts. Applications to the ECtHR must be made within six months of the final domestic decision.

5

ARTICLE 4: PROHIBITION OF SLAVERY AND FORCED LABOUR

Article 4
Prohibition of slavery and forced labour

1. No one shall be held in slavery or servitude.
2. No one shall be required to perform forced or compulsory labour.
3. For the purpose of this Article the term 'forced or compulsory labour' shall not include:
   (a) any work required to be done in the ordinary course of detention imposed according to the provisions of Article 5 of this Convention or during conditional release from such detention;
   (b) any service of a military character or, in the case of conscientious objectors in countries where they are recognised, service exacted instead of compulsory military service;

(c) any service exacted in case of an emergency or calamity threatening the life or well-being of the community;

(d) any work or service which forms part of normal civic obligations.

A. Introduction

5.01 While slavery and servitude have long been outlawed in domestic law this Article is still relevant, though in practice the prohibition on slavery is less likely to be relevant than the prohibition on servitude and forced and compulsory labour, since slavery occurs when a person is treated as a chattel rather than a person.

5.02 Newspapers continue to report occasions in which individuals are treated incredibly badly and seem almost to exist in a form of slavery. Such treatment can be analysed either as a form of servitude or slavery and in either case there is a positive obligation on the state to protect the individual. Also, from time to time, circumstances still arise in which persons are compelled to enter into arrangements which involve forced labour. Again Article 4 ECHR will be relevant.

5.03 While in the six years since the HRA 1998 came into effect, Article 4 has not given rise to any domestic reported cases of importance[1] in the ordinary employment context, it has played an important role in the background. Thus, it lies behind the new Council of Europe Convention on Action against Trafficking in Human Beings,[2] and it has been under consideration in new legislation to protect employees from abuse by gangmasters.

5.04 This chapter discusses the nature of the prohibition on slavery and servitude, and what is forced or compulsory labour. It considers the domestic approach to harsh employment conditions, and the impact of Article 4 on private employment. Lastly, it considers the effect of the Article on work required by the state.

B. Exceptions and derogations

5.05 There are no exceptions to and can be no derogation from the prohibition on slavery and servitude in Article 4(1) ECHR.[3] It should be noted that Article 4(3) does not provide an exception to Article 4(2) but 'delimits' the meaning of forced

---

[1] In *Kopel v Safeway Stores* [2003] IRLR 753 the claimant's complaint of unfair dismissal to an employment tribunal included the allegation that her employers had infringed the prohibition against torture in Art 3 ECHR and the prohibition against slavery in Art 4 ECHR. However, the tribunal said these allegations were seriously misconceived and called them 'frankly ludicrous'.

[2] Warsaw, 16 May 2005; TS 197.

[3] *Zarb Adami v Malta* Application 17209/02 (Judgment 20 June 2006) para 43, (2007) 44 EHRR 3.

and compulsory labour. Derogations from Article 4(2) can take place only in time of war or other public emergency threatening the life of the nation (see Article 15(1)).

There is a special procedure for exercising such derogations under Article 15(3). **5.06** However, this has not been included in Schedule 1 to the HRA 1998. It is unlikely that there would be any derogation from this provision save in the gravest emergency, and only then by special legislation. Therefore this Article is essentially unqualified in its application.

C. International prohibition on slavery

Slavery has been unlawful under UK law since the seminal judgment of Lord **5.07** Mansfield CJ in *Somerset v Stewart*[4] (see also *The Slave Grace*[5]). That judgment is credited with ending the traffic in slaves in London.

In 1807, the slave trade was abolished in the British colonies, although it was not **5.08** until the Slavery Abolition Act 1833 that slavery was abolished altogether in the Dominions.[6] The legal consequences of the campaign to abolish slavery in the British Empire were felt late into the twentieth century (see, eg, *Buck v Attorney General*;[7] *Akar v Attorney General of Sierra Leone*[8]).

It was not until 1865 that the 13th Amendment to the Constitution of the United **5.09** States of America was ratified providing that:

> Neither slavery nor involuntary servitude, except as a punishment for crime whereof the party shall have been duly convicted, shall exist within the United States, or any place subject to their jurisdiction.

International common law now condemns all slavery. A change in common **5.10** understanding late in the nineteenth century was at the heart of this. Thus Lord Denning MR said:

> . . . International law does change . . . when the rules of international law were changed (by the force of public opinion) so as to condemn slavery, the English courts were justified in applying the modern rules of international law . . .[9]

---

[4] (1772) Lofft 1.

[5] (1827) 2 Hag Adm 94.

[6] See also *Halsbury's Laws* (4th edn, London: Butterworths, 1973), Vol 18, para 1708, for a further discussion.

[7] [1965] Ch 745.

[8] [1970] 1 AC 853.

[9] See *Trendtex Trading Corporation v Central Bank of Nigeria* [1977] 1 QB 529, at 554, where Lord Denning MR cites the 'Statement of Opinion' by Sir R Phillimore, Mr M Bernard, and Sir H.S. Maine, appended to the Report of the Royal Commission on Fugitive Slaves (1876), XXV, paras 4 and 5.

5.11 Numerous international treaties now condemn slavery and servitude and some of these are discussed below.

D. The general application of Article 4

5.12 The provisions of Article 4 ECHR speak generally to all who are in a position to impose slavery, servitude, or forced or compulsory labour. In practice the state will be involved either directly or indirectly. It must be remembered that the state is responsible under Article 13 ECHR for the duty to provide an effective remedy before national authorities. Article 13 is given effect in the UK through the HRA 1998, so if there is a situation in which Article 4 ECHR might be relevant, the HRA 1998 will be a major route for its implementation.

5.13 Thus employers will be affected by Article 4 ECHR when they impose conditions of employment which go well beyond what is reasonable and interfere with the liberty of the individual. The court or tribunal will be required by sections 3 and 6 of the HRA 1998 to look at the substantive nature of the arrangement. If in fact the individual is in a situation in which he or she is controlled by the wishes of the employer, or even another person such as a landlord or a person who has granted a loan, then this Article will be relevant.

(1) Positive obligations

5.14 Moreover there is no doubt that Article 4 imposes a positive obligation on the state to prohibit slavery, servitude, and compulsory and forced labour. In *Siliadin v France*,[10] the Applicant who was a minor from Togo who had been kept in servitude by a family living in France argued that the state was under a positive obligation to adopt tangible criminal law provisions that would deter such offences, backed up by law enforcement machinery for the prevention, detection, and punishment of breaches of such provisions.[11]

5.15 The ECtHR ruled in favour of this approach:

> 82. The Court considers that, together with Articles 2 and 3, Article 4 of the Convention enshrines one of the basic values of the democratic societies making up the Council of Europe.
>
> 83. It notes that the Commission had proposed in 1983 that it could be argued that a Government's responsibility was engaged to the extent that it was their duty to ensure that the rules adopted by a private association did not run contrary to the provisions of the Convention, in particular where the domestic courts had jurisdiction to

---

[10] Application 73316/01, judgment 26 July 2005, (2006) 43 EHRR 16.
[11] See para 71.

examine their application (*X. v the Netherlands*, no. 9327/81, Commission decision of 3 May 1983, Decisions and Reports (DR) 32, p. 180).

84. The Court notes that, in referring to the above-mentioned case, the Government accepted at the hearing that positive obligations did appear to exist in respect of Article 4.

85. In this connection, it notes that the Article 4 of the Forced Labour Convention, adopted by the International Labour Organisation on 28 June 1930 and ratified by France on 24 June 1937, provides:

> '1. The competent authority shall not impose or permit the imposition of forced or compulsory labour for the benefit of private individuals, companies or associations.'

86. Furthermore, Article 1 of the Supplementary Convention on the Abolition of Slavery, the Slave Trade, and Institutions and Practices Similar to Slavery, adopted on 30 April 1956, which entered into force in respect of France on 26 May 1964, states:

> 'Each of the States Parties to this Convention shall take all practicable and necessary legislative and other measures to bring about progressively and as soon as possible the complete abolition or abandonment of the following institutions and practices, where they still exist and whether or not they are covered by the definition of slavery contained in article 1 of the Slavery Convention signed at Geneva on 25 September 1926: . . . , [d]ebt bondage, . . . [a]ny institution or practice whereby a child or young person under the age of 18 years, is delivered by either or both of his natural parents or by his guardian to another person, whether for reward or not, with a view to the exploitation of the child or young person or of his labour.'

87. In addition, with particular regard to children, Article 19 of the International Convention on the Rights of the Child of 20 November 1989, which entered into force in respect of France on 6 September 1990, provides:

> '1. States Parties shall take all appropriate legislative, administrative, social and educational measures to protect the child from all forms of physical or mental violence, injury or abuse, . . . , maltreatment or exploitation, including sexual abuse, while in the care of parent(s), legal guardian(s) or any other person who has the care of the child;'

Article 32 provides:

> '1. States Parties recognize the right of the child to be protected from economic exploitation and from performing any work that is likely to be hazardous or to interfere with the child's education, or to be harmful to the child's health or physical, mental, spiritual, moral or social development.
>
> 2. States Parties shall take legislative, administrative, social and educational measures to ensure the implementation of the present article. To this end, and having regard to the relevant provisions of other international instruments, States Parties shall in particular:
>
> (a) Provide for a minimum age or minimum ages for admission to employment;
> (b) Provide for appropriate regulation of the hours and conditions of employment;

(c) Provide for appropriate penalties or other sanctions to ensure the effective enforcement of the present article.'

88. Finally, the Court notes that it appears from the Parliamentary Assembly's findings (see 'Relevant law' above) that 'today's slaves are predominantly female and usually work in private households, starting out as migrant domestic workers . . .'

89. In those circumstances, the Court considers that limiting compliance with Article 4 of the Convention only to direct action by the State authorities would be inconsistent with the international instruments specifically concerned with this issue and would amount to rendering it ineffective. Accordingly, it necessarily follows from this provision that Governments have positive obligations, in the same way as under Article 3 for example, to adopt criminal-law provisions which penalise the practices referred to in Article 4 and to apply them in practice (see *M.C. v Bulgaria*, cited above, paragraph 153).

5.16 The UK has strong criminal provisions outlawing human trafficking,[12] the critical issue, as in *Siliadin* is whether they are effectively used. In cases not involving trafficking there will still be a positive obligation on the state not to permit slavery, servitude or forced labour.

E. What is slavery?

5.17 Article 1(1) of the 1926 Slavery Convention[13] defines 'slavery' as:

. . . the status or condition of a person over whom any or all of the powers attaching to the right of ownership are exercised.

5.18 Pursuant to a further Convention on the Abolition of Slavery[14] made in 1956 under the auspices of the UN, states (including the UK) agreed to take all necessary measures to bring about the complete abolition of institutions similar to slavery, such as debt bondage, serfdom, bride-price, and exploitation of child labour.[15]

5.19 Protection from slavery has been the subject of very little case law of the ECHR. In 1999, the Commission dismissed a complaint by a Mauritanian who was the son of a slave, who did not wish to return from Sweden to Mauritania. He claimed that he would be forced into slavery on his return, but the Commission decided

---

[12] For a review of current UK laws concerned with trafficking see <http://www.coe.int/t/e/human_rights/trafficking/3_documents/national_laws/eg(2002)2volii_e.asp#P3806_294580>.

[13] International Convention with the object of securing the Abolition of Slavery and the Slave Trade (Geneva, 25 September 1926; TS 16 (1927); Cmd 2910), amended by the Protocol of 7 July 1953 (TS 24 (1956); Cmd 9797).

[14] United Nations, Supplementary Convention on the Abolition of Slavery, the Slave Trade and Institutions and Practices Similar to Slavery 1956 (Geneva, 7 September 1956; TS 59 (1957); Cmd 257).

[15] For a discussion of this Convention, see n 6 above, para 1705.

that his claim that he would be subjected to treatment contrary to Article 4 ECHR was not substantiated (see *Ould Barar v Sweden*[16]).

The Court has also dismissed a claim that working without being paid, in the **5.20** context in which a debt has been acknowledged, is slavery (see *Cherginets v Ukraine*[17]).

F. What is servitude?

Servitude differs from slavery in not involving ownership though coercion will **5.21** be present.[18] However, there is no bright line distinction between the two concepts. This human trafficking usually involves coercion and it has been condemned as a new form of slavery by the Council of Europe. In 2006, the Council of Europe launched a new campaign to end this.[19] The Human Trafficking Convention imposes obligations on member states of the Council of Europe in relation to all forms of servitude including abuse of women, and au pairs. The Convention was referred to in *Siliadin v France* in which the ECtHR held that France had failed to protect a young girl brought into France to work as an unpaid family maid (see above 5.14–5.15).

(1) Serfdom

Serfdom is also a form of servitude. Thus in *Van Droogenbroeck v Belgium*[20] the **5.22** Commission adopted the definition of serfdom in the Slavery Convention and stated that:

> . . . in addition to the obligation to provide another with certain services, the concept of servitude includes the obligation on the part of the 'serf' to live on another's property and the impossibility of changing his condition . . .

This might arise in a modern context where a person is bound by terms of a **5.23** mortgage or other loan to remain in a property owned by the other person, or over which the other has a charge (see *Horwood v Millar's Timber and Trading Company Limited*[21]).

---

[16] Application 42367/98, (1999) 28 EHRR CD 213.
[17] Application 37296/03 (Judgment 28 February 2006) para 1.
[18] See *Siliadin v France*, para 123.
[19] See <http://www.coe.int/T/E/human_rights/trafficking/>.
[20] (1982) 4 EHRR 443.
[21] [1917] 1 KB 307.

(2) Employment for life

5.24 Servitude can imply lifetime service. A contract binding an employee for life would undoubtedly be repugnant at law (*per* Dillon LJ in *Methodist Conference (President) v Parfitt*[22]). However, such a contract of employment for life (though very unusual; see *Malins v Post Office*[23]) has been enforced against employers (*McClelland v Northern Ireland General Health Services Board*[24]). It may be that if the court cannot enforce a contract for life against an employee, it should now consider if the same term can be enforced against the employer.

5.25 The practical implications of such a term will have to be considered on a case-by-case basis. It is suggested that in the context of modern employment law it will usually (though not always) be either repugnant at law, or contrary to the proper construction of the contract of employment for it to be construed as binding an employer for the life of the employee. An exceptional case might arise where there is a special relationship such as landlord and tenant (see, eg, *Ivory v Palmer*[25]). So far no case has been brought in which an employer has sought to be released from such a contract on the basis that it involves the employee being held in servitude.

G. What is forced or compulsory labour?

5.26 The prohibition on forced or compulsory labour is likely to be more important in contemporary employment law than the prohibition on slavery or servitude. The word 'labour' is not limited to manual labour; it covers other types of work equally (*Van der Mussele v Belgium*[26]).

5.27 The European Commission of Human Rights restated the two key elements of forced or compulsory labour in *Reitmayr v Austria*:[27]

(a) The labour or service must be performed by the person concerned against his will.
(b) The obligation to perform this labour or service must either be unjust or oppressive or must itself constitute an avoidable hardship.

5.28 What is unjust and oppressive must be objectively construed under the Convention. Since the HRA 1998 provides a floor, not a ceiling, to the rights enjoyed by individuals, it is worth bearing in mind the domestic approach to such situations (see 5.35–5.38).

---

[22] [1984] ICR 176, at 183.
[23] [1975] ICR 60.
[24] [1957] 1 WLR 594, [1957] 2 All ER 129 (HL) (NI).
[25] [1975] ICR 340.
[26] (1984) 6 EHRR 163, at 173.
[27] (1995) 20 EHRR CD 89.

In *Van der Mussele v Belgium*, the ECtHR adopted the approach of the ILO **5.29**
Forced Labour Convention[28] in deciding what was forced or compulsory labour.
The Court took as its 'starting point' Article 2(2) of the ILO Convention, which
said that:

> . . . forced or compulsory labour . . . [shall mean] . . . all work or service which is
> extracted from any person under the menace of a penalty and for which the said
> person has not offered himself voluntarily . . .

So the menace of a penalty is necessary to demonstrate that there is forced or **5.30**
compulsory labour. *Van der Mussele v Belgium* is discussed further at 5.44 below
in relation to private employment.

Many might consider that they are required to carry out something akin to forced **5.31**
or compulsory labour. Welfare to Work programmes might be thought to come
close to a kind of compulsory labour. A more current problem is the condition of
some Filipino or Indian au pairs, brought into this country to work as servants in
circumstances in which they are neither allowed any time off by the employer,
nor in some cases permitted to leave the employer's premises. Likewise, the
position of some immigrants who enter into relationships akin to slavery may be
covered by Article 4 ECHR.

In their 2005 report on Forced Labour and Migration to the UK,[29] Bridget **5.32**
Anderson and Ben Rogaly state:[30]

> The common sense view regards forced labour as one individual who is personally
> able to exercise control and power over another or others, and this often extends over
> aspects of their lives over and above their work. This is certainly the view that
> is reflected in much of the press coverage of trafficking of migrants in the UK and
> is probably in part what leads to the focus on commercial sex and domestic work.
> The kinds of relations that operate between clients/pimps and workers in commer-
> cial sex, and between employers and domestic workers, can be extremely personal-
> ized and particularistic. Workers in both these sectors may find employers, clients
> and third parties exercise considerable power over them, not just as an employee/
> service provider, but over their whole personhood (Anderson and O'Connell
> Davidson 2003 Is Trafficking in Human Beings Demand Driven? A Multi-Country
> Pilot Study Geneva: IOM Research Series). They are subject to the personal power
> and authority of individuals.

Article 4(3) ECHR delimits Article 4(2) so that certain kinds of labour are **5.33**
not treated as forced or compulsory labour. These exceptions are considered at
5.57–5.60 below.

---

[28] ILO Convention 1930 No 29. See also Convention 1957 No 105.
[29] 2005 Study prepared by COMPAS in collaboration with the TUC at p 10.
[30] See <http://www.tuc.org.uk/international/tuc-9317-f0.pdf>.

H. The common law and harsh employment conditions

5.34 In 1887, Bowen LJ said that:[31]

> ...The law of England allows a man to contract for his labour, or allows him to place himself in the service of a master, but it does not allow him to attach to his contract of service any servile incidents—any elements of servitude as distinguished from service...

5.35 More recently Sir John Donaldson MR took a similar approach in *President of the Methodist Conference v Parfitt*.[32]

5.36 This principle has been used to strike down as contrary to public policy contracts in which there is an undue and improper fetter on the liberty of action of an individual (*Horwood v Millar's Timber and Trading Company Limited*,[33] approved by Lord Pearce in *Esso Petroleum Co Ltd v Harper's Garage (Stourport) Limited*[34]). A fundamental rights approach can also be seen in other, earlier cases such as *Ottoman Bank v Chakarian*,[35] in which it was held that the risk to the life of an employee of obeying an order to serve in Istanbul was so great as to justify his refusal.

5.37 However, what has been accepted under domestic labour law as just or at least as not oppressive, will, or may, be a poor guide to what the Convention requires. This is because labour law in the UK during the twentieth century developed by way of statutory accretion of rights on to the doctrine of common employment, which worked from the premise that a servant bargains equally with his master and is free to accept or refuse the terms of employment offered. Even though it has long been recognised that gross exploitation has existed in many industries at different times, Sir Otto Kahn-Freund declared in 1972 that:

> I know of no case in which a court invalidated a contract by reason of gross exploitation, but neither can I recall a case in which a court was given the opportunity of doing so.[36]

---

[31] *Davies v Davies* (1887) 36 Ch Div 359, at 393.
[32] [1984] 1 QB 368, at 376.
[33] [1917] 1 KB 307.
[34] [1968] 1 AC 269, at 326.
[35] [1930] 1 AC 277.
[36] See the Hamlyn Lecture *Labour and the Law*, by Sir Otto Kahn-Freund, P Davies and M Freedland (eds) (2nd edn, London: Stevens, 1977), 3.

(1) Domestic prohibition on excessive hours and low pay

It is now widely, but not uniformly,[37] accepted that statutory protection may be **5.38** necessary to avoid excessive hours or conditions. Rather than the courts invalidating contracts as unconscionable, statutory constraints have been imposed on the content of, and work done under, contracts of employment. In many cases, abuses amounting to unjust or oppressive labour conditions have been dealt with under statutory provisions such as the Factories Acts or the Truck Acts. The Truck Acts have now been repealed[38] and replaced by provisions of the ERA 1996. The Factories Acts legislation continues, and other employment protection legislation has been added.[39] The Working Time Regulations 1998[40] and the National Minimum Wage Act 1998 are now the twin pillars of the modern protection against excessive hours and oppressive pay conditions.

One of the first modern cases in which the court was given an opportunity **5.39** to treat the terms of a contract of employment as unconscionable was *Johnstone v Bloomsbury Health Authority*,[41] where the requirement for junior hospital doctors to work without adequate sleep for periods in excess of 88 hours per week was under consideration in a striking-out application. The Court of Appeal dealt with the case under the Unfair Contract Terms Act 1977 rather than from the point of view of fundamental rights. See also *Barber v RJB Mining (UK) Ltd*.[42]

The Unfair Contract Terms Act 1977 (UCTA 1977) restricts the extent to which **5.40** a person can limit liability for negligence (s 2) and imposes restraints on contractual terms where one party deals as a consumer, or in 'written standard terms of business' (s 3). The 1977 Act prohibits reliance by the party who is responsible for such terms on any term to exclude or restrict liability, to render contractual performance which is substantially different from that reasonably expected or no performance, except to the extent that 'the contract term satisfies the requirement of reasonableness'.[43] Schedule 1, paragraph 4 to the Act states that 'Section 2(1)

---

[37] The challenge by the UK to the Working Time Directive, demonstrated the extent to which the then Conservative Administration was prepared to go to try to retain the freedom to contract for any working hours; see Case C-84/94 *UK v Council of the European Union* [1996] ECR I-5755, [1996] 3 CMLR 671, [1997] ICR 443.

[38] See *Bristow v City Petroleum Ltd* [1988] ICR 165 for the last case heard by the House of Lords under the Truck Acts. The abuse in that case, forced and unlimited deductions from wages, led to the enacting of ss 2 and 3 of the Wages Act 1986, now ss 30 and 21 of the ERA 1996.

[39] See, eg, the ERA 1996 and the Health and Safety at Work etc Act 1974.

[40] SI 1998/1833.

[41] [1991] 1 ICR 269.

[42] [1999] 1 ICR 679.

[43] As to the standard of reasonableness, see UCTA 1977, s 11 and Sch 2.

and (2) do not extend to a contract of employment except in favour of the employee', which suggests that the Act may apply in respect of employment contracts. In *Brigden v American Express Bank Ltd*,[44] Morland J decided that employment contracts could be regarded as consumer contracts, and thus as covered by the Act. However, in a recent decision, *Commerzbank AG v Keen*,[45] the Court of Appeal has held that employment contracts do not readily fit into the categories of consumer contracts or standard form contracts, as to allow such an interpretation would involve treating workers as users or recipients of goods or services when in truth they are providers of their services. The Court therefore held that the Act did not apply in respect of a term concerned with the payment of discretionary bonuses (and also said that it was artificial and unconvincing to read section 3 as extending to any payment provisions in respect of personal services rendered by the employee to the employer). The Law Commission has considered this issue, and in February 2005, published a report and a draft Unfair Contract Terms Bill, recommending that the legislation should apply to employees where employment is on the employer's standard terms of employment.[46] The Law Commission's website states that the government accepted these recommendations, subject to a regulatory impact assessment, in July 2006, so new legislation may be forthcoming shortly. However, it is noteworthy that, as noted by the Court of Appeal in *Keen* in reaching its conclusions, the report focuses on additional services provided by the employer, such as health plans and holidays. This may mean that the result in *Keen* would remain the same under any new legislation, and that the legislation will be of little use in challenging unconscionable terms of employment.

I. Private employment and the prohibition on forced or compulsory labour

5.41   In *X v Netherlands*,[47] the European Commission of Human Rights clearly stated that Article 4 ECHR requires the state to prevent employers from imposing forced labour on employees. This case concerned a transfer system for professional footballers that was organised by a private football association.[48] Although the

---

[44] [2000] IRLR 94.
[45] [2007] IRLR 132.
[46] The report can be found at <http://www.lawcom.gov.uk/docs/lc292(1).pdf>, paras 6.2–6.10, and the draft bill at <http://www.lawcom.gov.uk/docs/lc292bill.pdf>.
[47] (1983) 5 EHRR 598.
[48] See also the discussion by the ECJ in Case C-415/93 *Union Royale Belge des Sociétés de Football Association Asb v Bosman* [1995] ECR I-4921, [1996] All ER (EC) 97 (ECJ).

Commission concluded that the situation in which the applicant found himself could not be considered as 'forced or compulsory work', it added that:[49]

> In the Commission's view it could be argued that the responsibility of The Netherlands government is engaged to the extent that it is its duty to ensure that the rules, adopted, it is true, by a private association, do not run contrary to the provisions of the Convention . . .

Article 4(3) ECHR excludes certain types of state-imposed requirements to work **5.42** from the ambit of Article 4. Where the complaint is principally in respect of the acts of a private employer, the exceptions under Article 4(3) will not apply directly, although they may be used to indicate the scope of the Article. Accordingly, private employment is considered first.

The Court reminded itself in *Van der Mussele* (see 5.30 above) that the Conven- **5.43** tion was a living instrument (see *Tyrer v UK*[50]) and that Article 4 had to be interpreted in the light of notions currently prevailing in member states. However, it will usually be argued that the worker has given prior consent to the conditions of work, ie that he or she has a choice as to whether to continue in such employment, so that the element of force or compulsion is lacking. Although this is undoubtedly an important factor and must be given relative weight, it is not by itself decisive.[51]

(1) Balancing business aims and worker's obligations

The basic requirement is a reasonable and considerable balance between the aim **5.44** pursued by the employer and the obligations accepted by the worker.[52] In *Van der Mussele* the Court, while rejecting the complaint, which concerned an obligation on pupil barristers to undertake pro bono work, added that work could amount to forced labour:[53]

> . . . in the case of a service required in order to gain access to a given profession if the service imposed a burden which was so disproportionate to the advantages attached to the future exercise of that profession that the service could not be treated as having been voluntarily accepted beforehand; this could apply for example in the case of a service unconnected with the profession in question . . .

Accordingly, it is at least arguable that in a gross case the state is in breach where it has failed to take steps to protect immigrant or other workers from having to

---

[49] At para 2.
[50] (1979–80) 2 EHRR 1, para 31.
[51] See *Van der Mussele*, at 174.
[52] In *Van der Mussele v Belgium*, the Court considered the social aspects of the exceptions under Art 4(3) ECHR as indicators of the kinds of matter that might be brought into the balance.
[53] *Van der Mussele*, at 175.

engage in forced labour. It may even be arguable that this applies to cases where illegal immigrants have accepted employment which, by reason of their special vulnerability, exposes them to particularly ruthless employment regimes.[54]

5.45   Some steps by the state have been taken in this respect in the UK; for instance, it is an offence to employ a person subject to immigration control (see Asylum and Immigration Act 1996, s 8).

5.46   The Gangmasters (Licensing) Act 2004 establishes an obligatory licensing structure for employment agencies and gangmasters who use or supply workers in processing and packaging industries such as gathering shellfish as well as agricultural work. The 2004 Morecombe Bay tragedy when 21 illegal Chinese cocklers drowned added force to the need for this legislation.

5.47   While these statutes go some way to prevent the exploitation of those without work permits,[55] it does not address the issue of the virtual enslavement of those immigrants who do have work permits but who find themselves restrained from leaving their employers' premises.[56]

J. Irregular immigration status

5.48   The protection provided by UK employment law is even more limited for those with irregular immigration status due to its exclusive application to those working under legal contracts. Immigration offences prove far more useful for the vulnerable workers in this position. New laws on trafficking were passed in 2002 and 2004: see section 145 of the Immigration Nationality and Asylum Act 2002 which created a new immigration offence of trafficking in prostitution. Similarly, section 4 of the Immigration and Asylum (Treatment of Claimants) Act 2004 created a new offence of trafficking people for exploitation. The maximum sentence on conviction for both offences is 14 years.

5.49   The HRA 1998 has enabled some successful trafficking and forced domestic labour Article 4 claims before immigration adjudicators and the Immigration Appeal Tribunal. A breach of Article 4 was found by an immigration adjudicator where a female Nigerian citizen had been 'kept in conditions of virtual slavery'.

---

[54] See *Siliadin v France*.

[55] See the Home Office Guidance for Employers, *Prevention of Illegal Working*.

[56] The situation of migrant domestic workers, in particular, is likely to be worsened by new government proposals which will, amongst other things, remove their current right to change their employer (see for a summary of the proposals <http://www.kalayaan.org.uk/>). These proposals may fall foul of Art 4.

Her employer had brought her to London, retained her travel documentation, forced her to work long hours without wages and beaten her.[57]

Whilst employment cases could be brought in cases of suspected forced labour **5.50** for those with work permits (the suspect sectors include residential care, contract cleaning, construction, and agriculture and horticulture),[58] irregular migrants will frequently be too fearful to denounce the agent under whose exploitation they are forced to work, and further risk having their complaints defeated by the existence of illegal contracts.

The best hope for such cases if brought in the employment law arena is to attempt **5.51** to emphasise the injustice to the worker. Thus Bingham LJ said in *Saunders v Edwards*:[59]

> Where issues of illegality are raised, the courts have (as it seems to me) to steer a middle course between two unacceptable positions. On the one hand it is unacceptable that any court of law should aid or lend its authority to a party seeking to pursue or enforce an object or agreement which the law prohibits. On the other hand, it is unacceptable that the court should, on the first indication of unlawfulness affecting any aspect of a transaction, draw up its skirts and refuse all assistance to the plaintiff, no matter how serious his loss nor how disproportionate his loss to the unlawfulness of his conduct.

Unfortunately, international human rights are not able to fill the gap in protec- **5.52** tion for irregular migrant workers in the UK, particularly as no section 6 (HRA 1998) claim could be brought directly against a gangmaster employer who is a private person, even if Article 4 is read as applying to private persons. In such circumstances the steps the state takes become all the more significant.

Such steps taken to protect vulnerable workers will differ from situation to **5.53** situation, but when it can be shown that such steps should have been taken then a violation of Article 4 ECHR might be established. If the circumstances of such 'forced' labour were to become increasingly notorious, with certain typical patterns, such as the employer retaining possession of the employee's passport, it might be argued that the state had taken inadequate steps within this Article.

---

[57] See adjudicator determination, *Miss T v SSHD* (AS/03637/2004), in which a police apology for failing to investigate is also discussed (para 75). See also Immigration Appeals Authority decisions: *Miss AB v SSHD* (CC/64057/2002); *Ms Tam Thi Dao v SSHD* (HX/28801/2003).
[58] See p 23 of the AS/TUC study n 29.
[59] [1987] 1 WLR 1116 at 1143B.

K. Working for state benefits

5.54 At the margin between public and private labour are schemes which require a person to accept work in order not to lose state benefits. In *X v Netherlands* (see 5.42 above), the European Commission of Human Rights held that this was not in breach of Article 4 ECHR.

5.55 Similarly, in *Talmon v Netherlands*,[60] the Commission found there was no breach of Article 4 where a man's benefits were reduced following his refusal to look for work other than as an 'independent scientist and social critic', as he was not forced to take up any work. Further, his refusal to look for employment (other than as independent scientist and social critic) did not make him liable to any other measures than the reduction of his unemployment benefits.

L. Work under compulsion by the state: the impact of Article 4(3)

5.56 The state itself requires persons to perform forced or compulsory labour in numerous circumstances under 'the menace of a penalty and for which the said person has not offered himself voluntarily'.[61]

5.57 The most common example is prison work. However, such work will usually not fall within the ambit of Article 4(2) because of Article 4(3). This does not limit the exercise of the rights guaranteed by Article 4(2) but 'delimits' it. It provides an interpretative tool for Article 4(2). Thus the ECtHR said in *Schmidt v Germany*:[62]

> . . . This being so, paragraph 3 serves as an aid to the interpretation of paragraph 2. The four sub-paragraphs of paragraph 3, notwithstanding their diversity, are grounded on the governing ideas of the general interest, social solidarity and what is normal in the ordinary course of affairs.

5.58 One key question will be whether there is a reasonable degree of proportionality between the obligation imposed by the state and the burden on the individual. The Commission have applied a two-stage test after *Van der Mussele*, asking whether the work was undertaken against the employee's will, or whether the person concerned entered the service in question voluntarily. Secondly, it should be asked whether the obligation to do the work was itself unjust in the sense of

---

[60] (1997) EHRLR 448.
[61] Article 2(2) of ILO Convention 1930 No 29.
[62] (1994) 18 EHRR 513, at para 22.

imposing a disproportionate burden on the individual, and whether it was required in the general interest. In applying this test it is necessary to consider whether the work in question falls within the ambit of the worker's normal activities.

Article 4(3) provides exceptions to Article 4(2) in the following areas:[63]   **5.59**

(a) *Work required to be done in the ordinary course of detention imposed according to the provisions of Article 5 or during conditional release from such detention.*
   Article 4(3)(a) specifically refers to Article 5, which limits the circumstances in which there may be an interference with the right to liberty and security. Accordingly, prison work will not normally be within the scope of Article 4 ECHR.[64] The fact that very small sums are usually paid to prisoners is not inconsistent with this provision (*Twenty-One Detained Prisoners v Germany*[65]). Subsequent claims by prisoners in relation to the amount of pay that they have received have been dismissed as manifestly unfounded.
   The word 'ordinary' limits the kind of work that can be required. Work aimed at rehabilitation based on general standards found among members of the Council of Europe will be 'ordinary' (*De Wilde, Ooms and Versyp*;[66] see also *Van Droogenbroeck v Belgium*[67]). A community service order imposed as an alternative to detention is probably covered directly by this delimitation. Formerly such orders were in one sense voluntary, depending on the willingness of the offender to accept such a punishment.[68]

(b) *Service of a military character.*
   Voluntary enlistment is within this exception, as well as compulsory military service (*W, X, Y and Z v UK*[69]).

(c) *Service exacted in case of an emergency or calamity threatening the life or well-being of the community.*

---

[63] For a wider discussion of the Commission's case law, see J Simor and B Emmerson, *Human Rights Practice* (London: Sweet & Maxwell, 2000), Ch 4.

[64] Indeed, even though there may have been a breach of part of Art 5, it does not necessarily follow that there has been a breach of Art 4; see *De Wilde, Ooms and Versyp v Belgium* (1979–80) 1 EHRR 373, para 89.

[65] Application 3134/67, 3172/67 and 3188 to 3206/67 (joined), 6 April 1968, 11 *Yearbook* 528.

[66] (1979–80) 1 EHRR 373, above, para 90.

[67] (1982) 4 EHRR 443, paras 59–60.

[68] The consent of the offender was an essential condition for the imposition of a community service order: see Powers of Criminal Courts Act 1973, s 14(2). However, for offences committed on or after 1 October 1997 this is no longer so. The court can now impose the order as a sentence without the consent of the defendant.

[69] Applications 3435/67, 3436/67, 3437/67 and 3438/67, 19 July 1968, 28 CD 109.

This exception may include work in the public service where there is a short-age of volunteers (*Johansen v Norway*[70]). This exception relates to the power of states to create derogations from Article 4 under Article 15.

(d) *Work or service which forms part of normal civic obligations.*

The ECtHR has held that a financial contribution payable to the state in lieu of what would otherwise be compulsory service in the fire brigade in a German state was within this exception (*Schmidt v Germany*[71]). In the UK, a person who fails without reasonable cause to comply with a summons for jury service is liable to a fine pursuant to section 20 of the Juries Act 1974. It is highly likely that such a fine would also fall within the Article 4(3)(d) exception, but the discriminatory imposition of that fine would be a breach of Article 4 taken with Article 14 (see *Zarb Adami v Malta*, above).

M. Frequently asked questions

5.60 **What is the scope of Article 4?**

This Article prohibits slavery, servitude, forced or compulsory labour. Derogations can only take place in the most serious emergency and would have to be enacted by special legislation. Where employers impose employment conditions which could attract the provisions within Article 4, the court or tribunal must examine the working arrangement in question in order to comply with sections 3 and 6 of the HRA 1998.

Does Article 4 impose any obligations upon the state?

The state is positively obliged to prohibit slavery, servitude, and forced or compulsory labour. It is not sufficient to have statutory provisions outlawing such behaviour; what matters is whether the provisions are effectively used.

What do slavery, servitude, and serfdom mean today?

Working without being paid does not amount to slavery. There needs to be some power of ownership over a person exercised. Servitude does not require the element of ownership but a measure of coercion. Serfdom is a form of servitude which ties a person to the owner's property.

---

[70] (1985) 44 DR 155.
[71] (1994) 18 EHRR 513, paras 22–23.

What is forced or compulsory labour?

The service must be performed by the individual against his will and the obligation to carry it out must be oppressive or constitute an unavoidable hardship. Further forced labour is not undertaken voluntarily. Servants who are not given any time off nor permitted to leave their employers' premises may be viewed as carrying out compulsory labour.

To what extent are harsh employment conditions prohibited under the common law?

Statutory protection has been enacted to prevent excessive hours or conditions of labour.

How does Article 4 impact upon private employment?

Complaints relating to private employers are difficult to argue where an illegal contract is involved. Vulnerable workers are all the more in need of state protection in such circumstances. It would be particularly difficult to argue that the state was liable for a one-off case of forced labour.

Do the exceptions within Article 4(3) relate to complaints about employers?

That prison work will not normally be within the scope of Article 4 means it would be very difficult to bring a complaint about the small sums of money paid to prisoners for the work they carry out. A community service order would probably fall within the meaning of Article 4(3)(a) although no pay is received for such work undertaken.

Voluntary enlistment and compulsory military service fall within the Article 4(3)(b) exception. Article 4(3)(c) makes an exception for service exacted in case of an emergency or calamity threatening the life or well-being of the community. In such circumstances public service work could be compelled. An example of the type of exception falling within Article 4(3)(d) is a fine imposed for a failure without reasonable cause to comply with a summons for jury service.

6

THE SCOPE OF ARTICLE 6: THE RIGHT
TO A FAIR TRIAL

Article 6
Right to a fair trial

1. In the determination of his civil rights and obligations or of any criminal charge against him, everyone is entitled to a fair and public hearing within a reasonable time by an independent and impartial tribunal established by law. Judgment shall be pronounced publicly but the press and public may be excluded from all or part of the trial in the interest of morals, public order or national security in a democratic society, where the interests of juveniles or the protection of the private life of the parties so require, or to the extent strictly necessary in the opinion of the court in special circumstances where publicity would prejudice the interests of justice.

2. Everyone charged with a criminal offence shall be presumed innocent until proved guilty according to law.
3. Everyone charged with a criminal offence has the following minimum rights:
    (a) to be informed promptly, in a language which he understands and in detail, of the nature and cause of the accusation against him;
    (b) to have adequate time and facilities for the preparation of his defence;
    (c) to defend himself in person or through legal assistance of his own choosing or, if he has not sufficient means to pay for legal assistance, to be given it free when the interests of justice so require;
    (d) to examine or have examined witnesses against him and to obtain the attendance and examination of witnesses on his behalf under the same conditions as witnesses against him;
    (e) to have the free assistance of an interpreter if he cannot understand or speak the language used in court.

A. Introduction

6.01   The impact of Article 6 ECHR on employment law is discussed in two chapters. This chapter discusses the scope of the right to a fair trial; the next chapter discusses its substantive content.

6.02   Article 6 sets the basic requirements for both civil and criminal trials. They are inevitably more extensive for criminal trials. This chapter therefore starts by considering the extent to which the criminal aspect of Article 6 ECHR is relevant to employment law. It then identifies the preconditions for Article 6 to apply in the determination of civil rights and obligations.

6.03   The difficult question as to when employees in the public sector are protected under this Article is discussed. Comparisons are drawn with the more generous approach taken by Community law.

B. Criminal provisions not usually relevant to employment law

6.04   Article 6 ECHR concerns both civil and criminal proceedings, but its content is more detailed and specific in setting requirements for criminal proceedings. The first paragraph of the Article relates to both types of proceedings, whereas Article 6(2) and (3) apply only to the criminal process. These provisions will not usually be relevant to employment lawyers but their content should not be wholly ignored.

6.05   Some situations that arise in employment may lead to proceedings that incur a criminal burden of proof. Others may seem so serious for the reputation of the persons concerned that they may 'feel' like criminal proceedings. However, the Commission has resisted treating employment proceedings as criminal even if they are very serious and can lead to harsh penalties. Thus, in *Wickramsinghe v UK*,[1] the Commission declared inadmissible a complaint that proceedings leading to the removal of a doctor's registration by a decision of the General Medical Council were criminal proceedings. On the other hand such proceedings are certainly within the scope of the civil aspects of Article 6 ECHR. It is for this reason that right of appeal to the Privy Council is by way of a rehearing rather than a supervisory review (see *Ghosh v General Medical Council*[2]), but despite their seriousness they remain civil proceedings (see also 7.12 *et seq*).

C. The relationship between civil and criminal requirements in Article 6

The protections in Article 6(2) cannot simply be transposed to civil trials, but they do have some relevance to a consideration of the content of Article 6(1). Thus, while in Article 6(3)(e) there is a right to an interpreter in a criminal trial, it does not follow that such a right is automatically applicable to employment tribunal proceedings (see *Williams v Cowell*[3]). **6.06**

On the other hand, since the HRA 1998 requires the jurisprudence of the ECHR to provide a floor of rights, it is possible that the protections in the criminal aspect of this Article could be appropriate in the domestic application of Article 6 through the Act. Practitioners therefore need to be aware of the minimum standards imposed by this Article in relation to the criminal process. **6.07**

A right to silence may not be appropriate in civil proceedings before professional disciplinary bodies (*R v Securities and Futures Authority Limited, ex parte Fleurose*[4]). However, where conflicts arise between civil and criminal proceedings so that a person might wish to stay silent in civil or disciplinary proceedings because of the stage that the criminal proceedings have reached the first part of Article 6 might well be very important. **6.08**

The common law has held that individuals have no right to silence in civil or disciplinary proceedings where a defendant's 'right to silence' in a criminal trial conflicts with the obligation to provide an explanation in a prior civil disciplinary or civil matter. However, in the court's discretion and in order to do justice the civil matter may be postponed (see *R v BBC ex parte Lavelle*[5]). This discretionary **6.09**

---

[1] [1998] EHRLR 338.
[2] [2001] 1 WLR 1915, [2001] UKPC 29.
[3] [2000] ICR 85.
[4] [2001] IRLR 764; aff'd on other grounds [2002] IRLR 297.
[5] [1983] ICR 99.

approach must at least be informed and may have to give way to the defendant's rights under Article 6(1).

6.10 Practitioners should, however, take note of the recent EAT decision in *Ali v Sovereign Buses (London) Ltd*,[6] dealing with a situation where the employer decided to proceed with the disciplinary hearing whilst criminal proceedings were pending. The employee refused to say anything during the hearing on the ground that his right to silence was being infringed. The EAT held that the employer's approach did not breach Article 6 where there was no compulsion on the employee to give answers during the disciplinary proceedings, where he had not in any event utilised his right to silence during the criminal proceedings, and where the employer was not a public authority. In relation to the latter point, the EAT held that section 98(4) of ERA 1996 provided satisfactory recognition of the standards of fairness required by the ECtHR for the purpose of internal disciplinary hearings, and that there was no need, in the circumstances of Mr Ali's case, to 'read across' the right to silence which would have been applicable in criminal proceedings. The EAT further held that insofar as the criminal law provided insufficient safeguards against inappropriate use of information vouchsafed by an employee during internal disciplinary hearings, that was a matter for the Crown Court.[7]

6.11 More generally, in criminal proceedings which are regulatory,[8] the reversal of the legal burden of proof (a common feature in civil proceedings) might be appropriate and proportionate (*R v Davies (David Janway)*[9]). However, this would not always be inconsistent with the presumption of innocence (*Salabiaku v France*[10]).

D. The conditions for Article 6 to apply in civil proceedings

(1) Is there a dispute over a right?

6.12 The first question whenever an issue is raised about the application of Article 6 ECHR, is whether there is a dispute about a right. This is because Article 6 is

---

[6] 26 October 2006 [2007] All ER (D) 51 (Jan).

[7] The case was remitted to the employment tribunal on other grounds, namely that the tribunal had failed properly to interpret the authorities dealing with the employer's duty to consider adjourning disciplinary hearings where criminal proceedings are pending.

[8] The fact that the proceedings are regulatory ought not to make any difference to the approach to Art 6 because of the rights in relation to Art 6(2), yet in practice the approach to regulatory matters can be very different.

[9] [2003] EWCA Crim 2949, [2003] ICR 586.

[10] (1988) 13 EHRR 379, 388, para 28.

concerned solely with the determination of rights. However, not all aspects of the employment relationship will engage the language of civil rights. It is therefore important to identify whether there is a right which is recognised as such under the Convention. On this the case law of the Commission and the Court is consistent in holding that there has to be a process which will be decisive of a dispute (in French a '*contestation*') over a 'right' which it can be said is 'at least on arguable grounds to be recognised under domestic law'. In these circumstances the dispute must be genuine and serious; it may relate not only to the actual existence of a right but also its scope and the manner of its exercise; and finally the result of the proceedings must be directly decisive for the right in question (*Zander v Sweden*[11]).

(2) Administrative decisions about qualifications

Administrative decisions about qualifications do not usually concern disputes **6.13** about rights within Article 6 ECHR. However, disputes can arise in relation to the consequences of such decisions and these usually will be within Article 6. Thus, when proceedings were held under the Insurance Companies Act 1982 to decide whether a person was a fit or proper person to hold a responsible position with an insurance company, it was held that these did not concern a dispute within Article 6 (*X v UK*[12]), but when there was a consequential intervention by the state a dispute arose.

The way in which the Commission considered this problem can be seen from the **6.14** following extract from *X v UK*,[13] in which it set out its decision on admissibility:

> The Commission drew a distinction between the acts of a body which is engaged in the resolution of a dispute ('contestation') and the acts of an administrative or other body purporting merely to exercise or apply a legal power vested in it and not to resolve a legal claim or dispute. Article 6(1) was held to apply to the acts of the former but not to acts of the latter even if they affected civil rights. The Commission found that, in taking his decision, the Secretary of State had exercised legal powers which affected civil rights but was not engaged in the determination of a dispute or 'contestation' concerning civil rights and obligations.

> The Commission considers that the civil rights of the present applicant were similarly affected by the decision of the Secretary of State. The applicant had been offered the post of chief executive of the company on terms which had been agreed between him and the company. The effect of the decision was to prevent him from taking up that post and had clear pecuniary implications for the applicant. It is true that any agreement could only become operative once notice had been served on the Secretary

---

[11] (1994) 18 EHRR 175, para 22.
[12] (1998) 25 EHRR CD 88
[13] At 96.

of State and the Secretary of State had either stated that he had no objection to the appointment or had failed to serve a notice of objection. Thus, the Secretary of State's decision did not as such directly affect any existing right of the applicant to conduct the business of the company as its chief executive. However, the fact that the applicant's contractual right to occupy the post of chief executive was made subject to there being no objection from the Secretary of State did not in the view of the Commission alter its character as a civil right for the purposes of Article 6(1) of the Convention. Further, the decision of the Secretary of State directly affected the exercise of that right, even though the Applicant had not yet taken up the post as chief executive.

The Commission is further unable to accept the Government's argument that the Secretary of State's decision did not affect the civil rights of the applicant, first, because the decision only related to his ability to take up a specific post and not his right to be employed in the insurance industry generally and, secondly, because during his interview with the officials of the DTI, the applicant indicated that he would probably not have taken up the post in the company in any event. The undisputed effect of the decision of the Secretary of State was to deprive him of the opportunity of accepting a specific post which had been offered on terms which had been agreed. In the view of the Commission the applicant's civil rights were affected by the decision, irrespective of whether the decision had wider ramifications for the employment prospects of the applicant in the insurance industry and irrespective of whether, in the result, he would have declined the particular post in question.

The Commission further considers that the procedure by which the Secretary of State actively intervened to prevent the appointment of the applicant to the post which he had been offered amounted to a 'determination of [the] civil rights' of the applicant for the purpose of Article 6 para. 1 (Art. 6-1). In the view of the Commission a dispute or 'contestation' arose from the moment when the Secretary of State indicated that he was considering issuing a notice on the ground that the applicant was not a fit and proper person and that preliminary view was contested by the applicant. This dispute was determined in the proceedings which followed, culminating in the decision of the Secretary of State that the applicant was not a fit and proper person, with the consequence that the applicant was precluded from taking up the post offered to him. The proceedings therefore determined the applicant's 'civil rights and obligations'.[14]

(3) Is there a dispute about 'civil' rights?

6.15 The word 'civil' is important to a proper understanding of this Article. Article 6 ECHR applies only to the determination of 'civil' rights and obligations. If the dispute is not about 'civil' rights then it will not be strictly within Article 6. The ECtHR has repeatedly held (*König v Germany*[15]) that the word 'civil' has an

---

[14] The Commission referred to *Le Compte, Van Leuven and De Meyere v Belgium* (1983) 5 EHRR 133, paras 44–50.

[15] (1980) 2 EHRR 170, para 88.

autonomous Convention meaning. Thus the classification of a right in a particular country will not be decisive.

In particular, it should be noted that the distinction made by the Commission **6.16** and the Court between public and private law is by no means the same as that in use in the field of employment law in England and Wales. (See, for example, *R v East Berkshire Health Authority, ex parte Walsh*;[16] *R v Derbyshire County Council, ex parte Noble*;[17] *R v Lord Chancellor's Department, ex parte Nangle*;[18] *R v Secretary of State for Education, ex parte Prior.*[19])[20]

E. Public sector employees

This may be important in a particular case and is most likely to be of importance **6.17** in relation to employees in the public sector. It is only in Article 11 that the ECHR specifically identifies that certain types of civil servants may be excluded from the scope of the Convention. The history of the ECHR and its ambiguous approach to state employees was pointed out in *Vogt v Germany*,[21] where the ECtHR said that although recruitment to the civil service was intentionally omitted from the ECHR, that did not mean that civil servants were generally excluded from its application. The ECtHR said:[22]

> The Court reiterates that the right of recruitment to the civil service was deliberately omitted from the Convention. Consequently the refusal to appoint a person as a civil servant cannot as such provide the basis for a complaint under the Convention. This does not mean, however that a person who has been appointed as a civil servant cannot complain on being dismissed if that dismissal violates one of his or her rights under the Convention . . .

While for some time there has been no doubt that employment in the private **6.18** sector may be considered within Article 6 (eg *Buchholz v Germany*[23]), employment in the public sector has been much more problematical.

---

[16] [1984] ICR 743.
[17] [1990] ICR 808.
[18] [1991] ICR 743.
[19] [1994] ICR 877.
[20] See also S De Smith, H Woolf, and J Jowell, *Judicial Review of Administrative Action* (6th edn, London: Sweet & Maxwell, 2006).
[21] (1996) 21 EHRR 205. Though it should be noted that this was not a case in which Art 6 ECHR was invoked.
[22] At para 43.
[23] (1981) 3 EHRR 597: delay in disposing of a claim by a dismissed employee of unfair dismissal by a dry cleaning firm.

6.19   The Court had refrained in the past from formulating any abstract definition of the civil rights, beyond distinguishing between private and public law (*Benthem v Netherlands*[24]). This has led to much uncertainty, leaving the interpretation to be discovered on a case-by-case basis. This has been very unsatisfactory and has led to many surprising results. However, in its decision in *Eskelinen v Finland* (Application 63235/00, Judgment 19 April 2007) the Court has largely done away with these distinctions.

6.20   Since the approach of the ECHR involved distinctions that were not readily recognisable in UK law, and since the Convention jurisprudence provides a floor of rights only, it was always arguable that this limited approach should not be applied domestically. After all, the protection from unfair dismissal applies generally to civil servants (see ERA 1996, s 191 and Part XIII).

6.21   However in the jurisprudence of the ECHR, complaints of violation of Article 6 by public employees in civil law (in contradistinction to common law) systems, concerning appointment, dismissal, conditions of service, and discipline, have been rejected at the admissibility stage in significant cases, including:

- *Saraiva de Carvalho v Portugal* (members of the armed forces);[25]
- *Leander v Sweden* (civil servants);[26]
- *X v Portugal* (judges);[27]
- *X v Germany* (clergymen in a state-regulated church);[28]
- *X v Italy* (state school teachers);[29] and
- *X v Belgium* (public corporation employees).[30]

(1) An example of the historic lack of protection for public sector employees in the UK

6.22   From a UK perspective, one of the most surprising examples of the reluctance of the European Commission of Human Rights to become involved in cases concerning the determination of employment issues is *Neigel v France*.[31] Miss Neigel was an auxiliary shorthand typist for Biarritz Town Council. She was denied

---

[24] (1986) 8 EHRR 1, para 34.
[25] (1981) 26 DR 262 (see also *Matthews v Ministry of Defence* [2002] 1 WLR 2621 (CA); [2003] 1 AC 1163.
[26] (1987) 9 EHRR 433, para 45.
[27] (1983) 32 DR 258.
[28] (1981) 27 DR 249.
[29] (1980) 21 DR 208.
[30] Application 3937/69, (12 December 1969) 32 CD 61.
[31] (2000) 30 EHRR 310.

reinstatement following leave of absence for personal reasons. The Commission held that although there was a dispute over a right, it was not a 'civil' right within Article 6(1) ECHR because the dispute concerned the exercise of an administrative discretion. This is most easily understood by noting that the dispute went through the French administrative law courts.

The Commission relied on *Neigel* in determining its approach to *Balfour v UK*,[32] **6.23** which directly concerned proceedings in a British industrial tribunal. Mr Balfour was dismissed from the Foreign and Commonwealth Office and brought a complaint of unfair dismissal to the industrial tribunal. As the case progressed, he sought discovery of certain documents. However, both the Home and Foreign Secretaries claimed public interest immunity, and neither the industrial tribunal nor the superior courts were prepared to go behind those certificates.

Although Mr Balfour cited *Darnell v UK*,[33] in which it was accepted that delay in **6.24** unfair dismissal proceedings brought by an NHS doctor breached Article 6 ECHR, the Commission rejected the complaint, relying directly on *Neigel*. It may be that the national security issues in the case played a subconscious part in the reluctance of the Commission to accept this application. However, *Neigel* is now unlikely to be followed (see 6.26 *et seq*).

F. The need for a changed approach

In *Huber v France*,[34] the difficulty in applying Article 6 ECHR in relation to **6.25** the civil service was obvious, and the need for a clearer test became ever more apparent. In *Huber*, the applicant complained of the time taken by the administrative court to quash a decision to send him on forced leave and suspend payment of his salary. The Court drew the distinction between disputes in relation to recruitment, careers, and termination of civil servants, and disputes over purely economic rights. By a majority of only 5:4, the Court held that this dispute was essentially about the applicant's career, and that although the consequences were pecuniary this did not bring the case within Article 6 ECHR. There were, however, strong dissenting judgments which underlined the need for reconsideration.

---

[32] Decision on admissibility given 2 July 1997, Application 30976/96, see [1997] EHRLR 665n. For a fuller discussion of the facts of this case, see *Balfour v Foreign and Commonwealth Office* [1994] ICR 277.
[33] (1994) 18 EHRR 205.
[34] (1998) 26 EHRR 457.

(1) The *Pellegrin* and *Martinie* jurisprudence

6.26 The ECtHR addressed these difficulties afresh in *Pellegrin v France*[35] and reached a radically different view. From this point the old case law is of only marginal relevance. The Court reviewed some of the old case law:[36]

> . . . Article 6(1) applies where the claim in issue relates to a 'purely economic' right—such as payment of salary (see the *De Santa v Italy, Lapalorcia v Italy and Abenavoli v Italy* judgments of 2 September 1997, Reports 1997-V, at p. 1663, paragraph 18, p. 1677, paragraph 21, and p. 1690, paragraph 16, respectively)—or an 'essentially economic' one (see the *Nicodemo v Italy* judgment of 2 September 1997, Reports 1997-V, p. 1703, paragraph 18) and does not mainly call in question 'the authorities' discretionary powers' (see the following judgments: *Benkessiouer v France*, 24 August 1998, Reports 1998-V, p. 2287, §§ 29-30; *Couez v France*, 24 August 1998, Reports 1998-V, p. 2265, paragraph 25; *Le Calvez v France*, judgment of 29 July 1998 (Reports of Judgments and Decisions 1998-V, pp. 1900–01, § 58), cited above, pp. 1900-01, § 58; and *Cazenave de la Roche v France*, judgment of 9 June 1998, Reports of Judgments and Decisions 1998-III, p. 1327, § 43), cited above, p. 1327, § 43).

6.27 The Court decided that it should reconsider its approach and that there should be a functional criterion for deciding whether Article 6(1) ECHR was applicable to employees in the public sector. This was based on the nature of the employee's duties and responsibilities. The critical ruling was:[37]

> The Court therefore rules that the only disputes excluded from the scope of Article 6(1) of the Convention are those which are raised by public servants whose duties typify the specific activities of the public service in so far as the latter is acting as the depositary of public authority responsible for protecting the general interests of the State or other public authorities. A manifest example of such activities is provided by the armed forces and the police. In practice, the Court will ascertain, in each case, whether the applicant's post entails—in the light of the nature of the duties and responsibilities appertaining to it—direct or indirect participation in the exercise of powers conferred by public law and duties designed to safeguard the general interests of the State or of other public authorities . . .

6.28 This clear interpretation of Article 6(1) was stated by the Court in the same judgment to be subject to limits:[38]

> . . . Accordingly, no disputes between administrative authorities and employees who occupy posts involving participation in the exercise of powers conferred by public law attract the application of Article 6(1) since the Court intends to establish a functional criterion (see paragraph 64 above). Disputes concerning pensions all come within the ambit of Article 6(1) because on retirement employees break the special

---

[35] (1999) 31 EHRR 651.
[36] At para 59.
[37] At para 66.
[38] At para 67.

bond between themselves and the authorities; they, and a fortiori those entitled through them, then find themselves in a situation exactly comparable to that of employees under private law in that the special relationship of trust and loyalty binding them to the State has ceased to exist and the employee can no longer wield a portion of the State's sovereign power (see paragraph 65 above)

More recently in *Frydlender v France*,[39] where the economic development depart-   **6.29**
ment of the French Ministry for Economic Affairs had failed to renew the contract of an employee, the European Court held that Article 6(1) ECHR did apply and had been breached in the case because of the failure to provide a hearing within a reasonable time. The applicant had been responsible for promoting the sale of French wines and spirits in New York. The Court examined whether, on account of the nature of his duties and the level of his responsibilities, the applicant might in practice have participated in activities designed to safeguard the general interests of the state, and so come within the exception to Article 6(1). In view of the nature of the duties performed by the applicant and the relatively low level of his responsibilities, the Court considered that he was not carrying out any task which could be said to entail, either directly or indirectly, duties designed to safeguard the general interests of the state. The Court observed that the *Pellegrin* judgment had been intended to restrict cases in which public servants could be denied the practical and effective protection afforded to them, as to any other person, by the Convention, and in particular by Article 6. The Court held that it had to adopt a restrictive interpretation, in accordance with the object and purpose of the Convention, of the exceptions to the safeguards afforded by Article 6(1). But such a restrictive interpretation would be too seriously weakened if the Court were to find that the activities of the staff of the economic development offices as a whole, whatever the nature of their duties and their level of responsibility, entailed the exercise of powers conferred by public law.

In *Devlin v UK*,[40] Devlin complained that the issue by the Secretary of State of a   **6.30**
security certificate under section 42 of the Fair Employment (Northern Ireland) Act 1976, certifying that the refusal to employ him as an administrative assistant in the Northern Ireland Civil Service was on national security grounds, constituted a breach of Article 6. The Court applied *Pellegrin* and found that Article 6 of the Convention was applicable as the employment was at the lowest grade in the non-industrial Civil Service. The Court also applied *Tinnelly & Sons Ltd v UK*[41] (see 7.60 below) and found that the issue of the certificate had been a disproportionate restriction on Devlin's right of access to a court.

---

[39] (2001) 31 EHRR 52.
[40] (2002) 34 EHRR 43.
[41] (1999) 27 EHRR 249.

6.31   In *Deveney v UK*,[42] the issue of a certificate preventing access to an employment tribunal on the ground of public safety or public order was held to be a disproportionate restriction on an applicant's right of access to a court in violation of Article 6(1). This is obviously contrary to the Commission's ruling in *Balfour v UK* (see 6.23).

6.32   Thus the old jurisprudence[43] must always be re-assessed for their relevance by reference to the ECtHR's judgment in *Pellegrin* and subsequent cases. More recently in a judgment of the Grand Chamber in *Martinie v France*,[44] the ECtHR said:

> 1. The Court would emphasise that the issue raised in the present case is, specifically, the applicability of Article 6 § 1 of the Convention to proceedings before the Court of Audit on an appeal from a judgment of a regional audit office levying a surcharge against a public accountant.
>
> It points out in this connection that it is common ground that there was a 'dispute' (*contestation*) regarding an 'obligation' of the applicant. The question that therefore needs to be determined is whether the 'obligation' in question is a 'civil' one within the meaning of Article 6 § 1. In order to determine that question, the proper approach, in theory, is to weigh the features of private law and public law present in the case against each other (see, for example, *Feldbrugge v the Netherlands*, judgment of 29 May 1986, Series A no. 99, §§ 26-40).
>
> 2. In the case of *Pellegrin*, to which the Government referred, the Court was confronted with the issue of the applicability of Article 6 § 1 of the Convention to a dispute between a non-established civil service employee under contract and the administrative authority employing him. Mr Pellegrin had complained before the domestic courts of the decision removing his name from the establishment list of the Ministry concerned.
>
> In *Pellegrin* the Court began by reiterating the position under the earlier case-law (see paragraph 59 of the judgment).
>
> According to that case-law, the principle was that 'disputes relating to the recruitment, careers and termination of service of civil servants are as a general rule outside the scope of Article 6 § 1'. However, this principle of exclusion, the Court observed, had been limited and clarified in a number of cases. In particular, Article 6 § 1 had been considered to apply where the claim in issue related to a 'purely economic' or 'essentially economic' right and did not mainly call in question 'the authorities' discretionary powers'.
>
> The Court held (see paragraph 60): 'as it stands, the above case-law contains a margin of uncertainty for Contracting States as to the scope of their obligations

---

[42] Application 24265/94 (19 March 2002).
[43] For an analysis of the position before the case of *Pellegrin v France*, discussed at 6.37–6.45 below, see G Morris, 'The European Convention on Human Rights and Employment: To which Acts does it apply' [1999] EHRLR 496.
[44] Application 58675/00 (judgment 12 April 2006).

under Article 6 § 1 in disputes raised by employees in the public sector over their conditions of service'.

In the circumstances the Court wished to 'put an end to the uncertainty which surrounds application of the guarantees of Article 6 § 1 to disputes between States and their servants' (see paragraph 61). It considered that it should 'adopt a functional criterion based on the nature of the employee's duties and responsibilities' (see paragraph 64). In its view, 'the only disputes excluded from the scope of Article 6 § 1 of the Convention are those which are raised by public servants whose duties typify the specific activities of the public service in so far as the latter is acting as the depositary of public authority responsible for protecting the general interests of the State or of other public authorities' (see paragraph 66). 'In practice, the Court will ascertain, in each case, whether the applicant's post entails – in the light of the nature of the duties and responsibilities appertaining to it – direct or indirect participation in the exercise of powers conferred by public law and duties designed to safeguard the general interests of the State or of other public authorities' (ibid.).

3. The *Pellegrin* judgment was thus a departure from precedent, and has since been confirmed, regarding the principles it established and the criterion of applicability of Article 6 § 1 it laid down, by a large number of judgments and decisions of the Court (see, for example, among other authorities, *Frydlender v France*, judgment of 27 June 2000 [GC], ECHR 2000–VII; *Linde Falero v Spain*, no. 51535/99, decision of 21 June 2000; *Rey and Others v France*, judgment of 5 October 2004, no. 68406/01; and *Czech v Poland*, judgment of 15 November 2005, no. 49034/99).

4. It therefore needs to be ascertained whether the applicant's post entailed – within the meaning of that case-law – direct or indirect participation in the exercise of powers conferred by public law and duties designed to safeguard the general interests of the State or of other public authorities.

5. The Grand Chamber concludes that Article 6 § 1 is applicable, as did the Chamber in its above-mentioned admissibility decision, but by different reasoning. The Chamber mainly had regard to the special nature of the dispute between the applicant and the State in reaching the conclusion that the obligations on the applicant were 'civil' ones within the meaning of Article 6 § 1 of the Convention, with private-law features predominating in this case. In the Grand Chamber's view, in the light of the *Pellegrin* judgment regard should rather be had to the applicant's post, the nature of his duties and the responsibilities attached to the post. The case involved a civil servant in the employ of the State education service who had been appointed by the Director of Education as accountant of a school and was responsible, in that capacity, for the accounts of a secondary school and of those of a centre attached to it that had no separate legal personality. Neither the nature of the duties carried out by the applicant, nor the responsibilities attached to them, support the view that he 'participated in the exercise of powers conferred by public law and duties designed to safeguard the general interests of the State or of other public authorities', unless these concepts are to be construed broadly. The correct approach, however, in accordance with the object and purpose of the Convention, is to adopt a restrictive interpretation of the exceptions to the safeguards afforded by Article 6 § 1 (see *Pellegrin*, cited above, § 64).

> Accordingly, the Court concludes that, having regard to the nature of his post, the dispute between the applicant and the State does come within the scope of Article 6 § 1 of the Convention.

6.33 Now the approach to the question whether there is a dispute about civil rights in the context of employment by an arm of the state will normally lead to the answer yes. Only if the dispute concerns the employment or dismissal of a public servant whose duties typify the specific activities of the public service insofar as the latter is acting as the depositary of public authority responsible for protecting the general interests of the state or of other public authorities is there likely to be a more intense inquiry. Even in such a case it is not a foregone conclusion that the ECtHR would rule inadmissible a complaint of breach of Article 6.

(2) How important is the distinction in the jurisprudence of the ECtHR between civil rights and other rights?

6.34 This approach is to be welcomed as it tends to eliminate the difficult conceptual difficulties that arise when common lawyers must address what is essentially a civil law concept. But it should also be noted that the limits to the scope of Article 6 which still remain are by no means beyond further re-appraisal. Thus, three judges of the Grand Chamber in a concurring joint Opinion argued by reference inter alia to norms set out in the Charter of Fundamental Rights of the European Union that the *Pellegrin* jurisprudence and the last remaining constraints on its application in an employment context would have to be reconsidered soon.[45]

6.35 So the answer to the headline question is that after the judgment in *Martinie* it may not be very important at all. Indeed it is likely that British courts and tribunals will not be very concerned with the old distinction. It had been paradoxical that sections 6 and 7 of the HRA 1998 give extra rights to employees of exclusively public authorities to enforce Convention rights, when, in respect of Article 6 ECHR, those same employees might have found that they had fewer rights than employees in the exclusively private sector. Yet this is no longer likely to be such a problem. *Martinie* makes it clear that the ECtHR is moving to decrease rather than increase this constraint on the reach of Article 6. See also *Eskelinen* referred to at 6.19.

(3) Should British courts and tribunals ever discriminate against civil servants in the application of Article 6?

6.36 It has been pointed out that the Court's approach in *Pellegrin* seems to contravene Article 14 ECHR which prevents discrimination on grounds of 'other status'.

---

[45] See the joint concurring opinion of Judges Tulkens, Maruste, and Fura-Sandström at the conclusion of the judgment in *Martinie v France*.

The rhetorical question might therefore be asked: why should a policeman not be protected under Article 6 ECHR when an employee of a private security firm is protected? There is no obvious answer to this question, especially when it is recalled that Article 1 ECHR requires that the rights and freedoms are to be secured to 'everyone'. However, the judgment in *Martinie* means this is now unlikely to be important.

In *Eskelinen v Finland* (Application no 63235/00, Judgment 19 April 2007) the ECtHR adopted this argument in minimising the differences.

G. Pre-*Pellegrin* case law

It may still be worth considering a few of the cases that were dealt with by the **6.37** Commission and the Court before *Pellegrin*, where they may still point to the approach that will be taken. However, they will need to be considered from the point of view of the functional test set out at above, but see also *Eskelinen v Finland* at 6.19.

(1) Actions against employees for reimbursement

In *Muyldermans v Belgium*,[46] the determination of the employee's obligation to **6.38** reimburse certain sums was held by the Commission to be within the scope of Article 6 ECHR. Mrs Muyldermans worked as an accountant in a post office. The Audit Court found that the applicant had failed to perform properly several of her duties and ordered her to make reimbursement to the post office. The Commission stated that:[47]

> . . . Finding that the applicant . . . had been guilty of negligence, the Court . . . ordered the applicant not to 'return' the sums for which she was accountable but to pay the National Post Office the sum of 2 Million Belgian Francs. The basis for determining *responsabilité* the scope of which may, according to the Court of Cassation, be assessed on the basis of certain rules inferred from the general principles set forth in the Civil Code, is thus not the settlement of the account but the assessment of the faults committed by the applicant. That being the case, . . . even though some of the facts might lead one to suppose that the obligation in question is to some extent public in nature, the Commission considers, that the obligation is mixed, with the private aspects predominating. The dispute (*contestation*) concerned a civil obligation within the meaning of Article 6 of the Convention. The Commission consequently considers that Article 6(1) of the Convention is applicable to the proceedings followed in the present case before the Audit Court.

---

[46] (1993) 15 EHRR 204.
[47] At paras 55–57.

(2) Claims for pensions

6.39 In *Lombardo v Italy*,[48] the ECtHR held that Article 6 ECHR applied to a police-man's claim to a public service pension which was clearly not linked to a private contract of employment. The Court stated:[49]

> Notwithstanding the public law aspects pointed out by the Government, what is concerned here is essentially an obligation on the State to pay a pension to a public servant in accordance with the legislation in force. In performing this obligation the State is not using discretionary powers and may be compared, in this respect, with an employer who is a party to a contract of employment governed by private law. Consequently, the right of a carabiniere to receive an 'enhanced ordinary pension' if he fulfils the necessary conditions of injury and disability is to be regarded as a 'civil right' within the meaning of Article 6(1), which is therefore applicable in the present case.

6.40 This approach was followed in *Massa v Italy*.[50] Mr Massa claimed a reversionary pension in respect of his deceased wife's employment as a headmistress of a state school. The Court held that although disputes relating to the recruitment, careers, and termination of service of public servants were, as a general rule, outside the scope of Article 6(1) ECHR, statutory intervention by the state had not always prevented the Court from finding that rights in issue were 'civil'. It held that:[51]

> . . . Notwithstanding the public law aspects pointed out by the Government, the . . . dispute arises from an obligation on the state to pay a reversionary pension to the husband of a public servant in accordance with legislation in force. In performing this obligation, the state is not using discretionary powers and may be compared in this respect to an employer who is party to a contract of employment governed by private law. Accordingly the applicant's rights to a reversionary pension is a civil one within the meaning of Article 6(1) . . .

(3) National Health Service workers

6.41 In *Darnell v UK*,[52] Dr Darnell had brought proceedings for unfair dismissal against his health authority. The unfair dismissal proceedings were heavily delayed. He complained to Strasbourg. At the admissibility stage the Commission stated:[53]

> The Commission notes that the applicant, although employed by a public authority, was not a civil servant. His employment and dismissal were based on a written

---

[48] (1992) 21 EHRR 188.
[49] At para 17.
[50] (1994) 18 EHRR 266
[51] (at para 26).
[52] (1994) 18 EHRR 205.
[53] (1991) 69 DR 306, at 308.

contract setting out the terms of his employment . . . Moreover, the applicant's contract and conditions of employment gave him access to the ordinary courts to determine his claims as to the legality and fairness of his dismissal . . . .

Before the Court it was conceded by the UK that there was a breach of Article 6(1) ECHR. This case might be compared with *Cazenave de la Roche v France*,[54] where, when a civil servant was dismissed and held to be entitled to compensation for that dismissal, the delay in the proceedings determining the amount of the compensation was held to amount to a breach of Article 6 ECHR.

(4) Police officers

In *X v UK*,[55] a claim by an English policeman was held not to fall within Article 6   **6.42** ECHR, because police officers 'are exclusively subordinated to governmental authorities and do not enter into contractual relationships'.[56]

(5) Payments of social security contributions

In what may seem a surprising decision to British lawyers, in *Schouten and*   **6.43** *Meldrum v Netherlands*,[57] the Court held that an employer's obligation to pay social security contributions[58] on behalf of his employees was a civil right or obligation. The judgment of the Court includes a detailed analysis of the public and private law elements.[59] The private law considerations covered the personal and economic nature of the rights in question, the link with the contract of employment, and the similarity to private insurance. The last consideration was ultimately decisive.

(6) Wages claims by civil servants

There had already been some signs that the Court was taking a more liberal   **6.44** approach to disputes about the wages of civil servants. Applicants in *De Santa, Lapalorca, Abnavoli and Nicodemo v Italy*,[60] were all civil servants who were complaining that there had been a breach of Article 6(1) ECHR in respect of complaints brought by them in relation to calculation of remuneration. The Court held that Article 6(1) was applicable because the discretionary powers of administrative authorities were not in issue and the individuals had asserted 'economic rights', so that the private law features predominated. It is questionable whether

---

[54] (2001) 33 EHRR 7.
[55] (1980) 21 DR 168.
[56] At 170.
[57] (1995) 19 EHRR 432.
[58] There had already been a number of cases in which the Court had held that Art 6 ECHR applied to social insurance: see, eg, *Schuler-Zgraggen v Switzerland* (1993) 16 EHRR 405.
[59] See paras 49–60.
[60] [1997] HRCD, vol VIII, 678.

these cases would be decided in the same way now since the Court has attempted to give clear guidance over the whole of this area of law.

6.45 This approach has been confirmed in *Ahmet Kılıç v Turkey*[61] where the ECtHR considered that it was the nature of the post held by a watchman employed by a local authority that was determinative in determining whether Article 6 applied to a dispute about wages. It held that:[62]

> . . . The Court sees no reason to hold [Article 6 does not apply], it being noted that, despite his status, the applicant did not occupy a post involving direct or indirect participation in the exercise of powers conferred by public law and duties designed to safeguard the general interests of the State or of other public authorities

H. Frequently asked questions

6.46 What rights do individuals have under Article 6?

Article 6 gives every individual the right to a fair and public hearing, within a reasonable time, by an independent and impartial tribunal established by law in the determination of his or her civil rights and obligations, or of any criminal charge against him/her. It also provides that judgment will be pronounced publicly (subject to certain specific qualifications), and makes specific provision in relation to the rights of those charged with criminal offences.

Do the rights relating to criminal proceedings have any relevance to employment lawyers?

Not directly. Even disciplinary proceedings before a regulatory body, which may remove an individual's right to work in a particular field, are not regarded by the ECtHR as criminal proceedings. However, the specific rights for those charged with criminal offences should be borne in mind by practitioners in considering the content of the floor of basic rights provided to individuals by the HRA 1998. Further, the different types of protection provided in relation to civil and criminal proceedings may require a stay of particular civil proceedings where there are contemporaneous criminal proceedings dealing with the same issues.

What is a 'right' for the purposes of Article 6?

The right must be one which can be said, at least on arguable grounds, to be recognised under domestic law. The dispute about the right must be genuine and serious; it may

---

[61] Application no. 38473/02 (judgment 25 July 2006).
[62] At para 21.

relate not only to the existence of the right, but also to its scope and exercise, but the result of the proceedings must be directly decisive of the right in question.

Can disputes arising out of any employment relationship give rise to the determination of civil rights?

Disputes over rights arising out of employment in the private sector may amount to civil rights within Article 6. It was initially thought that disputes relating to public sector employees would not be covered by Article 6. However, since *Eskelinen v Finland* (Application no 63235/00, Judgment 19 April 2007) these distinctions seem to have been removed, though how the guarantees in Article 6 should be applied to civil servants will be reviewed by the ECtHR: see *Eskelinen* at [64].

7

THE CONTENT OF ARTICLE 6: THE RIGHT TO A FAIR TRIAL

A. Introduction

7.01 This chapter discusses the substantive content of the right to a fair trial under Article 6 ECHR. For a discussion of the application of Article 6 to a particular set of facts, reference should be made to Chapter 6.

7.02 The content of Article 6 ECHR is readily recognisable since it encompasses the basic concepts of a fair trial. However, practitioners cannot take for granted that they know what it entails. The jurisprudence of the Court and the Commission in relation to this Article goes further than might perhaps be expected at first glance.

7.03 The common law has a long history of considering what is necessary for a fair civil trial. So, Article 6 jurisprudence will inform this but is unlikely to make a radical difference. However, there are at least two aspects of the employment tribunal jurisdiction for which Article 6 may be more significant.

- **Legal aid**
  For example, the historical absence of legal aid for tribunal proceedings which has led the tribunal to develop its own particular ways of dealing with issues of access to justice. The impact of the Article has been felt in relation to the provision of legal assistance to those who appear in the employment tribunals.
- **Sensitive proceedings**
  Secondly, the subject matter of tribunal proceedings is often very sensitive. Key business decisions and delicate personal matters may arise for discussion. These are constant themes in the discussion of the application of Article 6 in employment law.

These are considered in detail at 7.74 and 7.53 *et seq*.

7.04 Whilst this Article has not led to sudden and dramatic changes in the way that tribunals conduct cases, it has changed some of the ways that tribunals do their work. This chapter sets out what has occurred to date, but it should be noted that further developments will be forthcoming and the case law on this topic is constantly growing.

7.05 This chapter considers, first, the right to a court and how Article 6 ECHR applies to professional bodies that make decisions which affect employment. It then considers in detail the four minimum requirements for compliance with Article 6:

(a) an independent and impartial tribunal;
(b) a fair and public hearing;
(c) reasonable expedition of the hearing; and
(d) a public judgment.

It examines certain procedural rules which are affected by Article 6 under the heading 'fair and public hearing'. Lastly, the effect that Article 6 has on appeals is discussed.

B. The right to a court

(1) Which courts and tribunals are involved?

Article 6 ECHR requires that employment rights are subject to determination **7.06** under the rule of law. This is sometimes described as a 'right to a court'. Most employment disputes, but not all, are resolved in courts or tribunals to which Article 6 obviously applies.

(2) Ordinary courts and tribunals

Employment tribunals are the forum in which most employment rights are **7.07** determined initially. The High Court and county court will have jurisdiction in cases which give rise to contractual or tortious claims and/or where an equitable remedy is appropriate. Appeals lie from the employment tribunal to the Employment Appeal Tribunal (EAT). From both the EAT and the High Court and county courts appeals lie, with permission, to the Court of Appeal, and with leave, to the House of Lords. These are all courts for the purposes of Article 6 ECHR.

(3) Internal and professional bodies

Independence and impartiality can be an issue in relation to other tribunals which **7.08** are set up ad hoc, or which are internal to professional or other bodies. Some professional tribunals may be subject to Article 6 (*P (A Barrister) v General Council of the Bar*[1] and *Tehrani v UK Central Council for Nursing, Midwifery and Health Visiting*[2]). Where such tribunals do not comply with Article 6, the deficiency may be made good by an effective appeal, or by an effective judicial review procedure.

(4) The importance of judicial supervision of internal and professional bodies

Many decisions that are determinative of an individual's civil rights and obliga- **7.09** tions are taken by an administrative authority or the jurisdictional organ of a professional association, or by some other body that is not a tribunal in the sense of Article 6 ECHR, or which does not comply with the right to a fair trial

---

[1] [2005] 1 WLR 3019.
[2] [2001] IRLR 208.

(for example, in the absence of a public hearing). Where this is so, Article 6 is satisfied if there is an appeal to a body with 'full jurisdiction' that does comply with it.

7.10 This principle was stated by the Court most notably in the case of *Albert and Le Compte v Belgium*.[3] It has been restated by the Court in a planning case, *Bryan v UK*,[4] and by the Commission in an insurance case, *X v UK*.[5]

7.11 More recently in *R (on the application of Holding & Barnes Plc) v Secretary of State for the Environment, Transport and the Regions*,[6] the House of Lords held that the courts were able to exercise sufficient control over the decision-making portion of the Secretary of State's role by means of judicial review. The Court could not review the policy-making aspect of the Secretary of State's role, only the part concerned with the lawfulness of the decision and the adequacy of the procedural steps involved. So, whilst the reference to 'full jurisdiction' in *Albert and Le Compte v Belgium* might be thought to require a review of the substantive decision, this would amount to stepping into the Secretary of State's shoes in a manner contrary to established European jurisprudence.

(5) Minimum standards for disciplinary offences

7.12 In many member states, the duty of adjudicating disciplinary offences is conferred on professional associations. In these cases, at least one of the two following systems must apply to meet Article 6 ECHR:

(a) the jurisdictional organs of the professional associations themselves comply with the requirements of Article 6(1);

(b) the jurisdictional organs of the professional associations are subject to subsequent control by a judicial body that has full jurisdiction and provides the guarantees of Article 6(1).

7.13 In *Le Compte, Van Leuven and De Meyere v Belgium*,[7] the Court stated that:[8]

[W]hilst Article 6(1) embodies the 'right to a court' . . . it nevertheless does not oblige the Contracting States to submit '*contestations*' (disputes) [see 6.12 above] over 'civil rights and obligations' to a procedure conducted at each of its stages before 'tribunals' meeting the Article's various requirements. Demands of flexibility and efficiency, which are fully compatible with the protection of human rights, may

---

[3] (1991) 13 EHRR 415.
[4] (1996) 21 EHRR 342, paras 44 and 46.
[5] Application 28530/95, 19 January 1998.
[6] [2003] 2 AC 295.
[7] (1982) 4 EHRR 1.
[8] (para. 51).

justify the prior intervention of administrative or professional bodies and, a fortiori, of judicial bodies which do not satisfy the said requirements in every respect . . .

In some cases deficiencies at the first stage will be remedied at a full rehearing on appeal. Thus in *Wickramsinghe v UK*,[9] the Commission rejected an application by a doctor who complained that the procedure before the General Medical Council was in breach of Article 6 ECHR. While agreeing that the procedure that he was afforded had been in breach of the requirements, the Commission considered that the appellate role of the Privy Council (as opposed to a full factual review) which had full jurisdiction was sufficient to provide the rights guaranteed under Article 6. **7.14**

In *Ghosh v General Medical Council*,[10] the Privy Council held that the appellate, rather than the merely supervisory role of the Privy Council in relation to a disciplinary decision of the General Medical Council ensured Article 6 compliance. **7.15**

Accordingly, it can be seen from the above cases that the minimum standard for the safeguarding of fairness is set quite low. For example, in the planning case *Adlard v Secretary of State for the Environment*,[11] the judgment reiterated the House of Lords in *R v Secretary of State for the Environment, ex parte Alconbury Developments Ltd and Ors*,[12] by emphasising that safeguards are irrelevant to questions of policy or expediency. This stems from the principle set down in *Zumtobel v Austria*[13] of respect for the decision of an administrative authority on questions of expediency. So in *Adlard* it was acceptable for the local planning authority to make findings of fact. **7.16**

(6) Examples of how judicial review can provide a right to a court

This approach was applied in *Kingsley v UK*.[14] That case concerned a decision by the Gaming Board that the applicant, who had been the managing director of a gaming company, was not a fit and proper person to be involved in gaming pursuant to section 19 of the Gaming Act 1968. The effect of the decision was that the applicant was unable to obtain employment in any sector of the gaming industry in the UK, or in any jurisdiction which had a relationship with the UK gaming authorities. **7.17**

However, a member of the Gaming Board had already expressed views about the conduct of the company which had employed Mr Kingsley and had already taken **7.18**

---

[9] [1998] EHRLR 338.
[10] [2001] 1 WLR 1915, [2001] UKPC 29.
[11] [2002] 1 WLR 2515, CA, [2002] EWHC 7 (Admin), at para 117.
[12] [2001] UKHL 23, [2003] 2 AC 295.
[13] (1993) 17 EHRR 116.
[14] (2001) 33 EHRR 13.

steps in relation to it. Prior to the section 19 proceedings in relation to Mr Kingsley, his solicitors had suggested that an independent tribunal should be set up to investigate the matter. The Gaming Board had disagreed, saying that they were required to take the decision and that the matter could not be delegated. This argument succeeded on a judicial review and leave to appeal was refused.

7.19 The ECtHR considered first whether Article 6 ECHR applied:

> . . . the Court notes the parties' agreement that Article 6(1) is applicable and recalls the European Commission of Human Rights' decision in the case of *X v United Kingdom* where the applicant was prevented from taking up the position of chief executive of a large insurance company because of the Secretary of State's decision that he was not a 'fit and proper' person to hold such a position. The Commission found that the Secretary of State's decision deprived him of the opportunity of accepting a specific post which had been offered on terms which had been agreed and that the procedure by which the Secretary of State actively intervened to prevent the appointment of the applicant to the post which he had been offered amounted to a 'determination of [the] civil rights' of the applicant for the purpose of Article 6(1).
>
> In the present case, the withdrawal of the applicant's Section 19 certificates, although relating to specific premises, in effect prevents him from holding any management position in the gaming industry, as he would not be granted the requisite Section 19 certificate necessary for a management post at any other premises.
>
> The Court considers that the proceedings before the Panel and the High Court determined the applicant's 'civil rights and obligations'.

7.20 The Court then went on to consider whether there had been a breach by the Gaming Board, and held that there had. The government argued that the possibility of judicial review of the decision by the Gaming Board was sufficient to ensure that Article 6 ECHR was complied with. However, the Court noted that on the judicial review application the judge had felt that he could not remit the matter to the Gaming Board since only the Board could take the decision under the Gaming Act, and accordingly it could not be delegated to an independent and impartial tribunal. On this ground the Court held that there had been a breach of Article 6:

> The Court considers that it is generally inherent in the notion of judicial review that, if a ground of challenge is upheld, the reviewing court has power to quash the impugned decision, and that either the decision will then be taken by the review court, or the case will be remitted for a fresh decision by the same or a different body. Thus where, as here, complaint is made of a lack of impartiality on the part of the decision-making body, the concept of 'full jurisdiction' involves that the reviewing court not only considers the complaint but has the ability to quash the impugned decision and to remit the case for a new decision by an impartial body.
>
> In the present case the domestic courts were unable to remit the case for a first decision by the Board or by another independent tribunal. The Court thus finds that, in the particular circumstances of the case, the High Court and the Court of Appeal did

not have 'full jurisdiction' within the meaning of the case-law on Article 6 when they reviewed the Panel's decision.

In *R v United Kingdom Central Council for Nursing, Midwifery & Health Visiting,* **7.21** *ex parte Margaret Yvonne Simpson Tehrani,*[15] the Outer House of the Court of Session considered the application of Article 6 ECHR to nurses' disciplinary proceedings. The Court of Session found that proposed disciplinary proceedings before a professional conduct committee would lead to a determination of Ms Tehrani's civil rights and obligations, because an order striking her name from the UK Central Council register would exclude her from certain nursing posts, either as a matter of law or as the result of the application of criteria imposed by prospective employers. Hence, Article 6 applied to the proceedings.

However, it was not necessary that the UK Central Council's professional con- **7.22** duct committee should itself meet all the requirements of an independent and impartial tribunal, within the meaning of Article 6(1), given that an automatic right of appeal to the Court of Session lay from any order striking the name of one of its members (nurses or midwives) from the register. In the absence of any right of appeal, the Court (applying the case of *Le Compte, Van Leuven and De Meyere v Belgium*; see 7.13 above) entertained considerable doubt as to whether the conduct committee was an independent and impartial tribunal.

There remain unresolved issues as to how intrusive the judicial review or appeal **7.23** must be. The House of Lords ruled on Article 6 compliance in *R v Secretary of State for the Environment, ex parte Alconbury Developments Ltd and Ors,*[16] which involved the personal decision-making role of the Secretary of State for the Environment in planning inquiries. The Divisional Court had held that judicial review was not sufficient to cure the Secretary of State's lack of independence where he had made a planning decision in a case involving his own planning policy. A declaration of incompatibility was made under the HRA 1998. This was overturned on appeal to the House of Lords, where it was found that judicial review of the decision was sufficient to cure any infringements of the right to a fair trial caused by the lack of independence and impartiality of the Secretary of State. Their Lordships' decision appears to bow to the decisions of the Executive on the basis that 'Parliament, democratically elected, has entrusted the making of planning decisions to local authorities and to the Secretary of State with a general power of supervision and control in the latter'.[17]

---

[15] [2001] IRLR 208.
[16] [2001] UKHL 23, [2003] 2 AC 295.
[17] *Per* Lord Clyde.

7.24 This decision gives greater weight to the decision-making powers of the government than that of the Divisional Court when considering the protection of Article 6 rights, and suggests that the greater the political safeguards and democratic legitimacy below, the less intrusive the reviewing court need be (see also *R v Department for Environment and others, ex parte Langton and Allen*;[18] *Country Properties Ltd v The Scottish Ministers*;[19] but see in contrast *R (Wright and others) v Secretary of State for Health and another*,[20] where Stanley Burnton J held that the procedure for provisional listing on the Protection of Vulnerable Adults list was unfair because there was no right of appeal to an independent, impartial tribunal until nine months after the provisional listing, and the other independent remedy, judicial review, would not permit determination of the vital question of whether or not the individual had committed the misconduct.

(7) Implications for unfair dismissal cases

7.25 There will frequently be unfair dismissal cases before the employment tribunal, where the disciplinary hearing leading to dismissal did not amount to a fair hearing. However, that does not mean that there was a breach of Article 6 ECHR at the first stage. The interesting question is whether there could be an argument about the second stage—the review by the employment tribunal. Thus it might be argued that the rehearing of the case by the employment tribunal was not a decision in which the employment tribunal had full jurisdiction since the tribunal may only decide if the decision to dismiss was in the band of reasonable responses (*Foley v Post Office*[21]).

7.26 It is likely that such an argument would be considered to confuse substantive rights and procedure. The substantive right is not to be unfairly dismissed. That means not to be dismissed in consequence of a decision that was outside the range of reasonable responses to the facts in issue. That the employer has taken a decision that was not impartial will be a consequence of the relationship between the employer and the employee. The decision to dismiss then gives rise to the right to complain, and hence to the legal context to which Article 6 ECHR applies. Further, since Article 6(1) extends not to the content of a civil right and obligation but to *disputes* over such rights, it is legitimate for a domestic legal system to define the *Foley* unfair dismissal test.

---

[18] QBD, 17 December 2001.
[19] 2001 SLT 1125.
[20] [2006] EWHC 2886 (Admin), [2007] 1 All ER 825.
[21] [2000] ICR 1283.

(8) Implications where there is no right not to be unfairly dismissed

An employee may not have the right not to be unfairly dismissed. An example **7.27** would be where an employee who has less than one year's service is dismissed on grounds of misconduct. In these circumstances it will be necessary to ask whether the employee has any relevant civil rights for the purposes of the ECHR, and therefore for the HRA 1998. In many cases there will be a disciplinary code which applies to the employee. Where the employer is a public authority within section 6 of the HRA 1998 then it is arguable that the employer will be in breach of section 6 if it does not apply the standards required by Article 6 ECHR. The question that will first have to be asked is: Does the disciplinary code in question provide a civil right to the employee? On this see Chapter 6 generally.

An example where it did was *R v Civil Service Appeal Board, ex parte Cunningham*,[22] **7.28** where it was held that there was an obligation to give reasons for the decision of the Civil Service Appeal Board.[23] Although the ECHR was not referred to in the judgments of the Court of Appeal, it is likely that this case would have been argued now as requiring compliance with Article 6. This does not mean that the HRA 1998 would require the employment tribunal to disregard its statutory jurisdiction; rather, the employee would be able to bring a claim against the public authority for breach of section 6 of the HRA 1998. All possible remedies would be available. It seems unlikely that the Court would order specific performance of the contract of employment if that meant that the employer was required to provide work, but specific performance of disciplinary procedures is possible: *Irani v Southampton and South West Hampshire Health Authority*.[24] Additionally, damages might be awarded where an injunction was not appropriate because, for instance, of the passage of time or an irremediable breakdown of trust and confidence.

C. The four minimum requirements

It is important to note that Article 6 ECHR provides more than mere access to a **7.29** court. Rather, it requires a process before the court which meets four minimum standards (subject to the exceptions stated in Article 6(1)) for the resolution of such disputes:

(a) an independent and impartial tribunal;
(b) a fair and public hearing;

---

[22] [1992] ICR 816.
[23] For the right to a public judgment see below at 7.156.
[24] [1985] ICR 590. Though specific performance is unusual. See also *Powell v Brent London Borough Council* [1988] ICR 176, CA and *Alexander and others v Standard Telephones & Cables Plc* [1990] ICR 291.

(c)   reasonable expedition of the hearing;

(d)   a public judgment.

The requirements for a fair and public hearing overlap (as, for instance, in the area of immunities), but they are discussed separately in reverse order at 7.49 and 7.72 below.

7.30   In most cases the resolution of employment disputes is subject to determination under the rule of law and the process for that determination will meet these standards, but issues in relation to each of them can arise. These are addressed in the following paragraphs.

D. An independent and impartial tribunal

7.31   This requirement is one in which the ECHR has made a major impact, since in the UK issues of impartiality have been seen as much more important than independence. Scrutiny of independence had been viewed as a political rather than as a legal issue.

7.32   The impact of the HRA 1998 was brought home almost immediately when the independence of temporary sheriffs was challenged in Scotland very soon after it came into force (see *Starrs v Ruxton*[25]). The importance of this issue was emphasised when the Privy Council held that there could be no tacit waiver of the right to an independent court, even where no unfairness was apparent, in the way that the proceedings were conducted (*Millar v Procurator Fiscal, Elgin; Payne, Stewart and Tracey v Procurator Fiscal, Dundee*[26]).

7.33   The requirement of independence is very strict. Thus, in *Langborger v Sweden*,[27] the Court determined that two professional judges did not render a Swedish Housing and Tenancy Court, which included two lay assessors, one from a landlords' association and one from a tenants' association, independent. The point was that the two assessors had been nominated by their respective associations. (This is similar to the position of lay members in an employment tribunal nominated by either side of the industry.)

7.34   Each was appointed by the government for a term of three years which was renewable, as with lay members of an employment tribunal. There was no reason to doubt the personal integrity or impartiality of the tribunal. However, the Court noted the possibility that both assessors might be perceived to have a common

---

[25]   The Times, 17 November 1999, [2000] UKHRR 78, [2000] HRLR 191.

[26]   [2001] UKHRR 999, [2001] UKPC D4.

[27]   (1989) 12 EHRR 416.

interest contrary to the applicant's. The applicant was in dispute about the incorporation of a clause in a lease which required the parties to the lease to be bound by the current agreement made between the two associations. The Court held that there was an infringement of Article 6(1) because of this factor.

Practitioners should, however, compare the more recent case of *Ab Kurt* **7.35** *Kellermann v Sweden*,[28] where the Court held that the presence of lay assessors, representing employer and employee interests, in the Swedish Labour Court, did not breach the employer's right to an independent and impartial tribunal. The Court distinguished *Langborger* because there was no basis on which the lay assessors could be said to have a common interest contrary to that of the applicant, or interests which, whilst not common, were nevertheless opposed to those of the applicant. The assessors' interests were simply to interpret the terms of the relevant employment, and apply the principles of Swedish law.

Impartiality was considered in *Director General of Fair Trading v (1) Proprietary* **7.36** *Association of Great Britain (2) Proprietary Articles Trade Association sub nom in Re Medicaments & Related Classes of Goods (No 2)*,[29] where the Court of Appeal adjusted the test for bias as set out in *R v Gough*[30] to take account of the Convention jurisprudence. The difference between the domestic and the Strasbourg approach was that when the ECtHR considered whether the material circumstances gave rise to a reasonable apprehension of bias, it made it plain that it was applying an objective test to the circumstances, not passing judgment on the likelihood that the particular tribunal under review was in fact biased.

Thus, the approach to this question is as follows: **7.37**

(a) The court must first ascertain all the circumstances which have a bearing on the suggestion that the judge was biased.
(b) It must then ask whether those circumstances would lead a fair-minded and informed observer to conclude that there was a real possibility, or a real danger (the two being the same), that the tribunal was biased.

In the case of *Porter and Weeks v Magill*,[31] the House of Lords considered impartiality, bias, and delay. Dame Shirley Porter, having been accused of corruption over the sale of Westminster Council property in the 1980s, herself accused the auditor involved of partiality and lack of independence in his findings of wilful misconduct against her and another councillor, David Weeks. The House of

---

[28] Application 41579/98, ECtHR, 26 January 2005.
[29] [2001] 1 WLR 700.
[30] [1993] AC 646.
[31] [2001] UKHL 67, [2002] 2 AC 357.

Lords found there was some force in the criticism that where there were accusations of wilful misconduct, the auditor was required to act not only as investigator but also as prosecutor and judge. However, that problem was recognised and met by section 20(3) of the Local Government Finance Act 1982, which provided for an appeal and a complete rehearing by the Divisional Court which could exercise afresh all the auditor's decision-making powers. Hence, the Article 6(1) rights were fully protected by the Divisional Court proceedings.

7.39 The House of Lords also asked itself whether there was a real danger of bias by the auditor. The period under consideration was from 1989 to 1997. Their Lordships adopted the test put forward in *In re Medicaments and Related Classes of Goods (No 2)*,[32] with its adjustment of the *Gough* test to harmonise the Strasbourg jurisprudence. They considered that the real danger element of the test served no useful purpose and defined the question as whether the fair-minded and informed observer, having considered the facts, would conclude that there was a real possibility that the tribunal was biased. Here there was nothing in the auditor's words to indicate that there was a real possibility that he was biased.

(1) Impartiality and communication between tribunals

7.40 An issue that can arise is where there is communication between two different tribunals. It is not that this is impermissible in itself, rather that it is necessary that the communication is disclosed to all parties (*Nideröst-Huber v Switzerland*[33]), otherwise impartiality may be compromised.

(2) Employment tribunals and the EAT

7.41 Normally these tribunals and courts would be considered independent and impartial, but this is not necessarily so. At the hearing of a complaint, issues could arise about individual members of tribunals and courts by reason of some connection or past activity (*Locabail (UK) Ltd v Bayfield Properties Ltd*[34]).

7.42 While the impartiality of members was not in doubt in *Smith v Secretary of State for Trade and Industry*[35] (see also *Link v Secretary of State for Trade and Industry*[36]), the EAT queried whether an employment tribunal, whose members were appointed by the Secretary of State for Trade and Industry, was independent in a case in which he was a respondent. Leave was granted to appeal to the Court of Appeal, specifically because the judges of the Court of Appeal are independent and impartial.

---

[32] [2001] 1 WLR 700.
[33] (1997) 25 EHRR 709.
[34] [2000] 2 WLR 870.
[35] [2000] ICR 69.
[36] [2001] IRLR 416.

Since then the rules for the appointment of members of tribunals have been **7.43** changed.[37] Following this change, the EAT held that new procedures for appointing lay members of employment tribunals meant that those tribunals were now compliant with the Convention. Under the old procedure they were contrary to Convention provisions guaranteeing the right to a fair trial where the Secretary of State for Trade and Industry had an interest (*Scanfuture UK Ltd v Secretary of State for Trade and Industry; Link v Secretary of State for Trade and Industry*[38]). The EAT said that under the old system a fair-minded and informed litigant would have harboured an objectively justifiable fear that the employment tribunal lacked both impartiality and independence within the meaning of those expressions in Article 6.[39]

The House of Lords held in *Lawal v Northern Spirit Ltd*[40] that there is a real pos- **7.44** sibility of bias where counsel appears before an EAT which includes one or two lay members with whom he has previously sat as part-time judge.

It was the practice of the Lord Chancellor's department to appoint leading coun- **7.45** sel with experience of employment law to sit as part-time judges in the EAT and there were no restrictions on the freedom of such individuals to appear as counsel before the EAT of which they were part-time members. Whilst the EAT and the Court of Appeal both found that the fact that a lay member had sat with a part-time judge who was acting as counsel did not give rise to a real possibility of bias, the House of Lords applied the *Porter v Magill* test and found that a fair-minded and informed observer, having considered the given facts, would conclude that there was a real possibility that the EAT was biased and that the practice tended to undermine public confidence in the administration of justice and ought to be discontinued.

Practitioners should also note in this connection the comments of the Court of **7.46** Appeal in *Smith v Kvaerner Cementation Foundations Ltd (Bar Council Intervening)*.[41] The case concerned the decision of a recorder, who was the head of chambers of both counsel in the original trial. The result turned on a question of waiver, but the Court did comment that:

> . . . the changes in the way some chambers fund their expenses [this in reference to the practice of contributing a percentage of income to chambers] and the fact that

---

[37] See the announcement by the Lord Chancellor in the House of Lords: *Hansard*, HL, cols WA 71–72 (27 July 2000).
[38] [2001] ICR 1096, [2001] IRLR 416.
[39] See the application of the right to impartiality by the House of Lords in *Shirley Porter v Magill* [2002] 1 All ER 465, [2001] UKHL, at 7.38–7.39 above.
[40] [2003] ICR 856.
[41] [2006] 3 All ER 593.

counsel can now act under a conditional fee agreement mean that, in some cases at least, there may be grounds for arguing that a Recorder should not sit in a case in which one or more of the advocates are members of his chambers. Indeed we understand that the Bar Council is currently considering the implications of conditional fee agreements in this context.

Similar considerations are likely to apply where conditional fee agreements are used to fund employment cases.

7.47 In *Jiminez v Southwark LBC*,[42] an employment tribunal chairman had given the parties a forcefully expressed preliminary indication of the tribunal's view of the merits shortly before an eight-week adjournment. This was done with a view to encouraging settlement. The employer eventually lost as the chairman had predicted. The Court of Appeal overturned the EAT finding that there was a real possibility of a perception of bias and ruled that whilst it can be helpful in some cases for a chairman to let the parties' representatives know the tribunal's preliminary views, this must be done with great care, emphasising the provisional nature of the view expressed.

7.48 *Stansbury v Datapulse Plc*[43] also involved the concept of the appearance of fairness. Here a claimant argued he had been denied a fair trial where he had alleged that one of two employment tribunal lay members had been under the influence of alcohol and had fallen asleep during the hearing. The Court of Appeal found the allegations about the tribunal members' behaviour had been made out on a balance of probabilities. It was the duty of the employment tribunal to be alert and to appear to be so. The requirement that the hearing be seen to be fair was not satisfied in the present case. The fact that the claimant's objection had not been raised before the employment tribunal should not disentitle him from raising it before the EAT on appeal.

E. A public hearing

7.49 Public justice has been a fundamental rule of the common law for many years (*Scott v Scott*[44]). Employment tribunals are normally required to sit in public.[45] Accordingly, this requirement does not readily conflict with existing jurisprudence.

---

[42] [2003] EWCA Civ 502, [2003] ICR 1176.
[43] [2003] EWCA Civ 1951, [2004] ICR 523.
[44] [1913] AC 417.
[45] See Employment Tribunal (Constitution and Rules of Procedure) Regulations 2004, SI 2004/1861, Sch 1, r 16, and the similar rules found in subsequent schedules.

The ECHR recognises that sometimes there will have to be exceptions to this **7.50**
requirement. Thus, Article 6(1) provides:

> . . . the press and public may be excluded from all or part of the trial in the interest of
> morals, public order or national security in a democratic society, where the interests
> of juveniles or the protection of the private life of the parties so require, or to the
> extent strictly necessary in the opinion of the court in special circumstances where
> publicity would prejudice the interests of justice.

Accordingly, sometimes the hearing may not be public. However, this exception
to the requirement is obviously to be construed very narrowly and applied very
restrictively.

The Court of Appeal held in *Storer v British Gas Plc*[46] that a hearing cannot take **7.51**
place in private for want of space at the tribunal. Where a tribunal was sitting
behind a locked door it was sitting in private. This was outside its jurisdiction
since the obligation to sit in public was mandatory.[47]

The obligation to sit in public was both fundamental to the function of the tribu- **7.52**
nal and important in its own right, so that a failure to so sit rendered the tribunal's
decision unlawful and required that it be quashed. In this case only the convenience of the tribunal was in issue. However, sometimes there are competing
human rights considerations. These are examined below.

(1) Restricted reporting

While there are powers to make restricted reporting orders,[48] or to order that iden- **7.53**
tifying details are omitted from the register,[49] these powers are strictly construed
(*R v London North Industrial Tribunal, ex parte Associated Newspapers Ltd*[50]).

They should only be applied in a way that is consistent with the exceptions to this **7.54**
rule in Article 6 ECHR itself. It seems more likely this rule will be broken by professional disciplinary tribunals than by employment tribunals (see, eg, *Gautrim v
France*[51]).

However, the strict application of the rule that restricted reporting orders **7.55**
could be made only where there was an allegation of sexual misconduct was
widened in *Chief Constable of West Yorkshire v A*,[52] where a transsexual bringing a

---

[46] [2000] ICR 603.
[47] SI 2004/1861, Sch 1, r 16.
[48] See SI 2004/1861, Sch 1, r 50.
[49] Under SI 2004/1861, Sch 1, r 49.
[50] [1998] ICR 1212.
[51] (1998) 28 EHRR 196.
[52] [2002] ICR 128.

sexual discrimination case under the Equal Treatment Directive[53] successfully argued that her fear of publicity would prevent her from bringing the claim. The EAT held that it had jurisdiction to make a restricted reporting order in such circumstances, since the refusal of such an order would make it virtually impossible for this applicant to exercise her Community law rights. The EAT said that a balance had to be found between competing interests, including access to an effective remedy, the due administration of justice, and the respect for privacy.

7.56 In a later decision, *X v Commissioner Metropolitan Police Service*,[54] the EAT was satisfied that both employment tribunals and the EAT are able to make orders analogous to Restricted Reporting Orders and Register Deletion Orders where there are factual findings or concessions that a claimant would otherwise be deterred from bringing a claim. Such action is in line with the power and duty to enforce Article 6 of the Equal Treatment Directive by use of their powers to regulate their own procedure in this way. The EAT in *X* advised that applications for such orders should be made at the earliest opportunity, ideally with the originating application and, if the respondent has given consent, this should be indicated.

7.57 Employment tribunals must also take heed of arguments which rely on Article 6 ECHR. Thus the employment tribunal's general power in the procedure rules to regulate its own procedure should be interpreted to allow compliance with the ECHR right. Whether an order is made or not in any particular case would depend upon balancing the public interest in a public hearing with the right to a fair trial. Any restriction should be as limited as possible and as necessary to secure the particular aim in question.

7.58 An employment tribunal should sit in private if sitting in public would lead to an infringement of human rights: *XXX v YYY*.[55] Where a child appeared in video footage which the claimant wished to play before the tribunal, the EAT found if played in a public hearing it would infringe the child's right to protection of his private and family life. The tribunal was empowered to sit in private by virtue of rule 10(3) of the Rules of Procedure which permits a tribunal to sit in private to hear evidence from any person which is likely to consist of 'information which he could not disclose without contravening a prohibition imposed by or by virtue of any enactment'. Of course Article 6 expressly allows for a case to be heard in private where this is in 'the interests of juveniles or the protection of the private life

---

[53] Council Directive (EEC) 76/207 on the implementation of the principle of equal treatment for men and women as regards access to employment, vocational training and promotion, and working conditions [1976] OJ L39.
[54] [2003] IRLR 411.
[55] [2004] IRLR 137.

of the parties'. This decision arguably widens the usually narrow construction of exceptions to the public hearing requirement.

(2) Public interest immunity certificates

Sometimes the government seeks to interfere more fundamentally in the process **7.59** of the case in front of a court by issuing public interest immunity (PII) certificates. These should always be scrutinised most carefully to ensure that they comply with the government's stated position on their use after the 'Arms to Iraq' inquiry (see *R v Chief Constable of West Midlands Police, ex parte Wiley*[56]).[57]

In *Tinnelly & Sons Ltd v UK*,[58] a Northern Irish firm failed to win a tender and **7.60** complained of discrimination on grounds of political belief and religion to the Fair Employment Agency. A PII certificate was issued by the Northern Ireland Secretary of State, seeking to deny access to evidence sought by the Tinnelly firm in relation to the tender, in a judicial review application. The Court held that the certificate had a disproportionate effect on the limiting of the firm's request for disclosure of documents which went to whether they had been discriminated against. The balance to be struck here was between national security and access to justice. Similar conflicts could arise under UK domestic legislation: thus, section 52 of the Sex Discrimination Act 1975:

Acts safeguarding national security
(1) Nothing in Parts II to IV shall render unlawful an act done for the purpose of safeguarding national security.
(2) A certificate purporting to be signed by or on behalf of a Minister of the Crown and certifying that an act specified in the certificate was done for the purpose of safeguarding national security shall be conclusive evidence that it was done for that purpose.
(3) A document purporting to be a certificate such as is mentioned in subsection (2) shall be received in evidence and, unless the contrary is proved, shall be deemed to be such a certificate.

Following *Johnston v Chief Constable of the Royal Ulster Constabulary*,[59] the Sex **7.61** Discrimination (Amendment) Order 1988[60] was passed, which, with effect from 25 February 1988, disapplied section 52(2) and (3) of the Sex Discrimination Act 1975 in the context of employment law. Article 2 of the 1988 Order provides:

---

[56] [1995] 1 AC 274.
[57] See also the statement made by the Attorney General to the House of Commons and by the Lord Chancellor in the House of Lords: *Hansard* 287 HC Deb, col 949 and *Hansard* 576 HL Deb, col 1507, [1997] PL 177. This set out the ambit of the government's position on PII certificates.
[58] (1999) 27 EHRR 249.
[59] [1987] QB 129 (ECJ).
[60] SI 1988/249.

Subsections (2) and (3) of section 52 of the Sex Discrimination Act 1975 (certificate that act done for purpose of safeguarding national security to be conclusive evidence of that fact) shall cease to have effect in relation to the determination of that question whether any act is rendered unlawful by Part II of that Act, by Part III of that Act, so far as it applies to vocational training, or by Part IV of that Act taken with Part II or with Part III so far as it so applies.

7.62 Hence, these subsections do not permit a Minister to issue a conclusive certificate stating that the reason for the derogation from the principle of equal treatment for men and women was national security. Mrs Johnson had complained of sex discrimination after her fixed-term contract as an RUC officer was not renewed. A certificate was issued which said that the refusal to offer her further employment was a matter of safeguarding national security and protecting public safety and public order. This could not be repeated in an employment discrimination context.

7.63 The ECJ held that the principle of effective judicial control laid down in Article 6 of the Equal Treatment Directive did not allow a PII certificate such as the one issued in this case to be treated as conclusive evidence leading to the exclusion of the Court's reviewing process. Acts of sex discrimination which were done for reasons which were related to the protection of public safety, had to be examined in the light of the exceptions to the principle of equal treatment of men and women laid down in the Directive.

7.64 Section 69(2)(b) of the Race Relations Act 1976 (which had provided for the use of PII certificates) was repealed by virtue of section 7 of the Race Relations (Amendment) Act 2000, which limits the circumstances in which 'safeguarding national security' can be used to justify discrimination (see also the Employment Relations Act 1999, Sch 8).

While section 59 of the Disability Discrimination Act 1995 (containing similar provisions to section 52 of the Sex Discrimination Act 1975, but without the *Johnston* amendments) preserves the provisions permitting PII certificates to stand as conclusive evidence, which could lead to the application of the *Tinnelly* principles in UK employment tribunals, it should be noted that Schedule 8 to the Employment Relations Act 1999 repeals the certification process under paragraph 4(1)(b) of Schedule 3 to the Disability Discrimination Act 1995. Further, it seems likely that the HRA 1998 would require that a similar approach be taken in relation to all employment Acts of Parliament.

(3) Witness statements

7.65 Employment tribunal chairs have rightly taken the public hearing obligation under Article 6 ECHR very seriously. Thus, when, as frequently happens, an order is made that evidence-in-chief should be given by witness statement, it is usually directed that there should be enough copies of the witness statements produced to ensure that any member of the public present at the tribunal may read a copy. This approach has much to commend it.

The problem of reconciling the effect of reforms aimed at speedier justice with **7.66** the need to ensure that there really is a public hearing was considered by the Court of Appeal in another context in *Barings Plc (in liquidation) v Coopers and Lybrand*.[61] That case concerned the issue whether documents had entered the public domain. Where documents are annexed or scheduled to the witness statement it may be argued that they form part of the witness statement, and therefore are possibly in (or ought to be treated as in) the public domain (see *GIO Personal Investment Services Ltd v Liverpool and London Steamship Protection and Indemnity Association Ltd*[62]), so this consideration may have considerable impact on the way that evidence is given in the tribunal. Lord Woolf MR was concerned about the relationship between changes in civil litigation which had led to an increasing amount of pre-reading by judges and to the HRA 1998. He said:[63]

> The tension between the need for a public hearing of court proceedings and what happens in practice in the courts will be increased when the Human Rights Act 1998 comes into force and the courts will be under an obligation to comply with Article 6. The practice in relation to witness statements already referred to shows that some tribunal chairs are taking these issues appropriately seriously in relation to such statements, but the same points may be made in relation to skeleton arguments and other documents that are read silently by the tribunal.

(4) Arbitration

If a case is referred to arbitration, parties may not have their cases heard at all. The **7.67** idea of greater use of arbitration in unfair dismissal cases was put forward by a Green Paper, *Resolving employment rights disputes: options for reform*,[64] and adopted with the hope of stemming the ever-increasing numbers of tribunal applications.

The ACAS arbitration scheme under the Employment Rights (Disputes **7.68** Resolution) Act 1998, is intended for unfair dismissal claims which do not achieve a settlement. It is intended to be an informal and speedy means of resolving these disputes. Parties will agree to opt into it voluntarily. The scheme is distinct from the arbitration which has always been available in dismissal cases

---

[61] [2000] 1 WLR 2353.
[62] [1991] 1 WLR 984, *per* Potter LJ at 994–95.
[63] At para 51.
[64] Cm 2707, 1994.

under section 212 of the Trade Union and Labour Relations (Consolidation) Act 1992, which is entered into on a voluntary basis yet retains the right for a disappointed applicant to go to a tribunal. The difference with this ACAS scheme is that it is intended to operate as an *alternative* to tribunal proceedings. Once parties have agreed to refer their dispute to arbitration in accordance with the scheme, they cannot then return to the employment tribunal. The scheme provides that at any stage of the arbitration process the applicant may withdraw, but such a withdrawal shall constitute a dismissal of the claim. The respondent cannot unilaterally withdraw from the scheme once it has agreed to participate.

7.69   In 2004 a revised scheme was published by ACAS, providing a voluntary alternative to the employment tribunal for the resolution of claims arising out of an application for flexible working. The scheme also provides for certain provisions of the Arbitration Act 1996 to apply to arbitrations conducted in accordance with the Scheme, where the parties have agreed that the arbitration will be determined according to the law of England and Wales.

7.70   What are the implications for Article 6 where parties waive their rights to a public hearing by agreeing to arbitrate? In *Suovaniemi v Finland*,[65] the Court stated whilst a voluntary waiver of court proceedings in favour of arbitration is permissible under Article 6, it should not necessarily be considered as a waiver of all rights under that Article. Therefore, arbitrators should be independent and impartial; they must apply the domestic law compatibly with Strasbourg jurisprudence and adjudicate within a reasonable time.

7.71   That the operation of the scheme is dependent on the agreement of both sides means that it is unlikely that a party could be forced to comply with it and be denied a tribunal hearing. However, it is possible to envisage a situation where an applicant might feel compelled to go to arbitration due to lack of funds for legal representation, and consequently might complain that his or her Article 6 rights had been violated on grounds of no access to a hearing and inequality of arms. Inequality of arms is discussed at 7.72 *et seq*, and see also 7.97 below.

F. A fair hearing

(1) Equality of arms—fairness between represented and unrepresented parties

7.72   Issues about the fairness of a trial can arise where there is an inequality of arms. Inequality of arms most commonly occurs where one party is unrepresented and

---

[65] Application 31737/96, 23 February 1999.

the other is represented, but it can also arise where the parties' level of resources are very different, for instance, where one party has the assistance of solicitors, a QC, and a junior, and the other simply has a friend to help.

Human rights law affects situations where there is an inequality of arms at two **7.73** levels. First, there may be a requirement on the state to provide legal assistance for representation. Secondly, even if this is not required by Article 6 ECHR, nevertheless the tribunal is under a duty to ensure that the actual inequality does not lead to unfairness in the conduct of the trial.

(2) Legal aid and assistance

There is no doubt that there may be an inequality of arms in breach of Article 6 **7.74** unless legal assistance for representation is available (*Airey v Ireland*;[66] see also *Artico v Italy*[67]). However, the standard for disciplinary tribunals may be different from that for employment tribunals (*R v Securities and Futures Authority Limited, ex parte Fleurose*[68]).

The principle of equality of arms does not go far. In *R v Secretary of State for the* **7.75** *Environment, Transport and the Regions, ex parte Challenger*,[69] *Airey* was distinguished on its facts when an attempt was made to use it to argue a general right to legal aid. In *ex parte Challenger* reference was made to *X v UK*,[70] where the Commission held to be manifestly unfounded a complaint under Article 6(1) based on an inability to pursue a remedy before an industrial tribunal due to the unobtainability of legal aid. The Commission held that only in exceptional circumstances, such as where the withholding of legal aid would make the assertion of a civil claim practically impossible, could the right under Article 6(1) be invoked. The Commission held that there were no exceptional circumstances in the instant case requiring the applicant to be legally represented, referring to the lack of emphasis on formalities in proceedings before an employment tribunal.

The most recent decisions of the ECtHR on this subject have focused on defend- **7.76** ants to libel actions in the UK. In *McVicar v United Kingdom*,[71] the Court held, following the *Airey* line, that the failure to provide the applicant, a 'well-educated and experienced' journalist, with legal aid did not breach Article 6. In so finding, the Court relied upon the relative lack of complexity of the proceedings, the character and background of the applicant as discussed above, and the clarity of

---

[66] (1979–80) 2 EHRR 305.
[67] (1980) 3 EHRR 1.
[68] [2001] IRLR 764.
[69] [2000] HRLR 630 (QBD).
[70] Application 9444/81, 9 July 1983.
[71] Application 46311/99, 7 May 2002.

the disclosure rules (with which the applicant had not complied, resulting in the exclusion of some evidence). The Court also pointed to the applicant's relative lack of emotional involvement, in contrast to the applicant in *Airey* (which concerned divorce proceedings); see also the importance attributed to this factor by the Court in *P, C and S v United Kingdom*,[72] which concerned contact with a child.

7.77 However, a different decision was reached in *Steel and Morris v United Kingdom*,[73] where the Court concluded that the two applicants, who were the defendants in the much-publicised '*McLibel*' litigation, should have been granted legal aid to fund their defence against McDonald's libel claim. The Court held, summarising the earlier jurisprudence, that:

> The question whether the provision of legal aid is necessary for a fair hearing must be determined on the basis of the particular facts and circumstances of each case and will depend inter alia upon the importance of what is at stake for the applicant in the proceedings, the complexity of the relevant law and procedure, and the applicant's capacity to represent him or herself effectively.

7.78 The Court's decision that the failure to grant legal aid amounted to a breach of Article 6 was based on several factors, in particular: the high financial consequences to the applicants of failing to verify the defamatory statements made, the complexity of the proceedings (which included the longest trial in English legal history, large numbers of expert witnesses, and several interlocutory applications and appeals), and the legal issues involved, and the background of the applicants considered in conjunction with this complexity.

7.79 It is certainly arguable that the decision in *Steel and Morris*, and in particular the summary of the law quoted above, suggest a more open, practical approach on the part of the ECtHR as to the circumstances in which failure to grant legal aid may breach Article 6. It is, however, unlikely that this stance will have any general impact on the provision of legal aid for tribunal hearings.

7.80 It must be remembered that the employment tribunal was established as a venue where a party could litigate informally and without lawyers, meaning that an argument in favour of a general right to legal aid is unlikely to find favour under the *Steel and Morris* test.[74] The Commission in *X v UK* (above) made this point when rejecting the complaint.

---

[72] Application 56547/00, 16 July 2002.

[73] Application 68416/01, 15 February 2005.

[74] See also the case of *Pine v Law Society* (CA, 25 October 2001), where a solicitor had failed to convince a Solicitor's Disciplinary Tribunal that his lack of legal representation had barred him from adequately presenting his case. The Court of Appeal held that only where the withholding of legal aid would make the assertion of a civil claim practically impossible, or where it would lead to an obvious unfairness of the proceedings, could a right to free legal aid in civil cases be invoked by virtue of Art 6(1) ECHR.

What the approach in *Steel and Morris* does is to make it clear that this is an inad- **7.81**
equate basis on which to reject all such appeals to Article 6 ECHR. Present-day
employment law issues, from transfer of undertakings to disability discrimination law and working time regulations, require analysis and argument which are
simply beyond the scope of many litigants.

Moreover, some employment cases are so sensitive that it is not practicable to **7.82**
expect a party to conduct his or her own case. For instance, in a sexual harassment
case it may be practically impossible for the applicant to put all the allegations to
the alleged harasser. The conduct of the trial might lead to repeated interruptions
as the applicant sought to compose herself. Other examples might include parties
who were too physically weak or otherwise disabled to conduct the proceedings
themselves. This issue is considered in more detail in the section on exceptional
funding, at 7.88 *et seq*.

(3) Opportunities for legal assistance

When he was Lord Chancellor, Lord Irvine of Lairg, indicated that he would like **7.83**
to extend legal aid to tribunals in England and Wales; but, unlike the announcement in late 2000 by Scottish Ministers that legal aid would be extended to Scottish tribunals, the rise in tribunal claims since the unfair dismissal limit was
substantially increased, which has probably put these earlier plans on hold. In
England and Wales legal assistance for representation is therefore not normally
available. The Funding Code presently prohibits the Legal Services Commission
from granting legal aid for representation in employment tribunals save in the
circumstances set out at 7.88 *et seq* below.

(4) Equality Commissions

There are other sources of financial assistance. In discrimination cases it may **7.84**
be available from the respective Commissions under the Sex Discrimination
Act 1975, the Race Relations Act 1976, and the Disability Discrimination
Act 1995 (see s 7 of the Disability Rights Commission Act 1999, which brought
the 1999 Act into line with the earlier Acts).

The new Commission for Equality and Human Rights (CEHR), which has been **7.85**
set up under the Equality Act 2006, to promote equality in each of the areas covered by discrimination legislation, and the Convention rights, will shortly take
over the role of these separate bodies. The new Chair of the CEHR has indicated
that it will support strategic litigation.[75]

---

[75] Speech to Employment Lawyers Association, Employment Law Bar Association and
Discrimination Law Association on 24 April 2007.

(5) Free Representation Unit and Bar Pro Bono Unit

7.86 The possibility of free legal assistance may also exist through schemes such as the Free Representation Unit and the Bar Pro Bono Unit, though complex, long cases will rarely be undertaken on an entirely voluntary basis. Law centres provide free legal advice and representation in some cases. Trade union funding assists many union members, and a growing number of persons have legal insurance policies. However, there remain many non-unionised applicants who must either use their own funds, or attempt to find pro bono assistance, or find lawyers to take cases on a contingency fee basis if they want legal representation.

(6) Conditional fee agreements

7.87 In a particular case the possibility of a conditional agreement or free legal representa-tion could defeat an argument that the absence of legal assistance in employment tribunals involves a breach of Article 6 ECHR in denying a litigant access to the court: see *McTear v UK*.[76] This admissibility decision was concerned with the need for public funding in complex cases and the right to access to a court under Article 6. The case involved a negligence action against Imperial Tobacco, brought by the widow of a man whose death was caused by smoking. The applicant had been able to secure the assistance of counsel, experts, and an anti-smoking pres-sure group to date, and there was no indication that the representatives would not continue to act on a pro bono basis, or that she would be unable to obtain support-ing evidence for her claims. Consequently, the Court ruled that no interference with her rights was demonstrated. On the other hand, conditional fee agreements remain rare in relation to employment tribunal cases simply because the expected benefits are often relatively small compared with the cost of the litigation.

(7) Community Legal Service

7.88 Under the Community Legal Service, public interest cases may secure funding, and the Lord Chancellor has reserved the power to authorise funding in excep-tional individual cases before tribunals.[77] Accordingly, where a case is of a kind which by reason, individually or in combination, of length, complexity, or the nature of the forensic enquiry, is such that justice could not be done without legal assistance, it is strongly arguable that it would be breach of Article 6 ECHR to fail to provide that assistance.

---

[76] Application 40291/98, 7 September 1999.
[77] See s 6(8)(b) of the Access to Justice Act 1999 and the Lord Chancellor's Revised Guidance on Applications for Exceptional Funding, applying from December 2005. This may be accessed on the Legal Services Commission website at <http://www.legalservices.gov.uk/civil/guidance/funding_code.asp#>.

The Lord Chancellor has considered generally the discretion he has to grant **7.89**
assistance at the request of the Legal Services Commission in exceptional cases.
In the Revised Guidance on Applications for Exceptional Funding, he has said
that if the client is financially eligible for legal representation, if the relevant criteria in the Funding Code are satisfied, and if the client has produced evidence that
no alternative means of funding are available, then, if there is:

- a significant wider public interest (ie the case has real potential to benefit individuals other than the client); or
- the case is of overwhelming importance to the client; or
- there is convincing evidence that there are other exceptional circumstances
  such that, without public funding for representation, it would be practically
  impossible for the client to bring or defend the proceedings, or the lack of public
  funding would lead to obvious unfairness in the proceedings,

funding will be considered.

In the Revised Guidance the Lord Chancellor states:[78]   **7.90**

> . . . the fact that the opponent is represented or has substantial resources does not
> necessarily make the proceedings unfair. Courts are well used to assisting unrepre-
> sented parties in presenting or defending their cases. Similarly most tribunals are
> designed to be accessible to unrepresented clients . . . There must be something
> exceptional about the client or the case such that for the client to proceed without
> public funding would be practically impossible or would lead to obvious unfairness.
> I will use as a benchmark those very exceptional cases where the ECHR at Strasbourg
> has indicated that the right of access to the courts has effectively been denied because
> of the lack of public funding.[79]

As is apparent from the above quotation, the Revised Guidance was in existence **7.91**
in almost precisely the same form when *Steel and Morris* came before the ECtHR,
although when McDonalds first commenced their claim, libel cases were completely excluded from the public funding provisions. The Court passed no comment
on the Guidance as then formulated.

In a letter to the Joint Committee on Human Rights,[80] Lord Falconer confirmed **7.92**
that he did not consider it necessary to make any specific legislative amendments
or remedial orders to implement the *Steel and Morris* judgment as the law had
changed since the facts giving rise to the application. He considered the Exceptional Funding rules to give sufficient safeguards to prevent further violations
of Article 6.

---

[78] At 3C-268, para 15.
[79] This paragraph appeared at paragraph 10 of the 2001 Guidance, and was quoted in the previous edition of this work.
[80] Reproduced in its Thirteenth Report, 2005/06 session.

7.93   One reference to *Steel and Morris* has been included in the Guidance,[81] which deals with the third means of qualifying for exceptional funding, ie the 'other exceptional circumstances' clause, otherwise referred to in the Guidance as 'Jarrett complexity'. The Guidance states that this clause allows the Commission to take into account the particular circumstances of the client, but adds that:

> . . . there must be something exceptional about the client or the case [this must go above and beyond mere non-representation where the other side is represented] such that for the client to proceed without public funding would be practically impossible, or would lead to general unfairness.

7.94   Whilst the extract from *Steel and Morris* quoted at 7.90 above is reproduced in this section as a guide to the correct approach in considering the 'other exceptional circumstances' clause, the wording of this clause as set out above suggests that a more restrictive approach will still be applied. On the basis of the Guidance, it is likely to be extremely difficult for a claimant in the employment tribunal to persuade the Legal Services Commission to grant exceptional funding under this clause.

7.95   Similarly, the criterion of 'overwhelming importance' is very restrictive. It is defined as meaning:

> . . . affecting the life, liberty or physical safety of the client or his or her immediate family or the roof over their heads.[82]

It is obvious that few employment tribunal cases would meet this test, though no doubt the Lord Chancellor could exercise this discretion in a case which, while not exactly meeting the test, nevertheless was of a similar importance.[83]

7.96   As a result of the restrictive wording of the Guidance, it is likely to be extremely difficult for claimants to obtain exceptional funding unless their cases are of 'significant wider public interest'. Unfortunately—and for obvious reasons—the vast majority of claimants are unlikely to be able to fulfil this criterion.

(8) Equal treatment of the parties in tribunal

7.97   Issues about equality of arms may arise where one party is unrepresented and the other has the assistance of legal representation. For instance, a procedural requirement in relation to witness statements may be much easier for the represented party to meet. Care will need to be taken in relation to equality of arms in all cases in which there is a represented *and* an unrepresented party.

---

[81] At 3C-270, paras 4–8 .

[82] See 3C-037, para 4.10 of the Guidance.

[83] See the Report of the Review of Tribunals by Sir Andrew Leggatt at <http://www.tribunals-review.org.uk/leggatthtm/leg-00.htm> in particular paras 4.21–4.28, in which it is strongly argued that human rights require that the state should pay for representation in certain cases.

Issues could arise in relation to any of the following:　　　　　　　　　　**7.98**

(a) The time needed to comply with a direction or to prepare written documents.
(b) The consideration given to a witness statement which has been written by an individual rather than by a lawyer.
(c) The way in which examination of witnesses takes place.
(d) Knowledge of, or access to, the relevant law.
(e) The length of time given to each party to adduce evidence, cross-examine or make speeches or representations.

The duty to secure equality of arms insofar as possible is one which employment tribunal chairs rightly take very seriously. It has formed a key part of their training in relation to the HRA 1998.[84] The procedures that have been developed over the years in both tribunals have sought to ensure that as much assistance as possible is given to the unrepresented, provided that it is consistent with the judicial role of the tribunal.

Difficulties arising from unequal levels of representation were lessened by the　**7.99** Employment Tribunals (Constitution and Rules of Procedure) Regulations 2001,[85] which have now been succeeded by the 2004 Regulations of the same title.[86] Regulation 10 of the 2001 Regulations, re-enacted at regulation 3 of the 2004 Regulations, inserted an overriding objective into the rules of procedure to enable tribunals to deal with cases justly. This includes dealing with parties fairly and having in mind the funds they have at their disposal, as well as acting expeditiously and in proportion with the complexity of the case. Tribunals must also ensure that the parties are on an equal footing.

Like the 2001 Regulations, the 2004 Regulations contain costs provisions which　**7.100** might deter parties from bringing cases they previously would have attempted to litigate (see Sch. 1, rr 40–41), although the effect of these provisions on unrepresented litigants is somewhat mitigated by the rule allowing the Tribunal to take the paying party's means into account (r 41(2), reversing the Court of Appeal's decision in *Kovacs v Queen Mary and Westfield College and another*[87]). Unrepresented litigants may themselves now claim 'costs' in the form of a preparation time order (rr 42–47).

Rule 20 of Sch 1 to the 2004 Regulations permits the Tribunal to make a deposit　**7.101** order of up to £500 following a pre-hearing review where it is determined that a

---

[84] One of the co-authors, Robin Allen QC, was partly responsible for both devising and providing this training.
[85] SI 2001/1171.
[86] SI 2004/1861.
[87] [2002] IRLR 414.

claim or defence has little reasonable prospect of success. If this will debar the applicant from continuing with his or her claim, it is possible an HRA 1998, section 7 claim could be made against the tribunal claiming a breach of Article 6 ECHR. The Court found that such a breach had occurred in *Ait-Mouhub v France*,[88] where the claimant did not have the means to pay the required sum (see also *R v Lord Chancellor, ex parte Witham*[89]).

7.102 In *Uruakpa v Royal College of Veterinary Surgeons*,[90] the EAT addressed some of these issues. Dr Uruakpa had been represented at tribunal stage by her husband. As part of her appeal she argued that the availability of legal representation for the College and not for her was a denial of equality of arms before the employment tribunal and hence a violation of Article 6 ECHR. The EAT, dismissing her appeal, relied on factors such as the tribunal's emphasis on assisting and encouraging litigants in person and the duty on tribunal chairs to assist unrepresented parties. The appellant had therefore not suffered an inequality of arms. It was also noted that the failure of the appellant's case was not due in any way to any failing on the part of her representative.

(9) Procedural rules

7.103 There are numerous procedural provisions that cause access to tribunals to be limited, such as the exclusion of certain disputes involving national security issues.[91] These will often raise issues under Article 6 ECHR, and must be examined against the exceptions permitted under the Article.

7.104 Practitioners should note at the outset, however, that there is a distinction between situations where there is a procedural bar restricting a claimant's access to the court, which may engage Article 6, and situations where the claimant has no actionable civil right to which Article 6 can attach at all. The line between such cases can be narrow, as is illustrated by *Matthews v Ministry of Defence*,[92] a case concerning section 10 of the Crown Proceedings Act 1947, which exempted the Crown from liability in tort for injuries suffered by members of the armed forces as a consequence of events occurring prior to 1987. The House of Lords in *Matthews* held that the claimant had no actionable civil right as a result of section 10.

---

[88] (2000) 30 EHRR 382.
[89] [1998] QB 575.
[90] Unreported, 18 June 2001.
[91] See, for example, s 202 of the ERA 1996, which limits disclosure of information contrary to national security, and s 10 of the Industrial Tribunals Act 1996, which empowers the Minister to direct an employment tribunal to sit in private when hearing cases that concern national security.
[92] [2003] 1 AC 1163, [2003] UKHL 4.

(10) Language of proceedings

There is no right under Article 6 ECHR to have the proceedings in any special **7.105**
language (see *Williams v Cowell,*[93] where a bilingual appellant's access to the EAT
was said not to be impeded by the fact he was not permitted to have his appeal
heard in Welsh—although under section 22 of the Welsh Language Act 1993,
Welsh may be spoken in any legal proceedings taking place in Wales by any person who desires to use it). The Commission has also held that Article 6 does not
guarantee that witnesses who are familiar with the language of the court are entitled to speak in whatever language they may choose (*Bideault v France*[94]).

(11) Time limits in the employment tribunal

Subject to the new statutory disciplinary and grievance procedures discussed at **7.106**
7.114 below, the majority of claims to the employment tribunal must be made
within three months of the act complained of, be it dismissal or discrimination
(see, eg, s 111 of the ERA 1996, s 76 of the Sex Discrimination Act 1975, and s 68
of the Race Relations Act 1976, and Sch 3, para 3 to the Disability Discrimination
Act 1995).

Any argument that the three-month time limit for unfair dismissal and discrimi- **7.107**
nation claims breaches a litigant's right to a fair trial must be tested against the
principles set out in *Stubbings v UK*:[95]

 (a) The limitation must pursue a legitimate aim such as restricting the burden on
 employers.
 (b) The aim must be proportionate to the means used to achieve it.
 (c) The essence of the right itself must not be impaired by the reduced degree of
 access to the court.

The tests of reasonable practicability under section 111 of the ERA 1996, and of **7.108**
'just and equitable' extensions under the discrimination legislation, probably
comply with the above test, making it unlikely that domestic law on time limits
would be found incompatible with the requirements of Article 6 ECHR.

However, usually those claiming personal injury have three years in which to take **7.109**
their claims to the county courts. Following the case of *Sheriff v Klyne Tugs,*[96] if a
person has a claim for personal injury arising out of discrimination, he or she must
bring the personal injury claim at the same time as bringing the discrimination

---

[93] [2000] 1 WLR 187 (CA).
[94] (1986) 48 DR 232.
[95] (1996) 23 EHRR 213.
[96] [1999] ICR 1170.

complaint, that is, within three months to the employment tribunal. The impact of this judgment may well be in breach of both Articles 14 and 6 ECHR, although there still appear to be no appellate cases in which this point has been taken.

7.110 Another related timing aspect of the right to a fair hearing involves limitation bars. Rules which prevent claimants taking advantage of their implied right of access to a court by changing the law before they could be expected to know about such changes may be in breach of Article 6: see *Neshev v Bulgaria*.[97] Although time limits are able to exist as legitimate procedural limits in practice they can result in violations of the right to access, such as where compensation claims were rejected as being out of time because the time limit was calculated as starting from the date of delivery of the relevant judgment, rather than from the date on which the judgment was published: see *Escolano v Spain*.[98]

(12) Strike outs for lack of merits

7.111 In *Osman v UK*,[99] the Court warned against blanket strike outs on the grounds of public policy. When considering what type of impact this ruling and the cases of *Barrett v Enfield LBC*[100] and *Waters v Commissioner of Police for the Metropolis*[101] will have, it should be remembered that the employment tribunal strikes out complaints at a preliminary stage only in very specific, clearly delineated circumstances. Notice is always required, and it has recently been held that the right of a tribunal to govern its own procedure does not extend to its ability to strike out a claim that has no reasonable prospects of success (*Care First Partnership Ltd v Roffey and others*[102]). The Court of Appeal there found that the workers were entitled to a full hearing on the merits and that there was no need to raise the issue of the right to a fair hearing granted under the HRA 1998; applications to strike out not expressly covered by the statutory tribunal rules of procedure could not be countenanced.

7.112 In the case of *Z v UK*,[103] the Strasbourg Court held that *Osman* was wrongly decided and based on a misunderstanding of English tort law. The Court stated:[104]

> The Court considers that its reasoning in the Osman judgment [indicating that the exclusion of liability in negligence acted as a restriction on access to court judgment] was based on an understanding of the law of negligence (see, in particular,

---

[97] Application 40897/98, 28 October 2004.
[98] Application 38366/97, 25 April 2004.
[99] (2000) 29 EHRR 245.
[100] [1998] QB 367.
[101] [2000] ICR 1064.
[102] [2001] IRLR 85, [2001] ICR 87.
[103] [2001] 2 FLR 612.
[104] At para 100.

paragraphs 138 and 139 of the Osman judgment) which has to be reviewed in the light of the clarifications subsequently made by the domestic courts and notably the House of Lords. The Court is satisfied that the law of negligence as developed in the domestic courts since the case of Caparo ([Caparo Industries v Dickman [1990] 2 AC 605]) and as recently analysed in the case of Barrett v Enfield LBC (loc. cit.) includes the fair, just and reasonable criterion as an intrinsic element of the duty of care and that the ruling of law concerning that element in this case does not disclose the operation of an immunity. In the present case, the Court is led to the conclusion that the inability of the applicants to sue the local authority flowed not from an immunity but from the applicable principles governing the substantive right of action in domestic law. There was no restriction on access to court . . .

The Court of Appeal has recently reconsidered the tribunal's power to strike out claims under rule 18(7) of Schedule 1 to the Employment Tribunals (Constitution and Rules) Regulations 2004 in *Blockbuster Entertainment Ltd v James*.[105] Sedley LJ, giving the judgment of the Court, explicitly referred to Article 6 in this context, stating that claims should only be struck out by reason of scandalous, unreasonable or vexatious conduct where: **7.113**

(a) the conduct has taken the form of deliberate and persistent disregard of required procedural steps; or

(b) the conduct has made a fair trial impossible,

and (assuming that one or both of these conditions is fulfilled), striking out is a proportionate response in all the circumstances.

(13) Statutory Grievance Procedures

In October 2004, the statutory grievance and disciplinary procedures set out at Schedules 1 and 2 to the Employment Act 2002 (EA 2002), came into force. The grievance procedures in particular raise important Article 6 issues, as section 32(2)–(4) of EA 2002 (subject to some caveats contained at s 32(6)) prevents an employee from presenting most types of complaint to an employment tribunal if he/she has failed to comply with certain aspects of the relevant statutory procedure. In order to ensure that his or her complaint of, for example, discrimination, constructive unfair dismissal, unlawful deductions from wages, or failure to pay holiday pay or the national minimum wage is accepted by the tribunal, the employee must send a written statement of his or her grievance to the employer, and must then wait 28 days before sending any claim (on the same subject) to the tribunal. Complaints of actual (as opposed to constructive) unfair dismissal do not fall within the section. **7.114**

---

105 [2006] IRLR 630, [2006] EWCA Civ 684.

7.115 These provisions aroused adverse comment even before the Act had come into force, in particular from HHJ Prophet, who wrote a forceful memorandum criticising aspects of the Bill.[106] Before the Joint Committee came to consider HHJ Prophet's arguments, the government had tabled amendments which dealt with some of the issues raised.

7.116 In particular, the Bill as redrafted removed the wide power given to the Secretary of State to set out in regulations the circumstances in which employees would be prevented from making a claim to the tribunal. These circumstances were set out on the face of the Act as described at 7.114 above. The Joint Committee expressed its approval of these amendments.

7.117 However, a practical difficulty remained, in that section 32(4) provides that an employee will not be able to present a claim to the employment tribunal if he or she only complies with the required elements of the statutory grievance procedure 'more than one month after the end of the original time limit for making the complaint'. The Joint Committee commented at the time that it was 'regrettable' that under what is now section 32(5), the circumstances in which this requirement would be disapplied were left to be determined by the Secretary of State. A more serious problem arose when the provision was applied in practice as, taken at face value, it appeared to many Tribunals to impose a complete bar to, for example, discrimination or constructive unfair dismissal claims where the claimant first entered a grievance over four months after the event(s) complained of. This interpretation led tribunals to disapply the usual discretionary provisions on extending time where 'just and equitable' (in discrimination cases) or where it was 'not reasonably practicable' to submit the claim within the time limit (constructive unfair dismissal cases).

7.118 This wholly undesirable position, which may well have caused breaches of Article 6 in individual cases, was finally resolved some 16 months after the Act came into force, in *Bupa Care Homes (BNH) Ltd v Cann; Spillett v Tesco Stores Ltd*.[107] The EAT held that the words 'original time limit' in section 32(4) encompassed the tribunal's usual power to extend time beyond the primary limitation period. The Secretary of State has yet to make any regulations under section 33(5).

7.119 The Joint Committee also raised concerns as to who would decide whether a claimant had failed to comply with the section 32 requirements. In particular, it was worried that the decision would be made by a member of the secretariat, denying the claimant a right to a hearing by an independent tribunal. This concern was addressed by the government in the Employment Tribunals (Constitution and

---

[106] Appended to the Twelfth Report of the Joint Committee on Human Rights, 2001/02 session.
[107] [2006] IRLR 248.

Rules) Regulations 2004, which provide that a Secretary is to consider whether section 32 has been complied with, and if he or she feels it has not, must refer the claim on to a Chairman, who will make the final decision.[108]

In her response to the Joint Committee, the then Secretary of State for Trade **7.120** (Patricia Hewitt) recognised that the whole of what is now section 32 might restrict a claimant's access to the tribunal and thus lead to breaches of Article 6. However, she argued that the right of access under Article 6 was not absolute, and could be restricted as long as the restriction did not impair the very essence of the right. Section 32 was a means of regulating access to the tribunal 'according to the needs and resources of the community and of individuals', and of preventing unnecessary litigation.

The Joint Committee concluded that the Secretary of State was entitled to take **7.121** this view. However, in reaching this conclusion, it took into account several points that she said would mitigate the harshness of the section. In particular, she said that employees who failed to meet the requirements of the section before making their initial application would be allowed to make a fresh application after having a fresh opportunity to do so (this *is* provided for at reg 15 of the Employment Act 2002 (Dispute Resolution) Regulations 2004), and further that in certain circumstances, the tribunal would be permitted to dispense with the requirement to send a statement of grievance to the employer if it would be impractical for an employee to comply.

It is arguable that the latter promise has not been implemented as envisaged by **7.122** the Joint Committee. Regulation 6 of the Dispute Resolution Regulations provides that the grievance procedure will not apply where the employee is no longer employed by the employer, and, since the end of his employment, it has ceased to be 'reasonably practicable' for him to comply with step 1 of the procedure. Reasonable practicability, as interpreted in the context of extensions of time in unfair dismissal cases, is a stringent test—more stringent than a test based on the word 'impractical', used in the Twelfth Report, would be. There is as yet no case law on this point, and it is to be hoped that the words will be interpreted less strictly in this context, but this appears unlikely. Further, the exception applies only after employment has ceased. Further circumstances in which the statutory procedures will not apply, which mainly relate to potential threats or harassment arising out of the procedure, are set out at regulation 11. Regulation 11 also states that the procedures will not apply where 'it is not practicable for the party to commence the procedure or comply with the subsequent requirement within a

---

[108] Sch 1, r 3.

reasonable period'; but the word 'practicable' is likely to be still more stringently interpreted than the phrase 'reasonably practicable' in regulation 6.

7.123 So far, no Article 6 based challenge has been raised against section 32. This may be in part because the harsh effect of the section has been mitigated somewhat by the liberal interpretation given to the words 'written statement of grievance' by the EAT in recent cases such as *Shergold v Fieldway Medical Centre*[109] and *Canary Wharf Management Ltd v Edebi*.[110] The employee is only required to set out the *complaint* in writing, not the basis thereof, at this stage. In *Edebi*, Elias J summarised the requirement under step 1 of the procedure as follows:

> . . . the objective of the statute can fairly be met if the employers, on a fair reading of the statement and having regard to the particular context in which it is made, can be expected to appreciate that the relevant complaint is being made.

7.124 If the courts continue to interpret the statute in this way, it is to be hoped that, in most cases, section 32 will not act as a barrier to access for claimants. However, it is strongly arguable that a wider 'escape route' is still required to make the section Article 6 compliant, particularly for litigants in person. The Department of Trade and Industry undertook a further review of these rules in 2006. The Gibbons Review recommended in March 2007 that the rules be repealed and consultation followed, making legislative reform likely in 2008.

(14) Hearing a claim where a party is absent owing to illness

7.125 In addition to the power to strike out a claim, under rule 27(5) and (6) of Schedule 1 to the Employment Tribunals (Constitution and Rules) Regulations 2004, the tribunal has the power to dismiss or dispose of particular proceedings, or alternatively adjourn the proceedings, if a party fails to attend or be represented at a substantive hearing.

7.126 In *Teinaz v London Borough of Wandsworth*,[111] the Court of Appeal held that the right to a fair trial under Article 6 ECHR will usually require a court to grant an adjournment to any litigant whose presence is needed for the fair trial of a case, but who is unable to be present through no fault of his own. However, it is for the litigant to prove the genuine need for such an adjournment. If, as in *Teinaz*, the reason for the litigant's absence is a medical one, adequate evidence of the medical grounds preventing the party from attending must be provided. Where there are doubts as to whether the medical evidence is genuine or sufficient, the court has a discretion to give further directions to enable the doubts to be resolved.

---

[109] [2006] IRLR 76.
[110] [2006] IRLR 416.
[111] [2002] IRLR 721, [2002] EWCA Civ 1040.

However, in a similar case decided shortly after *Teinaz*, the Court of Appeal held   **7.127**
that, as it is for the party seeking the adjournment on medical grounds to produce
evidence of his/her condition, a tribunal could 'arguably' strike a claim out without
allowing the party a further opportunity to obtain sufficient medical evidence
(*Andreou v Lord Chancellor's Department*[112]). In fact, the claimant in that case had
been granted a short adjournment to produce satisfactory medical evidence, and
had failed to do so. In the circumstances, the Court of Appeal upheld the tribunal's
decision to strike her claim out.

(15) Lack of jurisdiction due to applicant's age

The 2006 Employment (Equality) Regulations repealed these sections which   **7.128**
barred employees aged over 65 from taking unfair dismissal and redundancy protection cases to the tribunal (ERA 1996, ss 109 and 156). Whilst Regulation 30
of the Age Regulations 2006 replaces this bar, it is under challenge by means of
the 'Heyday' case; judgment in which is expected from the ECJ in 2008. If such
exclusion were challenged on the basis of Article 6 ECHR (with or without
Article 14), the complainants would not have to rely on the disproportionate
impact of the provision on grounds of sex, as has been done in recent cases before
the tribunal (see *Rutherford v Secretary of State for Trade and Industry*[113] and
Nash v Mash/Roe Group Limited;[114] both cases relied on the equal pay for equal
work principle under Article 141 of the EC Treaty). The government would have
to justify the bar, and its arguments under Article 6(2) would be similar to those
justifying the indirect discrimination; none of which were put forward in the first
instance tribunal cases which led to *Rutherford*.

However, there may be an argument that the statutory position is already unsus-   **7.129**
tainable in the light of the ECJ's decision in *Mangold v Helm*.[115] Following the
implementation of the age discrimination provisions (see Chapter 14), employers
will have to comply with new procedures when dismissing employees aged 65 or
over, and where the reason for dismissal is not retirement, the usual unfair dismissal
laws will apply.

(16) Vexatious litigants

The domestic courts have rules on the applicability of the HRA 1998 to UK law on   **7.130**
barring litigants from the courts. In *Ebert v Official Receiver & Ors*,[116] the Court of

---

[112] [2002] IRLR 728, [2002] EWCA Civ 1192.
[113] [2006] UKHL 19, [2006] IRLR 551.
[114] [1998] IRLR 168.
[115] Case C-144/04 [2006] IRLR 143.
[116] [2001] 3 All ER 942.

Appeal held that the HRA 1998 and the ECHR had no effect on the general principles relating to the grant or refusal of leave to appeal to vexatious litigants under section 42 of the Supreme Court Act 1981. (See also *HM Attorney-General v Covey & Matthew*,[117] where a similar decision was reached.)

7.131 The Court considered whether section 42(4) of the Supreme Court Act 1981 (which restricted the applicant, a vexatious litigant, from appealing to the Court of Appeal) infringed the Convention and whether the High Court judge was inhibited by the Convention's provisions. It applied the reasoning in *Golder v UK*[118] and *H v UK*,[119] which upheld the UK approach to vexatious litigants. The procedure under section 42 of the 1981 Act respected, amongst other factors, proportionality in the general access to public resources, since it sought to prevent the monopolisation of court services by a few litigants. Section 42 also ensured the maintenance of the Convention values that:

(a) procedures concerning the assertion of rights should be under judicial rather than administrative control;

(b) an order inhibiting a citizen's freedoms should not be made without detailed enquiry;

(c) the citizen should be able to revisit the issue in the context of new facts; and

(d) new complaints that he wished to make, and each step, should be the subject of a separate judicial decision (see para 9).

(17) Immunities

7.132 There are many examples where a party to a claim has argued it is immune from challenge. In cases involving, for example, state immunity or immunity from suit, the court or tribunal will have to determine whether the claimant's access to a fair hearing has been unlawfully impeded. It must be noted that the right of access to a court or tribunal is confined to overcoming procedural bars and immunities as opposed to upholding substantive rights: see further *Matthews v MOD*.[120]

(i) State immunity

7.133 This was considered in *Fogarty v United Kingdom*.[121] Mary Fogarty was an Irish national living in London. She worked at the US Embassy as an administrative assistant for the foreign broadcasting information service, a subsidiary of the CIA. After being dismissed she successfully took a sex discrimination claim

---

117 [2001] EWCA Civ 254.
118 (1979–80) 1 EHRR 524.
119 (1985) 45 DR 281.
120 [2003] 1 AC 1163.
121 Application 37112/97, [2001] ECHR 762 (21 November 2001).

against her former employers. Thereafter she applied unsuccessfully for two posts at the US Embassy. The latter claimed immunity from the tribunal under the UK's State Immunity Act 1978.

The tribunal accepted the Embassy's claim of immunity from suit in relation to **7.134** staff of a diplomatic mission seeking to bring proceedings concerning their contract of employment. The applicant took her case to the ECtHR, arguing breaches of Article 6 and Article 14. While the government argued that the need for respect for other states amounted to a legitimate aim justifying any breach (which they did not accept existed), Ms Fogarty maintained that since her case did not involve sovereign acts of states the immunity went too far, and asked how, on the facts, the victimisation claim would constitute interference with the functioning of the US government.

When the Strasbourg Court delivered its judgment it found that grant of sovereign **7.135** immunity to a state in domestic proceedings did not exceed the margin of appreciation permitted when proscribing the party's access to court. Such limitation was said to reflect recognised rules of public international law (see further discussion at 7.136 below). But despite the breach being justified, it is significant that the Article was found to apply to Ms Fogarty's claim. This was due to the Court finding that she did have a substantive right under domestic law: the statutory right to bring a victimisation claim created by the Sex Discrimination Act. It is useful to note that a 'civil right' will exist where the dispute is over a claim for damages arising from a statutory cause of action—this would appear to include any discrimination claim.

The Court in Strasbourg considered that international practice was divided on **7.136** the question of whether state immunity did apply to employment in a foreign embassy; and if it did, whether it only covered disputes in relation to senior employees rather than administrative assistants. The UK's practice in affording such immunity could not be said to fall outside any currently accepted international standards. That Ms Fogarty's complaint related to discrimination in recruitment was also relevant, since questions regarding recruitment to embassies by their very nature involved issues of confidence. Since the UK's position could not be said to have exceeded the margin of appreciation afforded to states in limiting an individual's access to court, the Court found (by 16:1) that the Article 6(1) rights had not been breached.

The immunity applied to all employment-related disputes. Ms Fogarty was not **7.137** treated any differently from others trying to bring employment-related disputes against an embassy. Accordingly, the restriction placed on her access to court was not discriminatory and the Court unanimously found that there was no violation of Article 14 in conjunction with Article 6.

7.138 In *Holland v Lampen-Wolfe* (a defamation claim against a colleague employed by the US government),[122] the House of Lords stated that what distinguished this case from the attitude towards immunity in cases like *Osman* was that those cases were not concerned with international obligations. Lord Hope stated:[123]

> The immunity is an attribute of the state itself under international law which all other states are obliged by international law to recognise. Cases such as *Fayed v United Kingdom* (1994) 18 EHRR 393 and *Osman v United Kingdom* (2000) 29 EHRR 245 can readily be distinguished as they were concerned with the granting of immunities under domestic law in circumstances that did not involve any international law obligation. Those cases may be contrasted with *Waite v Germany* (1999) 6 BHRC 499, where the European Court of Human Rights held that the grant of immunity from the jurisdiction of the national court to an international organisation according to a long-standing practice essential for ensuring the proper functioning of these organisations free from unilateral interference by individual governments had a legitimate aim, measured up to the test of proportionality and did not involve a violation of Article 6, and with *NCF and AG v Italy* (1995) 111 ILR 153 where the Commission held the application inadmissible on the ground, among others, that Article 6 should be interpreted with due regard to parliamentary and diplomatic immunities as traditionally recognised. In the absence of any directly relevant authority to the contrary, I would hold that Article 6 of the Convention does not preclude a state from granting immunity to a foreign state in accordance with its international law obligations in respect of acts which can properly be characterised as jure imperii.

Consequently, the way forward is still unclear on the issue of diplomatic immunity and whether a strike out on this ground amounts to a breach of Article 6 ECHR.

(ii) Judicial proceedings immunity

7.139 It has been argued there should be immunity from action on judicial proceedings.[124] In *Heath v Commissioner of Police for the Metropolis*,[125] the Court of Appeal found that the inability of a claimant to refer to a disciplinary hearing at her tribunal hearing for sex discrimination, due to the rule of absolute immunity from suit for quasi judicial proceedings, did not violate her right to a fair hearing. As in *Fogarty*, the Court also had to consider whether the claim engaged Article 6 at all, but here the potential bar was the fact the claimant was a public

---

[122] [2000] 1 WLR 1573.

[123] At 1578.

[124] However, in *General Medical Council (Appellant) v Roy Meadow (Respondent) & Attorney General (Intervenor)* [2006] EWCA Civ 1390, [2007] 2 WLR 286, the Court of Appeal held that there was no principled reason why immunity should extend to regulatory proceedings.

[125] [2005] IRLR 270.

sector worker. The Court reminded itself of the *Pellegrin* principle confirmed in *Devlin v UK*:[126]

> Under this test the only disputes excluded from Article 6.1 are those which are raised by public servants 'whose duties typify the specific activities of the public service in so far as the latter is acting as the depository of public authority responsible for protecting the general interests of the State or other public authorities . . .'

As Ms Heath was a civilian station reception officer she was not deemed to wield **7.140** a sufficient portion of state sovereign power to cause her dispute to fall outside the ambit of Article 6.

(iii) The police and immunities

In two race discrimination cases concerning events which occurred prior to the **7.141** coming into force of the Race Relations (Amendment) Act 2000, it was held that the Chief Constable of a police force was not vicariously liable for actions of his constables (see *Farah v Commissioner of Police of the Metropolis*[127] and *Chief Constable of Bedfordshire Police v Liversedge*[128]). This situation was rectified in relation to race discrimination by the Race Relations (Amendment) Act 2000, by means of the insertion of a new section 76A into the Race Relations Act 1976. Similar provisions have now been included in the Sex Discrimination Act 1975 and the Disability Discrimination Act 1995, and were incorporated into the Sexual Orientation and Religion and Belief Regulations.

The Race Relations (Amendment) Act 2000 also outlawed discrimination by **7.142** any public authority (including the police) in carrying out any of its functions, by the introduction of new sections 19B–19F into the Race Relations Act 1976. It also imposed a positive racial equality duty on all public authorities by substituting a new section 71, having a much further reach, and including related sections 71A–71E. Similar provisions outlawing discrimination by public authorities have been included in the Disability Discrimination Act 1995 from 4 December 2006, and in the Sex Discrimination Act 1975 from 6 April 2007, as a result of the Equality Act 2006.

In addition to these general points, the Race Relations (Amendment) Act 2000 **7.143** made the following further changes:

(a) by section 3, it extended the reach of the Race Relations Act 1976 to government appointments outside the employment field;

---

[126] Application 29545/95 at para 25.
[127] [1998] QB 65.
[128] [2002] IRLR 15.

(b) by section 5 it made special provision about the interrelationship between the public interest in the effective pursuit of criminal investigations and the duty not to discriminate;

(c) by section 6, it made special provision in relation to discrimination in the immigration and asylum field;

(d) by section 7, it amended the way in which national security issues arising under the Race Relations Act 1976 are to be treated.

The widening of prohibited acts by statute reduces the likelihood of breaches of Article 6 ECHR as far as the police are concerned.

G. Reasonable expedition

7.144　The third requirement in Article 6(1) ECHR is reasonable expedition of the hearing. The approach of the Court is entirely objective. Thus, it said in *Styranowski v Poland*,[129] a case concerning a pension claim, that:

> [It] will assess the reasonableness of the length of the proceedings in the light of the circumstances of the case and having regard to the criteria laid down in its case-law, in particular the complexity of the case and the conduct of the applicant and of the relevant authorities, and the importance of what was at stake for the applicant in the litigation (see, among other authorities, *Süßmann v Germany* ((1997) 25 EHRR 64 at para. 48)) . . .

7.145　Outside issues about equality of arms, questions about Article 6 ECHR are most likely to arise where procedural or other rules limit the access to the tribunal or court, or where there has been inordinate delay. Delay can be a real problem, although the tribunals always try to ensure that there is a speedy hearing.

7.146　*Darnell v UK*[130] concerned the delay in dealing with Dr Darnell's complaints to the industrial tribunal of unfair dismissal by the Trent Regional Health Authority. The proceedings took nearly nine years before the EAT gave judgment. Not surprisingly, the Court held that there had been a breach. Shorter delays have also been held to be in breach of Article 6 ECHR (see *Mavronicihis v Cyprus*[131] where the Court held that four years was too long); however, there can be no tariff as the time must depend in part on the nature of the dispute.

---

[129]　(1998) 9 HRCD 1001, para 47.
[130]　(1994) 18 EHRR 205.
[131]　(1998) 9 HRCD 480.

The Court has held on numerous occasions that special diligence and efficiency **7.147** are necessary in employment disputes (see, eg, *Obermeier v Austria*[132] and *Trevisan v Italy*[133]).

(1) Typical periods of unacceptable delay

There is no one period beyond which delay becomes unacceptable. However, there are **7.148** many recent employment cases in which the Court has considered delay, including:

(a) *Stamoulakatos v Greece*,[134] where the Court held that a Greek Court of Audit case about an employee's pension was not concluded in reasonable time after nine years;

(b) *Papageorgiou v Greece*,[135] where the Court held that a trial to recover monies from a government electricity company as employer was not concluded in reasonable time;

(c) *SR v Italy*,[136] where it was held that a Court of Audit case about an employee pension was not concluded in reasonable time after four years;

(d) *Nemeth v Hungary*,[137] where the Commission declared admissible an allegation of breach of Article 6 ECHR in respect of labour court proceedings lasting over nine years;

(e) *Le Calvez v France*,[138] where the Court held that a delay of over six years in deciding on an employee's economic rights was not reasonable;

(f) *Benkessiouer v France*,[139] where the Court held that a delay in respect of an application for judicial review in relation to sick leave issues was a breach of Article 6 ECHR;

(g) *Janssen v Germany*,[140] where the Commission found no violation of Article 6 ECHR in relation to the conduct of a hearing of a social security claim for asbestosis suffered by the wife of the worker exposed, but declared a complaint as to the length of the proceedings to be admissible;

(h) *Nunes Violante v Portugal*,[141] where the Court held that nine years for the consideration of the applicant's claim from a union pension fund was not reasonable;

---

[132] Series A No 179, (judgment 28 June 1990).
[133] Series A No 257-F (judgment 26 February 1993).
[134] [1998] EHRLR 28.
[135] (1998) 9 HRCD 24.
[136] (1998) 9 HRCD 461.
[137] (1998) 26 EHRR CD 101.
[138] (2001) 32 EHRR 21.
[139] Application 95/1997/879/1091, 24 August 1998.
[140] (1999) 27 EHRR CD 91.
[141] (1999) 10 HRCD 116.

    (i) *Rajak v Croatia*,[142] where the Court held that a delay of three years and seven months in deciding the applicant's claim for payment for technical improvements and rationalisation of the working process at his workplace was not reasonable. This was against a background of a 25-year delay, most of which was not the subject of complaint to the Court;

    (j) *Somjee v The United Kingdom*,[143] where the Court held that delays of over eight years and nine months, seven years and eleven months and eight years and eight months in hearing three separate employment tribunal claims to conclusion were unreasonable, even though some of the delays were attributable to the applicant;

    (k) *Obasa v The United Kingdom*,[144] where the Court held that a delay of seven years, four months and 17 days in finally concluding race discrimination proceedings begun in the employment tribunal was unreasonable. The Court reached this conclusion despite the substantial contribution of the applicant to the delays, taking into account the fact that the three appeal levels consistently took a year or over to deal with the applicant's applications, and that whilst a year per instance may generally be taken as reasonable 'the overall length of time must be taken into account';

    (l) *Cocchiarella v Italy*[145] and *Ernestina Zullo v Italy*,[146] where the Court held that delays of just over eight years and eight months, and more than eight years eleven months to determine the right to an invalidity pension and an attendance allowance were unreasonable. In both cases, the claimants died during the course of proceedings;

    (m) *Apicella v Italy*,[147] where the Court held that a delay of twelve years and two months in determining the applicant's right to be re-registered on the list of farmers, on which her entitlement to maternity allowance depended, was unreasonable.

7.149 The three Italian cases referred to at (l) and (m) above each contain a useful discussion of the Court's approach to cases concerning delay in civil proceedings in respect of persistent 'offenders' such as Italy. Whilst Italy has now passed an Act to provide a remedy for applicants affected by delays, the Court made it clear in these decisions that it considered the remedies granted under the Act to be inadequate, particularly as the Italian government delayed in paying the compensation found to be owed, which was in any event too low. The Court therefore found that, despite the domestic remedy, it had jurisdiction to consider the applicants' cases, and awarded further compensation of between 5,000 and 8,000 euros in each case.

---

142 Application 49706/99, 28 June 2001.
143 (2003) 36 EHRR 16.
144 [2003] All ER (D) 84 (Jan); Application 50034/99, 16 January 2003.
145 Application 64886/01, 29 March 2006.
146 Application 64897/01, 29 March 2006.
147 Application 64890/01, 29 March 2006.

Since the decisions in *Somjee* and *Obasa*, the UK has taken a number measures to **7.150** ensure that cases are not unnecessarily delayed. For example, procedural changes have been introduced within the EAT to accelerate proceedings and the Employment Tribunals (Constitution and Rules) Regulations 2004 have introduced greater case management powers, and default judgments.[148]

In a domestic case decided after the HRA 1998 was in force, *Procurator Fiscal of* **7.151** *Linlithgow v Watson & Burrows*,[149] a seven-month delay without explanation was found to have violated a litigant's right to a fair trial within a reasonable time. That decision was overturned in the Privy Council, *Procurator Fiscal (Linlithgow) v (1) John Watson (2) Paul Burrows; HM Advocate v JK*,[150] where it was held that the total delay of 20 months between the charging of the defendant police officers and the proposed trial date did not violate Article 6(1). However, in the conjoined appeal (*JK*), a delay of 28 months between charging a child with serious sexual offences and bringing him to trial did give rise to a violation of his right to a fair trial within a reasonable time.

The Court of Appeal has recently considered the somewhat different, narrower **7.152** question of when a delay in reaching judgment in an employment tribunal claim will give grounds for appeal (*Bangs v Connex South Eastern Ltd*[151]).

The test applied in an 'ordinary' civil case, where there is a right of appeal on both **7.153** fact and law, was set out by the Privy Council in *Cobham v Frett*.[152] The Privy Council held that if delay is to be relied on in attacking a judgment, a fair case must be shown for believing that the judgment contains errors that are probably, or even possibly, attributable to the delay. The court must be satisfied that the judgment is not safe, and that to allow it to stand would be unfair to the complainant. However, the Court of Appeal in *Bangs* held that the situation is different where the decision appealed was made by an employment tribunal, essentially because appeal from a tribunal decision only lies on a point of law.

The Court set out the principles to be applied when determining an appeal from **7.154** an employment tribunal on the ground of unreasonable delay in promulgating the decision, as follows:

1. An appeal is confined to questions of law (s 21(1) of the Employment Tribunals Act 1996). In general, there is no appeal on the independent ground that the tribunal made erroneous findings of fact.

---

[148] See *Resolution ResDH* (2006) 29, adopted by the Committee of Ministers on 21 June 2006.
[149] High Ct Just, CA, 27 April 2001.
[150] *The Times*, 4 February 2002.
[151] [2005] IRLR 389, [2005] EWCA Civ 14.
[152] [2001] 1 WLR 1775.

2. No question of law arises from the decision itself just because it was not promulgated within a reasonable time. Unreasonable delay is a matter of fact, not a question of law, and does not in itself constitute an independent ground of appeal on the basis of which the correctness of the delayed decision can be challenged. However, it may result in a breach of Article 6 and possibly give rise to a state liability to pay compensation to the victim of the delay.

3. No question of law arises, and no independent ground of appeal exists simply because, by virtue of material factual errors and omissions resulting from delay, the decision is 'unsafe'. A challenge to the tribunal's findings of fact is not, in the absence of perversity, a valid ground of appeal, and there is no jurisdiction under section 21(1) of the Employment Tribunals Act 1996 to entertain it.

4. In order to succeed in a challenge to the facts found by the tribunal, it is necessary to establish that the decision is, as a result of the unreasonable delay, a perverse one either in its overall conclusion or on specific matters of material fact and credibility. The stringent *Yeboah v Crofton*[153] test will apply.

5. It is not incompatible with Article 6 of the Convention for domestic legislation to limit the right of appeal from an employment tribunal to questions of law. It was not argued that there was any such incompatibility.

6. Even if it were incompatible with Article 6 to limit appeals to questions of law, it is not possible by use of section 3(1) of the HRA 1998 or otherwise to interpret section 21(1) of the Employment Tribunals Act 1996 as expanding a right of appeal expressly limited to questions of law to cover questions of fact. This is what the Court of Appeal would have to do to allow appeals to be brought on the basis that the decision was 'unsafe', or that findings of fact were 'wrong', and this is outwith the limits of legitimate judicial interpretation.

7. There may, however, be exceptional cases in which unreasonable delay by the tribunal in promulgating its decision can properly be treated as a serious procedural error or material irregularity giving rise to a question of law in the 'proceedings before a tribunal'. That would fall within section 21(1), which is not confined to questions of law to be found in the substantive decision itself. Such a case could occur if the appellant established that the failure to promulgate the decision within a reasonable time gave rise to a real risk that, due to the delayed decision, the party complaining was deprived of the substance of his right to a fair trial under Article 6(1). As Article 6(1) guarantees a right to a fair trial, a point on whether or not a person has had a fair trial in the tribunal is capable of giving rise to a question of law. Section 21(1) does not expressly or impliedly exclude a right of appeal where, due to excessive delay, there is a real risk that the litigant has been denied or deprived of the benefit of a fair trial of

---

153 [2002] IRLR 634.

the proceedings and where it would be unfair or unjust to allow the delayed decision to stand, as this could give rise to a question of law. Although this interpretation of section 21(1) is more restrictive of the right of appeal than in an ordinary civil case, it would not be incompatible with Article 6(1).

The Court added that this test was 'less stringent' than the perversity ground **7.155** of appeal, but 'more stringent than the "unsafe" test formulated and applied by the Employment Appeal Tribunal as it excludes an appeal on fact'. In fact, the test set out by the Court of Appeal is difficult to distinguish from the 'unsafe' test in terms of wording, and, as a result, might cause some problems of practical application. However, the failure of the employer's appeal in *Bangs*, where the decision was not sent to the parties until over 13 months after the hearing, and counsel for the employer was able to point to significant omissions in the written reasons, suggests that successful appeals on grounds of delay will be very rare.

H. Public judgment

Tribunals normally provide a public judgment, and this requirement is unlikely **7.156** to be in issue. Judgments or decisions may be given in writing but must be available publicly (see *Campbell and Fell v UK* [154]).

(1) Reasons

Under domestic law, a tribunal must give sufficient reasons for a party to know why **7.157** he or she won or lost a case: see *Meek v City of Birmingham District Council* [155] and *English v Emery, Reimbold & Strick* [156]). Rule 30 of the Employment Tribunals (Constitution and Rules) Regulations 2004 now requires the following information to be included in all written reasons (which must be provided if requested):

(a) the issues which the tribunal or chairman identified as being relevant to the claim;
(b) if some identified issues were not determined, what those issues were and why they were not determined;
(c) findings of fact relevant to the issues which have been determined;
(d) a concise statement of the applicable law;
(e) how the relevant findings of fact and applicable law have been applied in order to determine the issues; and
(f) where the judgment includes an award of compensation or a determination that one party make a payment to the other, a table showing how the amount

---

[154] (1985) 7 EHRR 165, at paras 89–90.
[155] [1987] IRLR 250.
[156] [2002] 1 WLR 2409, [2002] EWCA Civ 605.

or sum has been calculated or a description of the manner in which it has been calculated.

It is unlikely that Article 6 ECHR adds significantly to these requirements.

7.158 An employer must give written reasons for a dismissal to an employee with more than one year's service, pursuant to section 92 of the ERA 1996. Public authority employers of workers who do not have such qualifying service may have to explain any failure to give reasons, because the decision to dismiss amounts to a decision on a civil right.

(2) Appeals

7.159 Article 6(1) ECHR does not guarantee a right of appeal in either criminal or non-criminal cases[157] from a decision of a lower court which itself has complied with Article 6. If a state, in its discretion, does provide a right of appeal, proceedings before the appellate court are governed by Article 6(1) ECHR.

7.160 In *Adolf v Austria*,[158] and *Edwards v UK*,[159] the Court accepted that a breach of Article 6 ECHR in the first instance court may be rectified by an appeal in compliance with Article 6. *Obermeier v Netherlands*[160] is an example, in an employment context, of the importance of rectification on appeal. In this case, there was no appeal to a tribunal on the merits against the decision of a government body to the effect that the applicant's dismissal had been 'socially justified'. It was ruled that:[161]

> . . . the Provincial Governor's decisions may, however, be the subject of an appeal to the Administrative Court. This appeal can be considered sufficient under Article 6 para. 1 only if the Administrative Court could be described as a 'a judicial body that has full jurisdiction' within the meaning of *Albert and Le Compte* [(1983) 5 EHRR 533] . . . In this respect it must be taken into account that the relevant legislation does not contain any substantial and precise provisions for the decisions to be taken by the Disabled Persons Board or the Provincial Governor. From this silence of the law, the Austrian Administrative Court has itself inferred that the Administrative Court can only determine whether the discretion enjoyed by the administrative authorities has been used in a manner compatible with the object and purpose of the law. This means, in the final result, that the decision taken by the administrative authorities, which declares the dismissal of a disabled person to

---

[157] A right of appeal in criminal cases is provided by Article 2 of Protocol 7 to the Convention. This has not been ratified by the UK and is not part of the HRA 1998.
[158] (1982) 4 EHRR 313, paras 38–41.
[159] (1993) 15 EHRR 417, para 39.
[160] (1991) 13 EHRR 290.
[161] At 23, para 70.

be socially justified, remains in the majority of cases, including the present one, without any effective review exercised by the courts. In disputes concerning civil rights, such a limited review cannot be considered to be an effective judicial review under Article 6 para 1.

Thus, where a public authority employs a person and holds a disciplinary inquiry which is or may be potentially within Article 6 ECHR, any defect can be cured by a substantive appeal which otherwise complies with the Article. If the public authority denies an appeal so that there is no body which complies with Article 6, the remedy would lie in an application to the Court for a breach of section 6 of the HRA 1998. However, if the employee has sufficient service to complain of unfair dismissal, it may be that that would be a better course. Only if the loss was likely to exceed the statutory maximum would it be more sensible in such a case to sue in the courts rather than to take the case to the tribunal.   **7.161**

I. Frequently asked questions

Do internal disciplinary proceedings, or those carried out by professional bodies, have to comply with Article 6?   **7.162**

Many determinations of individuals' employment rights may be taken by an administrative panel, or a body that is either not a tribunal within the sense of Article 6, or does not comply with the right to a fair trial. In such cases, Article 6 will be satisfied where there is an appeal to a body with 'full jurisdiction' that does comply with Article 6.

Where the original decision-making body in such cases is not Article 6 compliant, must the appeal constitute a full factual review in order to comply with Article 6?

No. For example, an appeal by a doctor from the GMC to the Privy Council need not involve a full rehearing in the sense of calling witnesses and re-examining the evidence. The appellate role of the Privy Council is sufficient to fulfil the requirements of Article 6. Judicial review may also be sufficient in certain circumstances, but not where the only remedy available to the reviewing judge is to remit the case to a body already impugned for lacking impartiality.

Does the 'band of reasonable responses' test applied in unfair dismissal cases contravene Article 6 as it prevents the tribunal from making its own decision on the facts?

Probably not. Article 6 applies to the determination of the legal right, ie the right not to be unfairly dismissed, which in turn means the right not to be dismissed in t consequence of a decision that was outside the range of reasonable responses. Article 6 does not determine the content of the legal right.

Can Article 6 assist an employee who is dismissed but is not entitled to claim unfair dismissal?

It is possible that employees of public authorities, to whom a disciplinary code applies, will be able to contend that the disciplinary code provides them with a 'civil right', and thus that the public authority will be in breach of section 6 of the HRA 1998 if it does not apply the standards required by Article 6 ECHR in its disciplinary procedures. The employee might then be able to bring a claim against the public authority for breach of section 6.

Will employment tribunals be considered 'independent and impartial' where counsel appears before an EAT including lay members with whom he has previously sat as a part-time judge?

No. The House of Lords has held that such a practice could lead to an objective perception of possible bias in the fair-minded and informed observer.

How does Article 6 affect barristers who sit in a judicial capacity when members of their chambers appear before them?

Whilst there is normally no difficulty in such a situation, the Court of Appeal has held that potential bias issues may arise where counsel is acting on a conditional fee agreement, given that many chambers fund their expenses using a percentage of members' income.

How stringent are the restrictions placed on tribunals' behaviour by the requirements of 'apparent fairness'?

This will inevitably depend on the specific facts of the case. To give two examples, the Court of Appeal has held that whilst a forcefully expressed preliminary indication of the tribunal's view of the merits of a case did not (in the circumstances of that case) lead to a real possibility of a perception of bias. However, where a lay member was found to have been under the influence of alcohol and to have fallen asleep during the hearing, it could not be said that the hearing gave the appearance of fairness.

How does Article 6 affect the tribunal's power to issue restricted reporting orders and register deletion orders?

Article 6 provides that the press and public may be excluded from all or part of a trial where the interest of juveniles or the protection of the private life or the parties so require. These exceptions have been interpreted to allow a restricted reporting order where there are factual findings or concessions that a claimant would otherwise be deterred from bringing a claim, or where a child's right to private and family life would be infringed.

Can parties waive their Article 6 rights by agreeing to go to arbitration?

Whilst parties can agree to waive their right to a hearing before the court by agreeing to arbitrate, they cannot thereby abandon all of their Article 6 rights. Arbitrators must be independent and impartial, apply the domestic law compatibly with Strasbourg jurisprudence and adjudicate within a reasonable time.

Does Article 6 require the state to grant legal aid to parties to employment disputes who would otherwise be unable to afford representation?

Legal aid is not available for the parties to the vast majority of employment disputes in the UK, and the ECtHR has said that Article 6 does not provide a general right to legal aid. However, the judgment of the ECtHR in the 'McLibel' case appears to require a more searching consideration of whether legal aid should be granted in a particular case, taking into account the importance of what is at stake for the claimant, the complexity of the relevant law and procedure, and the claimant's capacity to represent him/herself. There are provisions under which exceptional legal funding may be granted to parties in employment disputes (contained in the Revised Guidance on Applications for Exceptional Funding)*, but the criteria are stringent and arguably do not comply with the 'McLibel' guidelines.*

Does the usual three-month time limit for bringing employment tribunal claims conflict with the right to a fair hearing under Article 6?

Probably not, as the provisions are likely to pursue a legitimate aim, and are proportionate given that the time limits can be extended in appropriate cases. However, there may be an argument that the decision in Sheriff v Klyne Tugs, *which requires personal injury claims arising out of discrimination to be brought within the normal time limit, may breach Articles 6 and 14, given that the normal time limit for personal injury claims is three years.*

How does Article 6 affect the tribunal's ability to strike out claims?

The Court of Appeal has held that cases should only be struck out by reason of scandalous, unreasonable, or vexatious conduct where there has been deliberate and persistent disregard of required procedural steps, or the conduct has made a fair trial impossible and striking out is a proportionate response in all the circumstances. A similarly

*stringent approach is likely to be applied in other types of strike out or dismissal appli-
cation. For example, where there is evidence that a party is too ill to attend a hearing,
Article 6 will normally require that an adjournment be granted, although it is for the
party requesting an adjournment to prove that it is genuinely needed.*

Do the statutory grievance and disciplinary procedures comply with Article 6?

*Whilst the government is of the view that the procedures are Article 6 compliant, it is
arguable that the requirement that complainants lodge a grievance with their employer
prior to the commencement of proceedings amounts to an impermissible bar on access
to the courts. The harshest effects of this rule have been mitigated by the EAT's liberal
interpretation of the requirement for a 'written statement of grievance', but there may
be scope for Article 6 challenges in the future. The government has stated its intention
to overhaul the current rules in the light of stringent criticism from commentators, but
it is not yet clear when this will occur.*

Will a decision to strike out an employment case against a foreign embassy on grounds of state immunity infringe Article 6?

*On the current state of Strasbourg case law, probably not. The ECtHR's current posi-
tion is that, whilst other states may operate differently, the UK's practice of granting
immunity in respect of all such employment disputes does not fall outside any currently
accepted international standards.*

Is there a specific period which amounts to 'reasonable expedition' of a hearing in the employment context?

*The short answer is no, although the ECtHR has said that 'special diligence' is neces-
sary in resolving employment disputes. The question of what amounts to unacceptable
delay will always depend on the facts of the case; some examples are provided
at 7.148.*

When will excessive delay in reaching judgment in employment tribunal proceedings give grounds for appeal?

*The Court of Appeal has held that delay in promulgating judgment will not normally
give rise to grounds for appeal in employment cases unless it has led to an error of law,
or a perverse decision, as the right to appeal from employment tribunals is limited to
questions of law. However, the Court also held that there may be exceptional cases
where a litigant can establish that the delay gave rise to a real risk that he/she was
deprived of the substance of the right to a fair trial. This would amount to a question
of law, as Article 6 guarantees the right to a fair trial, and tribunals are obliged to*

comply with Article 6 under section 6 of the HRA 1998. However, such 'exceptional circumstances' are likely to arise extremely rarely in practice.

Does Article 6 guarantee a right of appeal in employment cases?

No, not where the lower court has itself complied with Article 6, although if an appeal is provided, it must also comply with Article 6.

8

ARTICLE 8: RESPECT FOR PRIVATE AND FAMILY LIFE

Article 8

Right to respect for private and family life

1 Everyone shall have the right to respect for his private and family life, his home and his correspondence.

2 There shall be no interference by a public authority with the exercise of this right except such as is in accordance with the law and is necessary in a democratic society in the interests of national security, public safety or the economic well-being of the country, for the prevention of disorder or crime, for the protection of health or morals, or for the protection of the rights and freedoms of others.

A. Introduction

8.01   This chapter considers first why Article 8 ECHR is so important to employment law, before looking in greater detail at the content of the right. It then discusses the circumstances in which an interference may be justified, and the positive obligations of the state and the role of the employment tribunal. The chapter surveys in detail the application of Article 8 in the workplace in a number of special situations, including workplace surveillance, data protection, security checks, compulsory medical testing, and dress codes. It then examines related domestic provisions, including those dealing with sexual orientation and the workplace and discrimination on grounds of family responsibilities.

8.02   The workplace can also give rise to privacy issues in relation to customers and others who are not employees or employers. These are considered briefly at the end of the chapter.

(1) Why Article 8 is important for employment law

When the employment tribunal chairmen received training in relation to the **8.03** HRA 1998, the scope of Article 8 ECHR was one of the most debated topics. The reason for this was not difficult to see. When a person accepts a job and goes to work, it had been natural to assume that he or she had left home and accepted in the contract of employment the right of the employer to control his or her time at work. As Article 8 seems to be concerned with home life and privacy it was asked rhetorically what has it to do with work life. The short answer is that human rights law shows that it has a good deal to do with it.

First, the boundary between work and home is often difficult to discern. After all, **8.04** many people now work exclusively at home as homeworkers or teleworkers. Many people mix work and home life almost seamlessly, for example, a corporate golf day, or the office party to which spouses are invited. With developments in technology many workers are on call even when they are not at work. Moreover, the moment they go to work no one loses their right to some privacy and few can completely shed their family obligations at the office door or factory gate. Telephone calls or correspondence with partners or family members may be necessary during the working day. Relationships at work can become more than working relationships. In any event, every person needs some private space during the day, if only to visit the lavatory. These are some of the reasons that Article 8 ECHR is so important in providing a controlling point of reference in relation to working life.

(2) New technology and its impact on private life

There are numerous and ever-increasing ways in which an employer may carry **8.05** out surveillance at work. All such surveillance has the capability of impacting on respect for privacy. Drug testing, psychometric testing, infrared badges, closed circuit television, telephone call monitoring and email are just some examples.[1] Technological change is making it ever more possible for an employee's every move to be scrutinised. Already employers are increasingly secretly monitoring employees' communications including emails, other web use, and voice telephony. They can, for example, use Internet 'cookies' to track employees' visits to different sites, and thereby generate and collate data on them.[2]

---

[1] See also M Ford, *Surveillance and Privacy at Work* (London: Institute of Employment Rights, 1998).

[2] See JB Sessler, 'Computer Cookie Control: Transaction Generated Information and Privacy Regulation on the Internet' (1997) 5 JL & Pol'y 627. For a consideration of the human rights implications of 'encryption' of Internet usage, see Y Akdeniz, 'Internet Privacy: Cyber-crime vs cyber-rights' (1999) Comp & Law Vol 10, Issue No 1, at 34–39.

8.06 There are many other examples of the way in which personal life interfaces with work life. For instance, there have been examples of employees being dismissed for extensive use of the Internet (see *Franxhi v Focus Management Consultants Ltd*[3]). Growing numbers of employees are also being monitored at work, for example, by CCTV in rest areas and by devices monitoring keyboard use. Workers have been arrested and suspended from work when alleged drug dealing had been caught on CCTV.[4] Personal health insurance policies at work require medical disclosures. Other records at work can contain important private information such as details about the workers' children (see, eg, *Paulík v Slovakia*[5]).

(3) Associated statutory protections

8.07 That is why Article 8 ECHR and associated Community law have been the inspiration for important statutory measures to protect specific invasions of privacy and so practitioners need to keep these measures in mind. The most important are:

(a) the Interception of Communications Act 1985;
(b) the Data Protection Act 1998;
(c) the Regulation of Investigatory Powers Act 2000;
(d) the Freedom of Information Act 2000.

Reference will be made below to the statutory provisions which may have relevance in relation to the protection of rights under Article 8 ECHR.

(4) Associated rights under the Convention

8.08 Article 8 comes into contact with many of the other Articles of the ECHR. Sometimes it underpins them and sometimes it is in conflict with them. Article 10, which protects freedom of expression, is the Article which is most frequently cited in opposition to Article 8 rights. This interface is discussed at 8.20 below.

8.09 Article 9, which protects the right to religion and belief, is one Article which is most closely associated with Article 8. In the jurisprudence of the ECtHR, Article 9 ECHR is sometimes described as a *lex specialis* of Article 8. That is to say that the rights in Article 8 are general, and those in Article 9 are specific examples of those general rights. Accordingly, some of the case law in relation to Article 9 can be relevant to understanding the content of Article 8. Article 9 is discussed in greater detail in Chapter 9. However, where issues concerned with religion and

---

[3] Application 2102862/98, 15 June 1999 (Liverpool Employment Tribunal).
[4] Alison Clarke, 'The monitoring of staff needs regulation' *The Times* (6 April 1999) 35.
[5] Application 10699/05, judgment 10 October 2006, at [19] and [42].

belief are concerned it is necessary to consider Article 9 first and then to consider whether reference to Article 8 will add anything of importance.

B. The content of Article 8

Article 8 ECHR covers private life, family life, the home, and correspondence. **8.10** These are considered in further detail below.

(1) Private life

The ECtHR has developed a very broad concept of 'private life', which is 'closely **8.11** linked with issues of personal autonomy and development, so it goes further than simply a right to privacy'. It includes:

(a) freedom in relation to appearance;
(b) sexual identity and choice of acquaintances;
(c) personal bodily integrity;
(d) protection from intrusive publications;
(e) a certain freedom to a 'private space' in a public place.

For instance, in *Mubilanzila Mayeka and Kaniki Mitunga v Belgium*,[6] the ECtHR **8.12** pointed out:[7]

> It has often said that the expression 'private life' is broad and does not lend itself to exhaustive definition. Thus, private life, in the Court's view, includes a person's physical and mental integrity. The guarantee afforded by Article 8 of the Convention is primarily intended to ensure the development, without outside interference, of the personality of each individual in his relations with other human beings (see, *mutatis mutandis, Niemietz v Germany*, judgment of 16 December 1992, Series A no. 251-B, p. 33, § 29; *Botta v Italy*, judgment of 24 February 1998, *Reports* 1998-I, p. 422, § 32; *Von Hannover v Germany*, judgment of 24 June 2004, no. 59320/00, § 50, ECHR 2004-VI).

The right to respect for private life can also include the right to have information **8.13** such as official records, photographs, letters, diaries, and medical records kept private and confidential. Indeed, the ECtHR has recently held that the state is under a positive obligation to protect aspects of private life such as the right of a person to control the use of his or her own image (see *Von Hannover v Germany*[8]).

---

[6] Application 13178/03, judgment 12 October 2006.
[7] At [83].
[8] Application 59320/00, judgment 24 June 2004, ECHR 2004-VI.

(2) Family life

8.14   The right to respect for family life includes the right of a family to live together and enjoy each other's company, and the right to have family relationships recognised by the law. Unmarried couples, foster families, and homosexual relationships may be covered by the Strasbourg concept of 'family', as long as there are continuing, and real ties. In *Üner v The Netherlands*,[9] the Grand Chamber pointed out:[10]

> Article 8 . . . protects the right to establish and develop relationships with other human beings and the outside world (see *Pretty v the United Kingdom*, no 2346/02, § 61, ECHR 2002-III) and can sometimes embrace aspects of an individual's social identity (see *Mikulić v Croatia*, no 53176/99, § 53, ECHR 2002-I).

(3) The home

8.15   The right to respect for the home protects individuals from arbitrary intrusions into the premises by, for example, agents of the state such as the police or court bailiffs (see also *Chappell v UK*[11]). The right under Article 8 ECHR is a right to peaceful enjoyment of the home, which can include a protection from intrusion by factors such as pollution and aircraft noise. As developed below, this includes professional premises.

(4) Correspondence

8.16   The right to respect for correspondence prevents the state from interrupting or censoring communications (by conventional or electronic means) without good reason. It has been held, for example, to restrict the police from 'tapping' people's telephones and prison officers from limiting correspondence between inmates and their lawyers. It also covers emails: *Copland v U.K.* (Application no 62617/00, Judgment 3 April 2007).

C. A qualified right

8.17   It is essential to remember that Article 8 ECHR is a qualified right, so that it may be lawful to interfere with this right in appropriate circumstances. However, any interference has to be justified strictly and on the grounds set out in Article 8(2).

---

[9] Application 46410/99, Judgment 18 October 2006.
[10] At [59].
[11] (1990) 12 EHRR 1.

Article 8(2) requires, first, that the interference is in accordance with law. This has **8.18**
been the subject of some argument in the employment law context. For instance,
it might be thought that it would not be permissible to receive evidence which
had been obtained against the law. This is not necessarily so as the rule as to
admissions of evidence are themselves legal rules and their interface with the
prohibition in question must be considered. See for instance *Jones v Warwick
University* and *Avocet Hardware Plc v Morrison*[12] discussed further at 8.27–8.28
below.

Secondly, the interference must be under the control of the courts. In the case of **8.19**
Lambert v France,[13] the Court found that phone tapping of calls in connection
with theft amounted to a breach of Article 8 rights. While the Court agreed with
the French government and the Commission that the interference with Mr Lambert's right to respect for his private life was designed to establish the truth in
connection with criminal proceedings (involving large-scale illicit dealing in fur-
niture), and therefore to prevent disorder, it criticised the domestic court for finding that a victim of the tapping of a telephone line that was not his own has no
standing to invoke the protection of national law or Article 8 of the Convention.
Since Mr Lambert had been found not to have standing, he did not have available
to him the 'effective control' to which citizens are entitled under the rule of law
and which would have been capable of restricting the interference in question to
what was 'necessary in a democratic society'.

(1) The inter-relationship between Article 8 and Article 10

It should also be remembered that Article 8 ECHR frequently comes into **8.20**
conflict with rights under Article 10 to freedom of expression. Practitioners
should be aware of the constraints under section 12 of the HRA 1998 on any
attempts to secure without notice or prior restraints on publicity (see Chapter 10).
However, it would be wrong to conclude that there is a hierarchy of rights.

The UK courts have held in a number of cases relating to the proposed publica- **8.21**
tion of private information that both articles are of equal value in a democratic
society (see in particular *Campbell v MGN Ltd*[14]). The court therefore has to balance the relevant Article 8 and Article 10 rights. This exercise will require an
intense focus upon the comparative importance of the specific rights being
claimed in each individual case. The court must take into account the justifications

---

[12] [2003] UKEAT 0417.
[13] (2000) 30 EHRR 346.
[14] [2004] 2 All ER 995, [2004] UKHL 22.

for interfering with or restricting each right, and the proportionality test must be applied to both (*Campbell v MGN Ltd*).

8.22 A detailed analysis of the facts is therefore required in all such cases, as illustrated by the first instance decisions in *McKennitt and others v Ash*,[15] where the former friend of a well-known folk singer was prevented from publishing certain details of the singer's private life in a book, and *HRH Prince of Wales v Associated News-papers Ltd*,[16] where the Prince of Wales was successful in obtaining an injunction to prevent publication of his private diaries, which had been disclosed to a news-paper by one of his former employees. Both cases were unsuccessfully appealed to the Court of Appeal,[17] and both (differently constituted) courts placed emphasis on the close relationships involved, and on the fact that the information concerned had been imparted in confidence. In the *Prince of Wales* case, the Lord Chief Justice pointed to the important public interest in the observance of duties of confidence, particularly in the employment context, and held that, in such cases, the question will be whether, in all the circumstances, it is in the public interest that the duty of confidence should be breached. A similar approach appears to have been taken in the earlier case of *Lady Archer v Jane Williams*,[18] where Lady Archer successfully restrained her former PA from revealing confidential information about her private life.

D. Positive obligations on the state to protect rights under Article 8

8.23 The ECtHR has repeatedly stated that Article 8 ECHR establishes a *positive* obligation on states to ensure respect for private and family life (*Marckx v Belgium*;[19] *W v UK*[20]). This was recognised explicitly in *Douglas v Hello Ltd*.[21] It has been repeated in many cases. The problem is not to establish the fact of a general positive obligation but to ascertain what is its extent in a particular situation. It must be noted first that the ECtHR has recognised that there is a margin of appreciation granted to states to determine how such obligations shall be met.

---

[15] [2005] EWHC 3003 (QB).
[16] [2006] EWHC 522 (Ch).
[17] *McKennitt* [2006] EWCA Civ 1714 and *HRH Prince of Wales* [2006] EWCA Civ 1776.
[18] [2003] EWHC 1670 (QB).
[19] (1979) 2 EHRR 330, at para 31.
[20] (1987) 10 EHRR 29.
[21] [2001] QB 967, para 130.

(1) The extent of the positive obligations

These positive obligations can require the adoption of measures designed to **8.24**
secure respect for the protected rights even in the sphere of relations between
individuals themselves (*X and Y v Netherlands*[22]). This notion of 'positive rights'
has been described as perhaps Article 8's most significant aspect. An 'interference'
with an Article 8 right will be made out not only by legal impediments, but also
by hindrances which in fact, even temporarily, interfere with the effective exercise
of the right (*Golder v UK*[23]).

(2) The tribunal's duty to ensure compliance with Article 8

So, whoever the parties to litigation before it, the tribunal as a public authority **8.25**
(see HRA 1998, s 6) will have to ensure that in exercising its jurisdiction it affords
appropriate respect to Article 8, and allows an interference with the rights provided only where there is a justification which is compliant with Article 8 or an
express statutory requirement.

It is therefore important always to remember that an employment tribunal is **8.26**
itself a public authority for the purposes of the HRA 1998 (see s 6(3)(a)).
Accordingly, it is under a duty to act compatibly with Article 8. This means
that in exercising any discretion in the conduct of the proceedings it will have to
consider whether there is likely to be an interference with the rights protected
under Article 8.

(3) Admissibility of evidence

Probably nowhere is this more important than in relation to the admission of **8.27**
evidence. The leading authority in this area is *Jones v University of Warwick*.[24]
In attempting to defend Ms Jones' personal injury claim, the defendant's insurers
instructed an inquiry agent to film her in her home using a hidden camera. It was
agreed that the filming was in breach of Article 8(1), and that the inquiry agent
who carried out the filming was guilty of trespass, meaning that the evidence had
not been obtained 'in accordance with the law'. The covert video evidence was
said by the defendant's medical expert to suggest that Ms Jones was not suffering
a continuing disability as she claimed. Ms Jones contended that, as the evidence
had been obtained in breach of Article 8, the court, which was bound to act compatibly with the claimant's Article 8 rights, could not admit the evidence unless
it was necessary in order to achieve justice in the case. The Court of Appeal held

---

[22] (1985) 8 EHRR 235.
[23] (1979–80) 1 EHRR 524, para 6.
[24] [2003] 3 All ER 760, [2003] EWCA Civ 151, [2003] 1 WLR 954.

that the evidence was admissible. The Convention did not itself decide what was to be the consequence of evidence being obtained in breach of Article 8; this was an issue for the domestic courts.[25] Once a court has decided the order which it should make in order to deal with the case justly, in accordance with the relevant provisions of the CPR, then it is required or necessary for the court to make that order. Accordingly, if the court could be said to be breaching Article 8(1) by making the order which it has decided the law requires, it would be acting within Article 8(2) in doing so. In Ms Jones' case, the Court of Appeal held that the judge had been entitled to exercise his discretion such as to admit the video evidence, because the conduct of the insurers was 'not so outrageous that the defence should be struck out', and it would be artificial and undesirable to exclude evidence which was relevant and admissible. The court did make it clear that it did not wish to condone the actions of the insurers and ordered the defendant to pay the costs of the admissibility proceedings. Arguably, however, this decision gives a green light to parties to obtain and rely on evidence obtained in blatant breach of Article 8; a costs order may be considered a small price to pay in high value litigation.

8.28   The *Jones* approach has since been followed in the employment context. In *Avocet Hardware Plc v Morrison*,[26] the EAT held that evidence of alleged gross misconduct obtained by intercepting the claimant's telephone call to a customer in contravention of section 1 of the Regulation of Investigatory Powers Act 2000, and regulation 3(2)(b) of the Telecommunications (Lawful Business Practice) Interception of Communication Regulations 2000[27] was admissible. The employment tribunal had concluded that, as the employer had acted in breach of Article 8 because the interference was not 'in accordance with the law', it would be interfering with the claimant's Article 8 rights if it were to admit the evidence. The EAT disapproved that approach. The employment tribunal has a discretion under the Civil Procedure Rules to deal with its procedure so as to avoid formality, and to apply the overriding objective. If, having considered the submissions of both parties, it exercises its discretion under the Rules so as to admit the evidence, it is acting in accordance with the law. It is not entirely clear from the judgment how the EAT reached the conclusion that the interference was 'proportionate', but the EAT seems to have balanced the importance of the defendant's right to a fair hearing against the interference with the claimant's Article 8 rights. It considered the claimant's case to be weaker than Ms Jones', apparently on the basis that the only breach of the statutory regime was the failure to inform the claimant that his business conversations with customers might be recorded.

---

[25] See para 27 of the judgment.
[26] [2003] UKEAT 0417, 17 February 2003.
[27] SI 2000/2699.

A slightly different example of the balancing exercise is set out in the EAT's deci- **8.29**
sion in *XXX v YYY*.[28] The Article 8 issue arose in the context of a live-in nanny's
(X) sex discrimination claim against her former employers. She contended that
she had been forced into a non-consensual relationship with Y, her charge's father.
She sought to rely upon covertly filmed video evidence in support of this claim.
The EAT held that the evidence would breach the Article 8 rights of J, Y's son
(who appeared in the video), but concluded that a fair balance of the relevant
Article 8 and Article 6 rights would be to allow the tape to be viewed in a private
employment tribunal hearing. This is only one example of the steps that may be
taken to minimise the invasion into an individual's private life; other potential
steps might include redacting relevant documents (see, eg, the approach taken
by the House of Lords in *Nassé v Science Research Council*[29]). The Court of Appeal
overturned the EAT's decision on the basis that it did not consider the evidence
to be relevant to the proceedings, meaning that it was inadmissible in any event.
However, the Court of Appeal apparently supported the EAT's adoption of the
Jones v Warwick type 'balancing exercise'.

(4) Disclosure

The proper disclosure of documents is an important tool of justice. Here too **8.30**
the obligation on the courts and tribunals will often engage Article 8. Thus, similar
issues to those concerned with the admission of evidence have arisen where a
party objects to disclosing documents on the basis that they reveal matters about
his or her private life or concern his or her correspondence.

In *De Keyser Ltd v Wilson*,[30] the first employment law case to focus on the **8.31**
HRA 1998 since its implementation, the claimant had brought a claim of
constructive dismissal arising from stress at work. The respondent sent a letter
of instruction to a doctor who it was proposed would examine the applicant.
This letter set out considerable details of the claimant's private life. The respondent believed such sensitive details to be the cause of the claimant's stress, but had
not received this information in confidential or privileged circumstances. Having
objected to the letter, the claimant asked the tribunal to direct that a fresh expert
be appointed.

Of its own motion, the tribunal announced there would be a hearing to deter- **8.32**
mine why the Notice of Appearance (ET3) should not be struck out. Following
the hearing, the tribunal struck out the ET3 on grounds that 'the manner in

---

[28] [2004] IRLR 127.
[29] [1979] ICR 921.
[30] [2001] IRLR 324.

which the proceedings have been conducted on behalf of the Respondent [have] been scandalous and in breach of Article 8 (right to respect for private and family life) ECHR and the Human Rights Act 1998'.

8.33 The respondent appealed on the issue of whether the employment tribunal was right to strike out the ET3 on the basis that the respondent had breached the applicant's Article 8 right to respect for her private life. In the EAT, Lindsay J found that the tribunal had acted wrongly, since:

(a) the letter was written before the HRA 1998 came into effect;

(b) the letter was written by an employment consultant acting for a company that could not be regarded as a public authority;

(c) it was written to a doctor who, it is assumed, would have to comply with confidentiality rules;

(d) the letter contained no reference to any information obtained surreptitiously, by deception or at all directly from Miss Wilson, nor any information derived by way of legal process, nor any given by Miss Wilson in confidence;

(e) Miss Wilson's solicitors were to see the instruction letter, and she was free to resist, as she did, its being acted upon in the sense of its leading to a requirement upon her to attend for examination;

(f) most importantly, the tribunal had not expressly considered whether a fair trial of the issues was still possible;

(g) there was no disobedience to a court order (although the relevance of this to an Article 8 argument is not entirely clear).

8.34 The most critical point (as in the later cases discussed above) was:

(h) the right to respect for private life is qualified by the right for both parties to have a just trial of the issues between them; and it must be borne in mind that it was the applicant who invoked the right to such a trial by bringing the claim.

Accordingly the EAT reinstated the ET3 and set out clear guidelines on the instruction of experts in the employment tribunals.

8.35 The issue arose again, in a slightly different context, in *Hanlon v Kirklees Metropolitan Council & others*.[31] In that case, the claimant, who was bringing a disability discrimination claim, refused to consent to the disclosure of certain medical records, or to provide further and better particulars ordered by the Tribunal. His claim was eventually struck out. Before the EAT, the claimant (who did not attend) apparently contended in a number of letters that the orders had breached his Article 8 right to privacy. The EAT held that the right to privacy was

---

[31] [2004] UKEAT 01119.

not absolute, but was subject to the protection of the rights of others. The EAT was satisfied that the Chairmen had performed the appropriate balancing exercise, and had not erred in concluding that a fair trial was not possible in the absence of the relevant medical evidence. In this case, as in others where the issue arises, the task for the Tribunal will be to see how the right to respect for private life can be protected in the context of a fair trial.

No rules of procedure have been made to enable claims for breach of Convention **8.36** rights to be advanced in tribunal proceedings. Consequently, a claim for a remedy for breach of Article 8 by a public authority under section 7 of the HRA 1998 would have to be made in a county court or the High Court, or possibly in the Administrative Court.

E. Use of Article 8 in substantive claims

In some cases, it may be arguable that a particular action taken by an employer **8.37** (eg dismissal) could amount to a breach of the employee's Article 8 rights. One possible example would be where an employee is dismissed not because of his performance or conduct at work, but because of a private activity he undertakes in his own time. The correct approach to such arguments has been considered in two cases.

In *Pay v Lancashire Probation Service*,[32] P was dismissed after his employer disc- **8.38** overed that he was involved in activities including merchandising of products connected with bondage, domination, sadomasochism, and that he performed shows in hedonist and fetish clubs. There were photographs of him engaged in such activities on the internet. P contended that his dismissal was unfair in that it entailed an infringement of his Article 8 and Article 10 rights. He did not bring any claim under section 6 of the HRA 1998, and relied only on section 98 of the ERA 1996. In relation to Article 8, the EAT held that P's claim failed as the Article was not engaged (see further 8.40–8.41 below), but said that, where Article 8 *is* engaged in a case of dismissal by a public authority employer, the employer 'will not act reasonably under Employment Rights Act 1996 s 98(4) if it violates its employee's Convention Rights'.

A more in-depth analysis of the issue was undertaken by the Court of Appeal **8.39** in *X v Y*,[33] a case which involved a *private* employer. X, a man who worked with young offenders, was dismissed as a result of his failure to disclose a caution he

---

[32] [2004] IRLR 129.
[33] [2004] IRLR 625, [2004] EWCA Civ 662.

had received for engaging in a sexual act with another man in a public toilet. The details of the case as it relates to an individual's right to a private sex life are dealt with further at 8.192 below, but the court also gave general guidance on the application of Article 8 in unfair dismissal claims.

8.40 As the respondent in *X v Y* was not a public authority, no Article 8 based action could be brought under section 6 of the HRA 1998. However, the state has a positive obligation under Article 8 to secure observance and enjoyment of the right to a private life as between private individuals. The employment tribunal, as a public authority, must act compatibly with Article 8 ECHR. The Court of Appeal held that this requirement to act compatibly strengthens the interpretative obligation under section 3 of the HRA 1998, requiring the tribunal to give effect to all legislation (including ERA 1996, s 98) in a way which is compatible with Article 8. The interpretative obligation applies regardless of whether the employer is a public or private sector body.

8.41 The Court of Appeal set out the following guidelines as to how section 3 affects unfair dismissal cases where the facts fall within the ambit of Article 8:

(1) In discharging its duty under s 3 of the HRA to read and give effect to s 98 of the ERA in a way which is, so far as it is possible, compatible with Article 8, the employment tribunal will be well aware that s 98 does two things: (a) it identifies reasons on which an employer is permitted to rely to justify a dismissal and (b) it sets the general objective standards to be applied by the employment tribunal in determining whether the dismissal was fair or unfair.

(2) That question of fairness depends on whether, in all the circumstances, the employer acted reasonably or unreasonably in treating the reason (eg. conduct) as a sufficient reason for the dismissal and on the equity and substantial merits of the case.

(3) Lord Woolf pointed out, in giving the judgment of the court in *Poplar Housing and Regeneration Community Association Ltd v Donoghue* [2002] QB 48 at paragraph 75, that
  '(a) unless the legislation would otherwise be in breach of the convention s 3 can be ignored (so courts should always first ascertain whether, absent s 3, there would be any breach of the convention);
  (b) if the court has to rely on s 3 it should limit the extent of the modified meaning to that which is necessary to achieve compatibility;
  (c) s 3 does not entitle the court to legislate (its task is still one of interpretation, but interpretation in accordance with the direction in s 3) . . .'

(4) It is not immediately obvious, on a reading of s 98 without reference to a particular set of facts, as to how it could be incompatible with or be applied so as to violate Article 8 and Article 14 and so attract the application of s 3. Considerations of fairness, the reasonable response of a reasonable employer, equity and substantial merits ought, when taken together, to be sufficiently flexible, without even minimal interpretative modification under s 3, to enable the employment tribunal to give effect to applicable Convention rights. How, it might be asked, could the proper application by the employment tribunal of the objective

standards of fairness, reasonableness, equity and the substantial merits of the case result in the determination of a claim for unfair dismissal that was incompatible with Article 8?

(5) In general, the reasonable expectation is that a decision that a dismissal was fair under s 98 would not be incompatible with Article 8 or Article 14. There would be no need to invoke s 3 in order to achieve a result compatible with Article 8 and 14. In such cases s 3 can be ignored.

(6) There may, however, be cases in which the HRA point could make a difference to the reasoning of the tribunal and even to the final outcome of the claim for unfair dismissal. I shall now consider the possible application and effect of s 3 of the HRA in such cases.

(7) As explained earlier, a dismissal for a conduct reason may fall within the ambit of Article 8. A reason for a dismissal is 'a set of facts known to the employer or beliefs held by him which cause him to dismiss the employee' *Abernethy v Mott Hay* [1974] IRLR 213. The relevant set of facts may relate to the employee's private life. Take, by way of example, an extreme case involving the more straightforward position of a public authority employer. An employee of a public authority is dismissed for eating cake at home or in his lunch break at work. That is the set of facts constituting the conduct of the employee within s 98(2)(b) of the ERA. The decision to eat cake is, in general, a private one. It is difficult, though not impossible, to conceive of a justification under Article 8(2) for the employer's interference with respect for private life by dismissal for that reason. It is possible that in some circumstances the interference with a person's right to eat cake is necessary, legitimate and proportionate.

(8) In the case of a public authority employer, who is unable to justify the interference, the dismissal of the employee for that conduct reason would be a violation of Article 8. It would be unlawful within ss 6 and 7 of the HRA. If the act of dismissal by the public authority is unlawful under the HRA, it must also be unfair within s 98, as there would be no permitted (lawful) reason in s 98 on which the public authority employer could rely to justify the dismissal. In that case no question of incompatibility between s 98 and the Convention right would arise.

(9) Taking the same set of facts, save for the substitution of a private sector employer, it would not be unlawful under the HRA for the private employer to dismiss the employee for eating cake, as a private employer is not bound by the terms of s 6 of the HRA not to act incompatibly with Article 8. It is, however, difficult to conceive of a case, in which the unjustified interference with respect for private life under Article 8 (by dismissal for eating cake) would not also be an unfair dismissal under s 98. Put another way, it would not normally be fair for a private sector employer to dismiss an employee for a reason, which was an unjustified interference with the employee's private life. If that is right, there would, in general, be no need for an applicant to invoke Article 8 in order to succeed on the unfair dismissal claim and there would be no question of incompatibility between s 98 of the ERA and Article 8 to attract the application of s 3 of the HRA.

(10) If, however, there was a possible justification under s 98 of the dismissal of the cake-eating employee, the tribunal ought to consider Article 8 in the context of the application of s 3 of the HRA to s 98 of the ERA. If it would be

incompatible with Article 8 to hold that the dismissal for that conduct reason was fair, then the employment tribunal must, in accordance with s 3, read and give effect to s 98 of the ERA so as to be compatible with Article 8. That should not be difficult, given the breadth and flexibility of the concepts of fairness used in s 98.

(11) As already indicated in the short answer, no question of incompatibility in fact arises in this case, whether the employer is a public authority or in the private sector. On the facts found by the employment tribunal the case does not fall within the ambit of Article 8. Issues of incompatibility with Article 8 and Article 14 do not arise. There is no obligation to apply s 3 or s 6 of the HRA. The employment tribunal was entitled to conclude that it 'did not have to go into the minutiae of whether there is or is not compliance with the Human Rights Act' ie whether there was justification or incompatibility.

8.42 Mummery LJ set out the following useful framework of questions to be asked by Tribunals in cases of unfair dismissal involving private litigants where Article 8 is invoked:

(a) Do the circumstances of the dismissal fall within the ambit of one or more of the Articles of the Convention? If they do not, the Convention right is not engaged and need not be considered.

(b) If they do, does the state have a positive obligation to secure enjoyment of the relevant Convention right between private persons? If it does not, the Convention right is unlikely to affect the outcome of an unfair dismissal claim against a private employer.

(c) If it does, is the interference with the employee's Convention right by dismissal justified? If it is, proceed to (e) below.

(d) If it is not, was there a permissible reason for the dismissal under the ERA 1996, which does not involve unjustified interference with a Convention right? If there was not, the dismissal will be unfair for the absence of a permissible reason to justify it.

(e) If there was, is the dismissal fair, tested by the provisions of section 98 of the ERA 1996 reading and giving effect to them under section 3 of the HRA 1998 so as to be compatible with the Convention right?

8.43 In *Copsey v WWB Devon Clays Ltd*,[34] a case concerning Article 9, Mummery LJ referred to the guidance given in *X v Y* as 'tentative'. He did not resile from the *X v Y* approach, but did give a two-stage summary of the questions to be asked where dismissal for a particular reason is said to amount to a breach of a Convention right:

(a) Do the circumstances of the dismissal fall within the ambit of the relevant article? If there has been no material interference with the right guaranteed

---

[34] [2005] IRLR 811.

by the relevant article, the article is not engaged and its impact on the dismissal need not be considered further.

(b) If the circumstances of the dismissal do engage the relevant article, is the dismissal justified? This involves considerations of (eg) Article 9(2) and its application to specific situations.

F. The connection between *domicile* and workplace

It might be thought that Article 8 ECHR had little to do with the workplace. **8.44**
However, ECHR law does not exclude all acts within the workplace. In *Niemietz v Germany*,[35] the Court held that a search of a lawyer's offices was in breach of the right to respect for private life in Article 8 ECHR. The Court pointed out that the word 'domicile', which was used in the French text of the Convention, was broader in meaning than 'home'.

It considered the extent to which the private and professional activities of prof- **8.45**
essional persons, such as lawyers, were intermingled, and concluded that:[36]

> ... to interpret the words 'private life' and 'home' as excluding certain professional or business activities or premises would *not* be consonant with the essential object and purpose of Article 8 ... (*emphasis added*)

To this extent the Court went further than the approach taken by the ECJ in **8.46**
Hoechst AG v Commission of the European Communities.[37] The case of *Halford v UK* (discussed below at 8.81–8.82)[38] is also an example of the Court finding a breach of Article 8 ECHR in relation to acts taking place in the office. (However, three excluded pupils failed to challenge their exclusion from school in *R v Head Teacher of Alperton Community School and others, ex parte B and others*,[39] where they had relied on *Niemietz* in arguing that Article 8(1) included the right to develop a personality in conjunction with others.) In *Copland v United Kingdom*[40] the ECtHR ruled that the collection and storage of personal information relating to the applicant's telephone (as well as to her e-mail and internet usage) without her knowledge amounted to an interference with her rights under Article 8 of the Convention. She was employed in a state-run college. Two interesting points about the case were that it made no difference that the college could have obtained

---

[35] (1993) 16 EHRR 97.
[36] At [31].
[37] Joined Cases C-46/87 and 227/88 [1989] ECR 2859; see also the Opinion of Advocate-General Warner to the contrary effect in Case 139/79 *National Panasonic v Commission* [1980] ECR 2033.
[38] (1997) 24 EHRR 523.
[39] [2001] ELR 359.
[40] Application 62617/00, judgment 3 April 2007.

from its telephone bills data such as date, length of conversation and number dialled nor that the employer had done nothing with the information it held, since the storing of personal data relating to the private life of an individual also came within the scope of Article 8(1). Arguments on justification failed: the interference could not be 'in accordance with law' for the purposes of Article 8(2) since no domestic law to regulate such monitoring existed at the relevant time.

8.47 The principles considered in *Niemietz* have also been applied in cases where individuals complain that their Article 8 rights have been breached by restrictions placed on their ability to work. In *Sidabras and another v Lithuania*,[41] the Court held that the restrictions preventing the applicants (who were former KGB officers) from engaging in professional activities in a variety of private sector spheres fell within the scope of Article 8, as they affected the applicants' ability to develop relationships with the outside world, and created serious difficulties for them as regards the possibility to earn their living, with obvious repercussions for their enjoyment of their private lives. The decision was followed in *Rainys and Gasparavicius v Lithuania*,[42] where the Court held that the scope of Article 8 was sufficiently wide to cover dismissal from a particular private sector job on these grounds, as well as the general impact on the applicants' ability to work. Both of these cases were dealt with using Article 14 in conjunction with Article 8, and the Court declined to consider the question of breach of Article 8 alone. However, a breach of Article 8 alone was found in the later case of *Turek v Slovakia*,[43] owing to a lack of procedural safeguards in the process for registering the applicant on a list of former Communist security agents, which restricted his employment opportunities.

8.48 The domestic courts have been diffident about applying these decisions to their fullest extent. In *R (Countryside Alliance and others) v Attorney General and another*,[44] the Court of Appeal held that the hunting ban did not engage Article 8 in the case of a man whose entire working and social life had revolved around a hunt for 14 years, and who had no other qualifications. He believed he would lose his job as a result of the ban. The Court based its decision partly on the impossibility of ascertaining whether this man and other claimants would in fact lose their livelihoods, but also distinguished *Sidabras*, on the basis that it concerned a blanket ban on employment in a wide swathe of alternative jobs. *Rainys* and *Turek* were not mentioned. However, in *R (on the application of Wright and others) v Secretary of State for Health and another* (discussed further at 8.130–8.131

---

[41] (2006) 42 EHRR 6.
[42] Applications 70665/01 and 74345/01, judgment 7 July 2005.
[43] Application 57986/00, judgment 13 September 2006.
[44] [2006] 3 WL 1017; [2006] EWHC 2886 (Admin).

below),[45] Stanley Burnton J held that a provisional listing on the Protection of Vulnerable Adults list would engage Article 8, as it indicated that a person constituted a risk to vulnerable persons, and was calculated to interfere with his personal relationships with colleagues, vulnerable persons with whom he had worked. He relied on *Turek v Slovakia* in reaching this conclusion, and distinguished the *Countryside Alliance* case.

(1) What kind of protection do employees have under Article 8?

Article 8 can have both vertical and horizontal effect. This means that it both **8.49** affects the way in which the state interferes with relationships between employer and employee and imposes obligations as to the way the employer treats the employee. It may also affect the way in which the employee treats the employer. Thus in *Douglas v Hello Ltd*,[46] the Court of Appeal was ready to consider that the breach of Article 8 involved in the taking of unauthorised photographs could have been committed by an employee.

(2) Arbitrary interference with Article 8 rights

Any arbitrary interference with the development of relationships between emp- **8.50** loyer and employee could be contrary to Article 8 ECHR. Certainly, business relationships are capable of being within Article 8 (*Niemietz v Germany*[47]). However, most statutory or administrative interferences in the employment relationship are a consequence of perceived or actual abuses, and accordingly are not likely to be arbitrary in origin. Thus, Sir Otto Kahn-Freund stated that:

> [T]he main object of labour law has always been, and I venture to say will always be, to be a countervailing force to counteract the inequality of bargaining power which is inherent in the employment relationship.[48]

Moreover there is a very exacting test for establishing that a legislative provision **8.51** is arbitrary in domestic law (see *Nottinghamshire County Council v Secretary of State for Employment*[49]), and the courts are unlikely to want to diminish their respect for the exercise of democratic power by lowering this standard.

Of course, even when intended to meet specific abuses, ill-drafted rules can have **8.52** arbitrary effects which may be in breach of Article 8, or changes in working

---

[45] [2006] EWHC 2886 (Admin).

[46] [2001] QB 967, but see also *Douglas v Hello Ltd (3)* [2007] UKHL 21, where the duty of confidence was considered.

[47] (1993) 16 EHRR 97, at para 19.

[48] See the Hamlyn Lecture by Sir Otto Kahn-Freund, P Davies and M Freedland (eds), *Labour and the Law* (2nd edn, London: Stevens, 1977) 6.

[49] [1986] AC 240.

patterns may render obsolete—and therefore arbitrary—old protective rules, such as those providing unnecessary limitations on the work that persons of a particular sex can do (see *Commission of the European Communities v UK*,[50] which led to amendments to the Sex Discrimination Act 1975). Thus rules excluding employment in security-sensitive jobs might be justified in a particular case where the employee is emotionally vulnerable, but have an arbitrary effect if applied in all cases.

(3) Limits to employees' rights in the workplace under Article 8

8.53 There are many ways in which Article 8 ECHR limits the rights of employers as regards the treatment of their employees. However, in taking up employment a person decides to engage with the world beyond the home. He or she makes a decision to accept rules and constraints which apply specifically within the workplace. Normally there is a choice whether to accept or refuse any employment. Likewise, when terms or conditions of employment are changed there is a fresh opportunity to choose whether to accept or refuse such changes. Though a worker may feel 'forced' into accepting changes for fear of the consequences of losing a job, or for other economic reasons, the fact of acceptance may prevent the Convention from applying. Issues regarding the waiver of Convention rights in a contract of employment are discussed at 8.114 below.

8.54 Economic choices about work are always inherent in any liberal democratic society. No one is immune from them. Choices about lifestyle, where to live, what career to pursue, what is an acceptable and what an unacceptable level of remuneration, and so on, inevitably impact on a person's private life. The ECtHR does not readily accept arguments that a specific job imposes unacceptable constraints on an employee's Article 8 rights. The respect required by Article 8 does not mean that an employee's private life is to be immunised from the impact of his or her choice of a particular job.

8.55 In *Knudsen v Norway*,[51] the applicant was a clergyman within a state church system who was concerned about the imposition on him of requirements in conflict with his convictions. The Commission decided that his freedom to relinquish his office was a satisfactory ultimate guarantee of his right to freedom of thought, conscience, and religion. The applicant's views on abortion were not found to have led to his dismissal; rather, it was his refusal to perform functions which were administrative roles of his office which led to his termination.

---

[50] Case 165/82 [1983] ECR 3431.
[51] (1985) 42 DR 247.

Article 8 may therefore provide little, in addition to statutory rights, in terms **8.56** of protection from merely onerous employment conditions. It is clear that it does not preclude work from having *any* impact on family life. The extent of its practical effect is now considered.

G. The practical impact of Article 8 in the workplace

(1) Employee records

Article 8 was the inspiration for the Data Protection legislation at both the **8.57** European and domestic levels. Now strict limits have been placed upon the way in which employers can store and utilise records relating to job applicants and employees by the Data Protection Act 1998 (DPA 1998), which regulates the processing of 'personal data' and, more stringently, 'sensitive personal data' by data controllers.

Whilst 'personal data' has a seemingly wide definition in the DPA 1998 as data **8.58** relating to a living individual who can be identified by such data, a rather narrow approach has been taken by the Court of Appeal in *Durant v Financial Services Authority*.[52] The Court put forward the following two tests to assist in deciding whether particular data falls within the definition in borderline cases, namely:

(a) whether the information is biographical in a significant sense, ie going beyond the recording of the subject's involvement in a matter or event which has no personal connotations and does not compromise his privacy;
(b) whether the information has the data subject as its focus, rather than some other person or event with whom or in which he has been involved.

Durant concerned a request to access particular data relating to Mr Durant's **8.59** complaint to the Financial Services Authority. The Court of Appeal held that the documents requested did not contain 'personal data', as the information therein related to Mr Durant's *complaint*, not to Mr Durant himself.

There is no reason to suggest, however, that any different definition would be **8.60** used in the context of a claim that personal data had been processed contrary to the provisions of the DPA 1998 (indeed, *Durant* has been referred to in the context of such a claim in *Johnson v The Medical Defence Union*[53]). The decision may well have the effect of narrowing parts of the Employment Practices Data Code discussed below.

---

[52] [2003] EWCA Civ 1746. See also S Lorber, 'Data Protection and Subject Access Requests' (2004) 33 ILJ 79.
[53] [2006] EWHC 321 (Ch).

8.61 'Sensitive personal data' covers a still narrower range of information, including racial or ethnic origins, political and religious beliefs, trade union membership, physical and mental health, sexual life, and criminal convictions or allegations.

8.62 'Processing' of data as defined in the Act again covers a wide range of activities, ranging from all automatic or computerised processing, to holding data in a 'relevant filing system'. Again, the potential width of the Act has been narrowed by the Court of Appeal in *Durant*, which held that to fulfil the definition, the files forming part of the system must be structured or referenced in such a way as to clearly indicate at the start of the search whether personal data is held within the system and if so, in which file or files; and which has a sufficiently sophisticated and detailed means of readily indicating whether and where in a particular file or files specific criteria or information about the subject can be readily located.

8.63 All personal data must be processed in accordance with the data protection principles set out in Schedules 1 and 2 to the DPA 1998. Sensitive personal data must be processed in accordance with Schedule 3.

8.64 Employees can enforce their rights under the DPA 1998 by asking the Information Commissioner to make an assessment as to whether or not personal data has been processed in accordance with the Act (s 42).

8.65 The Information Commissioner has the power to serve an Information Notice, requesting information from the employer in order to make such an assessment (s 43), and/or an Enforcement Notice, to prevent processing of personal data in contravention of the DPA 1998 (s 40).

8.66 It is an offence under the Act, punishable by a fine, to fail to comply with either of these types of notice (ss 47 and 60).

8.67 Individuals may also enforce their rights under the Act by sending a written notice directly to the employer requiring them to stop processing data on the grounds that it is causing the employee 'substantial unwarranted damage and/or distress'. This can be enforced by means of an application for an order from the court (s 10). Although these provisions do provide a remedy for individuals whose rights under the Act have been breached, they inevitably take some time to complete, and may not be appropriate to deal with one-off breaches.

8.68 The employee may also claim compensation under the DPA 1998 where unlawful processing of personal data has caused damage, including compensation for actual financial losses and, where financial losses have been caused, for distress (s 13). However, in many cases where personal data has been processed by employers in breach of the Act, there will have been no financial loss, leaving the employee without any compensatory remedy.

In June 2005, the Information Commissioner finally published the Employment **8.69** Practices Data Protection Code as a consolidated document. The Code, which is freely available on the Information Commissioner's website,[54] provides guidance on compliance with the Act, although it has no specific legal status.

A significant part of the Code gives guidance as to the appropriate way in which **8.70** to maintain and process records on job applicants and employees. Part 1 of the Code, which deals with recruitment and selection, is mostly concerned with 'good practice recommendations' ensuring that information obtained during the recruitment process is relevant to the recruitment decision to be made, used for that purpose only, and is retained only where necessary. Part 2 of the Code, which relates to records about existing employees, is more extensive. It contains guidance as to, amongst other things:

- the collection, retention and security of employment records, including sickness and absence records;
- use of personal data provided to pension or insurance schemes;
- equal opportunities monitoring;
- use of personal data for marketing or preventing fraud;
- providing and retaining references;
- responding to disclosure requests;
- disclosure of worker data in connection with mergers and acquisitions;
- accessing personal data to be used as evidence in support of grievance/ disciplinary proceedings, and keeping records of such proceedings; and
- outsourcing data processing.

Essentially, Part 2 of the Code is intended to ensure that personal data is collated **8.71** and retained only for as long as is necessary, anonymised where appropriate and practicable (eg in the case of information obtained through equal opportunities monitoring), and disclosed, as far as possible, only in accordance with a disclosure policy, and where it is fair to do so.

(2) Freedom of Information Act 2000

The UK Freedom of Information Act 2000 (FOIA 2000) came into full force **8.72** on 1 January 2005. It sets out an information right or a right of access by the public to all information held by public authorities. There are two ways to access

---

[54] At <http://www.ico.gov.uk>.

such information held by a public authority: via a publication scheme and via a right to request information. The information requested must be made available within a specific time period. There are also exemptions to the requirement to provide the information. The FOIA 2000 does not change the right of individuals to protection of the confidentiality of their personal information in accordance with Article 8 ECHR, the DPA 1998, and at common law. Accordingly, there are certain records which may not be disclosable in response to an access request. These often concern an individual's private or home life, or personal correspondence.

8.73 Whilst it may well be that the role of employees in carrying out their work is not generally a private one, situations involving physical privacy (changing rooms or work toilets), communication in non-working environments (staff restaurants or non-work emails or telephone calls), or personal information (such as intimate health matters recorded in a personal file) would be regarded as protected by virtue of Article 8 and a public authority employer who discloses such information risks breaching the HRA 1998.

8.74 The rights of workers to privacy whilst at work are narrower in scope than those protecting privacy in the home or family life and employees would be prudent to recognise the difference between their public role as employees and their personal role which involves their identity at home or in correspondence.

8.75 It is advisable for public authority employers to issue guidance or draw up policies clarifying how information about staff will be treated in respect to freedom of information (FOI) requests. For example, policies covering the use of work email accounts are now commonplace.

8.76 Some work records do not obviously contain personal information. Documents such as electronic diaries often contain a blend of personal and work-related dates and reminders. If an employer enacts a policy that they have the right to inspect all records maintained by workers in the course of their employment it will be far easier to determine FOI requests when they arise. If staff are aware that personal material contained in work documents of any kind will be inspected and potentially disclosed following an FOI request disputes are less likely to occur.

(3) Surveillance

8.77 Surveillance can occur at work for many reasons, not all of which are bad or unjustifiable. Employers gather information for many reasons, including defending claims at a later stage. Defendants in personal injury claims frequently rely on secretly obtained footage of claimants apparently displaying better health than their claim dictates (see the discussion of *Jones v Warwick* at 8.27). This can also apply to pension claims.

Thus, in *Law Debenture Trust Group (Appellant) v (1) Terence Malley (2) Pensions* **8.78**
Ombudsman (Respondents),[55] Alliott J considered the reliance by trustees of a pension scheme on evidence obtained by surveillance when refusing the applicant's ill-health early retirement request. He held that covert surveillance was a legitimate course to pursue on appropriate occasions in the investigations of claims.

Whilst such practices have been known for some time, recent studies suggest **8.79**
that day-to-day surveillance of employees during their ordinary working hours has increased hugely in the past five years.[56] New technologies have enabled more and more intrusive methods of surveillance, such as requiring supermarket and warehouse workers to wear computers on their arms and hands which direct and monitor their work.[57] The ways in which such surveillance can be carried out are ever-increasing, so it is not possible to address each of them here. However, some of the most common kinds of surveillance are considered below.

(i) Interception of telephone conversations, email, and the Internet

Most workers will wish to make personal calls from the workplace from time **8.80**
to time. The Court has readily accepted that secret surveillance of telephone calls can infringe the right to respect for private life. Thus, in *Malone v UK*,[58] the government failed to convince the Court that its power to intercept telephone conversations had a legal basis. The UK subsequently passed the Interception of Communications Act 1985.

Subsequently, in 1997, a senior police officer Alison Halford established a breach **8.81**
of Article 8 in relation to the tapping of her telephone at work (*Halford v UK*[59]). Her case is interesting both because of the Court's comments about the grounds

---

[55] [1999] OPLR 167.

[56] American Management Association e/Policy Institute Research, 2005 Electronic Monitoring and Surveillance Survey, available at <http://www.amanet.org/research> and Unison, *Privacy at Work Survey* (2004), available at <http://www.unison-scotland.org.uk/briefings/privacysurvey.html>, both cited in H Oliver, *Regulating Surveillance at Work* (London: Institute of Employment Rights), 4 and fn 5 and 6.

[57] See 'Firms Tag Workers to Improve Efficiency', *The Guardian* (7 June 2005) cited in H Oliver, *Regulating Surveillance at Work*, 5.

[58] (1985) 7 EHRR 14, para 79.

[59] (1997) 24 EHRR 523.

for attenuating this right and as showing the reach of Article 8 rights into the workplace. The Court found:[60]

> The evidence justifies the conclusion that there was a reasonable likelihood that calls made by Ms Halford from her office were intercepted by the Merseyside police with the primary aim of gathering material to assist in the defence of the sex discrimination proceedings brought against them. This interception constituted an 'interference by a public authority,' within the meaning of Article 8(2), with the exercise of Ms Halford's right to respect for her private life and correspondence . . . It cannot . . . be said that the interference was 'in accordance with the law' for the purposes of Article 8(2) of the Convention, since the domestic law did not provide adequate protection to Ms Halford against the interferences by the police with her right to respect for her private life and correspondence.

8.82 The Court held Article 8(1) applied because:[61]

> There is no evidence of any warning having been given to Ms Halford, as a user of the internal telecommunications system operated at the Merseyside police headquarters, that calls made on that system would be liable to interception. She would, the Court considers, have had a reasonable expectation of privacy for such calls, which expectation was moreover reinforced by a number of factors. As Assistant Chief Constable she had sole use of her office where there were two telephones, one of which was specifically designated for her private use. Furthermore, she had been given the assurance, in response to a memorandum, that she could use her office telephones for the purposes of her sex discrimination case.

8.83 This reasoning might imply that where the employer does not lead the employee to suppose that conversations over the phone will be confidential, there will be no breach of Article 8 ECHR. In some workplaces the employers make it explicit that telephone conversations may be monitored. The principles could equally apply to the use of email or the Internet, or even post from the office. However, employers need to recognise that even a general warning of the kind discussed may not be enough. The Court did not give a general licence to employers to invade employees' privacy. In each case the tests for attenuating the right under Article 8(2) must be met.

8.84 Accordingly, issues may still arise as to the nature of any such surveillance. Whereas there can be no reason why an employer should not listen to a conversation directly concerned with carrying out the employer's business, even a warning might not justify an employer listening to a conversation from the workplace which was concerned only with the private life of the worker, for instance arrangements for a sick relative.

---

[60] At paras 48 and 51.
[61] At para 45.

Such an invasion of privacy would almost certainly be disproportionate unless **8.85** there were very well-founded reasons such as doubting the genuineness of the phone call. The ECtHR has said that:

> [p]owers of secret surveillance of citizens, characterizing as they do the police state, are tolerable under the Convention only insofar as strictly necessary for safeguarding the democratic institutions.[62]

See also *Copland v United Kingdom* discussed at 8.46 above.

Different issues may arise where use of the Internet is involved, in particular **8.86** where employees use the Internet to publicise their social activities. Whilst not strictly a case about surveillance, *Pay v Lancashire Probation Service*[63] gives an idea of the approach of the EAT in this area. Mr Pay was a probation officer working predominantly with sex offenders. He was dismissed after his employers discovered that he was involved in activities including the merchandising of products connected with bondage, domination, and sadomasochism and that he performed shows in hedonist and fetish clubs. Photographs of him involved in these activities were available on the Internet. Mr Pay contended that his dismissal on grounds that these activities were incompatible with his role amounted to a breach of his rights under Articles 8 and 10 ECHR. The employment tribunal held that there was no interference with Mr Pay's Article 8 rights, as he had publicised his activities on the Internet and promoted them in public places and they were therefore no longer part of his private life. The EAT upheld that finding.

(4) Regulation of Investigatory Powers Act 2000

The Regulation of Investigatory Powers Act 2000 (RIPA 2000) was passed in **8.87** part to give effect to the judgment of the Court in *Halford* (see 8.81–8.82 above). Section 1(2) and (3) of this Act provide respectively for a criminal and civil remedy in cases of unlawful interception on a private telecommunications system.[64]

Section 2(1) of the RIPA 2000 defines a 'telecommunication system' and a **8.88** 'private telecommunications system'. The former is a system which exists 'for the purpose of facilitating the transmission of communications by any means involving the use of electrical or electro-magnetic energy', while a 'private telecommunication system' is:

> . . . any telecommunication system which, without itself being a public telecommunication system, is a system in relation to which the following conditions are

---

[62] *Klass v Germany* (1978) 2 EHRR 214, para 42. See further discussion of factors which might justify such surveillance in H Oliver, *Regulating Surveillance in the Workplace*, 28.

[63] [2004] IRLR 129.

[64] Criminal liability is subject to exclusions in the circumstances set out in s 1(6) of the Act. Such exclusions do not apply to the tortious claim in s 1(3) of the Act.

satisfied—(a) it is attached, directly or indirectly and whether or not for the purposes of the communication in question, to a public telecommunication system; and (b) there is apparatus comprised in the system which is both located in the United Kingdom and used (with or without other apparatus) for making the attachment to the public telecommunication system . . .

8.89 The Act therefore covers an office telephone system and any Internet email messaging system, however not all communications are equally covered. In particular, the Act does not cover all the communications that might be monitored by employers. In particular, it applies only to 'interceptions' of communications in the course of transmission. This means that although emails opened by the employer before they have been read by the employee will fall within the Act, emails which are read by the employer after they have been opened and stored by the employee will not (RIPA 2000, s 1).

8.90 The civil remedy created by section 1(3) of the RIPA 2000 is entirely new, because the Interception of Communications Act 1985 created neither a criminal offence nor a civil remedy for unlawful interception over a *private telecommunications system*, instead only covering communications over a public telecommunications system. Section 1(3) of the RIPA 2000 says:

> (3) Any interception of a communication which is carried out at any place in the United Kingdom by, or with the express or implied consent of, a person having the right to control the operation or the use of a private telecommunication system shall be actionable at the suit or instance of the sender or recipient, or intended recipient, of the communication if it is without lawful authority and is either—
>
>   (a) an interception of that communication in the course of its transmission by means of that private system; or
>
>   (b) an interception of that communication in the course of its transmission, by means of a public telecommunication system, to or from apparatus comprised in that private telecommunication system.

8.91 The requirement of the 'express or implied consent' of the controller of the private telecommunication system would seem to exclude a situation where an employee of the controller engages in interception activities which are clearly outside the scope of the employee's employment and authorisation.

8.92 What is less clear is whether mere acquiescence is sufficient to found an action under section 1(3). If a controller of a private telecommunications system knows that another individual may be using the system unlawfully to intercept communications and does not intervene, or indeed simply knows that the individual has the capacity to do so and does not adequately supervise, it may be asked whether the sender or recipient of the communication would still be afforded a remedy under section 1(3).

An action[65] under section 1(3) lies at the suit of either the sender, or the recipient **8.93** or the intended recipient of the communication. Thus, where an employee believes that his or her employer has unlawfully intercepted a telephone conversation with a third party, either the employee or the third party may sue the employer.

A cause of action under section 1(3) arises only where the interception is without **8.94** lawful authority. According to section 1(5) of the RIPA 2000, conduct will be lawful if one of the following provisions applies:

> (5) Conduct has lawful authority for the purposes of this section if, and only if—
> > (a) it is authorised by or under s. 3 or 4;[66]
> > (b) it takes place in accordance with a warrant under section 5 ('an interception warrant'); or
> > (c) it is in exercise, in relation to any stored communication, of any statutory power that is exercised (apart from this section) for the purpose of obtaining information or of taking possession of any document or other property . . .

(5) The Telecommunications (Lawful Business Practice) (Interception of Communications) Regulations 2000

The Telecommunications (Lawful Business Practice) (Interception of **8.95** Communications) Regulations 2000 (which are set out in Appendix 6)[67] define how interceptions may be made lawfully without consent. The Regulations were made under section 4(2) of the RIPA 2000 and came into force on 24 October 2000.

The DTI believes that the Regulations should offer business the greatest possible **8.96** scope for maximising the advantages of new ways of working with phone, email, and other electronic communications, consistent with a high degree of privacy for the users of communications services.

---

[65] However, a cause of action will lie only where both the conduct effecting the interception takes place within the UK and either the sender or the intended recipient of the communication is within the UK: s 2(4) of the Act.

[66] The full text of these exceptions is outside the scope of this book. However, for employers the most important exception is likely to be obtained by consent under s 3(1): '(1) Conduct by any person consisting in the interception of a communication is authorised by this section if the communication is one which, or which that person has reasonable grounds for believing, is both—(a) a communication sent by a person who has consented to the interception; and (b) a communication the intended recipient of which has so consented.' The Act is not precise as to whether the communication must relate to the specific communication, or can be more general (eg where an employee has signed a contract or workplace policy which permits the interception of email or telephone communications).

[67] SI 2000/2699.

8.97   These Regulations authorise businesses (in the widest sense of the word, which covers charities and other non-commercial bodies, and expressly includes public authorities) to monitor or record all communications transmitted over their systems without consent for the following purposes:

(a) establishing the existence of facts;

(b) ascertaining compliance with regulatory or self-regulatory practices or procedures;

(c) ascertaining or demonstrating standards which are achieved or ought to be achieved by persons using the system;

(d) in the interests of national security;

(e) preventing or detecting crime;

(f) investigating or detecting unauthorised use of the business's telecoms system;

(g) ensuring the effective operation of the system.

8.98   The Regulations also authorise businesses to monitor (but not record) communications for the following purposes:

(a) checking whether or not communications are relevant to the business;

(b) monitoring calls to confidential counselling helplines run free of charge.

8.99   The Regulations provide that interceptions will only be authorised where they are effected solely for the purpose of monitoring or keeping a record of 'communications relevant to the systems controller's business' (reg 3(2)(a)). This phrase covers communications by which business transactions are entered into, which otherwise relate to the business, or which take place in the course of carrying on the business (reg 2(b)).

8.100 Whilst this could be taken to mean that monitoring or recording of purely private communications will be unlawful, the government expressly confirmed during the consultation process that the ability to monitor to prevent unauthorised use could be used to intercept emails and internet use to prevent communication of offensive materials.[68] Such communications will of necessity have little or nothing to do with the employer's business. This suggests that the Regulations were intended to have a wider effect, allowing employers to monitor and record all communications occurring within working hours, or which might have any effect on the employer's business.

8.101 In cases of proposed interception, the Regulations require businesses to 'make all reasonable efforts' to inform those people who use the organisations' telecoms

---

[68] H Oliver, *Regulation of Surveillance at Work*, 48 citing the Lawful Business Practice Regulations – Response to Consultation (Department of Trade and Industry Communication and Information Industries Directorate, October 2000).

systems that interceptions may take place. This requirement is in the view of the authors vital, since it is the only way a party to a communication might know that an interception could take or had taken place.

In its paper responding to the consultation process over the draft Regulations, **8.102** the DTI stated that:[69]

> The Government is anxious to make clear and workable regulations and to avoid placing unreasonable burdens on business. We accept that, in many cases, a requirement to inform outside correspondents of interceptions would place an excessive burden on business. For that reason, we have removed the requirement to inform all parties to communications of interceptions. However we have retained a requirement for businesses to 'make all reasonable efforts' to inform the users of their own telecoms systems that interceptions might take place. This will ensure that, in accordance with current best practice, businesses inform employees that communications may be monitored or recorded. There is therefore no requirement to make any effort to inform external third parties that their communications may be monitored or recorded.

It is important for employment lawyers to remember that users of communica- **8.103** tion systems are usually not in control of what is sent to them, and hence should not be penalised for communications such as emails received, unless they have been reading such mail in unauthorised time.

In the response to the consultation mentioned above, civil liberties organisations **8.104** and trade unions commented that the draft Regulations did not go far enough to protect the right to privacy. The response was to make no amendments as a reaction to such concerns, but rather to widen the Regulations following submissions from businesses as to administrative and costs implications. For example, following consultation, the DTI expanded the Regulations in certain ways, including permitting businesses to record or monitor communications without consent so that their telecoms systems could operate effectively. Further, in response to the perceived need for businesses to be able to check voicemail systems and email accounts in order to access communications during the absence of staff, the Regulations were widened to allow the monitoring of communications without consent in order to determine whether they are relevant to the business. The government has said that this will achieve a balance between giving businesses free access to their own communications and protecting the privacy of non-business communications where these are permitted.

Some consultation responses suggested that the Regulations should include **8.105** a proportionality test to govern the extent of businesses' interception activities,

---

[69] At para 30–31.

in order to ensure that a business's interception activities were in proportion to the level of need for interception. The government has said that such a test would leave businesses and others unsure as to what interception activities were permitted and place them in a vulnerable legal position. It says that the proportionality test within the DPA 1998 is sufficient to ensure that businesses act in a proportionate manner when collecting and using personal information.

8.106 The adoption of such a test would make the Regulations more transparent. But despite the failure to amend the draft Regulations, a complaint to an employment tribunal would still require the tribunal to act in accordance with section 3 of the HRA 1998 and apply Article 8 ECHR even if the test of proportionality is not expressed in the Regulations themselves.

8.107 The only case in which the EAT has so far considered the Regulations is *Avocet Hardware Plc v Morrison* (see 8.28 above), where the employer sought to adduce evidence obtained in breach of the Regulations and the RIPA 2000. The EAT's approach in the *Avocet* case suggests that whilst tribunals are required to balance the relevant Article 6 and Article 8 rights before admitting such evidence, the balance may well often come down in favour of admitting 'relevant' evidence, even if obtained in breach of Article 8.

(6) Other forms of monitoring and surveillance

8.108 Though monitoring of employees is routine, it too can interfere with private life. For instance, it is not unknown for employers to place closed circuit television (CCTV) cameras in the lavatory. There may be ostensibly 'good' reasons for this where it is suspected that crime or health and safety issues arise. Yet obviously there is a very great risk that there will be an unacceptable breach of Article 8 rights, and indeed even criminal acts.[70]

8.109 Employers may also wish to monitor employees outside the workplace. In *McGowan v Scottish Water*,[71] the employer suspected that Mr McGowan, who lived in a tied house close to his workplace, was falsifying his time sheets with regard to call-out time and periods when it was necessary for him to attend the plant. They hired private investigators to undertake covert video surveillance of Mr McGowan's home. The footage confirmed the employer's suspicions, and Mr McGowan

---

[70] In *Choi* (7 May 1999, CA) No 9805975 Z4, the Court of Appeal dismissed an appeal against conviction for outraging public decency, for secretly video-recording women in a supermarket lavatory.

[71] [2005] IRLR 167.

was dismissed. Mr McGowan contended that the covert filming amounted to a breach of his Article 8 rights and rendered his dismissal unfair.

The employment tribunal held that, as what was filmed inside the house could **8.110** have been seen by anyone using the public road outside Mr McGowan's house, there was no 'reasonable expectation' of privacy. On appeal, the Scottish EAT suggested that it did not accept that finding, holding that:

> at least at first sight, covert surveillance of a person's home, unbeknown to him or her, which tracks all people coming and going from it . . . raises at least a strong presumption that the right to have one's private life respected is being invaded, and if the issue stopped there we might have considered that the Article was engaged.

However, the EAT went on to find that any interference was justified and proportionate because:

(a) the employer, a public corporation, was investigating what was effectively criminal activity in the sense of fraudulent timesheets;
(b) the employer had considered other means of dealing with the problem but had concluded that these would be impractical and ineffective;
(c) it could be argued that the tied house was part of the workplace;
(d) the aim of the surveillance (to quantify the number of times Mr McGowan left the house to go to the process plant) went to the heart of the investigation the employer needed to carry out to protect the assets of the company;
(e) the surveillance was therefore not undertaken for external or whimsical reasons.

This gives an indication of the type of factors employment tribunals will take into **8.111** account when considering whether surveillance is or was proportionate.

However, other tribunals may place more emphasis than did the Scottish EAT **8.112** in *McGowan* on the extent to which the employee's rights were breached in carrying out the Article 8(2) balancing exercises. For example, another tribunal might have paid more attention to the fact that Mr McGowan had recently been bereaved at the time the surveillance took place, which could be considered to render the interference into this family life more intrusive.

So far, there have been no reported cases in which a tribunal has been required **8.113** to consider the fairness of a dismissal based on surveillance evidence obtained in breach of Article 8. It is unlikely that the tribunal would exclude such relevant evidence in the light of the decisions in *Jones v University of Warwick* and *Avocet Hardware plc v Morrison* (see 8.27–8.28 above). However, in accordance with the principles outlined in *X v Y* (see 8.39–8.42 above), the tribunal will be required to interpret section 98's (of the ERA 1996) compatibility with Article 8.

Assuming that the dismissal was for a fair conduct-related reason, the *X v Y* approach should arguably lead the tribunal to conclude that, as the evidence was gained in breach of the employee's Article 8 rights, the dismissal should be considered procedurally unfair. However, the protection thus granted to the employee is likely to be limited, as the employer may be able to argue that had a fair procedure been followed, dismissal would have occurred on the balance of probabilities in any event and thus avoid a finding of unfair dismissal under section 98A(2) of the ERA 1996. Alternatively, there may well be a significant finding of contributory fault under section 123(6) of the ERA 1996.

8.114 As is evident from the discussion above, Mr McGowan was not informed of his employer's intention to place him under surveillance, but the EAT nevertheless found that his Article 8 rights had not been breached. The failure to obtain consent for specific monitoring will often be a factor in considering whether an employee's Article 8 rights have been breached. Employers may seek to obtain from their employees a general waiver of Article 8 rights in advance of the occasion in question. However, it may not be enough to simply ask the worker to sign a contract of employment containing such a general waiver (see *Rommelfanger v Germany*[72]). The ECtHR has distinguished between new employees, who can decide whether to accept an offer of employment having waived such rights (see *Glasenapp v Germany*[73]), and existing employees who are forced to sign a waiver under threat of dismissal. This is an example of the manner in which Convention jurisprudence recognises that economic choices are inherent in a liberal democracy.

8.115 Ultimately, the question whether Article 8 rights arise in the context of employer monitoring will largely depend on the nature of the expectation of privacy (which will obviously differ as between the open plan office and the staff toilet) and whether less intrusive ways exist for an employer to pursue a legitimate ground for surveillance. Even where an employee has accepted that the employer has powers to monitor and powers of surveillance, the impact of those powers is not irrelevant. At a certain point such action can go beyond what is necessary for the firm and/or the protection of the employees themselves. There may be an invasion of the human dignity of the individual. It would not be compatible with Article 8 ECHR to have a work regime in which the autonomy of the individual is so removed that employees' dignity is lost and they are

---

[72] (1989) 62 DR 151.
[73] (1986) 9 EHRR 25.

rendered mere robots. Thus an American judge referred to constant CCTV monitoring of workers as:[74]

> ... not only personally repugnant to employees but it has such an inhibiting effect as to prevent the employees from performing their work with confidence and ease. Every employee has occasion to pause in the course of their work, to take a breather, to scratch his head, to yawn or otherwise be himself without affecting his work. An employee, with reason would hesitate at all times to so behave, if his every action is being recorded on TV. To have workers constantly televised is . . . reminiscent of the era depicted by Charlie Chaplin in 'Modern Times' and constitutes an affront to the dignity of man.

(7) Monitoring and surveillance and the DPA 1998

Monitoring inevitably raises data protection issues. The DPA 1998 has already **8.116** been considered in part at 8.57–8.71 above, but further consideration is necessary here. Part 3 of the Information Commissioner's Employment Practices Data Protection Code deals solely with monitoring at work. It addresses the impact of the DPA 1998 on the monitoring by employers of telephone calls, emails, and Internet access involving their employees, as well as the use of CCTV and other devices to keep track of the conduct of employees, and the quality/ quantity of their work.

The Code deals with both overt and covert monitoring. In the introductory **8.117** section of this part of the Code, it is made clear that human rights issues are raised by most types of monitoring carried out by employers.

> Monitoring may, to varying degrees, have an adverse impact on workers. It may intrude into their private lives, undermine respect for their correspondence or interfere with the relationship of mutual trust and confidence that should exist between them and their employer. The extent to which it does this may not always be immediately obvious. It is not always easy to draw a distinction between work-place and private information. For example, monitoring email messages from a worker to an occupational health advisor, or messages between workers and their trade union representatives, can give rise to concern.
> In broad terms, what the [DPA 1998] requires is that any adverse impact on workers is justified by the benefits to the employer and others . . .

The general approach to monitoring employees is set out at paragraph 3.1 of **8.118** Part 3 of the Code. Employers should abide by the following core principles:

- it will usually be intrusive to monitor workers;
- workers have legitimate expectations that they can keep their personal lives private and that they are entitled to a degree of privacy in the work environment;

---

[74] *Re Electronics Instrument Company and the International Union of Electrical Workers* (1965) LA 563.

- if employers wish to monitor their workers, they should be clear about the purpose and satisfied that the particular monitoring arrangement is justified by real benefits that will be delivered;
- workers should be aware of the nature, extent, and reasons for any monitoring unless (*exceptionally*), covert monitoring is justified;
- workers' awareness will influence their expectations.

8.119 As is apparent from the general principles, the Code is particularly stringent in relation to covert monitoring, which should be authorised by senior management only where there are grounds for suspecting criminal activity or equivalent malpractice, and where advance notification would prejudice its prevention or detection. Such monitoring should be used only in the context of a specific investigation. Further, it should not be used in places which workers would genuinely and reasonably expect to be private, for example toilets or private offices. The approach taken in the Code suggests that an employee may have a greater chance of showing a breach of the DPA 1998 than of utilising Article 8 to prevent reliance on evidence such as that obtained in *McGowan* and *Jones*.

8.120 The Code also contains guidance as to monitoring in particular situations, for example, monitoring of electronic communications (including telephone calls, emails, and Internet access) and in-vehicle monitoring. The former section suggests that employers should set out a clear policy as to personal use of such communication systems, and inform employees of specific restrictions on internet material that may be viewed or copied.

8.121 In addition to the Employment Practices Data Protection Code, the Information Commissioner has produced a CCTV Code, which provides guidance as to situations in which this type of monitoring may breach the DPA 1998. While it is directed at the use of such equipment in public places rather than by employers to monitor workers' behaviour, some of its provisions are relevant to employee monitoring.

H. Security checks and disclosure of confidential information to employers/regulatory bodies

8.122 In *Hilton v UK*,[75] the Commission said that a security check per se did not interfere with respect for private life, but it might do so if it involved the collection of information about a person's private affairs.

---

[75] (1981) 3 EHRR 104.

However, in *Leander v Sweden*,[76] the Court confirmed that the retention and use of information about an individual in connection with employment in jobs which had a national security sensitivity, did not carry with it a positive obligation to allow the applicant to know the content of the files. Accordingly, provisions[77] within the ERA 1996 (see s 193) which exclude or limit the ordinary jurisdiction of the employment tribunal in national security cases may be difficult to challenge under this Article.   **8.123**

In the UK, before the HRA 1998 came into force, the Court of Appeal considered the competing public interests of confidentiality in a statement given to the police by a nurse and the need to protect public health and safety in *Woolgar v Chief Constable of Sussex Police*.[78] A patient had died in a nursing home, and the matron had thereafter been interviewed under caution by the police. She attempted to prevent the police from disclosing a transcript of an interview to her regulatory body, the United Kingdom Central Council. Upholding a refusal to grant the matron an injunction to prevent disclosure of the interview, the Court of Appeal said that this was a matter of balancing the public interest in protecting public health and safety (which entitled the police to disclose to a regulatory body operating in that field confidential information which the police reasonably believed was relevant to an inquiry being conducted by that body on the basis that confidentiality would be otherwise maintained) and the countervailing public interest in ensuring the free flow of information to the police for the purposes of criminal proceedings (which required that information given in confidence would not be used for some collateral purpose).   **8.124**

The Court of Appeal stated that in order to safeguard the interests of the individual, the person affected by the disclosure should be informed of the police's intentions. (See also *General Mediterranean Holdings v Patel*;[79] *R v Law Society ex parte Pamplin*;[80] *R v A Police Authority ex parte LM*;[81] and *Silver v UK*,[82] concerning disclosure of confidential documents and the interrelation between Articles 6 and 8 ECHR.)   **8.125**

The Court of Appeal has now considered the issues raised in *Woolgar* in a human rights context in *R (on the application of D) v Secretary of State for Health*.[83] D was   **8.126**

---

[76] (1987) 9 EHRR 443.
[77] See also the Employment Tribunal (Constitution and Rules of Procedure) Regulations 2004, SI 2004/1861, Sch 2.
[78] [2000] 1 WLR 25.
[79] [2001] 1 WLR 272.
[80] [2001] EWHC Admin 300.
[81] (2000) UKHRR 143.
[82] (1983) 5 EHRR 347.
[83] [2006] EWCA Civ 989, (2006) Lloyd's Rep Med 457.

a doctor who had been accused of indecent assault by six separate patients over a number of years, although he had been acquitted of all relevant offences in the criminal courts. In 1999, an 'alert letter' detailing the history of the allegations and court proceedings was issued to prospective employers of D by the Regional Director of Public Health (RDPH). The purpose of such letters is to make NHS bodies aware of registered health professionals whose performance and conduct could place patients or staff at serious risk. By 2004, all criminal proceedings had been concluded and there were no proceedings outstanding before the GMC, which would normally lead to the withdrawal of the alert letter. However, in December 2004, the letter was re-issued on the basis of the old allegations, as the RDPH felt that D still posed a serious risk to patients. D sought judicial review of the decision. Laws LJ held that the applicable test in domestic law and the proportionality test under Article 8(2) ECHR were the same: was there a 'pressing need' for the information to be disclosed to prospective employers? He concluded that in D's case the test for disclosure was satisfied. The possibility that D represented a danger to women in his care was 'plainly more than fanciful', which was a powerful factor in favour of disclosure. In the circumstances, the issuing of an alert letter was the least that could have been done.

I. Article 8 and the protection of vulnerable people

8.127   In recent years, there has been continuing expansion in the number of statutory measures designed to inform employers about potential or actual employees who may pose a risk to vulnerable people. In particular:

- Sections 113A–F of the Police Act 1997 place Chief Constables under a duty to provide criminal record certificates and/or enhanced criminal record certificates in particular situations. The latter certificates contain information which might be relevant to the question of a person's suitability for certain specified positions, and which need not relate to an actual conviction or caution.
- Section 1 of the Protection of Children Act 1999 requires the government to keep a list of individuals who are considered unsuitable to work with children (the POCA list).
- A similar provision at section 81 of the Care Standards Act 2000 requires the government to keep a list of individuals who are considered unsuitable to work with vulnerable adults (the POVA list).
- List 99, a register of individuals barred from working with children in schools, social work, and voluntary settings, is maintained under section 142 of the Education Act 2002.

(1) Enhanced criminal record certificates

The Article 8 implications of enhanced criminal record certificates (ECRCs) **8.128**
were considered in *R (on the application of X) v Chief Constable of the West
Midlands Police*.[84] The case concerned a social worker of good character who,
following a police interview during which he had made no admissions, was
charged in relation to two incidents of indecent exposure. No evidence was
offered at trial as the complainant failed to make a positive identification.
Information relating to the alleged incidents was included in the 'other relevant
information section' of the claimant's ECRC. On the claimant's application for
judicial review, both parties agreed that Article 8 applied to the information
disclosed on the ECRC. Wall J concluded that the disclosure was unlawful
because the decision-makers had failed to undertake the appropriate balancing
exercise required by Article 8(2). Before disclosing the information, the Chief
Constable should have formed the opinion that it was relevant because, viewed
objectively, it was as a whole reliable, and should also have identified and explained
his reasons for deciding to disclose. Further, in a case where the information did
not relate to an actual conviction, a fair procedure would give the individual
a chance to make representations on his own behalf prior to disclosure, and no
such opportunity had been given to X.

The Court of Appeal took a different view. The Court proceeded on the agreed **8.129**
basis that Article 8(1) was engaged, although no finding to that effect was made.
Lord Woolf CJ held that the Police Act 1997 required the Chief Constable to disclose the information unless there was a good reason not to do so. The statute was
enacted in order to serve a pressing social need, and so complied with Article 8(2).
Therefore, as long as the Chief Constable was entitled to form the opinion that
the information disclosed might be relevant, that information should be included
in the certificate; although Lord Woolf did accept that there might be situations
where it would be disproportionate to include the information in the certificate
(eg where it was trifling, or where the evidence made it very unlikely that the
information was correct). The court should not form its own opinion as to
the relevance of the disclosed information. Further, there was no requirement on
the Chief Constable to give X the opportunity to make representations on his
own behalf. X had been given the opportunity to give his account in the police
interview, and could also have used the procedure under section 117 of the Police
Act 1997 to correct the certificate, which he had not done.

---

[84] [2005] 1 All ER 610, [2004] EWCA Civ 1068, [2005] 1 WLR 65.

8.130   Clearly, this decision gives an extremely wide discretion to the Chief Constable in any particular case to determine the type of information that may be disclosed to a prospective employer, even where such information is likely to have a devastating effect on the individual's career. Further, the procedural 'safeguards' referred to by the Court of Appeal are likely to be of little value in a case such as X's, where the information will have been revealed to the subject's prospective employer before he has had a chance to comment on it. The decision of the ECtHR in *Turek v Slovakia* (discussed at 8.47–8.48 above), as considered in *R (on the application of Wright and others) v Secretary of State for Health and another*,[85] suggests that the procedure approved by the Court of Appeal may be insufficient to protect the subject's Article 8 rights.

8.131   Procedural safeguards are all the more important given the extremely wide ambit of the information that can be included in the ECRC as illustrated in *X* and further in the recent case of *R (on the application of L) v Metropolitan Police Commissioner; R (on the application of G) v Chief Constable of Staffordshire Police*.[86] There Munby J held that disclosure of information (in L's case) relating to neglect of L's son and his inclusion on the Child Protection Register, and (in G's case) showing that she had been charged with manslaughter through negligence of a child at her school and acquitted on the direction of the judge, engaged Article 8. However, he held that the disclosures were made in accordance with Article 8(2), and in particular that the 'other information' to be included in the ECRC was not limited to criminal conduct, but could include any relevant information, such as that showing incompetence, fecklessness, or negligence.

(2) The POCA and POVA lists

8.132   As has already been discussed at 8.130 above, in *R (on the application of Wright and others) v Secretary of State for Health and another*, Stanley Burnton J held that even provisional listing on the POVA list will engage Article 8. He went on to hold that there was a breach of Article 8 (and also Article 6) in the cases before him because the procedures surrounding provisional listing were unfair. There was no right of appeal to an independent, impartial tribunal (ie the Care Standards Tribunal) until nine months had passed since the provisional listing, and the other independent remedy, judicial review, would not permit determination of the vital question of whether or not the individual had committed the misconduct.

---

[85] [2006] EWHC 2886 (Admin), [2006] All ER (D) 216 Nov, [2005] 1 All ER 825.
[86] [2006] EWHC 482 (Admin), [2006] All ER (D) 262 (Mar).

(3) The Safeguarding of Vulnerable Groups Act 2006

Following widespread publicity about the employment in schools of certain **8.133** individuals who had been convicted of sexual offences, a Bill designed to consolidate the information contained in the various lists discussed above was passed through Parliament and received Royal Assent on 8 November 2006. The Safeguarding Vulnerable Groups Act 2006[87] is due to come into force in late 2007.

The Safeguarding of Vulnerable Groups Act is extremely wide-ranging. It pro- **8.134** vides for the establishment and maintenance of 'barred lists' in respect of children and adults by a new body corporate to be known as the Independent Barring Board (IBB). Individuals placed on the lists will be prevented from engaging in an extremely wide range of 'regulated activities' as defined in Schedule 4 to the Act. The Act also provides that it will be an offence to:

- engage in regulated activity whilst barred; or
- to do so when not subject to the Act's monitoring framework; or
- to use a barred person for regulated activity; or
- to use a person not subject to monitoring for regulated activity; or
- (in specified circumstances) to fail to check whether a person is on the barred list, or is subject to monitoring.

Whilst detailed consideration of these provisions is beyond the scope of this **8.135** work, disquiet has already been expressed about the lack of exemptions for, and resulting criminalisation of, individuals who are unaware of the full extent of the extremely wide range of activities covered by the Act and thus do not know that they are engaging in 'regulated activity'.[88]

Of most concern from an Article 8 perspective are the provisions providing for **8.136** automatic inclusion of individuals on the lists in circumstances to be specified by the Secretary of State (Sch 3, paras 1 and 7). These circumstances have yet to be defined. Whilst individuals included on the lists under other paragraphs of Schedule 3 will have the right to appeal either:

(a) against a refusal to remove them from the list following representations (paras 2 and 8, which also cover circumstances to be specified by the Secretary of State); or
(b) against their initial inclusion on the list at all (paras 3–5 and 9–11, which concern individuals who have engaged in specific types of behaviour, or who are thought to pose a risk of harm),

---

[87] Available at <http://www.opsi.gov.uk/ACTS/en2006/2006en47.htm>.
[88] See Liberty's briefing for the Second Reading of the Safeguarding Vulnerable Groups Bill in the House of Commons, June 2006, paras 17–21.

individuals automatically included under paragraphs 1 and 7 have only the right to request a review of the decision after a minimum period of time (also yet to be specified), which will be considered only in certain very narrow circumstances.[89]

8.137 The ECtHR decision in *Turek v Slovakia*, together with the recent decision of the High Court in *R (on the application of Wright and others) v Secretary of State for Health and another*, suggest that these procedural safeguards may well be insufficient to comply with Article 8 in view of the extremely wide range of activities covered by the Act.

J. Privacy of correspondence

8.138 An employer who opens a letter addressed to one of his employees (especially if it is marked 'private and confidential') may well be acting in breach of Article 8 ECHR, which includes the right to respect for correspondence. While there is no personal obligation on an employer who is not a public authority, statutory provisions are now in force to protect this kind of activity, and these will be read in the light of Article 8 (see also Postal Services Act 2000, s 84 which creates an offence in relation to unlawful opening of mail).

8.139 In *Petra v Romania*,[90] the Court found there had been a violation of Article 8 where a prisoner complained that his letters had been intercepted by prison authorities in circumstances where such monitoring was automatic, independent of any decision by a judicial authority and unappealable.

See also Copland discussed at 8.46.

K. Medical records

8.140 Employers collect medical information in a variety of ways, through sick notes delivered for sick pay, through doctors' reports, and even from family and friends explaining absences from work. Such information will not necessarily be limited to information about the worker but may include information about the worker's immediate or wider family.

8.141 The collection of medical data and the maintenance of medical records fall within the sphere of private life (*Chave neé Jullien v France*[91]).

---

[89] See s 4 and para 18 of Sch 13 to the Act and further Liberty's briefing, at para 7.
[90] (2001) 33 EHRR 5.
[91] Application 14461/88, 9 July 1991, 71 DR 141.

There may be an invasive intrusion into the private life of the employee when **8.142** the employer collects highly sensitive health-related information about its employees. The use of such information must be controlled. The three Acts which must be borne in mind are the Access to Personal Files Act 1987, the Access to Medical Records Act 1988, and the Access to Health Records Act 1990. Where the state fails to protect employees from the abuse by employers of the private or family life of workers, there will prima facie be a breach of Article 8 ECHR which will need to be justified. Thus the use of medical data for purposes other than those to which the employee has agreed may give rise to a breach of Article 8.

(1) Medical records and interferences with Article 8

Medical data must not be used in a way which undermines confidentiality, unless **8.143** it is in a situation which conforms strictly to Article 8(2).

In *MS v Sweden*,[92] the applicant had injured her back at work and made a claim **8.144** for compensation from the state under the Industrial Injury Insurance Act 1976. The clinic where she was treated disclosed her medical records in full to the Social Insurance Office at its request, but without her permission. The ECtHR held that there was a breach of Article 8 ECHR, but that it was justified under Article 8(2) because the disclosure was necessary for the determination of the applicant's claim to compensation, and the interference was in accordance with law and in pursuit of a legitimate aim of protecting the economic well-being of the country by ensuring that public funds were allocated only to deserving claimants. However, there was a continuing duty to protect the confidentiality of the informant. The Court ruled:[93]

> The domestic law must afford appropriate safeguards to prevent any such communication or disclosure of personal health data as maybe inconsistent with the guarantees in Article 8.

The Court has emphasised the need for 'limitations' and 'effective and adequate **8.145** safeguards against abuse' (*Z v Finland*[94]). In *A Health Authority v X and Others*,[95] it was held by the Family Division of the High Court that disclosure of medical records to a public body was an interference with a patient's rights under Article 8, which could be justified only where there were effective and adequate safeguards against abuse. The respondent general practitioners had done everything in their power to obtain the appropriate consents from the patients, only two of whom did not consent. Dr X did not dispute that his ultimate obligation was to comply

---

[92] 27 August 1997, RJD, 1997-IV, 1437 (1997) 3 BHRC 248.
[93] At (para 41).
[94] (1998) 25 EHRR 371, para 103.
[95] (2001) 2 FLR 673 affirmed by CA [2002] 1 FLR 1045.

with any court order for disclosure, but he asserted that, prior to any order being made, he had to comply with the duty of confidentiality owed to his patients.

8.146 It was held that patient records were confidential as between Dr X and the patients, and were equally confidential as between the patients and the health authority. That confidentiality was underscored by the guarantee of respect for the patients' private and family life in Article 8 ECHR.

8.147 The court found that the disclosure was necessary within the meaning of Article 8(2): there was a compelling public interest requiring the disclosure of some of the documents as the matters that the health authority wished to investigate were of considerable gravity. The disclosure could be justified by effective and adequate safeguards against abuse, including:

(a) the maintenance of the confidentiality of the documents themselves;
(b) the minimum public disclosure of any information derived from the documents; and
(c) the protection of the patient's anonymity.

8.148 Lastly, Munby J commented that the requirement to justify an interference with a patient's rights under Article 8 of the Convention arose not only when that patient's records passed from his doctor to a public authority, but also every time such records transferred from one public authority to another. It was the duty of every public body, including the court, to ensure that that confidentiality was preserved and that there were effective and adequate safeguards against abuse before authorising the transfer of medical records from a doctor to a public body, or from one public body to another. The Court of Appeal upheld his approach on 21 December 2001.[96]

8.149 The importance of the use of proper procedural safeguards when considering the disclosure of medical records has again been emphasised in the recent case of *R (on the application of TB) v Stafford Combined Court*.[97] In that case, the Crown Court summonsed TB, a 14-year-old girl, to appear before it to obtain her view on the disclosure of her psychiatric records, which were said to be relevant to a criminal case in which she was the complainant. She was given less than a day's notice and had no opportunity to obtain representation. On review, the court held that Article 8 was clearly engaged, and that Article 8(2) required that TB be given proper notice of the summons, and a real opportunity to make representations before the order was made.

---

[96] See [2002] 1 FLR 1045.
[97] [2006] EWHC 1645 (Admin), [2007] 1 All ER 102, [2006] 2 Cr App R 34.

(2) Medical records and data protection issues

There is a separate section of the Employment Practices Data Protection Code **8.150** (Part 4), which deals with information about workers' health. Such information is classified as sensitive personal data, and at least one of the additional conditions set out in Schedule 3 to the DPA 1998 must therefore be fulfilled before it can be processed. The Code sets out useful recommendations as to when and how information about workers' health may be collected and retained, and contains particular guidance as to the results of medical examination and testing, genetic testing, and drug/alcohol testing (see 8.152 below).

(3) Compulsory medical testing

Employers are increasingly adopting policies of random drug testing and medical **8.151** checks on employees; and in many personal injury cases, claimants must undergo medical examination or testing by the defendants' experts. A recent study into drug and alcohol testing by employers[98] found that of 200 companies polled in 2003, 4 per cent said that they currently conducted drug tests, and a further 9 per cent were likely to introduce tests in the next year.

Such tests inevitably raise issues under Article 8, as they clearly affect the subject's **8.152** physical integrity. Part 4 of the Employment Practices Data Protection Code recognises the intrusive nature of drug/alcohol testing and contains a section devoted to providing guidance on the circumstances in which testing may be appropriate. Essentially, it states that testing is only likely to be justified where it is for health and safety reasons. The Code is clear that very few employers will be justified in testing merely to detect illegal use, save where such use would not only breach the employee's contract/the employer's disciplinary code but also cause serious damage to the employer's business. There should be a clear policy on drug/alcohol testing, and samples should be obtained with the worker's knowledge. Post-incident testing is more likely to be justified than random testing, and, where possible, the least intrusive method of detecting drug/alcohol abuse should be utilised.

It is clear, however, that individuals required to undergo such testing will not **8.153** necessarily be able to rely on Article 8. In *X v Netherlands*,[99] the Court held that requiring a motorist who had failed a breathalyser test to submit to a blood test may be a violation of Article 8(1) but could be justified under Article 8(2).

---

[98] See the Independent Inquiry into Drug Testing at Work, reporting in June 2004; see summary conclusions at <http://www.jrf.org.uk/knowledge/findings/foundations/694.asp>.
[99] (1981) 16 DR 184.

See also the decision of the EAT in *O'Flynn v Airlinks*,[100] which concerned drug testing by an employer undertaken before the HRA 1998 came into force, but contains an interesting discussion about the potential arguments had the HRA 1998 applied.

8.154 A still more stringent approach was taken by the Privy Council in *Whitefield v General Medical Council*.[101] Dr Whitefield's fitness to practice was judged by the General Medical Council (GMC) to be seriously impaired by severe depression and harmful use of alcohol. Following various hearings before the GMC, conditions were placed upon Dr Whitefield's continued registration which, amongst other things, required him to abstain completely from the consumption of alcohol, to undergo random blood and urine tests when required, and to attend Alcoholics Anonymous. Dr Whitefield argued before the Privy Council that these conditions interfered with his right to a private life under Article 8. The ban prevented him from drinking even on social occasions, and was disproportionate. Random testing was a compulsory medical intervention which interfered with his right to private life.

8.155 The Privy Council held that a ban on the consumption of alcohol was not in itself an interference with the right to respect for private life under Article 8(1), as Dr Whitefield could still engage in his social life while drinking non-alcoholic drinks. Further, Dr Whitefield's claim for respect for his private life had to be reduced to the extent that, as a doctor, he had brought his private life into contact with public life, or into close connection with other potential interests. His right to a private life had to give way to the wider public interest in ensuring that he did not pose a risk to his patients. The Privy Council further held that, even if the condition did constitute an interference with private life, it was permissible under Article 8(2), as the conditions were lawfully made, pursued a legitimate aim (the protection of health and the rights and freedoms of others) and were necessary and proportionate. Similar reasoning applied to other conditions of which complaint was made.

(4) Workers suffering from AIDS/HIV

8.156 There is a growing body of cases in which workers suffering from HIV/AIDS have experienced adverse consequences at work. Generally, their cases need to be considered under the provisions of the Disability Discrimination Act 1995, since they are now deemed to be disabled even if they have not as yet developed any symptoms (see Sch 1, para 6A). Certainly Article 8 ECHR requires that the

---

[100] EAT, 15 March 2002.
[101] [2003] IRLR 39 (PC).

respect accorded to the private lives of such workers will need particular care,[102] see also *H v N*.[103]

8.157 The need for such care is reflected in the concerns of the Information Commissioner in Part 4 of the Employment Practices Data Protection Code (see 8.152 above).

L. Dress codes at work

8.158 Mostly, cases involving dress codes at work have been concerned with discrimination issues (*Smith v Safeway plc*[104]), since this was the only possible route to a remedy in the municipal courts. However, these cases may also raise issues which have to be considered under Article 8, and obviously they may also concern rights to freedom of expression and religion and belief (see also Chapters 9 and 10).

8.159 Cases such as *Schmidt v Austicks Bookshops Ltd*,[105] where the applicant was fairly dismissed for wearing trousers in contravention of a workplace rule that banned such clothing for women employees who came into contact with the public, and *Smith v Safeway plc* (above), where the Court of Appeal upheld the dismissal of a male employee who refused to cut long hair which offended the employer's appearance code, will fall to be reconsidered in the light of the employees' rights under Article 8.[106]

8.160 In *Stevens v UK*,[107] where a mother complained that her children had to wear school uniform, the Commission held that any constraint imposed by rules as to dress during school hours on school premises cannot be said to be so serious as to constitute an interference with the right to respect for private and family life contrary to Article 8 ECHR. The applicant's comparison of school uniform with prison uniform[108] was rejected. However, where the complaint is that school uniforms unreasonably discriminate between the sexes, an Article 8 claim may have more prospect of success.

---

[102] See B Watt, 'The Legal Protection of Health Care Workers and the Human Rights Jurisprudence of the European Court of Justice' [1998] EHRLR 301.

[103] [2002] EWCA 195.

[104] [1996] ICR 868.

[105] [1978] ICR 85.

[106] Although for a case where the Court found that the requirement to wear a school uniform on the premises was not an interference with family life, see *Stevens v UK* Application 11674/85, (1986) 46 DR 245, (1986) 83 LSG 1904.

[107] (1986) 46 DR 245.

[108] In *McFeeley v UK* Application 8317/78, (1980) 20 DR 44 and *X v UK* Application 8231/78, (1982) 28 DR 5, it was held that the requirement for prisoners to wear prison clothing was an interference with their rights under Art 8(1).

8.161 In 1999, the Equal Opportunities Commission backed the case of the schoolgirl, Jo Hale, who was not allowed to wear trousers as part of her school uniform. Following a settlement, the school agreed to change its uniform policy, allowing girls to wear trousers and (if they so wished) boys to wear skirts. While this case was brought under the Sex Discrimination Act 1975, after October 2000 a human rights argument based on Article 14 ECHR read along with Article 8 might have assisted the complainant. (But see *Cootes v John Lewis*.[109])

(1) The reason for the dress code

8.162 A tribunal considering whether a dismissal for failure to comply with such a code is reasonable, will certainly need to take into account factors such as the employer's reasons for the clothing or appearance requirement, whether the requirement forms part of the employment contract, the employee's reasons for objecting to the requirement, and the way in which the employer sets about enforcing the requirement (see, eg, *Boychuk v HJ Symons Holdings Ltd*[110]).

M. Sexual orientation

8.163 Article 8 ECHR may also raise questions about the right to an open sexual orientation in the workplace, following the decision of the ECtHR in the 'gays in the military' case of *Lustig-Prean and Beckett v United Kingdom*;[111] and *Smith & Grady v United Kingdom*.[112]

8.164 If a person were dismissed on the grounds that he or she displayed a particular sexual orientation at work, it would be arguable that the employment tribunal should hold that it was not reasonable to dismiss since it interfered with the employee's right to respect for his or her private life. However, it would be necessary to consider carefully the facts of the case in question. Certainly the tribunal could not ignore its obligation as a public authority to respect the applicant's private life.

8.165 Since the publication of the last edition of this work, the Employment Equality (Sexual Orientation) Regulations 2003 have been brought into force. The 2003 Regulations, which are discussed more fully in Chapter 14, make it illegal for employers to discriminate against workers on grounds of sexual orientation, whether directly or indirectly, or by means of victimisation or harassment. As such,

---

[109] EAT, 27 February 2001 (2001 WL 322168).
[110] [1977] IRLR 385.
[111] (2000) 29 EHRR 548, [1999] IRLR 734.
[112] (2000) 29 EHRR 493.

the Regulations will normally provide an easier means for protection for workers discriminated against on grounds of their sexual orientation than an Article 8 claim. They will need to be construed consistently with Article 8 rights but it is unlikely that there will be a major conflict between Article 8 obligations and the obligation to construe these Regulations consistently with Community law.

N. Family-friendly policies in the workplace

There are increasing numbers of cases before the employment tribunal, which **8.166** concern the difficulties in balancing home life and the workplace. Caring is a major issue and it is mostly but not exclusively a burden borne by women. In *London Underground v Edwards*,[113] judicial notice was taken of the fact that the broad national ratio of single parents with child care responsibilities was 10:1 as between men and women. Gender issues concerned with family-friendly policies will most easily be analysed under discrimination law and it will only be if there is some conflict with Article 8 rights or some question as to the substance of the right that Article 8 is likely to be relevant. Only limited comment on these issues is made below at 8.172–8.175.

However, it should not be assumed that there is no relevance. In *Petrovic v* **8.167** *Austria*,[114] legislation relating to parental leave allowances was deemed to fall within the scope of Article 8, although in this case the lack of a duty on the state to provide this kind of financial help meant that there was no breach.

The extent to which discrimination on grounds of family responsibilities, arising **8.168** out of, for example, inability to work certain shifts or days owing to parental or care duties at home, will be deemed contrary to Article 8 ECHR and the right to a family life is likely to depend on the horizontal effect of Convention rights as between private individuals.

The role of the tribunal will be engaged only if some other ground for its jurisdic- **8.169** tion is raised, thus the possibility of any remedy may depend on whether a dismissal has occurred or not. This is because the HRA 1998 does not provide directly for the horizontal effect of Convention rights but only requires public authorities to comply with the rights.

So, in a case where an employer who was not a 'public authority' dismissed **8.170** a worker for her refusal to work full-time after returning from maternity leave, the tribunal could not create a new cause of action for breach of Article 8 ECHR.

---

[113] [1998] IRLR 364.
[114] (1998) 5 BHRC 232.

It would have to interpret her contract of employment as containing an implied term that the employer would not invoke the contractual power to force her as a parent to work hours which unnecessarily interfered with her right to respect for family life. The tribunal must interpret and apply the law of contract in a way which is compatible with Article 8. In its application of the reasonableness test within any unfair dismissal claim, the tribunal would have to give consideration to Article 8. If the claim was one of indirect discrimination, Article 8 would limit any possible justification.

(1) Domestic protection against discrimination on grounds of family responsibilities

8.171 Since the publication of the last edition of this work, a raft of additional legislation has been introduced to provide further protection for workers with childcare responsibilities. Detailed consideration of this legislation is beyond the scope of this book, but a brief summary of the protection available is set out below. Obviously, this legislation is in addition to the pre-existing law prohibiting indirect discrimination. That legislation has been amended in recent years to rid the definition of some of its more restrictive concepts, as discussed in more detail in Chapter 13. However, this remains a gender-based right which does not directly address the fact that it is parental responsibilities which differentiate between those who can and cannot comply with the relevant 'provision, criterion or practice'.

(2) Flexible working

8.172 In the first edition of this book, reference was made to the 'flexible working' rights introduced from April 2003 at sections 80F–80I of the ERA 1996, and supplemented by the Flexible Working (Eligibility, Complaints and Remedies) Regulations 2002,[115] and the Flexible Working (Procedural Requirements) Regulations 2002.[116]

8.173 Section 80F gives employees with responsibility for young children the right to make an application to vary the terms and conditions of their contracts insofar as they relate to hours or times of work, and place of work. However, flexibility is not guaranteed; the employer may refuse the application for a fairly wide range of reasons (set out at s 80G), and the employee is only entitled to complain to a tribunal if the employer has failed to comply with the procedural requirements for dealing with an application, or if the decision to reject the application was based on incorrect facts.

---

[115] SI 2002/3236.
[116] SI 2002/3207.

The latter route has been broadly interpreted in *Commotion Ltd v Rutty*,[117] where **8.174** the EAT held that, in considering whether the employer has relied on incorrect facts, the tribunal must be entitled to look at the ground(s) for refusal on which the employer relies and see whether it is/they are factually correct. This will involve consideration of the circumstances surrounding the situation, and in particular a consideration of the likely effect of granting the application; for instance, would it have caused disruption; could the time have been made up; how would staff feel? *Rutty* suggests that the courts are likely to apply a wider construction of section 80H(1) than might be apparent from the text of the statute. This may mitigate against the relative weakness of the statutory provisions, which gave rise to much criticism from commentators when the legislation was first passed.

From 1 April 2007 the new Work and Families Act 2006 has widened the scope **8.175** of the existing law on flexible working to enable more people with caring responsibilities to request to work flexibly: see section 12.

(3) Part-time workers (Prevention of Less Favourable Treatment) Regulations 2000[118]

These Regulations were introduced to prevent discrimination against part-time **8.176** workers. However, they operate within a narrow ambit, with fairly restrictive conditions for eligibility. In particular, it is necessary for the employee to find an actual (rather than hypothetical) comparator who is employed by the same employer under the same type of contract and is engaged on 'the same or broadly similar work'.

The Regulations were initially restrictively interpreted by tribunals, which virtu- **8.177** ally extinguished their usefulness to workers. However, the House of Lords has reached a broader interpretation in the recent case of *Matthews and others v Kent and Medway Towns Fire Authority and others*.[119]

On the question of 'same type of contract', the House of Lords held that if **8.178** both part-time and full-time groups fall within the same category under regulation 2(3)—in this case employees employed under a contract that is not a contract of apprenticeship—the contracts are of the same type, regardless of differences in individual terms and conditions. Perhaps, more importantly, the House of Lords held that the test for 'the same or broadly similar work' requires the tribunal to look at the work done by both groups as a whole.

---

[117] [2006] IRLR 171.
[118] SI 2000/1551.
[119] [2006] UKHL 8, [2006] ICR 365.

Tribunals should concentrate particularly on the degree to which work done by the two groups is 'exactly the same', and on the centrality of that work to the job as a whole. If both groups spend a lot of time carrying out the core activity of the enterprise, their work is likely to be broadly similar regardless of any additional tasks full-timers may perform. Hopefully this decision will return some bite to the Regulations, but there remain a number of hurdles for claimants (including the requirement for an actual comparator) which limit the usefulness of the legislation.

(4) International prohibitions against discrimination on grounds of family responsibility

8.179 A variety of international instruments already exist which seek to provide for a right not to suffer discrimination: ILO Conventions No 111 on discrimination in employment and occupation, and No 156 on equal opportunities and treatment for men and women workers with family responsibilities. ILO Convention No 156 is the most relevant, but the UK has not yet ratified it. Article 3(1) of this Convention provides:

> With a view to creating effective equality of opportunity and treatment for men and women workers, each Member shall make it an aim of national policy to enable persons with family responsibilities who are engaged or wish to engage in employment to exercise their right to do so without being subject to discrimination and, to the extent possible, without conflict between their employment and family responsibilities . . .

(5) Associated new maternity and parental provisions

8.180 Domestic maternity rights were extended in 2000 and 2001, largely due to standards set by Community law. The rights of pregnant women at work, comprising maternity leave, time off for antenatal care, and protection against dismissal and detriment when pregnant, are substantially altered and enlarged by the Employment Relations Act 1999 and attendant Regulations which came into force on 15 December 1999. These rights were extended yet further by the Work and Families Act 2006 from 1 April 2007. It is hoped that these new rights will assist in rectifying the current situation whereby UK maternity pay is still the lowest in Western Europe.[120]

8.181 Amongst other important innovations, these provisions introduced the right to paid paternity leave for the first time in the UK (ERA 1996, sections 80A–80E). The right is for up to two weeks' leave paid at a rate of £112.75 per week, as

---

[120] Report published by Mercer HR Consulting, 10 May 2006.

of 2 April 2007. The 2006 Act also gives employed fathers a new right to up to six months Additional Paternity Leave some of which can be paid at the flat rate, if the mother returns to work before taking her full entitlement to maternity pay.

There have also been significant increases in the amount of maternity pay available to mothers. Prior to April 2007 all mothers who have worked continuously for at least 26 weeks ending with the fifteenth week before the expected week of childbirth were entitled to 90 per cent of normal weekly earnings for the first six weeks of maternity leave, and a flat weekly rate for the remainder of the 26-week period of ordinary maternity leave. The Work and Families Act 2006 abolishes the length of service threshold for ordinary maternity pay and extends the time (for female employees with babies due on or after 1 April 2007) over which statutory maternity pay will be payable to nine months, or 39 weeks. (In its Response to Consultation, the government stated that the maternity pay period would eventually be increased to 12 months, but has provided no time scale for this development.) There is now no length of service requirement for additional maternity leave (which is unpaid)—so anyone entitled to ordinary maternity leave is entitled to additional maternity leave, thus permitting them to take up to one year off work. It should be remembered that these provisions also apply to adoptive parents.

8.182

Parental leave is available to working parents (adoptive and natural) of both sexes who have one year's continuous employment with their employer, in respect of children who are under five years of age, or, in the case of adopted children, within five years of the date on which the placement began. The entitlement is to 13 weeks' unpaid leave for each child (see the Council Directive 96/34/EC on the framework agreement on parental leave[121] and the Maternity and Parental Leave etc Regulations 1999[122]).

8.183

These provisions concern the right to a private life in the context of relations with the newborn and with young children.

8.184

When the tribunal is construing the rights in relation to time off for domestic incidents and for maternity and parental leave granted under the Employment Relations Act 1999 (in particular ss 7 and 8), it will need to keep Article 8 ECHR in mind in order to comply with its duty under section 3 of the HRA 1998.

8.185

---

[121] Council Directive (EC) 96/34 on the framework agreement on parental leave concluded by UNICE, CEEP and the ETUC [1996] OJ L145.
[122] SI 1999/3312.

O. Health and Safety and Article 8

(1) Environmental pollution

8.186   Environmental issues can arise under Article 8 ECHR.[123] In *Lopez Ostra v Spain*,[124] the Court held that there was a breach of Article 8 as a result of a failure by the state to protect the applicant from environmental pollution. Accordingly, failures in the system of protection of health and safety at work could perhaps give rise to breaches of Article 8. In particular, there may be a positive obligation in relation to disclosure (*McGinley and Egan v UK*[125]).

(2) Monitoring and health and safety

8.187   There is also a relationship between health and safety and monitoring. Monitoring can take place ostensibly because the employer wishes to protect the employees' health and safety. However, the employer may then use that information not to protect the employees but to penalise them for their output. Community law has given some thought to this. Thus, the Health and Safety (Display Screen Equipment) Regulations 1992,[126] implementing Council Directive 90/270,[127] limit the abuse of such information by requiring the employer to disclose monitoring of computer work:[128]

> In designing, selecting, commissioning and modifying software, and in designing tasks using display screen equipment, the employer shall take into account the following principles: . . . (b) . . . no quantitative or qualitative checking facility may be used without the knowledge of the operators or users; (c) systems must provide feedback to operators or users on the performance of those systems . . .

(3) Environmental protection and positive obligations of disclosure

8.188   Disclosure of information by the government may also be in issue here. In *Guerra v Italy*,[129] the applicants lived close to a chemical factory that produced hazardous fumes. They contended that the failure to provide them with relevant information was an infringement of their right to respect for family life, and the Court unanimously found that Article 8 ECHR had been violated.

---

[123] They may also give rise to issues in relation to Art 10 ECHR on the freedom of expression; see Chapter 10.

[124] (1995) 20 EHRR 277.

[125] (1998) 27 EHRR 1, at para 101.

[126] SI 1992/2792.

[127] Council Directive (EEC) 90/270 on the minimum safety and health requirements for work with display screen equipment [1990] OJ L156.

[128] Reg 3 and Schedule, para 4.

[129] (1998) 26 EHRR 357.

(4) Health issues and Article 2

The disclosure of health risks may also give rise to issues under Article 2 ECHR   **8.189**
(the right to life). In *LCB v UK*,[130] the ECtHR accepted that employees and
their families who were exposed to high radiation levels would have been entitled
to be informed of this, had the state appreciated the health risk at the time.

There have been a few unsuccessful attempts in the ECtHR to enlarge the protec-   **8.190**
tion given to employees who work in dangerous workplaces: see, for instance,
Barrett v UK.[131] The applicant was the widow of a naval seaman who died when
he choked to death on his own vomit when intoxicated while at work. She complained that the naval base had an inadequate system of control of consumption
of alcohol, and argued that this, along with the inadequate care and attention
her husband had received after his collapse, amounted to a breach of Article 2
ECHR. The Commission accepted that issues under Article 2 were raised where
a state provided drinking facilities where there was a risk of excessive consumption, where there were no measures designed to discourage excessive drinking,
and where there was substandard care and treatment of an excessive drinker.
On the facts, though, there was held to be no evidence of the state condoning the
above factors. Neither were there signs which should have alerted the state to
the facts set out above. It is possible that a case on more serious facts could arise.

P. Employees' activities outside work

Activities undertaken by employees outside of the work environment are some-   **8.191**
times relied upon by employers as grounds for dismissal or other disciplinary
action. In such cases, it may be open to the employee to argue that the action
amounted to a breach of his/her Article 8 rights. As set out at 8.31–8.42 above,
the claimants in *X v Y* and *Pay v Lancashire Probation Service* relied upon Article 8
arguments in support of their unfair dismissal claims. Neither was successful.

In *X v Y*, the Court of Appeal held that Article 8(1) was not engaged at all.   **8.192**
The claimant was dismissed because he had failed to disclose a caution for committing a sex offence with another man in a transport cafe lavatory to which the
public had, and were permitted to have, access. This was not conduct falling
within the scope of Article 8 because it happened in a place to which the public
had access; it was a criminal offence, which is normally a matter of legitimate
concern to the public, and it led to a caution for the offence, which was relevant

---

[130]   (1999) 27 EHRR 212.
[131]   (1997) 23 EHRR CD 185.

to X's employment, and should have been disclosed to his employer as a matter of legitimate concern to it.

8.193 The EAT reached a similar conclusion in Mr Pay's case. Whilst it accepted that private life includes sexual activities, the Tribunal agreed with the reasoning of the employment tribunal below: that Mr Pay's activities had been publicised on the website of a company of which he was a director, and that he was present in bars and clubs to which the public was admitted promoting the interests of that company in bondage, domination, and sadomasochism. Therefore, Article 8 was not engaged.

8.194 This does not mean that Article 8 will never be engaged in cases involving an employee's social activities. However, it will be important for practitioners to consider whether the activity in question is truly private (or truly relates to the claimant's family life) before developing an argument along these lines.

Q. Rights of others under Article 8

8.195 In some employment contexts the private lives of persons who are neither employees nor employers can become an issue. Thus, in a disciplinary case, a health authority might be concerned to ensure that it does not breach Article 8 ECHR when seeking to justify a decision to terminate a health worker's employment on grounds of capability or conduct. Similar problems could arise in other contexts, such as social work. However, if the court ordered the discovery of the relevant documents after consideration of Article 8 and after taking the necessary steps to redact the document to protect the patient's privacy, there would be no breach of Article 8 (see, eg, the approach in *Nassé v Science Research Council*[132]). Since the privacy concerned is the patient's, the tribunal should be prepared to hear submissions on her or his behalf as to what steps are necessary (see also 8.138–8.142).

R. Is there a need for a workplace privacy code?

8.196 In Canada an employee privacy code has been adopted by the Federal Government which might serve as a useful model for the UK. The aim of the Code is to set out clearly what the employee might expect as protection by the employer of information about his or her private life. The regulations under the RIPA 2000 and the DPA 1998 show that in practice the bones of an integrated employee privacy code are being worked out in the UK. There would be real advantage in the publication of a consolidated privacy code for employees and employers.

---

132 [1979] ICR 921.

S. Frequently asked questions

What rights are protected by Article 8?   **8.197**

The right to respect for private and family life, home, and correspondence.

Does Article 8 give individuals absolute protection for those rights?

No. Article 8 provides qualified protection only. The exercise of Article 8 rights may be limited by the state where any limitation is in accordance with the law and necessary in a democratic society in the interests of national security, public safety, the economic well-being of the country, the prevention of crime and disorder, the protection of health or morals, or the protection of the rights and freedoms and others.

Does Article 8 apply to protect individuals whilst at work?

The protection granted by Article 8 has been interpreted widely by the ECtHR. Individuals' home and work lives are often closely intermingled. Many people use work resources for private correspondence on a daily basis. Some things people do at work (eg eating or visiting the lavatory) must be considered 'private' activities. Most employers will store some private information about each and every one of their employees. Employees' continued employment, or ability to work in particular spheres, may be affected by activities they undertake outside work. Issues arising out of these 'private' aspects of working life may well fall within the ambit of Article 8.

What happens when Article 8 rights conflict with rights provided under Article 10?

The right to respect for privacy and family life, home, and correspondence will often conflict with the right to freedom of expression. Where this occurs, neither right will be considered superior. The court must balance the relevant Article 8 and Article 10 rights, focusing on the comparative importance of the specific rights being claimed in each individual case, taking into account the justifications for interfering with or restricting each right, and applying the proportionality test to both. Where the full exercise of the right to freedom of expression will result in a breach of confidence, this will be an important factor for the court to take into account.

What effect does the 'positive obligation' on states to ensure respect for private and family life have on employment tribunals?

As tribunals are public authorities within the meaning of section 6 of the HRA 1998, they are under a duty to ensure that, in exercising their jurisdiction and their discretion in the conduct of proceedings, they are not acting in breach of parties' Article 8 rights.

Does Article 8 require employment tribunals to exclude evidence obtained in breach of Article 8?

Not necessarily. Even if particular evidence has been obtained in breach of Article 8(1), the tribunal has a discretion under the 2004 Procedure Regulations to deal with its procedure so as to avoid formality and to apply the overriding objective (as does the county court under the CPR). If it applies these rules so as to admit the evidence, it will be acting in accordance with the law and may well decide that any breach of Article 8(1) is proportionate (eg because the relevance of the evidence to the issues before it outweighs any interference with privacy or family life). The tribunal may take steps to limit the impact of the evidence on the party concerned, for example, by making a restricted reporting order, holding proceedings in private, or redacting documents.

Does Article 8 give parties to employment proceedings the right to refuse to disclose relevant medical records?

Where medical records are important for the determination of a claimant's claim (for example, in disability discrimination cases), a tribunal is likely to hold that any interference with Article 8 rights is justified, particularly as the claimant will have brought these issues before the tribunal themselves. However, once the records are disclosed, there will be a continuing duty to protect the confidentiality of the claimant so far as is possible.

What course should a tribunal take where the basis for the dismissal of a particular employee amounts to an interference with the employee's Article 8 rights?

Where the employer is a public authority, the dismissal of an employee for a reason which amounts to an unjustifiable interference with his Article 8 rights will be unlawful under section 6 of the HRA 1998, and thus cannot amount to a permitted (lawful) reason for dismissal under section 98 of the ERA 1996. Where the employer is a private authority section 6 HRA will not apply. However, the section 3 duty on the tribunal to interpret national legislation compatibly with the ECHR means that section 98 must be interpreted so as to be compatible with Article 8. If it would be incompatible with Article 8 to hold that dismissal for that particular reason was fair, section 98 must be interpreted accordingly.

Do employees have any means of control over the way in which employers use personal information retained in, for example, personnel files?

Article 8 (used in conjunction with HRA 1998, s 6) may provide a means of preventing public authority employers from disclosing confidential information to outside sources, or of obtaining compensation for any disclosure. However, employers are also subject to important duties under the DPA 1998, which require them to process personal data in accordance with certain data protection principles. Where these duties are breached, individuals may take legal action to prevent the processing of data, or claim compensation. Further guidance is contained in the Employment Practices Data Protection Code, published on the Information Commissioner's website.

Do employers have the right to intercept personal communications to or from employees at work?

Interception of telephone conversations, emails, or use of the Internet may well amount to an interference with an employee's Article 8 rights. If employers fail to abide by the legal limits imposed on such interception, as set out in the RIPA 2000 and the Telecommunications (Lawful Business Practice) (Interception of Communications) Regulations 2000, they will not be able to justify any breach of Article 8(1) under Article 8(2). However, practitioners should bear in mind that, even where evidence which provides grounds for dismissal has been obtained in breach of this legislation, that evidence may be admitted by a tribunal in accordance with the 2004 Procedure Regulations.

The DPA 1998 also covers monitoring of employees' communications whilst at work, and more general monitoring and surveillance. The Information Commissioner's Code suggests that it will be difficult to justify covert surveillance of workers, which may mean that the DPA 1998 provides greater protection in this respect than Article 8.

How does Article 8 affect the provision of information to employers or potential employers in the form of enhanced criminal record certificates?

The courts have held that a very wide range of information may be included on enhanced criminal record certificates, which need not relate to the commission or suspected commission of a crime, but need only be 'relevant' to the question of a person's suitability for certain specified positions. Findings of neglect or possibly even incompetence may be sufficient. Provision of such information to employers will not offend Article 8 as long as the relevant authority is entitled to form the opinion that the information disclosed might be relevant, and there will not necessarily be any obligation on the authority to give the subject of the information the opportunity to make representations about whether or not it should be included in the certificate. Arguably, this lack of procedural safeguards is incompatible with the ECtHR jurisprudence.

What impact will Article 8 have on decisions to include individuals in lists barring them from engaging in certain types of employment?

The High Court has held that provisional inclusion in the Protection of Vulnerable Adults list (which bars individuals from working with vulnerable adults) may engage

215

Article 8(1), and that the failure to provide an immediate right of appeal to an independent, impartial, fact-finding tribunal means that any interference cannot be justified under Article 8(2). This decision may mean that the listing provisions contained in the new Safeguarding of Vulnerable Groups Act 2006 (not yet in force) are not Article 8 compliant.

Will compulsory drug or alcohol testing of employees breach Article 8?

Whilst such testing may interfere with an employee's Article 8(1) rights, the domestic and European jurisprudence suggests that it will be considered justifiable under Article 8(2) where it is necessary to protect the health, rights, and freedoms of others.

Can Article 8 be used to challenge dress codes at work?

Article 8 challenges to the requirement that individuals wear school uniform have not thus far found much success. However, a challenge to differential dress rules for males and females may be possible using Articles 8 and 14.

Does Article 8 protect employees from disciplinary action or dismissal on the basis of activities undertaken outside work?

This will depend on the nature of the relevant activity. Indications from the courts suggest that the activity must be truly private, in a narrow sense, if it is to give rise to Article 8 protection. For example, dismissals on the basis of:

- *failure to disclose a caution for a sex offence with another man committed in a transport cafe lavatory to which the public had access; and*
- *sexual activities publicised on a website and forming part of shows in clubs and bars,*

were held not to engage Article 8 at all, as the activities in question were not truly private.

9

ARTICLE 9: FREEDOM OF THOUGHT, CONSCIENCE AND RELIGION

Article 9
Freedom of thought, conscience and religion

1. Everyone has the right to freedom of thought, conscience and religion; this right includes freedom to change his religion or belief and freedom, either alone or in community with others and in public or private, to manifest his religion or belief, in worship, teaching, practice and observance.
2. Freedom to manifest one's religion or beliefs shall be subject only to such limitations as are prescribed by law and are necessary in a democratic society in the interests of public safety, for the protection of public order, health or morals, or for the protection of the rights and freedoms of others.

A. Introduction

9.01   It has been said that the rights to freedom of thought, conscience, and religion are the foundations of Western human rights ideology.[1] The case law on Article 9 ECHR is closely linked with that under Article 10[2] which is equally concerned with the maintenance of a broad liberal democracy. It is important to also keep in mind its historical context. The right to hold and maintain religious and other opinions and beliefs has only been established across Europe after much religious conflict and the oppression of religious minorities.[3] The right comprises both an absolute right and a qualified right. It may be an element of equal treatment rights as well. It is also a right that can come into conflict with other rights.

---

[1] See D Gomien, D Harris, and L Zwaak, *Law and Practice of the European Convention on Human Rights and the European Social Charter* (Strasbourg: Council of Europe Publishing, 1996) 263.

[2] Article 9 is sometimes described as a specific example (or *lex specialis*) of Article 10, as to which see Chapter 10.

[3] For a fuller discussion of the historical and modern context of this Article, see MD Evans, *Religious Liberty and International Law in Europe* (Cambridge: Cambridge University Press, 1997).

Within the UK Article 9 rights are being taken increasingly seriously. Recently **9.02**
Lord Nicholls has commented:[4]

> Religious and other beliefs and convictions are part of the humanity of every individual. They are an integral part of his personality and individuality. In a civilised society individuals respect each others beliefs. This enables them to live in harmony. This is one of the hallmarks of a civilised society.

As people become more enthusiastic about identifying themselves with their reli- **9.03**
gious faith and adopting signs to reflect this, the scope and content of Article 9
has become increasingly topical. In the employment context, it is important to
bear in mind that both employers and employees may have Article 9 rights.
Indeed, the customers of employers may also have such rights.

It has long been recognised[5] that the demands of the workplace can come into **9.04**
conflict with both manifesting and changing religion in many different ways:
Muslims may wish to visit the mosque on Fridays; Jews may not wish to work on
Saturdays, Christians on Sundays; Sikhs may be unwilling to observe rules about
being clean shaven (see *Panesar v Nestle Co Ltd*[6]) or wearing safety helmets.[7]

Since religion and racial origin are often closely connected, there have been a **9.05**
number of occasions on which cases which are closely concerned with religious
discrimination in employment have been brought as cases of direct or indirect
race discrimination. (See, for example, *Mandla v Dowell Lee* (Sikhs are a racial
group);[8] *Dawkins v Department of Environment* (Rastafarians are a religious not a
racial group);[9] *Seide v Gillette Industries* (Jews are a religious and racial group);[10]
Commission for Racial Equality v Dutton (Gypsies are a racial group);[11] *Tariq v
Young* (Muslims are not a racial group).[12])

So Article 9 ECHR could be used as an adjunct to existing rights. Moreover, since **9.06**
Sikhs and Jews are racial groups, they have been able to assert religious rights
through the Race Relations Act 1976. The obvious inequality between such

---

[4] R *(on the application of Williamson) v Secretary of State for Education and Employment* [2005] 2 All ER 1, [15].
[5] This passage in the first edition of this book was noted with approval by the CA in *Copsey v WWB Devon Clays Ltd* [2005] IRLR 811 at p 812.
[6] [1980] IRLR 60.
[7] Sikhs are exempted from the requirement to wear safety helmets on construction sites (Employment Act 1989, ss 11 and 12); compare *Singh v British Rail Engineering Ltd* [1986] ICR 22. The Commission rejected a complaint that British motorcycling laws which did not allow a Sikh to wear a turban, were contrary to Art 9: *X v UK* Application 7992/77, 12 July 1978, 14 DR 234.
[8] [1983] 2 AC 548.
[9] [1993] IRLR 284.
[10] [1980] IRLR 427.
[11] [1989] 1 All ER 306.
[12] COIT 24773/88.

religious groups and Muslims and Christians has led to an increasingly loud clamour for change.

B. The elements of Article 9

9.07   Article 9 ECHR has four elements that need to be disentangled before any critical analysis of the effect it will have in domestic law can be undertaken.

(1) An absolute right

9.08   First, Article 9 contains an absolute right to freedom of thought, conscience, and religion. The absolute nature of this right reflects the importance that the Convention ascribes to freedom of thought. This is sometimes termed the 'internal aspect' of the freedom to believe. It is unlikely that this internal aspect of Article 9 will come under serious attack in the near future in the UK. Persecution or oppression of persons merely because of what they believe is mercifully much less common than in previous centuries.

(2) A qualified right

9.09   Secondly, Article 9 establishes a qualified right to manifest one's religion or belief, in worship, teaching, practice, and observance. This right is more complex, both in being qualified and in its content. This complexity requires some special consideration. This is sometimes called the 'external aspect' of the freedom to believe; and because it necessarily impacts on society, it has to be balanced against the other needs of society.

(3) Collective rights

9.10   The third aspect of Article 9 ECHR is often overlooked but may prove to be just as significant as any other aspect. It is that Article 9 concerns collective rights. Thus by Article 9(1), a right to manifest religion in public or private includes a right to do so in community with others.[13] Accordingly, Article 9 may be very important in relation to organisations, especially schools and housing associations, which are founded on religious or other belief grounds. They will be able collectively to assert their rights under Article 9 in defence of claims against them.

---

[13] For a fuller discussion of this, see J Rivers, 'From Toleration to Pluralism: Religious Liberty and Religious Establishment under the United Kingdom's Human Rights Act', in R Ahdar (ed), *Law and Religion* (Aldershot: Ashgate, 2000).

(4) Article 9 and equal treatment issues

The fourth aspect of Article 9 ECHR is a negative point. It concerns what it **9.11**
is not. It is not an equal treatment Article. The Convention deals with non-
discrimination in Article 14, which, as is well known, is an accessory (not a free-
standing) Article. The Council of Europe has agreed a new Protocol 12 to the
ECHR that will replace Article 14 with a free-standing non-discrimination
provision for those countries that have signed and ratified it. This Protocol
opened for signature on 4 November 2000, since then 35 member states have
signed it and 11 have ratified it. It came into effect in those countries that had
both signed and ratified it three months after ten ratifications were received.[14]
This occurred on 1 April 2005. Although the UK government has indicated at
present that it will not ratify it, it seems likely that in due course it will have to do
so (see Chapter 13). There have already been calls for its implementation.[15]

Employment practitioners will, however, need to be aware of the connections **9.12**
between this Article and the developing rights not to permit discrimination on
grounds of religion or belief (see 9.110–9.122).[16]

There is also no doubt that equal treatment issues can arise in relation to Article **9.13**
9 ECHR taken with Article 14. A striking example of this interrelationship can
be seen in the case of *Thlimmenos v Greece*,[17] where a rule in Greece prohibiting
those with a criminal record from becoming chartered accountants was held to be
contrary to Article 14 when taken with Article 9.

Though the rule was prima facie neutral it was found to be unjustifiably indir- **9.14**
ectly discriminatory on grounds of religion when applied to a Jehovah's Witness
(see, eg, *Tinnelly and Sons Ltd and others and McElduff and others v UK*[18]).

In *Thlimmenos*, the complainant had been convicted of the offence of refusing **9.15**
to wear military uniform; however, his refusal had been on grounds of his pacifist
religious beliefs. This case is all the more unusual since Article 9 is more often
successfully invoked on its own rather than with Article 14 (see Chapter 14).
The way in which the Convention treats discrimination is considered more fully
in Chapter 14.

---

[14] For current table of signatures and ratifications see <http://conventions.coe.int/Treaty/Commun/ChercheSig.asp?NT=177&CM=8&DF=19/02/2006&CL=ENG> (accessed 1 December 2006).
[15] See G Moon (ed), *Race Discrimination: Developing and Using a new Legal Framework* (Oxford: Hart Publishing, 2000). For an eloquent argument for its ratification, see David Pannick, 'Labour Intent on Spoiling Human Rights Party', *The Times* (17 October 2000).
[16] See G Moon and R Allen, 'Substantive Rights and Equal Treatment in Respect of Religion and Belief: Towards A Better Understanding of the Rights, and Their Implications' [2001] EHRR 580.
[17] (2001) 36 EHRR 15.
[18] (1999) 27 EHRR 249.

C. What is a religion or belief?

9.16 In order to determine when this Article is engaged it is necessary first to consider what is encompassed by 'religion or belief'. In *Kokkinakis v Greece*,[19] the Court considered the scope of Article 9 in relation to Jehovah's Witnesses. It pointed out:[20]

> As enshrined in Article 9, freedom of thought, conscience and religion is one of the foundations of a 'democratic society' within the meaning of the Convention. It is, in its religious dimension, one of the most vital elements that go to make up the identity of believers and their conception of life, but it is also a precious asset for atheists, agnostics, sceptics and the unconcerned. The pluralism indissociable from a democratic society, which has been dearly won over the centuries, depends on it.

> While religious freedom is primarily a matter of individual conscience, it also implies, inter alia, freedom to 'manifest [one's] religion'. Bearing witness in words and deeds is bound up with the existence of religious convictions. According to Article 9, freedom to manifest one's religion is not only exercisable in community with others, 'in public' and within the circle of those whose faith one shares, but can also be asserted 'alone' and 'in private'; furthermore, it includes in principle the right to try to convince one's neighbour, for example through 'teaching', failing which, moreover, 'freedom to change [one's] religion or belief', enshrined in Article 9, would be likely to remain a dead letter ...

> The fundamental nature of the rights guaranteed in Article 9 para. 1 (art 9–1) is also reflected in the wording of the paragraph providing for limitations on them. Unlike the second paragraphs of Articles 8, 10 and 11 (art 8–2, art 10–2, art 11–2) which cover all the rights mentioned in the first paragraphs of those Articles (art 8–1, art 10–1, art 11–1), that of Article 9 (art 9–1) refers only to 'freedom to manifest one's religion or belief'. In so doing, it recognises that in democratic societies, in which several religions co-exist within one and the same population, it may be necessary to place restrictions on this freedom in order to reconcile the interests of the various groups and ensure that everyone's beliefs are respected.

(1) No closed lists

9.17 The Court has never established a closed list of religions or beliefs to which Article 9 ECHR applies. All the main world religions are within its scope, as are a number of less well-known or established religions or beliefs such as the Krishna Consciousness movement, the Divine Light Centrum, the Church of Scientology, Druids, the Moon Sect, pacifism, and veganism.[21]

---

19 (1994) 17 EHRR 397.
20 See para 31.
21 Respectively, *Iskcon v UK* (1994) 76A DR 90; *Omkarananda and the Divine Light Zentrum v Switzerland* (1981) 25 DR 105; *X and Church of Scientology v Sweden* (1979) 16 DR 68; *ARM*

(2) A wide concept derived from the Universal Declaration of Human Rights

The width of the concept can be seen in its derivation from Article 18 of the **9.18** Universal Declaration of Human Rights, which states:

Everyone has the right to freedom of thought, conscience and religion; this right includes freedom to change his religion or belief, and freedom, either alone or in community with others and in public or private, to manifest his religion or belief in teaching, practice, worship and observance.

The origin of this wording lies in the negotiations leading up to the agreement on **9.19** Article 18, when a compromise was reached between those countries who wished to protect the right to follow a religion explicitly and those countries who did not accept the validity of any religion and therefore wished to protect the right to have no belief or religion.[22]

(3) A right not to believe or to hold unconventional beliefs

The right protected is thus not only the right to belong to a defined, traditional, **9.20** recognised, and established religion, but also the right not to believe or to hold unconventional beliefs that are not subscribed to by others.

Article 9 ECHR has been followed and developed in the later provisions dealing **9.21** with belief discrimination, notably Article 18 of the International Covenant on Civil and Political Rights in 1966.[23] In 1993, the UN Human Rights Committee, in commenting on Article 18, said:

The right to freedom of thought, conscience and religion (which includes the freedom to hold beliefs) in Article 18.1 is far-reaching and profound; it encompasses freedom of thought on all matters, personal conviction and the commitment to religion or belief, whether manifested individually or in community with others . . . Article 18 protects theistic, non-theistic and atheistic beliefs, as well as the right not

---

Chappell v UK (1987) 53 DR 241; *X v Austria* Application 8652/79, (1981) 26 DR 89; *Arrowsmith v UK* (1978) 19 DR 5; and *X v UK* (Commission) Application 18187/91, 10 February 1993.

[22] See BC Labuschagne, 'Religious Freedom and Newly-Established Religions in Dutch Law' (1997) *Netherlands International Law Review*, Vol XLIV, Issue 2, 168.

[23] This provides: '1. Everyone shall have the right to freedom of thought, conscience and religion. This right shall include freedom to have or adopt a religion or belief of his choice, and freedom, either individually or in community with others and in public or private, to manifest his religion or belief in worship, observance, practice or teaching. 2. No one shall be subject to coercion which would impair his freedom to have or to adopt a religion or belief of his choice. 3. Freedom to manifest one's religion or beliefs may be subject only to such limitations as are prescribed by law and are necessary to protect public safety, order, health, or morals or the fundamental rights and freedoms of others. 4. The States parties to the present Covenant undertake to have respect for the liberty of parents and, when applicable, legal guardians to ensure the religious and moral education of their children in conformity with their own convictions.'

to profess any religion or belief. The terms belief and religion are to be broadly construed. Article 18 is not limited in its application to traditional religions or to religions and beliefs with institutional characteristics or practices analogous to those of traditional religions.[24]

9.22 This has led to differing views about political opinions. In *Hazar and others v Turkey*,[25] a complaint concerning adverse treatment on grounds of membership of the Communist Party was found to be admissible under Article 9 ECHR. In *Gill v Northern Ireland Council for Ethnic Minorities*,[26] the use of the term 'political opinion' within the meaning of the Northern Ireland legislation prohibiting discrimination on grounds of religion and belief, was found not to encompass the applicant's views on anti-racism.

(4) The limits to the concept of religion and belief

9.23 The Strasbourg Court is not concerned with constraints to the ambit of religion or belief:[27]

> The right to freedom of religion as guaranteed under the Convention excludes any discretion on the part of the State to determine whether religious beliefs or the means used to express such beliefs are legitimate.

9.24 Thus, undoubtedly, the ECHR has shown a very marked reluctance to limit the concept of religion or belief, but it is also clear that some limits are inherent in the very fact that Article 9 ECHR is concerned with fundamental freedoms. It cannot be a wholly subjective test since rights are in issue. The affirmation of Article 9 rights must be subject to determination and control by law.

9.25 The limits to this concept lie in a requirement of a serious ideology, having some cogency and cohesion, though it is clear that it need not be approved by the state nor be of a traditional character. Thus, in *Campbell and Cosans v UK*,[28] a case concerned with Article 2 of Protocol 1 (which concerns the right to education), the Court said that:[29]

> The term 'beliefs'. . . denotes a certain level of cogency seriousness cohesion and importance

---

[24] General Comment no 22(48) (Art 18) adopted on 20 July 1993, CCPR/C/21/Rev 1/Add 4, 27 September 1993, p 1.
[25] Application 16311/90, (1990) 72 DR 200.
[26] [2002] IRLR 74.
[27] *Manoussakis v Greece* (1996) 23 EHRR 387, para 47.
[28] (1982) 4 EHRR 293.
[29] See para 36.

Beyond that, it is inappropriate to define what is 'religion or belief'. To extend the concept too far could undermine the fundamental nature of the right, but in practice Strasbourg has avoided this problem by a willing application of the Article 9(2) qualification where necessary. **9.26**

While Article 9(1) has been held to apply to Druids (*Chappell v UK*[30]), vegans (*W v UK*[31]), and atheists (*Kokkinakis v Greece*[32]), the concept of freedom of conscience does not extend to beliefs which are necessarily group beliefs, beyond the realm of the personal or private (see *Vereniging Rechtswinkels Utrecht v Netherlands*;[33] but see *Hazar v Turkey*, at 9.22 above). **9.27**

D. Manifestation

The next question to be considered is whether any particular act is in fact a 'manifestation', since if it cannot be so characterised it will not be necessary to test the justification for any particular interference. While Article 9(1) makes absolute provision for freedom of thought, conscience, and religion, the protections for the manifestation of such beliefs have been interpreted more narrowly. Questions have been raised as to whether a particular set of religious beliefs leads to a particular manifestation, and a distinction has been drawn between manifestation and motivation. **9.28**

However, some commentators have criticised the lack of rigour in the Court's failure to distinguish adequately between manifestation and justification, saying that the logical order of the questions to be answered has been practically inverted.[34] Carolyn Evans has commented:[35] **9.29**

> Cases that have raised less traditional manifestations have been dismissed in part through the development of a restrictive test of practice and in part through determinations that applicants have voluntarily agreed to restrictions on their religion or belief.

---

[30] (1987) 53 DR 241.
[31] Application 18187/91, 10 February 1993.
[32] (1994) 17 EHRR 397.
[33] (1986) 46 DR 200.
[34] See J Martinez-Torrón (with R Navarro-Valls) in Lindholm, Durham, Cole and Tahzib-Lie (eds), *Facilitating Freedom of Religion and Belief: Perspectives, Impulses and Recommendations from the Oslo Coalition* (The Hague: Kluwer, 2004).
[35] C Evans, *Freedom of Religion under the European Convention on Human Rights* (Oxford: OUP, 2001) 132.

9.30 Manifestation can be in private or in public. However, as the Commission said in *C v UK*,[36] a case concerning a Quaker's unwillingness to pay the proportion of his taxes that would be used to fund armament research:

> Article 9 primarily protects the sphere of personal beliefs and religious creeds, i.e. the area that is sometimes called the forum internum. In addition, it protects acts which are intimately linked to these attitudes, such as acts of worship or devotion which are aspects of the practice of a religion or belief in a generally recognised form.

9.31 Thus, in *Efstratiou v Greece*,[37] and *Valsamis v Greece*,[38] students who, as Jehovah's Witnesses, were pacifists, refused to take part in a parade to commemorate the Greek national day. The Court concluded that taking part in the parade did not have a particular ideological connotation and therefore was not contrary to the pacifist beliefs of the students. This decision clearly involved substituting the pupils' judgement of conscience with a judgment of the court.

9.32 Article 9 ECHR itself lists a number of forms that the manifestation of religion or belief can take, namely 'worship, teaching, practice and observance'.

(1) Worship

9.33 Worship is perhaps relatively uncontentious; it will encompass the acts, rites, or ceremonies of homage, reverence, or devotion shown to a deity. However, each of the other concepts is worth considering in a little greater depth.

(2) Observance

9.34 Observance has not been separately defined; however, it is often linked together with worship.

(3) Teaching

9.35 This clearly covers schools with a religious foundation as well as religious establishments, but is not limited to these. It includes 'teaching' of the unconverted as well as the converted, and hence proselytising (*Kokkinakis v Greece*[39]). However, this does not necessarily apply if there is a hierarchical relationship between the converter and the potential convertee, such as is found in the armed forces. (See *Larrisis v Greece*,[40] where the Greek Air Force was permitted to restrict officers attempting to convert junior officers to the Pentecostal religion.)

---

[36] Application 10358/83, 15 December 1983, (1983) 37 DR 142; re-affirmed in *X v UK* Application 10295/82, (1984) 6 EHRR 558.
[37] (1997) 24 EHRR 294.
[38] (1996) 24 EHRR 294.
[39] Series A No 260, (1994) 17 EHRR 397.
[40] (1999) 27 EHRR 329.

(4) Practice

It is perhaps understandable that this is the most contentious aspect of Article 9 **9.36**
ECHR, and indeed of any statement of the right to freedom of religion and
belief. Who is to judge whether a practice complies with a religion or belief? How
is it to be judged? Indeed, is this a justiciable concept? In the US there has been a
great reluctance to engage with these issues, partly because of the constitutional
importance attaching for historical reasons to religious freedom and partly
because of the inherent difficulty of these questions.

In Strasbourg the term 'practice' has been interpreted not to include each and **9.37**
every act motivated by religion or belief. Actions or behaviour merely motivated
by belief are not always within its scope. This has raised questions as to whether
the word 'practice' is to be interpreted as analogous to worship, or whether it can
include acts consequential on the belief.

Thus, in *Arrowsmith v UK*,[41] which concerned a pacifist who had been convicted **9.38**
for distributing leaflets encouraging the UK troops to refuse to serve in Northern
Ireland, the Commission held that:

> the term 'practice'. . . does not cover each act which is motivated and influenced by
> a religion or belief . . . [It added] . . . when the actions of individuals do not actually
> express the belief concerned they cannot be as such protected by Article 9(1), even
> when they are motivated or influenced by it.

A distinction between actions that are motivated by a religion and belief and **9.39**
those that express the religion or belief has therefore emerged. However, this is
not universally accepted, and is in any event difficult to apply. In a dissenting
opinion in *Arrowsmith*, Mr Klecker argued that it was not necessary for the views
actually to express the belief. He considered that:

> . . . if it is accepted that practical action is an important part of the philosophy of
> pacifism . . . it is not in dispute that the distribution of the leaflet in question repre-
> sented action in pursuance of her views . . . there could not be a clearer example of
> pacifist action than these appeals to both parties to stop fighting.

(5) Manifestation and a religious motive

Here a distinction has sometimes been made between manifestation and motiva- **9.40**
tion. It has repeatedly been said that 'Article 9 does not protect every act motivated or inspired by a religion or belief'.[42] This led Lord Bingham to observe in

---

[41] (1981) 3 EHRR 218, 12 June 1979.
[42] See *Kalaç v Turkey* (1997) 27 EHRR 552 at para 27.

R (on the application of Begum) v Headteacher and Governors of Denbigh High School:[43]

> The Strasbourg institutions have not been at all ready to find an interference with the right to manifest religious belief in practice or observance where a person has voluntarily accepted an employment or role which does not accommodate that practice or observance and there are other means open to the person to practise or observe his or her religion without hardship or inconvenience.

9.41 In this case, a Muslim schoolgirl sought to challenge her school's uniform requirements. The school permitted the wearing of a shalwar kameeze, however, they refused to allow her to wear a jilbab to school. She asserted that she was obliged by her religion to wear the jilbab and she challenged the school's refusal to admit her while she was wearing it. Lords Bingham, Scott, and Hoffmann considered that while they did not doubt the sincerity of her belief that she was obliged to wear the jilbab this action did not amount to a limitation on the manifestation of her belief. This was because she could have chosen to go to another school where she would have been permitted to wear the jilbab.

9.42 Lord Nicholls appeared to consider that it was a limitation of the manifestation of her religion or belief saying to deny this would be to over-estimate the ease with which she could move to another, more suitable school and to under-estimate the disruption that this would be likely to cause to her education. Baroness Hale agreed with him.

9.43 While the approach of the members of the House of Lords differed in the way that they resolved this issue it can be seen in each opinion that an assessment of the substantive extent of any alleged interference was important, even though one approach was to hold that there had been no interference with her religion practices whereas the other focused on the justification for that interference.

(6) Manifestation as a necessary expression of religious belief

9.44 Another approach is to look at whether the action was a 'necessary expression' of the religion or belief. In *X v UK*,[44] the Commission considered the case of a Buddhist prisoner who was allowed to write to a Buddhist minister once a week but was refused permission to send out religious articles for publication in a Buddhist magazine. He produced statements showing that communication with other Buddhists was an important part of his religious practice. The Commission found that:

> . . . he has failed to prove that it was a necessary part of this practice that he should publish articles in a religious magazine. However in our view it is important to

---

[43] [2007] 1 AC 100, para 23.
[44] Application 5442/72, 20 December 1974, 1 DR 41.

ensure that there should not be a conflation of the concepts of manifestation and the justification for an interference.

Thus, the ECtHR, in testing out Article 9 cases, asks whether the action in question is required by the religion or belief, not merely whether it is motivated or influenced by the religion or belief in question. It has been argued that the Court has used this distinction in order 'to exclude cases that the Court or Commission deemed unmeritorious'.[45]   **9.45**

(7) Is religious clothing a manifestation?

In recent years there have been a number of cases concerning the wearing of the Islamic headscarf for women as well as the wearing of the hijab and veil and the wearing of beards for men all of whom have regarded this as a requirement of their religion. In *Dahlab v Switzerland*,[46] the applicant was a Swiss primary school teacher who converted to Islam and wore long, loose clothing and a scarf for four years before the Director General of Education challenged her actions. The Swiss Court upheld her dismissal and her subsequent appeal to the European Court was refused as 'manifestly ill-founded'; they clearly did not consider that it was a matter that deserved their consideration.   **9.46**

In *Şahin v Turkey*,[47] a university medical student challenged a university circular that instructed lecturers to refuse access to lectures, tutorials, and examinations to students 'with a beard or wearing the Islamic headscarf'. The Grand Chamber of the ECtHR endorsed the Chamber judgment in *Şahin* when they said:[48]   **9.47**

> The applicant said that, by wearing the headscarf, she was obeying a religious precept and thereby manifesting her desire to comply strictly with the duties imposed by the Islamic faith. Accordingly, her decision to wear the headscarf may be regarded as motivated or inspired by a religion or belief and, without deciding whether such decisions are in every case taken to fulfil a religious duty, the Court proceeds on the assumption that the regulations in issue . . . constituted an interference with the applicant's right to manifest her religion.

Thus they appear to have accepted that the wearing of her scarf was a religious practice and was a manifestation of her religion.

---

[45] See C Evans, *Religious Freedom under the European Convention on Human Rights* (2001) 115–23 and C Evans, 'The Islamic Scarf in the European Convention on Human Rights' (2006) *Melbourne Journal of International Law*, 52–73.
[46] (2001) V Eur Court HR 449.
[47] Application 44774/98, Judgment (2005) 41 EHRR 8, 19 BHRC 590; Grand chamber (2007) 44 EHRR 5.
[48] Ibid, para 78.

9.48 In considering the correct approach to this case they reviewed the position of the 'Islamic headscarf' in state education across Europe noting that it is not permitted for pupils in French state schools (although there are no rules for state universities) while in other countries, such as Austria, Germany, the Netherlands, Spain, Switzerland, and the UK, pupils were permitted to wear the 'Islamic headscarf'. Sweden and Finland permit scarves to be worn at school however, they draw a distinction between the scarf and the wearing of a burka (a full veil covering the whole body and face) and the niqab (a veil covering the upper body with the exception of the eyes), permitting schools to prohibit the wearing of the burka and the niqab 'provided they do so in a spirit of dialogue on the common values of equality of the sexes and respect for the democratic principle on which the education system is based'.[49] The case of Aishah Azmi, a Muslim classroom assistant, came before the Employment Tribunal at the end of 2006 when she refused to remove her niqab when teaching children. The Tribunal dismissed her claims of discrimination and harassment on religious grounds and the EAT upheld the Tribunal's decision.[50]

(8) The continuum of religious expression

9.49 It is important to distinguish between the different ways in which religious practice may take place. Since prayer is a personal observance it is usually less prone to affect others and so more often tolerated. Accordingly, there will be a greater need to justify an interference with such observance. By contrast, proselytising at work may well involve pressure between workers at a different place in the hierarchy. It is likely to be permissible to prevent such activity (*Larissis v Greece*[51]).

9.50 There is, of course, a continuum between these events and there are an increasing number of actions motivated by religion or belief that come into conflict in the workplace. These may involve issues of attendance at work, or working hours, or dress requirements and restrictions on the wearing of 'jewellery'.

(9) Another approach to manifestation: when is Article 9 'engaged'?

9.51 There is a clear line of cases which assert that Article 9 is not engaged when the believer has an option of expressing his or her beliefs by not persisting in their desired action, for example, they can leave the job in question or move to another school, etc. These cases seem to confuse the issue of when Article 9 rights are engaged with the issues of when such interference can be justified.

---

[49] Ibid, para 63.
[50] *Azmi v Kirklees Metropolitan Borough Council*, Judgment 30 March 2007; [2007] All ER (D) 528 (Mar).
[51] (1999) 27 EHRR 329, at paras 53–54.

In *Ahmad v UK*,[52] Mr Ahmad, a Muslim teacher, wanted to attend prayers at **9.52** the mosque during school hours in circumstances that had been determined by the Court of Appeal to be in breach of his contract of employment. The European Commission of Human Rights held that the decision of his state employers not to release him had given 'due consideration' to his right under Article 9(1), taking into account the extent of the religious obligation and the measures of accommodation offered by the employer. It was not conclusively established that he had a binding obligation to attend the mosque, and the education authority had allowed him to be absent when the consequences for his school were not so great.

When the case was heard in the Court of Appeal as *Ahmad v Inner London Education* **9.53** *Authority*,[53] they dismissed his appeal. However, Scarman LJ gave a powerful dissenting judgment, holding that for Mr Ahmad to leave 45 minutes early on a Friday was no breach of his contract of employment. In his view the case turned on the effect that section 30 of the Education Act 1944 had on the contract of employment. This section provided that no one should be prohibited from being a teacher in a state school by reason of his religious convictions (see now s 59(2) of the School Standards and Framework Act 1998). Scarman LJ held that the choice before the Court was to construe the requirements of the contract of employment broadly or narrowly.

He held that a broad construction was necessary in the context of the **9.54** Convention:[54]

> A narrow construction . . . would mean that a Muslim, who took his religious duty seriously, could never accept employment as a full-time teacher, but must be content with the lesser emoluments of part-time service. In modern British society, with its elaborate statutory protection of the individual from discrimination arising from race, colour, religion or sex, and against the background of the European Convention, this is unacceptable, inconsistent with the policy of modern statute law, and almost certainly a breach of our international obligations.

In a later passage he considered the arguments of cost and administrative burden **9.55** which were advanced by the respondents and said:[55]

> Nor do I think there is any substance in the point that a broad construction of section 30 imposes an unfair burden upon the teacher's colleagues. The distribution of the teaching burden depends upon the staffing and timetable arrangements made by the authority. If the authority has made no arrangements to distribute the burden

---

[52] (1981) 4 EHRR 126.
[53] [1977] ICR 490.
[54] At 504.
[55] At 505.

fairly in the event of its Muslim teachers going to the mosque on Fridays, this must be because they have interpreted section 30 as enabling them to refuse teachers reasonable time off to attend public worship which it is their religious duty to attend. If, however, my view of section 30 is correct, all that is necessary is that the authority should make its administrative arrangements on the basis of that view. It may mean employing a few more teachers either part-time or full-time: but, when that cost is compared with the heavy expenditure already committed to the cause of non-discrimination in our society, expense would not in this context appear to be a sound reason for requiring a narrow meaning to be given to the words of the statute. The question, therefore, as to whether Mr Ahmad broke his contract ultimately depends upon an examination of the particular circumstances of his case. Ordinarily this would be a question of fact for the industrial tribunal. But the tribunal erred in law in ruling that the question, as it put it, of reasonableness had to be determined independently of section 30. In my judgment section 30 is vital not only in considering the reasonableness of the ILEA's ultimatum but also in determining Mr Ahmad's contractual rights. Once the full implications of the section in its contractual context are properly understood, I find it impossible to say that the 45 minutes' absence from class every Friday to go to the mosque constitutes a breach of this contract. In my judgment the industrial tribunal and the appeal tribunal misconstrued the statute and misunderstood the contract.

9.56 The Commission continued their line of argument in *Kontinnen v Finland*,[56] where a Seventh-Day Adventist was dismissed for taking time off work on Fridays for religious reasons. Since there was nothing preventing this complainant from resigning from his job, his right to freedom of religion was not deemed by the Commission to have been infringed and the Commission concluded that his application was 'manifestly ill-founded'.

> In these particular circumstances the Commission finds that the applicant was not dismissed because of his religious convictions but for having refused to respect his working hours. This refusal, even if motivated by his religious convictions, cannot as such be considered protected by Article 9 para. 1. Nor has the applicant shown that he was pressured to change his religious views or prevented from manifesting his religion or belief.

> The Commission would add that, having found his working hours to conflict with his religious convictions, the applicant was free to relinquish his post. The Commission regards this as the ultimate guarantee of his right to freedom of religion. In sum there is no indication that the applicant's dismissal interfered with the exercise of his rights under Article 9 para. 1.

9.57 In this case and another Commission decision—*Stedman v UK*[57]—the dismissals were deemed to be for refusing to work certain hours rather than for the employee's religious practices.

---

[56] Application 249/49/94, 3 December 1996; (1996) 87 DR 68.
[57] Application 29107/95, (1997) 23 EHRR CD 168.

In the UK context these cases were considered in detail in *Copsey v WWB Devon* **9.58**
Clays Ltd[58] when the Court of Appeal were dealing with the application of Article
9(2) to the case of a Christian worker who was not willing, on a regular basis, to
work on Sundays. He had worked for the company for 12 years on a shift system
that did not involve Sunday working before he was first asked to work on Sundays.
For two years his employer allowed him to work on a six-day shift basis. However,
the time came when his employer contended that the change in commercial
demand for their products meant that it was no longer possible to make special
arrangements to permit Mr Copsey and one or two of his colleagues to be omitted from the Sunday shift rota. Mr Copsey argued that his Article 9 rights had
been breached.

Mummery LJ, was critical of the ECtHR jurisprudence, however, he considered **9.59**
that he was bound by it. He set out the reasons for his concern as follows:[59]

(1) The Commission rulings on non-interference with the Article 9 right are repeated
assertions unsupported by the evidence or reasoning that would normally accom-
pany a judicial ruling.
(2) The rulings are difficult to square with the supposed fundamental character of
the rights. It hardly seems compatible with the fundamental character of Article 9
that a person can be told that his right has not been interfered with because he is free
to move on, for example, to another employer, who will not interfere with his fundamental right, or even to a condition of unemployment in order to manifest the
fundamental right.
(3) The argument that the complainant is free to resign and go to work elsewhere
was not deployed by the Strasbourg Court against the applicants in *Smith and Grady v
United Kingdom* [1999] IRLR 734. Their complaint that their discharge from the armed
forces was in breach of Articles 8 and 14 was upheld. The context of the complaint was
analogous to employment. (Indeed, there were proceedings in the industrial tribunal under the Sex Discrimination Act 1975 which were stayed and later withdrawn.)
No argument was advanced that the complaint fell outside the ambit of Article 8
because the applicants were free to resign from the armed forces and thereby avoid the
application to them of the Ministry of Defence policy on sexual orientation, to which
they objected and which was ultimately held to violate the Article 8 right to respect
for their private life, to be discriminatory contrary to Article 14 and to be unjustified. It was not argued that they had waived their Convention rights by joining the
armed forces in the knowledge of the policy of exclusion by the Ministry of Defence.
The only point against non-interference taken by the United Kingdom was that the
discharge would not have amounted to an interference in the case of those applicants
who were aware of the policy and of its application to them at the time when they were
recruited. The Court dealt with the case as one in which justification was required
for an exclusion policy, which interfered with the Convention rights.

---

[58] [2005] ICR 1789, [2005] IRLR 811.
[59] At para 35.

9.60 This led him to conclude:[60]

> In the absence of the Commission rulings, I would have regarded this as a case of material interference with Mr Copsey's Article 9 rights. The rights would be engaged and interference with them would require justification under Article 9(2). Under the 1998 Act, however, this court must take the Commission rulings into account, so far as they are relevant in determining a question which has arisen in connection with a Convention right: s.2(1)(c). They are relevant. It is not a case of an isolated ruling. So far as the Commission is concerned it seems to be well established that the qualified Article 9 right of a citizen in an employment relationship to manifest his belief is not engaged when the employer requires an employee to work hours which interfere with the manifestation of his religion or dismisses him for not working or agreeing to work those hours because he wishes to practise religious observances during normal working hours.

9.61 Rix LJ disagreed with his interpretation of these cases drawing a distinction between those cases where the applicant had agreed to comply with contractual rights and later sought to alter them on religious grounds and those where it was the employer who was seeking to alter the employee's contract, concluding that:

> an employee cannot complain of interference in his rights of religious freedom if he binds himself by his own contract in a way inconsistent with those rights.

9.62 In order to reach this analysis he held that both *Ahmad* and *Kontinnen* were correctly decided, but in *Stedman* the Commission 'incomprehensibly' reached the wrong conclusion as:

> There the applicant was a Christian who did not wish to work on Sundays. The facts are not well reported, but it seems that at some stage after she had been employed . . . she was asked to agree to work on Sundays and had refused, and had therefore been dismissed . . . her original contract had not involved Sunday working.

9.63 He therefore concluded that Mr Copsey's refusal to agree to a change in his contract of employment to include regular Sunday working could be a manifestation of his Article 9 rights:

> where an employer seeks to change the working hours and terms of his contract of employment with his employee in such a way as to interfere materially with the employee's right to manifest his religion, then Article 9(1) of the Convention is potentially engaged. One solution is to find a reasonable accommodation with the employee. If this is found, then there will in the event be no material interference. If a reasonable solution is offered to the employee, but not accepted by him, then I think it remains possible to say that there is no material interference; alternatively, one can speak of justification under Article 9(2). What is important to realise is that there is, as always (save in the case of absolute rights), a balance to be struck between the rights of the individual and the rights of all members of a

---

[60] At para 36.

democratic society. The latter rights will include the rights of the employer, who has a business or other form of undertaking to run, the rights of fellow-employees, and the rights of the public in general, mediated through parliament, who have an interest in fair but efficient employment laws. In the case of a private employee like Mr Copsey, the state's interest, and obligation, is in ensuring that employment laws allow room for an individual's Convention protected rights to be capable of being vindicated.

He went on to suggest that employers in this situation should consider whether **9.64** they need to make a reasonable accommodation for their employee's needs:

> it seems to me that if respect for the right to manifest one's religion is to have meaning in a democratic society, it is not possible to say that an employer who, in the given situation, would simply ignore any need to seek a reasonable accommodation would be acting fairly.

However, both Judges agreed that even if there had been a manifestation within **9.65** the terms of Article 9 the employer's actions would have been justified under the terms of Article 9(2) (see below). The third Judge, Neuberger LJ, considered that the Article 9 rights were irrelevant and the case could be decided on the basis of the relevant employment rights alone.

The outcome was that Mr Copsey lost each way round and the House of Lords **9.66** in declining permission to appeal must have concluded that the distinctions were of insufficient public importance on the facts or not adequate to explore those distinctions.

E. Justification of qualified rights

(1) The nature of the qualified right

Article 9(2) specifically limits the freedom to manifest religion or belief in a similar **9.67** way to the limitations under Articles 8, 10, and 11. Accordingly, the same rules apply as to assessment of any interference (see 2.15–2.17). Article 9(2) presents an important balance between an individual, or group's, interest in exercising their freedom to manifest a religion or belief and the state's interest in ensuring that such manifestation does not unjustifiably conflict with others' safety, public order, health or morals, or their rights and freedoms. Any conflict between the Article 9 rights of an employing body and the individual rights of an employee (whether under Article 9 or elsewhere) will have to be resolved by reference to Article 9(2). That is to say:

(a) any limitations must be prescribed by law; and

(b) they must be necessary in a democratic society on one or more of the given grounds in Article 9(2).

9.68 An example of how the European Commission on Human Rights balanced rights in Article 9(1) against permitted derogations can be seen in *Chappell v UK*.[61] Here the applicants had complained that the decision to close Stonehenge and the surrounding area during the summer solstice, and not to allow Druids to practise the midsummer solstice ceremony, infringed their right to freedom of religion as guaranteed by Article 9 ECHR. The Commission, treating Druidism as a religion, considered that the closing of Stonehenge and the surrounding area during the summer solstice period amounted to an interference with the applicants' rights under Article 9. However the Commission's reasons for finding that the implied interference with the applicants' rights was in accordance with the law and necessary in a democratic society in the interests of public safety, for the protection of public order or for the protection of the rights and freedoms of others, included the fact that the area had to be closed due to the threat to Stonehenge and the risk of harm to the public through disruption.

(2) Limitation prescribed by law

9.69 The nature of a limitation prescribed by law has been widely interpreted; it will include all statute law, regulation, and case law but also rules and regulations authorised by law. So that, for example, in the case of *Şahin v Turkey*[62] it encompassed the universities' rules and regulations. However, the law in question must be sufficiently certain and precise so that its application is predictable.

(3) Proportionality

9.70 In practice proportionality is likely to be very important in determining the right relationship between:

(a) the interests of public safety;
(b) the protection of public order, health, or morals;
(c) the protection of the rights and freedoms of others,

on the one hand, and the interference prescribed by law on the other. This will also be very important when Article 9 rights come into conflict with other rights. Such justifications might include rules concerned to ensure that staff at a police or customs establishment were sufficiently visible, or staff in a hospital complied with health requirements. There are a variety of limits that could arise when the protection of the rights and freedoms of others are concerned. One such example

---

[61] (1987) 53 DR 241.
[62] Application 44774/98, judgment 29 June 2004 (2005) 41 EHRR 8; 19 BHRC 590; opinion of Grand Chamber: 10 November 2005 (2007) 44 EHRR 5.

might be when a teacher in a state school is severely limited by religious observance in carrying out their tasks.

It seems likely that a case such as *O'Neill v Governors of St Thomas More School*[63] **9.71**
in which the religious rights of the employing organisation clashed with the sex discrimination rights of an employee (see 9.102 and 9.143) would have to be reconsidered in the light of this. It might be argued that in such circumstances a decision to dismiss was both fair and should not attract compensation under the Sex Discrimination Act 1975. The difficulty is that the Sex Discrimination Act 1975 currently does not allow for an exception which would have permitted such a decision. In this context the ECJ will no doubt be called on to resolve the conflicts inherent in anti-discrimination laws deriving from Europe which do not have any express mechanisms for dealing with such conflicts.

(4) An example of how the justification argument might be viewed

A limitation on Article 9 rights has to be defined by legal rules. There has to be a **9.72**
pressing social need for the limitation in question on one of the specified grounds; and above all there has to be a degree of proportionality between the limitation actually made and the need for it.

Perhaps a religious organisation might seek to recruit employees who have the **9.73**
same faith and that this could have the effect of causing religious or racial discrimination unless there was a defence under Article 9(2). However, the organisation would not have a defence if the job in question was not involved with the religious work of the community at all. There would have to be a pressing social need for the qualification for the job.

Take, for instance, a person who simply took the kitchen waste away, or stoked **9.74**
the boilers, or looked after the gardens. If an individual was a Sikh and applied for such a job, and was turned down because he was not of the same religion as the organisation, there would be a breach of Article 9 ECHR. A remedy would lie under the Race Relations Act 1976 and also under the Employment Equality (Religion or Belief) Regulations 2003.[64] Although the rights of the organisation under Article 9 would be affected, the interference under the Race Relations Act 1976 or the Religion or Belief Regulations 2003 would be justified by Article 9(2). The limitation on the organisation's Article 9 rights is prescribed by law, and it is necessary to ensure that there is no race or religion discrimination. There is no pressing social need for the person to be of any religious denomination. The ground for the limitation is to prevent an interference with the rights

---

[63] [1997] ICR 33.
[64] SI 2003/1660.

and freedoms of the job applicant not to suffer discrimination, and the means chosen are proportionate.

F. Collective rights under Article 9

9.75 The collective aspect of Article 9 ECHR must be considered separately. Its importance and the commitment to its use by religious groups should not to be underestimated.[65] There is an informal but powerful consensus among different faith groups of the general importance of religious beliefs that has enabled such groups to work collectively at a political level even though they may have severe doctrinal differences. The existence of section 13 of the HRA 1998, which requires the court to pay special heed to Article 9, is an eloquent statement of the power of this consensus since it was the result of concerted pressure on Parliament during the passage of the HRA 1998.

9.76 It was seen from the outset of discussions about the HRA 1998 as inevitable that an appeal to Article 9 would be made to resolve conflicts between individual employee rights and the rights of such religious organisations. It is for this reason that section 13 of the HRA 1998 was enacted to provide:

> (1) If a court's determination of any question arising under this Act might affect the exercise by a religious organisation (itself or its members collectively) of the Convention right to freedom of thought, conscience and religion, it must have particular regard to the importance of that right.
>
> (2) In this section 'court' includes a tribunal.

9.77 Typically section 13 will be relevant in cases concerned with religious institutions such as schools, housing associations, mosques, temples, churches, and synagogues. Commentators are by no means clear as to what 'particular regard' in section 13(1) may mean. It seems that the main effect of this section will be to emphasise the Court's own case law as to the importance of Article 9, but not to create any greater right over and beyond that which is found in Article 9 itself.

9.78 The political energy of this informal group of 'faith' bodies has been converted into a more proactive legal policy in pursuit of collective rights under Article 9. There has been some strong evidence of this in the activities of the Christian Institute in seeking to persuade the government on no account to agree to legislation under Article 13 EC in relation to sexual orientation.[66] This was not successful and was predicated on an erroneous assertion that collective Article 9 rights

---

[65] It is of course well established that a church body can possess and exercise an Art 9 right as a representative of its members: see, eg, *Holy Monasteries v Greece* (1995) 20 EHRR 1.

[66] See, eg, the Christian Institute, website at <http://www.christian.org.uk>.

would always trump individual rights. The case law of the Court shows this to be false, in that it requires a balance to be struck on a case-by-case basis[67] rather than an absolute ban. The government has used its power in Part 3 of the Equality Act 2006 to make Regulations prohibiting discrimination on the grounds of sexual orientation in the provision of goods, facilities and services, in education and in the exercise of public functions. Prior to April 2007, when these Regulations came into force,[68] the Catholic and Church of England Churches combined to oppose legislation preventing adoption agencies from discriminating against homosexuals. The government decided eventually that the exemption sought by religious organisations when performing public functions would not be granted. The Regulations therefore contain the same provision as in the Northern Ireland Regulations that no exemption applies where a religious organisation is performing a public function on behalf of a public authority. The public debate at the time included argument over whether the suggested exemption would provide a protection not for the holding of a religious belief but for the manifestation of the belief. The outcome of the debate has determined that it is necessary and justifiable to limit the right to manifest a religious belief where it conflicts with the right of homosexual couples not to be discriminated against in their access to services as important as those concerned with adoption.[69] However, adoption agencies have been given until the end of 2008 to make arrangements for the change in the way they must operate: see Regulation 15 of the Equality Act (Sexual Orientation) Regulations. During this transition period, faith based adoption and fostering agencies must refer lesbian, gay and bisexual couples to agencies who are able to assist, to minimise the potential negative impact of the exception upon such couples.

To understand the effect of Article 9 ECHR on employment law it is necessary to note that collective rights are especially relevant to organisations founded on religious grounds. The UK does already have some legislation in relation to schools and religion which may well have to be reconsidered in the light of this Article. Other obvious clashes between the rights of these kinds of employers and other rights are discussed at 9.101. **9.79**

---

[67] *Kala v Turkey* (1999) 27 EHRR 552, at para 30, and compare the objections to such blanket bans in *Smith and Grady v UK* [1999] IRLR 734 and *Vogt v Germany* (1996) 21 EHRR 205.
[68] The Equality Act (Sexual Orientation) Regulations 2007, SI 2007/5920.
[69] See further the 28 February report (HL Paper 58, HC350) of the Joint Committee On Human Rights upon the sought after opt out: <http://www.publications.parliament.uk/pa/jt/jtrights.htm>.

G. Article 9 rights in the workplace

9.80 Assuming that there is a manifestation of an Article 9 right and that therefore the Article is engaged how might it be relevant in the workplace?

9.81 Employees of public authorities, such as local authorities and central government, will be able to assert Article 9 rights directly against their employers. However, those who are employees of non-exclusively public bodies (see Chapter 4) will not be able to assert their rights quite so directly. They will have to rely on Article 9 indirectly. They may be able to argue that the default term of trust and confidence (see *Malik & Mahmud v BCCI*[70]) has to be construed consistently with Article 9 (see HRA 1998, s 2), or that any judicial discretion or statutory provision must take it into account (see s 3). It was this later point that arose in *Copsey* (see 9.58–9.66).

9.82 Other employees will be in the same position as those of non-exclusively public bodies.

(1) Recruitment

9.83 Although it should be emphasised that it was a deliberate decision to exclude from the Convention any right of recruitment to the public service (*Kala v Turkey*[71]), it does not follow that domestic courts, in using the Convention as a floor rather than a ceiling, would necessarily conclude that Article 9 was not engaged by a provision which interfered with these rights.

9.84 For example, in *Prais v Council of the European Communities*,[72] the claimant/applicant, who was a practising Jew, relied on Article 9 ECHR when she complained to the ECJ that the holding of examinations on a Saturday, to qualify for appointment to a weekday job (which she could not sit because of her religious obligations), was a violation of her rights. The ECJ dismissed her complaint only because she had raised the matter too late after the date for the examinations had been fixed. Had she raised the matter earlier and the examinations had then been set on a Saturday, it is likely that she would have established a violation of her rights.

(2) Dress and appearance requirements

9.85 Dress and appearance requirements are becoming an increasing focus of attention. Frequently, they will be considered as a discrimination issue coming

---

[70] [1998] AC 20.
[71] (1999) 27 EHRR 552, at para 35.
[72] Case 130/75, [1976] ECR 1589, [1976] 2 CMLR 708.

under the Employment Equality (Religion or Belief) Regulations 2003 (see 9.110 below); however, they can also give rise to Article 9 issues.

The cases of *Dahlab v Switzerland* and *Şahin v Turkey*[73] concerning the wearing of the 'Islamic scarf' are discussed above at 9.46–9.48. It is worth noting that the key justifications for prohibiting the women in these cases from wearing a scarf was that it could be seen as a form of proselytisation to others, that it was a sign of gender inequality and it is symbolic of intolerance. In summary the Court in *Şahin* decided that although the restrictions imposed on the wearing of the Islamic headscarf in Turkey's universities had interfered with the applicant's right to manifest her religion, this interference was prescribed by law and was, in fact, compatible with the Convention. The Grand Chamber of the Court in *Sahin* set out the context for its justification decision as follows:[74]

9.86

> In democratic societies, in which several religions coexist within one and the same population, it may be necessary to place restrictions on freedom to manifest one's religion or belief in order to reconcile the interests of the various groups and ensure that everyone's beliefs are respected . . . Pluralism, tolerance and broad-mindedness are hallmarks of a 'democratic society' . . . Pluralism and democracy must also be based on dialogue and a spirit of compromise necessarily entailing various concessions on the part of individuals or groups of individuals which are justified in order to maintain and promote the ideals and values of a democratic society.

The wearing of an 'Islamic scarf' is clearly a statement, and must be intended to be by the wearer, however, it is of an altogether different degree to that in issue in *Kokkinakis v Greece*[75] where Mr Kokkinakis visited his neighbours in order to attempt to convert them to his beliefs. It is hard to see why Mr Kokkinakis' actions were deemed to be justifiable whilst the mere wearing of a scarf is not. In the cases of *Dahlab* and *Şahin* the facts do not set out that women made any attempt to convert others, indeed, Ms Dahlab, when asked why she wore a scarf, always asserted that it was to keep her head warm.

9.87

Whilst the question of gender inequality can arise in the context of Islamic clothing, in these cases it seems that the two women had reached their own independent and clear determination about what they wanted to wear. So much so that they fought their cases to the ECtHR and in the case of Ms Şahin, a medical student, transferred her studies to a university in Austria so that she could continue to study and wear a scarf. Judge Tulkens in her powerful

9.88

---

[73] Application 44774/98, Judgment (2005) 41 EHRR 8; 19 BHRC 590; Grand Chamber (2007) 44 EHRR 5.
[74] Ibid, paras 106 and 108.
[75] (1994) 17 EHRR 397.

dissenting judgment in *Şahin* rightly says 'what is lacking in this debate is the opinion of the women, both those who wear the headscarf and those who choose not to'.

9.89 It is also hard to see how their actions were characterised by intolerance. It is clearly important as the Court sets out that everyone's beliefs must be respected and that society must operate in a spirit of dialogue and compromise. However, these cases do not appear to demonstrate that the authorities concerned operated in a spirit of dialogue and compromise.

9.90 This has led Carolyn Evans to comment:[76]

> Such judgments, justified on the basis of equality, tolerance and human rights, do harm to the very notion of neutrality that the Court claims to be central to proper adjudication in these areas. When those who are not Christians but whose rights have been violated can gain no relief from the Court because the Court employs stereotypes and refuses to engage with the complexity of modern religious pluralism, then religious freedom and pluralism are undermined and the notion of human rights degraded.

9.91 She rightly points to the words of the UN Human Rights Committee which when ruling on Article 18 of the International Covenant on Civil and Political Rights stated that:

> the freedom to manifest one's religion encompasses the right to wear clothes or attire in public which is in conformity with the individual's faith or religion. Furthermore, it considers that to prevent a person from wearing religious clothing in public or private may constitute a violation . . .[77]

(3) Dismissal

9.92 Usually there will be a pressing social need before a state employer dismisses on grounds of religious expression. The same is likely to be true in relation to beliefs. Certainly any dismissal on such grounds would have to be considered very carefully. In each case the exact nature of the manifestation of religion or belief would have to be weighed against the state's own requirements.

9.93 This can be seen perhaps most clearly from a case under Article 10 ECHR, *Vogt v Germany*.[78] This concerned the dismissal from the state teaching system of a teacher who was a member of the DKP, the German Communist party.

---

[76] C Evans '"The Islamic Scarf" in the European Court of Human Rights' (2006) *Melbourne Journal of International Law*, vol 7, 52–73, at 73.
[77] *Raihon Hudoyberganova v Uzbekistan*, Human Rights Committee, Communication No 931/2000, UN Doc CCPR/C/82/D/931/2000 (18 January 2005) [6.2].
[78] (1996) 21 EHRR 205.

The following extract from the Court's judgment[79] shows how an assessment of the relevant factors should be carried out:

> ... the Court ... will accordingly concentrate on Mrs Vogt's dismissal. In this connection it notes at the outset that there are several reasons for considering dismissal of a secondary-school teacher by way of disciplinary sanction for breach of duty to be a very severe measure. This is firstly because of the effect that such a measure has on the reputation of the person concerned and secondly because secondary-school teachers dismissed in this way lose their livelihood, at least in principle, as the disciplinary court may allow them to keep part of their salary. Finally, secondary-school teachers in this situation may find it well nigh impossible to find another job as a teacher, since in Germany teaching posts outside the civil service are scarce. Consequently, they will almost certainly be deprived of the opportunity to exercise the sole profession for which they have a calling, for which they have been trained and in which they have acquired skills and experience.

A second aspect that should be noted is that Mrs Vogt was a teacher of German **9.94** and French in a secondary school, a post which did not intrinsically involve any security risks.

The risk lay in the possibility that, contrary to the special duties and responsibil- **9.95** ities incumbent on teachers, she would take advantage of her position to indoctrinate or exert improper influence in another way on her pupils during lessons. Yet no criticism was levelled at her on this point. On the contrary, the applicant's work at school had been considered wholly satisfactory by her superiors and she was held in high regard by her pupils and their parents and also by her colleagues (see paragraph 10 of the judgment); the disciplinary courts recognised that she had always carried out her duties in a way that was beyond reproach (see paragraphs 20 and 22 of the judgment). Indeed the authorities only suspended the applicant more than four years after instituting disciplinary proceedings (see paragraphs 11 to 16 of the judgment), thereby showing that they did not consider the need to remove the pupils from her influence to be a very pressing one.

Since teachers are figures of authority to their pupils, their special duties **9.96** and responsibilities to a certain extent also apply to their activities outside school. However, there is no evidence that Mrs Vogt herself, even outside her work at school, actually made anti-constitutional statements or personally adopted an anti-constitutional stance. The only criticisms retained against her concerned her active membership of the DKP, the posts she had held in that party and her candidature in the elections for the Parliament of the Land. Mrs Vogt consistently maintained her personal conviction that these activities were

---

[79] At para 60.

compatible with upholding the principles of the German constitutional order. The disciplinary courts recognised that her conviction was genuine and sincere, while considering it to be of no legal significance, and indeed not even the prolonged investigations lasting several years were apparently capable of yielding any instance where Mrs Vogt had actually made specific pronouncements belying her emphatic assertion that she upheld the values of the German constitutional order.

9.97   A final consideration to be borne in mind is that the DKP had not been banned by the Federal Constitutional Court and that, consequently, the applicant's activities on its behalf were entirely lawful.

9.98   In the case of a non-state employee then the employment tribunal will be constrained by precedent to take an approach consistent with that taken by the Court of Appeal in *Copsey* (see 9.58–9.66). As explained above while the judges agreed on the outcome their reasoning was substantially different. It is suggested that the approach of Mummery LJ is to be preferred to that of Neuberger LJ. Moreover the approach of Rix LJ is closer to that of Mummery LJ and their approaches are both more obviously compliant with section 6 of the HRA 1998 (see, for example, paragraph 69 of the Court of Appeal judgment).

(4) The particular nature of the workplace

9.99   In *Kala v Turkey*,[80] a judge advocate in the Turkish armed forces complained of a breach of Article 9 ECHR when he was forced to retire in consequence of his fundamentalist Muslim beliefs. The Turkish government argued that the reason for his retirement was his lack of loyalty to the secularist foundation of the Turkish state which it was the duty of the armed forces to protect. The state said that facilities were granted for Muslims and others to practise their faiths while in the armed forces. However, it argued that the protection of Article 9 did not extend to membership of a fundamentalist movement whose activities were 'likely to upset the army's hierarchical equilibrium'.

9.100   While this case must be seen, first, as a case about army service,[81] its emphasis on the situation in which a person wishes to manifest religion or belief is highly relevant. In rejecting Kala's application the Court said:

> . . . Article 9 does not protect every act motivated or inspired by a religion or belief. Moreover in exercising his freedom to manifest his religion, an individual may need to take his specific situation into account.

---

[80] (1999) 27 EHRR 552.
[81] Note the reference to the case of *Engel and others v The Netherlands (No 1)* (1976) 1 EHRR 647 cited in the text.

In choosing to pursue a military career Kala was accepting of his own accord a system of military discipline that by its very nature implied the possibility of placing on certain of the rights and freedoms of members of the armed forces limitations incapable of being imposed on civilians.

(5) Religious schools

Under section 60 of the School Standards and Framework Act 1998, preference may be given to teachers whose religious opinions are in accordance with the tenets of the religion or religious denomination specified in relation to the school, and who attend religious worship in accordance with those tenets, or who give, or are willing to give, religious education at the school in accordance with those tenets. Moreover, regard may be had, in connection with the termination of the employment of any teacher at the school, to any conduct on his or her part which is incompatible with the precepts, or with the upholding of the tenets, of the religion or religious denomination so specified. **9.101**

This section is designed to ensure that the collective rights of the school under Article 9 ECHR are taken into consideration. However, while section 60 secures this result, it does not mean that the competing rights of the employee are irrelevant. In such cases the Northern Ireland approach to ordinary employment may be relevant (see 9.123–9.132 below). If the incompatible conduct is such that it has no impact on the running of the school then it is hard to see that section 60 would provide a complete answer in a claim for unfair dismissal. The approach taken by the Court in *Vogt* (see 9.93–9.97) will be in point. If the conduct which is incompatible is wholly external and does not, as in *O'Neill v Governors of St Thomas More School* (see 9.143 *et seq*),[82] touch on actual work responsibilities then it is possible that a dismissal could still be found to be unfair because it is in breach of Article 9 ECHR. **9.102**

In Northern Ireland there is no right for a teacher to complain of discrimination on grounds of religion (see Article 71 of the Fair Employment and Treatment (Northern Ireland) Order 1998). **9.103**

(6) Oaths of office and Article 9

It is not uncommon for the holder of a job in the public sector to be required to make an oath or affirmation. Provided any such requirement enables the individual to make an affirmation which is appropriate to his or her religion or belief, **9.104**

---

[82] [1997] ICR 33.

this is not likely to involve a breach of Article 9. (See, eg, *Buscarini v San Marino*;[83] *McGuinness v UK*.[84] See also *Re Treacy's Application*.[85])

9.105 Requirements of a religious affirmation in relation to private employment, or employment with a specific church or religious organisation may be justifiable since they will usually involve the rights of the members of the church or organisation to manifest their religion or belief collectively. While this might lead in some cases to religious or racial discrimination, such discrimination may be justified where it can be shown that there was an objective justification for the requirement of such an oath or affirmation.

(7) The established church

9.106 A few rules remain limiting the work which those who are not members of the Church of England may perform.[86] These rules may not be consistent with Article 9 ECHR. However, in *Knudsen v Norway*,[87] the European Commission of Human Rights rejected a complaint by a clergyman in the state church, stating that if the requirements imposed upon him by the state were in conflict with his convictions, he was free to relinquish his office. The Commission regarded this as an ultimate guarantee of his rights under Article 9 ECHR.

H. Other prohibitions on discrimination on grounds of religion or belief

9.107 Religious discrimination has been prohibited in Northern Ireland for over 30 years and discrimination on grounds of religion or belief is now prohibited in Great Britain. The laws are similar but different.

(1) New rights to non-discrimination on grounds of religion

9.108 In 2000 the European Council agreed an Employment Equality Directive under Article 13 EC, requiring member states to create a right not to be discriminated

---

[83] (2000) 30 EHRR 208.

[84] [1999] EHRLR 639.

[85] [2000] NI330.

[86] The description 'non-conformist' derives from the Act of Uniformity 1662. Most discrimination against Roman Catholics was removed by the Roman Catholic Relief Act 1829 and the Lord Chancellor (Tenure of Office and Discharge of Ecclesiastical Functions) Act 1974, which enabled Roman Catholics to become Lord Chancellor. However, it remains the law that a Roman Catholic may not occupy the throne (Bill of Rights 1688 and Act of Settlement 1700, s 2), or hold certain related offices (see Lord Chancellor (Tenure of Office and Discharge of Ecclesiastical Functions) Act 1974). See also *Halsbury's Laws of England* (4th edn, London: Butterworths, 1975), Vol 14, paras 1389 *et seq*.

[87] Application 11045/84, 8 March 1985, (1985) 42 DR 247.

against on grounds of religion or belief. This is an employee's right rather than an employer's right. The Employment Equality Directive enables an employer to argue a defence of genuine occupational qualification (see Article 4). Article 4(2) provides:

> Member States may maintain national legislation in force at the date of adoption of this Directive or provide for future legislation incorporating national practices existing at the date of adoption of this Directive pursuant to which, in the case of occupational activities within churches and other public or private organisations the ethos of which is based on religion or belief, a difference of treatment based on a person's religion or belief shall not constitute discrimination where, by reason of the nature of these activities or of the context in which they are carried out, a person's religion or belief constitute a genuine, legitimate and justified occupational requirement, having regard to the organisation's ethos. This difference of treatment shall be implemented taking account of Member States' constitutional provisions and principles, as well as the general principles of Community law, and should not justify discrimination on another ground.
>
> Provided that its provisions are otherwise complied with, this Directive shall thus not prejudice the right of churches and other public or private organisations, the ethos of which is based on religion or belief, acting in conformity with national constitutions and laws, to require individuals working for them to act in good faith and with loyalty to the organisation's ethos.

9.109 However, such a defence to a claim of religious discrimination will be of no use if it does not also, at least potentially, enable the religious organisation to defend an associated claim of discrimination on other grounds. These issues of conflict of rights are discussed at 9.134–9.148.

(2) Employment Equality (Religion or Belief) Regulations 2003

9.110 In 2003 the Employment Equality (Religion or Belief) Regulations 2003 were introduced in Great Britain to implement the Employment Equality Directive. The regulations prohibit discrimination in employment whether it is direct, indirect, or by way of victimisation or harassment.

9.111 There is a close relationship with Article 9. Thus 'religion or belief', for the purposes of the protection afforded against discrimination by the 2003 Regulations, was defined by regulation 2(1) as any religion, religious belief, or similar philosophical belief. This did not explicitly cover discrimination occurring because of a lack of religion or belief, although it was clear that Parliament had intended that this should be covered by the regulations. The Equality Act 2006 (EA 2006) introduced a new definition in order to make this explicit in section 77. 'Religion' is defined to mean any religion and 'belief' means any religious or philosophical belief. Any reference to 'religion' or 'belief' includes a reference to a lack of religion or 'belief'. This definition in section 44 of the EA 2006 replaces that which had originally applied to employment discrimination under the 2003 Regulations.

9.112   The explanatory note on the EA 2006 describes the word 'religion' as having 'a broad definition in line with the freedom of religion guaranteed by Article 9 of the ECHR'. Hence the definitions discussed earlier in 9.16–9.27 will be of real relevance in ascertaining how the definition in the Regulations is to be interpreted.

9.113   In discussing the meaning of 'belief' in the provisions in the EA 2006, the Home Office Minister, Baroness Scotland, explained:[88]

> . . . philosophical beliefs must therefore always be of a similar nature to religious beliefs. It will be for the courts to decide what constitutes a belief for the purposes of Part 2 of the Bill, but case law suggests that any philosophical belief must attain a certain level of cogency, seriousness, cohesion and importance, must be worthy of respect in a democratic society and must not be incompatible with human dignity. Therefore an example of a belief that might meet this description is humanism, and examples of something that might not – I hope I do not give any offence to anyone present in the Chamber – would be support of a political party or a belief in the supreme nature of the Jedi Knights.

9.114   ACAS has published Guidance[89] which has a useful Appendix setting out all the main religions and beliefs in Britain together with their main customs, needs, and festivals. However, it is clear that the scope of the Regulations is not limited to these religions; they cover any religion as discussed above (see 9.16–9.27).

9.115   Thus, it should be noted that in contrast to the position in Northern Ireland where there is explicit protection from discrimination on grounds of political belief,[90] the 2003 Regulations are not intended to cover political belief.[91] However, difficulties are likely to arise in the areas where political beliefs come close to religious beliefs, and both pacifism and vegetarianism might come into this category.[92]

9.116   Rather more difficult problems arise when fascism or racist political beliefs such as those of the British National Party (BNP) are in scope. Many anti-racist organisations might want to prohibit access to members wishing to espouse these views. The first case on this raised the situation of a member of the BNP who was refused a job interview on the grounds that he was an active member of

---

[88] *Hansard* HL Debates, col 1110 (13 July 2005).

[89] ACAS, *A Guide for Employers and Employees: Religion or Belief in the Workplace*, 2003 <http://www.acas.org.uk/media/pdf/f/l/religion_1.pdf>.

[90] See Fair Employment and Treatment (Northern Ireland) Order 1998, SI 1998/3162 (NI 21) (as amended).

[91] See DTI, *Explanatory Notes for the Employment Equality (Religion or Belief) Regulations 2003* pp 2–3.

[92] Both pacifism and veganism have been accepted as beliefs for the purpose of Art 9 ECHR; see *Arrowsmith v UK* (1978) 19 DR 5 and *X v UK* Application 18187/91, 10 February 1993 (unreported).

the BNP. The employment tribunal examined the constitution of the BNP which sets out that the party 'represents the collective National, Environmental, Political, Racial, Folkish, Social, Cultural, Religious and Economic interests of the indigenous Anglo-Saxon, Celtic and Norse folk communities of Britain and those we regard as closely related and ethnically assimilable aboriginal members of the European race also resident in Britain'. They concluded that the BNP is a political party as it has a political ethos and puts up political candidates in elections, so allegiance to it is therefore not a religion, religious belief, or similar philosophical belief within the terms of the 2003 Regulations.[93]

Difficulties are also likely to arise when religious beliefs include political beliefs, such as Roman Catholic liberation theology found in South America or the Dutch Reform Church of South Africa. Disentangling the political beliefs from the religious beliefs in such cases may not prove easy. **9.117**

(3) The right to act on a religion or belief

It is not yet clear how far these new provisions will go in protecting the right to express a belief in the way one behaves, particularly when those beliefs may be based on cultural practices and traditions. In circumstances where a person's religion or belief dictates certain behaviour, it is likely that less favourable treatment on grounds of that behaviour will be found to be discriminatory. However, whether it is less favourable treatment will depend on how those of a different religion or belief would be treated in similar circumstances. **9.118**

In a case concerning an employee's right to take time off after a family bereavement, the question was raised as to whether this was part of his Muslim faith.[94] The employment tribunal applied a wide and liberal interpretation to 'religion' and 'religious belief' and held that, if a person genuinely believes that his or her faith requires a particular course of action, that is sufficient to make it part of his or her religion. The employment tribunal concluded that trying to differentiate between cultural manifestation, traditions, and religious observance would lead to 'unnecessary complications and endless debate'. However, the employee's claim failed as he was unable to show that his employer would have treated a non-Muslim differently. Clearly, employment tribunal cases will not bind other tribunals or courts, but in the absence of other authority such cases **9.119**

---

[93] *Baggs v Fudge* ET case no 1400114/05, Judgment 23 March 2005. Although this case was decided on the basis of the older definition in the Regulations, the new definition in the EA 2006 is not likely to change the decision that was reached here. The point did not arise for consideration in *Redfearn v Serco Ltd* [2006] ICR 1367, [2006] IRLR 623 even though the case concerned the dismissal of a BNP bus driver.

[94] *Husain v Bhullar Bros t/a BB Supersave* ET case no 1806638/04.

may provide an indication of the way in which these provisions will be interpreted in future.

(4) Relevance of the discriminator's belief

9.120 The wording of the provisions of regulation 3 of the 2003 Regulations and section 77(2) of the EA 2006 in relation to direct discrimination prohibits actions or conduct which are shown to be 'on grounds of' religion or belief. Regulation 3(2) provides that such treatment must be on grounds of the religion or belief of the complainant, or any other person except the alleged discriminator. So where, on grounds of religion or belief, person A treats person B less favourably than he or she would treat others, the reference to 'religion or belief' does not include A's religion or belief.[95] The employer's religion will be relevant evidence that there has been discrimination, but treatment based on it will not constitute discrimination under the 2003 Regulations by itself.

9.121 The explanatory notes say that this means that the prohibition 'does not apply where the less favourable treatment occurs solely on grounds of A's religion or belief – for example, where A feels motivated to take particular action because of what his religion or belief requires'.[96] It is still unclear why this provision was added and different commentators have suggested differing meanings. It may mean that A does not discriminate against B when A has the same religion or belief as B. This would mean that a Hindu Brahmin is not discriminating unlawfully if he refuses to employ a Hindu untouchable.

9.122 Such a conclusion seems unjustified and inconsistent with the source of the Regulations in EC law. The government has said that this is not what this clause was intended to mean.[97] It may have been intended to mean that if an employer, on grounds of his or her religion or belief, discriminates against someone on grounds of their sexual orientation this will not amount to unlawful religious discrimination—however, such conduct would amount to unlawful sexual orientation discrimination under the Employment Equality (Sexual Orientation) Regulations 2003 unless one of the permitted exceptions applies. However, it can be very difficult to separate what is motivated by A's religion or belief and what is caused by B's religion or belief. The Employment Equality Directive makes no mention of any particular need to consider the position of the perpetrator, so it may be that this provision is contrary to the Directive.

---

[95] Employment Equality (Religion or Belief) Regulations 2003, reg 3(2).
[96] *Explanatory Notes to Equality Act 2006*, para 173.
[97] *Hansard* HL Debates, cols 1118–1119 (13 July 2005).

(5) Northern Ireland

In Northern Ireland, the Fair Employment Acts of 1976 and 1989[98] prohibit discrimination on grounds of religious belief. This legislation has provided an essential context for the development of the peace process. The Fair Employment Acts have now been replaced by the Fair Employment and Treatment (Northern Ireland) Order 1998.[99] However, this legislation is subject to a special limiting defence.   **9.123**

(6) The essential nature defence in Northern Ireland

By Article 70(3) of the 1998 Order, the employment provisions of that legislation do not apply: **9.124**

> . . . to or in relation to any employment or occupation where the essential nature of the job requires it to be done by a person holding, or not holding, a particular religious belief.

The essential nature defence was to be found in the previous Fair Employment Acts, and was the subject of guidance under the old Fair Employment Code of Practice issued by the Fair Employment Commission. The relevant part of the guidance said: **9.125**

> 7.2.2 If you are an employer who is considering recruiting for such a job then you should ensure that its essential nature is such that it must be done by someone of a particular religious belief, or none. It would be difficult to argue, for example, that the essential nature of cooking or gardening would require either the cook or the gardener to hold a particular religious belief even if that cooking or gardening was being done for the members of the particular religious group or church body. But when the cook or gardener had other duties of a religious or evangelising nature associated with their cooking or gardening functions—such as inducting members of a home hostel or community into a particular set of religious values—then you could reasonably claim that the essential nature of that particular job required to be done by someone of a specific religious belief.

It is plain that this guidance worked well, since neither the Fair Employment Commission nor its successor the Northern Ireland Equalities Commission[100] has been involved to date in litigation in relation to its scope, notwithstanding the fact that religious discrimination is more of an issue in Northern Ireland than anywhere else in the UK. This is the more remarkable since the Code came into effect on 31 December 1989.   **9.126**

---

[98] For a useful guide to these Acts, see C McCrudden (ed), *Fair Employment Handbook* (London: Industrial Relations Services, Eclipse Publications, 1991).

[99] SI 1998/3162 (NI 21).

[100] The successor body to the Fair Employment Commission.

(7) Exemption against protection for Northern Ireland teachers

9.127 The legislation also does not apply to teachers who, under the Northern Ireland legislation, cannot complain at all on grounds of religious discrimination.[101] It seems unlikely that in the long run a blanket exemption for teachers of the kind described above can survive. It may be asked: 'How can it meet the Article 9(2) tests?' Any answer to this question must lie in the special situation in Northern Ireland, which has been recognised more than once in the context of human rights.[102]

9.128 Indeed the Employment Equality Directive states at Recital 35:

> The need to promote peace and reconciliation between the major communities in Northern Ireland [which] necessitates the incorporation of particular provisions into this Directive.

9.129 It then specifically deals with employment as a teacher:[103]

> In order to maintain a balance of opportunity in employment for teachers in Northern Ireland while furthering the reconciliation of historical divisions between the major religious communities there, the provisions on religion or belief in this Directive shall not apply to the recruitment of teachers in schools in Northern Ireland in so far as this is expressly authorised by national legislation.

9.130 The plain aim of this provision is reconciliation, which is clearly a legitimate lever and necessary aim in Northern Ireland; but it must be asked whether it is achieved in this way. By now some objective evidence of the merits and effectiveness of this approach might be thought to be evident. More specifically, it must be expected that ultimately this provision, like all such derogations, will need to be removed.[104] In the field of policing the Employment Equality Directive creates a more obviously justified exemption:[105]

> In order to tackle the under-representation of one of the major religious communities in the police service in Northern Ireland, differences in treatment regarding recruitment into that service, including support staff, shall not constitute discrimination insofar as those differences in treatment are expressly authorised by national legislation.

---

[101] See Art 71 of the 1998 Order. This exclusion has been subject to a number of reviews but it has always been maintained.

[102] See, eg, the two Derogations (1988 and 1989) from the Convention set out in Sch 3 to the HRA 1998.

[103] See Art 18(2) of the Council Directive establishing a General Framework for Equal Treatment in Employment and Occupation.

[104] See J Cooper, 'Applying Equality and Non-Discrimination Rights', in G Moon (ed), *Race Discrimination Developing and Using a New Legal Framework* (Oxford: Hart Publishing, 2000), at 57 *et passim* for a discussion of the need to limit such action in time.

[105] See Art 18(1) of the Council Directive establishing a General Framework for Equal Treatment in Employment and Occupation; see also *Independent Commission on Policing for Northern Ireland*, September 1999.

The Northern Ireland Police Service now recruits one Catholic for each non- **9.131**
Catholic pursuant to the time-limited provisions of the Northern Ireland
(Policing) Act 1998.

Ultimately these exceptions will need to be reviewed against the jurisprudence of **9.132**
Article 9 and Article 14 ECHR (see Chapters 9 and 14).

There will continue to be cases where racial and religion discrimination co-exist. **9.133**
For instance, a Muslim might complain of Islamophobia, perhaps because of complaints about his wearing a beard or her wearing the shalwar kameez at work.
A dress code rule which in practice prohibits either of these might well be indirectly discriminatory against Asian employees. If it is a case of indirect discrimination the key question will be whether this practice is justified. In such a case it will
be possible to point to Article 9 ECHR and argue that it is not open to the employer
to justify on grounds which affect the religious rights of the individual. Indeed
even if the workplace was a Catholic school, it would probably not be permissible
for the school to seek to justify the exclusion of a Muslim employee simply because
she had manifested her religion in her clothing, or of the man for his decision not
to shave. In such a case it will be necessary to consider how Article 9(2) applies.

I. Conflicts

The 2000 Employment Equality Directive, which includes prohibitions on dis- **9.134**
crimination on grounds both of sexual orientation and religion or belief, anticipated that conflicts might arise. It dealt with this by permitting certain genuine
and determining requirements to overcome the rights in the Directive. Thus the
definition of discrimination in the Directive is subject to an exclusion set out in
Article 4, which provides that what would otherwise be discrimination for the
purposes of the Directive shall not be treated as such where:

> . . . by reason of the nature of the particular occupational activities concerned or the
> context in which they are carried out, such a characteristic[106] constitutes a genuine
> and determining occupational requirement, provided that the objective is legitimate
> and the requirement is proportionate.

(1) Conflicts between the protection from sexual orientation discrimination and Article 9

It now appears that the proposed protection for persons of a particular sexual **9.135**
orientation is seen by some groups as coming into conflict with the protection

---

106 That is, a particular sexual orientation, religion, disability, or age.

against discrimination on grounds of religion and, indeed, Article 9 of the Convention.

9.136 In 2000, the Christian Institute published a pamphlet entitled 'Ditch the Directive' which took a particularly strident approach to this issue. The authors of this pamphlet appear to think that the Directive would adversely affect the existing UK legislation. (See 9.78 above for discussion of section 60 of the School Standards and Framework Act 1998.) The pamphlet sets out a whole raft of concerns, including suggestions that a Roman Catholic school might wish to employ only Roman Catholics for religious education and might be acting unlawfully if 'it refused to employ non Roman Catholics, neo Nazis, atheists, communists, Seventh Day Adventists or practising homosexuals'.

9.137 A public authority may interfere with the rights guaranteeing respect for private life and for freedom of religion, provided such interference is 'prescribed by law' and 'necessary in a democratic society' for one of the aims set out in Article 8(2) or Article 9(2). Those aims include 'the rights and freedoms of others', and may include people's right to found and run religious associations reflecting and propagating their beliefs.

9.138 Some such bodies will be public authorities, particularly bodies carrying out educational functions, and in particular in countries where church and state institutions are not clearly separated. Accordingly, dismissing a person from employment with such a body on the ground of religion or sexual orientation may amount to an interference with his or her right to freedom of religion or right to respect for private life, and such interference needs to be justified. Where restrictions on the right to respect for private life concern 'a most intimate part of an individual's private life'—such as sexual orientation—only 'particularly convincing and weighty reasons' can provide such justification (*Smith & Grady v United Kingdom*[107]).

9.139 Any justification must be considered in the context of a 'democratic society', which is one characterised by 'pluralism, tolerance and broadmindedness'.[108] Justification must be assessed by reference to the particular circumstances of the person dismissed.

9.140 Blanket exclusions are most unlikely to be justified under Article 9 ECHR. Provisions which remove consideration of the merits of an alleged violation from the jurisdiction of a national authority would violate Article 13 ECHR. This provision requires that there must be an effective remedy allowing the competent

---

[107] (2000) 29 EHRR 493, para 94.
[108] Ibid, para 87.

national authority both to deal with the substance of the relevant Convention complaint and to grant appropriate relief.[109]

So a rule which banned all homosexuals from appointment in religious schools, either automatically, or at the option of the school, would not be consistent with Convention law. Any blanket exclusion of the kind proposed by the Christian Institute would have such effects and would inevitably lead in due course to a challenge in the ECtHR and (if it were rooted in the text of the proposed Directive) to an inevitable conflict between Community and Convention law or (if it were only in the domestic legislation) a conflict between domestic and Convention law. **9.141**

This approach would satisfy the requirements of both Articles 8 and 13 of the Convention since a balance has to be struck after consideration of the facts. Plainly, if a neo-Nazi or Communist sought to indoctrinate pupils at a school with his or her ideology the balance would be struck in a way which would lead to his or her dismissal. Likewise, if a head teacher at a Catholic school became a Muslim, the school would be able under the Employment Equality Directive (as it would under the current s 60 of the School Standards and Framework Act 1998) and under Convention law, to conclude that the balance was to be struck in favour of dismissal. In the context of the essential nature test in the Northern Ireland legislation it would no doubt be said that it was essential that the pastoral care of the school was in the hands of a Catholic. **9.142**

(2) Conflicts between the protection from sex discrimination and Article 9

One example of how Article 9 collective rights might come into conflict with other rights can be seen from the facts of a case that was decided before the HRA 1998 came into force. The case was *O'Neill v Governors of St Thomas More School*[110] where a Roman Catholic school dismissed an unmarried teacher who was pregnant by a priest on grounds that her position as a teacher of religious education was untenable. The school was found to have breached the Sex Discrimination Act 1975 and had to pay her compensation. This kind of conflict between the collective rights of persons manifesting a religion and belief, and others seeking to assert individual employment rights, creates a real problem for tribunals. **9.143**

(3) Conflicts between the protection from race discrimination and Article 9

It is not uncommon for a religious community such as a school to advertise for workers and to stipulate a requirement or condition that the worker be a member **9.144**

---

109 Ibid, para 135.
110 [1997] ICR 33.

of the same religion. Suppose it is a Christian community which has placed such an advertisement, it would certainly indirectly discriminate against Jews or Sikhs. So it will potentially be in breach of the Race Relations Act 1976, unless justified.

9.145 If it were a Jewish community, or a Sikh community, it might directly discriminate on grounds of race against non-Jews, or Sikhs. In that case, unless the school could show that the requirement was a genuine occupational qualification (see s 5 of the Race Relations Act 1976), it would not have a defence under the 1976 Act. This is because the Act does not permit an act of direct race discrimination to be justified.

9.146 However, if the case was argued as one of indirect discrimination, a further problem arises. Indirect discrimination can be justified, but the justification must be irrespective of the racial group of the person concerned (see the Race Relations Act 1976, s 1(1)(b)(ii)). If the justification for the requirement or condition is connected with the racial group who can comply with the requirement, it is tainted. So under the Race Relations Act 1976 it would not be possible to justify the decision.

9.147 Paradoxically this would not be the case if the school was a Christian organisation. Since under UK law persons might be Jewish or Sikh by race but Christian by religion (but not race), it would be possible to have a permissible justification solely concerned with the fact that the person was not a Christian.

9.148 This sort of problem will affect schools, housing associations, old people's homes, and other similar organisations. If proceedings are brought against the institution it will affect their rights under Article 9 (and possibly Article 14) ECHR. This is where the difficulty arises. The Race Relations Act 1976 will not permit such a justification. To this extent the 1976 Act may well be in breach of the HRA 1998 and the ECHR. These problems become even more complicated when the prohibitions on religious discrimination (see 9.108) are taken into account.

J. Frequently asked questions

9.149 **Does Article 9 grant absolute or qualified rights?**

The right to freedom of thought, conscience, and religion is absolute. This right is granted both to individuals and to those who are in community with others (ie it is a collective as well as an individual right). However, Article 9 also provides for a qualified right to manifest one's religion or belief in worship, teaching, practice, or observation.

How has the ECtHR defined 'religion' and 'belief'?

There is no closed list of religions or beliefs covered by Article 9. All the main world religions are within its scope, as are a number of less well known or established religions or beliefs such as the Krishna Consciousness movement, the Divine Light Centrum, the Church of Scientology, Druids, the Moon Sect, pacifism, and veganism. Article 9 also protects those who do not believe, and those who hold unconventional beliefs. However, there are limits to its scope: the religion or belief relied upon must have a serious ideology, with some cogency and cohesion.

What is a 'manifestation' of religion or belief?

This is a difficult question, to which the courts have provided no easy answer. Some guidance is provided in the wording of Article 9 itself, which refers to worship, teaching, practice, and observance. The ECtHR has drawn a distinction between actions that are motivated by a religion and belief and those that express the religion or belief. In considering whether something amounts to a manifestation of the religion or belief, it therefore asks whether the action is a 'necessary expression' of, or is required by the religion or belief.

Will Article 9 be engaged where the believer is able to continue to manifest his/her beliefs by, for example, moving workplaces?

Whilst this issue may seem to practitioners to be more one of justification, there is a line of authority to the effect that, in this situation, Article 9 may not be engaged at all as the individual has the option to avoid interference with his Article 9 rights by changing his job. The position under UK law is unclear following Copsey v WWB Devon Clays Ltd *(CA), where one judge felt that ECtHR authority required him to conclude that Article 9 was not engaged, and another was of the view that Article 9 was engaged in a case where terms of employment were altered post-contract to require the employee to work on Sundays. The issue has not gone to the House of Lords, probably because the Court of Appeal in* Copsey *considered that, had Article 9 been engaged, any interference would have been justified.*

When will interference with an individual's right to manifest his or her religion or belief be justified?

The justification provisions are the same as those set out, for example, in Articles 8 and 10. Interference will only be justified in accordance with limitations prescribed by law and necessary in a democratic society for the reasons set out in Article 9(2).

How will Article 9 affect decisions to dismiss individuals on grounds of manifestation of their religion or belief?

Practitioners are referred to Chapter 8 (at 8.41 for example) for a full consideration of the test to be applied where public authorities dismiss employees in contravention of their Convention rights. In cases involving private employees, the tribunal will have to follow the test laid down in Copsey v WWB Devon Clays Ltd. *The particular nature of the workplace will be relevant: for example:*

- *if an individual chooses to join the army, he or she will be considered to have accepted the strictures required by military life;*
- *there are specific provisions permitting faith schools to have regard to any conduct on a teacher's part which is incompatible with the precepts, or with the upholding of the tenets, of the relevant religion in connection with the termination of that teacher's employment. These provisions are designed to protect the collective rights of the school under Article 9, but may conflict with the rights of the individual, for example, where the relevant conduct has no impact on the running of the school.*

What happens where Article 9 rights come into conflict with rights not to be discriminated against on grounds of sexual orientation?

In the case of sexual orientation, where there are some exceptions in the domestic legislation in respect of religious organisations, it will be necessary to balance the Article 9 rights with, for example, the individual's Article 8 right to private and family life. This will require a similar balancing act to that often carried out where rights under Articles 8 and 10 conflict.

What happens where Article 9 rights come into conflict with rights not to be discriminated against on grounds of sex or race?

The position is more complicated in respect of conflicts involving discrimination on grounds of race or sex. Acts of direct race or sex discrimination cannot be justified under the domestic legislation, and acts of indirect race or sex discrimination can be justified only where the justification is irrespective or the sex or racial group of the person concerned. As a result, in many cases a requirement that an employee be of a particular religion, or a dismissal on grounds of particular religious beliefs could amount to a breach of the Sex Discrimination Act 1975 or Race Relations Act 1976. In such circumstances, the absence of any justification provisions may amount to a breach of an individual's, or an organisation's, Article 9 rights under the HRA 1998.

10

ARTICLE 10: FREEDOM OF EXPRESSION

Article 10
Freedom of expression

1. Everyone has the right to freedom of expression. This right shall include freedom to hold opinions and to receive and impart information and ideas without interference by public authority and regardless of frontiers. This Article shall not prevent States from requiring the licensing of broadcasting, television or cinema enterprises.

2. The exercise of these freedoms, since it carries with it duties and responsibilities, may be subject to such formalities, conditions, restrictions or penalties as are prescribed by law and are necessary in a democratic society, in accordance with interests of national security, territorial integrity or public safety, for the prevention of disorder or crime, for the protection of health or morals, for the protection of the reputation or rights of others, for preventing the

disclosure of information received in confidence, or for maintaining the authority and impartiality of the judiciary.

A. Introduction

10.01 The rights in this Article are sometimes considered to be the very backbone of democracy (see *Handyside v UK*[1]) since without freedom of expression there can be no basis for a genuine freedom of any kind.

10.02 This chapter considers the remit and extent of Article 10 ECHR and looks at the ways in which it can be limited, both in accordance with Article 10(2) and as a matter of contract. Freedom of expression always carries with it responsibilities since it is a freedom which can be abused and such abuse can at its worst even imperil democracy. That is why the right to freedom of expression is qualified.

10.03 Those qualifications need to be considered carefully by reference to the principles established in Chapter 2. They are discussed further below in the context of the specific application of Article 10 in the workplace.

10.04 Key areas at work where Article 10 arises are examined, including disciplinary proceedings, whistle-blowing, dress codes, media comment, and industrial disputes.

B. Dialogue: The right to hold, receive and impart

10.05 The main content of rights in Article 10 become clear from a consideration of these three words—'hold', 'receive', and 'impart'. It is not merely a right to hold and express ideas, but also a right to participate in dialogue. In that sense, although connected with, it is yet distinct from Article 9.

10.06 The right to participate in dialogue has consequences which may be very important in the context of employment law. Dialogue is necessarily, to some extent, uncontrolled. It is a simple truth that one participant cannot determine in advance precisely what another may say, and may easily be induced in turn to respond to the other by what the other says.

10.07 So, if one person uses inflammatory or rude language, that may be significant in considering a response of another which is induced by that language. The ECtHR has held that allowance must be made in disciplinary proceedings in respect of offensive language on the grounds that it was uttered in a rapid and

---

[1] (1976) 1 EHRR 737.

spontaneous exchange with a journalist (see *Fuentes Bobo v Spain;*[2] see 10.57). This could be important in the context of shop-floor banter.

However, it should not be assumed that this means that racist or sexist language **10.08** on the shop-floor is permissible (see *Jersild v Denmark*,[3] where restraints on racist language were considered by the Court). The Court's point in *Fuentes* is that the context is important in deciding how to deal with the disciplinary consequences of such language.

The interface between expressing ideas and the workplace was explored in **10.09** *Sidabras & Dziautas v Lithuania*.[4] The applicants had the status of 'former KGB officers' and were therefore subject to the employment restrictions imposed by Article 2 of the Lithuanian Law on the Evaluation of the USSR State Security Committee and the Present Activities of Permanent Employees of the Organization.

Both were dismissed from their posts, as respectively a tax inspector and a lawyer, **10.10** and banned from public-sector and various private-sector jobs from 1999 to 2009. They claimed violations of their Article 10, 8 and 14 rights. The European Court found that the dismissals and employment restrictions did not amount to a restriction on the applicants' ability to express their views or opinions and therefore did not fall within the ambit of Article 10.

The Court compared the facts of this case with three German cases, *Vogt v* **10.11** *Germany*,[5] *Volkmer v Germany*,[6] and *Petersen v Germany*.[7] In these three cases German states imposed restrictions on positions such as teaching posts, which by their nature involved the imparting of ideas and information on a daily basis, and the ECtHR held the cases came within the ambit of Article 10.

In contrast, neither the dismissal of Sidabras and Dziautas from their positions **10.12** as, respectively, a tax inspector and a prosecutor, nor their alleged inability to find employment in line with their academic qualifications were viewed as amounting to a restriction on their ability to express their views or opinions to the same extent as in the above-mentioned cases against Germany.

The contrast shows the importance of the context. The extent to which Article 10 **10.13** is engaged will therefore be decided on a case-specific basis.

---

2 (2001) 31 EHRR 50.
3 (1995) 19 EHRR 1.
4 Applications 55480/00 and 59330/00, 27 July 2004, (2006) 42 EHRR 6.
5 Series A No 323, (26 September 1995), (1996) 21 EHRR 205.
6 Application 39799/98, 22 November 2001.
7 Application 39793/98, ECHR 2001-XII.

C. The necessary conditions for the qualification of Article 10

10.14 There are two explicit conditions for an interference with this right. It must be prescribed by law and be necessary in a democratic society. These conditions are discussed in context below. It is important to emphasise that they are cumulative conditions. That is to say, it is not enough that an interference is in some sense prescribed by law if it is not necessary or is disproportionate.

10.15 An example of how the Court determines interferences with Article 10 occurred where it held that it was not justifiable to bind over protesters for protesting against fox hunting when such behaviour did not amount to a criminal offence. In *Hashman and Jarrup v UK*,[8] the protesters argued that the bind-overs constituted an interference with their Article 10 rights. The Court considered that despite the protest taking the form of impeding the activities of which the hunt saboteurs disapproved, such protest constituted an expression of opinion within the meaning of Article 10.

10.16 It was not accepted that it must have been evident to the applicants what they were being ordered not to do for the period of their binding over. The bind-over did not comply with the requirement of Article 10(2) of the Convention that it be 'prescribed by law'.

10.17 On the other hand, a restriction was found to be justified on the ground of being 'necessary in a democratic society' in *Ahmed v UK*.[9] Here the Court found that the restriction on standing for political office upon local government officers was justified, since the aim pursued by the restrictive Regulations was to ensure that the effectiveness of the system of local political democracy was not diminished through the corrosion of the political neutrality of certain categories of officers.[10]

10.18 Thus whether an interference is proportionate is likely to be a very important question (see *Carter v UK*,[11] regarding proportionate interference). Although an employment contract may directly or indirectly impose a restraint on the exercise of the right to freedom of expression, the penalty for the breach of such restraint will always need to be justified in this context.

---

[8] (2000) 30 EHRR 241.
[9] (2000) 29 EHRR 1.
[10] For an example of the infringement on an Article 10 right going beyond what is necessary in a democratic society, see *Barthold v Germany* (1985) 7 EHRR 383.
[11] Application 36417/97, 29 June 1999.

D. Horizontal effect

Article 10 has a wide horizontal effect. The Court stated in *Fuentes Bobo v Spain*   **10.19**
(see 10.07) that Article 10 is engaged whether or not the relationship between
employer and employee is governed by public or private law.[12]

In *Douglas v Hello! Ltd*,[13] Sedley LJ said[14] that section 12(4) of the HRA 1998   **10.20**
puts:

> . . . beyond question the direct applicability of at least one Article of the Convention
> as between one private party to the litigation and another—in the jargon, its hori-
> zontal effect.

It should be noted, though, that access to the civil service was specifically not   **10.21**
included in the Convention (*Vogt v Germany*;[15] and see 10.11 above).

Since the permitted grounds for a restriction in Article 10(2) have little or no rele-   **10.22**
vance to the relationship of employment, the possible grounds for a restriction on
this right by employers are considerably limited. This will be likely to be important in the context of post-termination restraints on former employees
discussing matters of concern to their former employers. These are discussed
further at 10.32–10.33 below.

E. Positive obligations

Like the other Articles referred to, there may be positive obligations inherent in   **10.23**
the rights to freedom of expression. The reasoning in *Plattform 'Ärzte für das
Leben' v Austria*,[16] that there was an obligation on a state under Article 11 ECHR
to prevent disruption of a demonstration by a hostile mob, would be equally
applicable to Article 10.

Article 10(1) prohibits 'interference by public authority', which itself suggests   **10.24**
that there are positive obligations on the state to take action where the material
threat to an individual's freedom of expression comes from a private source. The
existence of positive obligations on public authorities to protect rights under this

---

[12] See (2001) 31 EHRR 50, at [38]; note the Court referred *mutatis mutandis* to the position
under Article 11 in *Schmidt and Dahlström v Sweden* (1979–80) 1 EHRR 632, para 33.
[13] [2000] 1 QB 967.
[14] At para 133.
[15] (1996) 21 EHRR 205, para 43.
[16] (1991) 13 EHRR 204.

Article was confirmed by the Court in *Fuentes Bobo v Spain*[17] by reference to *Young, James and Webster v UK*.[18]

10.25 Perhaps the most obvious example of the UK taking positive steps to protect freedom of speech is in the Public Interest Disclosure Act 1998, discussed at 10.48–10.49 below. However, the old common law rules that confidence will be protected by the courts, save that there is no confidence that can be protected in relation to an iniquity (see, eg, *British Steel Corporation v Granada Television Ltd*;[19] and also *Initial Services Ltd v Putterill*[20])[21] may be too restrictive to comply with Article 10 ECHR.

F. Disciplinary proceedings and freedom of expression

10.26 Article 10 has important consequences for disciplinary proceedings in relation to the exercise of the right of freedom of expression, and likewise for the approach by an employment tribunal to such proceedings. The positive obligation must necessarily fall on any public authority which under the HRA 1998 has responsibilities to protect Article 10 rights; and accordingly, where a person has been subject to dismissal (or even a lesser disciplinary penalty which falls to be reviewed by a court or tribunal) it will be necessary to determine whether Article 10 rights have been breached.

10.27 In *Veraart v Netherlands*,[22] a lawyer was found guilty of misconduct by a disciplinary appeal tribunal in relation to public comments he had made questioning the standing of a therapist. He was issued with a warning. The ECtHR held that the tribunal had failed to carry out an acceptable assessment of the relevant facts enabling it to give an informed decision as to whether the applicant had overstepped the limits of acceptable professional behaviour. As it was, the tribunal's decision was based on an inadequate assessment of the facts and the reasons provided therefore lacked relevance. Accordingly, the imposition of a sanction by the tribunal amounted to a violation of Article 10. This case has important implications for disciplinary hearings and tribunals which criticise comments made by individuals.

---

[17] At para 33.
[18] (1982) 4 EHRR 38, para 55.
[19] [1981] 1 AC 1096.
[20] [1968] 1 QB 396, 405B *et seq*, 408G.
[21] For a further consideration of the principles in relation to confidentiality, see the Law Commission's Report *Breach of Confidence* (Law Com No 110, 1981); and see also, Y Cripps, *The Legal Implications of Disclosure in the Public Interest* (2nd edn, London: Sweet and Maxwell, 1994).
[22] Application 10807/04, (2006) ECHR 1018.

G. Contractual limitations on the exercise of freedom of expression

There are many examples of contracts of employment containing limits on one   **10.28**
party's freedom of expression. It is not to be assumed that such restrictions are
automatically unlawful. It may well be that they are consistent with Article 10(2).

(1) In what circumstances can rights be limited?

The precise content of the positive obligation is still in need of elaboration.   **10.29**
However, the Commission has stated that an individual may contract to limit his
expression rights and that the enforcement of the agreed restriction will not
amount to an interference with his rights under Article 10(1) (*Vereniging
Rechtswinkels Utrecht v Netherlands*[23]).

In another decision the Commission noted the positive duty on a state to take   **10.30**
steps to ensure that the exercise of an employee's freedom of expression should
not be subject to restrictions 'which would strike at the very substance of this
freedom'.[24] Here a doctor employed in a Catholic hospital was dismissed after
writing a letter about abortion. The Commission found that his contractual duty
of loyalty towards the Catholic Church did not mean that he had waived his right
to freedom of expression. (See, also, *Knudsen v Norway*,[25] for the impact of Article 9
on a church employee dismissed when he refused to change his views.)

(2) Waiver of rights and the HRA 1998

In principle there is no reason why an employer and his employee could not   **10.31**
decide to agree on a limitation of freedom of expression provided there was no
improper coercion of either party and the restriction did not interfere with other
legal obligations. For example, an employee of a gunsmith might agree not to
criticise the use of guns, without violating of the Convention. In the authors'
view, to establish that a waiver does not breach the Act, an employer must show
that such waiver is made in full awareness of the right, without compulsion, and
in full and unequivocal terms.

It remains to be seen what the effect will be on post-termination restraints on   **10.32**
freedom of expression. What is clear is that if a public authority employer dismissed his workforce and re-employed them on contracts which included waiver

---

[23] Application 11308/84, (1986) 46 DR 200.
[24] *Rommelfanger v Germany* (1989) 62 DR 151, at 161.
[25] (1985) 42 DR 247, at 258.

of Convention rights, an application could be brought by the workers under section 6 of the HRA 1998.

10.33 Clearly the competing legal obligation of disclosure will have to be weighed against the restrictions agreed by contract and is likely in almost all cases to displace them.

(3) Article 10 and restrictive covenants

10.34 The key question here is whether the action prohibited by the restrictive covenant is in accordance with the strict terms of the derogation pursuant to Article 10(2). In *Jacubowski v Germany*,[26] a news agency editor, after being dismissed, sent articles criticising his old employers to other journalists. When an injunction was issued forcing him to desist from the mailings, he complained that his right to freedom of expression under Article 10 ECHR had been breached. The Commission agreed, but the ECtHR came to a different conclusion. The interference was prescribed by law and pursued a legitimate aim under the Convention: 'the protection of the reputation or rights of others.'

10.35 It was necessary to ask whether the interference was necessary in a democratic society. The Court found that the margin of appreciation given to contracting states in assessing the degree of interference necessary was especially important in the commercial context of unfair competition. The Court confined its considerations to the question of whether the measures taken at national level were justifiable in principle and proportionate. In this case, the key feature of the circular was the competitive purpose of the exercise rather than the need for the applicant to defend himself against personal attacks in the press. Since all the injunction did was to prohibit distribution of the applicant's complaining circular, he remained at liberty to voice his opinions about his former employers through other means. Hence the interference with his Convention right was found (by a majority of 6:3) not to be disproportionate.

10.36 The dissenting opinion stated that exceptions to the principle of freedom of expression must be interpreted narrowly, and that it was crucial that the margin of appreciation remained subject to an effective European supervision.

10.37 When considering if a restrictive interference is justified, consideration must be given to the employer's legitimate aims, such as preventing disclosure of confidential information. The factors which go to determining whether the silencing is necessary in a democratic society will include the reasons for the employee's expression, the forum and method of the expression, its consequences, and its intended audience.

---

[26] (1995) 19 EHRR 64.

However it must be remembered that a Court considering such a question now **10.38**
will consider section 12 of the HRA 1998 to be relevant (see 10.61 onwards).
This may make it more difficult to get ex parte injunctive relief. For further
consideration of restrictive covenants, see 12.55–12.56.

(4) Scrutiny of contractual limits

An agreed limitation between employer and employee on the freedom of expres- **10.39**
sion is not, however, beyond scrutiny and is not itself without limits. It has even
been emphasised that the rights under Article 10 ECHR do not stop at the gates
of army barracks (*Grigoriades v Greece*[27]).

Perhaps the best known case in which the Court emphasised the need for a **10.40**
proper scrutiny is *Vogt v Germany*.[28] Here the applicant maintained that her dismissal from the German civil service on account of her political activities as a
member of the German Communist Party had infringed her right to freedom of
expression secured under Article 10 ECHR. The Court held that dismissal of
teachers for holding Communist beliefs was a breach of Article 10 (see, further,
Chapter 9 at 9.93–9.97). However, generally the Court has been reluctant to
interfere in this arena.

H. Tests for employment in the public sector

In two cases which concerned Article 10 (*Glasenapp v Germany*[29] and *Kosiek v* **10.41**
Germany[30]) the Court decided that 'tests' for holding public office concerned
with freedom of expression, if independent of the function of the job, are not
violations. In both instances, the Court treated such cases as claims for rights to
the office, a right not protected by the Convention. In *Glasenapp v Germany* the
Court ruled[31] that:

> . . . access to the Civil Service lies at the heart of the issue submitted to the Court.
> In refusing Mrs Glasenapp such access, the *Land* authority took account of her
> opinions and attitude merely in order to satisfy itself as to whether she possessed one
> of the necessary personal qualifications for the post in question. That being so, there
> has been no interference with the exercise of the right protected under paragraph 1
> of Article 10.

---

[27] (1997) 27 EHRR 464, at para 45.
[28] (1996) 21 EHRR 205.
[29] (1987) 9 EHRR 25.
[30] (1987) 9 EHRR 328.
[31] At para 53.

I. Freedom of expression in relation to health and safety at work

10.42 Just as the government may be under a positive duty under Article 8 ECHR in relation to disclosure of public health matters (as in *Lopez Ostra v Spain*[32]), so there may be a corresponding positive duty to ensure that there is freedom of expression in relation to such matters in and from the workplace.[33] (See also ERA 1996, ss 44 and 100.)

J. Freedom of expression and dress codes

10.43 Dress codes can be considered under Article 8 (where clothes are deemed to express one's personal autonomy, see 8.158–8.162), Article 9 (where clothes are pivotal to religious expression, see 9.40–9.48 and 9.133), and Article 10 (where clothes are a means of expressing beliefs by dressing in a particular way). While relevant to challenging dress codes, Article 10 does not appear to have been widely used in this way. Dress codes that differentiate on the basis of the sex of an employee and which cannot be justified by the employer can be challenged under the Sex Discrimination Act 1975 and may give rise to issues in relation to Article 14.[34]

10.44 That an outfit is simply 'fashionable' will not be enough to engage with Article 10. However, the imposition of a dress code by a public authority may constitute a violation of Article 10 ECHR if an employee can maintain that his appearance amounts to the expression of an 'idea or opinion', for example, in *Stevens v UK*.[35] Stevens complained that her children's school uniform prevented them from expressing themselves as they wished through their dress. The Commission found that although the right to freedom of expression may include the right for a person to express his ideas through the way he dresses, it had not been established on the facts of the case that the applicant's children had been prevented from expressing a particular opinion or idea by means of their clothing. Further, any

---

[32] (1995) 20 EHRR 277.

[33] For a comprehensive review of the law before the Public Interest Disclosure Act 1998 came into force, see Cripps, n 21, ch 11.

[34] In the employment tribunal case of *Moran v RBR International Ltd* ET Case No 2302546/00 the Tribunal considered whether Arts 10 and 14 were engaged when applying the Sex Discrimination Act 1975. It found that the employer, by prohibiting a female worker from wearing trousers, had unduly interfered with her freedom of expression under Article 10. The tribunal also ruled that since the restriction was a response to conventional differences between the sexes rather than any commercial need for the dress code, there was also a breach of Article 14. The case was not appealed.

[35] (1986) 46 DR 245.

rules regarding clothing affected the children only during their attendance at school, and they remained at liberty to express themselves as they wished outside. No violation of Article 10 had been demonstrated.

The DFES is currently consulting on new guidance for teachers regarding the **10.45** HRA 1998 and school uniform.[36] The suggested guidance provides:

> The Human Rights Act 1998 protects the right to 'manifest one's religion or beliefs'.
>
> Various religions require their adherents to conform to a particular dress code, or to otherwise outwardly manifest their belief. Some religions require adherents to wear or carry specific religious artefacts, others may hold a belief that they should not cut their hair, and a number of religions require their followers to dress modestly, for example, by wearing loose fitting clothing, or covering their head.
>
> It may be possible for many religious requirements to be met within a school uniform policy and schools should act reasonably in accommodating religious requirements.
>
> However, schools should note that the freedom to manifest a religion or belief does not mean that an individual has the right to manifest their religion at any time, in any place, or in any particular manner. A pupil might have the opportunity to attend a school whose uniform policy can accommodate his or her requirements: this will ensure that his/her religious beliefs are catered for even though the school may not be the one preferred for other reasons. Even if an alternative school is not available, a school uniform policy that restricts the freedom of pupils to manifest their religion may still be lawful, so long as this interference with pupils' rights is justified on grounds specified in the Human Rights Act. These include health, safety and the protection of the rights and freedoms of others. This has been confirmed in two recent court cases.[37]
>
> In fulfilling their obligations, schools may have to balance the rights of individual pupils against the best interests of the school community as a whole. Where schools have good reasons for restricting an individual's freedoms, for example, to ensure the effective delivery of teaching and learning, the promotion of cohesion and good order in a school, the prevention of bullying, or genuine health and safety or security considerations, then the restriction of an individual's rights to manifest their religion may be justified.

(Of course school uniforms which discriminate without justification against girls or boys may be deemed contrary to the Sex Discrimination Act 1975 in any case.) Employees may argue rights have been infringed by relying on both Articles 8 and 10 ECHR.

---

[36] http://www.dfes.gov.uk/consultations/conSection.cfm?consultationId=1468&dId=776&sId=4511&numbering=1&itemNumber=1

[37] *R (on the application of Begum) v Denbigh High School* [2006] UKHL 15 and *R (on the application of X) v Y School* [2007] EWHC 298 (Admin).

10.46   The lawfulness of a school dress code which did not allow for traditional Muslim dress was considered by the House of Lords in *Regina (SB) v Governors of Denbigh High School*[38] (see also 9.40–9.43).

10.47   Although the case was brought as an Article 9 challenge it could arguably also have been brought under Article 10. The ratio is relevant to both Convention rights and likely to apply to dress codes in the workplace as well as schools. Their Lordships held that a refusal to allow a pupil to attend school unless she wore the prescribed school uniform and not the jilbab did not amount to an interference with the pupil's right to manifest her religion since alternative educational facilities were available. The decision is in line with early ECHR cases where the court has not been prepared to find an interference with the right to manifest religious belief in practice or observance where a person has voluntarily accepted an employment or role which does not accommodate that practice or observance, and there are other means open to the person to practice or observe his or her religion without undue hardship or inconvenience (see *X v Denmark*[39] and *Kjeldsen, Busk Madsen and Pedersen v Denmark*[40])

K.   Public Interest Disclosure Act 1998

10.48   The Public Interest Disclosure Act 1998 (PIDA 1998) provides some protection to 'whistle-blowers' who disclose material wrong-doing by their employers. This Act is clearly designed as a positive intervention in a field in which expression of an opinion or disclosure of knowledge can have very dire consequences for an employee. The importance of protection was recently emphasised by the Court of Appeal when interpreting the legislation so as to protect employees from victimisation after dismissal. see *Woodword v Abbey National plc.* Case law from the Court can be relied on to ensure that the Act gives the necessary protection envisaged by Article 10, although it has been argued that the extent of the protection is not great.[41] Its provisions have been incorporated into Part IVA of the ERA 1996.

10.49   The Court has touched on the arena of public disclosures in cases such as *Gridgoriades* and *Rommelfanger* (see above 10.30, 10.39). In *Brown v UK*,[42] the claimant who was severely reprimanded for talking to the media about safety concerns at

---

[38] [2006] UKHL 15, [2007] 1 AC 100.
[39] (1976) 5 DR 157, 1 EHRR 711.
[40] Applications 5095/71, 5920/72 and 5926/72, (1976) 1 EHRR 711.
[41] See L Vickers, 'Whistleblowing in the public sector and the ECHR' [1997] PL 594; J Bowers and J Lewis, 'Whistleblowing: Freedom of Expression in the Workplace' [1996] EHRLR 637.
[42] Application 10293/83 (decision 12 December 1985).

Aldermaston, had his claim before the Commission declared inadmissible because the sanction was justified as protecting the rights of his employer and it was proportionate pursuant to Article 10(2). The key issue when determining whether whistle-blowing in the public sector can legitimately be qualified is whether the sanction is proportionate. Article 10 remains an important weapon for those working in sectors excluded by PIDA 1998 such as the army or the police.[43] A claim brought by workers in these sectors could lead to an extension of the protected categories of complainants within the legislation.

(1) Competing public interests

In some jobs there may be implied a restriction on the way in which freedom of expression is to be exercised because of competing public interests. In *Schopfer v Switzerland*,[44] the Court rejected a complaint by a barrister in relation to disciplinary proceedings brought against him for holding a press conference in which he made a number of highly critical remarks about the 'flagrant' disregard of the law. In particular he stated that he was speaking to the press because he had no other redress. In fact this was not correct.   **10.50**

The Court held that since lawyers held a central position in the administration of justice, restrictions on the conduct of members of the Bar might be justified (see also *Casado Coca v Spain*[45]). The Court recognised that lawyers had rights under Article 10 ECHR, but emphasised that there was a need to strike a balance between the interests involved, which included not only those of the applicant but also the need to maintain public confidence in the administration of justice. Here the Court ruled that the criticism could best be judged by the national authorities. Thus, the result in the end turned on the margin of appreciation (see 2.18 above as to the relevance of this doctrine to domestic courts and tribunals). In a domestic forum a court or tribunal might find a breach on slightly different facts.   **10.51**

It is easy to see that this approach might be applied to other employments where the right to freedom of expression has to be balanced against the effect that an intemperate use of that right might have on other important interests.   **10.52**

An example of this occurred in a 2004 case where a probation officer working predominantly with sex offenders argued his right to freedom of expression under Article 10 was engaged where he was dismissed after his employers discovered   **10.53**

---

[43] See further the website of the organisation Public Concern at Work (PCaW) at <http://www.pcaw.co.uk>.

[44] [1998] EHRLR 646.

[45] (1994) 18 EHRR 1, at para 54.

that he was involved in activities including the merchandising of products connected with bondage, domination, and sadomasochism and that he performed shows in hedonist and fetish clubs: *Pay v Lancashire Probation Service*.[46] Mr Pay complained that his dismissal was unfair in that it entailed an infringement of the HRA 1998 and in particular his Article 8 and Article 10 rights. The EAT found the tribunal was also entitled to find that, whilst the right to freedom of expression under Article 10 was engaged, balancing the competing interests of the employers' concern to protect their reputation and maintain public confidence as required by Article 10(2) with the applicant's right to freedom of expression, there was no unjustified interference with that right. Dismissal was a proportionate response given the indication that the applicant would not curtail his activities and that alternative employment was not a viable option.

L. Freedom of expression and industrial disputes

10.54   Another way in which Article 10 ECHR might be very relevant is in the context of industrial disputes. The Court has consistently protected the rights of journalists to report on issues of topical interest and importance (see *Jersild v Denmark*[47]). Sometimes that may involve information about what happens in the workplace.

10.55   In *Fressoz and Roire v France*,[48] the Court was concerned with the prosecution of two journalists from *Canard Enchaine*, a Parisian investigative magazine, who published information culled from the tax returns of the chairman of the Peugeot car company about his pay increases at a time when he was opposing such increases for his workers. The Court held that it was disproportionate to prosecute the journalists for publishing information which in itself was not confidential, and that there had been a breach of Article 10. It is important to note that the Court rejected the argument by France that the information was not a matter of general interest. Moreover, it held that the public had a right to receive this information.[49]

10.56   While in the UK information about directors' pay is readily available in annual reports, it is worth noting that this approach might apply to other information that is less readily available but which is equally relevant.

10.57   In *Fuentes Bobo v Spain*,[50] the ECtHR was concerned with disciplinary proceedings against a television producer who was in dispute with his employers, the state

---

46 [2004] 1 ICR 187.
47 (1995) 19 EHRR 1.
48 [1999] EHRLR 339.
49 At para 51.
50 (2001) 31 EHRR 50.

television company. He was first dismissed in relation to industrial action aimed at the directors of the company. However, the dismissal was revoked by the courts. Thereafter he was interviewed on radio, where he said that the managers were 'leeches' and that they 'shitted on' the workers.[51] This time the domestic courts upheld the dismissal. However, the Court disagreed, holding that while such offensive language certainly merited disciplinary action, dismissal was disproportionate.[52] It may well be that the Court was affected by the very poor treatment that Mr Bobo had received from the company. It was certainly affected by the fact that the remarks were relatively spontaneous and occurred during an unscripted conversation with a journalist.

M. Conflicts between Article 10 and Article 8

These two Articles frequently come into conflict, especially when newspapers **10.58** and journalists wish to exercise their rights to freedom of expression. In the workplace such conflict is possible but less likely than in the media, but see *H v N*.[53]

Douglas and others v Hello! Ltd and others (No.3)[54] was a breach of confidence **10.59** claim. Whilst it did not originate in the employment arena, the Article 10(2) principle it is concerned with, will apply across the board to include, for example, employees breaching confidentiality. The Court treated the parties' Article 8 and Article 10 rights as absorbed into an action for breach of confidence (which was held to extend to the protection of private or personal information) and confirmed that the correct test for whether information was private or not was whether the party seeking to disclose it knew or ought to have known that the owner of that information had a reasonable expectation that the information would remain private. This is the test set out in *Campbell v Mirror Group Newspapers Ltd*.[55] The court considered that the 'law of confidence' is sufficiently certain in UK law such that the restriction imposed on the newspaper groups' freedom of expression was compliant with the substantive safeguards of Article 10(2).

There are various cases involving former employees seeking to disclose informa- **10.60** tion gained as a direct consequence of their employment, where the courts are seen to balance the right to freedom of expression against the right to privacy.

---

[51] At para 25.
[52] At paras 49 and 50.
[53] [2002] EWCA 195.
[54] [2006] 1 QB 125.
[55] [2004] UKHL 22, [2004] 2 AC 457.

Thus in *Lady Archer v Williams*[56] the court was prepared to grant an injunction on the grounds that there was no overriding public interest in the disclosure of sensitive personal information about Lady Archer, so Williams' right to freedom of expression could not supersede Lady Archer's rights to respect for her private and family life. In *HRH Prince of Wales v Associated Newspapers Ltd*[57] it was held that the disclosure of private journals was not necessary in a democratic society for the protection of the rights and freedoms of others such that the applicant's right to confidentiality should be overridden. The decision of the High Court has recently been upheld by the Court of Appeal.[58]

N. Constraints on court action to limit freedom of expression

10.61 Section 12 of the HRA 1998 applies if a court[59] is 'considering whether to grant any relief which, if granted, might affect the exercise of the Convention right to freedom of expression', so as to restrain the use of the court's powers.

10.62 The Act imposes one procedural and three substantive safeguards on the right to freedom of expression. Their particular significance in the workplace may be that they will affect the way in which applications are made for preliminary relief in relation to restrictive covenants in respect of matters such as confidentiality or discussions with third parties. In any such case, it will be important for practitioners to ensure that they have considered and complied with section 12.

(1) Procedural safeguard

10.63 The procedural protection is that no relief is to be granted unless the person against whom the application for relief is made is present (see s 12(2)). Exceptionally, relief may be granted in the absence of the relevant party where the court 'is satisfied . . . that the applicant has taken all practicable steps to notify the respondent, or . . . that there are compelling reasons why the respondent should not be notified'.

(2) Substantive safeguards

10.64 The first substantive protection is that 'such relief is [not] to be granted so as to restrain publication before trial unless the court is satisfied that the applicant is

---

56 [2003] EWCA 1670 (QB).
57 [2006] EWHC 522 (Ch).
58 [2006] EWCA Civ 1776, [2007] 2 All ER 139.
59 This includes a tribunal: s 12(5).

likely to establish that publication should not be allowed'.[60] Accordingly, in such a case the practitioner will need to assert that it is likely that one of the specific exceptions to Article 10 ECHR will be established. These are contained in Article 10(2), which provides:

> 2. The exercise of these freedoms, since it carries with it duties and responsibilities, may be subject to such formalities, conditions, restrictions or penalties as are prescribed by law and are necessary in a democratic society, in the interests of national security, territorial integrity or public safety, for the prevention of disorder or crime, for the protection of health or morals, for the protection of the reputation or rights of others, for preventing the disclosure of information received in confidence, or for maintaining the authority and impartiality of the judiciary.

Secondly, section 12(4) requires the court to 'have particular regard to the importance of the Convention right to freedom of expression'. This refers to its central role in the maintenance of democratic freedoms (see 10.01 above).   **10.65**

The third and cumulative substantive safeguard applies 'to material which the respondent claims, or which appears to the court, to be journalistic, literary or artistic material (or to conduct connected with such material)'. In such circumstances the court must have particular regard to '(a) the extent to which . . . (i) the material has, or is about to, become available to the public; or (ii) it is, or would be, in the public interest for the material to be published; [and] (b) any relevant privacy code'.[61]   **10.66**

In *AG v Blake*,[62] the House of Lords decided that the ex-spy George Blake must account to Her Majesty's Government for the profits on his 1989 autobiography, thus preventing him from profiting from his freedom of expression. While this does not inhibit his free expression, rather it prevented him profiting from it. Blake had signed the Official Secrets Act and was now seeking to obtain a profit from 'the very thing' he contracted not to do. Post publication it was too late to prevent the disclosure of once confidential information and despite this being an exceptional remedy, in these circumstances it was just to grant an account of profits in response to the defendant's breach of contract in publishing his autobiography in flagrant disregard of the express undertaking he had given on joining the Secret Intelligence Service not to divulge any official information in book form, either during or after his service.   **10.67**

Section 12 of the HRA 1998 was considered in *HM Attorney-General v MGN Ltd*.[63] The claimant was seeking an interim injunction to prevent the defendant   **10.68**

---

[60] See s 12(3).
[61] See s 12(4).
[62] [2001] IRLR 36.
[63] [2002] EWHC 3201 (Ch).

from publishing further material obtained from a former employee of the royal household who had signed an undertaking of confidentiality. The Court stated that the correct test in section 12(3) of the HRA 1998 on an application to restrain publication prior to trial was whether the claimant had convincingly established a real prospect of success at trial (following *Cream Holdings Ltd & Ors v (1) Chumki Banerjee (2) Liverpool Daily Post (3) Echo Ltd*[64]). The Court also noted (considering *Campbell* below) that there was some mileage in the argument that a duty of confidentiality expressly assumed under a contract should be given greater weight than an implied duty arising under the general principles of equity.

10.69 Another case in which section 12 arose was *Naomi Campbell v Vanessa Frisbee*[65] where the Court held that it was arguable that express contractual undertakings of confidentiality carry more weight when balanced against the restriction of the right of freedom of expression than the implied duty. Further the Court acknowledged that section 12(4) of the HRA 1998 now gave statutory recognition to the common law principle that the right to confidentiality, whether founded on contract or not, must give way where it is in the public interest that the confidential information should be made public.

10.70 Lastly, in *Douglas and Zeta-Jones & OK! v Hello! Ltd*,[66] the Court of Appeal determined *Hello!*'s appeal examined the interrelationship between the couple's right to respect for private life in Article 8 and *Hello!*'s right to freedom of expression in Article 10 and also considered the impact of section 12 of the HRA 1998. In deciding whether to continue an injunction, it was held that section 12 did not give Article 10 a presumptive priority over Article 8 but required the Court to achieve a just balance between the two conflicting rights.

O. Restricted reporting orders

10.71 A party in the employment tribunal resisting an application for a restricted reporting order may remind the tribunal of section 12 of the HRA 1998. Such an application would involve a balancing of Articles 8 and 10, as mentioned above. When Lindsay J made a restricted reporting order in *Chief Constable of West Yorkshire Police v A*,[67] he commented that:

> . . . it has to be recognised that such matters as freedom of expression, freedom of the press and the right to a public hearing have, in some circumstances, such as those

---

[64] [2003] EWCA Civ 103, [2003] 3 WLR 999.
[65] [2002] EWCA Civ 1374, [2003] 1 ICR 141.
[66] [2001] 1 QB 967.
[67] [2001] ICR 128, at 140.

before me, countervailing factors operating, such as freedom from discrimination and respect for privacy and, perhaps most of all, most important in the case before me, the need for access to an effective remedy and the due administration of justice.

In *Associated Newspapers Ltd v London (North) Industrial Tribunal*,[68] Keene J **10.72** quashed a restricted reporting order, stating that the freedom of the Press to report fully and contemporaneously should be constrained only where and to the extent clearly necessary. He commented that:[69]

> It is difficult to see that Article 10 of the European Convention on Human Rights adds significantly to this, given that the principle to which I have referred is so firmly embedded in the English common law.

Despite this assurance, employment lawyers must be alert to the need to balance competing interests when freedom of expression arises as a live issue, in the course of a hearing as well as in the context of the workplace.

P. Article 10 and discrimination

In *Serco Ltd t/a West Yorkshire Transport Service v Redfearn*,[70] the Court of Appeal **10.73** rejected a race discrimination claim of an employee who planned to stand as a British National Party candidate and had been dismissed. (The discrimination claim failed as the appeal court found there had been no race discrimination within the meaning of the Race Relations Act 1976.) Mummery LJ commented that, if the employer had been a public authority, Mr Redfearn might have been able to bring a claim under the HRA 1998 in respect of a breach of his rights of freedom of expression (and association). Since Article 10 has 'horizontal effect' Mr Redfearn could have attempted to rely on it despite the respondent not being a public authority.

Mummery LJ also stated that employers will still need to be wary of dismissing or **10.74** disciplining employees for expressing political views, however repugnant, saying:[71]

> It is not, in general, fair to dismiss a person from employment for engaging in political activities or for being a member of a political party propagating policies that are unacceptable to his employer, to his fellow employees, to trade union officials and members, or even to most of the population. We aspire to live in peace with one another in a politically free and tolerant society. Unpopular political opinions are lawful, even if they are intolerant of others and give offence to many. The right to stand for political

---

[68] [1998] IRLR 569, HCQB.
[69] At para 39.
[70] [2006] EWCA Civ 659, [2006] IRLR 623.
[71] At para 10.

office in a democratic election and to engage in political debate is entitled to respect, however unpalatable the person's political convictions may be to many others.

10.75 The Court of Appeal did not determine the Article 10 point and therefore did not address the point as to whether Mr Redfearn was using the ECHR to protect views that are incompatible with the ECHR. It must be remembered that Article 17 ECHR states:

> Nothing in this Convention may be interpreted as implying for any state, group, or person any right to engage in any activity or perform any act aimed at the destruction of any of the rights and freedoms set forth herein or at their limitation to a greater extent than is provided for in the Convention.

10.76 In *Norwood v United Kingdom*,[72] a member of the BNP claimed that his freedom of expression under Article 10 was violated by criminal proceedings against him for displaying a racist poster (an attack on all Muslims in the UK) in the window of his flat. His claim was rejected as inadmissible on the ground that Article 17 ECHR prevented individuals or groups who acted in a way that was incompatible with the values proclaimed and guaranteed by the ECHR, notably tolerance, social peace, and non-discrimination, from exploiting in their own interests the principles enunciated by the ECHR. See also *Glimmerveen v The Netherlands*.[73]

Q. Frequently asked questions

10.77 What is the content of Article 10?

Article 10 encapsulates the right to hold and express ideas and to participate in dialogue. These are all highly relevant in an employment law context. One frequently occurring issue is that of responsibility for the consequences of dialogue; if a spontaneous exchange is occurring, the outcome could be unexpected and result in disciplinary proceedings. The right to express one's opinions could then be used as a defence to charges of misconduct brought, providing a sensible balance is achieved regarding permissible behaviour in the workplace.

How is the right qualified?

The right to freedom of expression can only be curtailed if prescribed by law and if necessary in a democratic society.

---

[72] (2004) 40 EHRR SE 11.1.
[73] Application 8348/78, [1979] 4 EHRR 260.

Does Article 10 just operate between the individual and the state?

No, Article 10 is engaged between two individuals such as employer and employee as well as having vertical effect. However, rights can be waived in an employment contract as long as consent is freely given.

What are the state's obligations under this Article?

The state has a positive obligation to take action to protect these rights where an individual's freedom of expression is threatened. Courts and tribunals, as part of their status as public authorities are also under a duty to uphold these rights. Even internal disciplinary hearings (particularly those in the public sector) need to be alert to whether Article 10 has been breached when subjecting workers to disciplinary penalties.

How does Article 10 operate on post-termination restraints?

ECtHR case law has said that restrictive covenants may be necessary in a democratic society in the commercial context of protection against unfair competition. Member states are given a margin of appreciation in determining the extent to which interference with Article 10 rights is prescribed by law and pursues a legitimate aim.

Whether a restrictive interference with the ex-employee's freedom of expression is justified, will be fact dependent, in a similar way to the common law approach to the legality of restrictive covenants.

What is the relevance of Article 10 to particular dress?

This Article covers the right to express beliefs by dressing in a particular way. It may be difficult to establish that individuals are prevented from expressing a particular opinion or idea via their clothing, especially if outside working hours those concerned remain able to dress as they please.

Dress codes laid down by employers or institutions such as schools need to be clearly understood by all and to be aware of where clashes with religious sensitivities may occur.

Do sanctions against whistle-blowers offend Article 10 rights?

The Public Interest Disclosure Act 1998 provides some protection to employees who disclose material wrong-doing by their employers. The carefully specified ways in which a complaint should be brought and the subject matter of protected disclosures probably means that whistle-blowers who fall foul of this domestic legislation will not have remedies under Article 10 as long as the employer can show the action taken is necessary in a democratic society and that the sanction is justified. These conditions are clearly fact specific.

What happens when Article 10 rights conflict with Article 8?

Courts and tribunals have often had to address this conflict where newspapers wish to exercise their rights to freedom of expression. Whilst in the workplace this clash will occur less frequently than it does in the media, employers need to be alert to the need to balance competing interests especially where issues of confidentiality arise.

How does section 12 of the HRA 1998 restrain courts from limiting freedom of expression?

Where a court is considering granting relief which might violate Article 10 rights, section 12 places safeguards upon such action of a procedural and substantive nature.

1. *The person against whom restrictive control may be placed must be present in court.*
2. *Relief can only be granted to restrain publication before trial if those who seek it can show it is likely that a specific derogation to Article 10 can be established.*
3. *The Court is obliged to have particular regard to Article 10 and lastly whether the relevant information is in the public domain already must be examined along with the public interest in publishing it and the existence of any privacy code.*

Section 12 will commonly be considered by tribunals who are asked to make restrictive reporting orders. Practitioners need to be familiar with such competing issues in the context of the workplace as well as in the course of a hearing.

Is Article 10 relevant to discrimination complaints?

Situations may arise in the workplace where a worker accused (for example) of race or sex discrimination asserts that s/he is simply exercising the right to express ideas. Employers may also refuse to employ individuals whom they feel hold unacceptable beliefs. Practitioners should be aware that, when examining if employers have acted lawfully in dismissing or disciplining employees for expression of political views, it will often be necessary to have regard to Article 17 which warns against the use of the ECHR to protect views which are incompatible with Convention rights.

As well as raising Article 10 issues, Article 14 may also be engaged where dress codes impact restrictively without justification.

11

ARTICLE 11: FREEDOM OF ASSEMBLY AND ASSOCIATION

Article 11
Freedom of assembly and association

1. Everyone has the right to freedom of peaceful assembly and to freedom of association with others, including the right to form and to join trade unions for the protection of his interests.

2. No restrictions shall be placed on the exercise of these rights other than such as are prescribed by law and are necessary in a democratic society in the interests of national security or public safety, for the prevention of disorder or crime, for the protection of health or morals or for the protection of the rights and freedoms of others. This Article shall not prevent the imposition of lawful restrictions on the exercise of these rights by members of the armed forces, of the police or of the administration of the State.

A. Introduction

11.01 In this chapter we give an overview of the importance of Article 11 ECHR, followed by a discussion of the basic content of the Article including consideration of the permitted interferences and the negative obligations that are implied by its text. A comparison is drawn with Article 12 of the European Charter of Fundamental Rights and Freedoms. We then discuss in greater detail the extent to which the Article gives rights to trade union activity, including the question as to whether a right to strike can arise in any circumstances and the extent to which the right affects picketing and other trade union activities.

B. The scope of Article 11 and its impact on UK employment law

11.02 Article 11 is not merely about joining trade unions; its scope is wider than that. Indeed, the right to form and join trade unions is a consequence of the principal aspects of the Article—the rights to freedom of peaceful assembly and to freedom of association with others.

11.03 In the context of employment law it is likely that these rights will be of most interest in cases where there are trade disputes, but it does not follow that this is the only aspect of importance. Plainly, if new labour laws were threatened or introduced which were unacceptable to either employers or workers, it is likely that the right to peaceful assembly or to freedom of association could be very important to anyone involved in campaigning around work-related issues. In this context, Article 11 is likely to be important in connection with the Article 10 right to freedom of expression (see Chapter 10).

11.04 However, the case law of the Convention in this area remains modest and this may reflect the extent to which reliance on this Article has been necessary.

11.05 The first major impact that Article 11 had in the UK has been to cause the death of the closed shop provisions in labour law (see *Young, James and Webster v UK*[1]). This litigation is important in that it established that the Article implied negative rights against being forced to join trade unions, and this will apply equally in relation to any attempt to force employers to join associations.

11.06 While UK domestic legislation protects the non-unionist worker to a large extent (see, eg, ss 137, 146 and 152 of the Trade Union and Labour Relations

---

[1] (1982) 4 EHRR 38.

(Consolidation) Act 1992), the HRA 1998 could provide such non-unionists with further ammunition against any attempt to introduce anything like a closed shop.

The principal obligation under Article 11 is on the state. Nevertheless, the pos- **11.07** sibility of horizontal effect remains real. Since so much of employment law depends on the exercise of judicial discretion, whether in respect of unfair dismissal, interim injunctions to restrain an alleged breach of covenant, or elsewhere, the Article may well be given horizontal effect between non-state litigants by the exercise of such discretions.

In *Plattform 'Ärzte für das Leben' v Austria*,[2] the Court found that the right to free- **11.08** dom of assembly went further than the state's obligation not to interfere and involved positive measures, 'even in the sphere of individuals if need be'.[3] Preventing the violence of counter-demonstrators against the original demonstrators involved balancing the rights of both groups.

Obviously, the state can interfere with freedom to associate by acting in a variety **11.09** of different ways. It could be liable as a lawmaker, as an employer, as an emanation of the state, or if its laws permit an employer to restrict the rights of an individual through an abuse of power (see *Cheall v UK*[4]). The exclusion of an employee from a trade union must have an objective basis, otherwise the state will not have provided an *effective* right to join a trade union.

(1) The rights in Article 11

Article 11 contains two general rights, one of which is said to contain a specific **11.10** right. The two rights are to freedom of peaceful assembly and to freedom of association with others. The latter right includes the right to form and to join trade unions for the protection of the individual's interests. There is no statement about the content of the rights, therefore it has been a matter for case law to flesh out.

(2) Peaceful assembly

In an employment context this right is likely to be of most relevance in relation **11.11** to the exercise of trade union rights. Peaceful mass meetings are likely to be protected under this part of Article 11. Equally, picketing can be a form of assembly and any restraint on picketing could be challenged by reference to Article 11. Thus, in any application for an injunction to stop picketing, the court would have to ensure that it was not unlawfully interfering with this right.

---

[2] (1991) 13 EHRR 204.
[3] At para 10.
[4] (1985) 8 EHRR 74.

(3) Freedom of association

11.12 The right to freedom of association affects not only workers who come together in trade unions, but also employers who come together in trade associations. It might also be of importance for professional groupings where persons come together for the purpose of advancing their common professional interests.

(4) Trade union rights

11.13 Article 11 specifically identifies the right to form and join trade unions. Its content is explored in greater detail at 11.39–11.51 below. It is significant at this stage to note that the Article does not say what a trade union must be permitted to do. It is of course a clear implication that trade unions must be permitted to function in some respects; if it were otherwise the right would fail the requirement of providing real and effective rights. This Article is therefore one of those in which the lack of content of the right must be seen as limiting the extent to which the Convention imposes any one, specific requirement. This has been a source of frustration to trade unionists.

11.14 It must be noted that freedom of association applies to trade unions and not to state-established professional associations such as medical or legal associations (see *Le Compte, Van Leuven and De Meyere v Belgium*[5]).

(5) Permitted interferences

11.15 Article 11(2) permits unspecified restrictions on the rights which meet strict criteria. They must be:
- (a) prescribed by law; and
- (b) necessary in a democratic society;
- (c) on one of the following, limited grounds—
    - (i) in the interests of national security or public safety,
    - (ii) for the prevention of disorder or crime,
    - (iii) for the protection of health or morals, or
    - (iv) for the protection of the rights and freedoms of others.

11.16 The Article also permits restrictions in certain specified cases; that is to say, in respect of:
- (a) members of the armed forces;
- (b) the police; or
- (c) the administration of the state,

---

[5] (1982) 4 EHRR 1, paras 64–65.

provided in each case that the restrictions are lawful. Therefore soldiers, the police and those in the state's administration can have their rights under Article 11 removed without a need to show that the restriction is necessary in a democratic society, though it must be a restriction that is imposed under the rule of law, which requires at least that the restriction's scope be certain. However, since the functions of the police and soldiers are essentially connected with the prevention of disorder and crime and the protection of the rights and freedoms of others, this aspect may be of little significance.

Who is included in the category 'administration of the state' is unclear, although it **11.17** should not be widely construed. In *CCSU v UK*[6] workers at GCHQ were deemed to be members of the administration of the state as their work included national security functions. It may be asked whether, for instance health workers, local authority employees, or ambulance drivers work within state administration.

In *Tum Haber Sen and Cinar v Turkey*,[7] the ECtHR held that the dissolution of a **11.18** trade union solely on the ground that it had been founded by civil servants, and that its members were civil servants amounted to an unjustifiable interference with Article 11(1). The civil servants in question were public sector staff working in the communications field. Whilst the court recognised that restrictions were permitted in the cases set out at 11.16 above, it went on to hold that the restrictions in Article 11(2) must be interpreted strictly, and that only 'convincing and compelling' reasons can justify restrictions on freedom of association.

Importantly, the Court accepted the Committee of Independent Experts' view **11.19** that Article 5 of the European Social Charter (which affords all workers the right to form trade unions) applies to civil servants. The Court further noted that as Article 5 sets out conditions for forming trade union organisations for members of the police and the armed forces, it should be considered as applying without restriction to other categories of state employees. There were no clear legislative provisions on the right of civil servants to form trade unions in Turkey, and the Turkish court had held that this meant there was an absolute prohibition on this activity. The Court held that, in the absence of any evidence to show that the activities of the union represented a threat to Turkish society or the Turkish state, this failure to secure the members' right to freedom of association was not justified.

The relevance of the closed shop to the restrictions under Article 11(2) is minimal. **11.20** On the basis of case law to date, it is hard to imagine the Court deeming a closed shop as necessary, that is, as a proportionate response to a pressing social need.

---

[6] (1987) 50 DR 228.
[7] Application 28602/95, ECtHR, 21 May 2006.

11.21   In every case the restriction must be proportionate to the purpose which it is intended to achieve. These restrictions have features in common with other Articles in the Convention, and their scope is discussed more generally in Chapter 2. Their application in specific cases is discussed further below.

(6) The state as employer

11.22   States have tried to argue that as an employer a government's activities are not susceptible to regulation under Article 11 ECHR. This narrow interpretation was rejected in *Swedish Engine Drivers' Union v Sweden*[8] and in *Schmidt and Dahlström v Sweden*.[9] Article 11 is accordingly binding upon the 'state as employer', whether the latter's relation with its employee is governed by public or private law.

(7) Negative as well as positive freedoms

11.23   The extent to which the Convention must be read as containing implied rights is exemplified by Article 11. Thus the Court stated in *Young, James and Webster v UK*,[10] that the freedom to join an association entailed the freedom not to join an association. However, this construction of the Article, implying a negative as well as a positive right, has its own consequential difficulties.

11.24   First, the Court has recognised that this negative freedom may need to be attenuated in the face of pressing social needs. This was explored in *Sigurður A Sigurjónsson v Iceland*,[11] where a taxi driver objected to a requirement to join a particular taxi association. The Court acknowledged the need for control of taxi drivers. However, in the end it held that it was not necessary to require taxi drivers to belong to a particular association in order to exercise sufficient control over their conduct. The Court ruled that 'membership was by no means the only conceivable way of compelling the licence-holders to carry out such duties and responsibilities as might be necessary for the relevant functions'.[12] The Court's view was that if it were necessary to regulate the supply of labour, it ought to be undertaken by government rather than by a trade union. Likewise, it suggested that the Convention recognises only a limited role for trade unions to maintain decent working conditions. Rather, it is for the modern state to ensure statutory protection for workers against unfair dismissals and unilateral variations of contracts.

---

[8] (1979–80) 1 EHRR 617.
[9] (1979–80) 1 EHRR 632, para 33.
[10] (1982) 4 EHRR 38.
[11] (1993) 16 EHRR 462.
[12] At para 41.

Secondly, such a negative obligation is more likely to arise where other funda- **11.25**
mental right considerations are involved. Thus in *Young, James & Webster*, the
Court was also aware that issues of conscience were involved. The applicants had
strong objections to trade unionism and had to choose between not joining the
union or joining it against their conscience. Freedom of conscience is specifically
guaranteed under Article 9 ECHR (see Chapter 9). On the other hand, freedom
to follow one's trade is an economic right, and such rights are not protected under
the ECHR.

It seems that where a negative right is relied upon but there are no issues of free- **11.26**
dom of conscience and a person's livelihood is not at stake, the Court is far less
likely to find an infringement of Article 11 than in factual situations akin to those
in *Young, James & Webster*. Thus in *Sibson v UK*,[13] the Court found that there was
no breach of Article 11 ECHR when an employer sought to redeploy an employee
who had changed unions. Suitable alternative employment had been offered, and
the employee had no objections to trade unionism per se.

However, recent case law suggests that the ECtHR may be growing more hostile **11.27**
to the general principle of the closed shop. In *Sorensen v Denmark; Rasmussen v
Denmark*,[14] the Court held that there was 'little support' in the contracting states
for the maintenance of closed shop agreements, and that the Community Charter
of the Fundamental Social Rights of Workers, and Article 12 of the Charter of
Fundamental Rights (see 11.33) showed that their use in the labour market was
not an indispensable tool for the effective enjoyment of trade union freedoms.
On the facts of the two cases, the Court held that the applicants' Article 11 rights
had been breached as they were/would have been dismissed had they resigned
from a particular union, even though they had been fully aware when accepting
their positions that trade union membership was a pre-condition of employment. The Court held that the distinction between pre- and post-entry closed
shops in terms of the scope of protection provided by Article 11 was not tenable;
it could 'at most' be seen as a consideration for the Court to take into account.

Of course the exercise of collective rights can come into conflict with the negative **11.28**
rights not to belong to an association. This was the issue which arose in *Gustafsson v
Sweden*.[15] The case concerned a restaurateur who complained when he suffered
from a boycott imposed by Swedish trade unions and the government failed
to intervene to help him. The reason for the boycott was that Mr Gustafsson
had not entered into collective agreements because he was not a member of

---

[13] (1993) 17 EHRR 193.
[14] Applications 52562/99 and 52620/99, ECtHR, 11 January 2006.
[15] (1996) 22 EHRR 409.

the relevant employers' association nor had he entered into substitute agreements. He held strong views against collective bargaining. The basis of Mr Gustafsson's complaint was that since Article 11 entailed a negative freedom of association, he should be protected from being forced into an association. The case therefore brought into conflict the rights of trade unions to take industrial action and the rights of an employer to refuse to join an association. The Court pointed out that Article 11 ECHR did not give the right not to enter into a collective agreement. It stated that such compulsion as operated in the circumstances did not significantly impinge upon the right of freedom of association, there was no doubt that the union collective agreement pursued legitimate aims within Article 11, and that bearing in mind the margin of appreciation (see Chapter 2) there was no violation.

11.29 This case emphasised the possibilities for the negative and positive aspects of this right to come into conflict, but it is interesting that the Court refused to say whether the negative rights were on an equal footing with the positive rights. The Court also refused to comment finally on this issue in *Sorensen* and *Rasmussen*; however, it did state that it:

> . . . does not in principle exclude that the negative and the positive aspects of the Article 11 right should be afforded the same level of protection in the area under consideration.

11.30 Arguably, the decision in *Sorensen* and *Rasmussen* itself (see 11.27 above) suggests that the Court is increasingly willing to place greater weight on negative freedoms.

11.31 The ECHR does not specifically refer to the freedom to form an employer's association, as opposed to a trade union, but as companies are recognised as having rights under the Convention as well as individuals (see *Autronic AG v Switzerland*[16]), the right of a company to form a voluntary association for a legitimate purpose should be viewed as part of the general right of association contained in Article 11.

C. Related Charter Rights

(1) Introduction

11.32 The Charter of Fundamental Rights of the European Union has some effect in relation to Article 11 ECHR. It is set out in full in Appendix 3. The effect of the Charter is discussed more generally in Chapter 14. Here its principal effect will be to limit further the extent to which derogations from Article 11 will

---

[16] (1990) 12 EHRR 485.

be permitted. Obviously, if some act which interferes with Article 11 is also contrary to any Charter Article then it may be argued that it is not a proportionate or otherwise permissible interference. However, as can be seen from the text of the relevant Charter Articles, the rights and limitations which they create and impose are in the main derived from other international provisions.

(2) Charter Article 12 in relation to freedom of assembly and association

This Article is most closely related to Article 11 ECHR. It is clear from its text **11.33** that it was modelled on Article 11. Thus Article 12 of the Charter of Fundamental Rights of the European Union provides:

1. Everyone has the right to freedom of peaceful assembly and to freedom of association at all levels, in particular in political, trade union and civic matters, which implies the right of everyone to form and to join trade unions for the protection of his or her interests.
2. Political parties at Union level contribute to expressing the political will of the citizens of the Union.

(3) Other Charter rights in relation to solidarity

Chapter IV of the Charter is entitled 'Solidarity'. It contains 14 Articles of **11.34** which Articles 27 ('Workers' Rights to Information and Consultation within the Undertaking') and 28 ('Right of Collective Bargaining and Action') are the most important in this context.

Charter Article 27 provides:

Workers or their representatives must, at the appropriate levels, be guaranteed information and consultation in good time in the cases and under the conditions provided for by Community law and national law and practices.

The second part of this Article limits its scope to the existing laws and practices **11.35** and so may not have much effect in relation to Article 11 ECHR. Nevertheless, the use of the prescriptive verb 'must' may suggest that the possibility for regression in relation to these rights is very limited.

Charter Article 28 is in a declaratory form. It states: **11.36**

Workers and employers, or their respective organisations, have, in accordance with Community law and national laws and practices, the right to negotiate and conclude collective agreements at the appropriate levels and, in cases of conflict of interest, to take collective action to defend their interests, including strike action.

This Article expressly states the right of collective organisations of workers (ie **11.37** trade unions) to take collective action including strike action. This is an important statement of principle. Again, its most likely effect is to limit the power of the union to legislate any regression from this principle. The European Commission requires its lawyers to scrutinise any draft legislation for compliance with the Charter. So from now on it is likely that any legislation from the Community in relation to employment should be construed as implying rights consistent with this Charter Article. Over time this is likely to mean that some of the debates over the content of Article 11 ECHR in relation to the right to strike may become less important.

11.38 It is also important to remember that the precursors to Article 11 ECHR were Articles 20 and 23(4) of the Universal Declaration of Human Rights. Collective rights are enshrined in Article 6 of the European Social Charter. There are similar provisions to Article 11 ECHR in Articles 21 and 22 of the International Covenant on Civil and Political Rights. ILO Conventions 87 and 98 also provide rights of collective bargaining and freedom of association.

D. What rights to trade union activity does Article 11 give?

(1) Indispensable rights

11.39 In a group of cases in the 1970s, the Court noted that Article 11 ECHR is phrased in very general terms and 'does not secure any particular treatment of trade unions, or their members' (*Swedish Engine Drivers' Union v Sweden*[17]). Apart from the specified rights to form and to join trade unions, Article 11 demands of states only that they protect rights that are 'indispensable for the effective enjoyment of trade union freedom'. These include the right of a trade union to choose its members and to expel members whose views are contrary to its constitution: *ASLEF v UK*, Application no 11002/05, Judgment 27 February 2007.

(2) A right to be heard

11.40 The Court has taken a very narrow view of what rights are indispensable. In *National Union of Belgian Police v Belgium*,[18] it was conceded that they included a right for the union to be heard by the employer on behalf of its members in order to function effectively. This included the union having such rights as are indispensable to protect an individual's interests, but did not, however, suppose a right to be consulted, which the applicants claimed and which in Belgium was allowed only to certain large trade unions.

---

[17] Series A No 20 (1979–80) 1 EHRR 617, para 39.
[18] (1979–80) 1 EHRR 578.

Similarly, in *Swedish Engine Drivers' Union v Sweden*, the Court held that the **11.41**
right to be heard, which remains the only indispensable right so far recognised,
did not entail that the applicant trade union be allowed to enter into a collective
agreement with an employer.

Most recently, in *Wilson and National Union of Journalists v United Kingdom*,[19] **11.42**
the Court has reiterated that the right to be heard does not extend to imposing on
an employer an obligation to recognise a trade union for the purpose of collective
bargaining, as this is not indispensable for the effective enjoyment of trade union
rights. All that is required is that the union and its members be free, in one way
or another, to seek to persuade the employer to listen to what it has to say on
behalf of its members. The Court confirmed that the contracting states still enjoy
a wide margin of appreciation as to how trade union freedom may be secured.

(3) An individual right to representation

It has been argued very strongly that 'there should be an *individual* right to repre- **11.43**
sentation by a union, a right which may be derived from the fundamental right
to join a union, i.e. from freedom of association'.[20]

The most significant development regarding collective rights within the Employ- **11.44**
ment Relations Act 1999 is the right for an independent trade union to demand
recognition from the employer when a majority of the workforce requires it. It
may be possible to utilise the Convention to challenge shortfalls in the recognition procedure. Should there be limitations in the range of recognition on a discriminatory basis, such as unions not having authority to enter into collective
bargaining negotiations on topics like conditions of employment where poor
conditions affect a disproportionate number of female workers, it could be argued
that the employer is in breach of Article 14 ECHR read with Article 11.[21] The
fact that employers with fewer than 21 workers are excluded from the statutory
recognition parts of the Employment Relations Act 1999[22] could be discriminatory if small workforces tend to carry out particular types of work.

---

[19] (2002) 35 EHRR 523.

[20] See J Hendy, QC, and M Walton, 'An individual Right to Union Representation in International
Law' (1997) 26 ILJ 205, 207; see also J Hendy, 'The Human Rights Act, Article 11 and the Right to
Strike' [1998] EHRLR 582.

[21] Although this route is unlikely to assist a union seeking to challenge an employer's decision to deny
it recognition in circumstances where another union has been granted rights of negotiation, as (quite
apart from the need to show a breach by the state, or which the state is under a duty to prevent) there will
not usually be a reason for the difference in treatment which falls within the ambit of Art 14: see *R (on
the application of the National Union of Journalists) v Central Arbitration Committee* [2006] IRLR 53.

[22] See para 7 of Sch 1 to the Employment Relation Act 1999.

(4) Does Article 11 give a right to strike?

11.45 In *Schmidt and Dahlström v Sweden*,[23] the Court commented:

> The grant of a right to strike represents without any doubt one of the most important
> . . . means [of an effective enjoyment of trade union freedoms], but there are others.
> Such a right, which is not expressly enshrined in Article 11, may be subject under
> national law to regulation of a kind that limits its exercise in certain instances. The
> Social Charter of 18 October 1961 only guarantees the right to strike subject to such
> regulation, as well as to 'further restrictions' compatible with its Article 31 . . .

11.46 The right to strike is therefore merely one of several ways in which a union
attempts to protect members' interests. It is not therefore seen as indispensable.
The facts of this case were considered by the Court to involve a permissible 'regulation' of the applicants' right to strike.

11.47 It has yet to be established whether the right to strike in its essentials is a specific
right that a state is required to secure under Article 11, for in *Schmidt and
Dahlström* it was found that the right to strike is not a *necessary* incident of the
right to form effective trade unions. See also *Unison v UK*.[24]

11.48 More encouragement for such a view is found in a Commission decision. The
requirement (now repealed) that a trade union had to inform the employer of
those intending to participate in a strike (Trade Union and Labour Relations
(Consolidation) Act 1992, ss 226A and 234A) was found by the Commission not
to breach Article 11: *NATFHE v UK*.[25] Although the Commission here found
that such a requirement was not detrimental to the members or the trade union,
it arrived at this conclusion by considering the issue of proportionality, after
seeming to accept that Article 11 included a right to take collective action.

(5) A right to picket

11.49 Picketing is lawful under section 220 of the Trade Union and Labour Relations
(Consolidation) Act 1992 if it amounts to peacefully persuading a person to work
or strike, or peacefully obtaining or acquiring information. There are domestic
limits to picketing rights, such as there being no rights for those picketing to stop
colleagues from working. The question the courts have considered is whether the
restrictions are proportionate to the action in question (see *Steel v UK*;[26] *Thomas v
NUM (South Wales Area) & Ors*[27]). Clearly the action of picketing is within
Article 11, but it may be the subject of lawful restriction.

---

[23] (1979–80) 1 EHRR 632, at para 36.
[24] [2002] IRLR 497.
[25] (1998) 25 EHRR CD 122.
[26] (1998) 28 EHRR 603.
[27] [1985] ICR 886.

In *Steel v UK*, it was held that the right of peaceful picketing which Article 11   **11.50**
guaranteed was that of mere peaceful demonstration in contrast to disruptive
obstruction. The goal of those protesting and their purpose in doing so will determine where the line is drawn. For this reason the HRA 1998 is unlikely to change
the common law regarding picketing rights. (See *Ezelin v France*;[28] *Rassemblement
Jurassien v Switzerland*;[29] and *G v Germany*[30] for further consideration of proportionality and margins of appreciation in relation to picketing rights.) In *DPP v
Jones*,[31] a case involving a protest near Stonehenge, the House of Lords accepted
the importance of the Convention with regard to the common law.[32] Lord Irvine
said (in a judgment predating the coming into force of the HRA 1998):[33]

> Unless the common law recognises that assembly on the public highway may be
> lawful, the right contained in Article 11(1) of the Convention is denied. Of course
> the right may be subject to restrictions, for example: the requirements that user of
> the highway for purposes of assembly must be reasonable and non-obstructive, and
> must not contravene the criminal law of wilful obstruction of the highway. But in
> my judgment our law will not comply with the Convention unless its starting-point
> is that assembly on the highway will not necessarily be unlawful.

E. Restraints on political activity by employees

Some restraint on the activities of employees is permissible as an interference with   **11.51**
Article 11 rights. In *Ahmed v UK*,[34] the Court found that restrictions on political
activities of British local government officers did not breach Articles 10 or 11
ECHR since they underpinned local democracy and the neutrality of local government officers. In *Rekveni v Hungary*,[35] the Court upheld restrictions on a
police force's political activities, again emphasising the need to consolidate and
maintain democracy. See also *Maestri v Italy*,[36] where the Court held that the
state was entitled to discipline judges who were or became freemasons, although
there was a breach of Article 11 in the particular case because the legislative provisions did not render such an outcome sufficiently foreseeable. These decisions
emphasise the balance that has to be struck between the rights granted by Article 11

---

[28] (1992) 14 EHRR 362.
[29] (1980) 17 DR 93, at 119.
[30] (1980) 60 DR 256.
[31] [1999] 2 All ER 256, [1999] 2 AC 240.
[32] Their Lordships' majority decision was that while there was no general right of assembly on the
highway, a peaceful and non-obstructive assembly did not necessarily exceed the public's right of access
to the highway, provided that such user was reasonable in duration, did not extend beyond the physical
limits of the highway, and was not the predominant purpose of the occupation of the highway.
[33] At 266.
[34] (2000) 29 EHRR 1.
[35] (2000) 30 EHRR 519.
[36] Application 39748/98, ECtHR, 17 February 2004.

ECHR and the overall purpose of the Convention to provide a framework for a modern democracy.

F. Recent impact of Article 11 on UK law

11.52   In the case of *Associated Newspapers Ltd v Wilson; Associated British Ports v Palmer*,[37] the House of Lords held that it was permissible to discriminate by omission against trade union members in the grant of pay increases. Lord Bridge, in the context of victimisation (Trade Union and Labour Relations (Consolidation) Act 1992, s 146) and unfair dismissal (s 152), insisted on the distinction between 'membership' and 'activities', and said that it was illegitimate to contend that 'membership' included making use of the 'essential' services of the union.

11.53   Should membership have a wider meaning than simply access to employment? This was addressed in the case of *Harrison v Kent County Council*,[38] where a union shop steward complained that he had been refused employment because of his union membership. The EAT held that it was 'a fallacy' to proceed by analogy with section 146 (victimisation) and section 152 (unfair dismissal), and to assume, because they specifically mentioned union activities whereas section 137 (access to employment) did not, that section 137 gave no remedy to a person refused a job on account of his union activity. The EAT said: 'In this context a divorce of the fact of membership and the incidents of membership is illusory.' The majority of the House of Lords in *Wilson* and *Palmer* did not support this line of argument, although the comments in *Wilson* and *Palmer* are *obiter dicta* only.

11.54   Since it is now necessary, so far as possible, to read and give effect to the Trade Union and Labour Relations (Consolidation) Act 1992 in a way which is compatible with the Convention pursuant to section 3 of the HRA 1998, it is arguable that the *effective* right provided for by Article 11 ECHR (endorsed in cases like *National Union of Belgian Police v Belgium*[39]) does not permit drawing a distinction between the fact of membership and the necessary incidents of membership.

11.55   In *Fairness at Work*,[40] the government made it clear that it would act to negate the effect of *Wilson* and *Palmer*:

> 4.24 The Government is also concerned that the law currently allows for some discrimination against those involved in trade union activities. The House of Lords ruled in *Wilson* and *Palmer* that the law allowed an employer to discriminate by

---

[37] [1995] 2 All ER 100, [1995] IRLR 258, [1995] ICR 406.
[38] [1995] ICR 434, EAT.
[39] (1979–80) 1 EHRR 578.
[40] Cm 3968, 1998.

omission against an employee on grounds of trade union membership, non-membership or activities.

4.25 The Government believes that such discrimination is contrary to its commitment to ensuring individuals are free to choose whether or not to join a trade union. In addition, when a company has recognised a trade union it is important that trade union representatives are active in promoting effective dialogue with employees. The current law may deter employees from being involved in such activity. The Government therefore proposes to make it unlawful to discriminate by omission on grounds of trade union membership, non-membership or activities. The law already provides protection against discrimination in recruitment on the basis of trade union membership. The Government also proposes to prohibit blacklisting of trade union members.

Schedule 2 to the Employment Relations Act 1999 amended section 146 of **11.56** the Trade Union and Labour Relations (Consolidation) Act 1992 so that section 146(1) now reads: 'An employee has the right not to [be subject to any detriment as an individual by any act, *or any deliberate failure to act*, by his employer if the act *or failure* takes place] for the purpose of . . . [*emphasis added*].' However, the Employment Relations Act 1999 failed to amend section 148(3)–(5) which legitimates the purpose of changing the employer's relationship with employees, even where the purpose also exists of preventing union activities or membership. It is arguable that, under these provisions (now repealed, and see s 145B of the Act), a sweetener payment for the purpose of moving away from collective bargaining could have remained lawful.

The ECtHR considered the legality of the 'inducements' offered in the *Wilson* **11.57** and *Palmer* cases to those who agreed to give up their rights to trade union recognition and representation in *Wilson and National Union of Journalists v UK*.[41] The Court held that a trade union must be free to protect the occupational interests of trade union members, which means that it must be free to strive for the protection of its members' interests, and the individual members have a right that the trade union should be heard. Whilst this did not oblige employers to recognise any union for collective bargaining purposes, the Court held[42] that:

> . . . it must be possible for a trade union which is not recognised by an employer to take steps including, if necessary, organising industrial action with a view to persuading the employer to enter into collective bargaining with it on those issues which the union believes are important for its members' interests. Furthermore, it is of the essence of the right to join a trade union for the protection of their interests that employees should be free to instruct or permit the union to make representations to their employer or to take action in support of their interests on their behalf. If workers are prevented from doing so, their freedom to belong to a trade union, for the

---

[41] (2002) 35 EHRR 523.
[42] At para 46.

protection of their interests, becomes illusory. It is the role of the State to ensure that trade union members are not prevented or restrained from using their union to represent them, in attempts to regulate their relations with their employers.

11.58 Relying on these principles, the Court held that the fact that the UK permitted employers to offer pay rises to those who acquiesced in the termination of collective bargaining meant that those employers were permitted to pre-empt protests by unions or members against the imposition of limits on voluntary collective bargaining. As a result, UK law permitted less favourable treatment of employees who were not prepared to renounce a freedom that was an essential feature of union membership, and allowed employers to undermine or frustrate trade unions' ability to strive for the protection of their members' interests. In allowing employers to use financial incentives to induce employees to surrender important union rights, the UK had failed in its positive obligation to secure the enjoyment of rights under Article 11.

11.59 *Wilson* thus makes it clear that Article 11 prohibits the House of Lords' construction of domestic law: it is not only 'membership' of a trade union that is protected, but also the member's ability to make use of the essential services of the union. As a result of the decision in *Wilson*, the Trade Union and Labour Relations (Consolidation) Act 1992 has been amended such that it is now unfair for an employer to dismiss an employee on grounds that he had made use, or proposed to make use, of trade union services at an appropriate time (s 152(1)(ba)).

11.60 Generally speaking, the HRA 1998 is unlikely to provide greater remedies to trade union members than those provided under domestic legislation. However, domestic courts must be alert to their positive role as regards Article 11 ECHR. Even where no public authorities are involved, rights such as that of freedom of assembly must be upheld to the extent that the actions of other individuals are weighed in the balance, and restrictions limiting the rights must be disallowed unless they can be justified.

G. Frequently asked questions

11.61 **What is the content of Article 11?**

It is not just concerned with trade unions but also concerns the rights of other associations including business associations. It is concerned with the freedom of association with others as well as freedom of assembly.

Does Article 11 give a right to strike?

No, it is not part of Article 11.

What rights do trade unions have under Article 11?

It is not so much a question of what rights trade unions have as what rights do persons have in trade unions. Trade unions have those rights which are indispensable for the effective enjoyment of trade union freedom including the right to exclude members whose views are inconsistent with union policy. This will also normally include a right to be heard and a right not to suffer discrimination for being a member of a trade union.

Is it permissible to impose restraints on political activity by employees?

Yes, it will be permissible to apply proportionate restraints on employees where they are designed to underpin democracy.

12

ARTICLE 1 OF PROTOCOL 1: PEACEFUL ENJOYMENT OF PROPERTY

PROTOCOL 1

Article 1
Protection of property

Every natural or legal person is entitled to the peaceful enjoyment of his possessions. No one shall be deprived of his possessions except in the public interest and subject to the conditions provided for by law and by the general principles of international law.

The preceding provision shall not, however, in any way impair the right of a state to enforce such laws as it deems necessary to control the use of property in accordance with the general interest or to secure the payment of taxes or other contributions or penalties.

A. Introduction

The enjoyment of property and possessions has a wider scope within Convention **12.01** jurisprudence than might initially be imagined. While the peaceful enjoyment of property and possessions is here guaranteed by Article 1 of Protocol 1, the state retains power to control such enjoyment and, further, to deprive people of their property in specific circumstances.

The meaning of 'possessions' and 'property' is considered at 12.02–12.03 below; and the test for control and deprivation is discussed at 12.05–12.09. The relevance of Article 1 of Protocol 1 in the employment law field is considered along with possible areas of challenge.

B. Outline of the scope of the right to enjoy one's property

(1) The meaning of 'property' or 'possessions'

12.02 Article 1 of Protocol 1 covers property, chattels, and rights which have accrued and which have an economic value. The following list of matters held to amount to 'property' or 'possessions' demonstrates the wide nature of the Article's scope:

(a) shares: *Bramelid & Malmstrom v Sweden*;[1]

(b) claims in negligence: *Pressos Companai Naviera v Belgium*;[2]

(c) claims under contract: *Stran Greek Refineries v Greece*;[3]

(d) debts: *Angneessens v Belgium*;[4]

(e) alcohol licences: *Tre Traktorer Aktiebolag v Sweden*;[5]

(f) patents: *Smith Kline and French Laboratories v Netherlands*;[6]

(g) fishing rights: *Baner v Sweden*;[7] *R (Quark Fishing) v Secretary of State for Foreign and Commonwealth Affairs*;[8]

(h) planning consents: *Pine Valley Developments v Ireland*;[9]

(i) restitutionary claims: *National Provincial Building Society v UK*;[10]

(j) goodwill, so long as it has reached a minimum level: see *Karni v Sweden*[11] and *Van Marle v Netherlands*;[12]

(k) pensions and welfare benefits (see 12.34–12.45).

---

[1] (1983) 5 EHRR 249.
[2] (1996) 21 EHRR 301.
[3] (1995) 19 EHRR 293.
[4] (1988) 58 DR 63.
[5] (1991) 13 EHRR 309.
[6] (1990) 66 DR 70.
[7] (1989) 60 DR 128.
[8] [2003] EWHC 1743 (Admin).
[9] (1992) 14 EHRR 319.
[10] (1996) 21 EHRR 301.
[11] Application 11540, (1988) 55 DR 157.
[12] (1986) 8 EHRR 48.

(l)   licences: *Crompton T/A David Crompton Haulage v Department of Transport North Western Area.*[13]

Article 1 of Protocol 1 does not apply to rights which have not yet accrued, except **12.03** where there is an existing cause of action. Its scope does not extend as far as an expectation of work, although it may be possible for a legitimate expectation to amount to a property right: see *Gudmundsson v Iceland.*[14] In this case the legitimate expectation of taxi drivers that they could continue driving regardless of age (unless a conditional licence was withdrawn upon such conditions not being met), was held to amount to a property right. It is worth noting that the French text of the Convention refers to '*biens*'. This is broader in meaning than the English 'possessions' and denotes any property right.

(2) Positive obligations

There are circumstances in which an individual cannot exercise his or her rights **12.04** under Article 1 of Protocol 1 unless the state takes positive steps. This could include moving an obstruction to a building (see *Loizidou v Turkey*[15]). However, where a dispute concerns the private relationship between two parties it may be difficult to bring state responsibility into play. Situations where legislation protects against loss in such relationships, such as where one party dismisses another (in breach of contract), will generally impose a positive obligation and the Article will be engaged (see the Commission's comments on cases where the Article is breached in *Fenzel & Kollner v Austria*).[16]

C. Key principles

(1) Three rules within the Article

Three rules were said to be encapsulated within Article 1 of Protocol 1 in *Sporrong &* **12.05** *Lönnroth v Sweden*:[17]

(a)   the right to peaceful enjoyment of property;
(b)   deprivation of property must be in the public interest, subject to the conditions provided by law and by the general principles of international law;

---

[13] [2003] EWCA Civ 64; [2003] RTR 517.
[14] Application 23285/94, 17 January 1996 (Commission); (1996) 21 EHRR CD 89, E COM HR.
[15] (1996) 23 EHRR 513.
[16] Application 22351/93, 15 May 1996.
[17] (1982) 5 EHRR 35, at para 61.

(c) states may limit the above rights in accordance with the general interest and in specific ways such as securing the payment of taxes.

The rules are closely connected, the last two being concerned with permitted interference with the right.

(2) Assessing deprivation of property

12.06 Deprivation of property is permitted if in accordance with international law and in the public interest (see *Wiggins v UK*[18]). To be in the public interest:

(a) any deprivation of property must be for a legitimate purpose; and

(b) when achieving that purpose a fair balance must be struck between the need to protect individual rights and the demands of the general interest of the community (*James v UK*[19]).

The requirement of being in the public interest requires a high test.

(3) International law

12.07 The reference to 'the general principles of international law' in the latter part of the second sentence of Article 1 of Protocol 1 has been held to have no application to the taking by a state of the property of its own nationals.[20] Interference with property which does not affect its financial value is not prohibited under Article 1 of Protocol 1. However, interference with property on a non-pecuniary basis, such as by noise, could be protected under another Convention provision, such as Article 8, if the circumstances are appropriate.

(4) The control of property

12.08 A wider range of interference is permissible here, commensurate with the assumed need for some control over property and possessions in our society, such as through taxation.

12.09 The questions to ask when ascertaining if the control of property is in line with Convention rights are:

(a) Do the controlling measures have a legitimate aim (that is, not 'manifestly without a reasonable foundation')?

(b) Is there a reasonably proportionate relationship between the means employed and the achievement of the end pursued?

---

[18] (1978) 13 DR 40.

[19] (1986) 8 EHRR 123.

[20] See para 66 in the judgment of the ECtHR in *James v UK*, at p 151.

Even in cases where there is no deprivation or control of use, an interference has occasionally been found. This residual category appears to operate as a catch-all.[21] As in cases of deprivation of property, a fair balance must be struck. It is important to consider the fair balance test in a little more detail (see 12.17–12.22 below).

(5) Compensation

In *Lithgow v UK*,[22] the importance of adequate compensation where a depriva-   **12.10**
tion has occurred was considered by the Court. There it was said that compensation should be 'reasonably related' to the value of property taken. Compensation which is less than the full value of the property may be justified in several ways (see *James v UK*[23]). However, this is not an overall limit on the size of the award. There have been cases where large awards have been given for interference with property. In *Pine Valley Developments v Ireland*,[24] the applicant was prevented from developing land and was awarded 1,200,000 Irish Pounds, as this would have been the value of the land but for the interference. In *Sporrong and Lönnroth v Sweden*,[25] a planning restriction prevented development for 20 years in breach of Article 1 of Protocol 1. Compensation to the equivalent of £100,000 was awarded. The Court pointed out that the applicants had borne 'an individual and excessive burden' as a result of the upsetting of the fair balance which should be struck between the protection of the right of property and the requirements of the general interest. The reduction of the possibility of disposing of the properties concerned had had several effects, such as difficulties of selling at normal market prices and of obtaining loans; there was also the prohibition on any 'new construction'. The damage suffered was viewed by the Court as being made up of a number of elements which could not be severed or explained by a process of precise calculation.[26]

A recent example of how the public interest test is determined is the case of   **12.11**
Krasner v Dennison.[27] This involved the question of whether Article 1 of Protocol 1 was breached by a bankrupt losing the benefits of his pension when his pension policies vested in a trustee in bankruptcy, without the court having jurisdiction

---

[21] This work cannot develop this third category of interference further: for a thorough summary, see Clayton and Tomlinson, *The Law of Human Rights* (Oxford: OUP 2000) at paras 18.49–18.52.

[22] (1986) 8 EHRR 329.

[23] (1986) 8 EHRR 123, at para 54.

[24] (1992) 14 EHRR 319.

[25] (1982) 5 EHRR 35.

[26] Compare this to complaints regarding control of property where there is not an inherent right to compensation: *Banér v Sweden* (1989) 60 DR 128, at 142.

[27] [2001] 1 Ch 76.

as to whether some or the entire the pension should be paid to the bankrupt. The Court considered whether the impact of the bankruptcy provisions here amounted to a deprivation of property. The alleged deprivation was clearly in accordance with law under the Bankruptcy Act 1986. The key question was whether the vesting in the trustee in bankruptcy of the bankrupt's rights was in the public interest. The Court of Appeal reminded themselves that the domestic court was better placed than an international judge to appreciate what was in the 'public interest', and so it must be allowed a certain margin of appreciation (see 2.18).

12.12   This approach had been adopted by the Court in *James v UK*:[28]

> the decision to enact laws expropriating property will commonly involve consideration of political, economic and social issues on which opinions within a democratic society may reasonably differ widely. The Court, finding it natural that the margin of appreciation available to the legislature in implementing social and economic policies should be a wide one, will respect the legislature's judgment as to what is 'in the public interest' unless that judgment be manifestly without reasonable foundation.

The Court of Appeal summarised the various statutory enactments whereby Parliament had legislated in the area of pension rights and bankruptcy law, and found that such activity denoted a response to a perception of what the public interest required in this field. Furthermore, there were many judicial decisions demonstrating that the public interest generally required that a bankrupt's property should be available to answer the claims of his creditors. Hence, the 'depriving' legislation was found to be in the public interest. There was no breach. This ruling was approved by the Court of Appeal in *Rowe v Sanders*,[29] and in *Malcolm v Mackenzie & Others*.[30]

12.13   In *Vajagić v Croatia*,[31] the applicants successfully argued that the continuing failure of the domestic authorities to decide on the amount of compensation payable to them for an expropriation measure that had occurred in 1976 violated their property rights as guaranteed by Article 1 of Protocol 1.[32]

(6) Taxation

12.14   A decision considering interference with property via taxation was *Wallbank v Aston Cantlow and Wilmcote with Billesley Parochial Church Council*,[33] where the

---

28 (1986) 8 EHRR 123, at 142 (para 46).
29 [2002] EWCA Civ 242, [48]–[50], [2002] BPIR 847, 858; [2002] 2 All ER 800.
30 [2004] EWCA Civ 1748 [2005] 1 WLR 1238; [2005] ICR 611.
31 Application 30431/03, 20 July 2006.
32 See also D Anderson, 'Compensation for Interference with Property' (1999) EHRLR 543.
33 [2001] EWCA Civ 713, [2002] Ch 51.

freeholders of land, which was previously the glebe lands of a rectory, argued that they were not liable to contribute to the costs of repair to the parish church. The Court of Appeal considered *Darby v Sweden*[34] and found that the liability of lay rectors to contribute to church repairs was a taxation that contravened the right to peaceful enjoyment of property under Article 1 of Protocol 1, on the basis that money could constitute property. While the state utilised many measures to control the use of property or redistribute wealth, a tax which was arbitrary in nature, where an indeterminate liability could arise at any time, failed to provide the basic standard for the protection of possessions from state demands and went beyond the limits of the state's power. The manner in which the common law imposed such liability upon certain landowners was unjustifiably discriminatory, and in breach of Article 14 ECHR.

On appeal to the House of Lords (*Aston Cantlow & Others v Wallbank and Another*[35]) their Lordships did not agree with the Court of Appeal's finding that Mr and Mrs Wallbank's right to peaceful enjoyment of their possessions under Article 1 of the First Protocol, read either alone or with Article 14 ECHR, had been violated.[36] The Court of Appeal had not followed the three-step guidance in *Sporrong* and accordingly it could not be said that the Wallbanks as lay rectors were being deprived of their possessions or being controlled in the use of their property, when those expressions must be understood in the light of the general principle of peaceful enjoyment set out in the first sentence of Article 1 of Protocol 1. Lord Nicholls said:[37] **12.15**

> The liability is simply an incident of the ownership of the land which gives rise to it. The peaceful enjoyment of land involves the discharge of burdens which are attached to it as well as the enjoyment of its rights and privileges.

Lord Scott commented[38] that the liability to repair the chancel satisfied the requirements of the Article 1 exception since: **12.16**

(a) it was a liability created by the common law;
(b) it operated in the narrow public interest of the parishioners in the parish concerned and in the general public interest in the maintenance of churches;
(c) it was created by common law;
(d) it was subject to the incidents attached to it by common law;

---

[34] (1991) 13 EHRR 774.
[35] [2004] 1 AC 546.
[36] See para 65.
[37] At para 72.
[38] At para 134.

(e) the Wallbanks acquired the rectorial property and became lay rectors with full knowledge of the potential liability for chancel repair that that acquisition would carry with it.

D. The fair balance test

12.17 A test has been developed to deal with cases of both deprivation and control of property or possessions. A balance is required between the rights of the individual in question and the interests of the community. When this balancing exercise is carried out, the circumstances in any particular case will be particularly important. Procedural safeguards, such as the right to consultation or the ability to challenge decisions regarding property, will be weighed up.

12.18 As the case of *Krasner* demonstrates above, it will be difficult to argue that the ends do not justify the means where the goal is linked to public policy. For this reason, taxation decisions are difficult to challenge under Article 1 of Protocol 1.

12.19 However, in the context of consumer credit legislation, a breach of Article 1 of Protocol 1 was found by the Court of Appeal in *Wilson v First County Trust*.[39] The background to this case was that agreements which are controlled by the provisions of the Consumer Credit Act 1974 must be in a specific form containing prescribed information. Without this an agreement can be enforced only by an order of the court. However, section 127(3) of the 1974 Act provides that it is not possible for a court order to do this where a consumer credit agreement is defective in that no document exists which records the size of the loan. Mrs Wilson had pawned her car as security for a loan. She did not repay the loan. The pawnbroker sought repayment, failing which the car would be sold. Mrs Wilson's response was to commence proceedings in the county court. She claimed the agreement was unenforceable because it did not contain all the prescribed terms. Neither the loan nor the agreement could be enforced by virtue of section 127(3). The Court of Appeal considered the impact of the HRA 1998 upon the Consumer Credit Act and found that section 127(3) deprived creditors of the benefit of contractual rights arising from the agreement. The section was so flexible that it did not strike a fair balance between the public interest and the rights of the individual.

12.20 The House of Lords in *Wilson v First County Trust (No 2)*[40] decided that the Court of Appeal had been wrong to declare section 127(3) of the Consumer Credit Act 1974 to be incompatible with the ECHR in a case in which the events

---

39 [2001] EWCA Civ 633, [2001] 3 All ER 229; [2002] QB 74.
40 [2003] UKHL 40, [2004] 1 AC 816.

occurred, and cause of action arose, before the HRA 1998 came into force. Their Lordships ruled that in any event if section 127(3) had the effect of interfering with Convention rights that interference was justified.

Lord Scott[41] rejected the argument that section 127(3) deprived the pawnbroker **12.21** of its right to enforce repayment of the £5,000 loan and thereby disproportionably deprived it of its 'possessions'. His reasons were that:

(a) Article 1 is concerned with existing possessions or property rights, whereas the pawnbroker never had the right to enforce against Mrs Wilson the repayment of the loan.
(b) As this right did not exist, neither the Consumer Credit Act nor section 127(3) constituted an interference with such a right.

These issues could arise in employment cases where compensation is sought for **12.22** loss of benefits such as company cars or free travel post-dismissal.

E. Enjoyment of possessions in employment relations

(1) Debts, compensation, and contractual entitlements

The contract takes priority over the Convention entitlement to property (*X v* **12.23** *UK*[42]). If, for example, the contract of employment states that on termination of the contract all travel passes must be handed in to the employer, the fact that the return of the travel pass would amount to a deprivation of property is trumped by the entitlement to take action provided in the contract. In such circumstances it is not possible to argue that one's property rights have been interfered with.

In an unfair dismissal claim the applicant's right to claim future loss of earnings **12.24** is underpinned by Article 1 of Protocol 1 if he or she can argue that, but for the dismissal, he or she would still be receiving that income. While the entitlement to such wages might not yet have accrued, the property right would attach to the applicant's claim for damages.

Sometimes an applicant has only a hope or expectation that, had he or she not **12.25** been dismissed, he or she would have received a performance bonus. Such bonuses, though discretionary, might still be actionable on the basis that an employer must act in good faith (see *Clark v Nomura International plc*[43]). Accordingly, such rights could amount to property under Article 1 of Protocol 1.

---

[41] At paras 167–68.
[42] (1978) 14 DR 234.
[43] [2000] IRLR 766.

12.26 If an employee has a claim for unfair dismissal, for unlawful deduction from wages, or for unlawful discrimination where it is alleged that the discrimination caused absence from work or the loss of a job, the loss involved is very likely to include lost income. To be denied the opportunity to litigate such a claim, or to be deprived of a remedies hearing, may breach Article 1 of Protocol 1 (see *Gudmondsson v Iceland* [44]). This Convention right may prove especially useful in the light of the non-incorporation of Article 13 ECHR, the right to an effective remedy. The overlap with the 'right to payment', said in *Gudmundsson* to fall within the meaning of Article 1 of Protocol 1, may aid any difficulties caused by the inability to directly rely upon Article 13 under the HRA 1998. Accordingly, tribunals and courts will need to consider Article 1 of Protocol 1 in circumstances where they have discretionary powers to terminate such claims.

12.27 An example of this type of problem may be found in *Nerva v UK* [45] which concerned the legal status of non-cash tips. The waiter applicants argued that the domestic courts were wrong to hold that such tips paid in addition to a cheque or credit card payment could be used by employers to count towards the National Minimum Wage. But the European Court found there was no legitimate expectation that tips should not be counted as remuneration, since the intention of the customer was too imprecise a basis on which to found a legitimate expectation amounting to a 'possession' within the meaning of Article 1 of Protocol 1. Furthermore it was for the applicants to come to a contractual arrangement with their employer as to how the tips at issue were to be dealt with from the point of view of their wage entitlement—they were not able to rely on Article 1 of Protocol 1 to base a claim to a higher level of earnings.

(2) Licences giving the right to work

12.28 Article 1 of Protocol 1 can be a valuable tool for maintaining the right to remain in the workplace where a profession is regulated by licences or a permission system. In *Malik v Waltham Forest PCT & Secretary of State for Health*, [46] Dr Malik applied for judicial review of decisions of a Primary Care Trust to suspend him from its 'performers list' pursuant to the NHS (Performers Lists) Regulations 2004. [47] The High Court held that his unlawful suspension amounted to an interference to the right to peaceful enjoyment of possessions. His right to practise a profession could be regarded as a possession (*Van Marle v Netherlands* [48]).

---

[44] Application 23285/94, 17 January 1996 (Commission); (1996) 21 EHRR 89 E COM HR.
[45] (2003) 36 EHRR 4, [2002] IRLR 815.
[46] [2006] EWHC 487; [2006] IRLR 526; [2006] ICR 1111.
[47] SI 2004/585, reg 13.
[48] (1986) 8 EHRR 483.

Since inclusion in the medical performers list was akin to the possession of a licence it had intrinsic value in that it enabled the doctor to practise. Although the goodwill of the practice was not marketable per se, it was decided that the doctor's suspension could affect the economic value of the practice since the amount of his remuneration would be affected by his patient numbers. Dr Malik's inclusion on the medical performers list had a present value apart from the right to future income, and therefore amounted to a possession.

However, the Court of Appeal[49] overturned Collins J's decision on the basis: **12.29**

(a) that Dr Malik had no marketable goodwill in his patient list, and was therefore effectively claiming that a hope or expectation of earning income in the future amounted to a 'possession', which it could not;
(b) that, where the possessory right claimed is to some intangible entitlement conferred by a licence or other form of permission to the grantee to continue to follow an activity to his advantage, on the basis of which a future monetary entitlement is claimed, the court has to consider whether the entitlement has a present monetary value to the claimant in the sense of being marketable by him. Dr Malik's inclusion in the performers list had no such present monetary value;
(c) that there was no evidence of 'interference' in Dr Malik's practice, and in particular no actual or prospective loss of patients.

Another case involving licences was *R (on the application of Nichols & Others) v*   **12.30**
Security Industry Authority & Secretary of State for the Home Department.[50] In this case doormen needed specific permission to work as door supervisors. Such permission was granted under licensing criteria controlled by the Security Industry Authority pursuant to section 7 of the Private Security Industry Act 2001. The permissions were held to constitute possessions under Article 1 of Protocol 1. But whilst the published criteria interfered with those rights of possession the defendant Secretary of State had acted proportionately in imposing a bar to permission if an applicant committed certain serious criminal offences.

These cases have implications for a whole range of workers including teachers   **12.31**
and nurses, for whom suspension from a register completely removes the ability to practise.

(3) Insolvency

An employee cannot take proceedings against an insolvent employer but must   **12.32**
claim against the state. The state guarantees to provide redundancy payments

---

[49] [2007] EWCA Civ 265, [2007] All ER (D) 462 (Mar).
[50] [2006] EWHC 1792, at para 81; [2006] All ER (D) 259 (July).

where the employer is insolvent, and guarantees the payment of wages and other specified debts (ERA 1996, Parts XI and XII including s 184). The statutory limit on such compensation excludes any more than eight weeks' pay or statutory notice pay. No compensatory award is payable. This legislation probably does not amount to an interference with Article 1 of Protocol 1 since the statutory provisions preventing the full amount being claimed are arguably not arbitrary and are not devoid of proportionality. Employees in this position do receive some compensation.

12.33 However, in *Rodriguez Caballero v Fondo de Garantia Salarial*,[51] the ECJ held that a Spanish provision only partially guaranteeing unfair dismissal compensation contravened the Insolvency Protection Directive 80/987. This might apply to section 184(1)(d) which guarantees a basic award but not a compensatory award.[52]

(4) Pensions and welfare benefits

12.34 While there is no Convention right to a pension per se, where an employee has contractual entitlements to a pension and has complied with making the requisite contributions, he or she may have a proprietary interest in either a state or private pension.[53] It is much more difficult to claim that the withholding of a state pension gives rise to an interference with property rights due to the connection with social policy.

12.35 It was said in *Müller v Austria*[54] that decreases in pensions due to inflation are linked to the state's financial considerations and 'have nothing to do with the guarantee of ownership as a human right'. The Commission held that a claim to contributory benefits was a 'possession' by analogy with the proprietary right of a contributor to a private pension fund. Where there is a significant impact on the amount of a pension an interference may be found.

12.36 The following benefits have been found to amount to property rights:

(a) payments under a SERPS scheme: *Szrabjer v UK*;[55]
(b) social benefits made up partly by contributions: *Gaygusuz v Austria*;[56]
(c) industrial injuries disability benefit: *Carlin v UK*;[57]

---

[51] C-442/00, [2003] IRLR 115.
[52] See *Fenzel & Kollner v Austria* Application 22351/93, 15 May 1996, where the Commission considered a similar set of circumstances.
[53] *X v Sweden* (1986) 8 EHRR 252.
[54] (1975) 3 DR 25.
[55] [1998] EHRLR 230.
[56] (1996) 23 EHRR 364.
[57] Application 27537/95, 3 December 1997; (1998) 25 EHRR CD 75.

(d) widow's pension and death benefit: *Deumeland v Germany*;[58]
(e) sickness benefit: *Feldebrugge v Netherlands*;[59]
(f) unemployment benefit: *Nahon v UK* (no special amount of payment guaranteed);[60] *KS v Finland* (here terminating unemployment benefit following a fair dismissal was deemed justified in that it was proportionate and followed a legitimate aim);[61]
(g) reduced earnings allowance: *Stec & Others v UK*.[62]

Recent cases concerned with social security and Article 1 of Protocol 1 have **12.37** tended towards a judicial reluctance to interfere with policy matters. Whilst the House of Lords in *Carson & Reynolds v Secretary of State for Work & Pensions*[63] accepted that a pension was capable of being a possession, a low bar was set for justifying interference with it.

Ms Carson was a British pensioner resident in South Africa who claimed she was **12.38** entitled to the annual increases to her pension which UK pensioners received. Lord Nicholls said:[64]

> Once it is accepted that the position of Ms Carson is relevantly different from that of a UK resident and that she therefore cannot claim equality of treatment, the amount (if any) which she receives must be a matter for Parliament.

Further, Lord Walker stated:[65]

> This is an issue of macro-economic policy which is eminently within the province of the legislature and the executive.

Ms Reynolds had complained about the lower rate of jobseeker's allowance and **12.39** income support she received because she was under the age of 25. The House of Lords did not say that age could not fall within the category of suspect grounds of discrimination prohibited by Article 14, but said that this was a case about a question of general social policy rather than one where the right to respect for the individuality of a human being is at stake. Since it was accepted that the necessary expenses of young people were lower than those of older people, the Court found they could properly be treated differently for the purpose of social security payments.

---

[58] (1985) 7 EHRR 409.
[59] (1994) 7 EHRR 279.
[60] Application 34190/96, 23 October 1997.
[61] Application 29346/95, 16 March 2000.
[62] Applications 65731/01 and 65900/01, 12 April 2006; 20 BHRC 348.
[63] [2006] 1 AC 173.
[64] At para 25.
[65] At para 80.

12.40 One problem with the analogy of state contributory schemes and a private pension scheme is that in the UK it is difficult to distinguish contributions from general taxation. The European Court has said that although a claim to a social security benefit is a possession it does not entitle one to anything in particular: see *Jankovic v Croatia*.[66] Yet in *Poirrez v France*[67] the weakness of this analogy was viewed as a reason enlarging rather than restricting the scope of Article 1 of Protocol 1 treating it as applicable to all social security benefits whether contributory or non-contributory.

12.41 In *Stec v UK*,[68] a key question at the admissibility hearing was whether non-contributory rights could amount to a 'possession' for the purpose of Article 1 of Protocol 1. The Grand Chamber of the European Court accepted that the *Gaygusuz* judgment was ambiguous on this point and that following it two distinct lines of authority emerged in the case law of the Convention organs. On the one hand, the Commission in particular had continued to find that a welfare benefit or pension fell within the scope of Article 1 of Protocol 1 only where contributions had been made to the fund that financed it (see, for example, *Szrabjer & Clarke v UK*;[69] *Carlin v UK*;[70] *Coke v UK*;[71] *Stawicki v Poland*;[72] *Jankovic v Croatia*;[73] *Kohls v Germany*;[74] and *Asmundsson v Iceland*[75]).

12.42 On the other hand, however, the Court held that even a welfare benefit in a non-contributory scheme could constitute a possession for the purposes of Article 1 of Protocol 1 (see *Buchen v Czech Republic*;[76] *Poirrez v France*;[77] *Wessels-Bergervoet v Netherlands*;[78] *Van den Bouwhuijsen & Schuring v Netherlands*[79]).

12.43 The Court in *Stec v UK* determined that non-contributory benefits should attract the protection of this Article since:

(a) its approach should reflect the reality of the way in which welfare provision is currently organised within the member states;

---

[66] (2000) 30 EHRR CD183.
[67] (2005) 40 EHRR 34, 45, para 37.
[68] (2005) 41 EHRR SE18.
[69] Applications 27004/95 and 27011/95, Commission Decision of 23 October 1997.
[70] Application 27537/95, Commission Decision of 3 December 1997, (1998) 25 EHRR CD 75.
[71] Application 38696/97, Commission Decision of 9 September 1998; [1999] EHRLR 130.
[72] Application 47711/99, 10 February 2000.
[73] Application 43440/98, 12 October 2000; (2000) 30 EHRR CD 183.
[74] Application 72719/01, 13 November 2003.
[75] Application 60669/00, judgment of 12 October 2004, (2005) 41 EHRR 42.
[76] Application 36541/97, s 46, 26 November 2000.
[77] Application 40892/98 (2005) 40 EHRR 34.
[78] Application 34462/97, ECHR 2002-IV; (2004) 38 EHRR 793.
[79] Application 44658/98, 16 December 2003.

(b) within most of these states there was a wide range of social security benefits designed to confer entitlements which arise as of right;

(c) the variety of funding methods make it increasingly artificial to hold that only benefits financed by contributions to a specific fund fall within the scope of Article 1 of Protocol 1;

(d) to exclude benefits paid for out of general taxation would be to disregard the fact that many claimants under this latter type of system also contribute to its financing, through the payment of tax;

(e) the mere fact that an interpretation of the Convention may extend into the sphere of social and economic rights should not be a decisive factor against such an interpretation: many Convention rights have social or economic implications despite being essentially of a civil and political nature.

The European Court usefully reiterated what Article 1 of Protocol 1 did not do **12.44** (see more generally *Kopecky v Slovakia*[80]): it did not create a right to acquire property nor restrict a contracting state's freedom to decide whether or not to have in place any form of social security scheme, or to choose the type or amount of benefits to provide under any such scheme. Yet, although Article 1 of Protocol 1 does not include the right to receive a social security payment of any kind, if a state does decide to create a benefits scheme, it must do so in a manner which is compatible with Article 14. These principles were confirmed in the final judgment in *Stec v UK*.[81]

Despite the significant development in *Stec v UK*, the significance accorded to **12.45** member states' margin of appreciation as regards social security policy means claimants are not often granted relief under this head of claim: see *Grant v UK*[82] and *Barrow v UK*.[83] However, assistance may be gleaned through reliance on Article 14 (see Chapter 14) or on the particular circumstances of a class of people, for example, those whose welfare benefits are to be removed: see *Asmundsson v Iceland*.[84] Here the removal of a disability pension from a small group of disabled people amounted to a breach which was not justified due to the disproportionate burden it caused.

(5) Statutory limits on compensation for unfair dismissal

Currently, the compensatory award element of unfair dismissal compensation in **12.46** the UK is capped at £60,600 (ERA 1996, s 124, as amended by the Employment

---

[80] Application 44912/98, s 35, ECHR 2004-IX [GC].
[81] See Applications 65731/01 and 65900/01, 12 April 2006, at para 53.
[82] Application 32570/03, 23 May 2006, (2007) 44 EHRR 1.
[83] Application 42735/02, 22 August 2006; (2006) Times, 11 September; [2006] All ER (D) 104 (Aug).
[84] (2005) 41 EHRR 42.

Relations Act 1999). In some cases where losses far exceed that limit an argument might be raised that the cap was in breach of Article 1 of Protocol 1.

12.47 The fact that the limit is set by statutory instrument is significant, because secondary legislation can be revoked by a court under the HRA 1998 where it is inconsistent with Convention rights.

12.48 The statutory cap discriminates against high-earning employees or those suffering the greatest losses after an unfair dismissal. Their position might be compared with that of those whose losses for unfair dismissal are smaller. Another comparison could be made with other applicants to employment tribunals.

12.49 The difference between applicants can be shown in two examples from domestic law: dismissal due to sex or race discrimination; and claims in relation to protected 'whistle-blowing' activities (see ERA 1996, s 127B, as amended by the Employment Relations Act 1999; and the Public Interest Disclosure (Compensation) Regulations 1999[85]). In these cases there is no statutory maximum to the award the tribunal can order for loss of earnings.

12.50 For a breach to be found, it would be necessary for there to be a difference of treatment (here, different provisions for the award of damages for loss of employment) and for there to be no objective and reasonable justification for that difference of treatment.

12.51 Can this difference of treatment be objectively and reasonably justified? Here, where the right to compensation is limited rather than completely removed, it must be asked whether the statutory cap has a legitimate aim and if there is a reasonably proportionate relationship between the cap itself and the impact it has on litigants seeking to claim damages for lost earnings.

12.52 Some assistance may be found in the initial suggestions in the 1998 White Paper *Fairness at Work* to remove the cap altogether.[86] There were some suggestions that compensation should be set according to the size of the business ordered to pay. The memoranda submitted to the Select Committee in relation to the abolition of the statutory cap included the arguments that the attractions in principle of completely removing the upper limit in unfair dismissal compensation were outweighed by practical and legal considerations, such as encouraging employers to avoid building up employment rights, and to substitute permanent contracts with fixed-term contracts. It was also argued that the lack of a statutory

---

[85] (SI 1999/1548).
[86] See Cm 3968, May 1998, para 3.5.

cap would cause more workers to submit originating applications to the tribunal after their dismissal.

In the authors' view these arguments are not persuasive. The entitlement to full **12.53** compensation for unfair dismissal would encourage employers to put proper systems in place to avoid unfair dismissals (see similar arguments in *Marshall v Southampton and SW Hampshire Area Health Authority*[87]).

It does not appear that the existence of a cap is proportionate to the bar it places **12.54** on all such litigants of the chance of obtaining their full pecuniary remedy. The public policy grounds put forward by business during the consultation period for the White Paper were not persuasive, although, it must be said, the government was persuaded to put the original £50,000 cap in place.

(6) Restrictive covenants and injunctions

Employers on occasion attempt to acquire injunctions to enforce restrictive cov- **12.55** enants. They may argue that without the protection of an injunction their property rights are damaged. The arguments put forward against the granting of an injunction would have to be in line with the permitted derogations under Article 1 of Protocol 1. If the restrictive covenant was found to be valid, when the balancing exercise was carried out it might well be found that the failure to grant an injunction (thus allowing the employee to compete unrestrained) would interfere with the employer's business or property.

An example of the balancing exercise in relation to a post-termination injunction **12.56** interfering with a former employee's rights to comment on his former employer, can be seen in *Jacubowski v Germany*,[88] discussed at 10.34–10.36 above.

(7) Discrimination in the enjoyment of property rights

The benefit to the applicant who relies upon Article 14 ECHR along with Article 1 **12.57** of Protocol 1, is that he need not show that there has been a violation of the later right, but simply that his complaint of discrimination falls within the ambit of a Convention right. Discrimination in relation to access to social security benefits could be in breach of these two Articles read together: see *Gaygusuz v Austria*[89] and *Matthews v UK*.[90] On the other hand, the justification for the different treatment will become the key area of focus.

---

[87] Case 152/84, [1986] ICR 335.
[88] (1995) 19 EHRR 64.
[89] (1996) 23 EHRR 364.
[90] Application 40302/98, 28 November 2000.

12.58 *Matthews* concerned the discriminatory impact of a rule refusing free bus passes to men under 65 years old. The government sought to argue that an entitlement to a bus pass was not a 'possession' within the scope of Article 1 of Protocol 1 since it was not conditional on the payment of national insurance or other contributions (see *Gaygusuz v Austria*); and further that if the Article was applicable, there was an objective and reasonable justification for the differential treatment: public policy considerations.

12.59 Mr Matthews argued that the government was incorrectly interpreting *Gaygusuz* on the grounds that it was his sex which caused him to be denied an otherwise enforceable right to a bus pass. He submitted that there was no justification for the interference with his right and that the period of time Parliament had declared necessary to equalise pension entitlement was irrelevant to the question of concessionary travel. However, the complaint was found to be admissible essentially on justification grounds.

12.60 There have been other cases where the more favourable treatment given to widows has been challenged but with little success.[91] Thus, in *Coke v UK*,[92] applications by widows in connection with the armed services pension scheme were dismissed since they had made no contributions to the relevant funds.

12.61 In *Carson & Reynolds v Secretary of State for Work & Pensions*,[93] it was held that differences of treatment based on living in a different country did not breach Article 14 and even if they did such a breach was justified by the need for legal certainty. However, in this case the House of Lords was prepared to assume that the fact of foreign residence was a 'personal characteristic' bringing the claimant within the 'or other status' scope of Article 14: see further *R (S) v Chief Constable of the South Yorkshire Police*.[94]

12.62 The House of Lords case of *Aston Cantlow & Others v Wallbank and Another*[95] also considered property rights and their interface with Article 14. Lord Scott said:[96]

> 135. Nor ... do Mr and Mrs Wallbank have any case of infringement of article 14. The comparators for article 14 purposes cannot possibly be persons who are not lay rectors. A person who is sued for £1000 that he owes is not discriminated against for article 14 purposes because people who do not owe £1000 are not similarly sued. A person who

---

[91] See *Crossland v UK* Application 36120/97, 9 November 1999; *Fielding v UK* Application 36940/97, 8 June 1999; *Willis v UK* (1999) 27 CD EHRR 166; *Leary v UK* Application 38890/97, 11 May 1999, 25 April 2000; *Sawden v UK* Application 38550/97, 8 June 1999, 12 March 2002; *Cornwell v UK* (1999) 27 CD EHRR 62.

[92] [1999] EHRLR 130.

[93] [2005] UKHL 37, [2006] 1 AC 173.

[94] [2004] 1 WLR 2196, 2213, [48].

[95] [2004] 1 AC 546, see 12.14–12.16.

[96] At [135].

builds in breach of planning permission and has proceedings taken against him by the local planning authority is not discriminated against for article 14 purposes because a person who builds and has obtained planning permission is not sued. The comparators are not apt. The apt comparator in the present case would be a co lay rector who was liable for chancel repairs to the Aston Cantlow church but on whom no 1932 Act notice had been served. There is no case here of article 14 discrimination.

For further consideration of Article 14, see Chapters 13 and 14.

F. Frequently asked questions

How is Article 1 of Protocol 1 relevant to employment law?   **12.63**

Since this Article covers property, chattels, and accrued rights which have an economic value, disputes covering shares, contracts, debts, pension and welfare benefits, and issues of goodwill may raise the topic of the right to a possession.

In what circumstances can someone be deprived of the right to the peaceful enjoyment of property?

Deprivation of property must be in accordance with international law and in the public interest. This requires a high threshold of being for a legitimate purpose and when achieving that purpose a fair balance must be struck between the need to protect individual rights and the demands of the general interest of the community. The state may limit the above rights in accordance with the general interest and in specific ways such as securing the payment of taxes.

What remedies can the courts order where a deprivation of property has occurred?

The Courts may order adequate compensation where a deprivation of property is proven. They are obliged to achieve a fair balance between the rights of the individual and the interests of the community. Where public policy issues are involved, for example, with tax questions, it will be difficult to argue that the ends do not justify the means.

Where the value of lost benefits such as a company car or free travel is sought before an employment tribunal the conditions within the contract will have to be balanced against the individual's rights to the accrued possessions she or he is seeking. Where a contract is lawfully terminated the right to such possession will have likewise ended, but if the employer is in breach of contract the right will attach to the ex-employee's claim for damages.

How can Article 1 of Protocol 1 protect the right to work?

Increasingly professions are regulated by licences or a permission system. Suspension or removal from a register may completely remove the ability to practise one's profession.

If such action is unlawful or if a bar to obtaining such a licence (such as a blanket ban on those with criminal convictions entering a particular profession) is deemed disproportionate or contrary to the public interest a violation of Article 1 of Protocol 1 may be found.

Can claims for pensions and other benefits utilise the rights within Article 1 of Protocol 1?

There has been an ongoing debate about whether non-contributory rights can amount to a possession for the purpose of Article 1 of Protocol 1. The ECtHR case of Stec v UK has established that non-contributory benefits fall within the remit of this Article.

The margin of appreciation accorded to member states means that as a matter of social security policy claimants are not often granted relief under this head of claim.

If welfare benefits are to be removed from a particular class of people reliance may usefully be placed upon Article 14. So whilst Article 1 of Protocol 1 does not include the right to receive a social security payment of any kind, if a state does decide to create a benefits scheme, it must do so in a manner which is compatible with Article 14. When relying upon Article 14 an individual only needs to show that his complaint of discrimination falls within the ambit of a Convention right.

Could Article 1 of Protocol 1 be used to dislodge the statutory cap on unfair dismissal compensation?

The limit on compensation is set by statutory instrument; this is relevant as courts can use the HRA 1998 to revoke secondary legislation. Whether the cap could be removed depends upon if the cap can be said to have a legitimate aim and whether there is a proportionate relationship between the cap and the impact upon litigants seeking compensation for lost earnings. There are strong arguments for suggesting that the public policy grounds for the cap are not persuasive; likewise the cap itself is arguably not proportionate to the blanket bar which deprives litigants of the chance to obtain their full pecuniary remedy.

Do injunctions protect property rights?

Employers may argue that without injunctions to enforce restrictive covenants, possessions such as client lists or confidential information risk being damaged or lost. Ex-employees can argue that granting an injunction would not be for a legitimate purpose (fact-specific) and/or would fail to achieve a fair balance between the individual rights and those of the community.

13

EQUALITY, ARTICLE 14, AND THE CONCEPT OF DISCRIMINATION

A. Introduction

13.01 The right to equal treatment has long been held to be a fundamental right though it is not so expressed in the ECHR and its content is the subject of much judicial exposition. Moreover, Article 14 ECHR, which is considered below and in Chapter 14, and which provides some non-discrimination protection, is well known to be limited. The Council of Europe has itself said that:[1]

> . . . the protection provided by Article 14 of the Convention with regard to equality and non-discrimination is limited in comparison with those provisions of other international instruments. The principal reason for this is the fact that Article 14 . . . does not contain an independent prohibition of discrimination, that is, it prohibits discrimination only with regard to the 'enjoyment of the rights and freedoms' set forth in the Convention.

13.02 The other international human rights instruments to which the Council of Europe made reference have had and it is likely will continue to have a greater impact on employment law in the UK than Article 14. Accordingly, the focus of this chapter is on those instruments, and on equality and discrimination in a more general human rights context than that found in Article 14 ECHR. Additionally, reference will be made to other provisions of the ECHR which might provide some protection in relation to discrimination and equality.

13.03 While this chapter addresses Article 14 ECHR in general context, in order to enable practitioners to apply general human rights principles to discrimination law,

---

[1] Explanatory Report to Protocol 12, para 1.

Chapter 14 considers the effect that Article 14 might have in the field of employment law with specific reference to new discrimination law in the UK.

This approach is necessary because, under the HRA 1998, the many provisions **13.04** concerning equality and non-discrimination in domestic law will have to be construed in a way which is consistent with the ECHR. Likewise the international provisions discussed in this chapter will have an increasing impact upon domestic legislation originating from the European equality agenda.

B. Equality, the Universal Declaration of Human Rights, and the International Covenant on Civil and Political Rights

(1) Article 1 UDHR

The starting point for a consideration of equality is to be found in the most **13.05** important general provisions approved by the United Nations. Article 1 of the Universal Declaration of Human Rights (UDHR) proclaims:

> All human beings are born free and equal in dignity[2] and rights.

From this principle the United Nations has developed a general principle of equality and non-discrimination as a fundamental element of international human rights law.[3]

This can be seen clearly in the guarantees of equality in Article 7 UDHR, and **13.06** Article 26 of the International Covenant on Civil and Political Rights (ICCPR). These two Articles are not directly applicable in domestic law, but both have had and continue to have an important effect on the development of equality law in Europe and in the UK (see, eg, Recital 3 to the Race Directive, and Recital 4 to the Employment Equality Directive).

(2) Article 7 UDHR

Article 7 UDHR provides: **13.07**

> All are equal before the law and are entitled without any discrimination to equal protection of the law. All are entitled to equal protection against any discrimination in violation of this Declaration and against any incitement to such discrimination.

---

[2] The relationship between equality and dignity in international human rights law is a close one. While they are not the same concepts, it can be said that dignity informs many of the harder points of equality jurisprudence. Dignity is discussed shortly at 13.21–13.29; for a more detailed discussion see Moon and Allen, 'Dignity Discourse in Discrimination Law: A Better Route to Equality?' [2006] EHRLR 610.

[3] Council of Europe Explanatory Report to Protocol 12, para 1: see 13.129–13.141.

(3) Article 26 ICCPR

13.08 Article 26 ICCPR provides:

> All persons are equal before the law and are entitled without any discrimination to the equal protection of the law. In this respect, the law shall prohibit any discrimination and guarantee to all persons equal and effective protection against discrimination on any ground such as race, colour, sex, language, religion, political or other opinion, national or social origin, property, birth or other status.

(4) The effect of these Articles

13.09 Article 7 UDHR has been the inspiration for other important non-discrimination human rights instruments, such as the International Convention on the Elimination of All Forms of Racial Discrimination (ICERD) 1966 and the Convention on the Elimination of All Forms of Discrimination Against Women (CEDAW) 1979. These Conventions have their own reviewing committees under UN auspices: the Committee on the Elimination of Racial Discrimination (see Article 8 ICERD) and the Committee on the Elimination of Discrimination Against Women (Article 17 CEDAW).

13.10 Article 7 UDHR sets out the important provisions of equality before the law and equal protection of the law (see 13.86–13.93 and 13.94–13.95 below). It establishes the universality of the rule that there should be protection against discrimination. These provisions are not found in Article 14 ECHR but are in Article 26 ICCPR, where they are amplified by the second sentence. This states what the law must guarantee in respect of non-discrimination.

13.11 Article 26 ICCPR is free-standing and comprehensive (see *R (Pretty) v DPP*[4]); by contrast, Article 14 ECHR only provides for a right not to suffer discrimination which is parasitic on other rights within the ECHR (see, eg, *Van Raalte v Netherlands*;[5] *Botta v Italy*[6]). There is a body of jurisprudence which has grown up around Article 26 ICCPR, since some countries have permitted a right of individual complaint to the United Nations Human Rights Committee set up under Article 28 ICCPR in relation to alleged breaches of Article 26.[7] Additionally,

---

[4] [2002] 1 AC 800.
[5] (1997) 24 EHRR 503, at 516–17.
[6] (1998) 26 EHRR 241, at 250 (para 39).
[7] In *MacDonald v The Ministry of Defence* [2000] IRLR 748, [2001] ICR 1, the EAT considered one such case, *Toonen v Australia* (1994) 1–3 IHRR 97, in deciding that the Sex Discrimination Act 1975 should be construed so as to prohibit discrimination on grounds of sexuality. The case was subsequently overturned on appeal, and the House of Lords agreed with the Court of Session that the meaning of 'sex' in the Act could not be construed to include sexuality.

some European countries, most notably the Netherlands, have incorporated Article 26 ICCPR into their constitutions.

Because the ECHR provides only a weak right to protection against discrimin- **13.12** ation, the Council of Europe has agreed Protocol 12 to the ECHR which gives much stronger protection. This is discussed below at 13.129–13.141.

(5) The effect of those limits outside the Council of Europe

There is a broad range and variety of steps that have been or are due to be taken **13.13** outside the Council of Europe. Some of these will be well known to lawyers and advisers who are familiar with employment law such as the domestic anti-discrimination Acts. This legislation has undergone great change in the last five years as the Race Directive[8] and the Employment Equality Directive[9] (which draw on the UDHR, ICCPR, ICERD, and CEDAW, as well as on other inter-national human rights instruments such as the ILO Conventions) have been implemented in full into UK law.

Accordingly, practitioners need to understand not just the growing complexity of **13.14** new equality provisions, but how they interrelate, and what are the themes com-mon to the new provisions. The impact of these new Directives on employment law is discussed in Chapter 14.

C. Equality in a general human rights context

(1) Equality as an axiom for rational behaviour

It has been said that the principle of equal treatment is one of the premises on **13.15** which a modern liberal democracy is built. It is a first principle of law and a prin-ciple of rational behaviour by the state. Thus, Lord Hoffmann giving the judgment of the Privy Council in *Matadeen v Pointu*,[10] said that 'treating like cases alike and unlike cases differently is a general axiom of rational behaviour'.

In the context of developing equality and non-discrimination provisions this is **13.16** very important. Courts and tribunals often feel uncomfortable with, and even startled by, the reach of new equality laws. It can help them to be reminded that the social purpose of new legislation is based on this axiom of rational behaviour. Indeed, it is clear that public policy in the UK courts will support equal treatment

---

[8] 2000/43/EC.
[9] 2000/78/EC.
[10] [1999] 1 AC 98, at 109. Though this case concerned a construction of the constitution of Mauritius, these views were clearly expressed as having universal relevance.

in relation to the right to work. (See *Nagle v Fielden*,[11] where it was held that public policy would prevent the striking out of a claim by a woman trainer to be permitted to train under Jockey Club rules.)

(2) Equality as a superior rule of law

13.17 Equality is also described as a general principle of Community law; indeed, it has been described as a part of the foundation of the Community (see, eg, *Brunnhofer v Bank der Österreichischen Postsparkasse*[12]).

13.18 The ECJ developed non-discrimination principles from a very early stage of its existence in order to secure competitiveness (see *United Brands v Commission of the European Communities*[13]) and eliminate obstacles to free movement,[14] and has applied these principles very widely. It has described equality as a 'superior rule of law', because it is one of the general principles common to the laws of the member states. This is because it is one of the general principles common to the laws of the member states. (See *Aktien Zuckerfabrik Schšppenstedt v Council of the European Communities*,[15] where this concept first emerged as a touchstone for liability to make good damage caused by community institutions and servants pursuant to Article 288 (ex 215) EC.)

13.19 In fact it is not widely appreciated that the ECJ had developed a concept of indirect discrimination well before the idea was brought to the UK from the US (*Geitling Selling Agency for Ruhr Coal v European Coal and Steel Community*,[16] and *Compagnie des Hauts Fourneaux de Chasse v High Authority of the European Coal and Steel Community*[17]).[18]

13.20 Because equality is a superior rule of law, it is a principle which is applied by the ECJ in any relevant case, whether or not there is a black letter provision that requires its application. Thus, in *Prais v Council of the European Communities*,[19] a case in which an applicant for a job within the EC who was Jewish complained about exams taking place on a Saturday, the ECJ readily recognised that there was such a right of equality even though there was no express relevant provision.

---

[11] [1966] 2 QB 633.

[12] Case C-381/99, [2001] IRLR 271, at para 28.

[13] Case 27/76, [1978] ECR 207.

[14] See E Guild, *European Community Law from a Migrant's Perspective* (Deventer: Kluwer, 2000).

[15] Case 5/71, [1971] ECR 975, at para 11.

[16] Case 2/56, [1957] ECR 9.

[17] Case 15/57, [1957] and [1958] ECR 211.

[18] For a description of the fortuitous events that led to this change, see D Pannick, *The Concept of Discrimination* (Oxford: OUP, 1985), at 39 *et seq.*

[19] Case 130/75, [1976] ECR 1589.

(3) Equality as a consequence of respect for human dignity

There is a close relationship between equality and respect for human dignity. The **13.21**
concepts are not the same but are frequently conjoined as in Article 1 UDHR.
A recognition of the importance of the obligation to respect human dignity is
likely to inform the following problematic areas:

- Understanding what is harassment on protected grounds.
- Considering when it is appropriate to treat two persons as being in an analogous or comparable situation.
- Identifying what is permissible differential treatment. The equal treatment rule tells us that when two persons are not in an analogous position they should be treated differently. The rule does not say what should be the nature of that different treatment. A reference to dignity may help.
- Resolving confusion in relation to the test for justification.
- Deciding when reasonable accommodation or adjustment should be required. The UK is beginning to get to grips with this concept in relation to disability rights but across the Atlantic the concept appears to have a wider utility both as a means of addressing individuated problems of disadvantage and as a method for mediating conflicts of rights.[20]
- Resolving conflicts of rights between competing equality claims. Religion and sex provide particularly fertile grounds but others have also arisen.[21] At present it is not at all clear how, that is to say by what mechanism or juridical principle, such disputes should be resolved.[22] Either the European legislator or domestic

---

[20] See *Copsey v WWB Devon Clays Ltd* [2005] ICR 1789.

[21] The relationship between age rules and sex discrimination may prove to be the most difficult in the future but this relationship, while recognised as existing (see *Price v Civil Service Commission* [1978] ICR 27), is only now beginning to lead to more developed case law, see, eg, Case C-187/00 *Kutz-Bauer v Freie und Hansestadt Hamburg* [2003] ECR I-2741.

[22] It is only in Art 4(2) of Directive 2000/78/EC establishing a general framework for equal treatment in employment and occupation that we find any attempt to offer a resolution of a possible conflict of right between religion and other matters addressed: '2. Member states may maintain national legislation in force at the date of adoption of this Directive or provide for future legislation incorporating national practices existing at the date of adoption of this Directive pursuant to which, in the case of occupational activities within churches and other public or private organisations the ethos of which is based on religion or belief, a difference of treatment based on a person's religion or belief shall not constitute discrimination where, by reason of the nature of these activities or of the context in which they are carried out, a person's religion or belief constitute a genuine, legitimate and justified occupational requirement, having regard to the organisation's ethos. This difference of treatment shall be implemented taking account of Member States' constitutional provisions and principles, as well as the general principles of Community law, and should not justify discrimination on another ground.'

Provided that its provisions are otherwise complied with, this Directive shall thus not prejudice the right of churches and other public or private organisations, the ethos of which is based on religion or belief, acting in conformity with national constitutions and laws, to require individuals working for them to act in good faith and with loyalty to the organisation's ethos.

legislature will have to address them or else judges will have to cope on a case-by-case basis.[23] Legal uncertainty is rife and needs to be removed.

- Helping with a contrasting problem: the proper way to address what is sometimes called intersectional discrimination or discrimination which arises from multiple grounds. This issue is one which is now increasingly apparent as requiring special consideration.[24]

- Securing substantive equality: overarching all this is the desire to see a development in the benefits from equality law. The demand for substantive equality is repeated wherever disadvantaged groups or their advocates meet. The question that remains unanswered is whether this means equality of outcome or whether it means that there is a need for greater equality in the starting position of those to whom the equal treatment principle is applied.

13.22   There are at least three different roles[25] that dignity can play—as a value, as a principle, and as the basis for defined rights.[26] Dignity as a value or principle can help with the task of establishing equality.

13.23   Its importance as a moral right was emphasised in *Ghaidan v Godin-Mendoza*.[27] When discussing whether a gay man could succeed to a tenancy of his deceased partner, Baroness Hale of Richmond pointed out:

> Democracy is founded on the principle that each individual has equal value. Treating some as automatically having less value than others not only causes pain and distress to that person but also violates his or her dignity as a human being. . . . such treatment is damaging to society as a whole. Wrongly to assume that some people have talent and others do not is a huge waste of human resources. It also damages social cohesion, creating not only an under-class, but an under-class with a rational grievance. Third, it is the reverse of the rational behaviour we now expect of government and the state. Power must not be exercised arbitrarily. If distinctions are to be drawn, particularly upon a group basis, it is an important discipline to look for a rational basis for those distinctions. Finally, it is a purpose of all human rights instruments to secure the protection of the essential rights of members of minority groups, even

---

[23] For an example of the kinds of difficulties that can occur see *O'Neill v Governors of St Thomas More Roman Catholic Voluntarily Aided Upper School* [1997] ICR 33.

[24] Thus, the Equal Opportunities Commission has recently launched an investigation into the position of ethnic minority women at work. See '*Moving on up? ethnic minority women at work,*' at <http://www.eoc.org.uk/Default.aspx?page=17696&lang=en>.

[25] This point has been noted elsewhere in relation to the jurisprudence in Germany on human dignity: J Jones, 'Common Constitutional Traditions: Can the Meaning of Human Dignity under German Law Guide the European Court of Justice?' [2004] Public Law, Spring, 182.

[26] Sometimes described as 'moral' rights, a terminology used by Advocate-General Francis Jacobs in his classic Opinion in Case C-168/91 *Konstantinidis* [1993] ECR I-1191 at [18].

[27] [2004] 2 AC 557.

when they are unpopular with the majority. Democracy values everyone equally even if the majority does not . . . [28]

In this way, human dignity was found to be a key concept for determining when a law which distinguished between heterosexual and homosexual persons should be held not to comply with the right to equality in the ECHR. **13.24**

Sometimes the ECtHR refers to equal dignity. In *Gündüz v Turkey*,[29] the ECtHR described *equal dignity* as a foundation value of democracy. Later, Council of Europe conventions have made the connection explicit, as in the 1997 Convention on Human Rights and Biomedicine.[30] **13.25**

Commenting on the inviolability of human dignity the Praesidium responsible for drafting the European Charter of Fundamental Rights made it clear that it considered dignity to be at the core of human rights: **13.26**

> The dignity of the human person is not only a fundamental right in itself but constitutes the real basis of fundamental rights. The 1948 Universal Declaration of Human Rights enshrined this principle in its preamble . . . It results that none of the rights laid down in this Charter may be used to harm the dignity of another person, and that the dignity of the human person is part of the substance of the rights laid down in this Charter. It must therefore be respected, even where a right is restricted.[31]

Dignity is also at the centre of much common law. Thus, Munby J recently said in *R (A, B, X and Y) v East Sussex CC and the Disability Rights Commission (No 2)* that respect for human dignity 'is a core value of the common law, long pre-dating the [European Convention on Human Rights]'.[32] This is more fully discussed in Moon and Allen (see footnote 2 above). **13.27**

Further, Newman J pointed out how the common law would develop in *Horkulak v Cantor Fitzgerald International*[33] when discussing whether an employee must put up with foul abuse from a boss, thus: **13.28**

> The law has developed so as to recognise an employment contract as engaging obligations in connection with the self esteem and dignity of the employee.[34]

---

[28] [2004] 2 AC 557 at para 132. See also Baroness Hale of Richmond, 'The Quest for Equal Treatment' [2005] Public Law, Autumn, 571.

[29] *Gündüz v Turkey* Application 35071/97, 4 December 2003, (2005) 41 EHRR 5. At [40] the Court held that '. . . tolerance and respect for the equal dignity of all human beings constitute the foundations of a democratic, pluralistic society'.

[30] The Convention for the Protection of Human Rights and Dignity of the Human Being with regard to the Application of Biology and Medicine, Oviedo, 4.IV.1997. See also by way of a wider example principle 2 in the appendix to recommendation no r (97) 20 of the Committee of Ministers to Member States on 'Hate Speech' adopted on 30 October 1997, at the 607th meeting of the Minister's Deputies.

[31] <http://www.europarl.eu.int/charter/pdf/04473_en.pdf>.

[32] [2003] EWHC 167 (Admin), at para 86.

[33] [2004] ICR 697, [2003] EWHC 1918.

[34] See para 17.

13.29 It seems likely that the close relationship between dignity and equality will develop in the light of the obligation on the Commission for Equality and Human Rights to exercise its functions:

> . . . with a view to encouraging and supporting the development of a society in which — there is respect for the dignity and worth of each individual.[35]

D. Identifying prima facie discrimination in a human rights context

(1) The basic test for discrimination

13.30 In *Abdulaziz, Cabales and Balkandali v UK*,[36] the European Court stated that a difference of treatment was discriminatory if it 'has no objective and reasonable justification', that is, if it does not pursue a 'legitimate aim' or if there is not a 'reasonable relationship of proportionality' between the means employed and the aim sought to be realised.

13.31 The approach of the ECJ has been similar, though historically perhaps rather more prescriptive. It has said that the prohibition on unlawful discrimination requires that:

> comparable situations are not to be treated differently and . . . different situations are not to be treated alike.[37]

The European Court has used a similar formulation to that cited from the ECJ: *Thlimmenos v Greece* (see below at 13.110–13.118 for further discussion of this case).[38]

13.32 Of course, the ECJ, like the European Court, recognises that there may be an objective justification for such discrimination. It is well established that discrimination may be justifiable on objective grounds (see *Bilka-Kaufhaus GmbH v Karin Weber von Hartz*,[39] and the discussion at 13.114–13.118 below).

---

[35] See EA 2006, s 3(c).

[36] (1985) 7 EHRR 471, at para 72.

[37] See, eg, Case 203/86 *Spain v Council of the European Communities* [1988] ECR 4563, para 25. In *Re Colgan and Others* [1997] 1 CMLR 53, this principle was held to apply (at para 51). It has added that '. . . discrimination can arise only through the application of different rules to comparable situations or the application of the same rule to different situations' (see, eg, Case C-279/93 *Finanzamt Koeln-altstadt v Roland Schumacker* [1995] ECR I-225 and Case C-220/02 *Österreichischer Gewerkschaftsbund, Gewerkschaft der Privatangestellten v Wirtschaftskammer Österreich* [2004] ECR I-5907; see also C-17/05 *Cadman v HSE* [2006] ICR 1623).

[38] (2001) 36 EHRR 15, at para 44.

[39] Case 170/84, [1986] ECR 1607.

(2) Identifying direct and indirect discrimination

The phrases cited from the European Court and the ECJ at 13.30–13.31 above **13.33** may seem unusual to employment lawyers whose first familiarity is with domestic law definitions of discrimination. For them direct discrimination will occur when there is less favourable treatment on a specific ground; and indirect discrimination will occur where there are statistics which show that there is a group which has suffered a specific relative disadvantage. But these concepts, though useful in themselves, are really just applications of this approach.

Thus, direct discrimination will occur where persons in comparable circum- **13.34** stances are treated differently; and indirect discrimination will occur when persons in different situations are treated in the same way. In the one case the direct discrimination occurs because there is less favourable treatment; and in the other, the indirect discrimination occurs because the same requirement is applied to persons who have very different characteristics.

However, the difference between this human rights law approach to indirect dis- **13.35** crimination and the domestic law approach, in for instance section 1(1)(b) of the Race Relations Act 1976, is that the domestic law approach has been based on discrimination against a group.[40] In human rights law, it is enough if the same rule is applied to one person who is in a different situation.

Thus, in human rights law, indirect discrimination is not concerned only, or even **13.36** predominantly, with discrimination against groups. Of course groups of persons may suffer discrimination (see, eg, *Belgian Linguistics (No. 2)*[41]), and in those cases it may be easier to prove, but it is not necessary that there be a disadvantaged group. It is for this reason that the definition of indirect discrimination in the Race and Framework Directives is less concerned with proof of discrimination against a group (see Chapter 14).

(3) A comparison with domestic law discrimination concepts

Domestic law approaches discrimination principally in two ways: first, as a mat- **13.37** ter for statutory law; and, secondly, as an issue in relation to good administration. These two different ways are not wholly mutually distinct since good non-discriminatory administration will always involve the promotion of equal opportunities at work, though it will also go further and be concerned with matters such as tax and the distribution of benefits.

---

[40] However, the new definition of indirect discrimination in s 1(1A) of the Race Relations Act 1976, deriving from the Race Directive, is less 'group' focused and more concerned with disguised discrimination.

[41] (1979–80) 1 EHRR 252.

13.38   However, for the employment lawyer the concept of discrimination tends to arise in the context of discrete statutory provisions such as the Equal Pay Act 1970, the Sex Discrimination Act 1975, the Race Relations Act 1976, and the Disability Discrimination Act 1995, and the Fair Employment and Treatment (Northern Ireland) Order 1998.[42] It is from those measures that we tend to derive our concept of non-discrimination and equal treatment.

13.39   In this way it may seem misleading to talk of *the* concept of discrimination in domestic law. Practitioners will know that the definitions in the Equal Pay Act and the Disability Discrimination Act are not the same as those in the Sex Discrimination Act, Race Relations Act, and Fair Employment and Treatment Order. These differences reflect the different subject matter of each piece of legislation.

13.40   However, it is important to understand that conceptually they are indeed linked. Once this is realised, the link with human rights law is much easier to grasp, since in human rights law it is the links between the concepts which are particularly important. A firm understanding of the links between these different enactments will help practitioners to understand what the HRA 1998 can do in relation to domestic law. This chapter simply states enough for these links to become clear rather than aiming to give a complete overview of domestic discrimination law.

13.41   The Sex Discrimination Act, Race Relations Act, and Fair Employment and Treatment Order are all based explicitly on two different types of discrimination known to lawyers as direct and indirect discrimination. Direct discrimination occurs when one person is treated less favourably than another on some proscribed ground (see, eg, s 1(1)(a) of the Sex Discrimination Act 1975 and the Race Relations Act 1976). However, it is well known that the definition of discrimination in the Disability Discrimination Act 1995 does not fall neatly in line with these definitions. Thus under the 1995 Act, the definition of discrimination starts with the concept of disability (s 1; see also *Goodwin v Patent Office*[43]) and sets special tests for the assessment of the discrimination (previously s 5, now s 3A; see also *Clark v Novacold Ltd*[44]), which are obviously not the same as the direct and indirect tests. What is the reason for this different approach?

13.42   The reason for this difference is that in cases of sex, race, or religion and belief discrimination, the law starts with the assumption that a person's sex, race, religion, or belief is or ought to be irrelevant to the treatment that he or she receives.

---

[42] SI 1998/3162 (NI 21).
[43] [1999] ICR 302.
[44] [1999] ICR 951.

By contrast, a person who is within the definition of disability is most certainly not in the same position. The fact of disability is highly relevant. The legislation recognises that such a person may need special assistance to achieve substantive equality.[45]

Similarly, the law recognises that pregnant women or women who have just **13.43** given birth are in a special situation. It is inappropriate to treat them in exactly the same way as men, or indeed other women. Accordingly, special protections to ensure their fair treatment have been developed. These must be applied unless there is a justification for not so acting.

These differences in our own domestic statutes reflect a human rights approach **13.44** which concentrates on the context. In some cases persons are in exactly the same context, and in some they are not. Equality and non-discrimination require different kinds of treatment according to the context.

The Equal Pay Act 1970 is not expressly concerned with the concept of discrimin- **13.45** ation but it is in practice very much so. Equality is merely the opposite of discrimination. In proceedings under the Equal Pay Act 1970, the concern is always with establishing the relative positions of the relevant woman and man. However, in some cases where the positions are found to be truly comparable, it may be said that there is some special consideration which it is said justifies unequal pay. The process that human rights law (and therefore the HRA 1998) requires is therefore an analysis of the relevant context and of any justifications that may be advanced. Under the Equal Pay Act it is possible to justify overt direct discrimination.[46]

Of course, under domestic statutory provisions dealing with indirect discrimin- **13.46** ation it is possible to justify the discrimination. The tests for justification have been held to be the same (*Rainey v Greater Glasgow Health Board*;[47] *Hampson v Department of Education and Science*[48]). Discrimination lawyers often say that it is not possible to justify acts of direct sex or race discrimination. However, this conclusion does not bear closer analysis. Each piece of legislation makes special provision for genuine occupational qualifications which justify acts of direct discrimination. Thus in the Race Relations Act 1976 it is permissible to have as a genuine occupational requirement for a part in a play that a person be of a

---

[45] These points were made explicit by the House of Lords in *Archibald v Fife Council* [2004] UKHL 32, [2005] 1 ICR 954.
[46] The importance of this was recognised by the ECJ when considering the EPA in *Cadman v HSE* [2006] ICR 1623.
[47] [1987] ICR 129.
[48] [1989] ICR 179 (CA), [1990] ICR 511, [1991] 1 AC 171 (HL).

particular colour for reasons of authenticity (s 5(2)(a)). In such a case a person who is white, might be just as capable of acting as the Moor in *Othello* as someone who is black, but it is justifiable to require a black actor for reasons of authenticity. In this case the freedom of expression of the producer and playwright are engaged. So it is not surprising that here the Race Relations Act 1976 actually defines when it is justifiable to discriminate directly.[49] There are other areas where the reach of these Acts is specifically limited. In some cases these too are based on a principle of justification.

13.47   Although domestic legislation does not normally give an open-ended right to justify direct discrimination (as opposed to indirect discrimination), it does recognise that some such direct discrimination is justified. By contrast, human rights law is not so prescriptive in relation to such justifications. It recognises that not all possible occasions when a justification should be recognised can be stated. Its concern is to state the principles to be applied to test the justification when one is advanced. When the non-discrimination rights which were enjoyed domestically were so limited it was possible to attempt to catalogue the situations in which an act of discrimination might be justified. However, as these rights become more extensive this will be less and less possible. The interactions between differing rights will be so varied that it is unlikely that they could be reduced to a single section in an Act.

13.48   These themes of context or situation and justification are at the heart of Community law and the jurisprudence of the ECHR. Indeed, they are more important than the precise labels—direct or indirect—that practitioners tend to use. They help to ensure that the right to equality is an effective fundamental right which has sufficient utility to be able to respond to the effects of interaction with other fundamental rights.

(4) The three-stage analysis of discrimination and equality issues

13.49   Accordingly, the statements set out in 13.30–13.31 above should be seen as emphasising how important it is to identify what are the relevant circumstances so that the treatment in question can be appropriately analysed. This is as true for discrimination contrary to the ECHR as it is for discrimination contrary to Community law, or other human rights instruments. Plainly, if the situations of two or more persons are not comparable then different treatment is not only appropriate but necessary, whereas if the circumstances are the same then the

---

[49] Other possible genuine occupational requirements include work in a restaurant, as a photographic model, and providing personal welfare services. For genuine occupational qualifications under the Sex Discrimination Act 1975, s 7.

same treatment is both appropriate and necessary, unless in either case there is some objective justification. In this sense, all discrimination cases are concerned with a three-part analysis:

(a) What is the treatment in issue?
(b) What are the relevant circumstances?
(c) What, if any, justification for such treatment is advanced?

In practice the facts relevant to the different parts of the analysis may, and usually will, overlap.

(5) The importance of identifying the whole context

The importance of identifying the whole context cannot be over-emphasised. **13.50** The analysis of a situation that is said to be discriminatory requires a careful consideration of all the relevant circumstances since the way in which the circumstances are considered may ultimately be determinative as to whether there is a need for any assessment of objective justification. Thus in *Re Colgan*,[50] the Northern Ireland High Court applied the above principles in deciding whether a decision of the Northern Ireland Civil Service Commission not to permit Irish nationals to be appointed to the Civil Service was discriminatory. The court accepted that there was considerable sensitivity in the work of a civil servant, and that potentially it was justifiable to discriminate against foreign nationals. However, this policy did not operate in relation to recruitment into the UK Civil Service and in some parts of the Northern Ireland Civil Service. Accordingly, once the relevant situations were identified the reason for the different treatment fell away.

(6) Disguised discrimination

Community case law does not simply analyse discrimination as direct or indirect. **13.51** It also analyses disguised discrimination. Disguised discrimination is often considered in the context of indirect discrimination (see, eg, *Defrenne v Sabena*[51]), but it may be considered separately where, for instance, a distinction based on residence is thought to mask an impermissible distinction which is in truth based on nationality (see, eg, *Biehl v Administration des Contributions du Grand-Duché de Luxembourg*;[52] *Bachmann v Belgian State*[53]). Such an approach looks to see if less favourable treatment has been disguised under different terminology.

---

[50] [1997] 1 CMLR 53.
[51] Case 43/75, [1976] ICR 547, at para 18.
[52] Case C-175/88, [1990] ECR I-1779, 1793, para 14.
[53] Case C-204/90, [1992] ECR I-249.

The approach is always concerned with substantive equality: see 13.57–13.85 below. It is in this way that the division into direct and indirect discrimination can become a hindrance rather than a help.

13.52 This can be seen domestically in *James v Eastleigh Borough Council*,[54] which, though a case brought under domestic legislation as direct discrimination, is better seen as a case of disguised discrimination between men and women. Mr James, who was under 65, wished to use the Council's leisure centre for free. The Council granted free access to those over pensionable age.

13.53 However, since pensionable age for a man was 65 and for a woman 60, the rule was discriminatory. The use of pensionable age as the test for free access disguised (if only poorly) the discriminatory nature of the provision. The question for English domestic law was in what way could this provision be found to be unlawful under the Sex Discrimination Act 1975; was it directly or indirectly discriminatory?

Mr James's case was brought as one of direct discrimination in the county court. When the case reached the Court of Appeal, it was held that the discrimination was indirect and not direct. At that stage, the case was lost. On further appeal, the House of Lords held that a rule which though on its face is neutral is in fact a disguised sex-based criterion and is directly discriminatory. The approach of the House of Lords was to hold that but for the sex differential in pension age there would have been no discrimination.[55] Had this case been approached using the Community law concept of disguised discrimination, it is doubtful whether it would have been litigated so far.

(7) Justification

13.54 The approach to issues of justification in respect of discrimination is very much case specific. Different degrees of justification may be required according to the context. Thus, it has been said that race and sex discrimination require a very high degree of justification (*Abdulaziz, Cabales and Balkandali v UK*;[56] see also *Schuler-Zgraggen v Switzerland*;[57] and *Burgharz v Switzerland*[58]). Moreover,

---

[54] [1990] 1 QB 61 (CA), [1990] 2 AC 751 (HL).
[55] The use of the 'but for' test requires care, however, as the House of Lords explained in *Chief Constable of West Yorkshire v Khan* [2001] UKHL 48, [2001] IRLR 830. See also *St Helens Borough Council v Derbyshire* [2007] UKHL 16.
[56] (1985) 7 EHRR 471, para 78.
[57] (1993) 16 EHRR 405, para 67.
[58] (1994) 18 EHRR 101, para 27.

where the issue concerns indirect discrimination by the state in the process of lawmaking, a broader margin may be permissible (see *R v Secretary of State for Employment, ex parte Seymour-Smith*[59]).

As always in relation to justifications for breach of human rights principles, a test **13.55** of proportionality will be applied. Accordingly, it will normally be necessary for the party seeking to justify the discriminatory or unequal treatment to show that they have a permissible objective and the means taken to obtain that objective are proportionate. Usually this will require it to be shown that it is necessary to take the steps in question to obtain that objective.

(8) Formal equality and substantive equality

Equality as a concept has different meanings. In the UK and in Europe, equal **13.56** treatment has usually been discussed as a special kind of formal equality in the context of *equality of opportunity* rather than *substantive equality* or *equality of outcome*, although sometimes the two concepts become mixed up. Thus, Lord Denning MR said in *Edwards v SOGAT*,[60] that the courts would not allow 'a power to be exercised arbitrarily or capriciously or with unfair discrimination, neither in the making of rules nor in the enforcement of them'.

Consequently, equality of opportunity, in the sense of merely a right to an objec- **13.57** tive assessment against defined job criteria, is of little use to a disabled person if in fact the disabled person can never meet those job requirements. Likewise, equality of opportunity in a recruitment exercise is of little assistance to a person who, by reason of gross educational inequalities as a result of living in a deprived and racially segregated area, lacks the necessary skills to succeed.[61]

This limited concept of equality is slowly changing and giving way to a more **13.58** proactive pursuit of substantive equality. The main reasons for this change in Europe have been a consideration of the nature of inequality suffered by the disabled, and a recognition of the fact that merely to secure equality of opportunity (in the sense of equal and objective recruitment exercises) has not produced a result which is truly socially inclusive. Most critically, the decision of the Fourth World Conference on Women, in Beijing, underlined the importance of

---

[59] [1999] ICR 447, at paras 66–67.
[60] [1971] Ch 354.
[61] To some extent the existing legislation has addressed some of the issues associated with inequalities of training: see Sex Discrimination Act 1975, s 47; Race Relations Act 1976, ss 35–37.

mainstreaming equality for women,[62] as did the government's Equality Statement of 30 November 1999, in which it was said:

> . . . we (will) continue to tackle discrimination in all institutions, we will champion equality in every sense and at every level. Public bodies must take the lead in promoting equal opportunities and the Government will put this obligation in legislation as soon as Parliamentary time permits. Together with our commitment to implement the Stephen Lawrence Inquiry action plan, this will help ensure public institutions and services are free from discriminatory procedures and practices and should improve the position of disadvantaged groups, both as employees and users of public services . . . . We will also build on existing mainstreaming and appraisal guidance to ensure that policies are inclusive, and take full account of the needs and experience of all those likely to be affected by them, and of the impact on particular groups in society. We will continue to take action to meet our commitment to remove the under-representation of women, members of minority ethnic groups and disabled people on public bodies; and to meet the challenging targets set for representation of these groups in the Civil Service . . .[63]

13.59   Thus, action to secure positive discrimination in favour of a disadvantaged group has led to litigation and a sharper focus on these issues. Once equality of outcome is accepted as the main social aim, it becomes necessary to consider more deeply what equality requires. This in turn has led to a greater consideration of the necessity to take positive action to secure what might be called substantive equality, without giving rise to objectionable positive discrimination. These are sometimes called special measures.

(9) Substantive equality through special measures

13.60   Article 2(2) ICERD permits states parties:

> . . . when the circumstances so warrant [to] take in the social economic cultural and other fields special and concrete measures to ensure the adequate development and protection of certain racial groups or individuals belonging to them, for the purpose of guaranteeing them the full and equal enjoyment of human rights and fundamental freedoms. These measures shall in no case entail as a consequence the maintenance of unequal or separate rights for different racial groups after the objective for which they were taken has been achieved.

13.61   There are similar provisions in Article 4 CEDAW:

> Adoption by states parties of temporary special measures aimed at accelerating de facto equality between men and women shall not be considered discrimination as defined in the present Convention but shall in no way entail as a consequence the

---

[62] See Platform for Action and the Beijing Declaration, the Report of the Fourth World Conference on Women (UN Dept of Public Information, 1996), at 204.
[63] *Hansard*, col 175W (30 November 1999).

maintenance of unequal or separate standards; these measures shall be discontinued when the objectives of equality of opportunity and treatment have been achieved.

This interpretation of the concept of discrimination recognises that sometimes **13.62** women are not in the same position as men, and that therefore different treatment of them is necessary and justified and therefore not discriminatory.

The Committee on the Elimination of Discrimination Against Women considers **13.63** this a very important aspect of CEDAW. It has issued Recommendations which underline the importance of Article 4. Thus, it has recommended in relation to politics that:

> . . . States parties take further direct measures in accordance with Article 4 of the Convention to ensure . . . to women on equal terms with men and without any discrimination the opportunities to represent their Government at the international level and to participate in the work of international organizations.[64]

The UN committees which are concerned with maintaining an overview of its **13.64** equality provisions are particularly concerned to ensure that equality means more than just procedural equality. Thus the Human Rights Committee of the United Nations has said that states parties may take positive measures under Article 26 ICCPR[65] to ensure the equal enjoyment of rights without discrimination, and this may include affirmative action measures including legislation.[66]

European law has been less keen on such positive action. Article 2(4) of the Equal **13.65** Treatment Directive clearly anticipates that some positive action measures may be necessary. It states: 'This Directive shall be without prejudice to measures to promote equal opportunity for men and women in particular by removing existing inequalities which affect women's opportunities . . .'

Article 141 EC (ex Article 119), as amended by the Amsterdam Treaty, seemed **13.66** to permit positive action in relation to sex equality. Article 141(4) EC provided:

> 4. With a view to ensuring full equality in practice between men and women in working life, the principle of equal treatment shall not prevent any Member State from maintaining or adopting measures providing for specific advantages in order to make it easier for the under-represented sex to pursue a vocational activity or to prevent or compensate for disadvantages in professional career.

Four judgments of the ECJ in relation to positive action under the Equal **13.67** Treatment Directive came in quick succession: *Kalanke v Bremen*;[67] *Marschall v*

---

[64] CEDAW General Recommendation 8, A/43/38, 04/03/88.
[65] This provision is closely analogous to Art 14 ECHR, though it is a free-standing provision. It also formed the basis for Art 21 in Chapter III of the European Charter of Fundamental Rights.
[66] General Comment 18, CCPR/C/SR 901.
[67] Case C-450/93, [1995] ECR I-3051.

Land Nordrhein-Westfalen;[68] *Badeck and others*;[69] and *Katarina Abrahamsson, Leif Anderson v Elisabet Fogelqvist.*[70] The effect of these decisions can be taken from the third ruling of the last case:

> 3. Article 2(1) and (4) of Directive 76/207 does not preclude a rule of national case-law under which a candidate belonging to the under-represented sex may be granted preference over a competitor of the opposite sex, provided that the candidates possess equivalent or substantially equivalent merits, where the candidatures are subjected to an objective assessment which takes account of the specific personal situations of all the candidates.

13.68 The ruling in this last case seemed decisively to reject the view that had been prevalent, that the amendments to Article 141 EC (ex Article 119), now contained in Article 141(4), had the effect of permitting positive discrimination.[71] However, the later judgment of the ECJ in *Serge Briheche v Ministre de l'Intérieur, Ministre de l'Éducation Nationale and Ministre de la Justice*[72] has reopened this debate.

13.69 In this case the Court had to consider whether a French law, which prohibited recruitment to employment in the Civil Service for anyone aged over 45 unless the applicant was a widow or an unmarried man with childcare responsibilities, was discriminatory against a widower.

13.70 After reviewing the weaker provisions of Article 2(4) of the Equal Treatment Directive and noting that they were designed to enable measures to secure substantive equality the ECJ continued to state that both provisions were designed to help prevent or compensate for disadvantages in the professional career of the persons concerned.

13.71 However, it must be noted that the Court of Justice held that the French provision in question was *not* consistent with the limits to permissible positive action. The reasons of the Court of Justice are also helpful in explaining more about the concept of 'full equality in practice'. The argument of the French government was:

> 26 In its observations, the French Government maintains that the national provision in question in the main proceedings was adopted with a view to reducing actual instances of inequality between men and women, in particular due to the fact that

---

[68] Case C-409/95, [1997] ECR I-6363.
[69] Case C-158/97, [2000] ECR I-1875.
[70] Case C-407/98, [2000] IRLR 732.
[71] See also the comments of the editor of the IRLR at [2000] IRLR 676 as well as the more recent cases of Case C-366/99 *Griesmar*, Case C-476/99 *Lommers* and Case C-319/03 *Briheche*.
[72] Case C-319/03, judgment 3 July 2004, [2004] ECR I-8807.

women take on most of the housework, above all when there are children in the family, and with a view to facilitating the integration of women into work.

The Court of Justice then held that it was insufficient on the facts to justify the **13.72** step taken. The *automatic and unconditional disapplication* of the relevant conditions to certain women was crucial.

The Advocate General's Opinion is also helpful in explaining why no solution **13.73** would emerge from the Equal Treatment Directive:

30 . . . Three categories of positive measures can be distinguished.[73] A first category includes measures which are not directly discriminatory in nature but aim simply at improving the training and qualifications of women (for instance the allocation of training places to women). The underlying idea is that equality of opportunities requires the provision of means to allow the individual talents of women to be displayed. A second category contains measures which aim at enabling women to better reconcile their role as parent and their professional activity (such as the possibility to benefit from nursery places offered by the employer). Men can also benefit from the latter kind of measures, which can be neutrally designed in favour of parents. The third category includes measures which also aim at achieving equality between men and women on the labour market but are discriminatory in nature in that they favour women in order to reduce their under-representation in professional life. The third category includes measures having a direct impact on employment, which give preference to women in selection processes or set targets or quotas to be achieved. The previous case-law of the Court has had to deal mainly with positive measures in the third category, implying potential discrimination against men. In *Badeck* and *Lommers*, the Court had to judge whether and on what conditions measures belonging respectively to the first and second categories were compatible with Article 2(4) of Directive 76/207. All categories of positive measures are submitted to a threefold test.

31. To be compatible with Article 2(4) of Directive 76/207, a national measure should aim at remedying an existing situation of imbalance between men and women. For a positive measure to fall under Article 2(4) of Directive 76/207, it must thus first be demonstrated that women are under-represented in a specific sector or career grade. The measure is thus aimed at removing the inequalities existing in that sector or career grade. One could also imagine the adoption of a positive measure in the public sector in order for instance to make up for the difficulties encountered by older women in the private sector. A measure of this second type would not, however, be aimed at removing discrimination but at compensating for it. In any event, in the absence of any evidence, no action aimed at remedying the situation whether directly or indirectly can be justified under Article 2(4) of Directive 76/207.

32. Second, the Court will verify the likelihood that the measure taken will remedy the concrete situation. This adequacy test will however be superfluous for measures in the third category since they expressly prescribe the results they seek to achieve.

---

73 The Advocate-General noted: 'A similar distinction has already been advanced by Advocate General Tesauro, in *Kalanke*, cited above, at point 9.'

33. Finally, in order to be justified under Article 2(4) of Directive 76/207, the positive measure taken must be reconciled as far as possible with the equal treatment principle. This appears to exclude measures which establish automatic or absolute preferences for women and requires an analysis of the proportionality of the measure. Such an analysis of proportionality will have different consequences depending on the type of measure in question and its possible reconciliation with the principle of equal treatment.

13.74 The Court of Justice having noted that the provisions of Articles 2(4) and 141(4) were not identical and that Article 2(4) did not help added:

29 In those circumstances, it is necessary to establish whether a provision such as that in question in the main proceedings is nevertheless allowed under Article 141(4) EC.

30 Article 141(4) EC authorises the Member States to maintain or adopt measures providing for specific advantages in order, inter alia, to prevent or compensate for disadvantages in professional careers, with a view to ensuring full equality in practice between men and women in working life.

31 Irrespective of whether positive action which is not allowed under Article 2(4) of the Directive could perhaps be allowed under Article 141(4) EC, it is sufficient to state that the latter provision cannot permit the Member States to adopt conditions for obtaining access to public-sector employment of the kind in question in the main proceedings which prove in any event to be disproportionate to the aim pursued (see, to that effect, *Abrahamsson and Anderson*, cited above, paragraph 55).

13.75 Again the Advocate-General dealt with this point more fully than the Court and his reasoning, which is likely to have been taken into account by the Court in formulating its decision, is very important:

48 . . . It cannot be ruled out that positive measures which do not fall within the scope of Directive 76/207 could be authorised under this provision. In effect, as I have highlighted, one could argue that there is a distinction between measures aimed at reducing inequalities and measures aimed at compensating for past or existing inequalities suffered by a social group. It cannot be excluded that the reference in Article 141(4) EC to compensatory purposes is intended to provide the Member States with a broader discretion in adopting measures of positive discrimination. Such an interpretation must, however, always remain within the boundaries authorised by the general principle of equality. The question for the Court is not whether certain forms of positive discrimination would or would not lead to a more equal and just society but whether such forms of positive discrimination, if adopted by the legislature, can be reconciled with the general principle of equality and non-discrimination.[74]

---

74 The Advocate-General added: 'In assessing national legislature choices, the Court should also take into account the fact that allowing some diversity of national political choices, in an area where there is great uncertainty and debate as to the exact effects and benefits of measures of positive discrimination, may provide for some useful degree of experimentation and learning among the different Member States. Another factor to take into account is whether, in the instances where measures

49. In this respect, the reference to compensation in Article 141(4) EC could be read as meaning either that the need to compensate for past or existing social inequalities can justify favouring individuals in those groups at the expense of discriminating against members of the over-represented groups or that the adoption of measures of a compensatory type is necessary in view of the fact that the non-discriminatory application of the current societal rules is structurally biased in favour of the members of the over-represented groups.[75] The first reading makes individuals' rights not to be discriminated against subordinate to achieving equality between groups which is justified by the aim of compensating the members of the under-represented groups for the past discrimination to which they were subject. Such a reading is hardly compatible with the priority which the Court has given to equality of opportunities and to its traditional understanding of the general principle of equal treatment.

50. The second reading may however be more easily reconciled with the principle of equal treatment as interpreted and applied by the Court. According to this view, equality of results is not the goal. Nor do the aims of positive discrimination necessarily justify discrimination between individuals. What is believed is that measures often associated with substantive equality which compensate for the under-representation of certain groups (for example quotas, automatic preferences) are the only ones that can effectively bring about long-term equality of opportunities. Measures favouring the members of certain groups are therefore not conceived as a means to achieve equality among groups or equality of results but, instead, as an instrument to bring about effective equality of opportunities. The purpose of compensatory measures of this type becomes that of re-establishing equality of opportunities by removing the effects of discrimination and promoting long-term maximisation of equality of opportunities.[76] Compensation refers in this case to reinstating a balance between the opportunities given by society to the members of the different groups.

51. To base the acceptance of compensatory forms of positive discrimination on equality of opportunities and not on equality of results would still make equality among individuals prevail over equality among groups but would, in turn, impose certain limits and conditions on the forms of compensatory positive discrimination

---

of positive discrimination are adopted, the members of the over-represented group have sufficient representation and participation to express their views in the political process.'

75 This is at the core of the critiques made of formal equality which is said to reinforce discrimination existing in society.

76 The Advocate-General added: 'Two main reasons can be given in this regard. First, positive discrimination is conceived as simply improving the prospects of victims of discrimination to the point where they would have been without any such discrimination. Second, positive discrimination is supposed to be the only effective means to generate the right incentives for the under-represented groups to invest in human capital (breaking the cycle of discrimination) and to address market failures (social monopolies and information costs) that, by reinforcing current societal discrimination, actually prevent the best persons from being chosen. It should be noted that the causality between these reasons and the effects of positive discrimination is often contested and the subject of many alternative strategies. It is not, however, for the Court to assess the merits of these policies but only whether, and to what extent, they can be regarded as compatible with the principle of equal treatment.'

that could be acceptable in the light of Article 141(4) EC. The acceptability of such forms of positive discrimination would, for example, be closely linked to its transitional nature. Otherwise, such forms of positive discrimination may, in the long run, create entrenched rights even when the original conditions justifying them are no longer present. As a consequence, the purpose of creating long-term effective equality of opportunities would be compromised. Other conditions may be linked to the nature and extent of the burden imposed on the individuals of the over-represented group, the likelihood that increased prospects for the members of the under-represented group can lead to real equality of opportunities and the requirement to show under-representation not only in general but in the specific sector or institution subject to forms of positive discrimination.

52. In the present case, in the absence of evidence as to the aim pursued by the legislation, a provision such as Article 8 of the relevant law cannot be justified under Article 141(4) EC, so that it is not necessary to determine whether such conditions are fulfilled.

13.76 Although Article 5 of the Race Directive has not been transposed directly into the Race Relations Act 1976, the latter Act wherever possible must be interpreted in the light of it: see *Pfeiffer v Deutsches Rotes Kreuz, Kreisverband Waldshut e V.*[77] So this jurisprudence will have to be applied in that way at least to existing domestic provisions which deal with the possibilities for positive action. Accordingly it must be wary of any practice or scheme of positive action that *automatically and unconditionally* gives priority to persons of a particular racial group. In any such case it must be very careful to ensure that such a practice is at least *wholly proportionate*. Even then it is not entirely clear that what is obviously a clear breach of the equal treatment principle is definitely permitted and not in breach of the Race Directive.

(10) Substantive equality in practice

13.77 A good example of this change of emphasis to substantive equality can be seen in section 2 of the Race Relations (Amendment) Act 2000. This imposes a new positive racial equality duty on all public authorities by substituting a new provision for what was section 71 of the Race Relations Act 1976, and new duties under section 71 to make and carry out race equality schemes. Equivalent equality duties in relation to disability and sex discrimination have also been introduced.

13.78 Under section 71 specified public authorities are under a duty:

(a) to eliminate unlawful racial discrimination; and
(b) to promote equality of opportunity, and good relations, between persons of different racial groups.

---

[77] Joined cases C-397/01 to C-403/01, [2005] IRLR 137 at para 110 *et seq*.

The bodies to whom this duty applies are set out in Schedule 1A to the Race **13.79** Relations Act 1976. It is a substantial list, including, for example, all ministers and central government departments, local authorities, health authorities, the Housing Corporation, the Police Complaints Authority, the Legal Services Commission, and regulatory bodies such as the Law Society and the Bar Council. The list has been substantially extended on several occasions since the Race Relations (Amendment) Act 2000 was passed. Moreover, these bodies will have to construct and implement race equality schemes, which should ensure that they assess not merely whether there is equality of opportunity, in the sense of processes and procedures, but also whether they are achieving substantive equality.

A second place where this focus on outcomes rather than just processes can be **13.80** seen is in the accelerating debate about inequality in relation to women's representation in Parliament, following the decision of the employment tribunal in *Jepson and Dyas v Labour Party*[78] that it was unlawful to have single-sex shortlists for the selection of Labour Party parliamentary candidates.[79]

The Sex Discrimination (Election Candidates) Act 2002 came into force in **13.81** 2002 and reverses *Jepson and Dyas v Labour Party* by permitting such shortlists. This Act amends the 1975 Act to provide that Parts II to IV of the 1975 Act do not apply to measures adopted by a party to reduce inequality in the numbers of men and women elected as its candidates. Equivalent amendments are made to the Sex Discrimination (Northern Ireland) Order 1976, which covers Northern Ireland.

These are temporary special measures in the sense used in Article 4 CEDAW. **13.82**

A major driving force for this change in the law was the simple fact that though there had been ostensible equality of opportunity to become a prospective candidate, there were very few women MPs,[80] even though women were granted full equality of franchise in 1928.[81]

---

[78] [1996] IRLR 116.

[79] In *Sawyer v Ahsan* [2000] ICR 1, the EAT affirmed the decision of the tribunal in *Jepson and Dyas v Labour Party*, that discrimination on grounds of sex or race by political parties in relation to the selection of candidates for council by-elections was a breach of the Sex Discrimination Act 1975 and the Race Relations Act 1976. *Sawyer v Ahsan* was overruled by the Court of Appeal on 7 February 2002 in the decision in *Triesman v Ali and Sohal* [2002] EWCA Civ 93, [2002] IRLR 489. (Permission to appeal to the House of Lords was refused in November 2002, however, the matter will be revisited in the summer of 2007 when this case will go to the House of Lords on a subsequent matter.)

[80] In the election of 1997 only 18% of MPs were women. The percentage fell at the next election.

[81] Women over 30 obtained the vote in 1918, but it was not until 1928 that women obtained the vote at 21: AW Bradley, and KD Ewing, *Constitutional and Administrative Law* (London: Addison, Wesley, Longman Ltd, 1997), 169.

13.83 This new focus on outcomes rather than merely processes will become increasingly important. It is rooted in human rights law, and also connects with existing provisions in relation to positive action. This measure is of course only permissive. It does not require political parties to take advantage of it.

13.84 However, in some situations a minority group can never achieve full participation because of the entrenched nature of the organisation; the only way to remove the barriers is to be on the inside of the organisation, and it is never possible to reach the inside because of the barriers. In these circumstances stronger mandatory action may be necessary. A recent example of this situation can be seen in the problem of chronic and massive under-representation of Roman Catholics in the Royal Ulster Constabulary. These difficulties were identified in the Patten Report.[82] The Police (Northern Ireland) Act 2000 now requires[83] the appointment of equal numbers of Roman Catholics and non-Roman Catholics (s 46). This too is a temporary provision which will last for three years unless renewed, and so accords with the human rights requirement that such special measures should not continue indefinitely.

(11) The relationship of discrimination to equality

13.85 It is sometimes easier to consider a problem from the point of view of equality rather than from the point of view of discrimination. However, the concept of discrimination is the very opposite of equality. Thus, for instance, the Equal Treatment Directive[84] states that 'the principle of equal treatment shall mean that there shall be no discrimination whatsoever whether direct or indirect'.[85] While laws phrased by reference to discrimination emphasise the consideration of differences, it is always important to consider what equality requires. This is particularly so in relation to remedies. Case law tends to use the two terms interchangeably.

E. Other aspects of equality

(1) Equality before the law

13.86 Equality before the law goes back at least as far as section 3 of the French Declaration of the Rights of Man (*La Déclaration des Droits de l'Homme et du*

---

[82] The Independent Commission on Policing for Northern Ireland, September 1999.

[83] When the Framework Directive was made it specifically excluded policing in Northern Ireland from its provisions by Article 18(1), stating: 'In order to tackle the under-representation of one of the major religious communities in the police service in Northern Ireland, differences in treatment regarding recruitment into that service, including support staff, shall not constitute discrimination insofar as those differences in treatment are expressly authorised by national legislation.'

[84] 76/207/EEC.

[85] Art 2(1).

Citoyen 1793). It is a concept which, though ancient in origin, has taken its time to take a firm hold.[86]

This principle requires the consistent treatment of similar cases. Thus, in *Police v Rose*,[87] Rault J said that 'Equality before the law requires that persons should be uniformly treated, unless there is some valid reason to treat them differently'. In a criminal case it has been said that all that it requires is that 'the cases of all potential defendants to criminal charges shall be given unbiased consideration by the prosecuting authority and that decisions whether or not to prosecute in a particular case for a particular offence should not be dictated by some irrelevant consideration'.[88] **13.87**

However, these passages beg the all-important question as to what is relevant, or what is a valid reason for different treatment. All that can be said with certainty is that mere convenience cannot be a sufficient reason for different treatment. On what is relevant, views will undoubtedly change over time. **13.88**

Thus it was pointed out in *R v Home Secretary, ex parte Venables and Thompson*,[89] that the principle of equality before the law was once used to justify hanging, transporting, and imprisoning children on the same principles applicable to adults. Of course it is now well-recognised that children are not in the same position as adults in terms of their criminal responsibility, and that therefore it is quite valid to treat them differently. **13.89**

In *Matadeen v Pointu*,[90] Lord Hoffmann, approving the passage from *Police v Rose* cited above, stated that 'such a principle is one of the building blocks of democracy and necessarily permeates any democratic constitution'. In *Grant v South West Trains*,[91] Advocate-General Elmer stated that 'Equality before the law is a fundamental principle in every community governed by the rule of law and accordingly in the Community as well'.[92] It has certainly been a fundamental right under the common law for many years. **13.90**

The concept requires at least uniform treatment of employer and employee by the legal process. In the employment tribunal this is partly recognised by the way **13.91**

---

[86] It can now be seen in legislative provisions such as s 18 of the Competition Act 1998, which states that applying dissimilar provisions to equivalent transactions may amount to abuse of a dominant position in a market. See also s 2.

[87] [1976] *Mauritian Reports* 79, at 81.

[88] *Per* Lord Diplock in *Teh Cheng Poh v Public Prosecutor* [1979] 2 WLR 623, at 635.

[89] [1998] 1 AC 407 at 522.

[90] [1999] 1 AC 98.

[91] [1998] ICR 449.

[92] At para 42.

in which the wing members are drawn from both sides of industry (see reg 5(1)(b) and (c) of the Employment Tribunals Rules of Procedure 2001).

13.92 In the past it has been held that though wing members are to be drawn from the two panels of those selected after consultation with both sides of industry, the actual selection should be random and not on the basis of expert knowledge (*Halford v Sharples*[93]).

13.93 However, in discrimination cases it has been the practice of the President of Employment Tribunals to appoint at least one member having experience of race relations[94] or at least one member of each sex. Nevertheless, it has been held that this does not require that the person be of the same racial group (*Habib v Elkington & Co Ltd*[95]). There is a lack of consistency in this approach since it does not apparently extend to the disabled. Moreover, no clear guidance has been given with respect to the grounds of discrimination encompassing age, sexuality, religion, and belief. Yet the arguments for having some specialised knowledge of the issues before the tribunal when such cases are being litigated are as strong in such cases as those in relation to sex or race discrimination. Accordingly, it is arguable that if specialised race knowledge is relevant and appropriate, it is equally appropriate and relevant for disability and other such cases, and that the President ought to make similar arrangements. It is worth stating though that when advertising for wing members in 2002 a diverse mix of applicants was sought by government by writing to women's, disabled, and ethnic groups.

(2) Equal protection of the law

13.94 This principle has a long pedigree.[96] It was set out in terms in the 14th Amendment to the American Constitution, and can be found in many constitutional and human rights provisions usually associated with equality before the law. Indeed it is difficult to imagine how it could be justified to provide equality before the law and yet to deny equal protection of the law. Yet it has come to be recognised that this involves more than merely appropriate process. That is why Article 26 ICCPR goes further than Article 7 UDHR and states 'in this respect the law shall prohibit any discrimination and guarantee to all persons equal and effective protection against any discrimination'.

---

[93] [1992] ICR 146.

[94] In race discrimination cases this practice follows an undertaking given by Lord Jacques in the House of Lords on 15 October 1976: *Habib v Elkington & Co Ltd* [1981] ICR 435, at 438.

[95] [1981] ICR 435.

[96] In *Kruse v Johnson* [1889] 2 QB 291, Lord Russell considered that by-laws could be held unreasonable because of unequal treatment as between different classes.

An application of this principle might be considered in relation to those who are **13.95**
deaf and dumb. Both the requirement of equal protection of the law and equality
before the law would suggest that the state should ensure that they have the benefit of signers to ensure that they can be understood and heard. Both these two
principles have a close relationship with the rights which have been developed
under Article 6 ECHR in relation to equality of arms: see 7.72–7.102.

(3) Equality in state and administrative action

It has long been a principle of good administration that there should be no unjus- **13.96**
tified discrimination in relation to state action or the provision of social goods
to inhabitants or citizens of the state. Thus, in *R v Inland Revenue Commissioners,*
ex parte National Federation of Self-employed,[97] Lord Scarman held that the Inland
Revenue could not discriminate between one group of taxpayers and another.
It has been held to be a principle of good administration that all persons in a similar situation should be treated similarly (*R v Herefordshire CC, ex parte Cheung*;[98]
see also *Re Colgan*[99]). It is unlikely that there will need to be an appeal to international human rights norms in such matters. Either the discrimination will be
justified, or it will be subject to review on grounds of poor administration or
because it is contrary to existing non-discrimination provisions. See more generally the discussion on equal treatment in *Judicial Review of Administrative Action.*[100]
In an appropriate case such action may be reviewed under Article 14 ECHR too:
see Chapter 14.

F. Introduction to Article 14: Prohibition of Discrimination

Article 14 ECHR states: **13.97**

> The enjoyment of the rights and freedoms set forth in this Convention shall be
> secured without discrimination on any ground such as sex, race, colour, language,
> religion, political or other opinion, national or social origin, association with a
> national minority, property, birth or other status.

This Article gives a different kind of right to those found in the other Articles **13.98**
in the Convention. Below the concept of discrimination in the Convention is
explained along with the possible effect of Protocol 12 to the ECHR, which is
designed to replace Article 14 despite not having been ratified by the UK to date.

---

[97] [1982] 1 AC 617 at 651.
[98] The Times (4 April 1986), *per* Lord Donaldson MR.
[99] [1997] 1 CMLR 53.
[100] S De Smith, H Woolf, and J Jowell, *Judicial Review of Administrative Action* (5th edn, London:
Sweet & Maxwell, 1995), paras 13–036.

In Chapter 14 Article 14 is discussed in the context of what it might add in relation to existing employment law rights.

(1) The accessory rights

13.99 The first words of Article 14 ECHR state that 'The enjoyment of the rights and freedoms set forth in this Convention shall be secured without discrimination'. These words show that it is not like the other Articles discussed in this book. It is not a free-standing non-discrimination right. It only operates in situations where other Articles of the Convention are already engaged.

13.100 Thus, the Article has been described as having an 'accessory nature and autonomous status',[101] and as having 'no independent existence' (see, eg, the *Belgian Linguistics Case (No 1)*,[102] and *Airey v Ireland*[103]).

(2) An undeveloped concept of discrimination

13.101 One consequence of its accessory nature is that there are not many cases decided by the European Court, or even the Commission, by reference to Article 14 ECHR alone. Usually when the Court or Commission has found a violation of a substantive right, it has not found it necessary to decide whether there has been a violation of Article 14 with that particular right. Thus, in a discrimination case brought against the UK the Court declined to consider whether there had been a breach of Article 14 even though the case considered the proper conduct of discrimination legislation in Northern Ireland (see *Tinnelly and Sons Ltd and others and McElduff and others v UK*[104]). As a result the concept of discrimination in the case law of the ECHR is under-developed and has not until recently (*Thlimmenos v Greece*;[105] see 13.110–13.118 below) included any discussion of the concept of indirect or disguised discrimination.

13.102 One example of such discussion can be found in *Wessels-Bergervoet v The Netherlands*,[106] where the European Court found that an applicant's benefits under the Netherlands' General Old Age Pensions Act were reduced solely due to her being a married woman. A married man in the same situation as the applicant would not have been excluded from the insurance scheme in this manner. This inequality in treatment materialised in 1989 when, given the prevailing

---

[101] Aee Gomien, Harris, and Zwaak, *Law and Practice in the European Convention of Human Rights and the European Social Charter* (Strasbourg: Council of Europe, 1996), at 346.
[102] (1979–80) 1 EHRR 241, 1 EHRR 252.
[103] (1979–80) 2 EHRR 305, para 30, (No 2) (1979–80).
[104] (1999) 27 EHRR 249.
[105] (2001) 36 EHRR 15.
[106] Application 34462/97, judgment 4 June 2002.

social attitudes at that time, the aim pursued by the legal provisions concerned could no longer be upheld. The difference in treatment was not found to be on any 'objective and reasonable justification' and accordingly there was found to be a violation of Article 14 of the Convention taken in conjunction with Article 1 of Protocol No 1. (For another pension case concerning Article 14 see *Zeman v Austria*[107] and further *Koua Poirrez v France*[108] regarding discriminatory application of welfare rights.)

G. The grounds of discrimination prohibited by Article 14

(1) The stated grounds

Article 14 ECHR enumerates ten specific grounds for discrimination which are prohibited: sex, race, colour, language, religion, political or other opinion, national or social origin, association with a national minority, property, and birth or other status. The width of these specific grounds shows how important the non-discrimination principle is.   **13.103**

(2) Grounds of discrimination to be broadly interpreted

In contrast to the approach taken by domestic and EC law, the range of grounds of discrimination prohibited by Article 14 is completely open-ended. The words 'on any ground such as' and 'or other status' have been broadly interpreted. Moreover, since the ECHR is a living instrument, which reflects changing social standards (*Tyrer v UK*[109]), it must be assumed that the known scope of Article 14 will be enlarged as new forms of discrimination are identified.   **13.104**

Protocol 12 (discussed below) has adopted the same formulation. The Explanatory Report to Protocol 12 commented that: **13.105**

> . . . The list of non-discrimination grounds in Article 1 [of Protocol 12] is identical to that in Article 14 of the Convention. This solution was considered preferable over others, such as expressly including certain additional non-discrimination grounds (for example, physical or mental disability, sexual orientation or age), not because of a lack of awareness that such grounds have become particularly important in today's societies as compared with the time of drafting of Article 14 of the Convention, but because such an inclusion was considered unnecessary from a legal point of view since the list of non-discrimination grounds is not exhaustive, and because inclusion of any particular additional ground might give rise to unwarranted *a contrario* interpretations as regards discrimination based on grounds not so included. It is recalled

---

[107] Application 23960/02, judgment 29 September 2006.
[108] Application 40892/98, judgment 30 December 2003, (2005) 40 EHRR 34.
[109] (1979–80) 2 EHRR 1.

that the European Court of Human Rights has already applied Article 14 in relation to discrimination grounds not explicitly mentioned in that provision (see, for example, as concerns the ground of sexual orientation, in the case of *Salgueiro da Silva Mouta v Portugal*).

(3) Other status

13.106 Article 14 also concerns discrimination on grounds of other status. As well as the stated grounds, Article 14 has been held to cover discrimination on grounds of:

(a) age (*Nelson v UK*[110]);

(b) sexuality (*Salgueiro Da Silva Mouta v Portugal;*[111] *Sutherland v UK*[112]);

(c) illegitimacy (*Marckx v Belgium*[113]);

(d) marital status (*Rasmussen v Denmark*[114]);

(e) conscientious objection (*X v Netherlands*[115]);

(f) professional status (*Van der Mussele v Belgium*[116]);

(g) military status (*Engel and others v The Netherlands (No 1)*[117] and *Bucheň v République Tchèque*[118]);

(h) membership of a trade union (*National Union of Belgian Police v Belgium*[119]);

(i) KGB status (*Sidabras and Džiautas v Lithuania*[120]);

(j) adoption (*Pla v Puncernau v Andorra*[121]);

(k) residence (*Darby v Sweden*[122]);

(l) type of tenancy (*Larkos v Cyprus*[123]);

(m) coastal fishermen (*Posti v Finland*[124]).

The words 'other status' which appear at the end of the list in Article 14 are therefore not to be treated as words having any implied limitation.

---

[110] Application 11077/84, 49 DR 170.

[111] (2001) 31 EHRR 47.

[112] [1997] EHRLR 117.

[113] (1979) 2 EHRR 330.

[114] (1984) 7 EHRR 371.

[115] (1965) 8 YB 266.

[116] (1984) 6 EHRR 163.

[117] (1976) 1 EHRR 647.

[118] Application 36541/97, judgment 26 November 2002.

[119] (1979–80) 1 EHRR 578.

[120] (2006) 42 EHRR 6.

[121] Application 69498/01, [2005] 18 BHRC 120.

[122] [1990] 13 EHRR 744.

[123] [1999] 30 EHRR 587.

[124] Application 27824/95, judgment 24 September 2002, at [79]–[87], (2003) 37 EHRR 6.

(4) Any other ground

Discrimination on grounds which could or might be described as status are **13.107** equally covered, 'any ground' of discrimination is not limited in scope. This would seem to permit arguments on the basis of discrimination by reason of physical attributes, geographical location, or even education. In *Pine Valley Developments v Ireland*,[125] it was found to cover differential treatment for no apparent reason. This open text has the merit of allowing the provision to respond to new or deepening understanding of the nature of inequality, and has the capability to set the agenda for such an analysis.

For example, if a public authority refused to recruit someone on grounds of her **13.108** childcare responsibilities, or because she had an invalid husband, that individual might be able to pursue a section 6 claim against the authority on the grounds of discrimination contrary to Articles 8 and 14 ECHR. The argument would be that the reason for not offering a job amounted to discrimination in contravention of a Convention right. It also ought to enable complaints based on association with a person within a protected class, or where a person is perceived as belonging to a protected class. These concepts of associative and perceived discrimination are already understood in UK law (see 14.137–14.139).

H. The concept of discrimination in the ECHR

(1) The basic concept

The basic concept of discrimination in Article 14 ECHR has been construed **13.109** quite simply by asserting that the principle of equality of treatment is violated if a distinction has no reasonable and objective justification: *Belgian Linguistics (No 2)*[126] and see *Inze v Austria*.[127] However, more recently it has been extended to take a similar approach to that adopted by the ECJ, as described earlier in this chapter. The wider concept of discrimination in human rights law has already been discussed above.

(2) Indirect discrimination

The concept of indirect discrimination in human rights law has been considered **13.110** above at 13.34–13.37. It had been queried whether the concept of discrimination in Article 14 ECHR included indirect discrimination, but it has now been

---

[125] [1991] 14 EHRR 319.
[126] (1979–1980) 1 EHRR 252.
[127] (1988) 10 EHRR 394, para 41.

351

authoritatively determined that it does by the judgment of the European Court in *Thlimmenos v Greece*.[128] The Court said:

> 44. The Court has so far considered that the right under Article 14 not to be discriminated against in the enjoyment of the rights guaranteed under the Convention is violated when States treat differently persons in analogous situations without providing an objective and reasonable justification (see *Inze v Austria* . . . paragraph 41). However, the Court considers that this is not the only facet of the prohibition of discrimination in Article 14. The right not to be discriminated against in the enjoyment of the rights guaranteed under the Convention is also violated when States without an objective and reasonable justification fail to treat differently persons whose situations are significantly different.

13.111 In this case a Jehovah's Witness was convicted of a criminal offence for refusing to wear (on moral grounds) an army uniform while on national service. This conviction later led to his being barred from practising as an accountant because of a rule prohibiting convicted persons from holding this professional qualification. He argued to the European Court that this rule discriminated against him under Articles 14 and 9 ECHR, on grounds of his conscientious objection. His complaint was upheld. The Court avoided the problem of comparing the complainant with others in analogous positions, by finding that rights could also be violated where persons are not treated differently if their situations are significantly different.

13.112 This principle was later relied on in *Nachova & Others v Bulgaria*.[129] There, in the context of contracting states ensuring that in the investigation of incidents involving the use of force a distinction is made both in their legal systems and in practice between cases of excessive use of force and of racist killing, the Strasbourg Court said:

> A failure to make a distinction in the way in which situations that are essentially different are handled may constitute unjustified treatment irreconcilable with Article 14 of the Convention (see, mutatis mutandis, *Thlimmenos v Greece* [GC], no. 34369/97, § 44, ECHR 2000-IV).

However, it is important to note that this concept of indirect discrimination is as described in 13.110 and not the more complicated statistics-based concept of indirect discrimination found in the original provisions of the Race Relations Act 1976 or the Sex Discrimination Act 1975.

(3) What discrimination is protected and what discrimination is permitted?

13.113 It is vital to understand that the protection afforded by Article 14 ECHR is equality in the enjoyment of Convention rights. Thus, in *Thlimmenos*, the Court decided

---

[128] (2001) 36 EHRR 15.
[129] Applications 43577/98 and 43579/98, judgment 26 February 2004, at para 158.

that it was not necessary to decide whether there had been a breach of Article 9 rights in relation to religion and belief. It was sufficient that the issue concerned the enjoyment of those rights.[130] Obviously the Jehovah's Witnesses' enjoyment of their rights to freedom of religion was affected when they had the consequence that a barrier to a later professional career was erected by the conviction.

I. Objective justification

(1) Introduction

Many British employment lawyers are unfamiliar with the fact that direct dis‑ **13.114** crimination can be justified under the ECHR. The concept of justification is essentially similar to that found in domestic indirect discrimination law. It is based on the identification of a legitimate aim, which is attained by the distinc‑ tion in question by a means which is proportional.

The concept of objective justification is at the heart of ECHR discrimination law. **13.115** It also bears a close relationship to the concept of justification for indirect dis‑ crimination under Community law (see, eg, *Hampson v Department of Education and Science*,[131] and *Bilka-Kaufhaus GmbH v Karin Weber von Hartz*[132]). In *Belgian Linguistics (No 2)*,[133] the Court said that:

> . . . the principle of equality of treatment is violated if the distinction has no reason‑ able and objective justification. The existence of such a justification must be assessed in relation to the aim and effect of the measure under consideration, regard being had to the principles which normally prevail in democratic societies. A difference of treatment in the exercise of a right laid down by the Convention must not only pur‑ sue a legitimate aim; Article 14 is likewise violated when it is clearly established that there is no reasonable relationship of proportionality between the means employed and the aim sought to be realised.[134]

(2) The key requirements for justification under Article 14

Thus, for discrimination to be objectively justified it must be: **13.116**

(a) reasonable;
(b) assessed according to its aims and effects;
(c) considered against prevailing principles of normality in democratic societies;

---

130 See judgment, para 43.
131 [1991] 1 AC 171.
132 Case 170/84, [1987] ICR 110.
133 (1979–80) 1 EHRR 252.
134 At para 10, p 284.

(d)   seen to pursue a legitimate aim;

(e)   established that there is a relationship of proportionality between the means
      employed and the aim sought.

(3) An example of the reasoning of the ECtHR

13.117   The way these tests are applied by the European Court can be seen in its judgment in *Thlimmenos v Greece*,[135] where there was found to be no justification for
the barrier discriminating against Mr Thlimmenos since his conviction was not
linked to dishonesty or misconduct which could have a bearing on his profes-
sionalism. The European Court recalled that the Commission found:

> 38. . . . In the circumstances of the case, there was no objective and reasonable justi-
> fication for the failure of the drafters of the rules governing access to the profession
> of chartered accountants to treat differently persons convicted for refusing to serve
> in the armed forces on religious grounds from persons convicted of other felonies.

13.118   It then reached a similar conclusion. Its reasoning shows clearly how objective
justification is assessed:

> 1 . . . According to its case-law, the Court will have to examine whether the failure
> to treat the applicant differently . . . pursued a legitimate aim. If it did the Court will
> have to examine whether there was a reasonable relationship of proportionality
> between the means employed and the aim sought to be realised (see the *Inze* judgment
> cited above, ibid.).
>
> 2 The Court considers that, as a matter of principle, States have a legitimate interest
> to exclude some offenders from the profession of chartered accountant. However,
> the Court also considers that, unlike other convictions for serious criminal offences,
> a conviction for refusing on religious or philosophical grounds to wear the military
> uniform cannot imply any dishonesty or moral turpitude likely to undermine the
> offender's ability to exercise this profession. Excluding the applicant on the ground
> that he was an unfit person was not, therefore, justified. The Court takes note of the
> Government's argument that persons who refuse to serve their country must be
> appropriately punished. However, it also notes that the applicant did serve a prison
> sentence for his refusal to wear the military uniform. In these circumstances, the
> Court considers that imposing a further sanction on the applicant was dispropor-
> tionate. It follows that the applicant's exclusion from the profession of chartered
> accountant did not pursue a legitimate aim. As a result, the Court finds that there
> existed no objective and reasonable justification for not treating the applicant differ-
> ently from other persons convicted of a felony.
>
> 3 It is true that the authorities had no option under the law but to refuse to appoint
> the applicant a chartered accountant. However, . . . this cannot absolve the respond-
> ent State from responsibility under the Convention. The Court has never excluded
> that legislation may be found to be in direct breach of the Convention (see, *inter alia*,

---

[135]   (2001) 36 EHRR 15.

Chassagnou and others v France (2000) 29 EHRR 615). In the present case the Court considers that it was the State . . . which violated the applicant's right not to be discriminated against in the enjoyment of his right under Article 9 of the Convention, . . . by failing to introduce appropriate exceptions to the rule barring persons convicted of a felony from the profession of chartered accountants.

(4) Suspect classes

Obviously, discrimination which is exclusively on the grounds of sex or race will rarely be compatible with the ECHR (see *Schmidt v Germany*[136]). These are sometimes described as suspect classes of discrimination. **13.119**

This approach resonates with, but is not the same as, that of domestic law. Thus, under domestic law, it is normal to state that such direct discrimination is not permitted in the fields of sex and race discrimination, since it is only expressly permitted to justify indirect discrimination (see ss 1(1)(b)(ii) of the Sex Discrimination Act 1975 and Race Relations Act 1976). By contrast, the Disability Discrimination Act 1995 has only recently been amended to include a narrowly defined concept which can loosely be called direct disability discrimination (s 3A(5)), and to remove the justification provisions from the duty to make reasonable adjustments (s 3A(2)); disability-related discrimination (s 3A(1)) can still be justified. In this respect, the original structure of the 1995 Act (ie the old s 5) was closer to the general (ie non-suspect class) jurisprudence of the ECHR. However, in practice the Sex Discrimination Act and Race Relations Act along with the Employment Equality (Sexual Orientation) and (Religion or Belief) Regulations 2003 and the Employment Equality (Age) Regulations 2006 permit a limited class of genuine occupational qualifications (GOQs) as statutory defences to what would otherwise be acts of discrimination. **13.120**

For instance, reasons of decency may be a GOQ, and therefore justify some restrictions on the employment of either males or females (s 7 of the Sex Discrimination Act 1975), and reasons of promoting the welfare of a particular racial group may be a GOQ and justify restrictions on the employment of persons from a particular racial group (s 5 of the Race Relations Act 1976; see *Tottenham Under Fives Centre v Marshall*[137] for an example of how this section works). See also regulation 8 of the Age Regulations and regulation 7 of both the Religion and Belief and Sexual Orientation Regulations. (The same point can be made regarding the new disability legislation brought in as a result of the Framework Directive 2000/78.) In this respect it may be said that the municipal legislation acknowledges that there are some justified acts of discrimination. **13.121**

---

[136] (1994) 18 EHRR 513.
[137] [1989] ICR 214.

13.122 The ECHR has left open the possibility of reasons which, though exclusively concerned with gender or race, are nevertheless 'very weighty reasons' (*Petrovic v Austria*;[138] *Schuler-Zgraggen v Switzerland*;[139] *Van Raalte v Netherlands*;[140] *Gaygusuz v Austria*;[141] and most recently *Walker v UK*[142]). Such reasons therefore might be permitted to justify objectively what would otherwise be acts of discrimination.

(5) Special measures and positive action

13.123 As discussed above (see 13.60–13.84) special measures and positive action can sometimes be necessary to achieve substantive equality. Human rights law does not treat such special measures or positive action, where justified, as discrimination. This can raise important issues in respect of remedies where a court or tribunal has a measure of discretion as to what should happen (discussed in 13.124–13.128 below).

(6) Article 14 and remedies under domestic legislation

13.124 A proper remedy for past discrimination ought not to be seen as an act of discrimination but as positive remedial action. What is called positive discrimination in the UK may sometimes be permissible (*DG and DW Lindsay v UK*[143]) and may indeed be necessary. The Sex Discrimination Act 1975 and Race Relations Act 1976 permit some positive action in education and training (see s 37 of the Race Relations Act 1976). These Acts also permit an employment tribunal to make a recommendation as to future action as a remedy for past discrimination (s 56(1)(c) of the Race Relations Act 1976).

13.125 This remedy has been held to exclude a recommendation of effective equality, such as a direction that the next job should go to the person who has suffered unlawful discrimination: *Noone v North West Thames Regional Health Authority (No 2)*[144] and *British Gas v Sharma*.[145] These decisions have been criticised, and are very likely to be re-examined in the light of the HRA 1998, on the basis the remedial action is not discrimination but rather appropriate recompense for the wrong that has been done. In this way the Court could demonstrate its ability to deliver effective and proportionate remedies.

---

[138] (2001) 33 EHRR 14, para 37.
[139] (1993) 16 EHRR 405, para 67.
[140] (1997) 24 EHRR 503, para 39.
[141] (1997) 23 EHRR 364, para 42.
[142] Application 37212/02, judgment 22 August 2006, [2006] All ER (D) 102 (Aug).
[143] [1986] 48 DR 181.
[144] [1988] IRLR 530.
[145] [1991] ICR 19.

In the fields of discrimination based on sex, race, religion and belief, disability **13.126** and sexual orientation the court or tribunal would still have to apply EC law. (While Community law does not permit positive action (save in a very limited sense, see 13.66–13.77) in relation to recruitment, the ECJ has not yet had to rule on positive action to remedy a finding of discrimination.)

The ECJ has consistently ruled that remedies for discrimination must guarantee **13.127** real and effective judicial protection (see *Marshall v Southampton and South West Hampshire Health Authority*[146]), and the ECJ has stated (in *Von Colson v Land Nordrhein-Westfalen*,[147] and *Harz v Deutsche Tradax GmbH*[148]):

> Such measures may include, for example, provisions requiring the employer to offer a post to the candidate discriminated against or giving the candidate adequate financial compensation, backed up where necessary by a system of fines.

Accordingly, it is likely that positive action such as requiring the next job to go **13.128** to a person who has been denied a job by reason of discrimination would be held to be lawful under EC law. Similarly, it seems likely that where Article 14 ECHR applies the European Court would permit such a result.

J. The impact of Protocol 12

Because of Article 14's accessory nature there has been much pressure on the **13.129** Council of Europe to agree a free-standing non-discrimination right appropriate to a modern age. On 26 June 2000, the Committee of Ministers of the Council of Europe adopted Protocol 12. This new Protocol has created a free-standing right to non-discrimination which, though relating to Article 14 ECHR, is much more extensive in its reach. Unfortunately this provision has not yet been included in Schedule 1 to the HRA 1998. The importance of this change has been recognised by the European Court. It gave an Advisory Opinion in relation to Article 14, in which it stated that:

> . . . certain forms of discrimination cannot be brought within the ambit of Article 14 . . . Protocol 12 provides a clear legal basis for examining discrimination issues not covered by Article 14.[149]

---

[146] Case 271/91, [1993] ICR 893.
[147] Case 14/83, [1984] ECR 1891, at 1907, para 18.
[148] Case 79/83, [1984] ECR 1921, at 1940, para 18.
[149] Council of Europe, Steering Committee for Human Rights (CDDH), Strasbourg, 1 February 2000, cddh\2000\48.

13.130 The Council of Europe has authorised publication of an Explanatory Report[150] giving the purpose and aim of the Protocol. This explanatory memorandum contains much useful comparative comment on the scope and effect of Article 14.

(1) The key provisions of Protocol 12

13.131 The key provisions of Protocol 12 to the ECHR are the Preamble and the first Article. The Preamble states:

> . . . Having regard to the fundamental principle according to which all persons are equal before the law and are entitled to the equal protection of the law;
>
> Being resolved to take further steps to promote the equality of all persons through the collective enforcement of a general prohibition of discrimination by means of the Convention for the Protection of Human Rights and Fundamental Freedoms signed at Rome on 4 November 1950 . . .;
>
> Reaffirming that the principle of non-discrimination does not prevent States Parties from taking measures in order to promote full and effective equality, provided that there is an objective and reasonable justification for those measures,
>
> [The signatory member states] Have agreed as follows:

Article 1 provides:

> 1 The enjoyment of any right set forth by law shall be secured without discrimination on any ground such as sex, race, colour, language, religion, political or other opinion, national or social origin, association with a national minority, property, birth or other status.
>
> 2 No one shall be discriminated against by any public authority on any ground such as those mentioned in paragraph 1.[151]

(2) Ratification and coming into force

13.132 Protocol 12 opened for signature on 4 November 2000: 35 states have signed it, and the following 14 states have ratified it: Albania, Armenia, Bosnia and Herzegovina; Croatia; Cyprus; Finland; Georgia; Luxembourg; the Netherlands; Romania, San Marino; Serbia and Montenegro, the former Yugoslav Republic of Macedonia; and the Ukraine. It came into force for those states on 1 April 2005. Accordingly, it is now binding on those countries that have ratified it and people from those countries are able to take cases to the European Court arguing a breach of the Protocol. Member states who have not ratified to date include Andorra, Bulgaria, Denmark,

---

[150] See <http://conventions.coe.int/Treaty/en/Reports/Html/177.htm>.

[151] Arts 2–6 deal with the Protocol's territorial application, relationship to the Convention, signature and ratification, entry into force, and depository functions. The Protocol is in Appendix 2.

France, Lithuania, Malta, Poland, Sweden, Switzerland, and the UK. It is likely that some of these states will ratify the Protocol in the next few years.

(3) Relationship of Protocol 12 to Article 14 ECHR

The relationship of Protocol 12 to Article 14 ECHR was described in the **13.133** Explanatory Memorandum as follows:

1 The purpose of this article [Article 3 of Protocol 12] is to clarify the relationship of this Protocol to the Convention by indicating that all the provisions of the latter shall apply in respect of Articles 1 and 2 of the Protocol. . . .

2 . . . Article 1 of the Protocol encompasses, but is wider in scope than the protection offered by Article 14 of the Convention. As an additional Protocol, it does not amend or abrogate Article 14 of the Convention, which will therefore continue to apply, also in respect of States Parties to the Protocol. There is thus an overlap between the two provisions. In accordance with Article 32 of the Convention, any further questions of interpretation concerning the precise relationship between these provisions fall within the jurisdiction of the Court.

(4) Ratification and the UK

It is to be hoped that the UK will eventually ratify the Protocol since it recognises **13.134** a fundamental right to equality and non-discrimination. Such ratification would mean that the HRA 1998 would have to be amended (see s 1(4), by which the Lord Chancellor is specifically empowered to amend the Act to reflect the effect in relation to the UK of a Protocol). However, it seems that this is still some way off. Although in March 2002 the Lord Chancellor announced a review of the UK's position on international human rights instruments, raising the possibility that the government might be willing to consider ratifying Protocol 12, the position of the government continues to be reluctant to commit to signing or ratification, despite being urged to so do by various bodies including the Joint Committee On Human Rights (see Seventeenth Report).

The government has expressed a number of concerns about Protocol 12. First, it **13.135** has been said that the grounds for discrimination are too general and open-ended. The counter-argument is that open-ended grounds for discrimination enable the courts to accommodate the changing needs of society, and no unjustified discrimination should be permitted to continue. Should the government decide to legislate against these forms of discrimination, similar open wording could be used to ensure the appropriate flexibility. It is worth noting that as these grounds already replicate the existing grounds of Article 14 ECHR, they are already to some extent incorporated into our law through the HRA 1998.

The government has also argued that the Protocol does not make specific **13.136** provision for 'objective and reasonably justified distinctions' to be permitted.

The government is concerned that as the Court is not bound by previous judgments and its interpretations of the Convention do evolve, so the concept of 'discrimination' under the Convention may change and the provisions on justification may be removed. However, the provisions enabling discrimination to be justified if there are 'objective and reasonable' grounds for the differential treatment are well established under the ECHR (see 13.47 and 13.54–13.55 above). It is extremely unlikely that the Court will abandon this principle.

13.137 A further apprehension of the government relates to the wording of the Protocol, which it is said does not make clear whether the reference to 'any right set forth by law' in Article 1 includes international law as well as domestic law. The government is particularly concerned that provisions in international treaties, such as the International Covenant on Economic, Social and Cultural Rights, which were not considered appropriate to incorporate into UK law, will be covered by the Protocol. As Protocol 12 would not create independent rights to substantive benefits, it is only when the government chooses to provide benefits, whether under national or international law, that it is placed under an obligation not to discriminate. This clearly does not allow for the incorporation of entire international treaties.

13.138 Rather curiously, the government has also argued that Protocol 12 'does not make provision for positive measures'. The government considers that there should be a specific provision within the Protocol stating that action to overcome the effects of past discrimination does not constitute discrimination. However, this is not necessary, as the third paragraph of the Preamble to the Protocol makes it clear that member states can take positive measures in order to promote full and effective equality. So long as there is an objective and reasonable justification for any such measures they are consistent with the aim of the Protocol, namely to eliminate discrimination.[152]

(5) Indirect impact of Protocol 12

13.139 Meanwhile, it must be expected that there will be cases from other countries brought to the European Court under Protocol 12. These will help to determine the utility of this newly ratified Protocol. It is likely that these cases will also affect the interpretation of Article 14 ECHR, as well as that of Protocol 12. Moreover, as part of the inspiration for the Equality Chapter of the European Charter of Fundamental Rights, it is probable that decisions under Protocol 12 by the European Court will affect the way in which Community law develops (see 13.26).

---

[152] See *Hansard*, col WA14 (23 October 2000).

(6) Positive obligations and Protocol 12

One interesting possibility is that Protocol 12 will be construed as conferring **13.140** positive obligations. The Explanatory Memorandum states that:

> 24. The wording of Article 1 reflects a balanced approach to possible positive obliga-
> tions of the Parties under this provision. This concerns the question to what extent
> Article 1 obliges the Parties to take measures to prevent discrimination, even where
> discrimination occurs in relations between private persons (so-called 'indirect hori-
> zontal effects'). The same question arises as regards measures to remedy instances
> of discrimination. While such positive obligations cannot be excluded altogether,
> the prime objective of Article 1 is to embody a negative obligation for the Parties: the
> obligation not to discriminate against individuals.

Accordingly, if ratified by the UK, once in force, it is possible that Protocol 12 **13.141** could lead to actions for special measures being taken. The standards for such special measures have already been discussed (see 13.61–13.85). While special measures in relation to sex and race discrimination are already under way, it is possible that this provision might encourage other special measures in relation to disability or discrimination on grounds of age.

(7) The use of Article 14 as a tool in the UK courts

The next chapter considers further the interface between Article 14 and relevant **13.142** strands of domestic legislation. Despite recent developments in UK discrimination law, Article 14 remains a useful means of extending human rights jurisprudence.

K. Frequently asked questions

Is the principle of equal treatment a human right?   **13.143**

The ECHR does not contain a principle of equal treatment. However, major human rights texts do recognise such a principle. The first of these in importance is the Universal Declaration of Human Rights. It is also a key component of the European Charter of Fundamental Rights.

What does equality mean?

Equality means a number of things. It is not possible to ascribe a single legal meaning to it. As well as the principle of equal treatment it is a principle for rational behaviour and a superior rule of law. It has a close relationship with the duty to respect human dignity. It also concerns positive action to secure substantive equality and therefore to ensure that equal opportunity is real.

How does the ECtHR address discrimination?

Any difference of treatment which has no objective and reasonable justification will be discrimination.

Does the concept of indirect discrimination apply in the ECtHR?

Yes. The ECtHR has begun to recognise explicitly that there is indirect discrimination and to approach it in much the same way that it is considered in the domestic courts and tribunals when considering domestic legislation.

What are the three stages of analysis?

Discrimination cases are usually analysed by reference to the treatment under scrutiny, the circumstances in which it was afforded, and the justification, if any, for the distinctions or treatment that has been given.

What is the difference between formal and substantive equality?

Rules which provide for equality of opportunity are formal rules, but they may not lead to substantive equality because of the circumstances in which they are applied. Substantive equality looks to the effect that such rules have on a person or group of persons.

Can there be special measures?

Human rights law recognises that special measures may be necessary to ensure that a group of persons can enjoy substantive equality. Measures such as those in relation to the selection of candidates for election or the selection of police officers are examples.

Does the European Union permit positive action or discrimination?

European law does permit positive action in principle but the circumstances in which it may be allowed are very limited and the law in relation to this is only at an early stage of development.

When is Article 14 engaged?

It is not a free-standing Article. It operates in circumstances where other Articles are engaged. That does not mean that there has to be a breach of those Articles but they must be relevant and provide a context to the matter under scrutiny.

What grounds of discrimination are prohibited by Article 14?

Article 14 specifically lists sex, race, colour, language, religion, political or other opinion, national or social origin, association with a national minority, property and birth or other status. A very wide range of grounds have been identified as being possibly within scope by reference to the other status provision.

What are principles by which justification is assessed?

The key requirements are that the distinction must be:
(a) *reasonable;*
(b) *assessed according to its aims and effects;*
(c) *considered against prevailing principles of normality in democratic societies;*
(d) *seen to pursue a legitimate aim;*
(e) *established that there is a relationship of proportionality between the means employed and the aim sought.*

14

THE INTERFACE BETWEEN EUROPEAN
AND DOMESTIC EQUALITY LAW

14.01　This chapter considers aspects of the interface between Article 14 and UK discrimination law intended to give effect to European discrimination law. It will consider the extent to which Article 14 might still be useful notwithstanding the extension of domestic protection against discrimination as a result of the European law such as the Race Directive and the Employment Equality Directive. The extent to which these Directives may not have been fully implemented is also examined. First it considers the impact of Article 14 on other non-discrimination areas of employment law such as unfair dismissal.

A. How might Article 14 relate to the law of unfair dismissal?

14.02　Article 14 ECHR may be relevant to unfair dismissal cases where the reason for dismissal can be linked to the status of the employee in question. This status could include a broad range of factors, see Chapter 13 at 13.106 above.

14.03　An employment tribunal has a duty to interpret domestic law in accordance with the Convention pursuant to section 3(1) of the HRA 1998. Accordingly, provided it is properly engaged, it should apply Article 14 to the common law as well as to statute law.

14.04　Thus in an appropriate case a tribunal must also take the Convention, including Article 14, into account when determining 'reasonableness' under section 98(4) of the ERA 1996. In this way, the HRA 1998 can have a 'horizontal effect' on the review of conduct between private parties by an employment tribunal, which is of course a public authority under section 6(3) of the HRA 1998. This is not to suggest that as a norm employees of public employers should be seen as having greater rights. Rather, public and private employees[1] should be treated identically in respect of unfair dismissal. In any event a tribunal would have to read section 98(4) of the ERA 1996 in a way which is, so far as possible, compatible with the Convention including Article 14.

14.05　The Court of Appeal set out guidelines in *X v Y*[2] as to how section 3 of the HRA 1998 affects the assessment of unfair dismissal cases where the facts fell within Articles 8 and 14. This case concerned a dismissal for the offence of gross indecency in toilets to which the public had access. The complainant was eventually

---

[1] It must also be remembered that s 7 of the HRA 1998 provides for a free-standing right of action against a public authority.

[2] [2004] IRLR 625, at para 58.

found not to amount to engage the right to a private life (see Chapter 8). Mummery LJ said that by:

> a process of interpretation the Article 8 right is blended with the law on unfair dismissal in the ERA, but without creating new private law causes of action against private sector employers under the HRA or the ERA.

The guidelines, though drafted to deal with cases where Article 14 was engaged, **14.06** will be relevant to other cases where other Articles of the ECHR are engaged, and are very useful. They are set out in full in Chapter 8 at 8.41.

The EAT had already given guidance as to the impact of the HRA 1998 on unfair **14.07** dismissal cases in *Pay v Lancashire Probation Service*.[3] There a probation officer working with sex offenders was dismissed following the discovery by his employers that he was involved in the sale of sadomasochistic merchandise and performed in fetish clubs.

The Court of Appeal commented in *X v Y*[4] that an employee of the Probation **14.08** Service could bring an unfair dismissal claim against it and could also rely directly on Article 8 pursuant to section 6 of the HRA 1998 since the Probation Service is a public authority. However, it is unlikely that the HRA 1998 was intended to produce different results depending on whether the employer was in the private sector or a public authority.

When considering whether Mr Pay's dismissal for these reasons breached his **14.09** Article 8 and 10 rights, the EAT in *Pay* recognised that 'primary legislation and subordinate legislation must be read and given effect in a way which is compatible with the Convention rights' because of the interpretative requirement upon tribunals and courts pursuant to section 3(1) of the HRA 1998.

This section applies to private as well as public employers. However, the EAT **14.10** recognised that a public authority employer will not act reasonably within the meaning of section 98(4) in dismissing an employee if it violates his or her Convention rights. In order to apply the section 98(4) test correctly, the statutory words 'reasonably or unreasonably' should be interpreted as having regard to the claimant's Convention rights. In this case, Mr Pay's activities were held not to be private and hence Article 8 was not engaged. Further, any interference with his freedom of expression was justified.

Even had Article 8(1) been engaged in *X v Y*, the Court of Appeal would have **14.11** found that the dismissal was justified under Article 8(2), since any interference

---

[3] [2004] IRLR 129.
[4] At para 56.

would have been in accordance with the law (as based on offences under the Sexual Offences Act 1956 and the ERA 1996). Further, the interference was needed for the employer's legitimate interests including the requirement for employees to behave in such a way which ensured the success of its activities and the importance of bearing in mind that this employee was a role model to the vulnerable children and young adults in his care.

14.12 It seems clear that pre-HRA cases such as *Notts County Council v Bowly*[5] and *Wiseman v Salford City Council*[6] (where the employees who worked with young people were found to have been fairly dismissed following their being cautioned for offences of gross indecency) would be approached in this way if heard today. On the other hand a case such as *Saunders v Scottish National Camps*,[7] where a handyman at a children's camp was dismissed on the grounds that he 'indulged' in homosexuality, which the employer felt rendered him totally unsuitable for employment in a camp accommodating schoolchildren and teenagers, might well be decided differently. Bar any suggestion of a real risk to children or a relevant criminal offence, this dismissal fairly clearly interfered with Mr Saunders' Article 8(1) rights on a non-justified basis. In any event the facts would probably amount to a discrimination against him which would be addressed under the Sexual Orientation Regulations.

B. Existing employment equality provisions in Community Law

14.13 Before considering the contribution that Article 14 might make in cases where there is a protection from discrimination, it is necessary to set out briefly what are the rights, and their relationship with European Law, which is always construed in a way which is consistent with human rights principles.

14.14 A key provision in Community Law is the protection of women in relation to discrimination in respect of pay. From the outset, the Treaty of Rome has stated explicitly the requirement of equal pay for equal work. The ECJ has held that this provision had direct effect and could be relied on by individuals against their employers (*Defrenne v Sabena*[8]).

---

5 [1978] IRLR 252.
6 [1981] IRLR 202.
7 [1980] IRLR 174.
8 Case 43/75, [1976] ECR 455.

Article 141 EC (ex Article 119) now states that: **14.15**

1. Each Member State shall ensure that the principle of equal pay for male and female workers for equal work or work of equal value is applied.

2. For the purpose of this Article, 'pay' means the ordinary basic or minimum wage or salary and any other consideration, whether in cash or in kind, which the worker receives directly or indirectly, in respect of his employment, from his employer.

Equal pay without discrimination based on sex means:

(a) that pay for the same work at piece rates shall be calculated on the basis of the same unit of measurement;

(b) that pay for work at time rates shall be the same for the same job.

3. The Council, acting in accordance with the procedure referred to in Article 251, and after consulting the Economic and Social Committee, shall adopt measures to ensure the application of the principle of equal opportunities and equal treatment of men and women in matters of employment and occupation, including the principle of equal pay for equal work or work of equal value.

4. With a view to ensuring full equality in practice between men and women in working life, the principle of equal treatment shall not prevent any Member State from maintaining or adopting measures providing for specific advantages in order to make it easier for the under-represented sex to pursue a vocational activity or to prevent or compensate for disadvantages in professional careers.

Article 141(4) strongly suggests that positive action may be taken in relation to   **14.16**
pay inequality, but the extent of this is not clear. On this see 13.123–13.128
above where this is discussed further.

Likewise, free movement of workers has been provided for in Community   **14.17**
Law from the outset so that there should be no discrimination on grounds of
nationality of a member state. The ECJ has also held that this provision has direct
effect and can be relied on by individuals against their employers (*Van Duyn v
Home Office*;[9] *Walrave v Association Union Cycliste Internationale, Koninklijke
Nederlandsche Wielren Unie*;[10] *Union Royale Belge des Sociétés de Football Association
Asbl v Bosman*;[11] *Bossa v Nordstress Ltd*[12]).

This provision is now found in Article 39 EC and requires that: **14.18**

1. Freedom of movement for workers shall be secured within the Community.

2. Such freedom of movement shall entail the abolition of any discrimination based on nationality between workers of the Member States as regards employment, remuneration and other conditions of work and employment.

3. It shall entail the right, subject to limitations justified on grounds of public policy, public security or public health:

(a) to accept offers of employment actually made;

---

9 Case 41/74, [1975] Ch 358.
10 Case 36/74, [1974] ECR 1405, at 1424 (*per* Advocate-General Warner), 1418, para 17.
11 Case C-415/93, [1995] ECR I-4921, at 5066, para 83.
12 [1998] ICR 694.

(b) to move freely within the territory of Member States for this purpose;

(c) to stay in a Member State for the purpose of employment in accordance with the provisions governing the employment of nationals of that State laid down by law, regulation or administrative action;

(d) to remain in the territory of a Member State after having been employed in that State, subject to conditions which shall be embodied in implementing regulations to be drawn up by the Commission.

4. The provisions of this Article shall not apply to employment in the public service.

14.19 This has had a vital effect on securing free movement without discrimination.[13] It was supplemented at an early stage by Council Regulation No 1612/68 on Freedom of Movement for Workers within the Community which provides more precise individual rights to workers to be able to move throughout the Community without discrimination. As a Regulation, this is a more powerful provision than a Directive. It gives individuals direct rights against all.

14.20 The Equal Value[14] and Equal Treatment Directives[15] enlarged the area of European non-discrimination in 1975 and 1976 respectively. These were followed by the Equal Treatment in Social Security Directive in 1979,[16] and the Equal Treatment in Occupational Social Security Schemes Directive in 1986.[17]

14.21 Meanwhile a number of recommendations in relation to equality were made which, while lacking the same legislative force, have had an important impact in determining how equality is viewed in Europe. Perhaps the most important of these was the Recommendation and Code of Practice on the Protection of Dignity at Work[18] which has helped to explain the concept of harassment in the work context and to define the Community law approach to harassment issues.

14.22 Other Directives have addressed the burden of proof in relation to sex discrimination cases, the protection of part-time and fixed-term workers, pregnancy, and

---

[13] It should be noted that the reservations (in particular Art 39(4)) have been very restrictively interpreted: see, eg, Case 152/73 *Sotgiu v Deutsche Bundespost* [1974] ECR 153; Case 66/85 *Lawrie-Blum v Land Baden-Württemberg* [1986] ECR 2121.

[14] Council Directive (EEC) 75/117 on the approximation of the laws of the member states relating to the application of the principle of equal pay for men and women [1975] OJ L45.

[15] Council Directive (EEC) 76/207 on the implementation of the principle of equal treatment for men and women as regards access to employment, vocational training and promotion and working conditions [1976] OJ L39. This Directive has been recast as a result of European Parliament and Council Directive 2002/73.

[16] Council Directive (EEC) 79/7 on the progressive implementation of the principle of equal treatment for men and women in matters of social security [1979] OJ L6.

[17] Council Directive (EEC) 86/378 on the implementation of the principle of equal treatment for men and women in occupational social security schemes [1986] OJ L225.

[18] Commission Recommendation 92/131.

parental leave. Moreover, the ECJ in *P v S and Cornwall County Council*,[19] extended Community law protection against sex discrimination to transsexuals. This in turn led to the amendment of the Sex Discrimination Act 1975 to extend domestic protection in the employment field against direct discrimination to transsexuals.

Parallel with these legislative acts, the Treaties have themselves been altered so that now in Article 2 of the EC Treaty it is provided that: **14.23**

> The Community shall have as its task . . . to promote throughout the Community . . . equality between men and women . . . and social cohesion . . .

and by Article 3(2) EC that in relation to the key activities set out in that Article:

> . . . the Community shall aim to eliminate inequalities and to promote equality between men and women.

while in Article 12 EC it is explicitly stated that:

> Within the scope of this Treaty and without prejudice to any special provisions contained therein any discrimination on grounds of nationality shall be prohibited.

(1) Article 13 EC

The wide-ranging and significant new equality Directives, passed in 2000, came about as a result of the 1997 Treaty of Amsterdam, which introduced new powers for the Community to legislate in relation to discrimination. Thus Article 13 EC provides: **14.24**

> Without prejudice to the other provisions of this Treaty and within the limits of the powers conferred upon it by the community, the Council, acting unanimously on a proposal from the Commission and after consulting the European Parliament, may take appropriate action to combat discrimination based on sex, racial or ethnic origin, religion or belief, disability, age or sexual orientation.

The background to this amendment lies in the work of the Starting Line Group, who had campaigned for many years for a Race Directive to be made but who had found that there was arguably an inadequate legislative basis in the earlier provisions of the European Treaties.[20] It was accelerated by the recognition that it was essential to get equality issues right in advance of any enlargement of the European Union, and by a recognition that broad equality and non-discrimination provisions are still far from being universally available across the European Union even **14.25**

---

[19] Case C-13/94, [1996] ICR 795.

[20] The difference in the degree to which member states have made any provision in relation to the different grounds of discrimination set out in Art 13 EC can be seen in Annex VI to the Communication from the Commission to the Council, the European Parliament, the Economic and Social Committee and the Committee of the Regions on Certain Community Measures to Combat Discrimination: COM (1999) 564.

if equality is a superior rule of law. Indeed, it can be said that equality has hitherto had an uncertain and developing place in many member states.

14.26 Once Article 13 EC was introduced, it was proposed to implement as the first new Directives under this Article a Race Directive[21] having an impact outside just employment, and a framework Employment Equality Directive.[22] These were proposed by the Commission in late 1999 and approved with remarkable speed in 2000. The importance of these Directives lies in the facts that they introduce new and more comprehensive definitions of discrimination; the Race Directive covers more than just employment and therefore required amendments to the Race Relations Act 1976 (RRA 1976); and, perhaps most importantly, the Employment Equality Directive required the introduction of new provisions to protect against discrimination in employment in relation to age, sexuality, and religion and belief. The approach taken to employment discrimination in the two 2000 Directives has now been mirrored in the field of sex discrimination as a result of Directive 2002/73/EC, which amends the Equal Treatment Directive. These new provisions have transformed equality law in both Great Britain and Northern Ireland.

14.27 Both Directives are expressly based on the international equality provisions to which reference has already been made in Chapter 13. This emphasises the importance of an understanding of the part that they play in relation to equality and discrimination law. The effect of the Directives on UK employment law is considered further at 14.35 *et seq* below.

(2) The Charter of Fundamental Rights of the European Union

14.28 The European Union agreed a Charter of Fundamental Rights at Nice on 7 December 2000.[23] This contains a chapter concerned specifically with equality: Chapter III (see Appendix 3). This part of the Charter is based on the other international human rights texts, including in particular the ICCPR, and Protocol 12 to the ECHR.

14.29 It was proposed to incorporate the Charter as Part II of the European Constitution, which would have made it a binding text. The Constitution has not yet been ratified as a result of referendum defeats in the Netherlands and France. The Charter therefore exists as a 'solemn proclamation' only, but it remains an important source of principle if not yet hard law. It is already being used by the European Commission to provide a foundation for the scrutiny of proposed European

---

[21] The Race Directive of 29 June 2000 (Council Directive (EC) 2000/43 implementing the principle of equal treatment between persons irrespective of racial or ethnic origin [2000] OJ L180).

[22] The Framework Directive for Equal Treatment in Employment and Occupation of 27 November 2000 (Council Directive (EC) 2000/78 establishing a general framework for equal treatment in employment and occupation [2000] OJ L303).

[23] [2000] OJ C364, p 1.

legislation and other administrative action. Equally importantly, it has already been used by the ECJ as an aid to the interpretation of all Community measures. Thus in the first such case Advocate-General Tizzano said in *Broadcasting, Entertainment, Cinematographic and Theatre Union (BECTU) v Secretary of State for Trade and Industry*,[24] that the Charter:

> 27. . . . includes statements which appear in large measure to reaffirm rights which are enshrined in other instruments. In its preamble, it is moreover stated that 'this Charter reaffirms, with due regard for the powers and tasks of the Community and the Union and the principle of subsidiarity, the rights as they result, in particular, from the constitutional traditions and international obligations common to the Member States, the Treaty on European Union, the Community Treaties, the European Convention for the Protection of Human Rights and Fundamental Freedoms, the Social Charters adopted by the Community and by the Council of Europe and the case-law of the Court of Justice of the European Communities and of the European Court of Human Rights'.
>
> 28. I think therefore that, in proceedings concerned with the nature and scope of a fundamental right, the relevant statements of the Charter cannot be ignored; in particular, we cannot ignore its clear purpose of serving, where its provisions so allow, as a substantive point of reference for all those involved—Member States, institutions, natural and legal persons—in the Community context.

It is certain that use of the Charter by the Commission, Council, European **14.30** Parliament, and even ECJ, will continue to occur despite the stated hopes of a former Foreign Office Minister that this is an aspirational document[25] rather than one having immediate effect, and despite the stalling of the project for a European Constitution. By way of example, the Court of First Instance relied heavily on the Charter in reaching its decision in *Max Mobil Telekommunikation Service GmbH v Commission*.[26]

The most important non-discrimination provision of the Charter is Article 21, **14.31** which establishes a free-standing principle of non-discrimination. Article 21 ('Non-discrimination') provides:

> 1. Any discrimination based on any ground such as sex, race, colour, ethnic or social origin, genetic features, language, religion or belief, political or any other opinion, membership of a national minority, property, birth, disability, age or sexual orientation shall be prohibited.
>
> 2. Within the scope of application of the Treaty establishing the European Community and of the Treaty on European Union, and without prejudice to the special provisions of those Treaties, any discrimination on grounds of nationality shall be prohibited.

---

[24] Case C-173/99, Opinion, 8 February 2001; [2001] ICR 1152.
[25] It was contemptuously described by the Junior Minister Keith Vaz MP as having no more relevance than the *Beano*.
[26] Case T-54/99, judgment 30 January 2002, paras 48 and 57.

C. The impact of Article 14 on sex and race discrimination law

14.32   Protection from discrimination and the concept of equal treatment in the employment field is already well entrenched and as a result it is likely that existing provisions in the SDA 1975 and RRA 1976 will continue to be of paramount importance. Article 14 is unlikely to have much direct relevance in enlarging the concepts contained in that legislation except perhaps in enabling cases of multiple discrimination to be addressed. At the moment the law in relation to discrimination where there is alleged to be a combination of grounds is very unsatisfactory. It has been held not to enable an analysis to be carried out on the basis that two or more grounds have combined to provide the basis for the treatment under scrutiny: *Law Society v Bahl*.[27]

14.33   However, in construing these provisions attention will have to be paid to the requirements of Article 14 if there is a context in which it is properly engaged with some other Article of the ECHR. Moreover it is doubtful that the result in *Bahl* is consistent with European law.

14.34   One such circumstance where Article 14 might be important is when interpreting the term 'racial group' in the RRA 1976. This could lead an employment tribunal to permit Rastafarians, for example, to define themselves as a racial and religious group although in the past they have failed to do so (see *Mandla v Dowell Lee*[28] and *Crown Suppliers (PSA) Ltd v Dawkins*[29]).

D. The impact of the new discrimination Directives on race and sex discrimination

14.35   The Race Directive concerns discrimination on grounds of racial or ethnic origin in a wide number of situations, from employment to social protection and access to goods and services. It operates as an instruction from the European Union to each member state to put in place directly enforceable legal measures to the minimum standard set out in the Directive. The Directive has been introduced into UK discrimination law by means of amendments to the RRA 1976, effected by the Race Relations Act 1976 (Amendment) Regulations 2003.[30]

---

[27] [2004] EWCA Civ 1070, [2004] IRLR 799.
[28] [1983] 2 AC 548.
[29] [1993] ICR 517, CA.
[30] SI 2003/1626.

The amendments to the Equal Treatment Directive are narrower in scope, but mirror the new approach to discrimination found in the Race and Framework Directives. These amendments were implemented in the UK by means of amendments to the SDA 1975, effected by the Employment Equality (Sex Discrimination) Regulations 2005.[31]

Although there are two separate Directives requiring changes to the existing **14.36** definitions of race and sex discrimination in the UK, both the Race Directive and the amendments to the Equal Treatment Directive employ the same definitions of discrimination in the employment context. These two long-established types of discrimination are therefore dealt with together below. Where distinct points arise in relation to either Directive, or where this text touches on issues outside the employment context which affect only the race provisions, these will be dealt with separately.

As will be seen from the discussion below, these Directives strengthen the domestic **14.37** protection against discrimination in a number of respects. However, there are still certain areas where Article 14 may be used to produce a wider interpretation of the statutory language, and these are also discussed below.

(1) Concepts of discrimination in the Directives

Historically, Community legislation did not define direct or indirect discrimin- **14.38** ation in a black letter text. However, this changed with the Burden of Proof Directive,[32] which in relation to sex discrimination used a formula for direct discrimination which was broadly comparable to section 1(1) of the SDA 1975. However, the formula for determining when indirect discrimination could occur was different. Article 2(2) of the Burden of Proof Directive said that:

> . . . indirect discrimination shall exist where an apparently neutral provision, criterion or practice disadvantages a substantially higher proportion of the members of one sex unless that provision criterion or practice is appropriate and necessary and can be justified by objective factors unrelated to sex.

When the Race and Framework Directives were published, they contained a yet **14.39** wider definition of indirect discrimination discussed below. For a time, sex discrimination therefore fell out of step with the other areas covered by European legislation; however, the position was harmonised as a result of the amendments to the Equal Treatment Directive.

---

[31] SI 2005/2467.
[32] Council Directive (EC) 97/80 on the burden of proof in cases of discrimination based on sex [1997] OJ L14 (applied in the UK by Council Directive (EC) 98/52).

14.40 The Directives prohibit both direct and indirect discrimination (on grounds of ethnic or racial origin only in the case of the Race Directive, and on grounds of sex, marital, or family status in the Equal Treatment Directive); they also recognise harassment and instructions to discriminate as forms of discrimination.

14.41 Direct discrimination occurs when one person is treated less favourably than another person is, has been, or would be treated in a comparable situation on grounds of his or her racial or ethnic origin, or on grounds of his or her sex, or marital/family status.

14.42 The definition of indirect discrimination contained in the Directives (see Article 2(2)(b) of both Directives) has been incorporated into the RRA 1976 using the following wording:

> (1A) A person also discriminates against another if, in any circumstances relevant for the purposes of any provision referred to in subsection 1B, he applies to that other a provision, criterion or practice which he applies or would apply equally to persons not of the same race or ethnic or national origins as that other, but –
>
>   (a) which puts or would put persons of the same race or ethnic or national origins as that other at a particular disadvantage when compared with other people;
>
>   (b) which puts that other at that disadvantage; and
>
>   (c) which he cannot show to be a proportionate means of achieving a legitimate aim.

14.43 The same wording (with the obvious adjustments to refer to men and women, as opposed to people of the same or different race or ethnic or national origins) has also now been incorporated into the SDA 1975 (s 1(2)(b) as amended).

14.44 This definition encompasses discriminatory practices which do not constitute a 'must'. Previously such practices or preferences had been interpreted as falling outside the RRA 1976 (see *Perera v Civil Service Commission*,[33] although this position had already been weakened in decisions such as that of the Scottish EAT in *Falkirk Council v Whyte*[34] and the EAT in *Chief Constable of Avon & Somerset Constabulary v Chew*[35]). In *British Airways Plc v Starmer*,[36] the EAT, considering the 'intermediate' definition of indirect discrimination used in the SDA 1975, held that the definition of a provision, criterion or practice (PCP) must be 'at least as wide' as to include anything that would previously have qualified as a requirement or condition, as a result of the non-regression principle contained in Article 6 of the Burden of Proof Directive. Burton P held that a PCP 'may allow for exceptions to be made'; and further that a PCP may be a 'one-off' or can involve

---

[33] [1982] ICR 350.
[34] [1997] IRLR 560.
[35] [2001] All ER (D) 101 (Sept).
[36] [2005] IRLR 862.

a discretionary decision. It does not have to be applied to others, as the question is whether the PCP is one which the employer '*would* apply equally to a man'. However, in reaching these conclusions, the EAT relied heavily on the pre-Burden of Proof Directive law.

On its face, the definition does not depend on statistical evidence about the **14.45** proportions affected by any disputed PCP. This is important, as relevant statistical evidence is not always available; clearly if it is available, it can be very helpful. This interpretation of the new provisions has been challenged by respondents to tribunal claims, but it is supported by case law from the ECJ, and in particular the following extract from the decision in *O' Flynn v Adjudication Officer*:[37]

> Accordingly, conditions imposed by national law must be regarded as indirectly discriminatory where, although applicable irrespective of nationality, they affect essentially migrant workers (see Case 41/84 *Pinna v Caisse d' Allocations Familiales de la Savoie* [1986] ECR 1, paragraph 24; Case 33/88 *Allué and Another v Università degli Studi di Venezia* [1989] ECR 1591, paragraph 12; and *Le Manoir*, paragraph 11) or the great majority of those affected are migrant workers (see Case C-279/89 *Commission v United Kingdom* [1992] ECR I-5785, paragraph 42, and Case C-272/92 *Spotti v Freistaat Bayern* [1993] ECR I-5185, paragraph 18), where they are indistinctly applicable but can more easily be satisfied by national workers than by migrant workers (see *Commission v Luxembourg*, paragraph 10, and Case C-349/87 *Paraschi v Landesversicherungsanstalt Wuerttemberg* [1991] ECR I-4501, paragraph 23) or where there is a risk that they may operate to the particular detriment of migrant workers (see Case C-175/88 *Biehl v Administration des Contributions* [1990] ECR I-1779, paragraph 14, and Case C-204/90 *Bachmann v Belgium* [1992] ECR I-249, paragraph 9).

However, there have as yet been no appellate cases fully exploring the meaning of **14.46** the words 'particular disadvantage', and the implications thereof. As sections 1(2)b SDA and 1(1A) RRA refer to a PCP that 'would put' persons at a disadvantage, the definition does not depend on proof that the disadvantage has already occurred.[38] Consequently, it can be used when a particular disadvantage is anticipated. It would be possible to call evidence from sociologists or economists to show the anticipated discriminatory effect of a provision. This new definition of indirect discrimination has been written to ensure that it is as widely drawn as possible. It does not have the same emphasis on group discrimination.

Harassment has now been given a separate section in both Acts (s 3A in the RRA **14.47** 1976 and s 4A in the SDA 1975). The provision in the RRA 1976 is fairly straightforward: harassment will occur where, on grounds of race or ethnic or national

---

[37] Case C-237/94, [1998] ICR 608.
[38] The section draws heavily on the judgment of the ECJ in Case C-237/94 *O'Flynn v Adjudication Officer* [1998] ICR 608, see 14.45.

origins (see 14.53 below on the exclusion of colour and nationality), a person engages in unwanted conduct which has the purpose or effect of:

(a) violating the other person's dignity; or
(b) creating an intimidating, hostile, degrading, humiliating, or offensive environment for him.

14.48 This provides greater protection than envisaged in the Directive, which requires that both (a) and (b) above be present in order to prove harassment, whilst they are disjunctive conditions in the Act. The definition in the Directive would have given less protection than the definition of harassment developed in UK case law, and would therefore have breached the non-regression clause in the Directive.

14.49 The provisions in the SDA 1975 are more complex, with section 4A(1)(a) mirroring the RRA 1976 protection above, section 4A(1)(b) providing protection where the unwanted conduct as defined was 'of a sexual nature' (which need not be meted out 'on the ground of sex') and section 4A(1)(c) prohibiting less favourable treatment of an individual on the ground that he/she has rejected or submitted to unwanted conduct as defined. This wider definition reflects the provisions of the Equal Treatment Directive as amended, although the definition of unwanted conduct is again disjunctive and thus more helpful to employees than that in the Directive.

(2) Exclusions

14.50 A number of specific exclusions in the RRA 1976 were eliminated by the 2003 Regulations, but only in relation to claims where the discrimination was on grounds of race, ethnic or national origins (see 14.53 below). These include exceptions for seamen recruited abroad (s 9 of the RRA 1976), training for people not ordinarily resident in the UK (s 6), charities as employers and providers of goods, facilities, and services (s 34), partnerships of less than six people (s 10), and the disposal and management of small dwellings (s 22).

14.51 There are no provisions in the SDA 1975 equivalent to the majority of the exclusions mentioned above, which are largely race-specific. However, there was no exclusion for partnerships of less than six people even prior to the 2003 Regulations; and the provisions relating to disposal and management of small dwellings, and charities, have not been amended. Some other exclusions which existed in the old SDA 1975 have been eliminated: for example, the Act now covers office holders (but not elected office holders or political officials: ss 10A and 10B); there is now some protection for ministers of religion insofar as they are office holders (although there are provisions permitting justification of discrimination in certain circumstances: s 19); the section on vocational training now covers all types of practical work experience, even where it is unpaid (s 14); and the section allowing discrimination in admission to the Cadet Forces administered by the MoD (s 85) has been repealed.

(3) The scope of the Race Directive

The Race Directive applies to both the public and private sector (Article 3). Its **14.52** scope is very wide, covering employment, self-employment and training, and social protection, including social security and healthcare, social advantages, education, and access to and supply of goods and services which are available to the public, including housing. As a result, amendments have been made to the RRA 1976 to import the new definitions of discrimination, including harassment, into both Part II and Part III of the Act.

However, differences of treatment based on nationality are expressly excluded from **14.53** the Directive, although they are covered by the RRA 1976. Additionally, provisions relating to the entry and residence of third country nationals and stateless persons, or treatment that arises from this legal status, are excluded (Article 3(2)). This exclusion is reflected in the amended provisions of the RRA 1976. Further, those provisions also exclude discrimination on grounds of colour. Although the Directive does not itself mention colour (stating at Article 2 that 'the principle of equal treatment shall mean that there shall be no direct or indirect discrimination based on racial or ethnic origin'), this latter point has proved particularly controversial. During the debate on the statutory amendments in the House of Lords, Lord Lester pointed out that the Race Directive refers to grounds of racial, national or ethnic origin, and that such grounds would, in common-sense language, include a person's colour. He further argued that the preamble to the Race Directive makes a reference to the International Convention on the Elimination of All Forms of Racial Discrimination, which includes colour, and argued that this plainly pointed to an intention that colour be included. Lord Filkin, having said that the simple answer to the discrepancy point was that the Directive did not cover discrimination on grounds of colour, agreed to look into the point. However, the anomaly remains.

As matters stand, there is therefore a 'two-tier' system of race discrimination **14.54** legislation, meaning that:

(a) those complaining of indirect discrimination on the basis of colour and nationality will be left to rely on the old definition of indirect discrimination (preserved in s 1(1)(b) of the RRA 1976);

(b) claimants may not complain of harassment on grounds of colour or nationality; and

(c) complaints of discrimination on grounds of colour or nationality will have to be dealt with under the old case law on the burden of proof (ie *King v Great Britain-China Centre*[39]).

---

[39] [1992] ICR 516.

14.55 There are various ways in which this difficulty may be met. As the new Code of Practice on Racial Equality in Employment points out, it should be possible to argue on practical grounds that almost anyone complaining of discrimination or harassment based on their colour is in truth also complaining of discrimination based on their race or national/ethnic origins.[40] Courts may well be ready to give a generous interpretation to those concepts so as to give effect to the true purpose of the Directive and the race relations legislation, although in practical terms, it would probably be most sensible for practitioners acting on behalf of claimants to draft all claim forms in terms of race and ethnic/national origins, as well as colour or nationality. Alternatively, it may be possible to undertake a purposive construction of the Directive and the legislation to include 'colour'. On this point, however, it is noteworthy that although five member states (Austria, Germany, Finland, Greece, and Luxembourg) were referred to the ECJ on 19 July 2004 for failing to pass all necessary legislation to bring national law in line with the Directive (*Commission v Luxembourg*;[41] *Commission v Greece*;[42] *Commission v Finland*;[43] *Commission v Germany*;[44] *Commission v Austria*[45]), no such referral was made in respect of the UK.

14.56 However, the apparent gap in the new legislation in terms of colour and nationality could also be challenged using the HRA 1998. The most obvious area for challenge would be for an individual whose claim has been pleaded only on the basis of colour or nationality to argue that the new provisions violate his right to a fair trial using Article 6 combined with Article 14 ECHR. It is, however, unlikely that such a person would be forced to formulate his case in this way since he or she is almost certain to be able to reformulate it in a way which would be adequately covered by the amended legislation.

14.57 The amendments to the Equal Treatment Directive do not have the wider scope of the Race Directive (compare Article 3 of each Directive). Thus, the changes to the SDA 1975 are limited to the employment sphere. However, the Equal Treatment Directive has required substantive alterations to the types of discrimination covered by the SDA 1975. In accordance with Article 2(7) of the Directive, the SDA 1975 now has a discrete section dealing with the special rules applicable to discrimination on the ground of pregnancy or maternity leave (s 3A). This gives effect to the law as it has developed, but removes the need to adopt the somewhat convoluted reasoning previously required in pregnancy discrimination cases.

---

[40] See, eg, para 2.10 of the Code.
[41] C-320/04.
[42] C-326/04.
[43] C-327/04.
[44] C-329/04.
[45] C-335/04.

(4) Genuine and determining occupational requirements

Although the provisions in the Directives relating to genuine and determining **14.58**
occupational requirements are virtually identical in wording, they have been
transposed into law in different ways in the two Acts. The RRA 1976 now provides
at section 4A that the discrimination provisions will not apply where, having
regard to the nature of the employment or the context in which it is carried out,
being of a particular race or of particular ethnic or national origins is a genuine
and determining occupational requirement; it is proportionate to apply that
requirement in the particular case, and either the person to whom the requirement is applied does not meet it, or the employer is not satisfied and in all the circumstances it is reasonable for him not to be satisfied, that that person meets it.
This is a more general provision than the old GOQ section (retained at s 5 for
claims based on colour or nationality), and it will be necessary for the courts to
interpret the new section in such a way as to avoid breaching the non-regression
clause of the Directive at Article 6(2).

The government decided not to use a similar general description in the SDA 1975. **14.59**
The provisions, set out at sections 7–7B of the Act, have largely remained the same,
save that the section relating to individuals who have undergone gender reassign-
ment (s 7B) has been amended so as to prevent employers from refusing to employ
such individuals where a job requires the holder to perform intimate searches, but
other employees can reasonably be employed on those duties instead.

(5) Positive action

Provisions in the Race Directive enable member states to maintain or adopt positive **14.60**
action measures to compensate for past disadvantage related to racial or ethnic
origin (Article 5). However, the Directive does not require member states to take
such action. It is doubtful whether these provisions go further (or much further)
than that which is permitted already in Community law. Article 2 of the Equal
Treatment Directive states that the Directive is without prejudice to provisions
concerning the protection of women, particularly as regards pregnancy and maternity, and the right of member states to recognise distinct rights to paternity and/
or adoption leave. Further, Article 2(8) states that member states may maintain
or adopt measures within the meaning of Article 141(4) of the Treaty with a view
to ensuring full equality in practice between men and women. These points are
discussed more fully at 13.60–13.84.

(6) Victimisation

In accordance with the Directives, both the SDA 1975 and RRA 1976 now con- **14.61**
tain specific sections forbidding any kind of discrimination against or harassment

of employees where the conduct in question arises out of and is closely connected to the employment relationship (s 27A of the RRA 1976; s 20A of the SDA 1975).

(7) Remedies

14.62 The Race Directive imposes on each member state the duty to provide for a right of redress for all victims of such discrimination (Article 15); the government has now provided that compensation for non-intentional indirect discrimination on grounds of race (see s 57(3) and 56(1)(b) of the RRA 1976). Equivalent compensation has been available under the SDA 1975 since 1996.

(8) Burden of proof

14.63 Article 4 of the Burden of Proof Directive[46] on the burden of proof in cases of discrimination based on sex, and Article 8 of the Race Directive provide that once an applicant establishes before a court or tribunal facts that indicate that there has been discrimination, it will be for the respondent to prove that no discrimination has occurred. This requirement has been implemented into the RRA 1976 by section 54A and the SDA 1975 by section 63A, and guidance on the interpretation of the relevant sections has since been provided by the Court of Appeal in *Igen Ltd v Wong*.[47] It should, however, be noted that for the reasons set out at 14.53–14.56 above, in cases under the RRA 1976, the new burden of proof provisions apply only where discrimination is said to have been on grounds of race, ethnic, or national origins, and *not* where the reason for the discrimination is colour or nationality.

(9) Bodies for the promotion of equal treatment

14.64 Member states must nominate an independent organisation to provide assistance to victims of discrimination; to undertake surveys about discrimination; to publish reports; and to make recommendations about such discrimination (Article 13). In Great Britain this duty is currently fulfilled by the CRE and the EOC, but from October 2007, these organisations will be replaced by the Commission for Equality and Human Rights (see 14.141–14.160 below). In Northern Ireland the Equality Commission for Northern Ireland will fulfil these functions.

---

[46] Council Directive (EC) 97/80.
[47] [2005] ICR 931, [2005] EWCA Civ 142.

E. The Employment Equality Directive

As discussed at 14.26 above, Article 13 of the EC Treaty also resulted in the **14.65** proposal for a new framework Employment Equality Directive. This prohibits direct and indirect discrimination in the areas of religion and belief, sexual orientation, age and disability, but only in the field of employment and occupation. The provisions on religion and belief and sexual orientation were implemented by the Employment Equality (Religion and Belief) Regulations 2003, and the Employment Equality (Sexual Orientation) Regulations 2003 respectively, and the provisions on age and disability in the Employment Equality (Age) Regulations 2006, and amendments to the Disability Discrimination Act 1995 (DDA 1995).

In relation to each of the four grounds of discrimination, an act which would other- **14.66** wise be unlawful will be permitted where the nature of the work or occupation, or the context in which it is to be carried out, creates a genuine and determining occupational need. There must be a legitimate objective and the requirement must be proportionate. The detail of the Directive is dealt with in the separate sections on each area of discrimination below, but the key provisions are summarised here.

The Employment Equality Directive prohibits both direct and indirect discrimin- **14.67** ation on grounds of religion and belief, sexual orientation, disability or age (Article 2). It recognises that harassment (Article 2(3)) and instructions to discriminate (Article 2(4)) are also forms of discrimination. Direct and indirect discrimination are defined in the same way as in the Race Directive discussed above, although in the case of persons with a particular disability, indirect discrimination will not be assumed to have occurred where the employer (or other organisation to whom the Directive applies) is obliged under national law to make reasonable accommodation for the disabled person (Article 2(2)(b)).

The Directive is stated to be without prejudice to national laws which, in a demo- **14.68** cratic society, are necessary for public security, the maintenance of public order and prevention of criminal offences, the protection of public health, and the protection of the rights and freedoms of others (Article 2(5)).

(1) Scope of the Employment Equality Directive

The Directive applies to both public and private sectors in relation to employ- **14.69** ment and conditions of work. These are defined very widely (Article 3) but do not cover goods, facilities, and services. The Directive specifically excludes differences of treatment on grounds of nationality and treatment that relates to the legal status of third country nationals or stateless persons (Article 3(2)). It also specifically excludes state social security and social protection schemes from its operation (Article 3(3)). The armed forces are excluded from the provisions of the Directive in relation to age and disability (Article 3(4)) (see 13.60–13.84 for a discussion of what is permitted of positive action).

(2) Genuine and determining occupational requirements

14.70 Member states may make provision for genuine and determining occupational requirements (Article 4(1)). National legislation can provide for an exception where the occupational activity or the context in which it is carried out means that a particular characteristic is a genuine and determining occupational requirement, provided that the objective is legitimate and the requirement is proportionate.

(3) Conflict of rights

14.71 There is also a specific exception in the case of employment by an organisation which has an ethos based on a particular religion or belief; see also the discussion of Article 9 ECHR at 9.67–9.74. In relation to churches and other public or private institutions whose ethos is based on a particular religion or belief, member states may maintain existing legislative provisions, or introduce new legislation based on existing national practices, to permit such organisations to discriminate in their occupational activities on the basis of religion or belief, but only where the nature of those activities, or the context in which they are carried out, constitutes a genuine, legitimate and justified occupational requirement, having regard to the organisation's ethos (Article 4(2)). This exception does not permit organisations with a particular religious ethos to discriminate on grounds of age, disability, or sexual orientation. In addition, churches and other public and private organisations whose ethos is based on a particular religion or belief may lawfully require individuals working for them to act in good faith and with loyalty to the organisation's ethos (Article 4(2)). See further 9.135–9.148.

14.72 Like the Race Directive, the Framework Directive contains provisions permitting a member state to maintain or adopt positive action measures to compensate for past disadvantage linked to any of the grounds or characteristics covered by the Directive. However, the Directive does not require member states to take such action (Article 7).

14.73 Once an applicant establishes before a court or tribunal facts that indicate that there has been discrimination, it will be for the respondent to prove that no discrimination has occurred (Article 10).

14.74 The Directive requires member states to introduce provisions to protect individuals from any adverse treatment or adverse consequences as a result of a complaint being made or proceedings being taken to enforce the principle of equal treatment (Article 11).

Member states have to put in place a system of sanctions that must be 'effective, **14.75** proportionate and dissuasive' (Article 17).

The Directive makes two specific provisions in relation to discrimination on **14.76** grounds of religion and belief for Northern Ireland, which reflect the lobbying done by the UK government prior to agreement on the Directive (Article 15(1)). These are considered at 9.123–9.133.

F. Article 14 and age discrimination in Employment Law

Whilst the Employment Equality (Age) Regulations 2006 are now in force, the **14.77** numerous exceptions in the new legislation mean there may yet be a continuing need to rely upon the possibility of the HRA 1998 assisting in this field. In order to assist to this end the protection offered prior to the 2006 Regulations coming into force is considered briefly below.

Age discrimination has long been known to be a problem in relation to employ- **14.78** ment. Measures short of legislation failed to have their desired aim: therefore whilst in 1999 a Code of Practice on Age Diversity was promulgated by the government, it did not adequately address the problem of age discrimination in the workplace. An evaluation of this Code was produced in October 2001 by National Opinion Polls (Consumer) for the Department of Work and Pensions which reported that age discrimination was frequently viewed as acceptable in the workplace, with older employees feeling under pressure to make way for younger workers.[48] There was also evidence suggesting a lack of understanding of age discrimination, despite as many as one in four people aged 50–69 experiencing it when working or seeking employment. It was found that there was little change to employers' often stereotypical views relating to older and younger workers since the Code was introduced.[49] The Report concluded that 'the level of change experienced and expected is still very low and many employers do not regard age discrimination as an issue for them',[50] and the researchers felt that the voluntary Code would not have sufficient impact upon awareness of age and workplace attitudes to it on its own without the added force of legislation. Although this

---

[48] At para 3.4.
[49] At para 4.8.
[50] At para 5.16.

voluntary approach has assisted employers in managing a more diverse work-force, it was clear that age discrimination is so ingrained that only legislation and litigation would ensure that practices which impact on older workers are eradicated.[51]

(1) Age discrimination case law preceding the 2006 Regulations

14.79 There are already a number of cases in which age or age bars have played a signifi-cant part in the treatment that an employee has received. In *Perera v Civil Service Commission and the Department of Customs and Excise*,[52] a barrister from Sri Lanka was turned down for a legal post in the Civil Service as candidates had to be under 32 years old. This applicant complained of race discrimination on the grounds that no Sri Lankan executive officers could comply with such a requirement as a high proportion of them were adults by the time they had moved to the UK. He was successful.

14.80 In *Price v Civil Service Commission*,[53] the Civil Service advertised for applicants aged 'at least 17 and under 28 years of age'. The applicant Mrs Price was 35 years old and complained that she had been unlawfully discriminated against on the ground of sex. The EAT held that the age limit of 28 was a condition which it was 'in practice' harder for women to comply with than men, since a large proportion of women are occupied with children at that age. The case was remitted to the tri-bunal, where the Civil Service failed to demonstrate that the limit was justifiable. The application of the upper age limit thus amounted to unlawful indirect discrimination.

14.81 Age bars on access to an employment tribunal to complain of unfair dismissal have been raised in a number of cases. The challenge arose out of the age limits for employment rights within domestic legislation, and in particular the absence of the right not to be unfairly dismissed if the employee has reached 65 or 'normal retiring age' (see s 109(1) of the ERA 1996). Statistics presented to tribunals have in several cases appeared to show that this provision is indirectly discrimin-atory against male employees. However, in *Rutherford v Secretary of State for Trade*

---

[51] A study by the Performance and Innovation Unit prepared for the Cabinet Office in 2000 called *Winning the Generation Game*, found that employers had changed their behaviour and put new procedures in place to avoid breaking the law when the other anti-discrimination legislation was introduced (see ch 6 of report). The study also found that under each Act behavioural change has occurred. While there was found to be no decisive international evidence on the effectiveness of age discrimination legislation, the study concluded that it was impossible to say that workplace partici-pation rates of older people would not have fallen further without legislation.

[52] [1982] ICR 350.

[53] [1978] ICR 27.

and Industry,[54] the House of Lords ruled that the men were not indirectly discriminated against as the statistics produced did not support a finding of adverse impact. The upper age limit was therefore found to be lawful. These issues have since been revisited in litigation about the new regulations (see 14.99 below).

(2) The Employment Equality (Age) Regulations 2006

When the Employment Equality (Age) Regulations 2006 came into force on **14.82** 1 October 2006, they implemented the age strand of the Employment Equality Directive. This book does not set out a full analysis of the contents of the Regulations[55] but summarises some of the key changes made and looks at where the Regulations may conflict with obligations under the HRA 1998. The key changes brought about by the Regulations are:

- A new default retirement age of 65.
- A duty imposed on employers to consider requests to work beyond retirement age.
- Direct and indirect age discrimination is unlawful unless objectively justified.
- No upper age limit for unfair dismissal but dismissal for reasons of retirement at or over the default retirement age of 65 will be a fair dismissal as long as the retirement is genuine.
- Harassment based on age is unlawful.
- Age-related elements of statutory redundancy pay are repealed.
- Service-related benefits are retained provided certain conditions are satisfied.
- Insurance benefits cannot be denied on grounds of age unless objectively justified.
- Occupational pensions are largely excluded from the impact of the Regulations.

The Age Regulations affect a wide number of parties including self-employed **14.83** people, paid office holders, and unpaid workers involved in vocational training.

Harassment is unlawful discrimination regardless of the need for a comparator. **14.84** With regard to the definition of harassment, the Directive required the conduct to be related to age, yet the Regulations simply say the conduct must be 'on the ground of' age. This may mean that a claimant has to show that age-related conduct led to an offensive working environment and that their age was the reason for the conduct. Such an interpretation may amount to a failure to properly implement the Directive.

---

[54] [2006] ICR 785.
[55] See O'Dempsey, Jolly and Harrop, *Age Discrimination Handbook* (LAG, 2007) for a comprehensive guide to these Regulations.

14.85 Initial drafts of the Regulations also included a non-exhaustive list of situations where direct age discrimination may, depending on the circumstances, pursue a legitimate aim:

- the setting of requirements as to age in order to ensure the protection or promote the vocational integration of people in a particular age group;
- the fixing of a minimum age to qualify for certain advantages linked to employment or occupation in order to recruit or retain older people; and
- the fixing of a maximum age for recruitment or promotion which is based on the training requirements of the post in question or the need for a reasonable period of employment before retirement.

The final version did not include such a list.

14.86 The examples within the draft Age Regulations were based on a list included in Article 6 of the Directive. Even if the Article 6 examples apply the employer would still have to show the practice pursues a legitimate aim, and is an appropriate and necessary (or proportionate) means of achieving that aim. Other legitimate aims mentioned in the July 2005 DTI Consultation Paper include:

- health, welfare, and safety (including protection of young or older people);
- facilitation of employment planning;
- particular training requirements;
- encouraging and rewarding loyalty;
- the need for a reasonable period of employment before retirement; and
- recruiting or retaining older people.

14.87 The legitimate aim cannot be related to age discrimination itself. So, taking the consultation document's example, it would not be lawful for a retailer of youthful fashion items to employ young shop assistants because it believes that this will further its aim of targeting young buyers. The DTI has indicated that trying to attract a young target group will not be a legitimate aim, because this has an age-discriminatory aspect. It is difficult to understand why 'trying to attract a young target group' is more age-discriminatory than establishing a maximum age for recruitment or even taking age into account for dramatic casting.

14.88 Economic factors such as business needs and considerations of efficiency may also be legitimate aims, but mere costs alone will not justify discrimination. See *Cross v British Airways plc*,[56] where a tribunal that had weighed up the cost implications of altering a retirement age that was indirectly discriminatory on grounds of sex was held not to have erred in law.

---

[56] [2005] IRLR 423, EAT.

Practitioners should note that the wording defining genuine occupational **14.89**
requirements in regulation 8 of the Age Regulations is broader than in the
Sexual Orientation Regulations. The latter contains reference to circumstances
where 'being of a particular sexual orientation is a genuine and determining
occupational requirement'. In contrast the age genuine occupational requirement provision uses a wider test of 'possessing a characteristic related to age'.

Whilst positive action could only be justified through the general test of objective **14.90**
justification, positive action includes giving persons of a particular age access to
vocational training; or encouraging persons of a particular age to use employment opportunities if this is reasonably expected to prevent or compensate for
disadvantages suffered by such persons.

Since the Employment Equality Directive covers employment relationships, an **14.91**
employer who discriminates in relation to the provision of employment-related
insurance will be guilty of unlawful direct or indirect discrimination, depending
on the circumstances, unless he can justify it.

Service-related pay and benefits will frequently amount to indirect age discrimin- **14.92**
ation as older age groups are more likely to have completed the required length of
service than younger employees. However, Article 6 of the Directive provides
that the fixing of conditions of age for access to employment advantages are capable of amounting to justified discrimination.

The Regulations contain a general provision and two specific exemptions on **14.93**
employment benefits, all of which cover the use of length of service as a criterion
for awarding or increasing benefits in specified circumstances. These exemptions
cover pay and non-pay benefits, such as annual leave and company cars. The benefits must reflect the higher level of experience of the employee, or reward the
loyalty of the employee, or increase or maintain the motivation of the employee
and result in a business benefit and be based on a length of service criterion which
is applied similarly to staff in similar situations.

When relying upon the general exemption provided by regulation 33 no evi- **14.94**
dence is required to demonstrate that the service-based benefits really achieve any
business advantage. The burden of proof is reached as long as the employer can
show it 'reasonably appears' to him that there is an advantage in awarding benefits
on this basis.

More specifically, any length-of-service requirement of five years or less will be **14.95**
exempted and lawful (reg 32) as will any length-of-service requirement that mir-
rors a similar requirement in a statutory benefit.

14.96   The age bands for younger employees under the national minimum wage will continue to be lawful where employees in the lower age group (those aged 16–17 or 18–21, as the case may be) are paid less than the adult minimum wage.

14.97   Article 6 of the Directive allows occupational pension schemes to set ages for admission or entitlement to retirement benefits. It is expected that under the Regulations pension schemes will continue to operate largely as before.

(3) A default retirement age

14.98   The most controversial part of the Regulations is the institution of a national default retirement age of 65 along with its consequent exemptions on the right to claim age discrimination over that age (see reg 33).[57] It is not possible to consider in full here the detailed and complex new provisions on age discrimination in dismissal and the right to claim unfair dismissal. The key intention is that there will be no right to claim either age discrimination or unfair dismissal in respect of a genuine retirement from age 65 onwards. There is nothing specifically in the Directive which authorises this removal of age discrimination rights nor any suggestion therein that the general prohibition on age discrimination was not intended to apply to workers who have reached age 65. The government has promised to review these provisions in 2011.

14.99   In late 2006, Heyday, an organisation backed by Age Concern brought a judicial review case[58] against the government arguing that the inclusion of a default retirement age of 65 years in the 2006 Regulations breached the Employment Equality Directive. The High Court did not itself determine whether forcing employees to retire at age 65 was discriminatory but has referred the issue to the ECJ (unopposed by government). If the UK is found to have implemented the Employment Equality Directive incorrectly, the statutory retirement age could be withdrawn well in advance of the 2011 review date.

14.100   The implications of this decision are different for the private and public sectors. Private employers can for now continue with the 'retirement procedure' whereas public employers which are 'emanations of the state' who compulsorily retire people at 65 could face retrospective challenges from such workers arguing that the exemption in the 2006 Regulations for compulsory retirement is inconsistent with EU law.

---

[57] It should be noted that those aged 65 and over will have no rights to claim age discrimination in recruitment (reg 7(4)). So once an employee reaches 65 s/he has the right not to be discriminated against in terms of recruitment on grounds of sex, sexual orientation, race, religion, or disability, but not age.

[58] *R (on the application of Incorporated Trustees of the National Council on Aging) v The Secretary of State for Trade and Industry* (Administrative Court CO/5485/2006).

Two references have been made from Spain to the ECJ on the issue of mandatory **14.101** retirement ages agreed as part of collective agreements: *Palacios de la Villa and Cortefield Sericios SA*[59] and *Garcia v Confederación Hidrográfica del Duero*.[60] The ECJ will consider the *Heyday* referral after these cases.

Recital 14 to the Directive provides that 'this Directive shall be without prejudice **14.102** to the national provisions laying down retirement ages'. It remains to be seen whether this recital alone justifies the blanket exclusion from the prohibition on discriminatory access to employment or dismissal after 65.

If a mandatory retirement age provision is permissible in this form at all, then the **14.103** provision in these Regulations will contravene Article 6[61] of the Framework Directive unless the government can show that the exclusion from age discrimination rights is 'objectively and reasonably justified by a legitimate aim, including legitimate employment policy, labour market and vocational training objectives, and if the means of achieving that aim are appropriate and necessary'. The key explanation given to date is that of retirement age playing a significant role in workforce planning. Yet Article 6 is surely concerned with individual acts of discrimination which can be objectively justified. It was not intended to be a provision qualifying the scope of application of the Directive which is defined very widely to include all dismissals in Article 3.

Under the Regulations, whilst the statutory age limit of 65 for claiming unfair **14.104** dismissal will no longer apply, the one-year qualifying length of service will be maintained and retirement at or over the default retirement age of 65 will be a fair dismissal as long as the retirement is genuine and any requests to continue working beyond retirement considered. Failure to comply with the duty-to-consider procedure will render a dismissal automatically unfair.

Like the right to request flexible working under section 80F of the ERA 1996, the **14.105** employer's right to request working beyond the intended date of retirement is procedural, not substantive. Most claims based on a refusal to allow flexible working can be brought alongside a complaint of indirect discrimination pursuant to the SDA 1975, compensation for which is not limited. In contrast there is no means by which an employee can substantively test the employer's refusal to allow a request to work past the planned retirement date.

---

[59] Case C-411/05.
[60] Case C-87/06.
[61] Article 6 of the Directive provides that: '. . . member states may provide that differences of treatment on grounds of age shall not constitute discrimination, if, within the context of national law, they are objectively and reasonably justified by a legitimate aim, including legitimate employment policy, labour market and vocational training objectives, and if the means of achieving that aim are appropriate and necessary.'

14.106   Article 14 ECHR may thus still be important in addressing age discrimination at work. Article 14 has been used already with Article 8 in cases concerning the age of sexual consent (see *Sutherland v UK*[62]). It might be possible to argue that the current rules which prevent an employment tribunal reviewing a dismissal on grounds of retirement after the necessary procedures have been followed are in breach of the HRA 1998. They certainly have the effect of discriminating against those of and over 65 in exercising a right of access to the court. However, it might be argued that the right itself was limited by the terms on which it was given and therefore that Article 6 was not engaged.

14.107   On the other hand, the European Court has held that it is not permissible for rules of civil procedure to differentiate as between women and men (*Schuler-Zgraggen v Switzerland*[63]). However, not all limitations on access to a court which differentiate between different groups are unlawful (see *Stubbings v UK*,[64] where the ECtHR said that contracting states enjoyed a margin of appreciation in assessing whether differences in otherwise similar situations justified a different treatment in law; and see also the discussion of *Matthews v Ministry of Defence*[65]).

G. Article 14 and sexual orientation

14.108   Prior to the Employment Equality (Sexual Orientation) Regulations 2003 coming into force in December 2003, Article 8 read with Article 14 was a key tool in challenging discrimination on grounds of sexual orientation. This has been discussed at 8.163. This section explores the contribution made by the 2003 Regulations as well as the continuing assistance of the HRA 1998 in relation to such discrimination.

(1) Sexual orientation as a right under Article 8

14.109   Since around the year 2000 it has been clear that ECHR does prohibit some discrimination on grounds of sexual orientation. In *Lustig-Prean and Beckett v United Kingdom*[66] and *Smith & Grady v United Kingdom*,[67] an infringement of the right to private life was found to have occurred when gay and lesbian service men and women were investigated and dismissed, but no finding was made in relation to Article 14 given that an Article 8 breach had already been found.

---

[62] [1998] EHRLR 117.
[63] (1993) 16 EHRR 405.
[64] (1997) 23 EHRR 213.
[65] [2003] 1 AC 1163, [2003] UKHL 4, at paras 33–53.
[66] (2000) 29 EHRR 548, [1999] IRLR 734.
[67] (2000) 29 EHRR 493.

However, it is implicit from the judgment of the European Court that discrimination on the ground of sexual orientation would breach Article 14. See also *Salguiro Da Silva Mouta v Portugal*[68] and *Mata Estevez v Spain*.[69] The extent of any right to protection in relation to sexual orientation in the workplace is discussed in Chapter 8 (see 8.163). This section considers the relevance of Article 14 ECHR prior to implementation of the Framework Directive. Whilst implementation of the Directive through these Regulations should mean that domestic legislation effectively protects against discrimination on grounds of sexual orientation in relation to employment, the exceptions to the protection given by the 2003 Regulations, discussed below, make it important to remain aware of the way in which Article 14 (and Article 8) arguments can assist when complaining of such discrimination. The issue of equality regarding workplace pension provision as between same-sex and married couples is considered at 14.112 *et seq* below.

First, it should be noted that the EAT in *X v Y*[70] confirmed that: **14.110**

> . . . the prohibition on discrimination contained in Article 14 extends to discrimination on the grounds of sexual orientation. See eg *Smith and Grady v UK* [1999] IRLR 231; *Salgueiro da Silva Mouta v Portugal* [2001] 1 FCR 653.[71]

But it by no means follows that all allegations of discrimination against gays and lesbians will be covered, since the ECtHR considers that Article 8 protects their private life rather than decisions on cohabitation or the way in which gays and lesbians have relationships (see further 14.116–14.124).

(2) The Civil Partnership Act 2004 and discrimination against gay and lesbian couples

That is why the Civil Partnership Act 2004 (CPA 2004) has been so important   **14.111** since it requires amendments to be made to the 2003 Regulations with regard to the status of partners in same-sex couples. From 5 December 2005, the status of a civil partner under the Regulations is comparable to that of a spouse (see reg 3(3)). Where a civil partner is treated less favourably than a married person they can bring a claim for sexual orientation discrimination. There will be no defence that heterosexual marriage is materially different from civil partnership. The only way to justify such less favourable treatment of a civil partner would be if an employer was able to demonstrate that heterosexual marriage was a genuine occupational requirement of the job: surely a most unlikely scenario.

---

[68] (2001) 31 EHRR 47.
[69] Reports of Judgments and Decisions 2001-VI, p 311.
[70] [2003] ICR 1138.
[71] At para 22.

14.112 Under the 2003 Regulations it is permissible to confer more favourable benefits such as survivor's benefit upon civil partners and spouses to the exclusion of those without this status (reg 25). This change to the Regulations has lessened the utility of the case of *Ghaidan v Mendoza*[72] within the employment field. In *Ghaidan* the House of Lords held that in the context of considering the terms on which a member of a family succeeded to a tenancy there was no fair or rational ground for distinguishing between a surviving homosexual partner and a surviving heterosexual partner.[73] Therefore, rights of a surviving partner in a same-sex relationship were infringed under Articles 8 and 14 of the ECHR.

14.113 But for the CPA 2004 it is also doubtful that this discrimination could be challenged by an extended reference to section 3 of the SDA 1975, which prohibits discrimination against married persons, since that provision does not protect against discrimination against single or unmarried persons (*Bick v Royal West of England Residential School for the Deaf*;[74] see also *McLeen v Paris Travel Services Ltd*[75] and *Coleman v Skyrail Oceanic Ltd*[76]).

14.114 It has been suggested that on a reference in relation to the Employment Equality Directive the ECJ might require member states to provide the same benefits to same-sex couples as are afforded to married persons. However, this might be contrary to the recitals to the Framework Directive, which suggest that such discrimination is justified: see also *R (Amicus) v Secretary of State for Trade and Industry* [2004] IRLR 430. Indeed, in the wider context of staff benefits within the Commission, the ECJ has declined to equate a stable single-sex relationship to marriage, even if that relationship is registered under the applicable laws of the member state (*D and Kingdom of Sweden v Council of the European Union*[77]).

14.115 However, benefits or pension schemes which provide for spouses, family members, or those who are 'living together as husband and wife' may be open to a statutory interpretation which assists same-sex couples. If 'family member' has been found to include the survivor of a same-sex couple (*Fitzpatrick v Sterling Housing Association*[78]), there should be scope for the judiciary and/or the legislature taking this development one step further and deciding that 'spouse' can be applied to a same-sex partner.

---

72 [2004] All ER 210.

73 See also *Fitzpatrick v Sterling Housing Association* [2001] 1 AC 27 where the House of Lords had decided that a same-sex cohabiting partner could succeed to an assured tenancy on the basis that the surviving partner was a member of the deceased's family.

74 [1976] IRLR 326.

75 [1976] IRLR 202.

76 [1981] ICR 864.

77 Joined Cases C-122/99 P and C-125/99 P, [2001] ECR I-4319.

78 [2001] 1 AC 27.

The jurisprudence of the ECHR in relation to discrimination on grounds of **14.116** marital status shows that a wide margin of appreciation has been acknowledged. But ironically, just as the momentum for the CPA 2004 was growing, Strasbourg jurisprudence, echoed by domestic judgments, has begun to move toward a more reluctant stance towards the margin of appreciation.

The initial position was demonstrated in *Saucedo Gomez v Spain*,[79] where no breach **14.117** of Article 14 with Article 8 ECHR was found to have occurred where a woman who had separated from the man she had cohabited with for many years was deprived of the financial and property benefits she would have attained were she married. The Court noted that the differences in treatment as to the allocation of the family home between spouses and cohabitants pursued a legitimate aim and were based on an objective and reasonable justification, namely the protection of the traditional family. It found that the defendant state had acted within the margin of appreciation in passing laws giving economic advantages to married couples. Moreover, the applicant had herself chosen not to profit from such advantages by remaining unmarried. From December 2005, this last argument could be applied to gays and lesbians as well as heterosexual cohabitees.

The wide margin of appreciation in Strasbourg law was also demonstrated in **14.118** *Smallwood v UK*,[80] where the applicant complained that he was discriminated against as a natural father because parental responsibility can be rescinded under section 4 of the Children Act 1989 only in the case of a natural father. The applicant claimed that, compared with married fathers and unmarried mothers, he had been the victim of a violation of Article 8 ECHR together with Article 14. The Commission found there existed an objective and reasonable justification for the difference in treatment between married and unmarried fathers with regard to the automatic acquisition of parental rights, and said that the relationship between natural fathers and their children varies from ignorance and indifference to a close stable relationship indistinguishable from the conventional family-based unit. No breach was found to have occurred. The Commission relied on and followed *McMichael v UK*.[81] Moreover, in *Re W: Re B (Child Abduction: Unmarried Fathers)*,[82] the Court found that the position of unmarried fathers did not breach Article 14 ECHR. (See also *Frette v France*[83].)

There have been cases, however, where quite apart from domestic legislation **14.119** the ECtHR has acknowledged that same-sex couples do enjoy a family life.

---

[79] Application 37784/97, admissibility decision 26 January 1999.
[80] (1998) EHRR CD 155, at 162.
[81] (1995) 20 EHRR 205.
[82] [1998] 2 FLR 146.
[83] Application 3651/97, decision 26 February 2002.

In *Karner v Austria*,[84] it was argued that a same-sex couple are a family and are entitled to the protection of Article 8 ECHR. Mr Karner claimed a breach of Article 14 ECHR in conjunction with Article 8. He argued that he had been discriminated against on the ground of sexual orientation in that the Supreme Court of Austria had denied him the status of 'life companion' of his deceased partner W, within the meaning of section 14 of the Rent Act, as a consequence of which he was not entitled to take over W's tenancy. The government submitted that the subject matter of the case did not come within the ambit of private and family life (*Rööslei v Germany*[85]). It was also argued that the justification for the differential treatment was the protection of the family in the traditional sense (see also *S v United Kingdom*[86]). The applicant's response to this was that the pertinent provision of the Austrian Rent Act merely aimed at providing social and financial protection from homelessness for a surviving cohabitant, but did not pursue any family or socio-political aims. In the light of this aim, the difference in treatment could not be justified. The Court declared the case admissible. When this case came to a full hearing[87] the Court said that in cases where the margin of appreciation is narrow, such as where the difference in treatment is based on sex or sexual orientation, the principle of proportionality requires that the government must show not only that the measure chosen is suitable for the aim sought, but also that it was necessary to exclude persons in a homosexual relationship from the domestic provisions. The government had not offered convincing and weighty reasons justifying the narrow interpretation of the domestic legislation. The Court therefore found a violation of Article 14 taken together with Article 8.

14.120   Sedley LJ commented on *Karner* in the Court of Appeal judgment of *M & Langley v Secretary of State for Work and Pensions* saying that:[88]

> . . . *Karner* heavily narrows the margin of appreciation [accorded by *Mata Estevez*] by bringing sexual preference within the grounds of discrimination prohibited, absent special justification, by Art 14 in relation to the enjoyment of Art 8 rights.

14.121   However, in *M v Secretary of State for Work and Pensions*,[89] the House of Lords took a more limited view of the extent that Articles 8 and 14 were engaged in a case in which the tax regime discriminated against a lesbian couple, one of whom was required to pay for the support of her child, who lived principally with the father.

---

84   Application 40016/98, found admissible on 11 September 2001.
85   Application 28318/95, Commission Decision 15 May, (1996) 85 DR 149.
86   Application 11716/85, (1986) DR 47, 274.
87   Judgment 24 July 2003, (2004) 38 EHRR 24.
88   [2005] 2 WLR 740, [2004] EWCA 1343, [46].
89   [2006] UKHL 11, [2006] 2 WLR 637.

It was accepted that under the then existing law if the mother's partner had been a male, whether she was married to him or not, a different and lesser payment would have been due. The case is complicated as the result was recognised to be 'anachronistic' but was said to be consistent with historic standards for dealing with gays and lesbians less well than heterosexual couples. The House held that although the statutory scheme drew a distinction based on sexual orientation that was not sufficient in itself to bring M's complaint within the ambit of discrimination under Article 14 or the right to respect for family and private life under Article 8. It held that having to pay higher child support contributions than she would have had to pay if she was living with a heterosexual partner was not an intrusion of M's right to respect for her private life and that her personal and sexual autonomy, which were the essence of private life, had not been invaded, nor had she been criminalised, threatened, or humiliated. Thus her right to respect for her continuing family life with her children had not been interfered with by her increased child support liability since it did not impair the love, trust, confidence, mutual dependence, and unconstrained social intercourse which were the essence of family life. The Lords added that the child support regime did no more than enforce the pre-existing obligation of absent parents to contribute towards the maintenance of their children, so that M's child support contributions could not amount to an interference with her right to protection of property under Article 1 of the First Protocol. Accordingly, the application of the relevant child support regulations did not come within the ambit of Article 14 as read in conjunction with Article 8 or Article 1 of the First Protocol.

14.122 This judgment emphasises the extent to which the recognition of the rights of gays and lesbians under the ECHR is seen domestically as novel and a development in human rights law. It also took a rather more limited view of *Karner*. Thus, Lord Nicholls held that the point had been decided in the earlier case of *Mata Estevez v Spain*[90] that same-sex partners do not fall within the scope of the protection of family life in Article 8. The point is of course different with respect to private life.

14.123 In *Lebbink v The Netherlands*,[91] the ECtHR found that the notion of 'family life' under Article 8 ECHR was not confined to marriage-based relationships and may encompass other de facto 'family' ties where the parties are living together out of wedlock. It appears that this latter case was not cited by the House of Lords in *M*. It is possible that it might have altered its approach.

---

[90] Reports of Judgments and Decisions 2001-VI, p 311.
[91] Application 45582/99, judgment 1 June 2004 (at paras 35 and 36).

14.124 At present, following the ruling of the House of Lords in *M*, the possibility of developing a human rights based jurisprudence to extend the protection against differential treatment of gay and lesbian couples as compared with heterosexual couples is not great.

H. Article 14 and disability rights

14.125 There have been significant advances with challenges relating to disability rights in Great Britain since the HRA 1998 came into force, particularly in the arena of mental health. These developments include a number of declarations of incompatibility. The subject matter of these claims has infrequently touched upon workplace issues to date, the more common facts involving living conditions or hospital treatment. However, if the threshold of suffering is high enough it may be possible to bring Article 3 challenges.

14.126 In *Price v UK* [92] the positive dimension of human rights was demonstrated in a right to life case. Ms Price was a disabled prisoner and a thalidomide victim. She was committed to prison for three days for contempt of court in the course of civil proceedings and endured conditions in prison which Judge Greve said were a violation of her rights to bodily integrity. The judgment emphasised that she had to be treated differently from other people because her situation was significantly different.

14.127 Further, the treatment of disabled people (including when at work) can give rise to Article 8 challenges. In *Botta v Italy*,[93] a physically disabled man was prevented from using a private beach due to lack of ramps and toilets. Relying on Article 8, Mr Botta argued that he was unable to enjoy a normal social life because of the state's failure to discharge its positive obligations and monitor compliance with domestic provisions relating to private beaches. In the process of dismissing the complaint on the facts the Court held that the state did have obligations of this sort where there is a direct and immediate link between the measures sought by the applicant and his or her private or family life, Judge Bratza stated:

> Although the object of Article 8 is essentially that of protecting the individual against arbitrary interference by the public authorities . . . this provision may nonetheless, in certain cases, impose on those States positive obligations inherent in an effective respect for private life even in the sphere of the relations of individuals between themselves . . . Such positive obligations may exceptionally arise in the case of the handicapped in order to ensure that they are not deprived of the possibility of developing social relations with others and thereby developing their own personalities. In this regard, the

---

[92] (2001) 34 EHRR 1285.
[93] (1998) 26 EHRR 241.

Commission observes that there is no water-tight division separating the sphere of social and economic rights from the field covered by the Convention. This is an area in which a wide discretion must inevitably be accorded to the national authorities. Nevertheless, the crucial factor is the extent to which a particular individual is so circumscribed and so isolated as to be deprived of the possibility of developing his personality.

This judgment established that Article 8 imposes positive obligations on the state **14.128** to facilitate access for disabled people to essential economic and social activities, and to a range of recreational and cultural activities as well. The *Botta* decision has begun to influence British courts in adopting a positive approach to Article 8 rights in relation to disabled people particularly with the concept of the right to dignity and the imposition of positive obligations on authorities.

R (A, B, X and Y) v East Sussex CC and the Disability Rights Commission (No 2)[94] **14.129** concerned two grown-up disabled sisters who had always lived in the family home with greatly impaired mobility. A long-running dispute with the local authority over the extent to which lifting and moving should be done manually caused the family great hardship because of the adoption of 'no lifting' policies.

The DRC intervened in the case and argued that the local authority's legitimate **14.130** concern for the safety of its staff had not been balanced against a recognition of the impact that the no-lifting policy had on the quality of disabled people's lives. The Health and Safety at Work etc Act 1974 imposes duties on employers to ensure, insofar as reasonably practical, the safety of employees. The Court ruled against the local authority's blanket ban on lifting and found that human dignity was at the heart of a person's 'physical and psychological integrity' protected by Article 8. It also ruled that:

> The other important concept embraced in the 'physical and psychological integrity' protected by Article 8 is the right of the disabled to participate in the life of the community . . . This is matched by the positive obligation of the State to take appropriate measures designed to ensure to the greatest extent feasible that a disabled person is not 'so circumscribed and so isolated as to be deprived of the possibility of developing his personality'.

It is possible that such issues could arise in workplace disputes and in such a situation **14.131** the Court would have to balance the computing rights along with the obligations of the State to give effect to the Article 8 rights. (See also *Bernard v London Borough of Enfield*[95].) It has been commented that these cases illustrate the:

> seamless coherence in the positive approach to equality realised in the reasonable adjustment provisions of the DDA, in the emerging popularity of the positive public

---

94 [2003] EWHC 167 (Admin).
95 [2002] EWHC 2282, [2003] UKHRR 452.

sector duty as a legislative device, and in the broad conception of human rights increasingly adopted by the Strasbourg and domestic courts when considering the situation of disabled people, and all this within a framework that prioritises the philosophical models of equality as redistribution and especially participation for social groups, not just discrete individuals.[96]

(1) Reasonable accommodation for disabled persons

14.132 Article 5 of the Framework Directive provides that in situations where a person with a disability is subject to indirect discrimination, member states must *either* make provision for a reasonable accommodation to be made for that person in order to ensure that he or she will receive equal treatment (obliging employers to take appropriate measures to enable a person with a disability 'to have access to, participate in, or advance in employment, or to undergo training unless such measures would impose a disproportionate burden on the employer' (Article 5)) *or* permit the treatment in question to be justified.

14.133 The Preamble states[97] that appropriate measures should be provided, for instance, effective and practical measures to adapt the workplace to the disability, for example, adapting premises and equipment, patterns of working time, the distribution of tasks, or the provision of training or integration of resources.

14.134 This obligation to make a reasonable adjustment is not derived from ECtHR jurisprudence but has its roots partly in the work of the International Labour Organisation[98] and partly in the development of such a concept in the US and Canada.

14.135 However, there is one issue which has not yet been fully considered in relation to the protection of the disabled. This is the question whether the Employment Equality Directive offers any protection to those who suffer discrimination because they associate with disabled persons. These are the carers and family members who support the disabled.

14.136 This associative discrimination occurs where a person (whether or not themselves disabled) is discriminated against on the grounds of his/her association with a disabled person. It has not yet been conclusively determined whether the terms of the Framework Directive are wide enough to prohibit associative dis-

---

[96] *Per* Nick O'Brien, Legal Director of the DRC in a speech at the Industrial Law Society Conference September 2004.

[97] At para 20.

[98] See also Arts 5, 6, 7, and 8 of the Declaration of the Rights of Disabled Persons 1975, adopted by the General Assembly of the United Nations, and the International Labour Organisation Convention 159, Vocational Rehabilitation and Employment (Disabled Persons) Convention 1983, see Arts 1(2), and 4.

crimination. A reference to the ECJ to decide this point is currently pending in *Attridge Law v Coleman*.[99]

14.137 If the Directive is held by the ECJ to prohibit associative discrimination in the context of disability, there is no obvious reason why it should not also do so in the context of age. However, domestic law at present does not outlaw associative discrimination in the context of age, at least as regards direct discrimination. The possibility of bringing claims of associative discrimination in the context of disability would have an enormous impact on the workplace and create greater consistency between the various types of discrimination legislation: the race and sexual orientation discrimination legislation already provide for protection from associative discrimination. The words 'on grounds of' have this wider meaning in relation to the RRA 1976 (*Weathersfield Ltd v Sargent*[100]).

(2) Discrimination through inhuman and degrading treatment

14.138 Discrimination which is inhuman and degrading treatment may be prohibited by Article 3 (*East African Asians v UK*[101]). So, the ECHR could be relevant in serious bullying and harassment cases based on sex, race (under the domestic provisions), or even possibly other grounds such as sexuality, disability, religion or belief.

14.139 However, there is no doubt at all that the bullying would have to be extremely severe to fall within Article 3 ECHR, and the victim would have to be an employee in an extremely subordinate or vulnerable position. In *Price v UK*,[102] the Strasbourg Court found that to detain a severely disabled person in conditions where she was dangerously cold and risked developing sores constituted degrading treatment contrary to Article 3. It is possible, but unlikely, that this use of Article 3 would add to the protections that are currently in place or which are due to be introduced.

I. The Equality Act 2006

(1) Introduction

14.140 In 2000, it was calculated that although there were (at the time) four principal Acts dealing with discrimination in Great Britain, to get a comprehensive picture of our discrimination laws you would have to consult 30 Acts, 38 statutory instruments,

---

[99] Case C-303/06.
[100] [1999] IRLR 94, [1999] ICR 425.
[101] (1973) 3 EHRR 76.
[102] Application 33394/96, 11 BHRC 401, [2001] Crim LR 916.

11 Codes of Practice, and 12 EC Directives and Recommendations.[103] This is the result of the law developing as a series of piecemeal reforms to remedy an immediate problem. Consequently, the law is notoriously complex and convoluted, and cannot be said to be easily accessible to the lay person.

14.141   In the last edition of this work, the authors expressed the hope that the government would take the opportunity to pass a single Equality Act and implement common standards across all strands of discrimination. Whilst the Equality Act 2006 has now been passed, and is coming into force incrementally, the Act has not achieved the latter aim. UK discrimination law still has to be considered in 'piecemeal' fashion as the various strands of discrimination are (as will be apparent from the above discussion) contained in various statutes and statutory instruments. However, the Equality Act does take some steps to unify those separate strands and, perhaps most importantly from the perspective of this book, creates a new Commission for Equality and Human Rights (CEHR), which will hopefully encourage some 'joined-up thinking' across these two strongly related areas of law. Meanwhile, the government published a Discrimination Law Review in June 2007 with an aim to producing a single Equality Bill before the end of the current Parliament: see www.communities.gov.uk.

(2) The main provisions of the Equality Act 2006

14.142   The main changes effected by the Equality Act are summarised below, followed by a discussion of the likely impact of the new CEHR on discrimination and human rights law.

14.143   Section 1 of the Act provides for the establishment of the CEHR. This body will bring together the established equality Commissions CRE, EOC, and DRC under a single umbrella, but will also have responsibility for issues relating to age, religion and belief, and sexual orientation, as well as providing support for human rights. It has now been determined that all the commissions will be incorporated into the CEHR in October 2007 (initially, the CRE had negotiated a delay in incorporation until 2009).

14.144   Under section 3 of the Act, the CEHR has a general duty to encourage and support the development of a society in which:

(a) people's ability to achieve their potential is not limited by prejudice and discrimination;

---

[103]   B Hepple, M Coussey, and T Choudhury, *The Cambridge University Report of the Independent Review of the Enforcement of UK Anti-Discrimination Legislation* (Oxford: Hart Publishing, 2000), at 21.

(b) there is respect for and protection of each individual's human rights;

(c) there is respect for the dignity and worth of each individual;

(d) each individual has an equal opportunity to participate in society; and

(e) there is mutual respect between groups based on understanding and valuing of diversity and on shared respect for equality and human rights.

14.145 In order to achieve these aims, specific duties are placed on the CEHR in sections 8 to 12 of the Act. Despite their name, the specific duties are fairly general in nature, requiring promotion of understanding, encouragement of good relations and practice, and elimination of discrimination and prejudice. There are specific duties in respect of equality and diversity (s 8), human rights (s 9), groups (ie relations between groups or classes of persons falling within the remit of the Act: s 10), monitoring the effectiveness of equality and human rights enactments (s 11), and monitoring progress in making the changes to society set out in the general duty (s 12). The specific duties in relation to human rights include promotion of understanding of the importance of human rights, and awareness, understanding and protection of human rights, and encouraging public authorities to comply with their duties under section 6 of the HRA 1998.

14.146 The Act grants the CEHR powers to assist it in complying with the specific duties. These consist of 'general powers' and 'enforcement powers'. The 'general powers' are similar to those already granted to the established Commissions, although some are slightly wider in scope. The CEHR has the power to:

(a) publish or disseminate ideas or information, undertake research, provide education or training, and give advice or guidance in pursuance of its duties under sections 8 to 10 (s 13);

(b) issue Codes of Practice in connection with equal pay, sex discrimination, race discrimination, disability discrimination, religion or belief, sexual orientation, and age (s 14); the Codes will have similar legal effect as the current Codes under the current legislation (s 15);

(c) conduct inquiries into a matter relating to any of the CEHR's duties under sections 8 to 10 of the Act (s 16);

(d) make grants to others (s 17; this power will no longer be limited to situations involving race discrimination as it was prior to the advent of the CEHR).

14.147 Section 19 also gives the CEHR the power to 'co-operate with persons interested in human rights' within the UK or elsewhere in pursuance of its human rights-related duties under section 9. The 'enforcement powers' do differ in a number of respects from the powers previously granted to the separate commissions. The new powers are summarised below, and differences from the old provisions discussed where appropriate.

14.148   The CEHR may investigate whether or not a person has committed an unlawful act if it has a reasonable suspicion that he has done so (s 20). If the investigation confirms that an unlawful act has taken place, the CEHR may issue an 'unlawful act notice', which may require the person to prepare an action plan for the purpose of avoiding repetition or continuation of the unlawful act, or alternatively may recommend action to be taken by the person for that purpose (s 21). Section 20 also allows investigations into whether or not a person has complied with a requirement imposed in such a notice (s 20(1)(b)).

14.149   The advantage of the requirement that a person prepare an action plan is that there is a fixed structure under section 22, under which the Commission can inspect and approve the action plan, or send it back for revision. The plan will normally come into force six weeks after the Commission has approved the plan or not required it to be revised. Further, the CEHR can apply to a county court for an order requiring a person to provide a first draft plan, or a further revised draft plan, or (within five years of the action plan coming into force) requiring the person to act in accordance with the action plan, or take certain specified actions (s 22(6)). This provision has teeth: failure to comply with such an order will be a criminal offence. No such provision existed in relation to the loose predecessor of the unlawful act notice: the non-discrimination notice.

14.150   The CEHR may enter into an agreement with a person under which the person undertakes not to commit an unlawful act of a specified kind, and to take, or refrain from taking other specific action (s 23). In return, the CEHR will undertake not to proceed against the person under sections 20 or 21 in respect of the specified Act. The CEHR may only enter into such an agreement if it thinks that the person has committed an unlawful act.

14.151   Under section 24 of the Act, the CEHR may apply to a county court for an injunction if it thinks a person is likely, if not restrained, to commit an unlawful act. This extends the power granted to the previous Commissions, which could only apply for an injunction where the person had previously had a non-discrimination notice served on him, or had been found to have discriminated by a tribunal or court (see, eg SDA 1975, s 71).

14.152   The CEHR may present a complaint to an employment tribunal or county court if it considers that a person has been involved in unlawful advertising, instructions, or pressure to discriminate (SDA 1975, RRA 1976, or DDA 1995, s 25). The CEHR may also apply for an injunction restraining such behaviour (s 25(5)). Section 27 of the Act allows the CEHR to make arrangements for the provision of conciliation services for disputes relating to all the grounds of discrimination covered by the Act.

The CEHR, like its predecessors, is able to provide legal assistance to individuals **14.153** who are or may become parties to legal proceedings which relate wholly or partly to a provision of the equality enactments, and who allege that they have been subject to behaviour contrary to a provision of the equality enactments (s 28). If the proceedings are initially concerned with one or more provisions of the equality enactments and another cause of action, and the former claim is discontinued, assistance must also be discontinued. This section can be disapplied in relation to cases which also concern ECHR rights (ie cases brought under the HRA 1998), but only where the Lord Chancellor so orders. Thus, it is likely to be difficult for individuals to obtain assistance from the CEHR in relation to human rights cases without an 'equality' element.[104]

In contrast to the situation with regard to the CEHR's predecessors, there is no **14.154** duty on the CEHR to consider every application for assistance it receives. However, the government has stated that, in practice, the CEHR will still have to consider all applications.[105]

The CEHR will have the power to institute or intervene in legal proceedings, **14.155** whether for judicial review or otherwise, if it appears to the Commission that the proceedings are relevant to a matter in connection with which it has a function (s 30). In relation to claims for breach of Convention rights, the CEHR may act only if there is or would be one or more victims of the unlawful act, although it need not be a victim itself.

The Commission will be responsible for enforcing the race, disability, and gender **14.156** equality duties (the latter imposed by Part IV of the Act). Under section 31, it may assess the extent to which a person has complied with one or more of the duties. Under section 32, it may issue a compliance notice requiring a public body to comply with either the general or a specific equality duty. The previous legislation only permitted service of a compliance notice in respect of the specific equality duties. If the CEHR considers that a person has failed to comply with a requirement of the notice, it may apply to the court for an order requiring the person to comply.

In addition to these general changes, the Act also makes some alterations to **14.157** specific strands of discrimination law. First, it amends the definition of 'religion' and 'belief' to include lack of religion or belief. The impact of this change is discussed further in the section on the Employment Equality (Religion and Belief)

---

[104] *Teeth and their Use: Enforcement Action by the Three Equality Commissions,* Public Interest Research Unit, 31 August 2006 and *Equality bodies failing to enforce discrimination law,* EOR No 157, 2–3.
[105] *Guide to the Equality Act 2006,* IDS Emp Law Brief 818, 13–17.

Regulations 2003 above. Secondly, as mentioned above, the Act also introduces a gender equality duty akin to the race equality and disability equality duties already imposed on public authorities carrying out public functions. Whilst the specific details of the duty go beyond the scope of this work, the two limbs of the general duty require public authorities when exercising their public functions to have due regard to the need (a) to eliminate unlawful discrimination and harassment, and (b) to promote equality of opportunity between men and women (SDA 1975, s 76A). The Secretary of State has the power under section 76B to make orders imposing specific duties on public authorities, and the Sex Discrimination Act 1975 (Public Authorities) (Statutory Duties) Order 2006[106] came into force in April 2007, requiring a number of specified public authorities to prepare and publish a gender equality scheme showing how they intend to fulfil their obligations under the general gender equality duty.

(3) The likely impact of the CEHR

14.158 In its report *Teeth and their use – enforcement action by the three equality commissions*, the Public Interest Research Unit expressed concern that the existing equality commissions were failing to use their direct enforcement powers to their full extent. During the 7½ years covered by the study, none of the commissions presented complaints about discriminatory advertisements, or about instructions or pressure to discriminate to tribunals. Further, only one non-discrimination notice was served throughout the whole period, and similarly, only one persistent discrimination injunction was sought. Particular concerns were raised about the CRE, which had instituted only three formal investigations in the first half of the current decade, as compared with 25 over the same period in the 1980s.

14.159 The report expressed concerns (already referred to above) about the possible dilution of certain indirect enforcement powers available to the CEHR (eg the absence of any requirement that the CEHR consider all applications for assistance, and the importance given to the Lord Chancellor in determining when assistance will be given in HRA 1998 cases). However, the direct enforcement powers given to the CEHR appear to have more 'teeth' than the equivalent powers available to its predecessors. The report suggests changes in the way the new CEHR will operate in order to ensure that maximum use is made of the powers available. Most radically, it suggests that the CEHR should test the assumptions on which the existing omissions appeared to have justified their approach (ie that strong enforcement action is counter-productive or otherwise damaging) and question whether alternative methods of promoting good practice might be

---

[106] SI 2006/2930.

more effective. It also suggests that Parliament should take a robust role in scrutinising the CEHR, and that there should be annual 'value for money' audits by the National Audit Office.

Certainly, the CEHR has an opportunity, using the significant powers which will **14.160** be available to it, to take more radical enforcement action in cases of discrimination if that appears to be the appropriate way forward. However, many of the bulked-up powers (eg investigations, unlawful act notices, action plans, powers in relation to unlawful advertising, etc) do not apply where the complaint is one of contravention of an ECHR right; the definition of 'unlawful act' which in turn defines the application of the relevant sections refers only to acts which are contrary to the provisions of the equality enactments (s 34(1)). In view of the corresponding dilution of the power to provide legal assistance in HRA 1998 cases, the institutional support for human rights provided under the Equality Act is comparatively weak. Whilst the provision of *any* such support is a new and welcome step in raising awareness of ECHR rights, it appears likely that stronger measures will be necessary if the CEHR is to play a major role in supporting individual claimants, or in preventing breaches of the HRA 1998.

J. Frequently asked questions

How does Article 14 affect the tribunal's consideration of unfair dismissal claims?

14.161

Where a tribunal considers an employer's action in dismissing an employee to have been in breach of Article 14, it must interpret section 98(4) of the ERA 1996 compatibly with the ECHR. Thus, the tribunal will need to consider the issues as set out in X v Y *and* Copsey v WWB Devon Clays *(discussed at 14.05 above and in Chapters 8 and 9), or, in the case of a public authority,* Pay v Lancashire Probation Service. *However, where apparently discriminatory conduct does not fall within the scope of another Convention article (eg on the facts in* X v Y, *the sexual activity in question occurred in a place to which the public had access, so did not engage Article 8), Article 14 will not assist the employee.*

Can Article 14 assist employees in cases covered by domestic/Community sex and race legislation?

Whilst the role of Article 14 is limited in such circumstances in view of the comprehensive legislation in these areas, it should not be discounted altogether. For example, it may be of assistance in cases where there is alleged to have been a combination of discriminatory grounds (eg sex and race) for the treatment in question, or in race discrimination cases where employees have claimed only discrimination on grounds of colour or nationality and therefore cannot rely on the new burden of proof or the harassment provisions.

Does any other provision of the ECHR have any relevance to discrimination cases?

Sometimes it is possible to argue that there has been a breach of Article 3 of the ECHR where there has been really serious harassment amounting to inhuman treatment.

What impact will the Commission for Equality and Human Rights have in relation to discrimination?

The Commission will have a broad remit which will cover the work of the existing Commissions but go a good deal further. It has a wide range of duties including to promote understanding between communities and also to protect dignity as well as to stop discrimination. Of course, it is also important that the CEHR will have a human rights function as well.

What is happening to reduce the complexity of the law?

There is currently a review of discrimination law with a view to producing a single Equality Bill in this Parliament. The work of the Discrimination Law Review will complement that of the CEHR and should, if the Bill becomes law, make it easier to deal with discrimination issues.

Appendices

Human Rights Act 1998

CHAPTER 42

An Act to give further effect to rights and freedoms guaranteed under the European Convention on Human Rights; to make provision with respect to holders of certain judicial offices who become judges of the European Court of Human Rights; and for connected purposes.

[9th November 1998]

BE IT ENACTED by the Queen's most Excellent Majesty, by and with the advice and consent of the Lords Spiritual and Temporal, and Commons, in this present Parliament assembled, and by the authority of the same, as follows:—

Introduction

1 The Convention rights

(1) In this Act "the Convention rights" means the rights and fundamental freedoms set out in—
- (a) Articles 2 to 12 and 14 of the Convention,
- (b) Articles 1 to 3 of the First Protocol, and
- (c) [Article 1 of the Thirteenth Protocol],

as read with Articles 16 to 18 of the Convention.

(2) Those Articles are to have effect for the purposes of this Act subject to any designated derogation or reservation (as to which see sections 14 and 15).

(3) The Articles are set out in Schedule 1.

(4) The [Secretary of State] may by order make such amendments to this Act as he considers appropriate to reflect the effect, in relation to the United Kingdom, of a protocol.

(5) In subsection (4) "protocol" means a protocol to the Convention—
- (a) which the United Kingdom has ratified; or
- (b) which the United Kingdom has signed with a view to ratification.

(6) No amendment may be made by an order under subsection (4) so as to come into force before the protocol concerned is in force in relation to the United Kingdom.

2 Interpretation of Convention rights

(1) A court or tribunal determining a question which has arisen in connection with a Convention right must take into account any—
- (a) judgment, decision, declaration or advisory opinion of the European Court of Human Rights,
- (b) opinion of the Commission given in a report adopted under Article 31 of the Convention,
- (c) decision of the Commission in connection with Article 26 or 27(2) of the Convention, or

(d) decision of the Committee of Ministers taken under Article 46 of the Convention, whenever made or given, so far as, in the opinion of the court or tribunal, it is relevant to the proceedings in which that question has arisen.

(2) Evidence of any judgment, decision, declaration or opinion of which account may have to be taken under this section is to be given in proceedings before any court or tribunal in such manner as may be provided by rules.

(3) In this section "rules" means rules of court or, in the case of proceedings before a tribunal, rules made for the purposes of this section—

    (a) by . . . [the Lord Chancellor or] the Secretary of State, in relation to any proceedings outside Scotland;

    (b) by the Secretary of State, in relation to proceedings in Scotland; or

    (c) by a Northern Ireland department, in relation to proceedings before a tribunal in Northern Ireland—

       (i) which deals with transferred matters; and

       (ii) for which no rules made under paragraph (a) are in force.

Legislation

3 Interpretation of legislation

(1) So far as it is possible to do so, primary legislation and subordinate legislation must be read and given effect in a way which is compatible with the Convention rights.

(2) This section—

    (a) applies to primary legislation and subordinate legislation whenever enacted;

    (b) does not affect the validity, continuing operation or enforcement of any incompatible primary legislation; and

    (c) does not affect the validity, continuing operation or enforcement of any incompatible subordinate legislation if (disregarding any possibility of revocation) primary legislation prevents removal of the incompatibility.

4 Declaration of incompatibility

(1) Subsection (2) applies in any proceedings in which a court determines whether a provision of primary legislation is compatible with a Convention right.

(2) If the court is satisfied that the provision is incompatible with a Convention right, it may make a declaration of that incompatibility.

(3) Subsection (4) applies in any proceedings in which a court determines whether a provision of subordinate legislation, made in the exercise of a power conferred by primary legislation, is compatible with a Convention right.

(4) If the court is satisfied—

    (a) that the provision is incompatible with a Convention right, and

    (b) that (disregarding any possibility of revocation) the primary legislation concerned prevents removal of the incompatibility,

it may make a declaration of that incompatibility.

(5) In this section "court" means—

    (a) the House of Lords;

    (b) the Judicial Committee of the Privy Council;

    (c) the Courts-Martial Appeal Court;

    (d) in Scotland, the High Court of Justiciary sitting otherwise than as a trial court or the Court of Session;

    (e) in England and Wales or Northern Ireland, the High Court or the Court of Appeal;

[(f) the Court of Protection, in any matter being dealt with by the President of the Family Division, the Vice-Chancellor or a puisne judge of the High Court].

(6) A declaration under this section ("a declaration of incompatibility")—

    (a) does not affect the validity, continuing operation or enforcement of the provision in respect of which it is given; and

    (b) is not binding on the parties to the proceedings in which it is made.

5 Right of Crown to intervene

(1) Where a court is considering whether to make a declaration of incompatibility, the Crown is entitled to notice in accordance with rules of court.

(2) In any case to which subsection (1) applies—

    (a) a Minister of the Crown (or a person nominated by him),

    (b) a member of the Scottish Executive,

    (c) a Northern Ireland Minister,

    (d) a Northern Ireland department,

is entitled, on giving notice in accordance with rules of court, to be joined as a party to the proceedings.

(3) Notice under subsection (2) may be given at any time during the proceedings.

(4) A person who has been made a party to criminal proceedings (other than in Scotland) as the result of a notice under subsection (2) may, with leave, appeal to the *House of Lords* [Supreme Court] against any declaration of incompatibility made in the proceedings.

(5) In subsection (4)—

"criminal proceedings" includes all proceedings before the Courts-Martial Appeal Court; and

"leave" means leave granted by the court making the declaration of incompatibility or by the House of Lords.

Public authorities

6 Acts of public authorities

(1) It is unlawful for a public authority to act in a way which is incompatible with a Convention right.

(2) Subsection (1) does not apply to an act if—

    (a) as the result of one or more provisions of primary legislation, the authority could not have acted differently; or

    (b) in the case of one or more provisions of, or made under, primary legislation which cannot be read or given effect in a way which is compatible with the Convention rights, the authority was acting so as to give effect to or enforce those provisions.

(3) In this section "public authority" includes—

    (a) a court or tribunal, and

    (b) any person certain of whose functions are functions of a public nature, but does not include either House of Parliament or a person exercising functions in connection with proceedings in Parliament.

(4) In subsection (3) "Parliament" does not include the House of Lords in its judicial capacity.

(5) In relation to a particular act, a person is not a public authority by virtue only of subsection (3)(b) if the nature of the act is private.

(6) "An act" includes a failure to act but does not include a failure to—

    (a) introduce in, or lay before, Parliament a proposal for legislation; or

    (b) make any primary legislation or remedial order.

7 Proceedings

(1) A person who claims that a public authority has acted (or proposes to act) in a way which is made unlawful by section 6(1) may—

    (a) bring proceedings against the authority under this Act in the appropriate court or tribunal, or

    (b) rely on the Convention right or rights concerned in any legal proceedings, but only if he is (or would be) a victim of the unlawful act.

(2) In subsection (1)(a) "appropriate court or tribunal" means such court or tribunal as may be determined in accordance with rules; and proceedings against an authority include a counterclaim or similar proceeding.

(3) If the proceedings are brought on an application for judicial review, the applicant is to be taken to have a sufficient interest in relation to the unlawful act only if he is, or would be, a victim of that act.

(4) If the proceedings are made by way of a petition for judicial review in Scotland, the applicant shall be taken to have title and interest to sue in relation to the unlawful act only if he is, or would be, a victim of that act.

(5) Proceedings under subsection (1)(a) must be brought before the end of—

    (a) the period of one year beginning with the date on which the act complained of took place; or

    (b) such longer period as the court or tribunal considers equitable having regard to all the circumstances,

but that is subject to any rule imposing a stricter time limit in relation to the procedure in question.

(6) In subsection (1)(b) "legal proceedings" includes—

    (a) proceedings brought by or at the instigation of a public authority; and

    (b) an appeal against the decision of a court or tribunal.

(7) For the purposes of this section, a person is a victim of an unlawful act only if he would be a victim for the purposes of Article 34 of the Convention if proceedings were brought in the European Court of Human Rights in respect of that act.

(8) Nothing in this Act creates a criminal offence.

(9) In this section "rules" means—

    (a) in relation to proceedings before a court or tribunal outside Scotland, rules made by . . . [the Lord Chancellor or] the Secretary of State for the purposes of this section or rules of court,

    (b) in relation to proceedings before a court or tribunal in Scotland, rules made by the Secretary of State for those purposes,

    (c) in relation to proceedings before a tribunal in Northern Ireland—

        (i) which deals with transferred matters; and

        (ii) for which no rules made under paragraph (a) are in force, rules made by a Northern Ireland department for those purposes, and includes provision made by order under section 1 of the Courts and Legal Services Act 1990.

(10) In making rules, regard must be had to section 9.

(11) The Minister who has power to make rules in relation to a particular tribunal may, to the extent he considers it necessary to ensure that the tribunal can provide an appropriate remedy in relation to an act (or proposed act) of a public authority which is (or would be) unlawful as a result of section 6(1), by order add to—

    (a) the relief or remedies which the tribunal may grant; or

    (b) the grounds on which it may grant any of them.

(12) An order made under subsection (11) may contain such incidental, supplemental, consequential or transitional provision as the Minister making it considers appropriate.

(13) "The Minister" includes the Northern Ireland department concerned.

8 Judicial remedies

(1) In relation to any act (or proposed act) of a public authority which the court finds is (or would be) unlawful, it may grant such relief or remedy, or make such order, within its powers as it considers just and appropriate.

(2) But damages may be awarded only by a court which has power to award damages, or to order the payment of compensation, in civil proceedings.

(3) No award of damages is to be made unless, taking account of all the circumstances of the case, including—

    (a) any other relief or remedy granted, or order made, in relation to the act in question (by that or any other court), and

    (b) the consequences of any decision (of that or any other court) in respect of that act, the court is satisfied that the award is necessary to afford just satisfaction to the person in whose favour it is made.

(4) In determining—

    (a) whether to award damages, or

    (b) the amount of an award,

the court must take into account the principles applied by the European Court of Human Rights in relation to the award of compensation under Article 41 of the Convention.

(5) A public authority against which damages are awarded is to be treated—

    (a) in Scotland, for the purposes of section 3 of the Law Reform (Miscellaneous Provisions) (Scotland) Act 1940 as if the award were made in an action of damages in which the authority has been found liable in respect of loss or damage to the person to whom the award is made;

    (b) for the purposes of the Civil Liability (Contribution) Act 1978 as liable in respect of damage suffered by the person to whom the award is made.

(6) In this section—

"court" includes a tribunal;

"damages" means damages for an unlawful act of a public authority; and

"unlawful" means unlawful under section 6(1).

9 Judicial acts

(1) Proceedings under section 7(1)(a) in respect of a judicial act may be brought only—

    (a) by exercising a right of appeal;

    (b) on an application (in Scotland a petition) for judicial review; or

    (c) in such other forum as may be prescribed by rules.

(2) That does not affect any rule of law which prevents a court from being the subject of judicial review.

(3) In proceedings under this Act in respect of a judicial act done in good faith, damages may not be awarded otherwise than to compensate a person to the extent required by Article 5(5) of the Convention.

(4) An award of damages permitted by subsection (3) is to be made against the Crown; but no award may be made unless the appropriate person, if not a party to the proceedings, is joined.

(5) In this section—

"appropriate person" means the Minister responsible for the court concerned, or a person or government department nominated by him;

"court" includes a tribunal;

"judge" includes a member of a tribunal, a justice of the peace [(or, in Northern Ireland, a lay magistrate)] and a clerk or other officer entitled to exercise the jurisdiction of a court;

"judicial act" means a judicial act of a court and includes an act done on the instructions, or on behalf, of a judge; and

"rules" has the same meaning as in section 7(9).

Remedial action

10 Power to take remedial action

(1) This section applies if—

  (a) a provision of legislation has been declared under section 4 to be incompatible with a Convention right and, if an appeal lies—

    (i) all persons who may appeal have stated in writing that they do not intend to do so;

    (ii) the time for bringing an appeal has expired and no appeal has been brought within that time; or

    (iii) an appeal brought within that time has been determined or abandoned; or

  (b) it appears to a Minister of the Crown or Her Majesty in Council that, having regard to a finding of the European Court of Human Rights made after the coming into force of this section in proceedings against the United Kingdom, a provision of legislation is incompatible with an obligation of the United Kingdom arising from the Convention.

(2) If a Minister of the Crown considers that there are compelling reasons for proceeding under this section, he may by order make such amendments to the legislation as he considers necessary to remove the incompatibility.

(3) If, in the case of subordinate legislation, a Minister of the Crown considers—

  (a) that it is necessary to amend the primary legislation under which the subordinate legislation in question was made, in order to enable the incompatibility to be removed, and

  (b) that there are compelling reasons for proceeding under this section, he may by order make such amendments to the primary legislation as he considers necessary.

(4) This section also applies where the provision in question is in subordinate legislation and has been quashed, or declared invalid, by reason of incompatibility with a Convention right and the Minister proposes to proceed under paragraph 2(b) of Schedule 2.

(5) If the legislation is an Order in Council, the power conferred by subsection (2) or (3) is exercisable by Her Majesty in Council.

(6) In this section "legislation" does not include a Measure of the Church Assembly or of the General Synod of the Church of England.

(7) Schedule 2 makes further provision about remedial orders.

Other rights and proceedings

11 Safeguard for existing human rights

A person's reliance on a Convention right does not restrict—

(a) any other right or freedom conferred on him by or under any law having effect in any part of the United Kingdom; or

(b) his right to make any claim or bring any proceedings which he could make or bring apart from sections 7 to 9.

12 Freedom of expression

(1) This section applies if a court is considering whether to grant any relief which, if granted, might affect the exercise of the Convention right to freedom of expression.

(2) If the person against whom the application for relief is made ("the respondent") is neither present nor represented, no such relief is to be granted unless the court is satisfied—

(a) that the applicant has taken all practicable steps to notify the respondent; or

(b) that there are compelling reasons why the respondent should not be notified.

(3) No such relief is to be granted so as to restrain publication before trial unless the court is satisfied that the applicant is likely to establish that publication should not be allowed.

(4) The court must have particular regard to the importance of the Convention right to freedom of expression and, where the proceedings relate to material which the respondent claims, or which appears to the court, to be journalistic, literary or artistic material (or to conduct connected with such material), to—

(a) the extent to which—

(i) the material has, or is about to, become available to the public; or

(ii) it is, or would be, in the public interest for the material to be published;

(b) any relevant privacy code.

(5) In this section—

"court" includes a tribunal; and

"relief" includes any remedy or order (other than in criminal proceedings).

13 Freedom of thought, conscience and religion

(1) If a court's determination of any question arising under this Act might affect the exercise by a religious organisation (itself or its members collectively) of the Convention right to freedom of thought, conscience and religion, it must have particular regard to the importance of that right.

(2) In this section "court" includes a tribunal.

Derogations and reservations

14 Derogations

(1) In this Act "designated derogation" means—

. . .

any derogation by the United Kingdom from an Article of the Convention, or of any protocol to the Convention, which is designated for the purposes of this Act in an order made by the [Secretary of State].

(2) . . .

(3) If a designated derogation is amended or replaced it ceases to be a designated derogation.

(4) But subsection (3) does not prevent the [Secretary of State] from exercising his power under subsection (1) . . . to make a fresh designation order in respect of the Article concerned.

(5) The [Secretary of State] must by order make such amendments to Schedule 3 as he considers appropriate to reflect—

(a) any designation order; or

(b) the effect of subsection (3).

(6) A designation order may be made in anticipation of the making by the United Kingdom of a proposed derogation.

15 Reservations

(1) In this Act "designated reservation" means—
  (a) the United Kingdom's reservation to Article 2 of the First Protocol to the Convention; and
  (b) any other reservation by the United Kingdom to an Article of the Convention, or of any protocol to the Convention, which is designated for the purposes of this Act in an order made by the [Secretary of State].

(2) The text of the reservation referred to in subsection (1)(a) is set out in Part II of Schedule 3.

(3) If a designated reservation is withdrawn wholly or in part it ceases to be a designated reservation.

(4) But subsection (3) does not prevent the [Secretary of State] from exercising his power under subsection (1)(b) to make a fresh designation order in respect of the Article concerned.

(5) The [Secretary of State] must by order make such amendments to this Act as he considers appropriate to reflect—
  (a) any designation order; or
  (b) the effect of subsection (3).

16 Period for which designated derogations have effect

(1) If it has not already been withdrawn by the United Kingdom, a designated derogation ceases to have effect for the purposes of this Act—

  ...

  at the end of the period of five years beginning with the date on which the order designating it was made.

(2) At any time before the period—
  (a) fixed by subsection (1) . . . , or
  (b) extended by an order under this subsection,
  comes to an end, the [Secretary of State] may by order extend it by a further period of five years.

(3) An order under section 14(1). . . ceases to have effect at the end of the period for consideration, unless a resolution has been passed by each House approving the order.

(4) Subsection (3) does not affect—
  (a) anything done in reliance on the order; or
  (b) the power to make a fresh order under section 14(1). . . .

(5) In subsection (3) "period for consideration" means the period of forty days beginning with the day on which the order was made.

(6) In calculating the period for consideration, no account is to be taken of any time during which—
  (a) Parliament is dissolved or prorogued; or
  (b) both Houses are adjourned for more than four days.

(7) If a designated derogation is withdrawn by the United Kingdom, the [Secretary of State] must by order make such amendments to this Act as he considers are required to reflect that withdrawal.

17 Periodic review of designated reservations

(1) The appropriate Minister must review the designated reservation referred to in section 15(1)(a)—

(a) before the end of the period of five years beginning with the date on which section 1(2) came into force; and

(b) if that designation is still in force, before the end of the period of five years beginning with the date on which the last report relating to it was laid under subsection (3).

(2) The appropriate Minister must review each of the other designated reservations (if any)—

(a) before the end of the period of five years beginning with the date on which the order designating the reservation first came into force; and

(b) if the designation is still in force, before the end of the period of five years beginning with the date on which the last report relating to it was laid under subsection (3).

(3) The Minister conducting a review under this section must prepare a report on the result of the review and lay a copy of it before each House of Parliament.

Judges of the European Court of Human Rights

18 Appointment to European Court of Human Rights

(1) In this section "judicial office" means the office of—

(a) Lord Justice of Appeal, Justice of the High Court or Circuit judge, in England and Wales;

(b) judge of the Court of Session or sheriff, in Scotland;

(c) Lord Justice of Appeal, judge of the High Court or county court judge, in Northern Ireland.

(2) The holder of a judicial office may become a judge of the European Court of Human Rights ("the Court") without being required to relinquish his office.

(3) But he is not required to perform the duties of his judicial office while he is a judge of the Court.

(4) In respect of any period during which he is a judge of the Court—

(a) a Lord Justice of Appeal or Justice of the High Court is not to count as a judge of the relevant court for the purposes of section 2(1) or 4(1) of the Supreme Court Act 1981 (maximum number of judges) nor as a judge of the Supreme Court for the purposes of section 12(1) to (6) of that Act (salaries etc);

(b) a judge of the Court of Session is not to count as a judge of that court for the purposes of section 1(1) of the Court of Session Act 1988 (maximum number of judges) or of section 9(1)(c) of the Administration of Justice Act 1973 ("the 1973 Act") (salaries etc);

(c) a Lord Justice of Appeal or judge of the High Court in Northern Ireland is not to count as a judge of the relevant court for the purposes of section 2(1) or 3(1) of the Judicature (Northern Ireland) Act 1978 (maximum number of judges) nor as a judge of the Supreme Court of Northern Ireland for the purposes of section 9(1)(d) of the 1973 Act (salaries etc);

(d) a Circuit judge is not to count as such for the purposes of section 18 of the Courts Act 1971 (salaries etc);

(e) a sheriff is not to count as such for the purposes of section 14 of the Sheriff Courts (Scotland) Act 1907 (salaries etc);

(f) a county court judge of Northern Ireland is not to count as such for the purposes of section 106 of the County Courts Act (Northern Ireland) 1959 (salaries etc).

(5) If a sheriff principal is appointed a judge of the Court, section 11(1) of the Sheriff Courts (Scotland) Act 1971 (temporary appointment of sheriff principal) applies, while he holds that appointment, as if his office is vacant.

(6) Schedule 4 makes provision about judicial pensions in relation to the holder of a judicial office who serves as a judge of the Court.

(7) The Lord Chancellor or the Secretary of State may by order make such transitional provision (including, in particular, provision for a temporary increase in the maximum number of judges) as he considers appropriate in relation to any holder of a judicial office who has completed his service as a judge of the Court.

[(7A) The following paragraphs apply to the making of an order under subsection (7) in relation to any holder of a judicial office listed in subsection (1)(a)—

    (a) before deciding what transitional provision it is appropriate to make, the person making the order must consult the Lord Chief Justice of England and Wales;

    (b) before making the order, that person must consult the Lord Chief Justice of England and Wales.

(7B) The following paragraphs apply to the making of an order under subsection (7) in relation to any holder of a judicial office listed in subsection (1)(c)—

    (a) before deciding what transitional provision it is appropriate to make, the person making the order must consult the Lord Chief Justice of Northern Ireland;

    (b) before making the order, that person must consult the Lord Chief Justice of Northern Ireland.

(7C) The Lord Chief Justice of England and Wales may nominate a judicial office holder (within the meaning of section 109(4) of the Constitutional Reform Act 2005) to exercise his functions under this section.

(7D) The Lord Chief Justice of Northern Ireland may nominate any of the following to exercise his functions under this section—

    (a) the holder of one of the offices listed in Schedule 1 to the Justice (Northern Ireland) Act 2002;

    (b) a Lord Justice of Appeal (as defined in section 88 of that Act).]

Parliamentary procedure

19 Statements of compatibility

(1) A Minister of the Crown in charge of a Bill in either House of Parliament must, before Second Reading of the Bill—

    (a) make a statement to the effect that in his view the provisions of the Bill are compatible with the Convention rights ("a statement of compatibility"); or

    (b) make a statement to the effect that although he is unable to make a statement of compatibility the government nevertheless wishes the House to proceed with the Bill.

(2) The statement must be in writing and be published in such manner as the Minister making it considers appropriate.

Supplemental

20 Orders etc under this Act

(1) Any power of a Minister of the Crown to make an order under this Act is exercisable by statutory instrument.

(2) The power of . . . [the Lord Chancellor or] the Secretary of State to make rules (other than rules of court) under section 2(3) or 7(9) is exercisable by statutory instrument.

(3) Any statutory instrument made under section 14, 15 or 16(7) must be laid before Parliament.

(4) No order may be made by . . . [the Lord Chancellor or] the Secretary of State under section 1(4), 7(11) or 16(2) unless a draft of the order has been laid before, and approved by, each House of Parliament.

(5) Any statutory instrument made under section 18(7) or Schedule 4, or to which subsection (2) applies, shall be subject to annulment in pursuance of a resolution of either House of Parliament.

(6) The power of a Northern Ireland department to make—

(a) rules under section 2(3)(c) or 7(9)(c), or

(b) an order under section 7(11),

is exercisable by statutory rule for the purposes of the Statutory Rules (Northern Ireland) Order 1979.

(7) Any rules made under section 2(3)(c) or 7(9)(c) shall be subject to negative resolution; and section 41(6) of the Interpretation Act (Northern Ireland) 1954 (meaning of "subject to negative resolution") shall apply as if the power to make the rules were conferred by an Act of the Northern Ireland Assembly.

(8) No order may be made by a Northern Ireland department under section 7(11) unless a draft of the order has been laid before, and approved by, the Northern Ireland Assembly.

21 Interpretation, etc

(1) In this Act—

"amend" includes repeal and apply (with or without modifications);

"the appropriate Minister" means the Minister of the Crown having charge of the appropriate authorised government department (within the meaning of the Crown Proceedings Act 1947);

"the Commission" means the European Commission of Human Rights;

"the Convention" means the Convention for the Protection of Human Rights and Fundamental Freedoms, agreed by the Council of Europe at Rome on 4th November 1950 as it has effect for the time being in relation to the United Kingdom;

"declaration of incompatibility" means a declaration under section 4;

"Minister of the Crown" has the same meaning as in the Ministers of the Crown Act 1975;

"Northern Ireland Minister" includes the First Minister and the deputy First Minister in Northern Ireland;

"primary legislation" means any—

(a) public general Act;

(b) local and personal Act;

(c) private Act;

(d) Measure of the Church Assembly;

(e) Measure of the General Synod of the Church of England;

(f) Order in Council—

(i) made in exercise of Her Majesty's Royal Prerogative;

(ii) made under section 38(1)(a) of the Northern Ireland Constitution Act 1973 or the corresponding provision of the Northern Ireland Act 1998; or

(iii) amending an Act of a kind mentioned in paragraph (a), (b) or (c);

and includes an order or other instrument made under primary legislation (otherwise than by the *National Assembly for Wales* [Welsh Ministers, the First Minister for Wales, the Counsel General to the Welsh Assembly Government], a member of the Scottish Executive, a Northern Ireland Minister or a Northern Ireland department) to the extent to which it operates to bring one or more provisions of that legislation into force or amends any primary legislation;

"the First Protocol" means the protocol to the Convention agreed at Paris on 20th March 1952;

. . .

"the Eleventh Protocol" means the protocol to the Convention (restructuring the control machinery established by the Convention) agreed at Strasbourg on 11th May 1994;

["the Thirteenth Protocol" means the protocol to the Convention (concerning the abolition of the death penalty in all circumstances) agreed at Vilnius on 3rd May 2002;]

"remedial order" means an order under section 10;

"subordinate legislation" means any—

    (a) Order in Council other than one—

        (i) made in exercise of Her Majesty's Royal Prerogative;

        (ii) made under section 38(1)(a) of the Northern Ireland Constitution Act 1973 or the corresponding provision of the Northern Ireland Act 1998; or

        (iii) amending an Act of a kind mentioned in the definition of primary legislation;

    (b) Act of the Scottish Parliament;

    [(ba) Measure of the National Assembly for Wales;

    (bb) Act of the National Assembly for Wales;]

    (c) Act of the Parliament of Northern Ireland;

    (d) Measure of the Assembly established under section 1 of the Northern Ireland Assembly Act 1973;

    (e) Act of the Northern Ireland Assembly;

    (f) order, rules, regulations, scheme, warrant, byelaw or other instrument made under primary legislation (except to the extent to which it operates to bring one or more provisions of that legislation into force or amends any primary legislation);

    (g) order, rules, regulations, scheme, warrant, byelaw or other instrument made under legislation mentioned in paragraph (b), (c), (d) or (e) or made under an Order in Council applying only to Northern Ireland;

    (h) order, rules, regulations, scheme, warrant, byelaw or other instrument made by a member of the Scottish Executive [Welsh Ministers, the First Minister for Wales, the Counsel General to the Welsh Assembly Government], a Northern Ireland Minister or a Northern Ireland department in exercise of prerogative or other executive functions of Her Majesty which are exercisable by such a person on behalf of Her Majesty;

"transferred matters" has the same meaning as in the Northern Ireland Act 1998; and

"tribunal" means any tribunal in which legal proceedings may be brought.

(2) The references in paragraphs (b) and (c) of section 2(1) to Articles are to Articles of the Convention as they had effect immediately before the coming into force of the Eleventh Protocol.

(3) The reference in paragraph (d) of section 2(1) to Article 46 includes a reference to Articles 32 and 54 of the Convention as they had effect immediately before the coming into force of the Eleventh Protocol.

(4) The references in section 2(1) to a report or decision of the Commission or a decision of the Committee of Ministers include references to a report or decision made as provided by paragraphs 3, 4 and 6 of Article 5 of the Eleventh Protocol (transitional provisions).

(5) Any liability under the Army Act 1955, the Air Force Act 1955 or the Naval Discipline Act 1957 to suffer death for an offence is replaced by a liability to imprisonment for life or any less punishment authorised by those Acts; and those Acts shall accordingly have effect with the necessary modifications.

22 Short title, commencement, application and extent

(1) This Act may be cited as the Human Rights Act 1998.

(2) Sections 18, 20 and 21(5) and this section come into force on the passing of this Act.

(3) The other provisions of this Act come into force on such day as the Secretary of State may by order appoint; and different days may be appointed for different purposes.

(4) Paragraph (b) of subsection (1) of section 7 applies to proceedings brought by or at the instigation of a public authority whenever the act in question took place; but otherwise that subsection does not apply to an act taking place before the coming into force of that section.

(5) This Act binds the Crown.

(6) This Act extends to Northern Ireland.

(7) Section 21(5), so far as it relates to any provision contained in the Army Act 1955, the Air Force Act 1955 or the Naval Discipline Act 1957, extends to any place to which that provision extends.

SCHEDULE I
THE ARTICLES

SECTION 1(3)

PART I
THE CONVENTION RIGHTS AND FREEDOMS

Article 2
Right to life

1 Everyone's right to life shall be protected by law. No one shall be deprived of his life intentionally save in the execution of a sentence of a court following his conviction of a crime for which this penalty is provided by law.

2 Deprivation of life shall not be regarded as inflicted in contravention of this Article when it results from the use of force which is no more than absolutely necessary:

(a) in defence of any person from unlawful violence;

(b) in order to effect a lawful arrest or to prevent the escape of a person lawfully detained;

(c) in action lawfully taken for the purpose of quelling a riot or insurrection.

Article 3
Prohibition of torture

No one shall be subjected to torture or to inhuman or degrading treatment or punishment.

Article 4
Prohibition of slavery and forced labour

1 No one shall be held in slavery or servitude.

2 No one shall be required to perform forced or compulsory labour.

3 For the purpose of this Article the term "forced or compulsory labour" shall not include:

(a) any work required to be done in the ordinary course of detention imposed according to the provisions of Article 5 of this Convention or during conditional release from such detention;

(b) any service of a military character or, in case of conscientious objectors in countries where they are recognised, service exacted instead of compulsory military service;

(c) any service exacted in case of an emergency or calamity threatening the life or well-being of the community;

(d) any work or service which forms part of normal civic obligations.

Article 5
Right to liberty and security

1 Everyone has the right to liberty and security of person. No one shall be deprived of his liberty save in the following cases and in accordance with a procedure prescribed by law:
  (a) the lawful detention of a person after conviction by a competent court;
  (b) the lawful arrest or detention of a person for non-compliance with the lawful order of a court or in order to secure the fulfilment of any obligation prescribed by law;
  (c) the lawful arrest or detention of a person effected for the purpose of bringing him before the competent legal authority on reasonable suspicion of having committed an offence or when it is reasonably considered necessary to prevent his committing an offence or fleeing after having done so;
  (d) the detention of a minor by lawful order for the purpose of educational supervision or his lawful detention for the purpose of bringing him before the competent legal authority;
  (e) the lawful detention of persons for the prevention of the spreading of infectious diseases, of persons of unsound mind, alcoholics or drug addicts or vagrants;
  (f) the lawful arrest or detention of a person to prevent his effecting an unauthorised entry into the country or of a person against whom action is being taken with a view to deportation or extradition.
2 Everyone who is arrested shall be informed promptly, in a language which he understands, of the reasons for his arrest and of any charge against him.
3 Everyone arrested or detained in accordance with the provisions of paragraph 1(c) of this Article shall be brought promptly before a judge or other officer authorised by law to exercise judicial power and shall be entitled to trial within a reasonable time or to release pending trial. Release may be conditioned by guarantees to appear for trial.
4 Everyone who is deprived of his liberty by arrest or detention shall be entitled to take proceedings by which the lawfulness of his detention shall be decided speedily by a court and his release ordered if the detention is not lawful.
5 Everyone who has been the victim of arrest or detention in contravention of the provisions of this Article shall have an enforceable right to compensation.

Article 6
Right to a fair trial

1 In the determination of his civil rights and obligations or of any criminal charge against him, everyone is entitled to a fair and public hearing within a reasonable time by an independent and impartial tribunal established by law. Judgment shall be pronounced publicly but the press and public may be excluded from all or part of the trial in the interest of morals, public order or national security in a democratic society, where the interests of juveniles or the protection of the private life of the parties so require, or to the extent strictly necessary in the opinion of the court in special circumstances where publicity would prejudice the interests of justice.
2 Everyone charged with a criminal offence shall be presumed innocent until proved guilty according to law.
3 Everyone charged with a criminal offence has the following minimum rights:
  (a) to be informed promptly, in a language which he understands and in detail, of the nature and cause of the accusation against him;
  (b) to have adequate time and facilities for the preparation of his defence;

(c) to defend himself in person or through legal assistance of his own choosing or, if he has not sufficient means to pay for legal assistance, to be given it free when the interests of justice so require;

(d) to examine or have examined witnesses against him and to obtain the attendance and examination of witnesses on his behalf under the same conditions as witnesses against him;

(e) to have the free assistance of an interpreter if he cannot understand or speak the language used in court.

Article 7
No punishment without law

1 No one shall be held guilty of any criminal offence on account of any act or omission which did not constitute a criminal offence under national or international law at the time when it was committed. Nor shall a heavier penalty be imposed than the one that was applicable at the time the criminal offence was committed.

2 This Article shall not prejudice the trial and punishment of any person for any act or omission which, at the time when it was committed, was criminal according to the general principles of law recognised by civilised nations.

Article 8
Right to respect for private and family life

1 Everyone has the right to respect for his private and family life, his home and his correspondence.

2 There shall be no interference by a public authority with the exercise of this right except such as is in accordance with the law and is necessary in a democratic society in the interests of national security, public safety or the economic well-being of the country, for the prevention of disorder or crime, for the protection of health or morals, or for the protection of the rights and freedoms of others.

Article 9
Freedom of thought, conscience and religion

1 Everyone has the right to freedom of thought, conscience and religion; this right includes freedom to change his religion or belief and freedom, either alone or in community with others and in public or private, to manifest his religion or belief, in worship, teaching, practice and observance.

2 Freedom to manifest one's religion or beliefs shall be subject only to such limitations as are prescribed by law and are necessary in a democratic society in the interests of public safety, for the protection of public order, health or morals, or for the protection of the rights and freedoms of others.

Article 10
Freedom of expression

1 Everyone has the right to freedom of expression. This right shall include freedom to hold opinions and to receive and impart information and ideas without interference by public authority and regardless of frontiers. This Article shall not prevent States from requiring the licensing of broadcasting, television or cinema enterprises.

2 The exercise of these freedoms, since it carries with it duties and responsibilities, may be subject to such formalities, conditions, restrictions or penalties as are prescribed by law and are necessary in a democratic society, in the interests of national security, territorial integrity

or public safety, for the prevention of disorder or crime, for the protection of health or morals, for the protection of the reputation or rights of others, for preventing the disclosure of information received in confidence, or for maintaining the authority and impartiality of the judiciary.

Article 11
Freedom of assembly and association

1 Everyone has the right to freedom of peaceful assembly and to freedom of association with others, including the right to form and to join trade unions for the protection of his interests.

2 No restrictions shall be placed on the exercise of these rights other than such as are prescribed by law and are necessary in a democratic society in the interests of national security or public safety, for the prevention of disorder or crime, for the protection of health or morals or for the protection of the rights and freedoms of others. This Article shall not prevent the imposition of lawful restrictions on the exercise of these rights by members of the armed forces, of the police or of the administration of the State.

Article 12
Right to marry

Men and women of marriageable age have the right to marry and to found a family, according to the national laws governing the exercise of this right.

Article 14
Prohibition of discrimination

The enjoyment of the rights and freedoms set forth in this Convention shall be secured without discrimination on any ground such as sex, race, colour, language, religion, political or other opinion, national or social origin, association with a national minority, property, birth or other status.

Article 16
Restrictions on political activity of aliens

Nothing in Articles 10, 11 and 14 shall be regarded as preventing the High Contracting Parties from imposing restrictions on the political activity of aliens.

Article 17
Prohibition of abuse of rights

Nothing in this Convention may be interpreted as implying for any State, group or person any right to engage in any activity or perform any act aimed at the destruction of any of the rights and freedoms set forth herein or at their limitation to a greater extent than is provided for in the Convention.

Article 18
Limitation on use of restrictions on rights

The restrictions permitted under this Convention to the said rights and freedoms shall not be applied for any purpose other than those for which they have been prescribed.

Part II
The First Protocol

Article 1
Protection of property

Every natural or legal person is entitled to the peaceful enjoyment of his possessions. No one shall be deprived of his possessions except in the public interest and subject to the conditions provided for by law and by the general principles of international law.

The preceding provisions shall not, however, in any way impair the right of a State to enforce such laws as it deems necessary to control the use of property in accordance with the general interest or to secure the payment of taxes or other contributions or penalties.

Article 2
Right to education

No person shall be denied the right to education. In the exercise of any functions which it assumes in relation to education and to teaching, the State shall respect the right of parents to ensure such education and teaching in conformity with their own religious and philosophical convictions.

Article 3
Right to free elections

The High Contracting Parties undertake to hold free elections at reasonable intervals by secret ballot, under conditions which will ensure the free expression of the opinion of the people in the choice of the legislature.

[Part III
Article 1 of the Thirteenth Protocol]

[Abolition of the Death Penalty
The death penalty shall be abolished. No one shall be condemned
to such penalty or executed.]

Schedule 2
Remedial Orders

Section 10

Orders

1 (1) A remedial order may—
    (a) contain such incidental, supplemental, consequential or transitional provision as the person making it considers appropriate;
    (b) be made so as to have effect from a date earlier than that on which it is made;
    (c) make provision for the delegation of specific functions;
    (d) make different provision for different cases.
  (2) The power conferred by sub-paragraph (1)(a) includes—
    (a) power to amend primary legislation (including primary legislation other than that which contains the incompatible provision); and
    (b) power to amend or revoke subordinate legislation (including subordinate legislation other than that which contains the incompatible provision).

(3) A remedial order may be made so as to have the same extent as the legislation which it affects.

(4) No person is to be guilty of an offence solely as a result of the retrospective effect of a remedial order.

Procedure

2   No remedial order may be made unless—
   (a) a draft of the order has been approved by a resolution of each House of Parliament made after the end of the period of 60 days beginning with the day on which the draft was laid; or
   (b) it is declared in the order that it appears to the person making it that, because of the urgency of the matter, it is necessary to make the order without a draft being so approved.

Orders laid in draft

3 (1)   No draft may be laid under paragraph 2(a) unless—
   (a) the person proposing to make the order has laid before Parliament a document which contains a draft of the proposed order and the required information; and
   (b) the period of 60 days, beginning with the day on which the document required by this sub-paragraph was laid, has ended.
(2) If representations have been made during that period, the draft laid under paragraph 2(a) must be accompanied by a statement containing—
   (a) a summary of the representations; and
   (b) if, as a result of the representations, the proposed order has been changed, details of the changes.

Urgent cases

4 (1)   If a remedial order ("the original order") is made without being approved in draft, the person making it must lay it before Parliament, accompanied by the required information, after it is made.
(2) If representations have been made during the period of 60 days beginning with the day on which the original order was made, the person making it must (after the end of that period) lay before Parliament a statement containing—
   (a) a summary of the representations; and
   (b) if, as a result of the representations, he considers it appropriate to make changes to the original order, details of the changes.
(3) If sub-paragraph (2)(b) applies, the person making the statement must—
   (a) make a further remedial order replacing the original order; and
   (b) lay the replacement order before Parliament.
(4) If, at the end of the period of 120 days beginning with the day on which the original order was made, a resolution has not been passed by each House approving the original or replacement order, the order ceases to have effect (but without that affecting anything previously done under either order or the power to make a fresh remedial order).

Definitions

5   In this Schedule—
   "representations" means representations about a remedial order (or proposed remedial order) made to the person making (or proposing to make) it and includes any relevant Parliamentary report or resolution; and

"required information" means—
- (a) an explanation of the incompatibility which the order (or proposed order) seeks to remove, including particulars of the relevant declaration, finding or order; and
- (b) a statement of the reasons for proceeding under section 10 and for making an order in those terms.

Calculating periods

6   In calculating any period for the purposes of this Schedule, no account is to be taken of any time during which—
- (a) Parliament is dissolved or prorogued; or
- (b) both Houses are adjourned for more than four days.

[7 (1) This paragraph applies in relation to—
- (a) any remedial order made, and any draft of such an order proposed to be made—
  - (i) by the Scottish Ministers; or
  - (ii) within devolved competence (within the meaning of the Scotland Act 1998) by Her Majesty in Council; and
- (b) any document or statement to be laid in connection with such an order (or proposed order).

(2) This Schedule has effect in relation to any such order (or proposed order), document or statement subject to the following modifications.

(3) Any reference to Parliament, each House of Parliament or both Houses of Parliament shall be construed as a reference to the Scottish Parliament.

(4) Paragraph 6 does not apply and instead, in calculating any period for the purposes of this Schedule, no account is to be taken of any time during which the Scottish Parliament is dissolved or is in recess for more than four days.]

SCHEDULE 3
DEROGATION AND RESERVATION

Sections 14 and 15

PART I

. . . . .

PART II
RESERVATION

At the time of signing the present (First) Protocol, I declare that, in view of certain provisions of the Education Acts in the United Kingdom, the principle affirmed in the second sentence of Article 2 is accepted by the United Kingdom only so far as it is compatible with the provision of efficient instruction and training, and the avoidance of unreasonable public expenditure.

Dated 20 March 1952. Made by the United Kingdom Permanent Representative to the Council of Europe.

SCHEDULE 4
JUDICIAL PENSIONS

Section 18(6)

Duty to make orders about pensions

1 (1) The appropriate Minister must by order make provision with respect to pensions payable to or in respect of any holder of a judicial office who serves as an ECHR judge.

(2) A pensions order must include such provision as the Minister making it considers is necessary to secure that—

    (a) an ECHR judge who was, immediately before his appointment as an ECHR judge, a member of a judicial pension scheme is entitled to remain as a member of that scheme;

    (b) the terms on which he remains a member of the scheme are those which would have been applicable had he not been appointed as an ECHR judge; and

    (c) entitlement to benefits payable in accordance with the scheme continues to be determined as if, while serving as an ECHR judge, his salary was that which would (but for section 18(4)) have been payable to him in respect of his continuing service as the holder of his judicial office.

Contributions

2   A pensions order may, in particular, make provision—

    (a) for any contributions which are payable by a person who remains a member of a scheme as a result of the order, and which would otherwise be payable by deduction from his salary, to be made otherwise than by deduction from his salary as an ECHR judge; and

    (b) for such contributions to be collected in such manner as may be determined by the administrators of the scheme.

Amendments of other enactments

3   A pensions order may amend any provision of, or made under, a pensions Act in such manner and to such extent as the Minister making the order considers necessary or expedient to ensure the proper administration of any scheme to which it relates.

Definitions

4   In this Schedule—

"appropriate Minister" means—

    (a) in relation to any judicial office whose jurisdiction is exercisable exclusively in relation to Scotland, the Secretary of State; and

    (b) otherwise, the Lord Chancellor;

"ECHR judge" means the holder of a judicial office who is serving as a judge of the Court;

"judicial pension scheme" means a scheme established by and in accordance with a pensions Act;

"pensions Act" means—

    (a) the County Courts Act (Northern Ireland) 1959;

    (b) the Sheriffs' Pensions (Scotland) Act 1961;

    (c) the Judicial Pensions Act 1981; or

    (d) the Judicial Pensions and Retirement Act 1993; and

"pensions order" means an order made under paragraph 1.

APPENDIX TWO

European Convention on Human Rights

Convention for the Protection of Human Rights and Fundamental Freedoms as Amended by Protocol No. 11

(Date of entry into force 1 November 1998)

The governments signatory hereto, being members of the Council of Europe,

Considering the Universal Declaration of Human Rights proclaimed by the General Assembly of the United Nations on 10th December 1948;

Considering that this Declaration aims at securing the universal and effective recognition and observance of the Rights therein declared;

Considering that the aim of the Council of Europe is the achievement of greater unity between its members and that one of the methods by which that aim is to be pursued is the maintenance and further realisation of human rights and fundamental freedoms;

Reaffirming their profound belief in those fundamental freedoms which are the foundation of justice and peace in the world and are best maintained on the one hand by an effective political democracy and on the other by a common understanding and observance of the human rights upon which they depend;

Being resolved, as the governments of European countries which are like-minded and have a common heritage of political traditions, ideals, freedom and the rule of law, to take the first steps for the collective enforcement of certain of the rights stated in the Universal Declaration,

Have agreed as follows:

Article 1
Obligation to respect human rights

The High Contracting Parties shall secure to everyone within their jurisdiction the rights and freedoms defined in Section I of this Convention.

Section I — Rights and freedoms

Article 2
Right to life

1 Everyone's right to life shall be protected by law. No one shall be deprived of his life intentionally save in the execution of a sentence of a court following his conviction of a crime for which this penalty is provided by law.

2 Deprivation of life shall not be regarded as inflicted in contravention of this article when it results from the use of force which is no more than absolutely necessary:

(a) in defence of any person from unlawful violence;

(b) in order to effect a lawful arrest or to prevent the escape of a person lawfully detained;

(c) in action lawfully taken for the purpose of quelling a riot or insurrection.

Article 3
Prohibition of torture

No one shall be subjected to torture or to inhuman or degrading treatment or punishment.

Article 4
Prohibition of slavery and forced labour

1 No one shall be held in slavery or servitude.
2 No one shall be required to perform forced or compulsory labour.
3 For the purpose of this article the term 'forced or compulsory labour' shall not include:
   (a) any work required to be done in the ordinary course of detention imposed according to the provisions of Article 5 of this Convention or during conditional release from such detention;
   (b) any service of a military character or, in case of conscientious objectors in countries where they are recognised, service exacted instead of compulsory military service;
   (c) any service exacted in case of an emergency or calamity threatening the life or well-being of the community;
   (d) any work or service which forms part of normal civic obligations.

Article 5
Right to liberty and security

1. Everyone has the right to liberty and security of person. No one shall be deprived of his liberty save in the following cases and in accordance with a procedure prescribed by law:
   (a) the lawful detention of a person after conviction by a competent court;
   (b) the lawful arrest or detention of a person for non-compliance with the lawful order of a court or in order to secure the fulfilment of any obligation prescribed by law;
   (c) the lawful arrest or detention of a person effected for the purpose of bringing him before the competent legal authority on reasonable suspicion of having committed an offence or when it is reasonably considered necessary to prevent his committing an offence or fleeing after having done so;
   (d) the detention of a minor by lawful order for the purpose of educational supervision or his lawful detention for the purpose of bringing him before the competent legal authority;
   (e) the lawful detention of persons for the prevention of the spreading of infectious diseases, of persons of unsound mind, alcoholics or drug addicts or vagrants;
   (f) the lawful arrest or detention of a person to prevent his effecting an unauthorised entry into the country or of a person against whom action is being taken with a view to deportation or extradition.
1 Everyone who is arrested shall be informed promptly, in a language which he understands, of the reasons for his arrest and of any charge against him.
2 Everyone arrested or detained in accordance with the provisions of paragraph 1.c of this article shall be brought promptly before a judge or other officer authorised by law to exercise judicial power and shall be entitled to trial within a reasonable time or to release pending trial. Release may be conditioned by guarantees to appear for trial.
3 Everyone who is deprived of his liberty by arrest or detention shall be entitled to take proceedings by which the lawfulness of his detention shall be decided speedily by a court and his release ordered if the detention is not lawful.
4 Everyone who has been the victim of arrest or detention in contravention of the provisions of this article shall have an enforceable right to compensation.

Article 6
Right to a fair trial

1 In the determination of his civil rights and obligations or of any criminal charge against him, everyone is entitled to a fair and public hearing within a reasonable time by an independent and impartial tribunal established by law. Judgment shall be pronounced publicly but the press and public may be excluded from all or part of the trial in the interests of morals, public order or national security in a democratic society, where the interests of juveniles or the protection of the private life of the parties so require, or to the extent strictly necessary in the opinion of the court in special circumstances where publicity would prejudice the interests of justice.

2 Everyone charged with a criminal offence shall be presumed innocent until proved guilty according to law.

3 Everyone charged with a criminal offence has the following minimum rights:
   (a) to be informed promptly, in a language which he understands and in detail, of the nature and cause of the accusation against him;
   (b) to have adequate time and facilities for the preparation of his defence;
   (c) to defend himself in person or through legal assistance of his own choosing or, if he has not sufficient means to pay for legal assistance, to be given it free when the interests of justice so require;
   (d) to examine or have examined witnesses against him and to obtain the attendance and examination of witnesses on his behalf under the same conditions as witnesses against him;
   (e) to have the free assistance of an interpreter if he cannot understand or speak the language used in court.

Article 7
No punishment without law

1 No one shall be held guilty of any criminal offence on account of any act or omission which did not constitute a criminal offence under national or international law at the time when it was committed. Nor shall a heavier penalty be imposed than the one that was applicable at the time the criminal offence was committed.

2 This article shall not prejudice the trial and punishment of any person for any act or omission which, at the time when it was committed, was criminal according to the general principles of law recognised by civilised nations.

Article 8
Right to respect for private and family life

1 Everyone has the right to respect for his private and family life, his home and his correspondence.

2 There shall be no interference by a public authority with the exercise of this right except such as is in accordance with the law and is necessary in a democratic society in the interests of national security, public safety or the economic well-being of the country, for the prevention of disorder or crime, for the protection of health or morals, or for the protection of the rights and freedoms of others.

Article 9
Freedom of thought, conscience and religion

1 Everyone has the right to freedom of thought, conscience and religion; this right includes freedom to change his religion or belief and freedom, either alone or in community with

others and in public or private, to manifest his religion or belief, in worship, teaching, practice and observance.

2 Freedom to manifest one's religion or beliefs shall be subject only to such limitations as are prescribed by law and are necessary in a democratic society in the interests of public safety, for the protection of public order, health or morals, or for the protection of the rights and freedoms of others.

Article 10
Freedom of expression

1 Everyone has the right to freedom of expression. This right shall include freedom to hold opinions and to receive and impart information and ideas without interference by public authority and regardless of frontiers. This article shall not prevent States from requiring the licensing of broadcasting, television or cinema enterprises.

2 The exercise of these freedoms, since it carries with it duties and responsibilities, may be subject to such formalities, conditions, restrictions or penalties as are prescribed by law and are necessary in a democratic society, in the interests of national security, territorial integrity or public safety, for the prevention of disorder or crime, for the protection of health or morals, for the protection of the reputation or rights of others, for preventing the disclosure of information received in confidence, or for maintaining the authority and impartiality of the judiciary.

Article 11
Freedom of assembly and association

1 Everyone has the right to freedom of peaceful assembly and to freedom of association with others, including the right to form and to join trade unions for the protection of his interests.

2 No restrictions shall be placed on the exercise of these rights other than such as are prescribed by law and are necessary in a democratic society in the interests of national security or public safety, for the prevention of disorder or crime, for the protection of health or morals or for the protection of the rights and freedoms of others. This article shall not prevent the imposition of lawful restrictions on the exercise of these rights by members of the armed forces, of the police or of the administration of the State.

Article 12
Right to marry

Men and women of marriageable age have the right to marry and to found a family, according to the national laws governing the exercise of this right.

Article 13
Right to an effective remedy

Everyone whose rights and freedoms as set forth in this Convention are violated shall have an effective remedy before a national authority notwithstanding that the violation has been committed by persons acting in an official capacity.

Article 14
Prohibition of discrimination

The enjoyment of the rights and freedoms set forth in this Convention shall be secured without discrimination on any ground such as sex, race, colour, language, religion, political or other opinion, national or social origin, association with a national minority, property, birth or other status.

Article 15
Derogation in time of emergency

1 In time of war or other public emergency threatening the life of the nation any High Contracting Party may take measures derogating from its obligations under this Convention to the extent strictly required by the exigencies of the situation, provided that such measures are not inconsistent with its other obligations under international law.
2 No derogation from Article 2, except in respect of deaths resulting from lawful acts of war, or from Articles 3, 4 (paragraph 1) and 7 shall be made under this provision.
3 Any High Contracting Party availing itself of this right of derogation shall keep the Secretary General of the Council of Europe fully informed of the measures which it has taken and the reasons therefor. It shall also inform the Secretary General of the Council of Europe when such measures have ceased to operate and the provisions of the Convention are again being fully executed.

Article 16
Restrictions on political activity of aliens

Nothing in Articles 10, 11 and 14 shall be regarded as preventing the High Contracting Parties from imposing restrictions on the political activity of aliens.

Article 17
Prohibition of abuse of rights

Nothing in this Convention may be interpreted as implying for any State, group or person any right to engage in any activity or perform any act aimed at the destruction of any of the rights and freedoms set forth herein or at their limitation to a greater extent than is provided for in the Convention.

Article 18
Limitation on use of restrictions on rights

The restrictions permitted under this Convention to the said rights and freedoms shall not be applied for any purpose other than those for which they have been prescribed.

Section II—European Court of Human Rights

Article 19
Establishment of the Court

To ensure the observance of the engagements undertaken by the High Contracting Parties in the Convention and the Protocols thereto, there shall be set up a European Court of Human Rights, hereinafter referred to as 'the Court'. It shall function on a permanent basis.

Article 20
Number of judges

The Court shall consist of a number of judges equal to that of the High Contracting Parties.

Article 21
Criteria for office

1 The judges shall be of high moral character and must either possess the qualifications required for appointment to high judicial office or be jurisconsults of recognised competence.
2 The judges shall sit on the Court in their individual capacity.

3 During their term of office the judges shall not engage in any activity which is incompatible with their independence, impartiality or with the demands of a full-time office; all questions arising from the application of this paragraph shall be decided by the Court.

Article 22
Election of judges

1 The judges shall be elected by the Parliamentary Assembly with respect to each High Contracting Party by a majority of votes cast from a list of three candidates nominated by the High Contracting Party.
2 The same procedure shall be followed to complete the Court in the event of the accession of new High Contracting Parties and in filling casual vacancies.

Article 23
Terms of office

1 The judges shall be elected for a period of six years. They may be re-elected. However, the terms of office of one-half of the judges elected at the first election shall expire at the end of three years.
2 The judges whose terms of office are to expire at the end of the initial period of three years shall be chosen by lot by the Secretary General of the Council of Europe immediately after their election.
3 In order to ensure that, as far as possible, the terms of office of one-half of the judges are renewed every three years, the Parliamentary Assembly may decide, before proceeding to any subsequent election, that the term or terms of office of one or more judges to be elected shall be for a period other than six years but not more than nine and not less than three years.
4 In cases where more than one term of office is involved and where the Parliamentary Assembly applies the preceding paragraph, the allocation of the terms of office shall be effected by a drawing of lots by the Secretary General of the Council of Europe immediately after the election.
5 A judge elected to replace a judge whose term of office has not expired shall hold office for the remainder of his predecessor's term.
6 The terms of office of judges shall expire when they reach the age of 70.
7 The judges shall hold office until replaced. They shall, however, continue to deal with such cases as they already have under consideration.

Article 24
Dismissal

No judge may be dismissed from his office unless the other judges decide by a majority of two-thirds that he has ceased to fulfil the required conditions.

Article 25
Registry and legal secretaries

The Court shall have a registry, the functions and organisation of which shall be laid down in the rules of the Court. The Court shall be assisted by legal secretaries.

Article 26
Plenary Court

The plenary Court shall
(a) elect its President and one or two Vice-Presidents for a period of three years; they may be re-elected;

(b) set up Chambers, constituted for a fixed period of time;

(c) elect the Presidents of the Chambers of the Court; they may be re-elected;

(d) adopt the rules of the Court, and

(e) elect the Registrar and one or more Deputy Registrars.

Article 27
Committees, Chambers and Grand Chamber

1 To consider cases brought before it, the Court shall sit in committees of three judges, in Chambers of seven judges and in a Grand Chamber of seventeen judges. The Court's Chambers shall set up committees for a fixed period of time.

2 There shall sit as an *ex officio* member of the Chamber and the Grand Chamber the judge elected in respect of the State Party concerned or, if there is none or if he is unable to sit, a person of its choice who shall sit in the capacity of judge.

3 The Grand Chamber shall also include the President of the Court, the Vice-Presidents, the Presidents of the Chambers and other judges chosen in accordance with the rules of the Court. When a case is referred to the Grand Chamber under Article 43, no judge from the Chamber which rendered the judgment shall sit in the Grand Chamber, with the exception of the President of the Chamber and the judge who sat in respect of the State Party concerned.

Article 28
Declarations of inadmissibility by committees

A committee may, by a unanimous vote, declare inadmissible or strike out of its list of cases an application submitted under Article 34 where such a decision can be taken without further examination. The decision shall be final.

Article 29
Decisions by Chambers on admissibility and merits

1 If no decision is taken under Article 28, a Chamber shall decide on the admissibility and merits of individual applications submitted under Article 34.

2 A Chamber shall decide on the admissibility and merits of inter-State applications submitted under Article 33.

3 The decision on admissibility shall be taken separately unless the Court, in exceptional cases, decides otherwise.

Article 30
Relinquishment of jurisdiction to the Grand Chamber

Where a case pending before a Chamber raises a serious question affecting the interpretation of the Convention or the protocols thereto, or where the resolution of a question before the Chamber might have a result inconsistent with a judgment previously delivered by the Court, the Chamber may, at any time before it has rendered its judgment, relinquish jurisdiction in favour of the Grand Chamber, unless one of the parties to the case objects.

Article 31
Powers of the Grand Chamber

The Grand Chamber shall

(a) determine applications submitted either under Article 33 or Article 34 when a Chamber has relinquished jurisdiction under Article 30 or when the case has been referred to it under Article 43; and

(b) consider requests for advisory opinions submitted under Article 47.

Article 32
Jurisdiction of the Court

1 The jurisdiction of the Court shall extend to all matters concerning the interpretation and application of the Convention and the protocols thereto which are referred to it as provided in Articles 33, 34 and 47.
2 In the event of dispute as to whether the Court has jurisdiction, the Court shall decide.

Article 33
Inter-State cases

Any High Contracting Party may refer to the Court any alleged breach of the provisions of the Convention and the protocols thereto by another High Contracting Party.

Article 34
Individual applications

The Court may receive applications from any person, non-governmental organisation or group of individuals claiming to be the victim of a violation by one of the High Contracting Parties of the rights set forth in the Convention or the protocols thereto. The High Contracting Parties undertake not to hinder in any way the effective exercise of this right.

Article 35
Admissibility criteria

1 The Court may only deal with the matter after all domestic remedies have been exhausted, according to the generally recognised rules of international law, and within a period of six months from the date on which the final decision was taken.
2 The Court shall not deal with any application submitted under Article 34 that
   (a) is anonymous; or
   (b) is substantially the same as a matter that has already been examined by the Court or has already been submitted to another procedure of international investigation or settlement and contains no relevant new information.
1 The Court shall declare inadmissible any individual application submitted under Article 34 which it considers incompatible with the provisions of the Convention or the protocols thereto, manifestly ill-founded, or an abuse of the right of application.
2 The Court shall reject any application which it considers inadmissible under this Article. It may do so at any stage of the proceedings.

Article 36
Third party intervention

1 In all cases before a Chamber of the Grand Chamber, a High Contracting Party one of whose nationals is an applicant shall have the right to submit written comments and to take part in hearings.
2 The President of the Court may, in the interest of the proper administration of justice, invite any High Contracting Party which is not a party to the proceedings or any person concerned who is not the applicant to submit written comments or take part in hearings.

Article 37
Striking out applications

1 The Court may at any stage of the proceedings decide to strike an application out of its list of cases where the circumstances lead to the conclusion that
   (a) the applicant does not intend to pursue his application; or
   (b) the matter has been resolved; or

(c) for any other reason established by the Court, it is no longer justified to continue the examination of the application.

However, the Court shall continue the examination of the application if respect for human rights as defined in the Convention and the protocols thereto so requires.

2 The Court may decide to restore an application to its list of cases if it considers that the circumstances justify such a course.

Article 38
Examination of the case and friendly settlement proceedings

1 If the Court declares the application admissible, it shall
   (a) pursue the examination of the case, together with the representatives of the parties, and if need be, undertake an investigation, for the effective conduct of which the States concerned shall furnish all necessary facilities;
   (b) place itself at the disposal of the parties concerned with a view to securing a friendly settlement of the matter on the basis of respect for human rights as defined in the Convention and the protocols thereto.
2 Proceedings conducted under paragraph 1.b shall be confidential.

Article 39
Finding of a friendly settlement

If a friendly settlement is effected, the Court shall strike the case out of its list by means of a decision which shall be confined to a brief statement of the facts and of the solution reached.

Article 40
Public hearings and access to documents

1 Hearings shall be in public unless the Court in exceptional circumstances decides otherwise.
2 Documents deposited with the Registrar shall be accessible to the public unless the President of the Court decides otherwise.

Article 41
Just satisfaction

If the Court finds that there has been a violation of the Convention or the protocols thereto, and if the internal law of the High Contracting Party concerned allows only partial reparation to be made, the Court shall, if necessary afford just satisfaction to the injured party.

Article 42
Judgments of Chambers

Judgments of Chambers shall become final in accordance with the provisions of Article 44, paragraph 2.

Article 43
Referral to the Grand Chamber

1 Within a period of three months from the date of the judgment of the Chamber, any party to the case may, in exceptional cases, request that the case be referred to the Grand Chamber.
2 A panel of five judges of the Grand Chamber shall accept the request if the case raises a serious question affecting the interpretation or application of the Convention or the protocols thereto, or a serious issue of general importance.
3 If the panel accepts the request, the Grand Chamber shall decide the case by means of a judgment.

Article 44
Final judgments

1 The judgment of the Grand Chamber shall be final.
2 The judgment of a Chamber shall become final
   (a) when the parties declare that they will not request that the case be referred to the Grand Chamber; or
   (b) three months after the date of the judgment, if reference of the case to the Grand Chamber has not been requested; or
   (c) when the panel of the Grand Chamber rejects the request to refer under Article 43.
3 The final judgment shall be published.

Article 45
Reasons for judgments and decisions

1 Reasons shall be given for judgments as well as for decisions declaring applications admissible or inadmissible.
2 If a judgment does not represent, in whole or in part, the unanimous opinion of the judges, any judge shall be entitled to deliver a separate opinion.

Article 46
Binding force and execution of judgments

1 The High Contracting Parties undertake to abide by the final judgment of the Court in any case to which they are parties.
2 The final judgment of the Court shall be transmitted to the Committee of Ministers, which shall supervise its execution.

Article 47
Advisory opinions

1 The Court may, at the request of the Committee of Ministers, give advisory opinions on legal questions concerning the interpretation of the Convention and the protocols thereto.
2 Such opinions shall not deal with any question relating to the content or scope of the rights or freedoms defined in Section I of the Convention and the protocols thereto, or with any other question which the Court or the Committee of Ministers might have to consider in consequence of any such proceedings as could be instituted in accordance with the Convention.
3 Decisions of the Committee of Ministers to request an advisory opinion of the Court shall require a majority vote of the representatives entitled to sit on the Committee.

Article 48
Advisory jurisdiction of the Court

The Court shall decide whether a request for an advisory opinion submitted by the Committee of Ministers is within its competence as defined in Article 47.

Article 49
Reasons for advisory opinions

1 Reasons shall be given for advisory opinions of the Court.
2 If the advisory opinion does not represent, in whole or in part, the unanimous opinion of the judges, any judge shall be entitled to deliver a separate opinion.
3 Advisory opinions of the Court shall be communicated to the Committee of Ministers.

Article 50
Expenditure on the Court

The expenditure on the Court shall be borne by the Council of Europe.

Article 51
Privileges and immunities of judges

The judges shall be entitled, during the exercise of their functions, to the privileges and immunities provided for in Article 40 of the Statute of the Council of Europe and in the agreements made thereunder.

Section III — Miscellaneous provisions
Article 52
Inquiries by the Secretary General

On receipt of a request from the Secretary General of the Council of Europe any High Contracting Party shall furnish an explanation of the manner in which its internal law ensures the effective implementation of any of the provisions of the Convention.

Article 53
Safeguard for existing human rights

Nothing in this Convention shall be construed as limiting or derogating from any of the human rights and fundamental freedoms which may be ensured under the laws of any High Contracting Party or under any other agreement to which it is a Party.

Article 54
Powers of the Committee of Ministers

Nothing in this Convention shall prejudice the powers conferred on the Committee of Ministers by the Statute of the Council of Europe.

Article 55
Exclusion of other means of dispute settlement

The High Contracting Parties agree that, except by special agreement, they will not avail themselves of treaties, conventions or declarations in force between them for the purpose of submitting, by way of petition, a dispute arising out of the interpretation or application of this Convention to a means of settlement other than those provided for in this Convention.

Article 56
Territorial application

1. Any State may at the time of its ratification or at any time thereafter declare by notification addressed to the Secretary General of the Council of Europe that the present Convention shall, subject to paragraph 4 of this Article, extend to all or any of the territories for whose international relations it is responsible.

1 The Convention shall extend to the territory or territories named in the notification as from the thirtieth day after the receipt of this notification by the Secretary General of the Council of Europe.

2 The provisions of this Convention shall be applied in such territories with due regard, however, to local requirements.

3 Any State which has made a declaration in accordance with paragraph 1 of this Article may at any time thereafter declare on behalf of one or more of the territories to which

the declaration relates that it accepts the competence of the Court to receive applications from individuals, non-governmental organisations or groups of individuals as provided by Article 34 of the Convention.

Article 57
Reservations

1 Any State may, when signing this Convention or when depositing its instrument of ratification, make a reservation in respect of any particular provision of the Convention to the extent that any law then in force in its territory is not in conformity with the provision. Reservations of a general character shall not be permitted under this article.
2 Any reservation made under this article shall contain a brief statement of the law concerned.

Article 58
Denunciation

1 A High Contracting Party may denounce the present Convention only after the expiry of five years from the date on which it became a party to it and after six months' notice contained in a notification addressed to the Secretary General of the Council of Europe, who shall inform the other High Contracting Parties.
2 Such a denunciation shall not have the effect of releasing the High Contracting Party concerned from its obligations under this Convention in respect of any act which, being capable of constituting a violation of such obligations, may have been performed by it before the date at which the denunciation became effective.
3 Any High Contracting Party which shall cease to be a member of the Council of Europe shall cease to be a Party to this Convention under the same conditions.
4 The Convention may be denounced in accordance with the provisions of the preceding paragraphs in respect of any territory to which it has been declared to extend under the terms of Article 56.

Article 59
Signature and ratification

1 This Convention shall be open to the signature of the members of the Council of Europe. It shall be ratified. Ratifications shall be deposited with the Secretary General of the Council of Europe.
2 The present Convention shall come into force after the deposit of ten instruments of ratification.
3 As regards any signatory ratifying subsequently, the Convention shall come into force at the date of the deposit of its instrument of ratification.
4 The Secretary General of the Council of Europe shall notify all the members of the Council of Europe of the entry into force of the Convention, the names of the High Contracting Parties who have ratified it, and the deposit of all instruments of ratification which may be effected subsequently.

Done at Rome this 4th day of November 1950, in English and French, both texts being equally authentic, in a single copy which shall remain deposited in the archives of the Council of Europe.

The Secretary General shall transmit certified copies to each of the signatories.

PROTOCOL [NO. 1] TO THE CONVENTION FOR THE PROTECTION OF HUMAN RIGHTS AND FUNDAMENTAL FREEDOMS, AS AMENDED BY PROTOCOL NO. 11

The governments signatory hereto, being members of the Council of Europe,

Being resolved to take steps to ensure the collective enforcement of certain rights and freedoms other than those already included in Section I of the Convention for the Protection of Human Rights and Fundamental Freedoms signed at Rome on 4 November 1950 (hereinafter referred to as 'the Convention'),

Have agreed as follows:

Article 1
Protection of property

Every natural or legal person is entitled to the peaceful enjoyment of his possessions. No one shall be deprived of his possessions except in the public interest and subject to the conditions provided for by law and by the general principles of international law.

The preceding provisions shall not, however, in any way impair the right of a State to enforce such laws as it deems necessary to control the use of property in accordance with the general interest or to secure the payment of taxes or other contributions or penalties.

Article 2
Right to education

No person shall be denied the right to education. In the exercise of any functions which it assumes in relation to education and to teaching, the State shall respect the right of parents to ensure such education and teaching in conformity with their own religious and philosophical convictions.

Article 3
Right to free elections

The High Contracting Parties undertake to hold free elections at reasonable intervals by secret ballot, under conditions which will ensure the free expression of the opinion of the people in the choice of the legislature.

Article 4
Territorial application

Any High Contracting Party may at the time of signature or ratification or at any time thereafter communicate to the Secretary General of the Council of Europe a declaration stating the extent to which it undertakes that the provisions of the present Protocol shall apply to such of the territories for the international relations of which it is responsible as are named therein.

Any High Contracting Party which has communicated a declaration in virtue of the preceding paragraph may from time to time communicate a further declaration modifying the terms of any former declaration or terminating the application of the provisions of this Protocol in respect of any territory.

A declaration made in accordance with this article shall be deemed to have been made in accordance with paragraph 1 of Article 56 of the Convention.

Article 5
Relationship to the Convention

As between the High Contracting Parties the provisions of Articles 1, 2, 3 and 4 of this Protocol shall be regarded as additional articles to the Convention and all the provisions of the Convention shall apply accordingly.

Article 6
Signature and ratification

This Protocol shall be open for signature by the members of the Council of Europe, who are the signatories of the Convention; it shall be ratified at the same time as or after the ratification of the Convention. It shall enter into force after the deposit of ten instruments of ratification. As regards any signatory ratifying subsequently, the Protocol shall enter into force at the date of the deposit of its instrument of ratification.

The instruments of ratification shall be deposited with the Secretary General of the Council of Europe, who will notify all members of the names of those who have ratified.

Done at Paris on the 20th day of March 1952, in English and French, both texts being equally authentic, in a single copy which shall remain deposited in the archives of the Council of Europe. The Secretary General shall transmit certified copies to each of the signatory governments.

PROTOCOL NO. 4 TO THE CONVENTION FOR THE PROTECTION OF HUMAN RIGHTS AND FUNDAMENTAL FREEDOMS, SECURING CERTAIN RIGHTS AND FREEDOMS OTHER THAN THOSE ALREADY INCLUDED IN THE CONVENTION AND IN THE FIRST PROTOCOL THERETO, AS AMENDED BY PROTOCOL NO. 11

The governments signatory hereto, being members of the Council of Europe,

Being resolved to take steps to ensure the collective enforcement of certain rights and freedoms other than those already included in Section 1 of the Convention for the Protection of Human Rights and Fundamental Freedoms signed at Rome on 4th November 1950 (hereinafter referred to as the 'Convention') and in Articles 1 to 3 of the First Protocol to the Convention, signed at Paris on 20th March 1952,

Have agreed as follows:

Article 1
Prohibition of imprisonment for debt

No one shall be deprived of his liberty merely on the ground of inability to fulfil a contractual obligation.

Article 2
Freedom of movement

1 Everyone lawfully within the territory of a State shall, within that territory, have the right to liberty of movement and freedom to choose his residence.
2 Everyone shall be free to leave any country, including his own.
3 No restrictions shall be placed on the exercise of these rights other than such as are in accordance with law and are necessary in a democratic society in the interests of national security or public safety, for the maintenance of *ordre public*, for the prevention of crime, for the protection of health or morals, or for the protection of the rights and freedoms of others.

4 The rights set forth in paragraph 1 may also be subject, in particular areas, to restrictions imposed in accordance with law and justified by the public interest in a democratic society.

Article 3
Prohibition of expulsion of nationals

1 No one shall be expelled, by means either of an individual or of a collective measure, from the territory of the State of which he is a national.
2 No one shall be deprived of the right to enter the territory of the state of which he is a national.

Article 4
Prohibition of collective expulsion of aliens

Collective expulsion of aliens is prohibited.

Article 5
Territorial application

1 Any High Contracting Party may, at the time of signature or ratification of this Protocol, or at any time thereafter, communicate to the Secretary General of the Council of Europe a declaration stating the extent to which it undertakes that the provisions of this Protocol shall apply to such of the territories for the international relations of which it is responsible as are named therein.
2 Any High Contracting Party which has communicated a declaration in virtue of the preceding paragraph may, from time to time, communicate a further declaration modifying the terms of any former declaration or terminating the application of the provisions of this Protocol in respect of any territory.
3 A declaration made in accordance with this article shall be deemed to have been made in accordance with paragraph 1 of Article 56 of the Convention.
4 The territory of any State to which this Protocol applies by virtue of ratification or acceptance by that State, and each territory to which this Protocol is applied by virtue of a declaration by that State under this article, shall be treated as separate territories for the purpose of the references in Articles 2 and 3 to the territory of a State.
5 Any State which has made a declaration in accordance with paragraph 1 or 2 of this Article may at any time thereafter declare on behalf of one or more of the territories to which the declaration relates that it accepts the competence of the Court to receive applications from individuals, non-governmental organisations or groups of individuals as provided in Article 34 of the Convention in respect of all or any of Articles 1 to 4 of this Protocol.

Article 6
Relationship to the Convention

As between the High Contracting Parties the provisions of Articles 1 to 5 of this Protocol shall be regarded as additional Articles to the Convention, and all the provisions of the Convention shall apply accordingly.

Article 7
Signature and ratification

1 This Protocol shall be open for signature by the members of the Council of Europe who are the signatories of the Convention; it shall be ratified at the same time as or after the ratification of the Convention. It shall enter into force after the deposit of five instruments of ratification. As regards any signatory ratifying subsequently, the Protocol shall enter into force at the date of the deposit of its instrument of ratification.

2 The instruments of ratification shall be deposited with the Secretary General of the Council of Europe, who will notify all members of the names of those who have ratified.

In witness whereof the undersigned, being duly authorised thereto, have signed this Protocol.

Done at Strasbourg, this 16th day of September 1963, in English and in French, both texts being equally authoritative, in a single copy which shall remain deposited in the archives of the Council of Europe. The Secretary General shall transmit certified copies to each of the signatory states.

PROTOCOL NO. 6 TO THE CONVENTION FOR THE PROTECTION OF HUMAN RIGHTS AND FUNDAMENTAL FREEDOMS CONCERNING THE ABOLITION OF THE DEATH PENALTY, AS AMENDED BY PROTOCOL NO. 11

The member States of the Council of Europe, signatory to this Protocol to the Convention for the Protection of Human Rights and Fundamental Freedoms, signed at Rome on 4 November 1950 (hereinafter referred to as 'the Convention'),

Considering that the evolution that has occurred in several member States of the Council of Europe expresses a general tendency in favour of abolition of the death penalty;

Have agreed as follows:

Article 1
Abolition of the death penalty

The death penalty shall be abolished. No-one shall be condemned to such penalty or executed.

Article 2
Death penalty in time of war

A State may make provision in its law for the death penalty in respect of acts committed in time of war or of imminent threat of war; such penalty shall be applied only in the instances laid down in the law and in accordance with its provisions. The State shall communicate to the Secretary General of the Council of Europe the relevant provisions of that law.

Article 3
Prohibition of derogations

No derogation from the provisions of this Protocol shall be made under Article 15 of the Convention.

Article 4
Prohibition of reservations

No reservation may be made under Article 57 of the Convention in respect of the provisions of this Protocol.

Article 5
Territorial application

1 Any State may at the time of signature or when depositing its instrument of ratification, acceptance or approval, specify the territory or territories to which this Protocol shall apply.
2 Any State may at any later date, by a declaration addressed to the Secretary General of the Council of Europe, extend the application of this Protocol to any other territory specified in the declaration. In respect of such territory the Protocol shall enter into force on the first day of the month following the date of receipt of such declaration by the Secretary General.

3 Any declaration made under the two preceding paragraphs may, in respect of any territory specified in such declaration, be withdrawn by a notification addressed to the Secretary General. The withdrawal shall become effective on the first day of the month following the date of receipt of such notification by the Secretary General.

Article 6
Relationship to the Convention

As between the States Parties the provisions of Articles 1 to 5 of this Protocol shall be regarded as additional articles to the Convention and all the provisions of the Convention shall apply accordingly.

Article 7
Signature and ratification

The Protocol shall be open for signature by the member States of the Council of Europe, signatories to the Convention. It shall be subject to ratification, acceptance or approval. A member State of the Council of Europe may not ratify, accept or approve this Protocol unless it has, simultaneously or previously, ratified the Convention. Instruments of ratification, acceptance or approval shall be deposited with the Secretary General of the Council of Europe.

Article 8
Entry into force

1 This Protocol shall enter into force on the first day of the month following the date on which five member States of the Council of Europe have expressed their consent to be bound by the Protocol in accordance with the provisions of Article 7.
2 In respect of any member State which subsequently expresses its consent to be bound by it, the Protocol shall enter into force on the first day of the month following the date of the deposit of the instrument of ratification, acceptance or approval.

Article 9
Depositary functions

The Secretary General of the Council of Europe shall notify the member States of the Council of:
(a) any signature;
(b) the deposit of any instrument of ratification, acceptance or approval;
(c) any date of entry into force of this Protocol in accordance with Articles 5 and 8;
(d) any other act, notification or communication relating to this Protocol.
In witness whereof the undersigned, being duly authorised thereto, have signed this Protocol.

Done at Strasbourg, this 28th day of April 1983, in English and in French, both texts being equally authentic, in a single copy which shall be deposited in the archives of the Council of Europe. The Secretary General of the Council of Europe shall transmit certified copies to each member State of the Council of Europe.

PROTOCOL NO. 7 TO THE CONVENTION FOR THE PROTECTION OF HUMAN RIGHTS AND FUNDAMENTAL FREEDOMS, AS AMENDED BY PROTOCOL NO. 11

The member States of the Council of Europe signatory hereto,

Being resolved to take further steps to ensure the collective enforcement of certain rights and freedoms by means of the Convention for the Protection of Human Rights and

Fundamental Freedoms signed at Rome on 4 November 1950 (hereinafter referred to as 'the Convention'),

Have agreed as follows:

Article 1
Procedural safeguards relating to expulsion of aliens

1 An alien lawfully resident in the territory of a State shall not be expelled therefrom except in pursuance of a decision reached in accordance with law and shall be allowed:
   (a) to submit reasons against his expulsion,
   (b) to have his case reviewed, and
   (c) to be represented for these purposes before the competent authority or a person or persons designated by that authority.
2 An alien may be expelled before the exercise of his rights under paragraph 1.a, b and c of this Article, when such expulsion is necessary in the interests of public order or is grounded on reasons of national security.

Article 2
Right of appeal in criminal matters

1 Everyone convicted of a criminal offence by a tribunal shall have the right to have his conviction or sentence reviewed by a higher tribunal. The exercise of this right, including the grounds on which it may be exercised, shall be governed by law.
2 This right may be subject to exceptions in regard to offences of a minor character, as prescribed by law, or in cases in which the person concerned was tried in the first instance by the highest tribunal or was convicted following an appeal against acquittal.

Article 3
Compensation for wrongful conviction

When a person has by a final decision been convicted of a criminal offence and when subsequently his conviction has been reversed, or he has been pardoned, on the ground that a new or newly discovered fact shows conclusively that there has been a miscarriage of justice, the person who has suffered punishment as a result of such conviction shall be compensated according to the law or the practice of the State concerned, unless it is proved that the non-disclosure of the unknown fact in time is wholly or partly attributable to him.

Article 4
Right not to be tried or punished twice

1 No one shall be liable to be tried or punished again in criminal proceedings under the jurisdiction of the same State for an offence for which he has already been finally acquitted or convicted in accordance with the law and penal procedure of that State.
2 The provisions of the preceding paragraph shall not prevent the reopening of the case in accordance with the law and penal procedure of the State concerned, if there is evidence of new or newly discovered facts, or if there has been a fundamental defect in the previous proceedings, which could affect the outcome of the case.
3 No derogation from this Article shall be made under Article 15 of the Convention.

Article 5
Equality between spouses

Spouses shall enjoy equality of rights and responsibilities of a private law character between them, and in their relations with their children, as to marriage, during marriage and in the event of its dissolution. This Article shall not prevent States from taking such measures as are necessary in the interests of the children.

Article 6
Territorial application

1 Any State may at the time of signature or when depositing its instrument of ratification, acceptance or approval, specify the territory or territories to which the Protocol shall apply and state the extent to which it undertakes that the provisions of this Protocol shall apply to such territory or territories.

2 Any State may at any later date, by a declaration addressed to the Secretary General of the Council of Europe, extend the application of this Protocol to any other territory specified in the declaration. In respect of such territory the Protocol shall enter into force on the first day of the month following the expiration of a period of two months after the date of receipt by the Secretary General of such declaration.

3 Any declaration made under the two preceding paragraphs may, in respect of any territory specified in such declaration, be withdrawn or modified by a notification addressed to the Secretary General. The withdrawal or modification shall become effective on the first day of the month following the expiration of a period of two months after the date of receipt of such notification by the Secretary General.

4 A declaration made in accordance with this Article shall be deemed to have been made in accordance with paragraph 1 of Article 56 of the Convention.

5 The territory of any State to which this Protocol applies by virtue of ratification, acceptance or approval by that State, and each territory to which this Protocol is applied by virtue of a declaration by that State under this Article, may be treated as separate territories for the purpose of the reference in Article 1 to the territory of a State.

6 Any State which has made a declaration in accordance with paragraph 1 or 2 of this Article may at any time thereafter declare on behalf of one or more of the territories to which the declaration relates that it accepts the competence of the Court to receive applications from individuals, non-governmental organisations or groups of individuals as provided in Article 34 of the Convention in respect of Articles 1 to 5 of this Protocol.

Article 7
Relationship to the Convention

As between the States Parties, the provisions of Article 1 to 6 of this Protocol shall be regarded as additional Articles to the Convention, and all the provisions of the Convention shall apply accordingly.

Article 8
Signature and ratification

This Protocol shall be open for signature by member States of the Council of Europe which have signed the Convention. It is subject to ratification, acceptance or approval. A member State of the Council of Europe may not ratify, accept or approve this Protocol without previously or simultaneously ratifying the Convention. Instruments of ratification, acceptance or approval shall be deposited with the Secretary General of the Council of Europe.

Article 9
Entry into force

1 This Protocol shall enter into force on the first day of the month following the expiration of a period of two months after the date on which seven member States of the Council of

Europe have expressed their consent to be bound by the Protocol in accordance with the provisions of Article 8.

2 In respect of any member State which subsequently expresses its consent to be bound by it, the Protocol shall enter into force on the first day of the month following the expiration of a period of two months after the date of the deposit of the instrument of ratification, acceptance or approval.

Article 10
Depositary functions

The Secretary General of the Council of Europe shall notify all the member States of the Council of Europe of:

(a) any signature;

(b) the deposit of any instrument of ratification, acceptance or approval;

(c) any date of entry into force of this Protocol in accordance with Articles 6 and 9;

(d) any other act, notification or declaration relating to this Protocol.

In witness whereof the undersigned, being duly authorised thereto, have signed this Protocol.

Done at Strasbourg, this 22nd day of November 1984, in English and French, both texts being equally authentic, in a single copy which shall be deposited in the archives of the Council of Europe. The Secretary General of the Council of Europe shall transmit certified copies to each member State of the Council of Europe.

PROTOCOL NO. 12 TO THE CONVENTION FOR THE PROTECTION OF HUMAN RIGHTS AND FUNDAMENTAL FREEDOMS

The member states of the Council of Europe signatory hereto,

Having regard to the fundamental principle according to which all persons are equal before the law and are entitled to the equal protection of the law;

Being resolved to take further steps to promote the equality of all persons through the collective enforcement of a general prohibition of discrimination by means of the Convention for the Protection of Human Rights and Fundamental Freedoms signed at Rome on 4 November 1950 (hereinafter referred to as 'the Convention');

Reaffirming that the principle of non-discrimination does not prevent States Parties from taking measures in order to promote full and effective equality, provided that there is an objective and reasonable justification for those measures,

Have agreed as follows:

Article 1
General prohibition of discrimination

1 The enjoyment of any right set forth by law shall be secured without discrimination on any ground such as sex, race, colour, language, religion, political or other opinion, national or social origin, association with a national minority, property, birth or other status.

2 No one shall be discriminated against by any public authority on any ground such as those mentioned in paragraph 1.

Article 2
Territorial application

1 Any state may, at the time of signature or when depositing its instrument of ratification, acceptance or approval, specify the territory or territories to which this Protocol shall apply.

2 Any state may at any later date, by a declaration addressed to the Secretary General of the Council of Europe, extend the application of this Protocol to any other territory specified in the declaration, in respect of such territory the Protocol shall enter into force on the first day of the month following the expiration of a period of three months after the date of receipt by the Secretary General of such declaration.

1 Any declaration made under the two preceding paragraphs may, in respect of any territory specified in such declaration, be withdrawn or modified by a notification addressed to the Secretary General. The withdrawal or modification shall become effective on the first day of the month following the expiration of a period of three months after the date of receipt of such notification by the Secretary General.

2 A declaration made in accordance with this article shall be deemed to have been made in accordance with paragraph 1 of Article 56 of the Convention.

3 Any state which has made a declaration in accordance with paragraph 1 or 2 of this article may at any time thereafter declare on behalf of one or more of the territories to which the declaration relates that it accepts the competence of the Court to receive applications from individuals, non-governmental organisations or groups of individuals as provided by Article 34 of the Convention in respect of Article 1 of this Protocol.

Article 3
Relationship to the Convention

As between the States Parties, the provisions of Articles 1 and 2 of this Protocol shall be regarded as additional articles to the Convention, and all the provisions of the Convention shall apply accordingly.

Article 4
Signature and ratification

This Protocol shall be open for signature by member states of the Council of Europe which have signed the Convention. It is subject to ratification, acceptance or approval. A member state of the Council of Europe may not ratify, accept or approve this Protocol without previously or simultaneously ratifying the Convention. Instruments of ratification, acceptance or approval shall be deposited with the Secretary General of the Council of Europe.

Article 5
Entry into force

1 This Protocol shall enter into force on the first day of the month following the expiration of a period of three months after the date on which ten member states of the Council of Europe have expressed their consent to be bound by the Protocol in accordance with the provisions of Article 4.

2 In respect of any member state which subsequently expresses its consent to be bound by it, the Protocol shall enter into force on the first day of the month following the expiration of a period of three months after the date of the deposit of the instrument of ratification, acceptance or approval.

Article 6
Depositary functions

The Secretary General of the Council of Europe shall notify all the member states of the Council of Europe of:

(a) any signature;

(b) the deposit of any instrument of ratification, acceptance or approval;

(c) any date of entry into force of this Protocol in accordance with Articles 2 and 5;

(d) any other act, notification or communication relating to this Protocol.

In witness whereof the undersigned, being duly authorised thereto, have signed this Protocol.

Done at _____, this _____ day of _____ 2000, in English and French, both texts being equally authentic, in a single copy which shall be deposited in the archives of the Council of Europe. The Secretary General of the Council of Europe shall transmit certified copies to each member state of the Council of Europe.

Charter of Fundamental Rights of the European Union

The peoples of Europe, in creating an ever closer union among them, are resolved to share a peaceful future based on common values.

Conscious of its spiritual and moral heritage, the Union is founded on the indivisible, universal values of human dignity, freedom, equality and solidarity; it is based on the principles of democracy and the rule of law. It places the individual at the heart of its activities, by establishing the citizenship of the Union and by creating an area of freedom, security and justice.

The Union contributes to the preservation and to the development of these common values while respecting the diversity of the cultures and traditions of the peoples of Europe as well as the national identities of the Member States and the organisation of their public authorities at national, regional and local levels; it seeks to promote balanced and sustainable development and ensures free movement of persons, goods, services and capital, and the freedom of establishment.

To this end, it is necessary to strengthen the protection of fundamental rights in the light of changes in society, social progress and scientific and technological developments by making those rights more visible in a Charter.

This Charter reaffirms, with due regard for the powers and tasks of the Community and the Union and the principle of subsidiarity, the rights as they result, in particular, from the constitutional traditions and international obligations common to the Member States, the Treaty on European Union, the Community Treaties, the European Convention for the Protection of Human Rights and Fundamental Freedoms, the Social Charters adopted by the Community and by the Council of Europe and the case-law of the Court of Justice of the European Communities and of the European Court of Human Rights.

Charter of Fundamental Rights of the European Union

Preamble

Enjoyment of these rights entails responsibilities and duties with regard to other persons, to the human community and to future generations. The Union therefore recognises the rights, freedoms and principles set out hereafter.

Chapter I
Dignity

Article 1
Human dignity

Human dignity is inviolable. It must be respected and protected.

Article 2
Right to life

1 Everyone has the right to life.
2 No one shall be condemned to the death penalty, or executed.

Article 3
Right to the integrity of the person

1 Everyone has the right to respect for his or her physical and mental integrity.
2 In the fields of medicine and biology, the following must be respected in particular:
— the free and informed consent of the person concerned, according to the procedures laid down by law,
— the prohibition of eugenic practices, in particular those aiming at the selection of persons,
— the prohibition on making the human body and its parts as such a source of financial gain,
— the prohibition of the reproductive cloning of human beings.

Article 4
Prohibition of torture and inhuman or degrading treatment or punishment

No one shall be subjected to torture or to inhuman or degrading treatment or punishment.

Article 5
Prohibition of slavery and forced labour

1 No one shall be held in slavery or servitude.
2 No one shall be required to perform forced or compulsory labour.
3 Trafficking in human beings is prohibited.

CHAPTER II
FREEDOMS

Article 6
Right to liberty and security

Everyone has the right to liberty and security of person.

Article 7
Respect for private and family life

Everyone has the right to respect for his or her private and family life, home and communications.

Article 8
Protection of personal data

1 Everyone has the right to the protection of personal data concerning him or her.
2 Such data must be processed fairly for specified purposes and on the basis of the consent of the person concerned or some other legitimate basis laid down by law. Everyone has the right of access to data which has been collected concerning him or her, and the right to have it rectified.
3 Compliance with these rules shall be subject to control by an independent authority.

Article 9
Right to marry and right to found a family

The right to marry and the right to found a family shall be guaranteed in accordance with the national laws governing the exercise of these rights.

Article 10
Freedom of thought, conscience and religion

1 Everyone has the right to freedom of thought, conscience and religion. This right includes freedom to change religion or belief and freedom, either alone or in community with others and in public or in private, to manifest religion or belief, in worship, teaching, practice and observance.
2 The right to conscientious objection is recognised, in accordance with the national laws governing the exercise of this right.

Article 11
Freedom of expression and information

1 Everyone has the right to freedom of expression. This right shall include freedom to hold opinions and to receive and impart information and ideas without interference by public authority and regardless of frontiers.
2 The freedom and pluralism of the media shall be respected.

Article 12
Freedom of assembly and of association

1 Everyone has the right to freedom of peaceful assembly and to freedom of association at all levels, in particular in political, trade union and civic matters, which implies the right of everyone to form and to join trade unions for the protection of his or her interests.
2 Political parties at Union level contribute to expressing the political will of the citizens of the Union.

Article 13
Freedom of the arts and sciences

The arts and scientific research shall be free of constraint. Academic freedom shall be respected.

Article 14
Right to education

1 Everyone has the right to education and to have access to vocational and continuing training.
2 This right includes the possibility to receive free compulsory education.
3 The freedom to found educational establishments with due respect for democratic principles and the right of parents to ensure the education and teaching of their children in conformity with their religious, philosophical and pedagogical convictions shall be respected, in accordance with the national laws governing the exercise of such freedom and right.

Article 15
Freedom to choose an occupation and right to engage in work

1 Everyone has the right to engage in work and to pursue a freely chosen or accepted occupation.
2 Every citizen of the Union has the freedom to seek employment, to work, to exercise the right of establishment and to provide services in any Member State.

3 Nationals of third countries who are authorised to work in the territories of the Member States are entitled to working conditions equivalent to those of citizens of the Union.

Article 16
Freedom to conduct a business

The freedom to conduct a business in accordance with Community law and national laws and practices is recognised.

Article 17
Right to property

1 Everyone has the right to own, use, dispose of and bequeath his or her lawfully acquired possessions. No one may be deprived of his or her possessions, except in the public interest and in the cases and under the conditions provided for by law, subject to fair compensation being paid in good time for their loss. The use of property may be regulated by law in so far as is necessary for the general interest.
2 Intellectual property shall be protected.

Article 18
Right to asylum

The right to asylum shall be guaranteed with due respect for the rules of the Geneva Convention of 28 July 1951 and the Protocol of 31 January 1967 relating to the status of refugees and in accordance with the Treaty establishing the European Community.

Article 19
Protection in the event of removal, expulsion or extradition

1 Collective expulsions are prohibited.
2 No one may be removed, expelled or extradited to a State where there is a serious risk that he or she would be subjected to the death penalty, torture or other inhuman or degrading treatment or punishment.

CHAPTER III
EQUALITY

Article 20
Equality before the law

Everyone is equal before the law.

Article 21
Non-discrimination

1 Any discrimination based on any ground such as sex, race, colour, ethnic or social origin, genetic features, language, religion or belief, political or any other opinion, membership of a national minority, property, birth, disability, age or sexual orientation shall be prohibited.
2 Within the scope of application of the Treaty establishing the European Community and of the Treaty on European Union, and without prejudice to the special provisions of those Treaties, any discrimination on grounds of nationality shall be prohibited.

Article 22
Cultural, religious and linguistic diversity

The Union shall respect cultural, religious and linguistic diversity.

Article 23
Equality between men and women

Equality between men and women must be ensured in all areas, including employment, work and pay. The principle of equality shall not prevent the maintenance or adoption of measures providing for specific advantages in favour of the under-represented sex.

Article 24
The rights of the child

1 Children shall have the right to such protection and care as is necessary for their well-being. They may express their views freely. Such views shall be taken into consideration on matters which concern them in accordance with their age and maturity.
2 In all actions relating to children, whether taken by public authorities or private institutions, the child's best interests must be a primary consideration.
3 Every child shall have the right to maintain on a regular basis a personal relationship and direct contact with both his or her parents, unless that is contrary to his or her interests.

Article 25
The rights of the elderly

The Union recognises and respects the rights of the elderly to lead a life of dignity and independence and to participate in social and cultural life.

Article 26
Integration of persons with disabilities

The Union recognises and respects the right of persons with disabilities to benefit from measures designed to ensure their independence, social and occupational integration and participation in the life of the community.

CHAPTER IV
SOLIDARITY

Article 27
Workers' right to information and consultation within the undertaking

Workers or their representatives must, at the appropriate levels, be guaranteed information and consultation in good time in the cases and under the conditions provided for by Community law and national laws and practices.

Article 28
Right of collective bargaining and action

Workers and employers, or their respective organisations, have, in accordance with Community law and national laws and practices, the right to negotiate and conclude collective agreements at the appropriate levels and, in cases of conflicts of interest, to take collective action to defend their interests, including strike action.

Article 29
Right of access to placement services

Everyone has the right of access to a free placement service.

Article 30
Protection in the event of unjustified dismissal

Every worker has the right to protection against unjustified dismissal, in accordance with Community law and national laws and practices.

Article 31
Fair and just working conditions

1 Every worker has the right to working conditions which respect his or her health, safety and dignity.
2 Every worker has the right to limitation of maximum working hours, to daily and weekly rest periods and to an annual period of paid leave.

Article 32
Prohibition of child labour and protection of young people at work

The employment of children is prohibited. The minimum age of admission to employment may not be lower than the minimum school-leaving age, without prejudice to such rules as may be more favourable to young people and except for limited derogations. Young people admitted to work must have working conditions appropriate to their age and be protected against economic exploitation and any work likely to harm their safety, health or physical, mental, moral or social development or to interfere with their education.

Article 33
Family and professional life

1 The family shall enjoy legal, economic and social protection.
2 To reconcile family and professional life, everyone shall have the right to protection from dismissal for a reason connected with maternity and the right to paid maternity leave and to parental leave following the birth or adoption of a child.

Article 34
Social security and social assistance

1 The Union recognises and respects the entitlement to social security benefits and social ser-vices providing protection in cases such as maternity, illness, industrial accidents, depend-ency or old age, and in the case of loss of employment, in accordance with the rules laid down by Community law and national laws and practices.
2 Everyone residing and moving legally within the European Union is entitled to social secur-ity benefits and social advantages in accordance with Community law and national laws and practices.
3 In order to combat social exclusion and poverty, the Union recognises and respects the right to social and housing assistance so as to ensure a decent existence for all those who lack suffi-cient resources, in accordance with the rules laid down by Community law and national laws and practices.

Article 35
Health care

Everyone has the right of access to preventive health care and the right to benefit from medical treatment under the conditions established by national laws and practices. A high level of human health protection shall be ensured in the definition and implementation of all Union policies and activities.

Article 36
Access to services of general economic interest

The Union recognises and respects access to services of general economic interest as provided for in national laws and practices, in accordance with the Treaty establishing the European Community, in order to promote the social and territorial cohesion of the Union.

Article 37
Environmental protection

A high level of environmental protection and the improvement of the quality of the environment must be integrated into the policies of the Union and ensured in accordance with the principle of sustainable development.

Article 38
Consumer protection

Union policies shall ensure a high level of consumer protection.

CHAPTER V
CITIZENS' RIGHTS

Article 39
Right to vote and to stand as a candidate at elections to the European Parliament

1 Every citizen of the Union has the right to vote and to stand as a candidate at elections to the European Parliament in the Member State in which he or she resides, under the same conditions as nationals of that State.
2 Members of the European Parliament shall be elected by direct universal suffrage in a free and secret ballot.

Article 40
Right to vote and to stand as a candidate at municipal elections

Every citizen of the Union has the right to vote and to stand as a candidate at municipal elections in the Member State in which he or she resides under the same conditions as nationals of that State.

Article 41
Right to good administration

1 Every person has the right to have his or her affairs handled impartially, fairly and within a reasonable time by the institutions and bodies of the Union.
2 This right includes:
   — the right of every person to be heard, before any individual measure which would affect him or her adversely is taken;
   — the right of every person to have access to his or her file, while respecting the legitimate interests of confidentiality and of professional and business secrecy;
   — the obligation of the administration to give reasons for its decisions.
1 Every person has the right to have the Community make good any damage caused by its institutions or by its servants in the performance of their duties, in accordance with the general principles common to the laws of the Member States.
2 Every person may write to the institutions of the Union in one of the languages of the Treaties and must have an answer in the same language.

459

Article 42
Right of access to documents

Any citizen of the Union, and any natural or legal person residing or having its registered office in a Member State, has a right of access to European Parliament, Council and Commission documents.

Article 43
Ombudsman

Any citizen of the Union and any natural or legal person residing or having its registered office in a Member State has the right to refer to the Ombudsman of the Union cases of maladministration in the activities of the Community institutions or bodies, with the exception of the Court of Justice and the Court of First Instance acting in their judicial role.

Article 44
Right to petition

Any citizen of the Union and any natural or legal person residing or having its registered office in a Member State has the right to petition the European Parliament.

Article 45
Freedom of movement and of residence

1 Every citizen of the Union has the right to move and reside freely within the territory of the Member States.
2 Freedom of movement and residence may be granted, in accordance with the Treaty establishing the European Community, to nationals of third countries legally resident in the territory of a Member State.

Article 46
Diplomatic and consular protection

Every citizen of the Union shall, in the territory of a third country in which the Member State of which he or she is a national is not represented, be entitled to protection by the diplomatic or consular authorities of any Member State, on the same conditions as the nationals of that Member State.

CHAPTER VI
JUSTICE

Article 47
Right to an effective remedy and to a fair trial

Everyone whose rights and freedoms guaranteed by the law of the Union are violated has the right to an effective remedy before a tribunal in compliance with the conditions laid down in this Article.

Everyone is entitled to a fair and public hearing within a reasonable time by an independent and impartial tribunal previously established by law. Everyone shall have the possibility of being advised, defended and represented.

Legal aid shall be made available to those who lack sufficient resources in so far as such aid is necessary to ensure effective access to justice.

Article 48
Presumption of innocence and right of defence

1 Everyone who has been charged shall be presumed innocent until proved guilty according to law.
2 Respect for the rights of the defence of anyone who has been charged shall be guaranteed.

Article 49
Principles of legality and proportionality of criminal offences and penalties

1 No one shall be held guilty of any criminal offence on account of any act or omission which did not constitute a criminal offence under national law or international law at the time when it was committed. Nor shall a heavier penalty be imposed than that which was applicable at the time the criminal offence was committed. If, subsequent to the commission of a criminal offence, the law provides for a lighter penalty, that penalty shall be applicable.
2 This Article shall not prejudice the trial and punishment of any person for any act or omission which, at the time when it was committed, was criminal according to the general principles recognised by the community of nations.
3 The severity of penalties must not be disproportionate to the criminal offence.

Article 50
Right not to be tried or punished twice in criminal proceedings for the same criminal offence

No one shall be liable to be tried or punished again in criminal proceedings for an offence for which he or she has already been finally acquitted or convicted within the Union in accordance with the law.

CHAPTER VII
GENERAL PROVISIONS

Article 51
Scope

1 The provisions of this Charter are addressed to the institutions and bodies of the Union with due regard for the principle of subsidiarity and to the Member States only when they are implementing Union law. They shall therefore respect the rights, observe the principles and promote the application thereof in accordance with their respective powers.
2 This Charter does not establish any new power or task for the Community or the Union, or modify powers and tasks defined by the Treaties.

Article 52
Scope of guaranteed rights

1 Any limitation on the exercise of the rights and freedoms recognised by this Charter must be provided for by law and respect the essence of those rights and freedoms. Subject to the principle of proportionality, limitations may be made only if they are necessary and genuinely meet objectives of general interest recognised by the Union or the need to protect the rights and freedoms of others.
2 Rights recognised by this Charter which are based on the Community Treaties or the Treaty on European Union shall be exercised under the conditions and within the limits defined by those Treaties.

3 In so far as this Charter contains rights which correspond to rights guaranteed by the Convention for the Protection of Human Rights and Fundamental Freedoms, the meaning and scope of those rights shall be the same as those laid down by the said Convention. This provision shall not prevent Union law providing more extensive protection.

Article 53
Level of protection

Nothing in this Charter shall be interpreted as restricting or adversely affecting human rights and fundamental freedoms as recognised, in their respective fields of application, by Union law and international law and by international agreements to which the Union, the Community or all the Member States are party, including the European Convention for the Protection of Human Rights and Fundamental Freedoms, and by the Member States' constitutions.

Article 54
Prohibition of abuse of rights

Nothing in this Charter shall be interpreted as implying any right to engage in any activity or to perform any act aimed at the destruction of any of the rights and freedoms recognised in this Charter or at their limitation to a greater extent than is provided for herein.

APPENDIX FOUR

Council Directive 2000/43/EC—The Race Directive

COUNCIL DIRECTIVE 2000/43/EC
of 29 June 2000 implementing the principle of equal treatment between persons irrespective of racial or ethnic origin

THE COUNCIL OF THE EUROPEAN UNION, Having regard to the Treaty establishing the European Community and in particular Article 13 thereof, Having regard to the proposal from the Commission, Having regard to the opinion of the European Parliament, Having regard to the opinion of the Economic and Social Committee, Having regard to the opinion of the Committee of the Regions, Whereas:

(1) The Treaty on European Union marks a new stage in the process of creating an ever closer union among the peoples of Europe.

(2) In accordance with Article 6 of the Treaty on European Union, the European Union is founded on the principles of liberty, democracy, respect for human rights and fundamental freedoms, and the rule of law, principles which are common to the Member States, and should respect fundamental rights as guaranteed by the European Convention for the protection of Human Rights and Fundamental Freedoms and as they result from the constitutional traditions common to the Member States, as general principles of Community Law.

(3) The right to equality before the law and protection against discrimination for all persons constitutes a universal right recognised by the Universal Declaration of Human Rights, the United Nations Convention on the Elimination of all Forms of Discrimination Against Women, the International Convention on the Elimination of all Forms of Racial Discrimination and the United Nations Covenants on Civil and Political Rights and on Economic, Social and Cultural Rights and by the European Convention for the Protection of Human Rights and Fundamental Freedoms, to which all Member States are signatories.

(4) It is important to respect such fundamental rights and freedoms, including the right to freedom of association. It is also important, in the context of the access to and provision of goods and services, to respect the protection of private and family life and transactions carried out in this context.

(5) The European Parliament has adopted a number of Resolutions on the fight against racism in the European Union.

(6) The European Union rejects theories which attempt to determine the existence of separate human races. The use of the term 'racial origin' in this Directive does not imply an acceptance of such theories.

(7) The European Council in Tampere, on 15 and 16 October 1999, invited the Commission to come forward as soon as possible with proposals implementing Article 13 of the EC Treaty as regards the fight against racism and xenophobia.

(8) The Employment Guidelines 2000 agreed by the European Council in Helsinki, on 10 and 11 December 1999, stress the need to foster conditions for a socially inclusive labour market by formulating a coherent set of policies aimed at combating discrimination against groups such as ethnic minorities.

(9) Discrimination based on racial or ethnic origin may undermine the achievement of the objectives of the EC Treaty, in particular the attainment of a high level of employment and of social protection, the raising of the standard of living and quality of life, economic and social cohesion and solidarity. It may also undermine the objective of developing the European Union as an area of freedom, security and justice.

(10) The Commission presented a communication on racism, xenophobia and anti-Semitism in December 1995.

(11) The Council adopted on 15 July 1996 Joint Action (96/443/JHA) concerning action to combat racism and xenophobia under which the Member States undertake to ensure effective judicial cooperation in respect of offences based on racist or xenophobic behaviour.

(12) To ensure the development of democratic and tolerant societies which allow the participation of all persons irrespective of racial or ethnic origin, specific action in the field of discrimination based on racial or ethnic origin should go beyond access to employed and self-employed activities and cover areas such as education, social protection including social security and healthcare, social advantages and access to and supply of goods and services.

(13) To this end, any direct or indirect discrimination based on racial or ethnic origin as regards the areas covered by this Directive should be prohibited throughout the Community. This prohibition of discrimination should also apply to nationals of third countries, but does not cover differences of treatment based on nationality and is without prejudice to provisions governing the entry and residence of third-country nationals and their access to employment and to occupation.

(14) In implementing the principle of equal treatment irrespective of racial or ethnic origin, the Community should, in accordance with Article 3(2) of the EC Treaty, aim to eliminate inequalities, and to promote equality between men and women, especially since women are often the victims of multiple discrimination.

(15) The appreciation of the facts from which it may be inferred that there has been direct or indirect discrimination is a matter for national judicial or other competent bodies, in accordance with rules of national law or practice. Such rules may provide in particular for indirect discrimination to be established by any means including on the basis of statistical evidence.

(16) It is important to protect all natural persons against discrimination on grounds of racial or ethnic origin. Member States should also provide, where appropriate and in accordance with their national traditions and practice, protection for legal persons where they suffer discrimination on grounds of the racial or ethnic origin of their members.

(17) The prohibition of discrimination should be without prejudice to the maintenance or adoption of measures intended to prevent or compensate for disadvantages suffered by a group of persons of a particular racial or ethnic origin, and such measures may permit organisations of persons of a particular racial or ethnic origin where their main object is the promotion of the special needs of those persons.

(18) In very limited circumstances, a difference of treatment may be justified where a characteristic related to racial or ethnic origin constitutes a genuine and determining occupational requirement, when the objective is legitimate and the requirement is proportionate. Such circumstances should be included in the information provided by the Member States to the Commission.

(19) Persons who have been subject to discrimination based on racial and ethnic origin should have adequate means of legal protection. To provide a more effective level of protection, associations or legal entities should also be empowered to engage, as the Member States so determine, either on behalf or in support of any victim, in proceedings, without prejudice to national rules of procedure concerning representation and defence before the courts.

(20) The effective implementation of the principle of equality requires adequate judicial protection against victimisation.

(21) The rules on the burden of proof must be adapted when there is a prima facie case of discrimination and, for the principle of equal treatment to be applied effectively, the burden of proof must shift back to the respondent when evidence of such discrimination is brought.

(22) Member States need not apply the rules on the burden of proof to proceedings in which it is for the court or other competent body to investigate the facts of the case. The procedures thus referred to are those in which the plaintiff is not required to prove the facts, which it is for the court or competent body to investigate.

(23) Member States should promote dialogue between the social partners and with non-governmental organisations to address different forms of discrimination and to combat them.

(24) Protection against discrimination based on racial or ethnic origin would itself be strengthened by the existence of a body or bodies in each Member State, with competence to analyse the problems involved, to study possible solutions and to provide concrete assistance for the victims.

(25) This Directive lays down minimum requirements, thus giving the Member States the option of introducing or maintaining more favourable provisions. The implementation of this Directive should not serve to justify any regression in relation to the situation which already prevails in each Member State.

(26) Member States should provide for effective, proportionate and dissuasive sanctions in case of breaches of the obligations under this Directive.

(27) The Member States may entrust management and labour, at their joint request, with the implementation of this Directive as regards provisions falling within the scope of collective agreements, provided that the Member States take all the necessary steps to ensure that they can at all times guarantee the results imposed by this Directive.

(28) In accordance with the principles of subsidiarity and proportionality as set out in Article 5 of the EC Treaty, the objective of this Directive, namely ensuring a common high level of protection against discrimination in all the Member States, cannot be sufficiently achieved by the Member States and can therefore, by reason of the scale and impact of the proposed action, be better achieved by the Community. This Directive does not go beyond what is necessary in order to achieve those objectives.

HAS ADOPTED THIS DIRECTIVE:

Chapter I
General Provisions

Article 1
Purpose

The purpose of this Directive is to lay down a framework for combating discrimination on the grounds of racial or ethnic origin, with a view to putting into effect in the Member States the principle of equal treatment.

Article 2
Concept of discrimination

1 For the purposes of this Directive, the principle of equal treatment shall mean that there shall be no direct or indirect discrimination based on racial or ethnic origin.

2 For the purposes of paragraph 1:

    (a) direct discrimination shall be taken to occur where one person is treated less favourably than another is, has been or would be treated in a comparable situation on grounds of racial or ethnic origin;

    (b) indirect discrimination shall be taken to occur where an apparently neutral provision, criterion or practice would put persons of a racial or ethnic origin at a particular disadvantage compared with other persons, unless that provision, criterion or practice is objectively justified by a legitimate aim and the means of achieving that aim are appropriate and necessary.

1 Harassment shall be deemed to be discrimination within the meaning of paragraph 1, when an unwanted conduct related to racial or ethnic origin takes place with the purpose or effect of violating the dignity of a person and of creating an intimidating, hostile, degrading, humiliating or offensive environment. In this context, the concept of harassment may be defined in accordance with the national laws and practice of the Member States.

2 An instruction to discriminate against persons on grounds of racial or ethnic origin shall be deemed to be discrimination within the meaning of paragraph 1.

Article 3
Scope

1. Within the limits of the powers conferred upon the Community, this Directive shall apply to all persons, as regards both the public and private sectors, including public bodies, in relation to:

    (a) conditions for access to employment, to self-employment and to occupation, including selection criteria and recruitment conditions, whatever the branch of activity and at all levels of the professional hierarchy, including promotion;

    (b) access to all types and to all levels of vocational guidance, vocational training, advanced vocational training and retraining, including practical work experience;

    (c) employment and working conditions, including dismissals and pay;

    (d) membership of and involvement in an organisation of workers or employers, or any organisation whose members carry on a particular profession, including the benefits provided for by such organisations;

    (e) social protection, including social security and healthcare;

    (f) social advantages;

(g) education;

(h) access to and supply of goods and services which are available to the public, including housing.

2. This Directive does not cover difference of treatment based on nationality and is without prejudice to provisions and conditions relating to the entry into and residence of third-country nationals and stateless persons on the territory of Member States, and to any treatment which arises from the legal status of the third-country nationals and stateless persons concerned.

Article 4
Genuine and determining occupational requirements

Notwithstanding Article 2(1) and (2), Member States may provide that a difference of treatment which is based on a characteristic related to racial or ethnic origin shall not constitute discrimination where, by reason of the nature of the particular occupational activities concerned or of the context in which they are carried out, such a characteristic constitutes a genuine and determining occupational requirement, provided that the objective is legitimate and the requirement is proportionate.

Article 5
Positive action

With a view to ensuring full equality in practice, the principle of equal treatment shall not prevent any Member State from maintaining or adopting specific measures to prevent or compensate for disadvantages linked to racial or ethnic origin.

Article 6
Minimum requirements

1 Member States may introduce or maintain provisions which are more favourable to the protection of the principle of equal treatment than those laid down in this Directive.

2 The implementation of this Directive shall under no circumstances constitute grounds for a reduction in the level of protection against discrimination already afforded by Member States in the fields covered by this Directive.

CHAPTER II
REMEDIES AND ENFORCEMENT

Article 7
Defence of rights

1. Member States shall ensure that judicial and/or administrative procedures, including where they deem it appropriate conciliation procedures, for the enforcement of obligations under this Directive are available to all persons who consider themselves wronged by failure to apply the principle of equal treatment to them, even after the relationship in which the discrimination is alleged to have occurred has ended.

1 Member States shall ensure that associations, organisations or other legal entities, which have, in accordance with the criteria laid down by their national law, a legitimate interest in ensuring that the provisions of this Directive are complied with, may engage, either on behalf or in support of the complainant, with his or her approval, in any judicial and/or administrative procedure provided for the enforcement of obligations under this Directive.

2 Paragraphs 1 and 2 are without prejudice to national rules relating to time limits for bringing actions as regards the principle of equality of treatment.

Article 8
Burden of proof

1 Member States shall take such measures as are necessary, in accordance with their national judicial systems, to ensure that, when persons who consider themselves wronged because the principle of equal treatment has not been applied to them establish, before a court or other competent authority, facts from which it may be presumed that there has been direct or indirect discrimination, it shall be for the respondent to prove that there has been no breach of the principle of equal treatment.

2 Paragraph 1 shall not prevent Member States from introducing rules of evidence which are more favourable to plaintiffs.

3 Paragraph 1 shall not apply to criminal procedures.

4 Paragraphs 1, 2 and 3 shall also apply to any proceedings brought in accordance with Article 7(2).

5 Member States need not apply paragraph 1 to proceedings in which it is for the court or competent body to investigate the facts of the case.

Article 9
Victimisation

Member States shall introduce into their national legal systems such measures as are necessary to protect individuals from any adverse treatment or adverse consequence as a reaction to a complaint or to proceedings aimed at enforcing compliance with the principle of equal treatment.

Article 10
Dissemination of information

Member States shall take care that the provisions adopted pursuant to this Directive, together with the relevant provisions already in force, are brought to the attention of the persons concerned by all appropriate means throughout their territory.

Article 11
Social dialogue

1 Member States shall, in accordance with national traditions and practice, take adequate measures to promote the social dialogue between the two sides of industry with a view to fostering equal treatment, including through the monitoring of workplace practices, collective agreements, codes of conduct, research or exchange of experiences and good practices.

2 Where consistent with national traditions and practice, Member States shall encourage the two sides of the industry without prejudice to their autonomy to conclude, at the appropriate level, agreements laying down anti-discrimination rules in the fields referred to in Article 3 which fall within the scope of collective bargaining. These agreements shall respect the minimum requirements laid down by this Directive and the relevant national implementing measures.

Article 12
Dialogue with non-governmental organisations

Member States shall encourage dialogue with appropriate non-governmental organisations which have, in accordance with their national law and practice, a legitimate interest in contributing to the fight against discrimination on grounds of racial and ethnic origin with a view to promoting the principle of equal treatment.

Chapter III
Bodies for the Promotion of Equal Treatment

Article 13

1 Member States shall designate a body or bodies for the promotion of equal treatment of all persons without discrimination on the grounds of racial or ethnic origin. These bodies may form part of agencies charged at national level with the defence of human rights or the safeguard of individuals' rights.

2 Member States shall ensure that the competences of these bodies include:
— without prejudice to the right of victims and of associations, organisations or other legal entities referred to in Article 7(2), providing independent assistance to victims of discrimination in pursuing their complaints about discrimination,
— conducting independent surveys concerning discrimination,
— publishing independent reports and making recommendations on any issue relating to such discrimination.

Chapter IV
Final Provisions

Article 14
Compliance

Member States shall take the necessary measures to ensure that:
(a) any laws, regulations and administrative provisions contrary to the principle of equal treatment are abolished;
(b) any provisions contrary to the principle of equal treatment which are included in individual or collective contracts or agreements, internal rules of undertakings, rules governing profit-making or non-profit-making associations, and rules governing the independent professions and workers' and employers' organisations, are or may be declared, null and void or are amended.

Article 15
Sanctions

Member States shall lay down the rules on sanctions applicable to infringements of the national provisions adopted pursuant to this Directive and shall take all measures necessary to ensure that they are applied. The sanctions, which may comprise the payment of compensation to the victim, must be effective, proportionate and dissuasive. The Member States shall notify those provisions to the Commission by 19 July 2003 at the latest and shall notify it without delay of any subsequent amendment affecting them.

Article 16
Implementation

Member States shall adopt the laws, regulations and administrative provisions necessary to comply with this Directive by 19 July 2003 or may entrust management and labour, at their joint request, with the implementation of this Directive as regards provisions falling within the scope of collective agreements. In such cases, Member States shall ensure that by 19 July 2003, management and labour introduce the necessary measures by agreement, Member States being required to take any necessary measures to enable them at any time to be in a position to guarantee the results imposed by this Directive. They shall forthwith inform the Commission thereof.

When Member States adopt these measures, they shall contain a reference to this Directive or be accompanied by such a reference on the occasion of their official publication. The methods of making such a reference shall be laid down by the Member States.

Article 17
Report

1 Member States shall communicate to the Commission by 19 July 2005, and every five years thereafter, all the information necessary for the Commission to draw up a report to the European Parliament and the Council on the application of this Directive.
2 The Commission's report shall take into account, as appropriate, the views of the European Monitoring Centre on Racism and Xenophobia, as well as the viewpoints of the social partners and relevant non-governmental organisations. In accordance with the principle of gender mainstreaming, this report shall, inter alia, provide an assessment of the impact of the measures taken on women and men. In the light of the information received, this report shall include, if necessary, proposals to revise and update this Directive.

Article 18
Entry into force

This Directive shall enter into force on the day of its publication in the Official Journal of the European Communities.

Article 19
Addressees

This Directive is addressed to the Member States.

Council Directive 2000/78/EC—The Framework Directive

COUNCIL DIRECTIVE 2000/78/EC
of 27 November 2000 establishing a general framework for equal treatment in employment and occupation

THE COUNCIL OF THE EUROPEAN UNION, Having regard to the Treaty establishing the European Community, and in particular Article 13 thereof, Having regard to the proposal from the Commission, Having regard to the Opinion of the European Parliament, Having regard to the Opinion of the Economic and Social Committee, Having regard to the Opinion of the Committee of the Regions, Whereas:

(1) In accordance with Article 6 of the Treaty on European Union, the European Union is founded on the principles of liberty, democracy, respect for human rights and fundamental freedoms, and the rule of law, principles which are common to all Member States and it respects fundamental rights, as guaranteed by the European Convention for the Protection of Human Rights and Fundamental Freedoms and as they result from the constitutional traditions common to the Member States, as general principles of Community law.

(2) The principle of equal treatment between women and men is well established by an important body of Community law, in particular in Council Directive 76/207/EEC of 9 February 1976 on the implementation of the principle of equal treatment for men and women as regards access to employment, vocational training and promotion, and working conditions.

(3) In implementing the principle of equal treatment, the Community should, in accordance with Article 3(2) of the EC Treaty, aim to eliminate inequalities, and to promote equality between men and women, especially since women are often the victims of multiple discrimination.

(4) The right of all persons to equality before the law and protection against discrimination constitutes a universal right recognised by the Universal Declaration of Human Rights, the United Nations Convention on the Elimination of All Forms of Discrimination against Women, United Nations Covenants on Civil and Political Rights and on Economic, Social and Cultural Rights and by the European Convention for the Protection of Human Rights and Fundamental Freedoms, to which all Member States are signatories. Convention No 111 of the International Labour Organisation (ILO) prohibits discrimination in the field of employment and occupation.

(5) It is important to respect such fundamental rights and freedoms. This Directive does not prejudice freedom of association, including the right to establish unions with others and to join unions to defend one's interests.

(6) The Community Charter of the Fundamental Social Rights of Workers recognises the importance of combating every form of discrimination, including the need to take appropriate action for the social and economic integration of elderly and disabled people.

(7) The EC Treaty includes among its objectives the promotion of coordination between employment policies of the Member States. To this end, a new employment chapter was incorporated in the EC Treaty as a means of developing a coordinated European strategy for employment to promote a skilled, trained and adaptable workforce.

(8) The Employment Guidelines for 2000 agreed by the European Council at Helsinki on 10 and 11 December 1999 stress the need to foster a labour market favourable to social integration by formulating a coherent set of policies aimed at combating discrimination against groups such as persons with disability. They also emphasise the need to pay particular attention to supporting older workers, in order to increase their participation in the labour force.

(9) Employment and occupation are key elements in guaranteeing equal opportunities for all and contribute strongly to the full participation of citizens in economic, cultural and social life and to realising their potential.

(10) On 29 June 2000 the Council adopted Directive 2000/43/EC implementing the principle of equal treatment between persons irrespective of racial or ethnic origin. That Directive already provides protection against such discrimination in the field of employment and occupation.

(11) Discrimination based on religion or belief, disability, age or sexual orientation may undermine the achievement of the objectives of the EC Treaty, in particular the attainment of a high level of employment and social protection, raising the standard of living and the quality of life, economic and social cohesion and solidarity, and the free movement of persons.

(12) To this end, any direct or indirect discrimination based on religion or belief, disability, age or sexual orientation as regards the areas covered by this Directive should be prohibited throughout the Community. This prohibition of discrimination should also apply to nationals of third countries but does not cover differences of treatment based on nationality and is without prejudice to provisions governing the entry and residence of third-country nationals and their access to employment and occupation.

(13) This Directive does not apply to social security and social protection schemes whose benefits are not treated as income within the meaning given to that term for the purpose of applying Article 141 of the EC Treaty, nor to any kind of payment by the State aimed at providing access to employment or maintaining employment.

(14) This Directive shall be without prejudice to national provisions laying down retirement ages.

(15) The appreciation of the facts from which it may be inferred that there has been direct or indirect discrimination is a matter for national judicial or other competent bodies, in accordance with rules of national law or practice. Such rules may provide, in particular, for indirect discrimination to be established by any means including on the basis of statistical evidence.

(16) The provision of measures to accommodate the needs of disabled people at the workplace plays an important role in combating discrimination on grounds of disability.

(17) This Directive does not require the recruitment, promotion, maintenance in employment or training of an individual who is not competent, capable and available to perform the essential functions of the post concerned or to undergo the relevant training, without prejudice to the obligation to provide reasonable accommodation for people with disabilities.

(18) This Directive does not require, in particular, the armed forces and the police, prison or emergency services to recruit or maintain in employment persons who do not have the

required capacity to carry out the range of functions that they may be called upon to perform with regard to the legitimate objective of preserving the operational capacity of those services.

(19) Moreover, in order that the Member States may continue to safeguard the combat effectiveness of their armed forces, they may choose not to apply the provisions of this Directive concerning disability and age to all or part of their armed forces. The Member States which make that choice must define the scope of that derogation.

(20) Appropriate measures should be provided, ie effective and practical measures to adapt the workplace to the disability, for example adapting premises and equipment, patterns of working time, the distribution of tasks or the provision of training or integration resources.

(21) To determine whether the measures in question give rise to a disproportionate burden, account should be taken in particular of the financial and other costs entailed, the scale and financial resources of the organisation or undertaking and the possibility of obtaining public funding or any other assistance.

(22) This Directive is without prejudice to national laws on marital status and the benefits dependent thereon.

(23) In very limited circumstances, a difference of treatment may be justified where a characteristic related to religion or belief, disability,age or sexual orientation constitutes a genuine and determining occupational requirement, when the objective is legitimate and the requirement is proportionate. Such circumstances should be included in the information provided by the Member States to the Commission.

(24) The European Union in its Declaration No 11 on the status of churches and non-confessional organisations, annexed to the Final Act of the Amsterdam Treaty, has explicitly recognised that it respects and does not prejudice the status under national law of churches and religious associations or communities in the Member States and that it equally respects the status of philosophical and non-confessional organisations. With this in view, Member States may maintain or lay down specific provisions on genuine, legitimate and justified occupational requirements which might be required for carrying out an occupational activity.

(25) The prohibition of age discrimination is an essential part of meeting the aims set out in the Employment Guidelines and encouraging diversity in the workforce. However, differences in treatment in connection with age may be justified under certain circumstances and therefore require specific provisions which may vary in accordance with the situation in Member States. It is therefore essential to distinguish between differences in treatment which are justified, in particular by legitimate employment policy, labour market and vocational training objectives, and discrimination which must be prohibited.

(26) The prohibition of discrimination should be without prejudice to the maintenance or adoption of measures intended to prevent or compensate for disadvantages suffered by a group of persons of a particular religion or belief, disability, age or sexual orientation, and such measures may permit organisations of persons of a particular religion or belief, disability, age or sexual orientation where their main object is the promotion of the special needs of those persons.

(27) In its Recommendation 86/379/EEC of 24 July 1986 on the employment of disabled people in the Community, the Council established a guideline framework setting out examples of positive action to promote the employment and training of disabled people, and in its Resolution of 17 June 1999 on equal employment opportunities for people

with disabilities, affirmed the importance of giving specific attention inter alia to recruitment, retention, training and lifelong learning with regard to disabled persons.

(28) This Directive lays down minimum requirements, thus giving the Member States the option of introducing or maintaining more favourable provisions. The implementation of this Directive should not serve to justify any regression in relation to the situation which already prevails in each Member State.

(29) Persons who have been subject to discrimination based on religion or belief, disability, age or sexual orientation should have adequate means of legal protection. To provide a more effective level of protection, associations or legal entities should also be empowered to engage in proceedings, as the Member States so determine, either on behalf or in support of any victim, without prejudice to national rules of procedure concerning representation and defence before the courts.

(30) The effective implementation of the principle of equality requires adequate judicial protection against victimisation.

(31) The rules on the burden of proof must be adapted when there is a prima facie case of discrimination and, for the principle of equal treatment to be applied effectively, the burden of proof must shift back to the respondent when evidence of such discrimination is brought. However, it is not for the respondent to prove that the plaintiff adheres to a particular religion or belief, has a particular disability, is of a particular age or has a particular sexual orientation.

(32) Member States need not apply the rules on the burden of proof to proceedings in which it is for the court or other competent body to investigate the facts of the case. The procedures thus referred to are those in which the plaintiff is not required to prove the facts, which it is for the court or competent body to investigate.

(33) Member States should promote dialogue between the social partners and, within the framework of national practice, with non-governmental organisations to address different forms of discrimination at the workplace and to combat them.

(34) The need to promote peace and reconciliation between the major communities in Northern Ireland necessitates the incorporation of particular provisions into this Directive.

(35) Member States should provide for effective, proportionate and dissuasive sanctions in case of breaches of the obligations under this Directive.

(36) Member States may entrust the social partners, at their joint request, with the implementation of this Directive, as regards the provisions concerning collective agreements, provided they take any necessary steps to ensure that they are at all times able to guarantee the results required by this Directive.

(37) In accordance with the principle of subsidiarity set out in Article 5 of the EC Treaty, the objective of this Directive, namely the creation within the Community of a level playing-field as regards equality in employment and occupation, cannot be sufficiently achieved by the Member States and can therefore, by reason of the scale and impact of the action, be better achieved at Community level. In accordance with the principle of proportionality, as set out in that Article, this Directive does not go beyond what is necessary in order to achieve that objective,

HAS ADOPTED THIS DIRECTIVE:

CHAPTER I
GENERAL PROVISIONS

Article 1
Purpose

The purpose of this Directive is to lay down a general framework for combating discrimination on the grounds of religion or belief, disability, age or sexual orientation as regards employment and occupation, with a view to putting into effect in the Member States the principle of equal treatment.

Article 2
Concept of discrimination

1 For the purposes of this Directive, the 'principle of equal treatment' shall mean that there shall be no direct or indirect discrimination whatsoever on any of the grounds referred to in Article 1.

2 For the purposes of paragraph 1:
   (a) direct discrimination shall be taken to occur where one person is treated less favourably than another is, has been or would be treated in a comparable situation, on any of the grounds referred to in Article 1;
   (b) indirect discrimination shall be taken to occur where an apparently neutral provision, criterion or practice would put persons having a particular religion or belief, a particular disability, a particular age, or a particular sexual orientation at a particular disadvantage compared with other persons unless:
      (i) that provision, criterion or practice is objectively justified by a legitimate aim and the means of achieving that aim are appropriate and necessary, or
      (ii) as regards persons with a particular disability, the employer or any person or organisation to whom this Directive applies, is obliged, under national legislation, to take appropriate measures in line with the principles contained in Article 5 in order to eliminate disadvantages entailed by such provision, criterion or practice.

1 Harassment shall be deemed to be a form of discrimination within the meaning of paragraph 1, when unwanted conduct related to any of the grounds referred to in Article 1 takes place with the purpose or effect of violating the dignity of a person and of creating an intimidating, hostile, degrading, humiliating or offensive environment. In this context, the concept of harassment may be defined in accordance with the national laws and practice of the Member States.

2 An instruction to discriminate against persons on any of the grounds referred to in Article 1 shall be deemed to be discrimination within the meaning of paragraph 1.

3 This Directive shall be without prejudice to measures laid down by national law which, in a democratic society, are necessary for public security, for the maintenance of public order and the prevention of criminal offences, for the protection of health and for the protection of the rights and freedoms of others.

Article 3
Scope

1. Within the limits of the areas of competence conferred on the Community, this Directive shall apply to all persons, as regards both the public and private sectors, including public bodies, in relation to:

(a) conditions for access to employment, to self-employment or to occupation, including selection criteria and recruitment conditions, whatever the branch of activity and at all levels of the professional hierarchy, including promotion;

(b) access to all types and to all levels of vocational guidance, vocational training, advanced vocational training and retraining, including practical work experience;

(c) employment and working conditions, including dismissals and pay;

(d) membership of, and involvement in, an organisation of workers or employers, or any organisation whose members carry on a particular profession, including the benefits provided for by such organisations.

1 This Directive does not cover differences of treatment based on nationality and is without prejudice to provisions and conditions relating to the entry into and residence of third-country nationals and stateless persons in the territory of Member States, and to any treatment which arises from the legal status of the third-country nationals and stateless persons concerned.

2 This Directive does not apply to payments of any kind made by state schemes or similar, including state social security or social protection schemes.

3 Member States may provide that this Directive, in so far as it relates to discrimination on the grounds of disability and age, shall not apply to the armed forces.

Article 4
Occupational requirements

1. Notwithstanding Article 2(1) and (2), Member States may provide that a difference of treatment which is based on a characteristic related to any of the grounds referred to in Article 1 shall not constitute discrimination where, by reason of the nature of the particular occupational activities concerned or of the context in which they are carried out, such a characteristic constitutes a genuine and determining occupational requirement, provided that the objective is legitimate and the requirement is proportionate.

2. Member States may maintain national legislation in force at the date of adoption of this Directive or provide for future legislation incorporating national practices existing at the date of adoption of this Directive pursuant to which, in the case of occupational activities within churches and other public or private organisations the ethos of which is based on religion or belief, a difference of treatment based on a person's religion or belief shall not constitute discrimination where, by reason of the nature of these activities or of the context in which they are carried out, a person's religion or belief constitute a genuine, legitimate and justified occupational requirement, having regard to the organisation's ethos. This difference of treatment shall be implemented taking account of Member States' constitutional provisions and principles, as well as the general principles of Community law, and should not justify discrimination on another ground.

Provided that its provisions are otherwise complied with, this Directive shall thus not prejudice the right of churches and other public or private organisations, the ethos of which is based on religion or belief, acting in conformity with national constitutions and laws, to require individuals working for them to act in good faith and with loyalty to the organisation's ethos.

Article 5
Reasonable accommodation for disabled persons

In order to guarantee compliance with the principle of equal treatment in relation to persons with disabilities, reasonable accommodation shall be provided. This means that employers shall take appropriate measures, where needed in a particular case, to enable a person with a disability to have access to, participate in, or advance in employment, or to undergo training, unless such measures would impose a disproportionate burden on the employer. This burden shall not be disproportionate when it is sufficiently remedied by measures existing within the framework of the disability policy of the Member State concerned.

Article 6
Justification of differences of treatment on grounds of age

1. Notwithstanding Article 2(2), Member States may provide that differences of treatment on grounds of age shall not constitute discrimination, if, within the context of national law, they are objectively and reasonably justified by a legitimate aim, including legitimate employment policy, labour market and vocational training objectives, and if the means of achieving that aim are appropriate and necessary.

Such differences of treatment may include, among others:

(a) the setting of special conditions on access to employment and vocational training, employment and occupation, including dismissal and remuneration conditions, for young people, older workers and persons with caring responsibilities in order to promote their vocational integration or ensure their protection;

(b) the fixing of minimum conditions of age, professional experience or seniority in service for access to employment or to certain advantages linked to employment;

(c) the fixing of a maximum age for recruitment which is based on the training requirements of the post in question or the need for a reasonable period of employment before retirement.

2. Notwithstanding Article 2(2), Member States may provide that the fixing for occupational social security schemes of ages for admission or entitlement to retirement or invalidity benefits, including the fixing under those schemes of different ages for employees or groups or categories of employees, and the use, in the context of such schemes, of age criteria in actuarial calculations, does not constitute discrimination on the grounds of age, provided this does not result in discrimination on the grounds of sex.

Article 7
Positive action

1 With a view to ensuring full equality in practice, the principle of equal treatment shall not prevent any Member State from maintaining or adopting specific measures to prevent or compensate for disadvantages linked to any of the grounds referred to in Article 1.

2 With regard to disabled persons, the principle of equal treatment shall be without prejudice to the right of Member States to maintain or adopt provisions on the protection of health and safety at work or to measures aimed at creating or maintaining provisions or facilities for safeguarding or promoting their integration into the working environment.

Article 8
Minimum requirements

1 Member States may introduce or maintain provisions which are more favourable to the protection of the principle of equal treatment than those laid down in this Directive.

2 The implementation of this Directive shall under no circumstances constitute grounds for a reduction in the level of protection against discrimination already afforded by Member States in the fields covered by this Directive.

Chapter II
Remedies and Enforcement

Article 9
Defence of rights

1 Member States shall ensure that judicial and/or administrative procedures, including where they deem it appropriate conciliation procedures, for the enforcement of obligations under this Directive are available to all persons who consider themselves wronged by failure to apply the principle of equal treatment to them, even after the relationship in which the discrimination is alleged to have occurred has ended.

2 Member States shall ensure that associations, organisations or other legal entities which have, in accordance with the criteria laid down by their national law, a legitimate interest in ensuring that the provisions of this Directive are complied with, may engage, either on behalf or in support of the complainant, with his or her approval, in any judicial and/or administrative procedure provided for the enforcement of obligations under this Directive.

3 Paragraphs 1 and 2 are without prejudice to national rules relating to time limits for bringing actions as regards the principle of equality of treatment.

Article 10
Burden of proof

1 Member States shall take such measures as are necessary, in accordance with their national judicial systems, to ensure that, when persons who consider themselves wronged because the principle of equal treatment has not been applied to them establish, before a court or other competent authority, facts from which it may be presumed that there has been direct or indirect discrimination, it shall be for the respondent to prove that there has been no breach of the principle of equal treatment.

2 Paragraph 1 shall not prevent Member States from introducing rules of evidence which are more favourable to plaintiffs.

3 Paragraph 1 shall not apply to criminal procedures.

4 Paragraphs 1, 2 and 3 shall also apply to any legal proceedings commenced in accordance with Article 9(2).

5 Member States need not apply paragraph 1 to proceedings in which it is for the court or competent body to investigate the facts of the case.

Article 11
Victimisation

Member States shall introduce into their national legal systems such measures as are necessary to protect employees against dismissal or other adverse treatment by the employer as a reaction to a complaint within the undertaking or to any legal proceedings aimed at enforcing compliance with the principle of equal treatment.

Article 12
Dissemination of information

Member States shall take care that the provisions adopted pursuant to this Directive, together with the relevant provisions already in force in this field, are brought to the attention of the persons concerned by all appropriate means, for example at the workplace, throughout their territory.

Article 13
Social dialogue

1 Member States shall, in accordance with their national traditions and practice, take adequate measures to promote dialogue between the social partners with a view to fostering equal treatment, including through the monitoring of workplace practices, collective agreements, codes of conduct and through research or exchange of experiences and good practices.

2 Where consistent with their national traditions and practice, Member States shall encourage the social partners, without prejudice to their autonomy, to conclude at the appropriate level agreements laying down anti-discrimination rules in the fields referred to in Article 3 which fall within the scope of collective bargaining. These agreements shall respect the minimum requirements laid down by this Directive and by the relevant national implementing measures.

Article 14
Dialogue with non-governmental organisations

Member States shall encourage dialogue with appropriate non-governmental organisations which have, in accordance with their national law and practice, a legitimate interest in contributing to the fight against discrimination on any of the grounds referred to in Article 1 with a view to promoting the principle of equal treatment.

CHAPTER III
PARTICULAR PROVISIONS

Article 15
Northern Ireland

1 In order to tackle the under-representation of one of the major religious communities in the police service of Northern Ireland, differences in treatment regarding recruitment into that service, including its support staff, shall not constitute discrimination insofar as those differences in treatment are expressly authorised by national legislation.

2 In order to maintain a balance of opportunity in employment for teachers in Northern Ireland while furthering the reconciliation of historical divisions between the major religious communities there, the provisions on religion or belief in this Directive shall not apply to the recruitment of teachers in schools in Northern Ireland in so far as this is expressly authorised by national legislation.

CHAPTER IV
FINAL PROVISIONS

Article 16
Compliance

Member States shall take the necessary measures to ensure that:

(a) any laws, regulations and administrative provisions contrary to the principle of equal treatment are abolished;

(b) any provisions contrary to the principle of equal treatment which are included in contracts or collective agreements, internal rules of undertakings or rules governing the independent occupations and professions and workers' and employers' organisations are, or may be, declared null and void or are amended.

Article 17
Sanctions

Member States shall lay down the rules on sanctions applicable to infringements of the national provisions adopted pursuant to this Directive and shall take all measures necessary to ensure that they are applied. The sanctions, which may comprise the payment of compensation to the victim, must be effective, proportionate and dissuasive. Member States shall notify those provisions to the Commission by 2 December 2003 at the latest and shall notify it without delay of any subsequent amendment affecting them.

Article 18
Implementation

Member States shall adopt the laws, regulations and administrative provisions necessary to comply with this Directive by 2 December 2003 at the latest or may entrust the social partners, at their joint request, with the implementation of this Directive as regards provisions concerning collective agreements. In such cases, Member States shall ensure that, no later than 2 December 2003, the social partners introduce the necessary measures by agreement, the Member States concerned being required to take any necessary measures to enable them at any time to be in a position to guarantee the results imposed by this Directive. They shall forthwith inform the Commission thereof.

In order to take account of particular conditions, Member States may, if necessary, have an additional period of 3 years from 2 December 2003, that is to say a total of 6 years, to implement the provisions of this Directive on age and disability discrimination. In that event they shall inform the Commission forthwith. Any Member State which chooses to use this additional period shall report annually to the Commission on the steps it is taking to tackle age and disability discrimination and on the progress it is making towards implementation. The Commission shall report annually to the Council.

When Member States adopt these measures, they shall contain a reference to this Directive or be accompanied by such reference on the occasion of their official publication. The methods of making such reference shall be laid down by Member States.

Article 19
Report

1 Member States shall communicate to the Commission, by 2 December 2005 at the latest and every five years thereafter, all the information necessary for the Commission to draw up a report to the European Parliament and the Council on the application of this Directive.
2 The Commission's report shall take into account, as appropriate, the viewpoints of the social partners and relevant non-governmental organisations. In accordance with the principle of gender mainstreaming, this report shall, inter alia, provide an assessment of the impact of the measures taken on women and men. In the light of the information received, this report shall include, if necessary, proposals to revise and update this Directive.

Article 20
Entry into force

This Directive shall enter into force on the day of its publication in the Official Journal of the European Communities.

Article 21
Addressees

This Directive is addressed to the Member States.

The Telecommunications (Lawful Business Practice) (Interception of Communications) Regulations 2000 (SI 2000/2699)

1. Citation and commencement

These Regulations may be cited as the Telecommunications (Lawful Business Practice) (Interception of Communications) Regulations 2000 and shall come into force on 24th October 2000.

2. Interpretation

In these Regulations—

(a) references to a business include references to activities of a government department, of any public authority or of any person or office holder on whom functions are conferred by or under any enactment;

(b) a reference to a communication as relevant to a business is a reference to—

    (i) a communication—(aa) by means of which a transaction is entered into in the course of that business, or (bb) which otherwise relates to that business, or

    (ii) a communication which otherwise takes place in the course of the carrying on of that business;

(c) 'regulatory or self-regulatory practices or procedures' means practices or procedures—

    (i) compliance with which is required or recommended by, under or by virtue of—

        (aa) any provision of the law of a Member State or other state within the European Economic Area, or

        (bb) any standard or code of practice published by or on behalf of a body established in a Member State or other state within the European Economic Area which includes amongst its objectives the publication of standards or codes of practice for the conduct of business, or

    (ii) which are otherwise applied for the purpose of ensuring compliance with anything so required or recommended;

(d) 'system controller' means, in relation to a particular telecommunication system, a person with a right to control its operation or use.

3. Lawful interception of a communication

(1) For the purpose of section 1(5)(a) of the Act, conduct is authorised, subject to paragraphs (2) and (3) below, if it consists of interception of a communication, in the course of its transmission by means of a telecommunication system, which is effected by or with the express or implied consent of the system controller for the purpose of—

(a) monitoring or keeping a record of communications—

    (i) in order to—(aa) establish the existence of facts, or

        (bb) ascertain compliance with regulatory or self-regulatory practices or procedures which are—applicable to the system controller in the carrying on of his business or applicable to another person in the carrying on of his business where that person is supervised by the system controller in respect of those practices or procedures, or

(cc) ascertain or demonstrate the standards which are achieved or ought to be achieved by persons using the system in the course of their duties, or

(ii) in the interests of national security, or

(iii) for the purpose of preventing or detecting crime, or

(iv) for the purpose of investigating or detecting the unauthorised use of that or any other telecommunication system, or

(v) where that is undertaken—

(aa) in order to secure, or (bb) as an inherent part of,

the effective operation of the system (including any monitoring or keeping of a record which would be authorised by section 3(3) of the Act if the conditions in paragraphs (a) and (b) thereof were satisfied); or

(b) monitoring communications for the purpose of determining whether they are communications relevant to the system controller's business which fall within regulation 2(b)(i) above; or

(c) monitoring communications made to a confidential voice-telephony counselling or support service which is free of charge (other than the cost, if any, of making a telephone call) and operated in such a way that users may remain anonymous if they so choose.

(2) Conduct is authorised by paragraph (1) of this regulation only if—

(a) the interception in question is effected solely for the purpose of monitoring or (where appropriate) keeping a record of communications relevant to the system controller's business;

(b) the telecommunication system in question is provided for use wholly or partly in connection with that business;

(c) the system controller has made all reasonable efforts to inform every person who may use the telecommunication system in question that communications transmitted by means thereof may be intercepted; and

(d) in a case falling within—

(i) paragraph (1)(a)(ii) above, the person by or on whose behalf the interception is effected is a person specified in section 6(2)(a) to (i) of the Act;

(ii) paragraph (1)(b) above, the communication is one which is intended to be received (whether or not it has been actually received) by a person using the telecommunication system in question.

(3) Conduct falling within paragraph (1)(a)(i) above is authorised only to the extent that Article 5 of Directive 97/66/EC of the European Parliament and of the Council of 15 December 1997 concerning the processing of personal data and the protection of privacy in the telecommunications sector so permits.

Numéro de dossier
File-number

COUR EUROPÉENNE DES DROITS DE L'HOMME
EUROPEAN COURT OF HUMAN RIGHTS

Conseil de l'Europe – *Council of Europe*
Strasbourg, France

REQUÊTE
APPLICATION

présentée en application de l'article 34 de la Convention européenne des Droits de l'Homme, ainsi que des articles 45 et 47 du règlement de la Cour

under Article 34 of the European Convention on Human Rights and Rules 45 and 47 of the Rules of Court

IMPORTANT: La présente requête est un document juridique et peut affecter vos droits et obligations.
This application is a formal legal document and may affect your rights and obligations.

I. LES PARTIES
THE PARTIES

A. LE REQUÉRANT/LA REQUÉRANTE
THE APPLICANT

(Renseignements à fournir concernant le/la requérant(e) et son/sa représentant(e) éventuel(le))
(Fill in the following details of the applicant and the representative, if any)

1. Nom de famille .... 2. Prénom(s)
   Surname   *First name(s)*

     Sexe : masculin / féminin   *Sex: male / female*

3. Nationalité .... 4. Profession
   Nationality   *Occupation*

5. Date et lieu de naissance
   Date and place of birth

6. Domicile
   Permanent address

7. Tel. No

8. Adresse actuelle (si différente de 6.)
   Present address (if different from 6.)

9. Nom et prénom du/de la représentant(e)[1]
   Name of representative*

10. Profession du/de la représentant(e)
    Occupation of representative

11. Adresse du/de la représentant(e)
    Address of representative

12. Tel. No .... Fax No

B. LA HAUTE PARTIE CONTRACTANTE
THE HIGH CONTRACTING PARTY

(Indiquer ci-après le nom de l'Etat/des Etats contre le(s)quel(s) la requête est dirigée)
(Fill in the name of the State(s) against which the application is directed)

13.

---

[1] Si le/la requérant(e) est représenté(e), joindre une procuration signée par le/la requérant(e) et son/sa représentant(e).

If the applicant appoints a representative, attach a form of authority signed by the applicant and his or her representative.

II. EXPOSÉ DES FAITS
STATEMENT OF THE FACTS

(Voir chapitre II de la note explicative)
(See Part II of the Explanatory Note)

14.

Si nécessaire, continuer sur une feuille séparée
Continue on a separate sheet if necessary

III. **EXPOSÉ DE LA OU DES VIOLATION(S) DE LA CONVENTION ET/OU DES PROTOCOLES ALLÉGUÉE(S), AINSI QUE DES ARGUMENTS À L'APPUI**
   STATEMENT OF ALLEGED VIOLATION(S) OF THE CONVENTION AND/OR PROTOCOLS AND OF RELEVANT ARGUMENTS

(Voir chapitre III de la note explicative)
(See Part III of the Explanatory Note)

15.

IV. EXPOSÉ RELATIF AUX PRESCRIPTIONS DE L'ARTICLE 35 § 1 DE LA CONVENTION
STATEMENT RELATIVE TO ARTICLE 35 § 1 OF THE CONVENTION

(Voir chapitre IV de la note explicative. Donner pour chaque grief, et au besoin sur une feuille séparée, les renseignements demandés sous les points 16 à 18 ci-après)
(See Part IV of the Explanatory Note. If necessary, give the details mentioned below under points 16 to 18 on a separate sheet for each separate complaint)

16. Décision interne définitive (date et nature de la décision, organe – judiciaire ou autre – l'ayant rendue)
    Final decision (date, court or authority and nature of decision)

17. Autres décisions (énumérées dans l'ordre chronologique en indiquant, pour chaque décision, sa date, sa nature et l'organe–judiciaire ou autre–l'ayant rendue)
    Other decisions (list in chronological order, giving date, court or authority and nature of decision for each of them)

18. Dispos(i)ez-vous d'un recours que vous n'avez pas exercé? Si oui, lequel et pour quel motif n'a-t-il pas été exercé?
    Is there or was there any other appeal or other remedy available to you which you have not used? If so, explain why you have not used it.

Si nécessaire, continuer sur une feuille séparée
Continue on a separate sheet if necessary

V. EXPOSÉ DE L'OBJET DE LA REQUÊTE
STATEMENT OF THE OBJECT OF THE APPLICATION

(Voir chapitre V de la note explicative)
See Part V of the Explanatory Note)

19.

VI. AUTRES INSTANCES INTERNATIONALES TRAITANT OU AYANT TRAITÉ L'AFFAIRE
STATEMENT CONCERNING OTHER INTERNATIONAL PROCEEDINGS

(Voir chapitre VI de la note explicative)
(See Part VI of the Explanatory Note)

20. Avez-vous soumis à une autre instance internationale d'enquête ou de règlement les griefs énoncés dans la présente requête? Si oui, fournir des indications détaillées à ce sujet.
Have you submitted the above complaints to any other procedure of international investigation or settlement? If so, give full details.

VII. PIÈCES ANNEXÉES　　　　　　　　　　(PAS D'ORIGINAUX,
　　　　　　　　　　　　　　　　　UNIQUEMENT DES COPIES ;
　　　　　　　　　　　　PRIÈRE DE N'UTILISER NI AGRAFE,
　　　　　　　　　　NI ADHÉSIF, NI LIEN D'AUCUNE SORTE)

LIST OF DOCUMENTS　　　　　　　*(NO ORIGINAL DOCUMENTS,*
　　　　　　　　　　　　　　　　ONLY PHOTOCOPIES,
　　　　　　　DO NOT STAPLE, TAPE OR BIND DOCUMENTS)

(Voir chapitre VII de la note explicative. Joindre copie de toutes les décisions mentionnées sous ch. IV et VI ci-dessus. Se procurer, au besoin, les copies nécessaires, et, en cas d'impossibilité, expliquer pourquoi celles-ci ne peuvent pas être obtenues. Ces documents ne vous seront pas retournés.)
(See Part VII of the Explanatory Note. Include copies of all decisions referred to in Parts IV and VI above. If you do not have copies, you should obtain them. If you cannot obtain them, explain why not. No documents will be returned to you.)

21.　a)

　　　b)

　　　c)

VIII. DÉCLARATION ET SIGNATURE
DECLARATION AND SIGNATURE

(Voir chapitre VIII de la note explicative)
(See Part VIII of the Explanatory Note)

Je déclare en toute conscience et loyauté que les renseignements qui figurent sur la présente formule de requite sont exacts.
I hereby declare that, to the best of my knowledge and belief, the information I have given in the present application form is correct.

Lieu/*Place*

Date/*Date*

(Signature du/de la requérant(e) ou du/de la représentant(e))
(Signature of the applicant or of the representative)

EXPLANATORY NOTE

for persons completing the Application Form
under Article 34 of the Convention

INTRODUCTION

These notes are intended to assist you in drawing up your application to the Court. **Please read them carefully before completing the form**, and then refer to them as you complete each section of the form.

The completed form will be your application to the Court under Article 34 of the Convention. It will be the basis for the Court's examination of your case. It is therefore important that you **complete it fully and accurately even if this means repeating information you have already given the Registry in previous correspondence.**

You will see that there are eight sections to the form. You should complete all of these so that your application contains all the information required under the Rules of Court. Below you will find an explanatory note relating to each section of the form. You will also find at the end of these notes the text of Rules 45 and 47 of the Rules of Court.

NOTES RELATING TO THE APPLICATION FORM

I. THE PARTIES – Rule 47 § 1 (a), (b) and (c)
(1-13)

If there is more than one applicant, you should give the required information for each one, on a separate sheet if necessary.

An applicant may appoint a person to represent him. Such representative shall be an advocate authorised to practise in any of the Contracting Parties and resident in the territory of one of them, or any other person approved by the Court. When an applicant is represented, relevant details should be given in this part of the application form, and the Registry will correspond only with the representative.

II. STATEMENT OF THE FACTS – Rule 47 § 1 (d)
(14)

You should give clear and concise details of the facts you are complaining about. Try to describe the events in the order in which they occurred. Give exact dates. If your complaints relate to a number of different matters (for instance different sets of court proceedings) you should deal with each matter separately.

III. STATEMENT OF ALLEGED VIOLATION(S) OF THE CONVENTION AND/ OR PROTOCOLS (15)
AND OF RELEVANT ARGUMENTS – Rule 47 § 1 (e)

In this section of the form you should explain as precisely as you can what your complaint **under the Convention** is. Say which provisions of the Convention you rely on and explain why you consider that the facts you have set out in Part II of the form involve a violation of these provisions.

You will see that some of the articles of the Convention permit interferences with the rights they guarantee in certain circumstances (see for instance sub-paragraphs (a) to (f) of Article 5 §§ 1 and 2 of Articles 8 to 11). If you are relying on such an article, try to explain why you consider the interference about which you are complaining is not justified.

IV. STATEMENT RELATIVE TO ARTICLE 35 § 1 OF THE CONVENTION –
Rule 47 § 2 (a)

(16-18)

In this section you should set out details of the remedies you have pursued before the national authorities.

You should fill in each of the three parts of this section and give the same information separately for each separate complaint. In part 18 you should say whether or not any other appeal or remedy is available which could redress your complaints and which you have not used. If such a remedy is available, you should say what it is (e.g. name the court or authority to which an appeal would lie) and explain why you have not used it.

V. STATEMENT OF THE OBJECT OF THE APPLICATION – Rule 47 § 1 (g)
(19)

Here you should state briefly what you want to achieve through your application to the Court.

VI. STATEMENT CONCERNING OTHER INTERNATIONAL PROCEEDINGS –
Rule 47 § 2 (b)

(20)

Here you should say whether or not you have ever submitted the complaints in your application to any other procedure of international investigation or settlement. If you have, you should give full details, including the name of the body to which you submitted your complaints, dates and details of any proceedings which took place and details of decisions taken. You should also submit copies of relevant decisions and other documents. Do not staple, seal with adhesive tape or bind documents.

VII. LIST OF DOCUMENTS – Rule 47 § 1 (h)
(21)   (NO ORIGINAL DOCUMENTS, ONLY PHOTOCOPIES)

Do not forget to enclose with your application and to mention on the list all judgments and decisions referred to in Sections IV and VI, as well as any other documents you wish the Court to take into consideration as evidence (transcripts, statements of witnesses, etc.). Include any documents giving the reasons for a court or other decision as well as the decision itself. Only submit documents which are relevant to the complaints you are making to the Court. Do not staple, seal with adhesive tape or bind documents.

VIII. DECLARATION AND SIGNATURE – Rule 45 § 3
(22)

If the application is signed by the representative of the applicant, it should be accompanied by a form of authority signed by the applicant and the representative (unless this has already been submitted).

Rules of the European Court of Human Rights

Chapter II
Institution of Proceedings

Rule 45
(Signatures)

1. Any application made under Articles 33 or 34 of the Convention shall be submitted in writing and shall be signed by the applicant or by the applicant's representative.
2. Where an application is made by a non-governmental organisation or by a group of individuals, it shall be signed by those persons competent to represent that organisation or group. The Chamber or Committee concerned shall determine any question as to whether the persons who have signed an application are competent to do so.
3. Where applicants are represented in accordance with Rule 36, a power of attorney or written authority to act shall be supplied by their representative or representatives.

Rule 47
(Contents of an individual application)

1. Any application under Article 34 of the Convention shall be made on the application form provided by the Registry, unless the President of the Section concerned decides otherwise. It shall set out
   (a) the name, date of birth, nationality, sex, occupation and address of the applicant;
   (b) the name, occupation and address of the representative, if any;
   (c) the name of the Contracting Party or Parties against which the application is made;
   (d) a succinct statement of the facts;
   (e) a succinct statement of the alleged violation(s) of the Convention and the relevant arguments;
   (f) a succinct statement on the applicant's compliance with the admissibility criteria (exhaustion of domestic remedies and the six-month rule) laid down in Article 35 § 1 of the Convention; and
   (g) the object of the application;
   and be accompanied by
   (h) copies of any relevant documents and in particular the decisions, whether judicial or not, relating to the object of the application.
2. Applicants shall furthermore
   (a) provide information, notably the documents and decisions referred to in paragraph 1 (h) of this Rule, enabling it to be shown that the admissibility criteria (exhaustion of domestic remedies and the six-month rule) laid down in Article 35 § 1 of the Convention have been satisfied; and
   (b) indicate whether they have submitted their complaints to any other procedure of international investigation or settlement.

3. Applicants who do not wish their identity to be disclosed to the public shall so indicate and shall submit a statement of the reasons justifying such a departure from the normal rule of public access to information in proceedings before the Court. The President of the Chamber may authorise anonymity in exceptional and duly justified cases.

4. Failure to comply with the requirements set out in paragraphs 1 and 2 of this Rule may result in the application not being examined by the Court.

5. The date of introduction of the application shall as a general rule be considered to be the date of the first communication from the applicant setting out, even summarily, the object of the application. The Court may for good cause nevertheless decide that a different date shall be considered to be the date of introduction.

6. Applicants shall keep the Court informed of any change of address and of all circumstances relevant to the application.

INDEX

age discrimination *see also* Employment
    Equality (Age) Regulations 2006
  case law 14.79–14.81
  Code of Practice 1999: 14.78
  Convention rights (ECHR) 14.106
  default retirement age
    age discrimination rights 14.98, 14.99
    dismissal 14.104
    employers' rights 14.105
    mandatory retirement age 14.101–14.103
    meaning 14.98
    private sector 14.100
    public sector 14.100
    statutory retirement age 14.99, 14.100
  fair trial 7.128, 7.129 *see also* fair trial
  Framework Employment Equality
    Directive 14.82, 14.91, 14.97 *see also*
    Framework Employment Equality
    Directive 2000
  Human Rights Act 1998 (HRA) 14.77, 14.82
  indirect discrimination 14.92
  margin of appreciation 14.107 *see also*
    margin of appreciation
  public perception 14.78
  voluntary approach 14.78
AIDS/HIV
  Convention rights (ECHR) 8.156
  disability legislation 8.156
  privacy 8.156 *see also* **medical records**
arbitration
  ACAS schemes 7.68, 7.69
  Convention rights (ECHR) 7.70, 7.71
    see also **European Convention on Human**
    Rights (ECHR)
  unfair dismissal 7.67, 7.68 *see also* **unfair**
    dismissal
Article 4 (ECHR) *see* **slavery and**
  forced labour
Article 6 (ECHR) *see* **fair trial**
Article 8 (ECHR) *see* **private and family life**
Article 9 (ECHR) *see* **thought, conscience**
  and religion
Article 10 (ECHR) *see* **freedom of expression**

Article 11 (ECHR) *see* **freedom of assembly and**
  association
Article 14 (ECHR) *see* **discrimination**

Charter of Fundamental Rights
  abuse of rights App 3
  child labour App 3
  consumer protection App 3
  environmental protection App 3
  equality under 14.28, 14.29, App 3
  European Constitutional Treaty 14.29, 14.30
  fair trial App 3
  freedom of assembly and association
    derogations 11.32
    permissible interference 11.32
    related rights, 11.32, 11.33, 11.38
    see also **Freedom of assembly and**
    association
  guaranteed rights App 3
  health care App 3
  human dignity App 3
  inhuman and degrading treatment App 3
  judicial notice 1.46
  non-discrimination 14.31
  ombudsman App 3
  principal freedoms App 3
  principal rights App 3
  services of general economic interest
    (SGEI) App 3
  significance 1.44, 1.45
  social security App 3
  solidarity
    collective bargaining 11.24, 11.36,
      11.37, App 3
    provisions App 3
    right to information 11.34, 11.35
    strike action 11.37
  status 1.43
children
  child care 8.166, 8.171
  child protection 8.127
  maternity rights 8.180, 8.182
  parental leave 8.167, 8.181, 8.183, 8.184

mental health 14.125
reasonable accommodation 14.132–14.137
right to life 14.126, App 1, App 2
workplace
    adaptation 14.133
    reasonable adjustments 14.134
discrimination
age discrimination *see* **age discrimination**
analysis of 13.49, 13.50
basic test 13.30, 13.31
context 13.50
Convention rights (ECHR) 13.12
difference of treatment 13.30, 13.31,
    13.34, 13.49
direct discrimination
    difference of treatment 13.34
    justification 13.46, 13.47
    less favourable treatment 13.33, 13.34
disguised discrimination 13.51–13.53
domestic law
    administrative approach 13.37
    conceptual relationships 13.38–13.40,
        13.45
    differences within 13.39–13.44
    fair treatment provisions 13.43
    human rights approach 13.44, 13.45
    international influences 13.13, 13.14
    justification under 13.46, 13.47
    statute law 13.37–13.39
dress code 8.158, 8.161
ECHR (Art 14)
    accessory nature 13.99–13.101, 13.129
    accessory rights 13.99, 13.100
    basic concept 13.109
    case law 13.101, 13.102
    discriminatory grounds 13.103–13.108
    domestic remedies 13.124, 13.125
    indirect discrimination 13.110–13.112
    justification 13.116
    permitted discrimination 13.113
    prohibition under 13.97, 13.98
    protection under 13.113
ECJ jurisprudence 13.31, 13.32, 13.48
EC law *see* **discrimination law (EC)**
equal treatment *see* **equal treatment**
equality distinguished 13.85 *see also* **equality**
freedom of expression 10.73–10.76 *see also*
    freedom of expression
indirect discrimination
    Convention rights (ECHR) 13.110–13.112
    definition 13.36
    domestic law approach 13.35
    human rights law 13.35, 13.36

justification 13.114, 13.115
    similar treatment 13.34
    specific relative disadvantage 13.33
justification
    degrees of 13.54
    direct discrimination 13.46, 13.47
    domestic law under 13.46, 13.47
    genuine occupational requirement 13.46
    objective justification 13.32, 13.49,
        13.114–13.128
    permissible objective 13.55
    proportionality 13.55
    tests for 13.46, 13.47
legitimate aim 13.30
multiple discrimination 14.32
objective justification
    ECtHR rulings 13.117, 13.118
    grounds for 13.32, 13.49
    indirect discrimination 13.114, 13.115
    legitimate aim 13.114
    positive action 13.123, 13.124,
        13.126, 13.128
    positive discrimination 13.124
    proportionality 13.114
    remedial action 13.125, 13.127
    requirements 13.116
    special measures 13.123
    suspect classes 13.119–13.122
political opinions 10.74
positive discrimination 13.124
proportionality 13.30
Protocol 12 (ECHR)
    adoption 13.129
    effect 13.98
    indirect impact 13.139
    non-discrimination grounds 13.105, 13.131
    non-discrimination right 13.129, 13.131
    positive obligations 13.140
    protection under 13.131
    provisions 13.98, 13.105, 13.129,
        13.131, 13.133
    public authorities 13.131
    purpose 13.130
    ratification 13.132, 13.134–13.138
    special measures 13.141
    UK position 13.129, 13.134–13.138,
        13.141, 13.142
provision/criteria/practice
    (PCP) 14.44–14.46
race discrimination 9.05, 9.144–9.148, 10.73,
    10.76 *see also* **race discrimination**
religious belief 9.108 *see also* **religion
    or belief**